# Hillier's

## Fundamentals of Automotive Electronics

BOOK 2

Sixth Edition

V. A. W. Hillier

Brian Devlin
Tommy Dodds
Steven Dufu-Chase
Andrew Gibson
Donald MacAndrew

Stephen Maidment
Hamza Munir
Tony Robinson
Josh Smith
Jon Sutherland and Diane Canwell

Series editor: John Taylor

Nelson Thornes

This edition published in 2012 by:
Nelson Thornes Ltd
Delta Place
27 Bath Road
CHELTENHAM
GL53 7TH
United Kingdom

12  13  14  15  16  /  10  9  8  7  6  5  4  3  2  1

A catalogue record for this book is available from the British Library

ISBN 978 1 4085 1537 2

Cover photograph: pagadesign/iStockphoto

Illustrations by GreenGate Publishing Services

Page make-up by GreenGate Publishing Services, Tonbridge, Kent

Printed and bound in Spain by GraphyCems

# Contents

# Preface

Since the last update of this publication, there has been a staggering increase and improvement in the electronic control of the systems fitted to motor vehicles. This improvement in electronic control has, in turn, led to a number of changes to systems that were previously operated by mechanical means; some of these systems are now operated 'by wire', with no mechanical contact between components.

The majority of improvements have been made to enhance the performance of driver and passenger safety systems, increase fuel economy and reduce toxic and greenhouse emissions. There are also a number of comfort systems available which have only been made possible through the development of on-board vehicle electronics.

The latest internal combustion, hybrid and electric vehicles now boast electronic systems and data transfer speeds which a few years ago were the domain of supercomputers, and there are now as many as 70 electronic control units (ECUs) fitted to some vehicles. We also have the first production hydrogen fuel celled vehicle (HFCV) on our roads.

This publication is directed at the vocational study area for apprentices, trainees and practising technicians, and because of the variety and differing operational characteristics, the contents will provide a generic view on the electronic operation of the systems available.

With this in mind and the fact that each system on the vehicle is no longer a stand-alone system, the vehicle technician now requires not only an understanding of individual system operation but also a knowledge of how the systems interact with each other to enhance the overall performance and operation of the vehicle and the safety of its occupants.

Another important consideration is one of health and safety. Modern vehicles are producing much higher operational voltages than in previous years, with capacitors in the latest electric vehicles (EVs) producing 600 volts (400 amps current) and electronic spark ignition systems producing in excess of 90,000 volts.

For the first time, the contents of the book are supplemented with online support for tutors, learners and apprentice technicians, which is designed to test and further enhance knowledge and understanding.

# 1

# Electrical principles

All electrical and electronic systems obey essential rules and laws. It is vital to understand the basic principles that need to be applied to all circuits and components. These principles help to understand how electricity behaves as well as electronics and circuits. Appreciating the fact that everything consists of atoms, it is easier to understand that electricity is a form of energy.

## 1.1 Circuit fundamentals

### 1.1.1 Electrical charge

The word 'electric' comes from the Greek word *electron*, which means amber. As long ago as 600 BC it was known that when this yellow translucent fossil resin was rubbed with a silk cloth, the amber was then able to attract to it particles of dust. Today, a similar effect can be produced after passing a plastic comb through your hair – the comb will attract small pieces of paper.

Experiments performed around the year 1600 showed that other materials could be 'charged' with electricity. Also, observations showed that when small objects, such as two pith balls, were charged from an electrified material, they would react in different ways when placed close together. When they were each charged from a similar source they would repel each other, but when one was charged from a resinous material and the other was charged from a vitreous substance (e.g. glass) the two charged objects would then be attracted together.

In 1747 Benjamin Franklin introduced the names **positive** and **negative** to distinguish between the two types of electrical charge. Vitreous materials were said to acquire a positive charge and resinous substances a negative charge. He thought the electrical flow (the flow of the charge) passed from a high potential positive source to a lower potential negative source. The choice was unfortunate because a later discovery proved that small electrical charges, called **electrons**, moved from negative to positive. However, by this time many electrical rules and laws had been established, so today the **conventional flow** from positive to negative is applied whenever basic laws have to be used. Actual flow from negative to positive is called **electron flow**. The unit of electrical charge is the coulomb. Matter is made up of atoms, which have positively charged nuclei and negatively charged electrons surrounding them.

The form of energy produced by rubbing a material is called **electrostatic** energy. In a motor vehicle this type of charge is generated at places where friction occurs (e.g. clutch and brake). These charges can build up in a vehicle, especially on a hot dry day, so the occupants can sometimes detect these static charges as they conduct or **discharge** the static electricity to the ground. Today, electrical energy is obtained normally from a battery or generator and this form of energy is called electric current to distinguish it from electrostatics. Although the energy is obtained from a different source, the behaviour of both forms is similar.

**Positive**: having an overall charge opposite to that of an electron.

**Negative**: having an overall charge of the same type as that carried by electrons.

**Electron**: a tiny, subatomic, negatively charged particle.

**Conventional flow**: electrical flow from positive to negative. This is, by convention, the direction of an electric current.

**Electron flow**: the flow of electrons from negative to positive. This is opposite to conventional flow.

**Electrostatic**: the type of electrical energy possessed by charged particles that are stationary (i.e. not in an electron flow).

**Discharge**: sparks caused by the build-up of static electricity (e.g. lightning).

## 1.1.2 Electrons and protons

Atoms are made up of a number of tiny particles. A hydrogen atom is the simplest, having just one **proton** as a nucleus at its centre and a single electron, which revolves around the proton at high speed (Figure 1.1).

In some materials, such as metals, the electrons are held less tightly by the nucleus, so they can move or drift in a random way from one atom to another (Figure 1.2). Materials like this, having these 'free' electrons, are good **conductors** of electricity. This is why copper is often used for electrical cables.

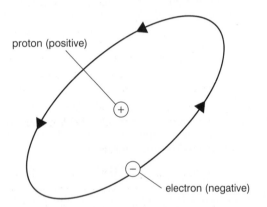

*Figure 1.1 Hydrogen atom*

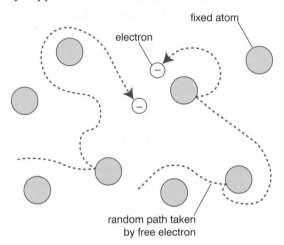

*Figure 1.2 Metal atoms*

Although electrons and protons are present in all atoms, it is the electrons that act as the primary carrier of electricity. The electron is the lightest of all particles, with a mass of just 0.0005 of the mass of the whole hydrogen atom. Each electron carries a tiny negative charge and this balances the positive charge in the proton. The charges on the electron and the proton are opposite and cancel one another out, making the atom electrically neutral.

**Proton**: a positively charged, subatomic particle. The charge is equal in magnitude to that of an electron but opposite in sign.

## 1.1.3 Conductors and insulators

Each different material has a different combination of electrons and protons. For example, copper atoms have 29 electrons, which move around in four different orbits around the atom's nucleus (the central part of the atom). The nucleus contains protons and also particles of another type, called neutrons, which do not have an electrical charge.

In comparison, some materials do not have any 'free' electrons, so electron flow from one atom to another is difficult. These materials are called **insulators**, as they tend not to conduct electricity. However, no material is absolutely resistant to electron flow and, if the voltage is high enough, some conduction of electricity occurs in insulators too.

**Conductor**: a material that allows electrons to flow easily from one atom to another.

**Insulator**: a material that makes it difficult for electrons to flow.

## 1.1.4 Attraction and repulsion

Two positive electrical charges repel one another, as do two negative ones. Negative charges attract positive ones and positive ones attract negative ones. You can think of the different polarities as being like the poles of a magnet: opposite poles attract, but the same poles repel. It is like this with electrons.

The French physicist Charles-Augustin de Coulomb studied the size of the force that was produced by electrically charged objects in 1775. In recognition for this, the unit of electrical charge is named after him: 1 C (coulomb) of charge passes through a conductor in 1 s (second) when the current is equal to 1 A (ampere).

## 1.1.5 Potential and potential difference

The potential is the amount that a body is electrically charged. If two bodies are charged with electrical energy of the same polarity, then a force is required to move those two bodies together. The application of this force over a given distance is called electrical potential.

**Potential difference (PD)** is rather like the pressure drop between two points in a water system. In an electrical circuit, the amount of work done will depend on the PD. The current, or rate of electron flow, will depend on the PD between two points in the circuit. Using conventional flow (positive to negative), electrical energy moves from a point of high potential to a point of lower potential. If point A has a higher potential than point B, then work is required to move a positive charge from B to A. This means that the PD between the two points A and B is 1 V if the work done in taking 1 C of positive charge from B to A is 1 J (joule).

**Potential difference (PD)**: measured in volts, is proportional to the charge on an object (measured in coulombs).

**Electromotive force (EMF)**: the voltage produced by a generator or battery in an electrical circuit.

## 1.1.6 Electromotive force

Both batteries and generators can create a difference in potential between two points. The electrical force that provides this increase in PD is known as the **electromotive force (EMF)**, which is measured in volts. A battery's or generator's terminals are marked positive and negative; these relate to the higher and lower potential, respectively.

EMF is a source of energy to drive charge around a circuit. The charge between different points in the circuit differs and it is this that allows electrons to move. In other words, at one point in the circuit there may be more electrons and at another there may be fewer. These charge differences are stored as EMF and it is this that allows the electrons to flow around the circuit.

| 1.2 | **Electrical symbols, units and terms** |
|---|---|

It makes sense that there is a commonly used set of symbols, units and terms that can be applied to all electrical systems. The symbols, units and terms used in the automotive industry are exactly the same as those that are used in electronics and other fields or industries.

## 1.2.1 Symbols and units

Electrical systems can be shown in a pictorial or theoretical form. There are various symbols used to identify items found in an electrical circuit. Automotive electrical systems can be complex so it is important to

### Hydraulic and electric circuits

Imagine that electrons move just like water in a pipe. To move, water needs to be under pressure, moving from a high pressure point to a lower pressure point. The water is under pressure in the pipes, but as soon as you turn a tap the water flows out as it is under a lower pressure. This is known as hydraulics and, in water systems, pumps create the water pressure. In electrical systems the 'pressure' is created by generators or batteries. A pump does not make water; it just gives energy (by applying pressure) to the water. Similarly, generators and batteries give energy to the electrons in the material that makes up the circuit.

Just as the flow of water can be measured in litres per second, so the flow of electrons is measured in amperes. In a water system, we can turn the flow on or off with a tap; in an electrical circuit we would use a switch. In both systems, the flow can be controlled: in a water system using a flow restrictor, which narrows the flow in the pipe; in an electrical system using a variable resistor, which controls the flow of electrons.

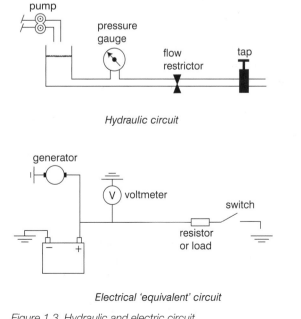

*Hydraulic circuit*

*Electrical 'equivalent' circuit*

Figure 1.3 Hydraulic and electric circuit

be able to identify each component using the standard symbols. The **British Standards Institution (BSI)** outlines a clear set of guidelines and electrotechnical symbols in BS 3939: 1985 that should always be used (corresponding to the International Electrotechnical Commission standards IEC 60617).

Electrical units each have their own symbol, as shown in Table 1.1.

*Table 1.1 Electrical symbols (BS 3939: 1985)*

| Description | Symbol |
|---|---|
| Direct current<br>Alternating current | |
| Positive polarity<br>Negative polarity | + <br> – |
| Current approaching<br>Current receding | |
| Battery 12 V<br>(Long line is positive) | |
| Earth, chassis frame<br>Earth, general | |

| Description | Symbol |
|---|---|
| Conductor (permanent)<br>Thickness denotes importance<br>Conductor (temporary) | |
| Conductors crossing without connecting | |
| Conductors joining | |
| Junction, separable<br>Junction, inseparable<br>Plug and socket | |

| Description | Symbol |
|---|---|
| Variability: applied to other symbols | |
| Resistor (fixed value) | |
| Resistor (variable) | |
| General winding (inductor, coil) | |
| Winding with core | |
| Transformer | |

| Description | Symbol |
|---|---|
| Diode, rectifying junction | |
| Light emitting diode | |
| Diode, breakdown:<br>Zener and avalanche | |
| Reverse blocking triode thyristor | |
| pnp<br>Transformer<br>npn | |

| Description | Symbol |
|---|---|
| Lamp | |
| Fuse | |
| Switch ('make' contact, normally open) | |
| Switch ('break' contact, normally closed) | |
| Switch (manually operated) | |
| Switch (two-way) | |
| Relay (single winding) | |
| Relay (thermal) | |
| Spark gap | |
| Generator AC and DC | |
| Motor DC | |
| Meters: ammeter, voltmeter, galvanometer | |

| Description | Symbol |
|---|---|
| Capacitor, general symbol | |
| Capacitor, polarised | |
| Amplifier | |

| Description | | Symbol |
|---|---|---|
| Junction FET | N-type channel | |
| | P-type channel | |
| Photodiode | | |
| Thyristor | | |

**British Standards Institution (BSI):** set up in 1901, BSI is a standard-setting organisation and the largest publisher of industrial and commercial standards. It operates across the world and publishes standards alongside the International Organization for Standardization (ISO).

*Table 1.2 Electrical units*

| Quantity | Usual symbol | Unit | Unit symbol |
|---|---|---|---|
| Voltage (PD or EMF) | V | Volt | V |
| Current | I | Ampere | A |
| Charge | Q | Coulomb | C |
| Resistance | R | Ohm | Ω |
| Capacitance | C | Farad | F |
| Battery capacity | Ah | Ampere hour | Ah |
| Frequency | f | Hertz | Hz |
| Power | P | Watt | W |

## 1.2.2 Electrical circuits

Electricity is conducted in metals as a result of the flow of free electrons from a higher to a lower potential (Figure 1.4). As the electrons move they collide with other atoms in their path; this causes the temperature of the metal conductor to increase.

In Figure 1.5 you can see a completed circuit with a battery. This is a closed circuit and the electrons are able to flow around the whole of the system. The electron flow is the electrical current.

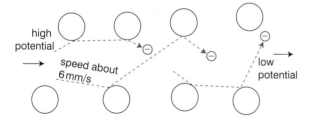

*Figure 1.4 Electron flow from high to low potential*

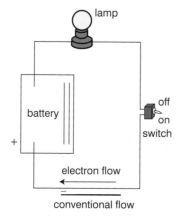

*Figure 1.5 Closed circuit*

## 1.2.3 Amperes

The **ampere (A)** is the unit of electric current. It was named after André-Marie Ampère, a French physicist (1775–1836). It is the measure of the rate of electron movement along a conductor. One ampere is equal to the quantity of electrons that have passed a given point when one coulomb passes that point in one second.

**Ampere (A):** the unit of electric current, or the rate of electron movement along a conductor; 1 A (ampere) of current represents a flow of electrical charge of 1 C/s (coulomb per second).

## 1.2.4 Watts

The **watt (W)** is a unit of power, the rate of work done (energy conversion). It was named after the Scottish engineer James Watt (1736–1819).

Power of 1 W is generated when a current of 1 A flows under the pressure (PD) of 1 V. Therefore:

$$\text{Power} = \frac{\text{Energy supplied (joules)}}{\text{Time (seconds)}}$$

This means:

$$\text{Power} = \frac{\text{Voltage} \times \text{Current} \times \text{Time}}{\text{Time}}$$

So:

Watts = Volts × Amperes

## 1.2.5 Ohm's law

In the 1820s the German physicist Georg Simon Ohm (1789–1854) began experimenting with the newly invented electrochemical cell (created by the Italian Alessandro Volta). Ohm managed to work out that there was a direct relationship between the PD (voltage) applied across a conductor and the resultant electric current. He discovered that the length of a wire in a circuit determines the current. When the length of the wire was increased, the current decreased. He came to the conclusion that, under constant temperature, the current in a conductor (the wire) is directly proportional to the PD between its ends – this became known as Ohm's law.

**Watt (W):** a unit of power, equivalent to a rate of 1 J/s (**joule** per second).

**Joule (J):** a unit of energy or work done. It is the energy expended by a force of 1 N (**newton**) when the force moves through a distance of 1 m; so 1 J = 1 Nm (newton meter).

**Newton (N):** a unit of force, equivalent to the force required to accelerate a mass of 1 kg at a rate of 1 m/s² (metres per second per second).

## 1.2.6 Resistance

Directly from Ohm's law we know about the relationship between PD, or voltage ($V$), and the current ($I$):

$$\frac{V}{I} = R$$

In the above equation, $R$ is the **resistance**, a constant that changes when the length (or the material) of the conductor is changed.

**Resistance**: measured in ohms ($\Omega$), it is the opposition to the current through a conductor.

Every material has some natural resistance to the flow of electron current. So far, no conductors have been created that do not have some amount of resistance. In order to compare materials for their resistivity, a 1 m length of 1 m² is used, as shown in Table 1.3.

*Table 1.3  Resistivity of selected materials*

| Material | Resistivity ($\Omega$m) at 20 °C |
|----------|-------------------------|
| Silver | $1.59 \times 10^{-8}$ |
| Copper | $1.7 \times 10^{-8}$ |
| Gold | $2.4 \times 10^{-8}$ |
| Aluminum | $2.8 \times 10^{-8}$ |
| Tungsten | $5.6 \times 10^{-8}$ |
| Iron | $10 \times 10^{-8}$ |
| Platinum | $11 \times 10^{-8}$ |
| Lead | $22 \times 10^{-8}$ |
| Nichrome | $150 \times 10^{-8}$ |
| Carbon | $3.5 \times 10^{5}$ |
| Polystyrene | $10^{7} - 10^{11}$ |
| Polyethylene | $10^{8} - 10^{9}$ |
| Glass | $10^{10} - 10^{14}$ |
| Hard rubber | $10^{13}$ |

Copper is the most common metal used for wiring and components as it is a relatively low-cost material that has a low resistance. Some other metals have lower resistance, but they are too expensive to be considered for most circuits. This is not to say that you will not see silver or gold components. It is also important to remember that, in most cases, when a material's temperature increases so too does its resistivity. This is of particular concern if cables are in an environment where the temperature will increase, such as under the carpet in a car where there is little airflow or in the engine compartment, which is subject to higher temperatures.

## 1.2.7 Circuit resistors

In the circuits found in a car there are a number of components that act like **resistors**. These components can carry out various functions, but they all affect voltage and current. Broadly speaking, resistors can be connected in **series**, **parallel** or a combination of the two.

**Resistor**: an electrical component whose main function is to provide resistance in a circuit.

As the name suggests, resistors act against the electrical current. When a current passes through a resistor, the voltage of the current drops as it flows across the terminals. Resistors are generally used in order to ensure that a known and safe current is flowing around the circuit.

**Series**: components are connected along a single path, which means that the same current is shared by all of them.

**Parallel**: components are connected so that the same voltage is applied to each of them.

In a car, many of the low-cost resistors are made from moulded carbon. Each of them can be identified by their resistance value and their tolerance.

Some resistors (or **potentiometers**) can be adjusted, which allows them to be set at a low value or up to the full rated value of the resistor. A potentiometer can be found in fuel level sensor units or pedal position sensors.

**Potentiometer**: a device for measuring an EMF. It does this by balancing it against the PD that is produced by passing a known current through a known variable resistance. In its role as a resistor it has an adjustable terminal.

### Resistance

In order to understand resistance, visualise a hose that is partially blocked with sand. The blockage slows down the flow of the water passing through the hose. This means that the blocked hose has more resistance to the water than a hose without a blockage. In order to force more water through the hose, you would have to increase the pressure by opening the tap connected to the hose. In the same way, some materials will have low resistance and will let electricity flow through them with ease, while others have a much higher resistance and a higher voltage (EMF) is needed to make the same current flow through them.

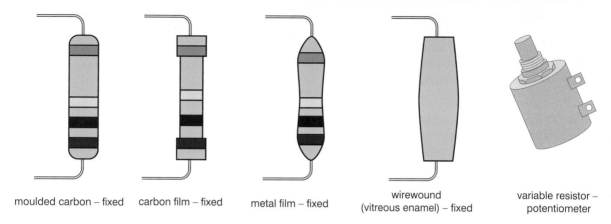

moulded carbon – fixed    carbon film – fixed    metal film – fixed    wirewound (vitreous enamel) – fixed    variable resistor – potentiometer

*Figure 1.6  Types of resistor*

As already mentioned, electrical circuits in cars can have a number of resistors. The resistance provided by these help to control the current into either a part of the circuit or into a component. Resistors are connected in series (Figure 1.7), in parallel (Figure 1.9) or in both (Figure 1.10).

Resistors that are placed in series means that the full current will pass through each of the resistors. In order to work out the total resistance in the circuit from the resistors all of the individual resistance values from each resistor have to be added up. Figure 1.7 shows a simple circuit with two resistors in series:

$$R = R_1 + R_2 = 2 + 4 = 6\,\Omega$$

$2\,\Omega$ $R_1$    $4\,\Omega$ $R_2$

conventional flow + to –

+    –

12 V
PD supply

*Figure 1.7  Resistors in series*

Using Ohm's law, we can work out the current in the circuit, assuming that the actual resistance in the cable or wiring is close to zero:

$$V = IR$$
$$I = \frac{V}{R}$$
$$\frac{12}{6} = 2\,A$$

If we position an **ammeter** and **voltmeter** to measure the current and the PD, we place the ammeter in series with the resistors. This means that the current has to pass through the ammeter no matter where we place the ammeter in the circuit. We will see that energy is expended as a result of driving the current through the resistors and that this causes the PD (voltage) to drop. Connecting the voltmeter will register that drop. In this particular case it will register 4 V, this means that the PD applied to $R_2$ is:

$$12\,V - 4\,V = 8\,V$$

**Ammeter**: an instrument that measures the current in amperes. There are various types and designs that allow the ammeter to be used to measure the amount and rate of current in a variety of circuits.

**Voltmeter**: an instrument that measures the voltage (PD) between two points in an electrical circuit. Originally they were called galvanometers. They are really ammeters, as they measure current rather than voltage. Current is measured in amperes but, using Ohm's law, they can be used to display a reading in volts.

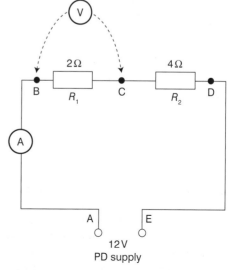

V

$2\,\Omega$ $R_1$    $4\,\Omega$ $R_2$

B    C    D

A

A    E

12 V
PD supply

*Figure 1.8  Voltage distribution*

Using the voltmeter, we can measure the voltages all around the circuit. This will show us how the voltage is distributed. This can be of particular value when checking a circuit to see if there are unexpected resistances which are often the cause of electrical faults.

When we connect resistors in parallel this ensures that the PD applied to each resistor is the same. The current that runs through an ammeter is shared between the two resistors. The amount of energy that flows through each of the resistors will depend on the resistance in that part of the circuit.

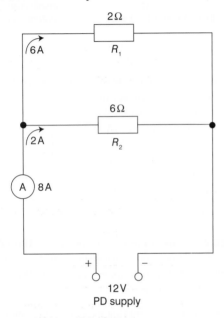

*Figure 1.9  Resistors in parallel*

Ohm's law applies again:

$$\text{Current at } R_1 = \frac{V}{R} = \frac{12}{2} = 6\,\text{A}$$

$$\text{Current at } R_2 = \frac{V}{R} = \frac{12}{6} = 2\,\text{A}$$

When calculated in this way, the current through each branch circuit can be found easily. Also it is possible to find the value of a single equivalent resistor ($R$), which would give the same total current as that which passes through both resistors. Working out the **equivalent resistance** is also straightforward:

$$\text{Equivalent } R = \frac{V}{I} = \frac{12}{8} = 1.5\,\Omega$$

**Equivalent resistance**: a single resistance that has the same value as two or more resistances in parallel.

In compound or series–parallel circuits, resistors or other components are connected in combination. In order to work out the current we have to imagine that the parallel resistors are replaced with a single resistor of equivalent value so that we can produce a single circuit (Figure 1.10).

The equivalent resistance of $R_1$ and $R_2$ is found by:

$$\frac{1}{R} = \frac{1}{R_1} + \frac{1}{R_2}$$

This can also be expressed as:

$$R = \frac{R_1 \times R_2}{R_1 + R_2} = \frac{16}{10} = 1.6\,\Omega$$

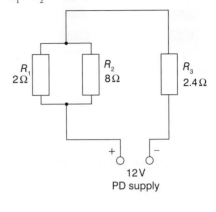

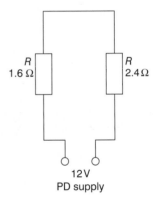

*Figure 1.10  Compound circuit*

The total resistance of the circuit is:

$$\text{Total } R = 1.6 + R_3 = 1.6 + 2.4 = 4\,\Omega$$

We can use Ohm's law in order to work out the current:

$$I = \frac{V}{R} = \frac{12}{4} = 3\,\text{A}$$

$R_1$ and $R_2$ share the 3 A current. The current divides according to the values of the resistors; the higher the value the smaller the current:

$$\text{Current at } R_1 = \frac{R_2}{R_1 + R_2} \times I = \frac{24}{10} = 2.4\,\text{A}$$

$$\text{Current at } R_2 = \frac{R_1}{R_1 + R_2} \times I = 2 \times \frac{3}{10} = \frac{6}{10} = 0.6\,\text{A}$$

By using this technique it is possible to examine complex circuits. Normally, even the most complex circuits are only a collection of simple circuits (sub-circuits) that have been connected together. By examining each of them in turn it is possible to determine the current and the voltage readings.

## 1.2.8 Circuit terms

### Insulated return

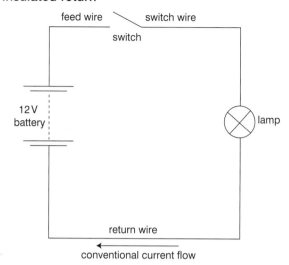

*Figure 1.11  Insulated return circuit for supply current*

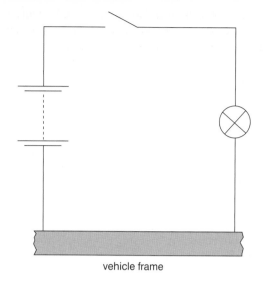

*Figure 1.12  Earth return circuit*

Figure 1.11 shows a simple circuit that connects a lamp to a battery. It has a switch to control the supply of electricity from the battery to the lamp via a 'feed wire'. To complete the circuit, the cable joining the lamp to the battery acts as a return for the 'supply current'. The term 'insulated return' is used whenever insulated cable provides the return path for the current.

### Earth return

In cars, few circuits look like Figure 1.11 as the feed wires supply components with current via switches and the return path is routed through the vehicle frame. In this case the vehicle frame or 'earth' provides the return path for the current (Figure 1.12). By not having a completely wired circuit, the amount of cabling required in the car is halved, cutting costs and weight. It also reduces the complexity of the overall wiring for the car and tends to mean that the electric circuitry as a whole is more reliable.

However, care must be taken as the feed wire could be compromised by abrasion as the wires rub against the metallic framework of the body of the car. This will conduct the supply current to earth and risk starting a fire. So most vehicles have an earth return system to reduce the likelihood of short circuits and improve safety. Exceptions include special-purpose vehicles with a high fire risk, such as petrol tankers, which use an insulated return layout (Figure 1.13) instead, to provide maximum protection.

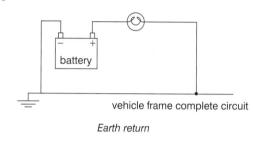

*Earth return*

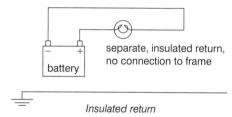

*Insulated return*

*Figure 1.13  Simple earth and insulated return circuit*

### Earth polarity

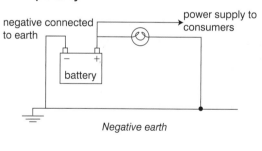

*Negative earth*

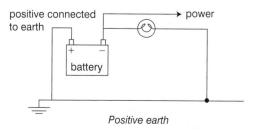

*Positive earth*

*Figure 1.14  Positive and negative earth systems*

Earthing connections also need to take polarity into account. In the majority of cases, the negative connection is connected to earth ('negative earth'). So all live cables have the same potential as the battery itself (12V for cars) and the earth connection will be 0V. The PD between the live cable and the body frame of the car is 12V (Figure 1.14).

## 1.2.9 Circuit faults

The failure of an electrical circuit is often caused by either open or short circuits. A complete circuit is needed if current is to flow around the system. An open circuit exists when the circuit is interrupted, either intentionally or unintentionally. A switch 'opens' the circuit by breaking the supply wire and a similar effect is produced when either a poor terminal connection or a broken cable stops the current.

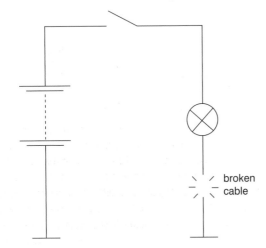

broken cable

*Figure 1.15  Open circuit*

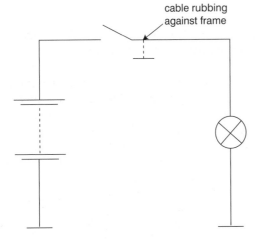

cable rubbing against frame

*Figure 1.16  Short circuit*

When the feed or switch wire insulation is damaged and the conductor touches the metal frame, some or all of the current will take this 'easy' path to earth. This alternative path offers the current a short path back to the battery, so the term 'short circuit' is used to describe this condition (Figure 1.16). The extent of the short-to-earth (i.e. the resistance of the alternative path), governs the PD that is left to act on the lamp in Figure 1.16. As the resistance in the short circuit path is reduced, the PD across the lamp is also reduced so the effect of the voltage reduction will be a proportional decrease in the lamp brilliance. A 'dead short' describes a very low resistance path to earth. When this happens, the very high current that results will soon make the cable glow red-hot. This melts the plastic covering of the cable and often starts a fire. With the insulation on fire the wiring could be destroyed, probably beyond repair. The common remedy to avoid this is to have a current-limiting device (fuse or circuit breaker), which effectively protects the wiring system from the worst damage that could be caused by a short circuit.

## 1.3    Magnetism and electromagnetism

### 1.3.1 Magnetism

As long ago as 600BC it was known that lodestone would always point in one direction when it was suspended. The name **magnet** was derived from the place where this magnetic iron was discovered – Magnesia in Asia. Because of its directional capabilities, the two ends of a magnet were called 'north' and 'south'. Perhaps the name 'north-seeking' would have been more appropriate in view of the fact that the Earth acts as a large magnet itself.

Later discoveries showed that the magnetic effect of lodestone was due to the iron deposits in the stone. Iron can be strongly magnetised, so this metal, along with nickel and cobalt, is called **ferro-magnetic**. While steel is also ferro-magnetic, it is more difficult to magnetise, although it retains its magnetism far better than iron.

**Magnet**: an object or device that gives off an external magnetic field. The magnetic field applies a force over a distance to magnets, electrical currents, circuits, or magnetic materials. Magnetism can be caused by electrical currents.

**Ferro-magnetic**: materials that retain their magnetic properties when the magnetic field is removed, such as iron and nickel.

A magnet made from a metal that retains its magnetism is called a permanent magnet (PM). Today, special steel alloys containing cobalt, nickel or aluminium are used to make strong PMs. Metals having no iron content (i.e. non-ferrous metals) are commonly described as being non-magnetic. However, some of these materials do show slight magnetic properties when exposed to a very powerful magnet.

Iron filings scattered on a sheet of paper placed over a magnet (Figure 1.17) form a pattern due to the presence of a magnetic field. This is an invisible region around a magnet that produces an external force on ferro-magnetic objects. The iron filings are more concentrated towards the ends of the magnet, so this shows that the field is strongest at these points. The two ends of the magnet are its 'poles': north pole (N) and south pole (S).

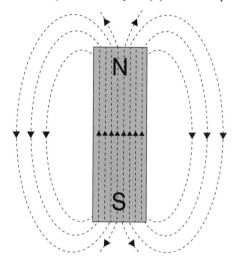

Figure 1.17 *Lines of force around a bar magnet*

The iron fillings arrange themselves to form a series of lines that extend from one pole to the other; these are known as 'lines of force'.

When a magnet is moved towards a second suspended magnet, the 'like' poles (e.g. N and N) repel one another, and the 'unlike' poles (N and S) attract one another (Figure 1.18). When this experiment is carried out under a sheet of paper containing iron filings, it is seen that the unlike poles of the magnets combine together to make a larger magnet and, as a result, the lines of force pass directly from one magnet to the other. This action produces an external force that makes it difficult to hold the magnets apart.

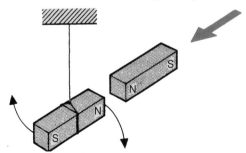

Figure 1.18 *Action when two opposing poles are brought together*

An opposite effect results when either N and N or S and S are brought together. In this case, the field of one magnet opposes the field of the other magnet and observation of the filings show that the lines of force are bent as the magnets come together. The external force pushing

the two magnets apart is related to the 'bending' of the lines of force; the greater the field distortion, the larger the magnetic force produced. The direction of a line of force can be found by using a small compass, which is a magnet pivoted at the centre for rotation purposes. By positioning the compass in various places in the field, the lines of force can be mapped out (Figure 1.19).

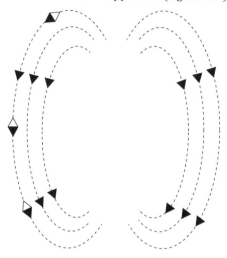

Figure 1.19 *Mapping a magnetic field*

Lines of force passing from N to S indicate a region of magnetic activity around a magnet. This activity is produced by a **magnetic flux**. The presence of this magnetic region is detected by the effects it produces. Sometimes it is said that magnetic flux flows around the magnet from the N pole to the S pole, where it then passes internally through the magnet to return to the N pole. This statement suggests movement but, unlike electricity, no flow actually takes place.

## 1.3.2 Electromagnetism

**Magnetic flux density** is the strength of a magnetic field at a given point. It is measured by the force that the field exerts on a conductor through which a given current is passed. A ferro-magnetic material, placed in a magnetic field (Figure 1.20), provides an easier path for the magnetic flux than through air. An iron frame concentrates the flux where it is required and gives an increased flux density. Iron accepts a magnetic flux easier than air, so iron is said to have a higher permeability than air.

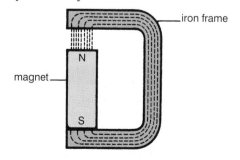

Figure 1.20 *Iron frame concentrates flux*

**Magnetic flux**: the lines of force around a magnet, measured in webers (Wb). A change in flux of 1 Wb/s (weber per second) induces an EMF of 1 V.

**Magnetic flux density**: the rate of flow of a magnetic field, shown as a ratio of the magnetic flux relative to the area. This is measured in tesla (T).

Magnetic **reluctance** is similar to resistance in an electrical circuit. In Figure 1.21 we can see that the air gap is reduced if the poles of a magnet are 'bridged' by a piece of iron.

*Figure 1.21  Reluctance*

**Reluctance**: the resistance of a material to a magnetic field. Reluctance is measured in henry (H), where 1 H is the reluctance of a circuit in which a rate of change of current of 1 A/s (ampere per second) creates an EMF of 1 V.

As current is passed through a conductor, a magnetic field is created around the conductor. The direction of the current determines the direction of the magnetic flux. The simplest way to visualise this is shown using Maxwell's screw rule (Figure 1.22).

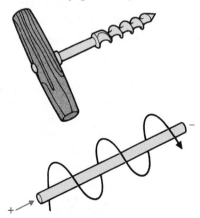

*Figure 1.22  Maxwell's screw rule*

## 1.3.3 Electromagnetic induction

In 1819 Oersted discovered that magnetism could be produced by an electric current. This would lead to some great breakthroughs in our understanding. However, it was not until 1831 that Michael Faraday showed that electricity could be produced from magnetism. He carried out a series of experiments in which he demonstrated the principles that allowed generators and many automotive parts to be developed.

### Faraday's discovery

British physicist and chemist Michael Faraday, born at the end of the 18th century, was a great inventor, known for his work on electromagnetic induction, electrolysis and the invention of the electric motor. He discovered electromagnetic induction in 1831 using an induction ring; he discovered that he could generate electricity in a wire by using the electromagnetic properties of a current in another wire. He created the first electric transformer using the induction ring. He attached a pair of wires using a sliding contact on to a copper disc and found that he could produce a continuous direct current by rotating a magnet's poles; in effect this was the first generator.

Faraday noticed that when he inserted a magnet into a coil, the needle on a **galvanometer** moved; when he took the magnet out, the needle went the other way (Figure 1.23). What this showed was that the current was only created when the magnet was moving. He also noted that the direction of the current depended on the direction he moved the magnet.

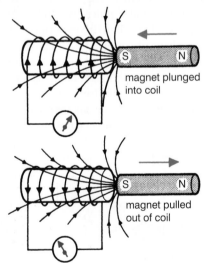

*Figure 1.23  Electromagnetic induction*

## Resistance

In an electromagnet, electrical charge will flow through a wire conductor (coil). The magnetic flux can be concentrated by a soft iron core in the centre. The coil is tightly wound so that the flux bends to create a common pattern around the core. The direction of the current determines the polarity of the magnet. The strength of the magnet is determined by the amount of current through the coil and the number of turns in that coil.

Galvanometer: a galvanometer is a type of ammeter used to measure small levels of current flow. It is an analogue device with a needle that deflects a set amount depending on the level of current detected.

This phenomenon is called electromagnetic induction. It showed that an EMF was induced in the coil when there was a change in magnetic flux close to the coil. Faraday could then prove that the strength of the EMF depended on the number of turns in the coil, the actual strength of the magnetic flux and the relative speed of movement between the coil and the flux.

## Mutual induction

Faraday went on to experiment with iron rings to show that a coil could be used to replace a magnet and still induce current in another coil. He connected the primary circuit (P) to a battery and the secondary circuit (S) to a galvanometer (Figure 1.24).

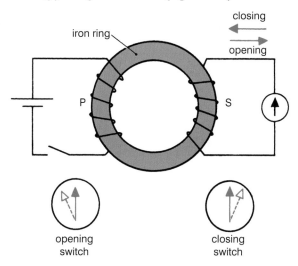

Figure 1.24 Mutual induction

Faraday saw that the galvanometer's needle moved every time the circuit was completed or broken, moving in opposite directions each time. He discovered that the induced current in the second coil depended on the strength of the primary current, the ratio of turns in the primary and secondary coils, and the speed of the collapse of the magnetic field.

This discovery became known as 'mutual induction'. It was an important experiment as it is the fundamental principle behind transformers and ignition coils.

## Lenz's law

Meanwhile, Lenz was looking at the direction of the induced current that came about from electromagnetic induction. He found that when a magnet was put into a coil, an induced current was created. The current created a magnetic field with a polarity opposite to the magnet; in effect the induced current was creating a north pole, which repelled the magnet.

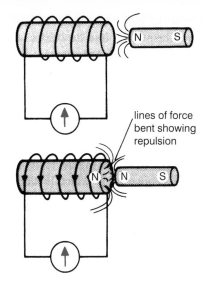

Figure 1.25 Apparatus for showing Lenz's law

Faraday's experiment into mutual induction matched Lenz's law. He noted that when the switch was closed, the magnetic field grew and produced an EMF in the primary circuit. This opposed the current that was flowing into the circuit and slowed down the growth of the current in the primary circuit (Figure 1.25).

## Self-induction

Faraday continued his experiments and discovered that when he opened the switch, the magnetic field collapsed and induced a current in the primary circuit. This caused arcing at the switch contacts. This phenomenon became known as self-induction. As a result of this, capacitors were connected across the contact breaker points in coil-ignition systems. This allows the EMF to be absorbed and the arcing is reduced. The net result is that the system lasts longer and has a better performance.

## Induction in a straight conductor

Faraday also discovered that EMF is created when the conductor is moved through a magnetic field. This can be seen in Figure 1.26. Faraday's discovery was later developed by Fleming who looked at the relationships between the direction of the magnetic field, the current and the conductor.

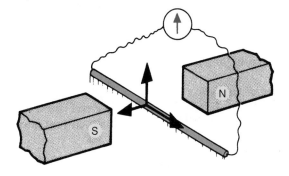

Figure 1.26 Induction in a straight conductor

## Fleming's right-hand and left-hand rules

Fleming's right-hand rule (Figure 1.27) has applications for dynamos and generators. It states:

'When the thumb and first two fingers of the right hand are all set at right angles to one another, then the forefinger points in the direction of the field, the thumb to the direction of the motion and the second finger points to the direction of the current.'

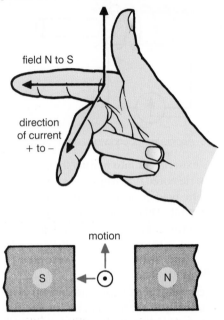

*Figure 1.27 Fleming's right-hand rule (dynamo rule)*

It is possible to summarise this:

- thu**M**b         **M**otion
- fore**F**inger     **F**ield
- se**C**ond finger   **C**urrent

Fleming's left-hand rule (Figure 1.28) has applications for motors. This gives the relationship between the field, current and motion. Similar fingers to those in the right-hand rule are used to give the directions:

- fore**F**inger     **F**ield
- thu**M**b         **M**otion
- se**C**ond finger   **C**urrent

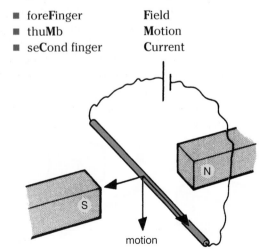

*Figure 1.28 Fleming's left-hand rule (motor rule)*

## Kirchhoff

Kirchhoff's two laws on current circuits are also basic principles. Kirchhoff was also working in the 19th century and he devised ways to look at the current in complex direct current networks that had EMF sources as well as load resistances.

His current law states that at any junction in an electrical circuit the total current that flows towards the junction is equal to the total current that is flowing away from that junction (Figure 1.29). This meant that:

$$I_1 + I_2 - I_3 - I_4 - I_5 = 0$$

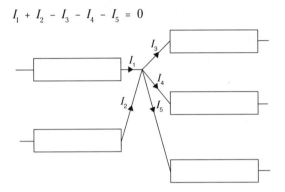

*Figure 1.29 Kirchhoff's current law*

His voltage law stated that in a closed-loop network the total of all of the drops in voltage around the loop are equal to the EMF that results and acts on that loop (Figure 1.30). This means:

$$E_1 - E_2 = IR_1 + IR_2 + IR_3$$

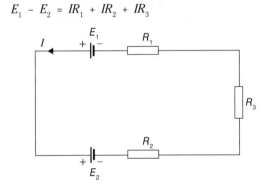

*Figure 1.30 Kirchhoff's voltage law*

## Alternating current

There are two types of current, direct current (DC) and alternating current (AC). A simple AC generator (or dynamo) consists of two magnetic poles of a field magnet and a loop conductor, which is rotated in the magnetic field that is generated (Figure 1.31).

Each end of the loop has a slip ring, which makes contact with a carbon brush. When the conductor loop is rotated in the magnetic field an EMF is generated. It is this force that drives the current around the circuit. The circuit consists of the loop, the slip rings, the carbon brushes and the connection wires to the resistor. It is the slip rings and the brushes that allow the loop to rotate while passing the current into the non-moving part of the circuit.

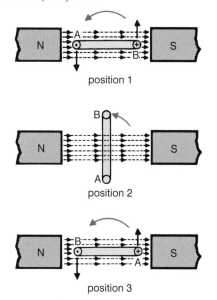

Figure 1.31 Simple dynamo

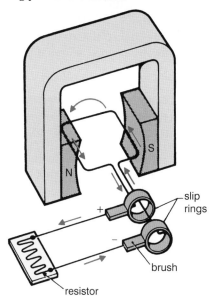

position 1

position 2

position 3

Figure 1.32 Coil position and current

Using Fleming's right-hand rule, the direction of the current can be worked out when the loop is in position 1. The arrows and symbols in Figure 1.32 show this.

When the loop rotates (position 2), the EMF output also falls; there is no output. When the loop rotates to reach position 3, the flux is cut by the conductors and the EMF is induced in the loop. This time, the EMF has an opposite polarity to the one it had in position 1. The current also flows in the opposite direction. In position 3, it conforms to Fleming's left-hand rule.

The EMF of the generator is shown in the graph in Figure 1.33. It can be seen that the EMF will cause the current to flow in one direction and then reverse

to flow in the opposite direction. This is an AC (alternating current).

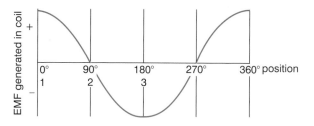

Figure 1.33 EMF generated in a coil

## AC circuits

If an AC is plotted on a graph comparing EMF and angle (Figure 1.34), it is possible to see that a curve is created, known as a sine wave (or sinusoidal wave).

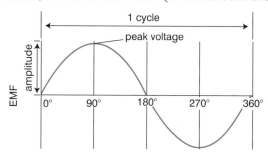

Figure 1.34 Sine wave

The graph shows that each complete turn produces a repeating pattern called a 'cycle'. The time it takes to create this cycle is called 'periodic time'. The maximum peak (positive or negative) on the $y$ axis is called the 'amplitude'. The 'peak-to-peak value' is the total distance from the positive to the negative peak.

Frequency is the number of complete cycles that take place each second; it is measured in hertz (Hz). So:

$$\text{Frequency} = \frac{1}{\text{Periodic time } (T)}$$

You will encounter ACs in power transmission networks. They are used to either step up or step down voltages in order to reduce the current and losses. In homes in Europe the AC is 230 V 50 Hz, but for motor vehicles the current flow must be unidirectional. A process known as rectification can allow the AC to be unidirectional or DC. The process involves converting the alternating waveforms so that the EMF is always in the same direction (Figure 1.35)

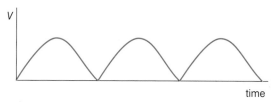

Figure 1.35 Full-wave rectification

### Root mean square (RMS) voltage

The peak value of an AC sine wave occurs twice in one cycle (once in each direction of flow). Therefore, the current flow is at a maximum, say 12 V, only twice, so there is less energy dissipated compared to a DC EMF, which would be at a constant voltage of 12 V.

Root mean square (RMS) values of sine waves are used to compare the AC and DC sine wave voltages. The AC is directly comparable to the DC in terms of power. The following example shows this:

RMS value of sine wave = Peak voltage × 0.707

Mean value of sine wave = Peak voltage × 0.637

The EMF provides a proportional current in a connected circuit with a given resistance ($R$). The power lost (as heat) can be found by:

Power (W) = $VI$ (or $I^2R$)

A multimeter will show the RMS value of a sine wave voltage. The RMS is used because the normal average voltage value of the sine wave is zero, regardless of the height of the peak voltage. A digital oscilloscope is also useful as it can measure sine waves and other more complex waves.

The concept of **impedance** is also important when analysing AC circuits. This is the opposition found in a circuit to the flow. A back EMF is caused by self-induction. This develops when the direction of the current is reversed. This effect prevents the AC from building up to that which would be obtained from a DC supply. Impedance of a circuit is the opposition it gives to the flow of the AC. It is expressed in ohms and calculated by:

Impedance = $\dfrac{\text{Voltage}}{\text{Current}}$

The frequency of the AC affects the impedance of the circuit. The current delivered by the conductor coil of a simple generator is a single-phase AC (Figure 1.36). This means that the output EMF and current corresponds to a single wave. It is a simple reversing current.

**Impedance**: a more general term for resistance. It is the total opposition to AC flow presented by a circuit. It is measured in ohms and is commonly used to rate input and output characteristics of components.

However, higher power is often needed and the single phase is not efficient enough, so a multi-phase supply is used. In practice this means three-phase; three conductor coils, each with a single-phase EMF (Figure 1.38), are connected with the peak voltage spaced at 120°. The net result is a smoother EMF, which has less ripples and a much higher current density.

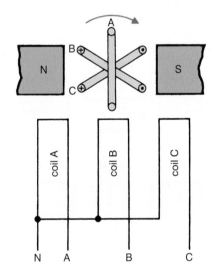

Figure 1.37 Three coils connected

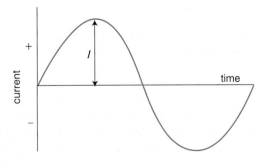

Figure 1.36 AC waveform

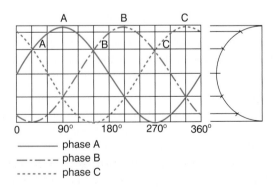

Figure 1.38 Three-phase output

## 1.4 Electromagnetic equipment

In an electrical machine the current is not only being induced in windings, but also in the components and the electrical frames. The conductor coils are normally wound on a soft iron former called an 'armature'. The iron concentrates the magnetic flux where it is needed and forms a part of the magnetic 'circuit'. If the cylindrical armature were made in one piece, rotation of the armature would cause an eddy current to be generated within its iron core. The direction of flow of the current can be obtained from Fleming's right-hand rule; Figure 1.39 shows how the current makes a path around the armature.

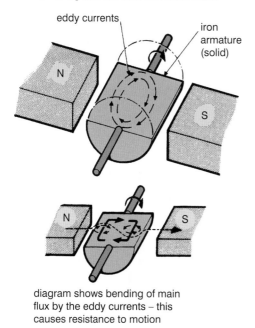

diagram shows bending of main flux by the eddy currents – this causes resistance to motion

*Figure 1.39  Eddy current*

In addition to the problem of heat created by the dissipation of electrical energy, the magnetic effect of the eddy current makes it more difficult to revolve the armature. This is because the eddy current sets up its own magnetic flux, as described in Lenz's law. Since the N pole of the flux from the eddy current is moving towards the N pole of the main field, repulsion action results.

Electric machines should have a high efficiency, so steps are taken to avoid the internal energy loss due to eddy currents. This is achieved by making the armature, or similar core devices, from thin iron stampings (Figure 1.40). Each is coated with varnish for insulation purposes.

Eddy currents can be usefully employed in a number of ways. They can be used to damp the needle movement of a test meter and as a brake retarder

to resist the rotation of a disc connected to the road wheels. The drag on the disc of a retarder is produced when the main field is energised; the stronger the field, the greater the drag on the disc.

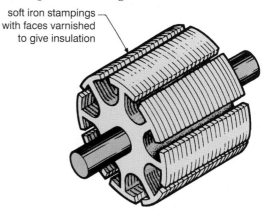

*Figure 1.40  Armature construction*

### 1.4.1 Transformer

A transformer is a device for stepping-up or stepping-down the voltage. It consists of two windings, a primary and a secondary, which are wound around a laminated iron core, as shown in Figure 1.41. If a higher voltage is required from the secondary, the secondary winding must have more turns than the primary. The relationship between turns and voltage is:

$$\frac{\text{Secondary voltage}}{\text{Primary voltage}} = \frac{\text{Secondary turns}}{\text{Primary turns}}$$

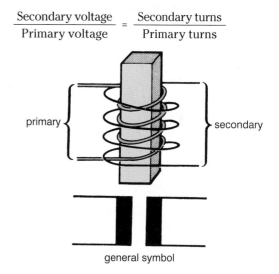

general symbol

*Figure 1.41  Transformer*

It has been stated that induction must be accompanied by a change in magnetic flux, so providing the primary receives an AC the output from the secondary will be AC at a voltage governed by the turns ratio, due to mutual induction. A transformer does not give 'something for nothing': an increase in voltage is balanced by a proportional decrease in current. Energy is lost in the iron core because of eddy currents, and the resistance of the copper also causes loss of energy by heating.

## 1.4.2 Simple DC motor

When current is supplied by a battery to a conductor placed in a magnetic flux, a force is produced that will move the conductor (Figure 1.42).

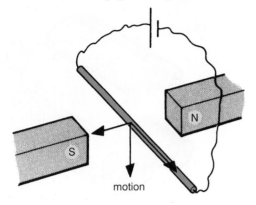

*Figure 1.42 Force on conductor*

The cause of the turning motion can be seen when the lines of magnetic force are mapped (Figure 1.43). This shows a current being passed through a conductor and the formation of a magnetic field around the conductor. This field causes the main field to be bent and the repulsion of the two opposing fields produces a force that gives the motion.

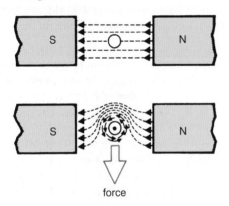

*Figure 1.43 Bending of main field*

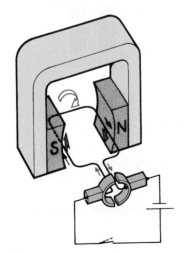

*Figure 1.44 DC motor*

Figure 1.44 shows the construction of a simple DC motor. The conductor is looped to form a coil and the ends of this coil are connected to a commutator (a device to reverse the current in the coil each cycle as it rotates). Carbon brushes rub on the commutator to supply the coil with current. Since the two sides of the coil in this construction act as two conductors, a greater turning moment (torque) is achieved. In Figure 1.43 the field distortion is shown and, if the lines of force in this diagram are considered to be rubber bands, then the principle of the motor movement can be seen.

### 1.4.3 Hall effect devices

In 1879 Edward Hall discovered that when a magnet was placed perpendicular to the face of a flat current carrying conductor, a difference in potential appeared across the other edges of the conductor. This event is called the Hall effect and the PD produced across the edges is termed the Hall voltage. Figure 1.45 shows the principle of the Hall effect. In Figure 1.45a the vertical edges of the plate have equal potential so the voltmeter registers zero. But when the plate is placed in a magnetic field (Figure 1.45b), a PD across the edges is shown as a steady reading on the meter.

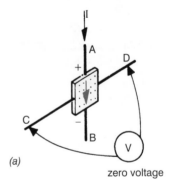

*(a)*

zero voltage

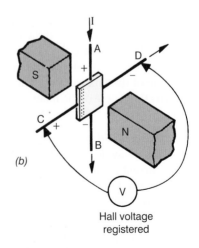

*(b)*

Hall voltage
registered

*Figure 1.45 Hall effect*

Hall voltage depends on the current flowing through the plate and on the strength of the magnetic field. When the current is constant, the Hall voltage is proportional to the field strength. Similarly, if the field strength is constant, the Hall voltage is proportional to the current flowing through the plate.

With common metals, such as copper, the Hall voltage is very low, but when a semiconductor is used a much higher voltage is achieved. The polarity of the plate edges depends on the type of semiconductor; a P-type has the opposite Hall voltage PD to an N-type. The magnetic field that gives the Hall effect does not act as a generator of energy; instead it acts in the form of a control or switch. An application of the Hall effect is for measuring the strength of a magnetic field.

## 1.4.4 Piezoelectric effect

In 1880 Pierre and Jacques Curie discovered a strange phenomenon that explained the interaction between the mechanical and electrical state in crystals. Some crystals had the property to exhibit electrical charges under certain mechanical loadings. At first, no one knew what to do with it or what it really meant. The discovery remained just that for some years until the practical applications became apparent in the 1950s. The charge amplifier was created in the 1950s and with it metal oxide semiconductor field effect transistors. This, in turn, led to the development of highly insulating materials such as Teflon. Piezoelectric sensors are now used everywhere.

What Pierre and Jacques had discovered was that tourmaline crystals, under pressure in particular directions, produced a reverse-poled electrical charge. This was proportional to the pressure that was being applied. They also discovered that quartz crystals created the same effect. The phenomenon became known as direct piezoelectric

effect (Figure 1.46). Today, it is used for sensors that measure pressure or acceleration.

There is also a reciprocal effect. The electrical field causes mechanical stresses in the crystals. The crystals actually alter in their physical size in proportion to the strength of the electrical field. When the crystals are subjected to a mechanical stress, charges on the surface of the piezoelectric material are generated. Electrodes can assess the effect. It is also the case that the charges do not remain: they leak away. Therefore piezoelectric materials are only useful for measuring dynamic or changing forces.

### Piezoelectric applications

Piezoelectric principles are used in sensors in order to measure the force or stress being applied to a material. It can be used to measure vibration. A combustion knock sensor measures the vibrations caused by an engine when it runs into detonation. It is likely that piezoelectric measurement will be used in sensors to measure combustion pressure. They would be ideal for this task as they are resistant to high temperatures as well as high pressure and forces found in the combustion chamber.

## 1.5  Measuring and test instruments

There is a huge range of different test equipment used in automotive work. Some of this equipment, such as multimeters, is used for basic fault finding. However, as vehicles become more technologically advanced, with on-board computer systems that provide diagnostic information, the computer is becoming an essential piece of equipment. Laptops or laptop notebooks can be used to read fault codes or display engine data, reducing the time it takes to identify and rectify a fault.

|  | Direct piezoelectric effect | Reciprocal piezoelectric effect |
|---|---|---|
| **Description** | A mechanical deformation of a piezoelectric body causes a charge in the electric polarisation that is proportional to the deformation. | An external electric Field E causes mechanical stresses proportional to the field, which alter the size of the piezo-crystal. |
|  | 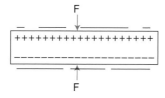 | 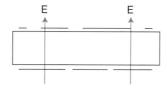 |
| **Application** | For measuring mechanical parameters, especially of forces, pressures and accelerations. | In ultrasonic and telecommunications engineering. |

*Figure 1.46 Piezoelectric effects*

## 1.5.1 Moving-coil meters

These are basic analogue electrical indicating devices that show the magnitude of what is being measured by means of a pointer moving along a scale.

Figure 1.47 shows the construction of this type of meter which resembles, in basic principle, the layout of a motor. There is a permanent magnet with two shaped pole pieces and between these is placed a fixed iron cylinder. This concentrates the magnetic field and makes the lines of force radiate from the cylinder centre.

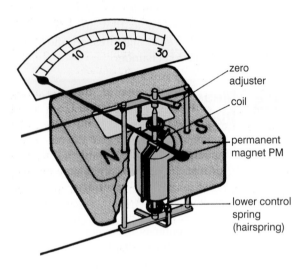

*Figure 1.47 Moving-coil meter*

The coil is wound on an aluminium former; this is pivoted on jewelled bearings and attached to a pointer, which registers on an evenly spaced scale. The actual number of turns of the coil and the gauge of the wire is governed by the purpose for which the instrument is to be used. By using an aluminium former, the damping effect of the eddy current allows the pointer to register a reading without oscillating to and fro. This 'dead beat' action is obtained by the opposition of the magnetic flux set up by the current induced into the former when it moves in the main field.

When current is passed through the coil (Figure 1.48), the flux distortion causes the coil to move. The angle of movement is controlled by two hairsprings, which are wound in opposite directions to compensate for thermal expansion. These control springs conduct the current to the coil and their strength governs the current required to give a full-scale deflection (FSD).

A moving-coil meter can be used only with DC and must be connected so as to give the correct polarity; terminals are marked + and –. This type of instrument is easily damaged by overload because excessive current damages the hairsprings.

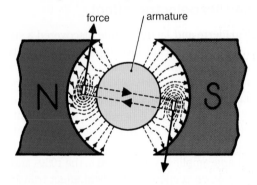

*Figure 1.48 Bending of magnetic flux by current*

## 1.5.2 Ammeters

Rather than scaling up a moving-coil meter to read amperes, which would result in a clumsy, inefficient meter, the moving-coil meter is modified to suit the range required by fitting a resistor of low value in parallel with the meter to shunt (by-pass) the major part of the current away from the meter (Figure 1.49).

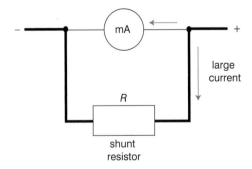

*Figure 1.49 Moving-coil ammeter*

By selecting a shunt resistor of suitable value, it is possible to vary the range of the meter to suit the application. The normal ammeter has an internally connected shunt to suit the range, but when this meter is to be used to measure a high current (e.g. a starter motor current of about 200 A) an external shunt may be fitted.

## 1.5.3 Voltmeters

The current flowing through a milliammeter is proportional to the PD, so by changing the scale it is possible to use the meter as a voltmeter. When a larger voltage is to be measured, a resistor is fitted in series with the meter to prevent damage from an excessive current. This high-value resistor, called a 'multiplier', is fitted internally and the meter is scaled accordingly (Figure 1.50).

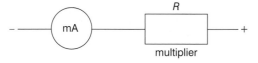

*Figure 1.50 Multiplier resistor for measuring voltage*

A voltmeter is used in parallel with a circuit component; it should have a high resistance across which the PD is to be measured, so as to give an accurate reading without influencing the circuit it is measuring.

## 1.5.4 Ohmmeters

Many multimeters incorporate a circuit for measuring the resistance of a component. To provide this feature, the milliammeter is switched into a circuit that incorporates a small battery and variable resistor (Figure 1.51). The zero on the ohms scale on the meter is set to coincide with the full deflection of the pointer. Before the instrument is used, the test leads are connected together and the variable resistor is adjusted to balance the battery voltage: this gives a zero reading on the ohms scale. After carrying out the initial setting, the test leads are connected to the resistance to be measured.

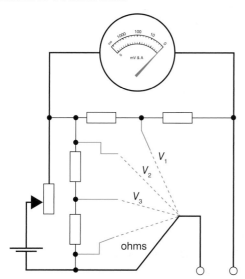

*Figure 1.51 Internal circuit of a multimeter*

The principle of the ohmmeter is based on Ohm's law ($R = V/I$). For a given voltage it is seen that the resistance

is inversely proportional to the current (i.e. as the current increases, the resistance decreases). By scaling the meter in the opposite direction to normal practice and calibrating the scale using known resistance values, it is possible to provide a meter that measures resistance in ohms. The range of an ohmmeter is increased by using a multi-point switch, which brings various multiplier resistors into the circuit.

## 1.5.5 Multimeters

Multimeters have the ability to measure:

- temperature, using a thermocouple input
- frequency, in the case of speed and pulse width
- dwell angle
- high currents, using shunts
- current, using inductive clamps
- rev count, with spark high-tension (HT) lead pick-up.

Ohmmeters are used to measure resistance, ammeters are used to measure current, and voltmeters are used to measure the voltage or PD between two points. However, multimeters (or AVO – amperes, volts and ohms) can combine all these functions (and others) in a single piece of measuring equipment.

Usually there is a single moving-coil measuring element that has all of the shunts, the multipliers and a battery. A dial is used to determine what is to be measured and in what range. There are connector sockets for test leads; a common return lead is used, but the red input lead is connected to different input jacks, depending on what is being measured (amperes, volts or ohms). The multimeter is also likely to have an internal fuse for protection.

## 1.5.6 Digital multimeters

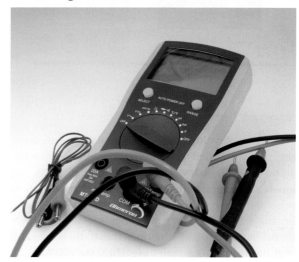

*Figure 1.52 Digital multimeter*

Moving-coil multimeters have all been replaced with digital versions (Figure 1.52). These devices are much easier to read and do not suffer from some of the potential errors that analogue meters can be prone to, such as the parallax error caused by the viewing angle.

The ease of use of digital multimeters has made them very popular for testing automotive systems. Compared with the analogue type, the modern digital multimeter, with a $10\,M\Omega$ high internal resistance (input impedance) and low operating voltage (3.5 V), draws less current from the device being tested so the meter is less likely to damage delicate computer circuits.

### 1.5.7 Oscilloscopes

Oscilloscopes are useful when analysing the complex waveforms common in automotive electrical systems, so can be of great help in diagnostic tests. Newer digital oscilloscopes can store data and also offer event trigger measurement and freeze frame. The digital versions can be linked to other handheld analysers.

Oscilloscopes are used for detailed analysis of the behaviour of a circuit. They used to be large pieces of equipment, used in laboratories; the original machines were analogue and had a large cathode ray tube, just like an old television (Figure 1.53). The problem was that they were too expensive for the car repair business and so were rarely used.

*Figure 1.53 Typical analogue scope*

With the development of digital oscilloscopes, the price dropped and their use increased in the automotive industry. The new screen displays are much clearer than the analogue versions and it is possible to freeze the screen display so that it can be analysed. The larger machines are still not ideal for automotive repair situations due to their size and that they often need mains electrical supply. Also, as they are not designed for the automotive industry, but for laboratory work, they are quite delicate.

However, as oscilloscopes are important pieces of test equipment for modern cars (most modern engine systems cannot be fully evaluated without one), handheld versions have been developed that are designed specifically for the industry (Figures 1.54 and 1.55).

*Figure 1.54 Handheld oscilloscope*

These new handheld versions are capable of a wide range of work. They have a 12 V battery (either their own or can be run from a vehicle), harnesses, adapters and clamps for HT and current measurement. Most importantly, they can also be hooked up to a computer in order to store data and analyse it.

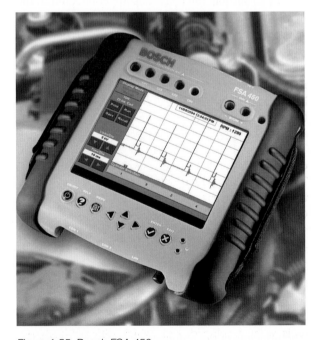

*Figure 1.55 Bosch FSA 450*

## 1.5.8 Logic probes

Logic probes were originally designed for the electronics industry, but they have clear applications for automotive repairs. Logic probes sense pulses and identify them as either being logic 1 (high) or logic 0 (low). The probe emits a bleep or shows a LED indication.

The logic probe is, therefore, ideal for checking signals from electronic systems or sensors. It can be applied in situations where there is a special voltage level, such as in the case of complementary metal oxide semiconductors (CMOS) or indeed transistor–transistor logic (TTL) devices (Figure 1.56).

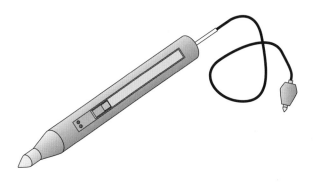

*Figure 1.56  TTL/CMOS logic probe*

Logic probes are routinely used to test camshaft position sensors, frequency signals, anti-lock braking system (ABS) wheel speeds, and a host of other pulses from both AC and DC speed sensors. Logical probes have high internal resistance, which makes them a safe option when being used on potentially sensitive circuits and components.

## 1.5.9 Fault code readers and scan tools

Fault code readers and scan tools (Figure 1.57) are also handheld devices. They are designed to be connected to the engine's electronic diagnostic interface. Once they are connected they can be used for a variety of purposes. The unit can access the fault memory to find stored fault codes, and erase them once they have been rectified. The unit can also transfer live data from sensors and the internal electronic control unit (ECU) as the engine operates, to aid fault finding. It is also possible for it to capture data during an event that causes an intermittent fault. Additionally, the units can be used to return settings to factory defaults or to program new parts.

In the past, many vehicle manufacturers developed their own scan tools that could only be used for their own makes and models. More recently, multi-use scan tools were developed, with which different software cartridges could be used, specific to the make and model. However, makes and models are so different that these multi-use scan tools still proved quite limited.

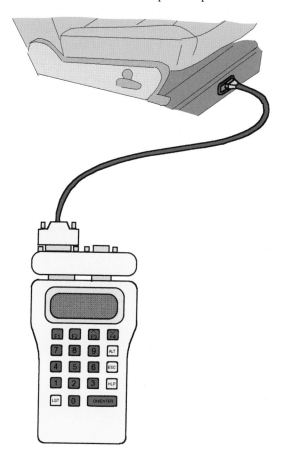

*Figure 1.57  Scan tool*

With the development of on-board diagnostics (OBD), steps were taken to introduce a standardisation in terms of data protocol and connection interfaces. This led to the development of truly universal scan tools, which are capable of accessing the fault memory to read and reset the fault codes. Recent legislation has also meant that these fault codes are being standardised. This allows anyone to understand the fault codes and reset the ECU. This legislation and the appropriate scan tools are designated OBD II certified (see page 205). In fact, this now means that, with the software freely available, any laptop is capable of being used as a diagnostic tool.

| 1.6 | **Resistance and capacitance** |
|-----|-------------------------------|

Another part of basic electronics is an understanding of resistance and capacitance. For the automotive industry, this means understanding the purpose and the functions of resistors and capacitors. A resistor is used to either divide voltage or to change it (by limiting current). A capacitor is basically a device that is used to store electricity for a limited period of time.

## 1.6.1 Fixed and variable resistors

### Fixed resistors

As we have seen, resistors are used in electrical systems to divide the voltage or to limit the current by changing it. In practical terms, the automotive industry tends to have two particular types of resistor, the fixed resistor and the variable resistor (Figure 1.58).

A fixed resistor is a low-cost alternative that is made from moulded carbon. There are three main types: wirewound, carbon film and metal oxide. There is a wide range of fixed resistors available on the market, from $10\,\Omega$ to $1\,M\Omega$. British Standards have set codes for each type of resistor in order to identify their resistance value and their tolerance. The most commonly used resistor values are shown in Table 1.4.

*Table 1.4 Commonly used resistor values*

| Resistance value | BS 1852 code |
|---|---|
| $0.47\,\Omega$ | R47 |
| $1\,\Omega$ | 1R0 |
| $4.7\,\Omega$ | 4R7 |
| $47\,\Omega$ | 47R |
| $100\,\Omega$ | 100R |
| $1\,k\Omega$ | 1K0 |
| $10\,k\Omega$ | 10K0 |
| $1\,M\Omega$ | 1M0 |

Letters after the resistance value indicate the tolerance of the resistor, as shown in Table 1.5.

*Table 1.5 Tolerance codes for resistors*

| Tolerance | Tolerance code |
|---|---|
| ±1% | F |
| ±2% | G |
| ±5% | J |
| ±10% | K |
| ±20% | M |

### Variable resistors and potentiometers

Variable resistors are also known as potentiometers. The idea is that they can be adjusted from a low value of resistance up to their fully rated value. In most cases these are either wirewound or carbon track. Variable resistors can be adjusted using a knob on a control panel or preset using a screwdriver. Each resistor is rated according to its maximum resistance and power.

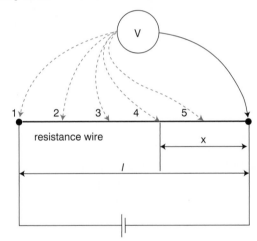

*Figure 1.59 Potentiometer*

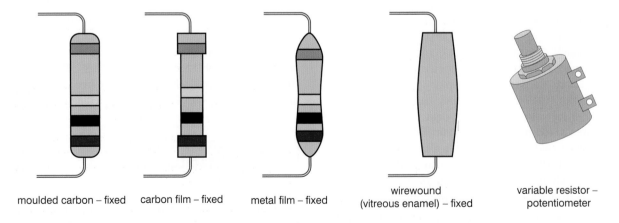

moulded carbon – fixed    carbon film – fixed    metal film – fixed    wirewound (vitreous enamel) – fixed    variable resistor – potentiometer

*Figure 1.58 Types of resistor*

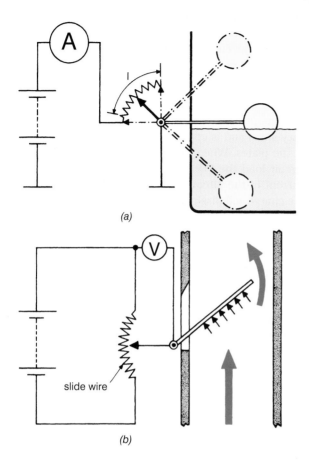

*(a)*

*(b)*

*Figure 1.60 Use of potentiometers*

Typical uses in the automotive industry include fuel level sensor (Figure 1.60a), throttle position sensor (Figure 1.60b) or pedal position sensor.

## 1.6.2 Resistors in series and parallel

You will find various components of an electrical circuit that will act just like resistors. Voltage drops and power loses are inevitable in some cases, but undesirable. Sometimes, the resistance deliberately controls the current in a part of the circuit or a component, or has a specific purpose, such as the resistance in a bulb's filament that causes heating to illuminate that bulb. It is important to have an understanding of the uses of resistors in circuits as well as appreciating the fact that they can be connected in various ways.

### Potential divider

Resistors in series and in parallel were covered earlier on pages 6–8. A circuit with a pair of resistors in series is called a potential divider. In fact, circuits such as this can be made up from a number of elements, with the voltages being taken from each of the connections between the elements (Figure 1.61).

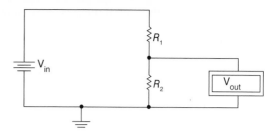

*Figure 1.61 Simple potential divider*

In order to work out the voltage output we carry out the following calculation:

$$V_{out} = R_2 \times \frac{V_{in}}{R_1} + R_2$$

This type of circuit could be used to provide a varying voltage signal as a result of a change in resistance. It is likely that you would find these in a coolant temperature sensor circuit with a thermistor, or in a throttle pedal position sensor circuit with a potentiometer.

### Bridge circuits

A bridge circuit (Figure 1.62) is used to find out the value of an unknown resistor. It can detect changes in resistance in a part of the circuit.

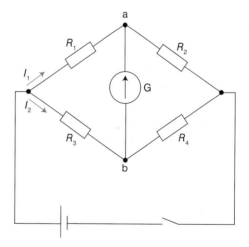

*Figure 1.62 Wheatstone bridge*

The idea is that the four resistors form four separate arms of the bridge. Current is passed across the bridge ($I_1$ and $I_2$). A centre zero voltmeter then measures the voltage across the bridge circuit (a to b). The resistance of the relevant section compared to the alternative section determines the currents in the two paths ($I_1$ and $I_2$).

Assuming that the resistors in the bridge are the same, the voltage (a to b) should be in balance. In other words:

$$\frac{R_1}{R_2} = \frac{R_3}{R_4}$$

A voltage change will show up if there is any change in resistance values of any of the resistors. This type of circuit is often used to test stress in materials. It is also used for hot-wire air-mass flow meters. The bridge circuit is used in this case as part of the measurement and compensation circuitry.

## 1.6.3 Capacitors

A capacitor, or condenser as it was called in the past, is a device for storing electricity for a limited period. The common type of capacitor consists of two electric plates separated by an insulator, called a 'dielectric'. The ability of a capacitor to hold a charge can be demonstrated by using a large capacitor. After charging the capacitor for a few seconds by connecting it to a high-voltage DC supply, it is possible to obtain a spark when the terminals are connected together. In the past, this storage ability made capacitors attractive for building up high-voltage electrical energy.

The actual amount of charge that the capacitor can handle is measured in terms of its capacitance. The unit of capacitance is the farad (F). More commonly, however, you will see microfarads (μF) or nanofarads (nF).

The most common types of capacitor can be seen in Figure 1.63; they have two parallel conducting plates that are separated by a layer of insulating material (dielectric). They have connecting leads attached to each of the plates and the whole set-up is inside a container.

At the times when the capacitor voltage is equal to the supplied voltage, no charge builds up on the plates, so there is no current in the capacitor. Essentially, the capacitor is charged up and will keep its PD even if the charging voltage stops; the capacitor is basically working just like a battery (Figure 1.64a).

The amount of charge that the capacitor can hold is very small and is completely dependent on the area of the plates. When the capacitor is connected to a circuit load the PD across the plates will force the current in the circuit, but only for a short while as the charge will dissipate very quickly (Figure 1.64b).

In order to work out the charge ($Q$) that a capacitor can store we use the following formula:

$$Q = C \text{(capacitance in farads)} \times V \text{(applied voltage)}$$

So $C = \dfrac{Q}{V}$

A 1F capacitor can store 1C (coulomb) of charge when 1V is applied. Capacitors can store energy at high voltage. A good example is the capacitor discharge ignition, where the energy for the spark is stored in the capacitor.

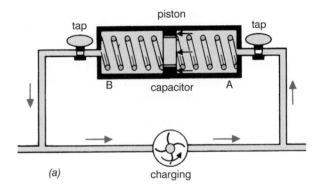

*(a)*   charging

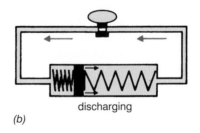

discharging

*(b)*

*Figure 1.64  Action of the capacitor*

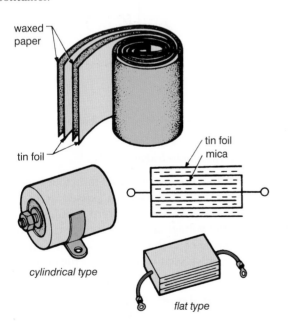

*Figure 1.63  Capacitor construction*

In order to work out the energy (W) stored in a capacitor we use:

$$W = Q \times \frac{V}{2}$$

## R–C time constant

The current flowing in or out of a capacitor is not constant when the capacitor is connected to a circuit (Figure 1.65). What is being shown in this figure is the charge voltage versus time. Voltage is measured as a percentage and time in constants. Figure 1.69b shows that the time (in seconds) to charge the capacitor to 63 per cent is the time constant ($t = C \times R$). In this formula $C$ is the capacitance (in farads) and $R$ is the resistance (in ohms).

The graph also shows that it takes around five time constants (5$t$) to either completely charge or completely discharge the capacitor. You will encounter resistor–capacitor networks in the automotive industry in some common places, such as the courtesy light when the door is opened and then closed, and the intermittent windscreen wiper, where a potentiometer in the R–C network allows a variable, adjustable delay.

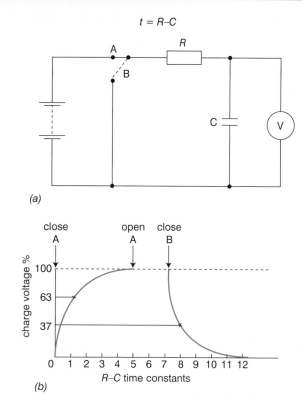

Figure 1.65 *Charging and discharging a capacitor*

## Capacitor construction

In automotive electronic circuits, capacitors can be made from a variety of materials, including tantalum, polyester and ceramics (Figure 1.66). Capacitors are

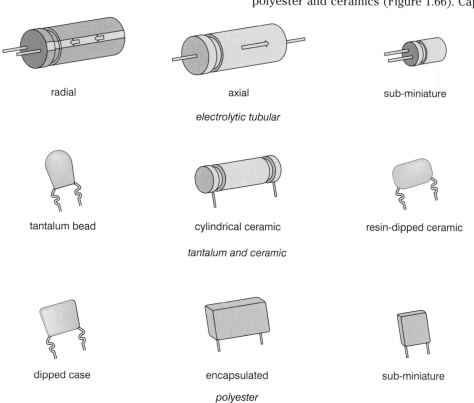

Figure 1.66 *Common types of capacitor*

coded according to colour, they also have numbers and letters which reveal their capacitance.

## Series and parallel connection of capacitors

Just like resistors, capacitors can be connected in series and in parallel. If two or more capacitors are connected in series, then the total capacitance will decrease. In practical terms this means that if you were to connect a $1.1\,\mu F$ capacitor and a $3.3\,\mu F$ capacitor in series, then the capacitance could be worked out using:

$$C = \frac{C_1 \times C_2}{C_1 + C_2}$$

So:

$$\frac{1.1 \times 3.3}{1.1 + 3.3} = \frac{3.63}{4.4} = 0.825\,\mu F$$

In comparison to the series connection, if you were to connect two or more capacitors in parallel, then the total capacitance would increase. We use the following formula to calculate this:

$$C = C_1 + C_2$$

So:

$$1.1 + 3.3 = 4.4\,\mu F$$

You may have noticed that the capacitors behave in completely the opposite way to resistors when they are connected in series or in parallel (see pages 6–8).

## 2.1 Semiconductor principles

### 2.1.1 Semiconductor materials

A conductor has a resistivity in the region of $0.000\,000\,01\,\Omega\text{m}$, and an insulator has a resistivity higher than about $10,000\,\Omega\text{m}$ (OHM metres). A **semiconductor** is a material whose resistivity comes between these values. There are many materials with these properties, but the most commonly used semiconductors are based on silicon.

**Semiconductor**: a material that conducts electricity with a resistivity between that of a conductor and an insulator.

In conductors, electric current is produced by the drift of free electrons, which are driven around a circuit by an applied potential difference. In insulators, however, electrons are bound tightly within the atoms of the material, so there are relatively few free electrons available to carry a current. This severely limits the amount of electron drift that can occur. Semiconductors come between these two extremes, and their ability to carry a current varies according to conditions.

### Electrons and holes

The atomic structure of silicon (Figure 2.1) has four electrons in its outermost shell (called the valence shell). These electrons, as well as being bonded to the nucleus of the atom, can be shared with adjacent atoms to form bonds. Bonds that are formed in this way are called covalent bonds. In silicon they form a crystal lattice.

### Current and electron flow

- In conventional current, charge flows from positive to negative, the same direction as a positive charge carrier, and is measured in amperes.

- Electron flow is in the opposite direction to the conventional current. The negatively charged electrons flow from negative to positive.
- Current can be the flow of positive or negative charges.

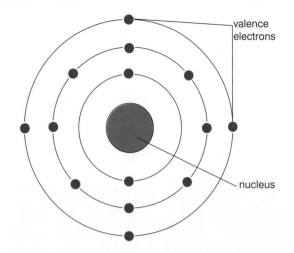

*Figure 2.1 Structure of the silicon atom showing the valence electrons*

At low temperatures the electrons are firmly bound to their nuclei, but as the temperature is raised, some electrons break free. When this happens the loss of an electron leaves a vacant space called a **hole** (Figure 2.2). The atom is now lacking a negatively charged electron, so it is no longer electrically neutral: the creation of a hole gives the atom a positive charge. This is because the positive charge of the nucleus is no longer balanced by the full number of negatively charged electrons.

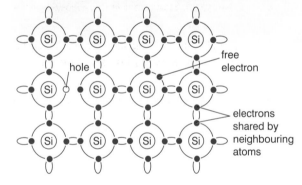

*Figure 2.2 Hole formed by creation of free electron*

When a hole exists, the positive charge of the atom attracts a valence electron from an adjoining atom and, after the transfer has taken place (as the electron drops into the hole), another hole is formed where the electron used to be. This transfer is called recombination. This movement of electrons and holes is random: there is no regular pattern of movement through the semiconductor material at this stage.

### The influence of potential difference

Potential difference (PD) is measured in volts from some reference point and, when this is established, the potentials of the two points can be compared to determine the difference. Using conventional flow, positive (+) to negative (−), electrical energy is considered to move from a point of high potential to

a point of lower potential. If a point A has a higher potential than a point B, then work is required to move a positive charge from B to A.

Connecting a battery to a semiconductor creates a PD to urge the electrons to move in one direction, towards the positive battery terminal. This electron movement effectively means there is a corresponding drift of holes in the opposite direction (Figure 2.3).

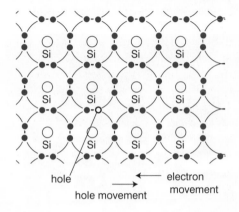

*Figure 2.3 Electron and hole movement under the influence of a PD*

Whereas the resistivity of good conductors increases as the temperature increases, the electrical resistance of a semiconductor decreases. This is one way in which a semiconductor can be distinguished from a pure metal. As the temperature of a pure metal is increased, the vibration of the atoms becomes more violent. This action causes the free electrons to collide more frequently with the atoms blocking their path, so in consequence the resistance to current is increased and extra heat is generated (a high resistance causes heat).

However, when the temperature of a semiconductor is raised, the increase in thermal energy causes more of the valence electrons to break free from their atomic bonds. These become free electrons and, because more current carriers are then available, the current through the material is increased (i.e. the resistance decreases as the semiconductor heats up). A semiconductor is said to have a **negative temperature coefficient** and this feature is used to sense temperature in automotive coolant, fuel, oil, ambient/cabin and engine intake air systems.

**Negative temperature coefficient**: a property of semiconductors, in which electrical resistance decreases as the material heats up.

### Semiconductor doping

**Doping** a semiconductor means adding a controlled amount of impurity atoms to a pure semiconductor crystal. This alters the behaviour by changing the number of charge carriers (electrons and holes) in the material.

**Doping**: the process of adding small impurities to a semiconductor to manipulate its electrical properties.

### N-type semiconductor (negative)

This type of semiconductor has a surplus of negatively charged electrons. It is made by adding a small trace (about one part in 10 billion – think of this as one grain of salt in a transit van full of sugar) of an impurity, such as arsenic or phosphorus, to a pure silicon crystal. Atoms of these elements have five valence electrons (one more than silicon), so when added to silicon, the extra electrons are not able to form bonds with the adjoining atoms. Instead, the surplus electrons remain free to drift at random through the crystal and act as extra charge carriers to those that already exist naturally (Figure 2.4). The name **N-type** is short for negative-type. In this case the arsenic or phosphorus is called a *donor* because the impurity donates extra (negatively charged) electrons to the semiconductor.

**N-type**: negative-type semiconductor that has an excess of negatively charged electrons.

### P-type semiconductor (positive)

This type is made by adding a trace of an impurity, such as boron or indium, to a pure crystal of silicon. The atoms of these elements have only three valence electrons (one fewer than silicon), so when added to silicon a number of holes are formed because of the incomplete bond between the impurity and the silicon. They have the effect of 'robbing' the semiconductor of some of its electrons and, for this reason, the boron or indium is called an *acceptor*. As the crystal becomes short of its full complement of valence electrons, this type of semiconductor is given the name **P-type**, which is short for positive-type.

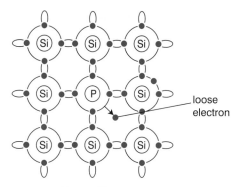

N-type silicon

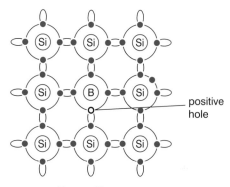

P-type silicon

*Figure 2.4 N-type semiconductor with extra (negative) electrons and P-type semiconductor with extra (positive) holes*

It can be thought of as being like a piece of Swiss cheese, full of electron-hungry holes (Figure 2.4).

**P-type**: positive-type semiconductor that has an excess of positively charged holes.

## 2.2 Diodes

Semiconductor diode — found in alternators to convert AC to DC

Breakdown diode — zener and avalanche, found in voltage stabilisation circuits

Light emitting diode — found in a host of automotive applications for illumination

 Light dependent resistor — used in rear-view mirrors for auto dimming

 Photodiode — applied to alarms, steering and ignition switching because of its fast operation

 Thermistor — the NTC type is most commonly found to measure temperature in coolant, fuel and air intake

*Figure 2.5 Diode symbols and automotive use*

## 2.2.1 PN junction diode

Diodes are the simplest forms of semiconductors. When P- and N-type semiconductors are joined together, the contact region is called a *junction*. At this point the surfaces diffuse together to give a thin region where the electrons and holes penetrate the P- and N-semiconductors respectively (Figure 2.6).

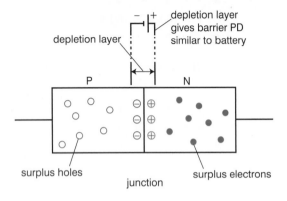

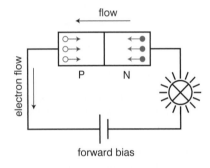

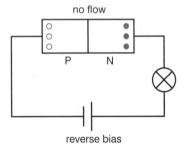

*Figure 2.6  PN junction diode*

After the initial electron and hole transfer has taken place, the negative charges on the P-side and the positive charges (holes) on the N-side build up to produce a *barrier PD* that opposes further diffusion. This occurs without the application of an external PD. This narrow region at the junction is called the *depletion layer*.

Figure 2.6 shows a PN junction diode placed in a circuit with a battery. With the positive battery terminal connected to the P-semiconductor, the electrons in the N-semiconductor readily flow to fill the holes in the P-semiconductor. The depletion layer collapses

and charge can now flow through the device. The PN junction is said to have a **forward bias** in this circuit and this will cause the lamp to illuminate.

**Forward bias**: connection so that a diode allows current to flow in a circuit.

Reversing the battery connections applies a **reverse bias** to the PN junction. Electrons on the P-side are in a minority since the surplus holes represent positive charges. The conditions will not allow electron flow from P to N at normal battery voltage as the depletion layer has expanded, creating a potential barrier. Temperature or high voltage affects this basic condition as, if either is increased, electrons will be forced across the junction from the P-semiconductor.

**Reverse bias**: connection so that a diode prevents current from flowing in a circuit.

The function of the PN junction describes the basic action of the semiconductor junction diode. The diode symbol and current properties are shown in Figure 2.7. (Remember that the convention for current direction is opposite to that of the electron flow.)

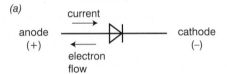

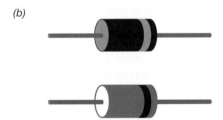

*Figure 2.7  Diode: (a) symbol and current, (b) typical appearance*

Assuming the applied voltage and temperature are not high, the diode will act as a one-way valve and will allow current in only one direction. This property makes it suitable for use as a **rectifier** and also in situations where a one-way flow is required (Figure 2.8). Direct current (DC) is required for charging a battery, so the alternating current (AC) generated by an alternator must be rectified.

**Rectifier**: an electrical device that converts AC, which periodically reverses direction, into DC, which travels in one direction only.

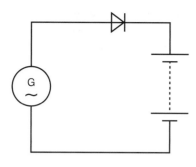

*Figure 2.8 Rectifier action of junction diode*

A single diode in the circuit shown in Figure 2.8 gives *half-wave rectification* of the AC generated, but this is wasteful because it loses half of the available energy (Figure 2.9). To achieve *full-wave rectification* a bridge circuit having four rectifier diodes is needed

(Figure 2.10). This circuit ensures that a DC flow is obtained irrespective of the direction of the AC being generated at the source. This type of rectification is used in the alternator circuit.

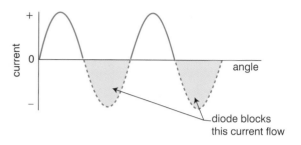

*Figure 2.9 Graph of half-wave rectification*

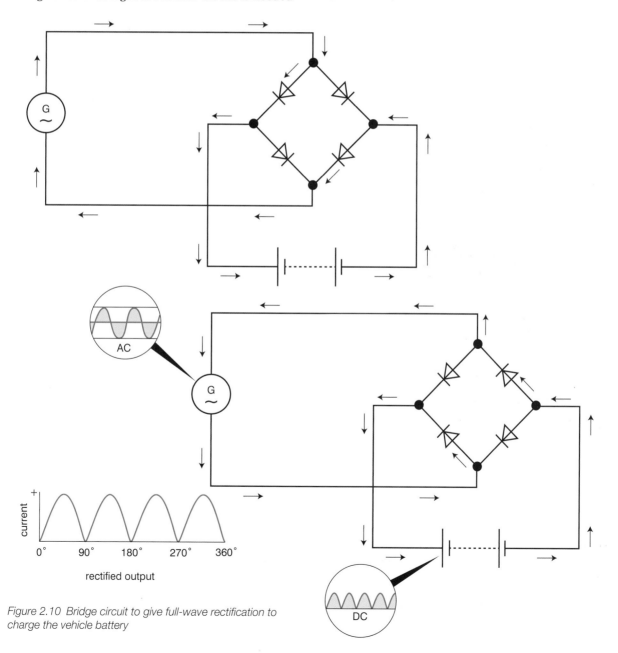

*Figure 2.10 Bridge circuit to give full-wave rectification to charge the vehicle battery*

## 2.2.2 Diode characteristic

Figure 2.11 shows the current–voltage characteristic typical of a silicon diode. This shows that when the forward bias (positive voltage applied to the P-side of the PN junction) is less than about 0.6 V, the diode passes very little current, but when this threshold voltage is raised to about 0.7–0.8 V the rate of current increase is substantially higher.

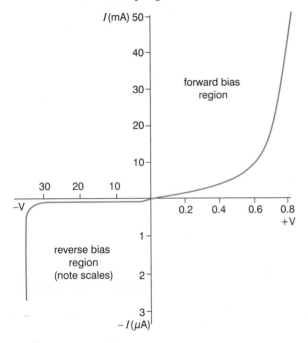

*Figure 2.11 Silicon diode characteristics*

When the polarity is reversed, the high impedance characteristic of the diode opposes current at normal temperatures and voltages, other than a slight **leakage current**, until it reaches its **breakdown voltage**; this varies from a few volts to many hundreds of volts.

**Leakage current**: a small charge that flows through diodes or transistors (even when switched off). This leads to some loss of electrical energy.

**Breakdown voltage**: the voltage at which a diode's threshold is reached, causing it to conduct.

### Voltage drop across a diode

The actual current in a circuit having a diode and series resistor is difficult to determine without using a load line. For practical purposes it is assumed that the voltage drop across a silicon diode is constant at about 0.6 V. It should be noted that this is different from a resistor: an increase in current through a resistor produces a proportional voltage drop, as indicated by Ohm's law in Chapter 1 on page 5.

## 2.2.3 Diode types

### Zener-type diode and avalanche diode

Clarence Zener discovered that when an increasing reverse bias PD was applied to a junction diode, a point was reached where the diode broke down and allowed charge to flow freely (Figure 2.13). This is called the **zener effect**. It is due to the high electric field that acts at the junction and causes electrons to break free from their atomic bonds at a particular voltage.

**Zener effect**: electrical breakdown in a reverse bias diode to increase current.

### Load line

A load line is used to graphically analyse a circuit in which a resistor, diode and power source are placed in a series. The current travelling through these components should be equal (Figure 2.12). The load line in the graph represents the relationship between current and voltage. The operating point of the circuit lies at the intersection of the load line (resistor response) and the exponentially rising curve (diode response). This is because the current must be the same through both linear and non-linear devices. Load lines can be used for AC and DC circuit analysis.

$$V = V_D + V_R$$

$$V = V_D + IR \quad \therefore I = \frac{V}{R} - \frac{V_D}{R}$$

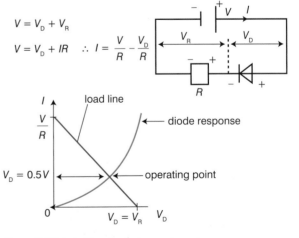

*Figure 2.12 Load line analysis graph*

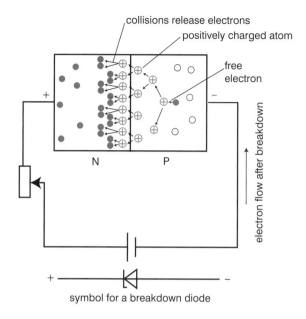

Figure 2.13 *Zener-type diode*

This feature makes the **zener-type diode** particularly suited for use as a voltage-conscious switch in a charging system regulator, or as a 'dump device' to act as a voltage stabiliser in a circuit subjected to a voltage surge (Figure 2.14).

**Zener-type diode**: a semiconductor device that conducts electrical current when its operating voltage is reached.

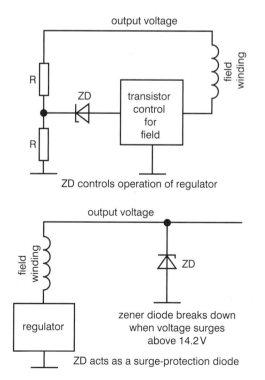

Figure 2.14 *Zener-type diode application*

The avalanche effect, when the zener voltage is reached, has resulted in this type being commonly called an **avalanche diode**, but from a scientific viewpoint the zener-type diode is different from a true avalanche diode. Whereas a zener-type diode achieves its voltage reference characteristic by 'tunnelling' of the charge carriers through the junction, the avalanche diode achieves the characteristic by producing a physical bulk breakdown across the junction.

**Avalanche diode**: a diode that breaks down at a specific reverse bias voltage.

### Voltage reference diode

A diode with a reverse breakdown characteristic below about 4.5 V is a zener-type diode and a diode having a breakdown voltage above 4.5 V is generally an avalanche type.

The voltage drop across a diode is constant irrespective of the current it is carrying, assuming it is operating within its specified range. This feature also applies to a zener-type diode, so this makes it particularly suitable for applications where a steady voltage is required instead of a varying one. PN junctions employed to give steady voltages above about 4.5 V are often called **voltage regulator diodes**.

**Voltage regulator diode**: a diode in which AC is converted to DC by reverse flow of the negative bias so that it is added to the forward bias electrical flow.

Figure 2.15 shows the use of an avalanche diode to stabilise the voltage in a circuit. When the input voltage exceeds the diode's breakdown voltage, the diode conducts and absorbs the excess voltage. During this stage, the output voltage remains constant because it represents the PD or voltage drop across the diode.

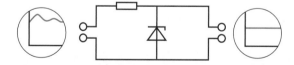

Figure 2.15 *Zener-type diode used as a regulator to stabilise voltage*

## 2.2.4 Diode testing

A test is necessary if it is suspected that a simple diode is failing to perform its one-way valve function. The removal or disconnection of one end of the diode for testing is carried out in a similar manner to that used for other discrete (separate) components.

First, the connections are noted, so that the new component can be correctly fitted, and then the solder from the joint is removed with a soldering iron and desoldering tool. Excessive heat will damage semiconductor devices, so pliers or a crocodile clip should be used as a heat shunt to absorb the heat and protect electronic components.

Digital multimeters incorporate a diode testing facility. In this mode, the red probe is connected to the anode end of the diode and the black probe to the cathode end (Figure 2.16). A reading of between 0.4 V and 0.8 V should be obtained. This is the minimum voltage that allows conduction through the diode. Then the diode is reversed and reconnected; the meter should not buzz, representing a closed circuit, or show an infinity reading.

An analogue ohmmeter can also be used to test a diode. For a good diode the needle will swing almost fully across the scale when connected to the diode in one direction and barely move when the connections are reversed. If the meter reading is equal for both directions, then the diode is faulty.

## 2.3   Other two-terminal devices

### 2.3.1 Light-emitting diode (LED)

In 1954 it was discovered that a diode made of gallium phosphide (GaP) emitted a red light when it was forward biased.

Since that time, experiments have shown that the colour of the emitted light can be altered by varying the impurity type or concentration in the material. LEDs are now commonly available in red, blue, orange, yellow and green (Figure 2.16). In addition, a radiation of near infra-red can be obtained: this is used with a phototransistor as a trigger on some optoelectronic ignition systems.

LEDs have a characteristic similar to a common P–N junction diode. To give a good light output a normal LED requires a voltage of about 2 V and currents of 10 mA for a red LED and 20 mA for other colours. Up to about 5 V no light is emitted when the diode is reverse biased, but if 5 V is exceeded the LED may be damaged.

LEDs are often used for automotive instrumentation systems, so it must be remembered when testing that each LED must have a resistor in series to limit the voltage to 2 V. For identification purposes, the cathode of a new LED has a short lead, as shown in Figure 2.16.

There has been a rapid increase in the use of LEDs in the automotive industry mainly due to their versatility and reliability. They can be used for dashboard, wheel arch, gear stick, number plate fixing screws, and washer jet illumination. Also, in comparison to incandescent bulbs, an LED will light faster, have a longer lifespan and be less easily damaged. It is also more economical because it generates significantly less heat when in operation.

There are, however, a few disadvantages of LEDs for automotive purposes. As well as having a high production cost, they generate some heat at their emitter if switched on for a prolonged period. Therefore, manufacturers have avoided using them for headlamps and daytime running lamps. Also, when light from LEDs is viewed at a slight angle, it becomes difficult to see, making them unsuitable for some information display systems.

*Figure 2.16 LEDs*

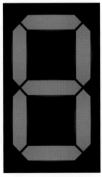

7-segment display

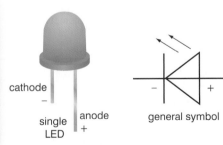

cathode
−

single
LED

anode
+

general symbol

− +

## 2.3.2 Light-dependent resistor (LDR)

This cadmium sulphide device changes its resistance in response to light energy. Figure 2.17 shows the appearance of an encapsulated LDR together with its symbol. As the light intensity passing through the clear end window increases, the resistance decreases. In total darkness the resistance of a typical LDR (type NORP-12) is $1\,M\Omega$ but this falls to about $400\,\Omega$ when the light is bright $(1000\,lx)$. LDRs are commonly found in rear-view mirrors for automatic dimming when an intense light is sensed from behind the vehicle.

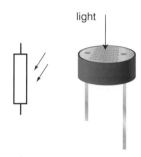

light

*Figure 2.17  LDR symbol and appearance*

## 2.3.3 Photodiode

This type of silicon junction diode (Figure 2.18) behaves in a similar manner to an LDR. The photodiode is much faster in operation, but it can only carry a current of a few microamperes. Terminated so that it is reverse biased, the leakage current increases proportionally with the incident light (i.e. as the light gets brighter the resistance decreases). The short switching time makes this device suitable for high-speed light pulse detection.

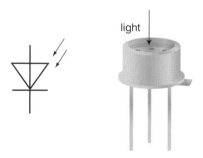

light

*Figure 2.18  Silicon junction photodiode*

In automotive systems LDRs are used in security alarms, automatic systems for parking light operation, self-dipping of headlamp beams, illumination of headlamps and some steering angle sensors.

## 2.3.4 Thermistor

A thermistor is a resistor whose resistance changes with temperature fluctuations. A thermistor is fitted in an electronic circuit to compensate for the alteration to resistance values of circuit components caused by temperature changes.

The resistance of common metals (good conductors) increases with temperature. Thermistors that have a sensing capsule that responds in a similar way are said to have a positive temperature coefficient (PTC). Conversely, a capsule made of a semiconductor material has a resistance that decreases with temperature. Such materials have a negative temperature coefficient (NTC) and are more commonly used. The hotter they get, the lower their resistance becomes, hence the larger the current in them. Figure 2.19 shows the relationship between resistance and temperature for an NTC thermistor.

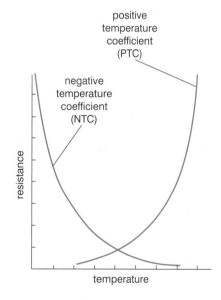

*Figure 2.19  Thermistor characteristics*

### Light measurement

When measuring light the following units may be used: lux, lumen and candela:

- Lux (lx) measures illumination per surface area.
- Lumen (lm) measures the total visible light emitted.
- Candela (cd) measures light intensity in a given direction.

From an automotive headlight, the number of lux will be a measure of how well an image is illuminated at a given distance. The number of lumens shows how much light is emitted in any direction. The number of candelas shows how bright the light is.

## Thermistor testing

Figure 2.20 shows a typical thermistor and the wiring for testing the thermistor *in situ*. The voltage supply from the electronic control unit (ECU) should be checked for 5 volts with a varying return signal proportional to engine temperature. Alternatively, remove the thermistor and place the sensing end in a water jug with a thermometer, then check the temperature against the resistance values. This type of coolant sensor can cause problems if it fails to illuminate a management light or record a trouble code. More information on sensor testing can be found in Chapter 5 on page 79.

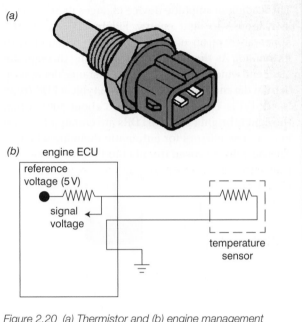

*Figure 2.20 (a) Thermistor and (b) engine management wiring*

The NTC type is used to sense temperature in many automotive systems, including the measurement of engine coolant temperature for instrumentation as well as engine management. Engine oil, fuel, air intake and ambient air are measured with the use of thermistors. A typical thermistor used to register coolant temperature measures resistance changes from $3000\,\Omega$ to $320\,\Omega$ as the temperature increases from $20\,°C$ to $100\,°C$.

The purpose of a transistor is to amplify current. A transistor can be used to amplify a logic integrated circuit's (IC) current so that a lamp can be operated.

This means that the transistor is being used to amplify voltage. Resistors, on the other hand, are used to convert changing current to changing voltage.

## 3.1   Transistors

Transistors are devices that are used to either switch or amplify the flow of electrons in a circuit. Typically, a transistorised ignition system uses the device in order for the transistor to switch the primary system on and off. An example of an amplifying application of a transistor would be in a music system where a radio signal might need strengthening.

As we will see, the transistor consists of three main elements: the emitter, the base and the collector. The transistor is made of two semiconductor materials; the collector and the emitter (known as the outer two elements) are made from the same material; and the base is made of another material. Each element has a conductor attached.

Importantly, the materials are labelled for their distinct properties. A 'P' means positive and therefore a lack of electrons. It has holes ready to receive electrons. An 'N' is used to label the negative, which means that the material has a surplus of electrons. The concept is a simple one: 'free' electrons move from one atom to another. This leaves a 'hole' in the atom that the electron has left. The hole is then filled with another electron. The movement of the electrons is transmitted throughout the conductor. The result is that an electrical current is created from negative to positive. Simultaneously, the

'hole' has been moved backwards in the conduction as each successive free electron takes it place. This means that the 'hole' flow is from positive to negative. Inside a transistor, the current can either be electron movement or hole flow. This will depend on the material from which the transistor is made.

### 3.1.1 Basic transistors

A basic transistor is formed when two PN junctions, or semiconductors, are placed back to back. As we have seen, the three connections necessary are a collector (C), a base (B) and an emitter (E). Figure 3.1 shows a transistor and the symbols that are commonly used.

The arrow in the symbol of each type points either to or from the base and is always placed on the emitter side. It is designed to show the direction of the current flow from P to N. A transistor can be used as a switch device or an amplifier. When they are used to amplify signals they are known as **active components**. This is in contrast to resistors, capacitors and diodes, which do not amplify and are known as **passive components**.

**Active component**: a component that can put power into the circuit, but still relies on a source of energy. It can amplify or increase the amplitude.

**Passive component**: a component that does not supply energy itself. It can change the electrical voltage and signal, but cannot amplify it.

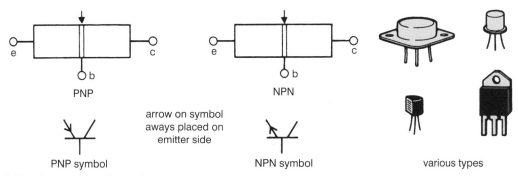

*Figure 3.1  Transistor construction and symbols*

As we will see, a transistor can broadly be broken down into two different types:

- bipolar – depending on the flow of electrons and holes
- unipolar – also known as field effect transistors, these depend on the flow of holes or electrons, but not both.

When an NPN transistor is connected in a simple circuit no current other than a slight leakage will pass the transistor from P to N. Electrons can be encouraged to cross the NP junction for the emitter to base but they will not pass to the collector because the collector has no spare holes for the electrons to fill.

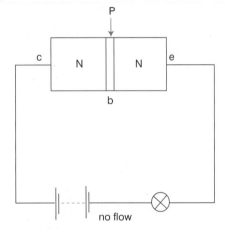

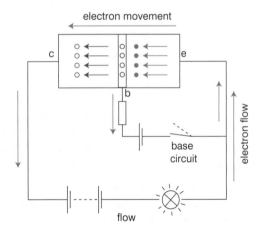

Figure 3.2 Switching action of transistor

The base circuit is used to influence and control the flow of electrons and give the switching action. When the switch in the base circuit is closed, a disturbance occurs at the PN junction. The very small current in the base circuit reduces the junction potential and this allows the electron charge carriers to bridge the PN base collector junction. This action closes the transistor switch and allows the current to flow freely in the main circuit. In Figure 3.2 the current is operating a lamp. Note that current is in the opposite direction to electron flow. Very little base current is needed to

switch the transistor, so this feature makes the device ideal for use as an alternative to an electromagnetic relay. The device, like other semiconductors, does not like heat and is damaged if the battery polarity is reversed. This is because a large electron flow from collector to base destroys the structure of the base.

The circuit for a PNP-type differs from a circuit for an NPN-type transistor. A PNP-type must have an emitter connected to a positive supply. Current through a PNP-type is opposite to an NPN-type. In both types of transistor the main current is controlled by the minute current in the base circuit. No physical movement occurs so the switching action is very rapid. The NPN-type operates faster than the PNP-type, which makes the former more suited for high-frequency switching operations.

### 3.1.2 Bipolar transistors

A bipolar transistor consists of three semiconductor regions that either create a PNP or an NPN configuration. Figure 3.2 shows a simple NPN transistor circuit and its switching action.

The bipolar transistor makes use of charge carriers of both holes and electrons. The emitter-collector current can be considerably greater than the base current that actually controls the flow. When the circuit is in operation the transistor is off and there is no current passing through the transistor, as a result of the reverse bias PN junction between the collector and the base.

The flow of electrons is controlled by the base circuit, which provides the switching action. When there is current in the base emitter, as a result of a disturbance in the PN junction, the potential is reduced, which allows electron charge carriers to bridge the junction and allows the current to flow from collector to emitter. Figure 3.3 shows a PNP transistor; this has to have its emitter connected to a positive supply. The current flows in the opposite direction to an NPN transistor.

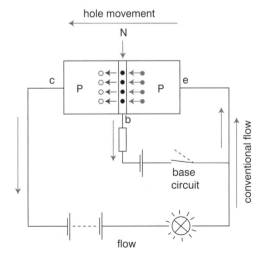

Figure 3.3 PNP transistor

## 3.2 Applications

Transistors form a major part of many circuits. Some of these key applications are looked at in this section. In fact both transistors and diodes are the building blocks of most electronic systems. We have already seen that the two main types of semiconductor material are used to construct these components.

### 3.2.1 Transistors and diodes

Both transistors and diodes are very important. There are two main types of semiconductor material that are used to make these components:

- **N-type** – this means that there is a surplus of negatively charged electrons. Arsenic is added to either the silicon or germanium crystal; this gives extra electrons to the semiconductor.
- **P-type** – boron is added to create a shortage of electrons and create a positive charge.

**N-type**: negatively charged.

**P-type**: positively charged.

Junctions are formed when these two types of semiconductor material are connected. At the junction point the surfaces fuse together and at that point there is an area where the electrons penetrate the P-semiconductor and holes penetrate the N-semiconductor. Once there has been an initial transfer, there is a negative charge build-up on the P side and a positive charge build-up on the N side. This creates a potential difference (PD), which prevents diffusion. This area is known as the depletion layer.

In Figure 3.4 we can see a PN junction diode. Diodes are electronic devices with terminals known as anodes and cathodes, which are created by a PN junction. They allow the current to flow in one direction only.

When a diode is connected in a particular way it will conduct and allow the current to flow; this is called **forward bias** condition. If the diode is connected in order to block current, then this is known as **reverse bias**.

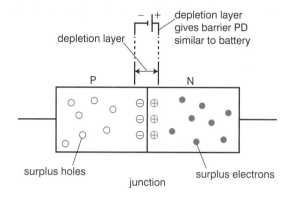

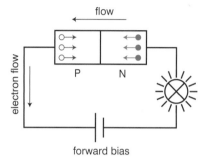

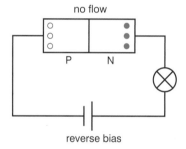

*Figure 3.4  PN junction diode*

**Forward bias**: holes are driven to the junction from the P-type and electrons are driven to the junction from the N-type. It is at the junction that the two are combined to produce a continuous current.

**Reverse bias**: a transient current is produced and both the electrons and holes are driven away from the junction. This is achieved by applying a reverse voltage to the junction. The current stops when the applied voltage is equal to potential at the depletion layer.

### Semiconductors

A semiconductor is a material that has a resistivity lower than that of an insulator, but higher than that of a conductor. A conductor has to have a resistivity of less than 0.00000001 Ωm (ohm metres). On the other hand, an insulator has to have a resistivity of greater than 10,000 Ωm. Semiconductors are usually made either of silicon or germanium. The conductivity can be varied by adding impurity atoms, such as boron, arsenic or phosphorus; this is known as doping. In effect, it alters the number of charge carriers in the material. (See Chapter 2.)

These properties of diodes make them ideal for applications when there is a need to convert from alternating current (AC) to direct current (DC). A component called a rectifier is used for this purpose. Figure 3.5 shows the current and voltage curves of a silicon diode in a circuit.

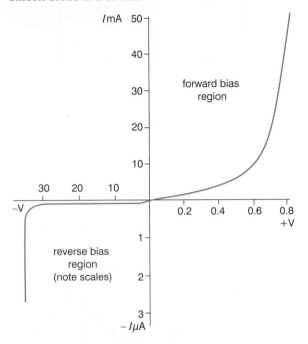

Figure 3.5 *Silicon diode characteristics*

As can be seen in the graph, the most important thing about a diode is that, when operating under forward bias conditions, it does not begin to conduct until a particular voltage has been applied across it. While the voltage depends on the semiconductor material, this is usually around 0.5 V. Once this has been reached the diode conducts. When there is a small increase in voltage there is a larger increase in the current.

When operating under reverse bias conditions, apart from a small leakage current, the diode will oppose current flow. As the reverse voltage increases, a point is reached where the diode begins to conduct and allows the current to flow in reverse. Once this critical point has been reached, the junction will overheat and usually the diode is destroyed. This level of voltage is known as breakdown or peak inverse voltage.

Diodes in certain conditions do not conform to Ohm's law. A resistor will comply because the voltage drop varies with current flow for a fixed resistance value. In a diode, the voltage drop will vary dependent on the material that the semiconductor is made from, but it is usually around 0.5 V.

## 3.2.2 Rectifiers

These are commonly used to convert AC to DC. In Figure 3.6 we can see a single diode in a circuit; this is known as a half-wave rectifier. In Figure 3.7 it is possible to see the half wave and its pulsing unidirectional DC current. It is not a very efficient system as it is clear that only half of the AC sine wave is allowed to pass through, so half of the energy is lost. There are ways in which this loss can be avoided, but this means setting up a network of four diodes connected in a bridge (Figure 3.8).

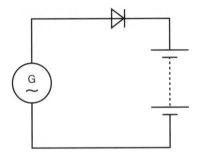

Figure 3.6 *Rectifier action of junction diode*

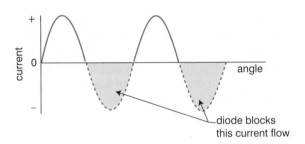

Figure 3.7 *Half-wave rectification of AC*

In this system the AC current is converted to unidirectional DC current. There is a minimal loss and, as a result, this is a configuration that is used in a large number of electrical circuits. In the automotive industry you are likely to find this in an alternator.

## 3.2.3 Zener diodes

A zener diode is designed to operate under conditions that would normally cause the diode to breakdown and begin to conduct under reverse bias conditions. This phenomenon is known as the zener effect, which is a high electrical field pressure at the PN junction.

The actual effect is reversible and zener diodes are designed precisely for this purpose. A diode that has a reverse breakdown voltage of below 4.5 V is known

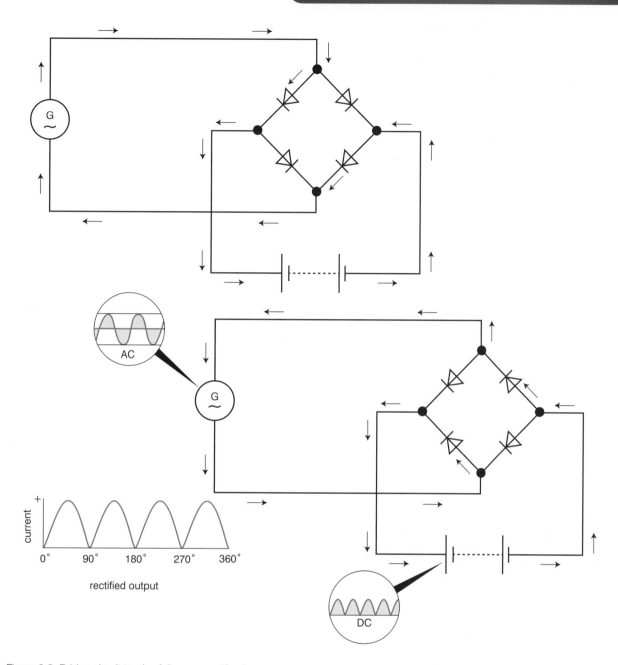

*Figure 3.8 Bridge circuit to give full-wave rectification*

as a zener diode. They are useful as voltage-conscious switches in a charging system regulator, where the circuit is potentially subject to voltage surges.

If the breakdown voltage is above 4.5 V, then the diode is known as an avalanche diode (Figure 3.11). These are used in voltage-stabilisation circuits. In cases when the voltage drop across the diode in a circuit is constant, the diode is designed to operate

as a voltage regulator (Figure 3.10). The diode will conduct and absorb any excess voltage once the input voltage exceeds the diode's breakdown voltage. The output voltage will remain constant, as it represents a voltage drop across the diode. It is possible to find this type of arrangement in the magnetic alternator charging system on smaller motorcycles.

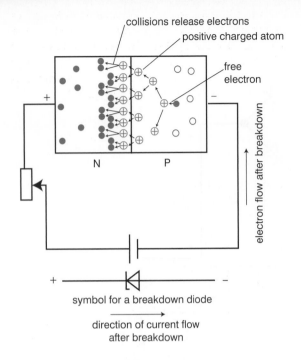

collisions release electrons

positive charged atom

free electron

electron flow after breakdown

N   P

symbol for a breakdown diode

direction of current flow after breakdown

*Figure 3.9  Zener-type diode*

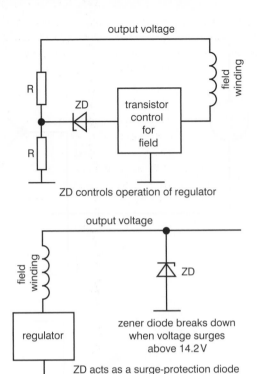

output voltage

R

ZD

transistor control for field

field winding

R

ZD controls operation of regulator

output voltage

field winding

ZD

regulator

zener diode breaks down when voltage surges above 14.2 V

ZD acts as a surge-protection diode

*Figure 3.11  Zener-type diode applications*

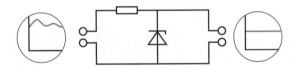

*Figure 3.10  Zener-type diode used as a regulator to stabilise voltage*

### 3.2.4 Light-emitting diodes (LEDs)

When forward biased, a diode made of gallium phosphide will emit a red light; this was the discovery of light-emitting diodes (LEDs). Since then LEDs, as they have become known, are available in many other colours, not just red. In electronic ignition systems LEDs are used for

---

**LED operation**

In many respects, the LED is the same as a PN junction diode. A 2 V red LED would require 2 V and a 10 mA current to light up. Other colours would need a current of 20 mA.

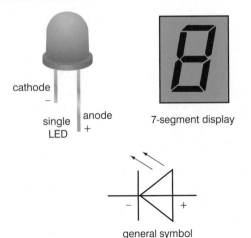

cathode
−

single LED

anode
+

7-segment display

−   +

general symbol

*Figure 3.12  Light-emitting diode (LED)*

You will find LEDs in most instrument panels.

To work out the polarity of an LED, the negative (or cathode) has a shorter connection lead. There is also a 'flat' on the casing of the LED on the cathode side. In order to test an LED it is necessary to use a series resistor in order to reduce the supply voltage to 2 V:

$$R = V_{supply} - \frac{V_{LED}}{I_{LED}}$$

$R$ is the series resistance, $V_{supply}$ is the supply voltage, $V_{LED}$ is the voltage required across the LED (less than 2 V), and $I_{LED}$ is the LED current.

the photoelectric properties in trigger circuits. They are also used for a vehicle's external lighting and signalling. They are very reliable and durable and have a low current draw compared to their light output.

## 3.2.5 Optoelectronics

Although an LED is an optoelectronic component, there are other more specialised versions, some of which are light-sensing and others that are light-sensitive. A resistor whose resistance decreases when it is exposed to light is known as a photoresistor, or light-dependent resistor (LDR) (Figure 3.13).

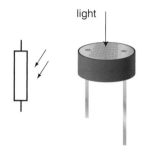

*Figure 3.13 Light-dependent resistor (LDR) symbol and appearance*

Many LDRs are made from cadmium sulphide; however, they can be made of other materials dependent on the light wavelength that the resistor is designed to be sensitive to.

There are other light-sensitive diodes that are similar to LDRs, but differ in respect of the fact that they can switch at higher frequencies; these are known as photodiodes. They are used as light meters or for photoelectric beams. In the automotive industry they are used for security systems or for panel light dimming and automatic switching systems for headlights. They are connected with a reverse bias. The leakage current increases as a result of incident light; in other words, if the light increases the resistance decreases.

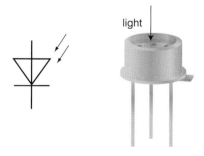

*Figure 3.14 Photodiode symbol and appearance*

## 3.2.6 Thermistors

Resistors whose resistance value changes when they are exposed to temperature changes are known as thermistors. The thermistor will have a negative temperature coefficient (NTC) or a positive temperature coefficient (PTC). The semiconductor material will increase the resistance as the temperature increases (PTC); another type of semiconductor material will reduce the resistance as the temperature increases (NTC) (Figure 3.15).

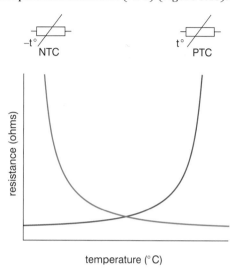

*Figure 3.15 Thermistor characteristics*

## 3.2.7 Thyristors

Thyristors are semiconductor devices that were developed out of transistors. Unlike transistors, which have two PN junctions, thyristors have three. More precisely, they are two interconnected transistors.

The most common type of thyristor is known as a reverse-blocking triode, or silicon-controlled rectifier. The term 'triode' indicates that it has three electrodes or connections, which are the anode, cathode and gate. The main feature is its switching action. By applying a small trigger current to the gate, the thyristor is switched on. This causes the current to flow from the anode to the cathode. Once the main current starts to flow the interruption of the gate current has no effect. Only when the anode to cathode voltage is reduced to zero, or its polarity is changed, is the thyristor switched off. The thyristor is useful in systems where a small trigger current of a limited duration is needed to start the flow of a large current. It is, therefore, likely that you will find a thyristor in electric motor speed controllers, rectifiers, inverters and converters. They are also used in capacitor discharge ignition systems, where the small current is used to start the larger current.

In Figure 3.16 a voltage is applied to the anode. No current will flow to the cathode because both $T_1$ and $T_2$ are switched off. Applying a voltage of similar polarity to the gate will switch on $T_2$. As a result $T_1$

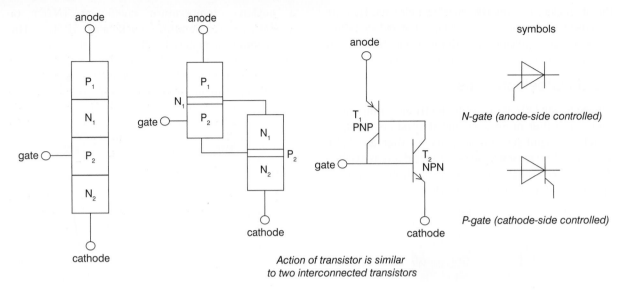

Figure 3.16 *Thyristor construction and symbols*

will also switch on. Current from the collector of $T_1$ to the base of $T_2$ will now keep $T_2$ switched on even if the gate current is discontinued.

## 3.2.8 Circuit applications

We have already seen that transistors are vital in many circuits. There are some specific circuit applications that relate to automotive electric circuits. The first is known as a Darlington pair (Figure 3.17). Because there is a limited current gain from a single transistor there is insufficient current to fully activate the component. This problem is overcome by using connected transistors so that the output from the first transistor is fed to the base of the second transistor. The transistors are mounted in a single package. They have three terminals, which are marked e (emitter), b (base) and c (collector). The gain of the two transistors is multiplied to give a combined gain. In other words, a high-gain low-power transistor can be coupled with a low-gain high-power transistor. This creates a unit that has both high gain and power and is ideal for switching low-voltage high-current that is found in many electrical circuits in vehicles.

Another use of transistors is what is known as the Schmitt trigger, as shown in Figure 3.18. This figure shows the circuit where the requirement is rapid switching and clear signal edges, relying on positive feedback. A higher base voltage is required to switch on the input transistor, $T_1$, than is needed to turn it off. When $T_1$ is off $T_2$ is switched on. The collector emitter current of $T_2$ passes through the resistor, $R_4$. This forms part of the base circuit of $T_1$. $T_1$ has to have a higher base emitter voltage than normal in order to

overcome the voltage at $R_4$ before $T_1$ can switch on. This means that if the input voltage is above 3.5V, then $T_1$ will switch on and $T_2$ will switch off. The output voltage will be high. If the input voltage is below 2.5V, $T_1$ will switch off and $T_2$ will switch on and there will be a low output voltage. Figure 3.19 shows a graph of the conversion of an analogue signal to a digital signal. A practical example is when the analogue sine wave signal from a crankshaft position sensor is converted into a digital signal that can be processed in the electronic control unit (ECU) timer circuit, in order to ascertain engine speed.

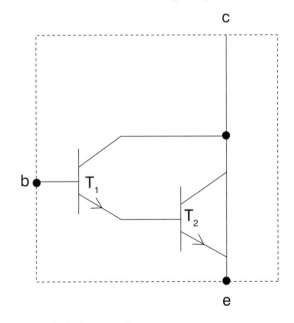

Figure 3.17 *Darlington pair*

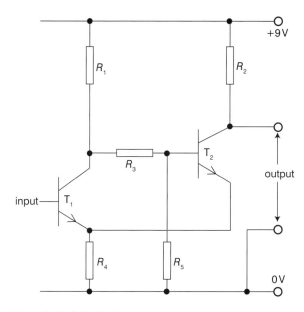

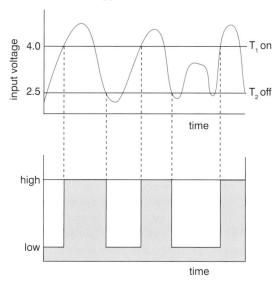

Figure 3.18  Schmitt trigger

Figure 3.19  Conversion of an analogue signal to a digital signal

## 3.3    Unipolar transistors

A transistor is called unipolar when it involves only one type of charge carrier, such as the majority type. Bipolar transistors involve the drift of **majority** and **minority carriers** through the base region. There are two basic types of unipolar field effect transistors. The first is known as a junction field effect transistor (JFET) and the second a metal oxide semiconductor field effect transistor (MOSFET).

> **Majority and minority carriers**: in N-type transistors the majority carriers are electrons and the minority carriers are holes; this is reversed for P-type transistors.

### 3.3.1 Junction field effect transistors (JFETs)

Figure 3.20 shows a JFET; it is made up of a single element of either a P- or N-type semiconductor. The connections for the main current are made across this single element. The connections are known as the drain (collector) or source (emitter). There is a third electrode on the side of this element, known as a gate (base). This is a thin conductor, electrically insulated.

When working, the electrons (or current) run from the source to the drain. The flow rate is controlled by the voltage that is applied to the gate. As the gate voltage increases relative to the source, the electron flow or current decreases in the source drain circuit until it stops. This happens because by raising the gate voltage the depletion region increases and thus reduces the width of the channel that allows the electrons to flow from drain to source. Basically, this means that an electrical field is being used to control the current. It also acts as a voltage control current source.

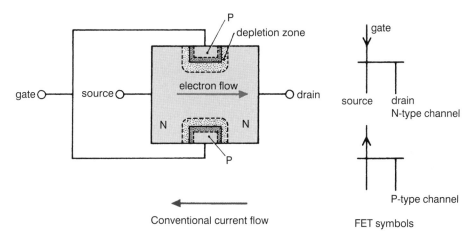

Figure 3.20  Junction field effect transistor (JFET)

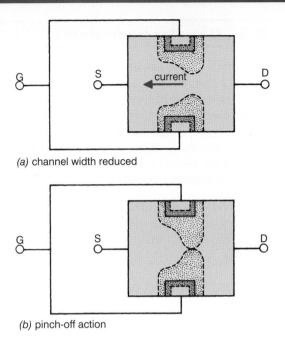

*(a) channel width reduced*

*(b) pinch-off action*

*Figure 3.21  JFET action*

## 3.3.2 Metal oxide semiconductor field effect transistors (MOSFETs)

This is a development of the field effect transistor. It is created by diffusing a pair of P+ regions into the side of an N-type silicon crystal (Figure 3.22).

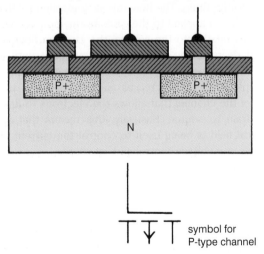

*Figure 3.22  MOSFET transistor, or insulated gate field effect transistor (IGFET)*

When a negative charge is applied to the gate, positive charges, or holes, are attracted to the N region adjacent to the gate. This builds up an **inversion layer**, which forms a P-type channel between the two P+ regions for the electrons to flow from the source to the drain. As the voltage is increased, the channel gets deeper and this allows a larger current.

**Inversion layer**: a layer in a semiconductor material where the type of majority carriers will change to its opposite under given conditions.

## 3.3.3 Field effect transistors and bipolar transistors

Field effect transistors, either as discrete or integrated components, are largely superior to bipolar transistors because:

- they have longer switching current
- they have a lower power requirement
- they have higher input impedance
- they have higher frequency response.

There is a low heat output as a result of the power requirement, which makes field effect transistors very suitable for use in ICs. Their superior thermal characteristics allow thousands of them to be fitted on to extremely small silicon chips that are used in ECUs or computers.

## 3.4  Integrated circuits (ICs)

ICs, or chips, are complex circuits that have been etched on to tiny chips of semiconductor material. ICs can be found in all computers, and microprocessors are in fact ICs that process information in a computer. The IC, for example, can keep track of which keys are being pressed.

Two inventors, completely unaware of one another's activity, invented what was to become an IC at virtually the same time. This was back in the late 1950s. The IC became vital as it opened the door to allow computers to become more sophisticated. The first ICs became commercially available in 1961.

### 3.4.1 Logic gates

ICs consist of a number of so-called logic gates on a single piece of silicon. Each of these logic gates is an individual switching transistor, diode, resistor and capacitor. By combining all of these individual components in such a way, small high-performance circuits, which were reliable and had relatively low power consumption, could be constructed. Over time, ICs have become more and more sophisticated. Originally, they were relatively simple devices, known as small-scale integration devices, with up to 12 gates. Nowadays, the circuits can have thousands of gate elements and are known as very large-scale integrated devices.

There are in fact three different types of logic circuits. The first is known as the transistor–transistor logic (TTL). These are widely used in relatively low-cost ICs. They are highly resistant to switching caused by interference.

The second group are faster than TTL circuits and are known as emitter coupled logic (ECL). However, these are more expensive and use more power.

The final group is the complementary metal oxide semiconductors (CMOS). Their switching speed is low when compared to TTL, but they can have a large number of gates as a result of low power consumption. They are vulnerable to static charges.

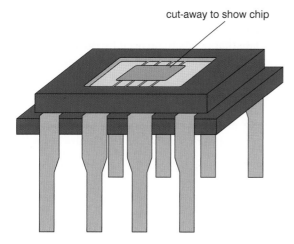

Figure 3.23  Eight-pin IC chip

## 3.4.2 Microprocessors

The Intel 4004 is generally regarded as being the first microprocessor. It appeared in an advertisement in November 1971. It originally arose out of the need to create a chip for a high-performance desk calculator.

A microprocessor incorporates many of the functions of a computer central processing unit (CPU) on a single IC. Essentially, it is a multipurpose and programmable device. It takes digital data as input, it then processes the data according to instructions, which are stored in its memory, and then it provides an output.

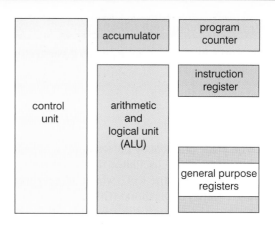

Figure 3.24  Parts of a microprocessor

The beauty of the microprocessor was that the hardware circuit was in two parts. One part processed the data and the other stored the data. In order for these two parts to work they needed instructions or a program, which would also be stored. These two key functions are now much better known as memory and software.

The function of the microprocessor is fairly straightforward. It uses a digital system with high- and low-voltage levels to transmit information from one part of the microprocessor to the other. These are binary signals. Each binary digit is known as a bit; there are most commonly 8 bits in 1 byte.

Originally the microprocessors could only sample limited instructions. In fact, in 1972 the Intel 8008 became the world's first 8-bit microprocessor. By the mid-1970s 16-bit designs were available. They had only been on the market for a short period of time, when in 1979 the 32-bit design arrived. In turn, this was replaced by the 64-bit in the early 1990s and there are now multi-core designs and high-performance, reduced instruction set computer microprocessors. The more bits of information that a processor can deal with at a given time, the faster it can use programs.

### Computer control

Many vehicle control systems in modern vehicles now incorporate microelectronic or computer control. The old analogue electronic circuits were just not up to the job. A prime example was the old way in which electric window systems worked compared to how they now operate:

- In the past, an electric motor drove the window regulator mechanism, which was controlled in turn by a motor reversing switch.
- Modern motors are now controlled by a digital control chip. It monitors the speed of the motor and the position of the window in order to ensure safety, as well as system protection. In other words, it prevents objects being trapped in the window mechanism. It also makes the motor stop when it is fully open or closed in order to prevent overheating.
- In the modern version, the window controller interacts with other systems, such as central locking, in order to achieve closure of doors and windows.

## Central processing unit (CPU)

A CPU works in a sequential manner; it carries out a cycle of operations:

1 It samples the data.
2 It carries out a calculation.
3 It returns a result.

This is all made possible by pulses from an oscillator. It is the speed of the oscillator that determines the processing speed of the CPU, which is measured in megahertz (MHz) or gigahertz (GHz).

Referring to Figure 3.24, we are able to see how the parts of the microprocessor actually interrelate with one another:

- Instructions are held in the register until they are needed.
- The program counter is the main register. It is there to record the location in the memory of any instructions that the CPU has to carry out.

- It is the CPU that collects data from the memory and carries out the instructions according to any information given to it in the form of the software or program.
- The arithmetic logic unit (ALU) does all the processing of information that either relates to arithmetic or logic functions.
- The data supplied to the CPU is directed to the ALU.
- Data that needs to be used by the ALU is stored in a temporary area called the accumulator.
- The command unit that directs all the processing operations is known as the control unit. This moves the data between the sections and provides control signals to activate each part as their contribution to the processing.

### 3.4.3 Microcomputers and microcontrollers

In the majority of cases as far as electronics in vehicles are concerned, microprocessors are to be found, along with other components, to create an embedded system, or an application specific computer. In these cases there will be a microprocessor (CPU), a memory to hold the program and data and an input output system, known as an I/O. There will also be peripherals, including switching devices. All of these are connected together via a Bus system. This creates a path so that data can be transmitted between each component. Each of these sub-systems forms a microcomputer on a single chip. Each microcomputer will be responsible for the monitoring and controlling of a variety of systems and components. This is now common practice, as the microcomputers and associated systems are not only high performance systems, but are also comparatively cheap.

Each microprocessor has a series of instructions that are programmed into it as part of the manufacturing process. These systems receive a variety of inputs, from specifically placed sensors (see Figure 3.25).

### 3.4.4 Bus systems

A bus system was originally designed so that there would be three computer buses in a computer system. One would be a data bus, which would carry information, the second an address bus, which would work out where the information needed to be sent and the third a control bus to determine the operations.

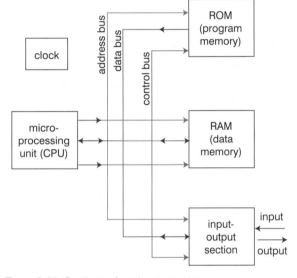

Figure 3.25  Sections of a microcomputer

Modern bus systems are now in effect multi-bus, or multi-lane, in order to carry information backwards and forwards as required. Again it was Intel that adopted the dual independent bus concept and it was introduced in the mid-1990s. The basics still remain the same:

- The data bus carries necessary data between the computer parts.
- The address bus holds the data address in a binary code and takes it from the CPU into the memory. It marks exactly where in the memory particular information is stored. Usually the address bus only works in one direction.

- The control bus controls the computer's functions. It reads and writes data. Reading means the data is passed for processing to the CPU. Writing means the data comes from the CPU and goes into storage.

### 3.4.5 Clock pulse generator

This is an electronic circuit, which is used to generate regular pulses. In effect, it controls the movement of data between parts of the microcomputer using a timing pulse. The pulse is generated by an oscillator, which is known as a system clock. By applying the clock pulse at the same time to two different parts of the microcomputer the data is able to travel between them. This makes the other parts of the microcomputer inactive. They are only activated if they are unlocked at the same time by the pulse. It is the clock pulse that allows the different parts of the microprocessor to be interconnected via the bus system.

### 3.4.6 Memory

In microcomputers 'memory' is a term used to describe devices that can store programs or data, either in a temporary or permanent state. There are three different types of memory:

- Operating memory – these store bits in binary form. They are read by the CPU when needed. For the microprocessor to perform particular functions a program has to be written that contains the necessary information. This information is translated into binary format and is held in the operating memory. The operating memory has two different parts; one of them stores the necessary programs that the CPU will need, and the other holds information in the form of an input to the CPU or an output from the microcomputer.
- Dedicated memory – read-only memory is a type of information that is held in the memory even if the microprocessor is switched off. This is information that has been specifically

designed to suit an application. Many vehicle manufacturers will use standardised chips for this kind of memory and data. They can program the chips themselves with specific information required for the operating system. The most common type is the erasable, programmable, read-only memory. This type of memory is ideal as the microprocessor cannot interfere with the memory or change it, but it can be rewritten externally, which allows for program upgrades.

- Temporary memory – additional memory, called random access memory (RAM), is memory that is lost if the power is switched off. In vehicles and in computers a battery is fitted to keep this information safe for short periods of time. This is usually used to store larger amounts of data.

### 3.4.7 Peripherals

Figure 3.26 shows how a CPU communicates with its external environment. In the automotive industry this function is vital, as it allows the user to interact with the CPU and the memory, such as in fault detection.

Peripheral modules connect to the microprocessor via the usual bus connection. They then have an external connection, which may be another microprocessor, a sensor or an actuator. This allows the microprocessor to receive or to send information and signals. The peripheral module communicates with the internal bus and it also communicates with the application environment, as well as being able to store data. It is often used for monitoring and timing.

### 3.4.8 Analogue input and output

A peripheral module known as an analogue to digital converter (ADC) is used to monitor the functions of vehicle components, which is carried out by sensors or **transducers**. These components convert physical quantities into electrical voltages. The ADC converts the analogue output into a digital form so that the CPU inside the ECU can process the information.

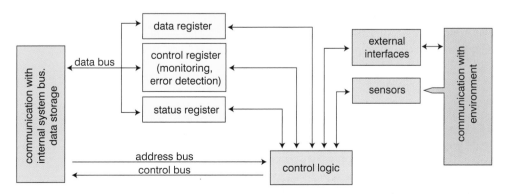

*Figure 3.26 CPU communication with external environment*

Analogue signals are converted to digital format and are sampled at regular intervals. These samples are then stored in the memory, along with a time stamp. The signal itself is not continually sampled, but regular sampling enables the memory to represent the original signal. This all relies on the sampling quality in terms of its frequency and **bit resolution**.

**Transducer**: a device that can convert energy from one type to another.

**Bit resolution**: the amount of data used to store information about each sample while sampling (i.e. converting from analogue to digital format).

When the CPU has received the data, it needs to make its calculations, which it then needs to pass on to the hardware, or actuator. With actuators that are driven by varying voltage, digital to analogue converters are used to handle the output from the microcontroller system. The module takes the digital input from the CPU; this is at a low switching level. It then uses a network of power-switching transistors to create a varying analogue voltage output, in order to drive the actuator. A prime example in a vehicle would be the idle speed control valve.

### 3.4.9 Driver modules

There may be a need for additional driver modules. These all interface to the microcontroller bus system and the actuators and components. An idle speed control would use what is known as stepper motor driver modules. An exhaust gas recirculation system would need on and off switching outputs for the solenoid valves.

These driver modules are also known as I/O peripheral modules and, in effect, there are two different types:

- Polled I/O – the peripheral acts independently and a buffer is used to store the data. The CPU then checks the module and transfers any data as needed. Each signal is monitored then processed and finally stored before the next signal is handled. The sequence is known as polling order.
- Interrupt driven I/O – the CPU carries out its routine tasks until an input signals a change. The processor is then interrupted. The I/O peripheral will process the operations independently and then signal the CPU. It will do this when there is new information or when the CPU needs to carry out an action.

### 3.4.10 Digital interfaces

The CPU will need to be able to send and retrieve data either to or from other control units using an external bus. The CPU can have a program that takes information from other controllers, such as the anti-lock braking system (ABS), and has the ability to send information to other control systems, such as the engine load signal. This is achieved either using controller area or local area networks (CAN or LAN).

### Bit resolution

Bit resolution has a power of 2. An 8-bit ADC has $2^8$ steps, which means 256 steps across the full voltage range. If the range of an ADC is 0 to +10V, then the lowest detectable change by the ADC is $10/256 = 0.039$, or 39 mV.

In the case of a knock sensor, the analogue to digital resolution needs to be high, so when the signal is converted from analogue to digital there is no loss in the high frequency detail.

# 4

# Digital circuit principles

Electric signals are of two fundamental types:

- Analogue signals – these have continuous values. An analogue signal shows a smooth continuous transition between its values. For example, if an analogue electrical signal changes value from 2 V to 2.5 V, it will do so continuously, holding all real values in the process (Figure 4.1a).
- Digital signals – these have a discrete set of values. A digital signal jumps between values in steps. For example, if a digital signal changes value from 0 V to 5 V, the change will be instantaneous, without the signal taking any value in between (Figure 4.1b).

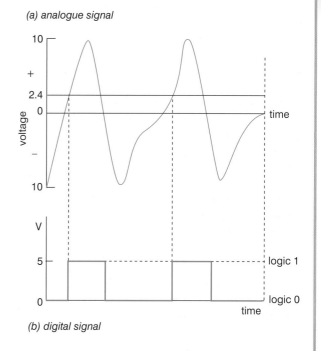

*(a) analogue signal*

*(b) digital signal*

*Figure 4.1 (a) Analogue signal and (b) digital signal*

## 4.1 Digital signals

Electronic sensors and components in motor vehicles communicate information using digital signals. Analogue signals from mechanical gauges are also transmitted as digital signals after being converted by an analogue to digital converter (ADC).

Digital quantities have discrete values, which can only change in multiples of a certain unit amount. This unit amount depends on the precision of the instrument producing the output. For example, a temperature sensor that measures in degrees Celsius to a precision of 0.1 °C will display a change in output only after a change greater than 0.1 °C occurs.

Digital quantities are expressed, stored, transmitted and processed using the binary number system.

This system involves representation using only two numbers, 0 and 1. A simple switch is a good example of a binary device. The switch has two possible states: ON and OFF. At any given instant it can only have one of the two. Such a variable, which can have only two values, is called a Boolean variable.

The use of Boolean variables makes it really easy to implement decision maps in the form of logic circuits. A large number of such circuits can be merged to make a computer. Digital signals in binary form have a number of advantages over analogue signals. They can be processed efficiently using cheap circuits and have no data loss during transmission. Binary data can also be stored compactly and accessed accurately from a memory device.

| | 128 | 64 | 32 | 16 | 8 | 4 | 2 | 1 | **Decimal digit (base 10)** |
|---|---|---|---|---|---|---|---|---|---|
| | $2^7$ | $2^6$ | $2^5$ | $2^4$ | $2^3$ | $2^2$ | $2^1$ | $2^0$ | **Binary digit (base 2)** |
| | 8 | 7 | 6 | 5 | 4 | 3 | 2 | 1 | **Bit sequence** |
| **Decimal number** | Binary number or code | | | | | | | | |
| 0 | 0 | 0 | 0 | 0 | 0 | 0 | 0 | 0 | |
| 1 | 0 | 0 | 0 | 0 | 0 | 0 | 0 | 1 | |
| 2 | 0 | 0 | 0 | 0 | 0 | 0 | 1 | 0 | |
| 3 | 0 | 0 | 0 | 0 | 0 | 0 | 1 | 1 | |
| 4 | 0 | 0 | 0 | 0 | 0 | 1 | 0 | 0 | |
| 5 | 0 | 0 | 0 | 0 | 0 | 1 | 0 | 1 | |
| 6 | 0 | 0 | 0 | 0 | 0 | 1 | 1 | 0 | |
| 7 | 0 | 0 | 0 | 0 | 0 | 1 | 1 | 1 | |
| 8 | 0 | 0 | 0 | 0 | 1 | 0 | 0 | 0 | |
| 9 | 0 | 0 | 0 | 0 | 1 | 0 | 0 | 1 | |
| 10 | 0 | 0 | 0 | 0 | 1 | 0 | 1 | 0 | |
| 11 | 0 | 0 | 0 | 0 | 1 | 0 | 1 | 1 | |
| 12 | 0 | 0 | 0 | 0 | 1 | 1 | 0 | 0 | |
| 13 | 0 | 0 | 0 | 0 | 1 | 1 | 0 | 1 | |
| 14 | 0 | 0 | 0 | 0 | 1 | 1 | 1 | 0 | |
| 15 | 0 | 0 | 0 | 0 | 1 | 1 | 1 | 1 | |
| 16 | 0 | 0 | 0 | 1 | 0 | 0 | 0 | 0 | |
| 17 | 0 | 0 | 0 | 1 | 0 | 0 | 0 | 1 | |
| 18 | 0 | 0 | 0 | 1 | 0 | 0 | 1 | 0 | |
| 19 | 0 | 0 | 0 | 1 | 0 | 0 | 1 | 1 | |
| 20 | 0 | 0 | 0 | 1 | 0 | 1 | 0 | 0 | |
| 21 | 0 | 0 | 0 | 1 | 0 | 1 | 0 | 1 | |
| 22 | 0 | 0 | 0 | 1 | 0 | 1 | 1 | 0 | |
| 23 | 0 | 0 | 0 | 1 | 0 | 1 | 1 | 1 | |
| 24 | 0 | 0 | 0 | 1 | 1 | 0 | 0 | 0 | |
| 25 | 0 | 0 | 0 | 1 | 1 | 0 | 0 | 1 | |
| 26 | 0 | 0 | 0 | 1 | 1 | 0 | 1 | 0 | |
| 27 | 0 | 0 | 0 | 1 | 1 | 0 | 1 | 1 | |
| 255 | 1 | 1 | 1 | 1 | 1 | 1 | 1 | 1 | |

Table 4.1 Decimal to binary conversion

## Binary and decimal numbers

The number system that we use most commonly is called the decimal system. This system uses base 10. For example, the number 15 can be expressed as:

$$1 \times 10^1 + 5 \times 10^0 = 10 + 5 = 15$$

The binary system uses base 2. So in terms of base 2, 15 can be expressed as:

$$1 \times 2^3 + 1 \times 2^2 + 1 \times 2^1 + 1 \times 2^0 = 8 + 4 + 2 + 1 = 15$$

and is written as 1111.

Table 4.1 shows several examples of binary and decimal equivalents.

## Logic circuits

Logic circuits use digital binary signals. The Boolean variables result in two logic states that translate to two voltage levels for the signal, as shown below:

| Logic | Voltage (V) | State |
|---|---|---|
| 0 | 0–0.8 | Low |
| 1 | 2.4–5.0 | High |

The switching between high and low states occurs at threshold voltages of 0.8V and 2.4V. A high state changes to a low state when the signal voltage falls below 0.8V. Similarly, a low state changes to a high state when the signal voltage exceeds 2.4V.

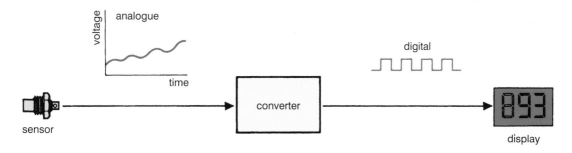

Figure 4.2 *Analogue signal to digital binary signal*

Signals from analogue sensors around the vehicle are converted to digital binary signals by an ADC before being transmitted. Figure 4.2 shows an analogue signal from a sensor being converted to a digital binary signal.

The digital signal has only two voltage levels. As mentioned before, this property of digital signals makes them easy to transmit, process, store and retrieve.

## 4.2  Logic gates and circuits

In its simplest form, a logic operation tells you whether a certain proposition is true if certain conditions are true. In electronics, a logic gate is a circuit that carries out such a logical operation.

A logic gate takes one or more Boolean variables as input and produces a Boolean output. As we saw before, digital signals are a combination of Boolean variables. Therefore, in electronic circuits, logic gates can be used to generate appropriate outputs in response to a given set of Boolean inputs.

The three basic logic gates are the NOT gate, the OR gate and the AND gate. Combinations of these basic gates can be used to construct more complex logic operations.

The NOT gate is also known as an inverter circuit; it gives an output of logic 1 when the input is logic 0 and vice versa.

The operation of a logic gate can be illustrated using a truth table. The truth table for the NOT gate is:

| Input | Output |
|-------|--------|
| 0     | 1      |
| 1     | 0      |

Truth tables for OR and AND gates are given in Figure 4.3. The rightmost column (labelled X) represents the logic state of the output. The columns to its left represent the logic state of the input(s).

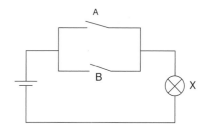

| A | B | X |
|---|---|---|
| 0 | 0 | 0 |
| 0 | 1 | 1 |
| 1 | 0 | 1 |
| 1 | 1 | 1 |

*(a) OR gate*

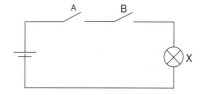

| A | B | X |
|---|---|---|
| 0 | 0 | 0 |
| 0 | 1 | 0 |
| 1 | 0 | 0 |
| 1 | 1 | 1 |

*(b) AND gate*

Figure 4.3 *Truth tables for (a) OR and (b) AND gates*

The NAND and NOR gates are two simple examples of logic operations made by combinations of the basic gates. The truth tables for NAND and NOR gates are given in Figure 4.4.

| A | B | X |
|---|---|---|
| 0 | 0 | 1 |
| 0 | 1 | 1 |
| 1 | 0 | 1 |
| 1 | 1 | 0 |

(a) NAND gate

| A | B | X |
|---|---|---|
| 0 | 0 | 1 |
| 0 | 1 | 0 |
| 1 | 0 | 0 |
| 1 | 1 | 0 |

(b) NOR gate

Figure 4.4 Truth tables for (a) NAND and (b) NOR gates

Boolean algebra is another method for expressing the operation of a logic gate. As with arithmetic, Boolean algebra has symbols for the basic operations of NOT, OR and AND. Figure 4.5 shows Boolean expressions for the basic logic operations.

The symbols used for representing logic gates either follow the American ANSI specifications or the European IEC specifications. In Britain, the IEC symbols are more common. These symbols are also given in Figure 4.5.

## 4.3   Applications of logic gates

There are hundreds of simple logic gate applications in a vehicle. Take the door warning light in a two-door car as an example. The light should be on as long as one of the doors is open. If we take an open door to be of logic state 0, we can construct the truth table for this application, as shown at the top of page 57.

| Logic element | British | American |
|---|---|---|
| AND | 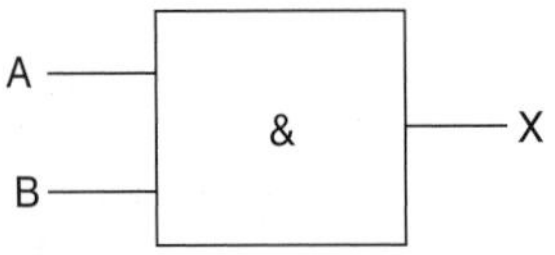 | 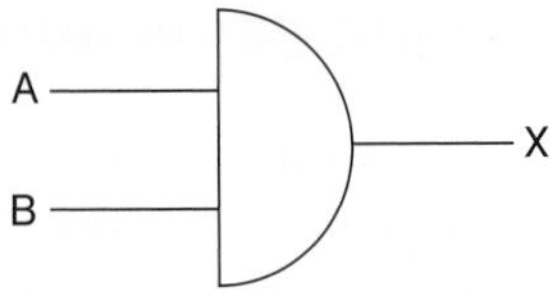 |
| OR | 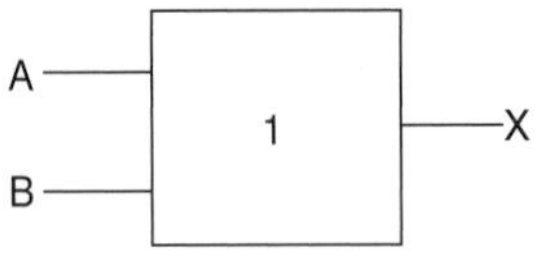 | 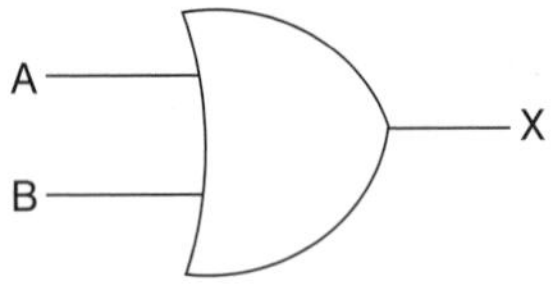 |
| NOT (inverter) | 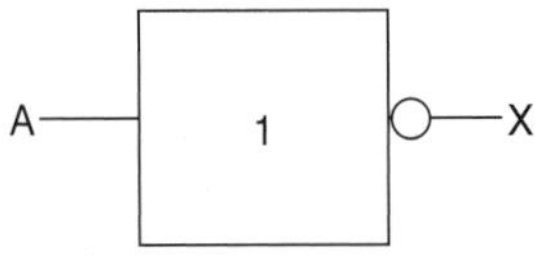 | 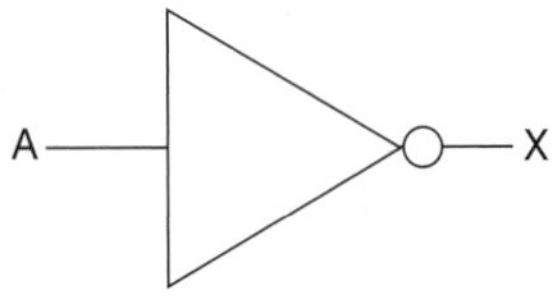 |
| NAND |  | 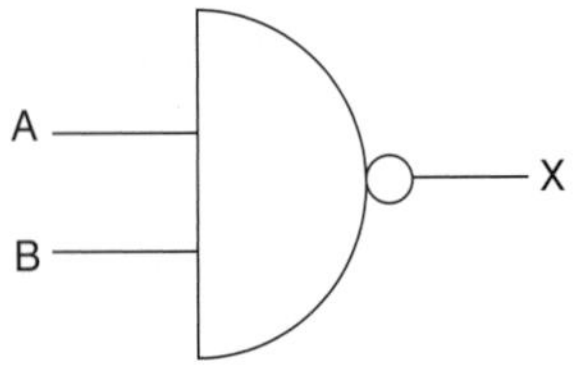 |
| NOR | 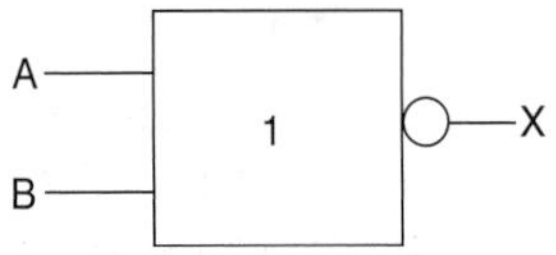 | 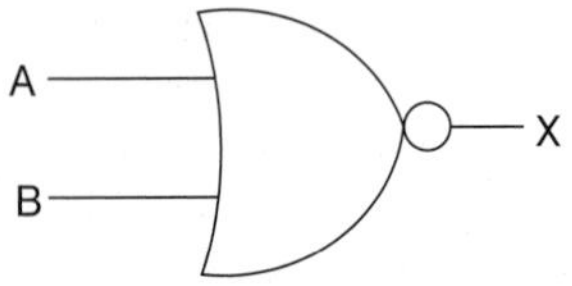 |

Figure 4.5 Boolean algebraic gate symbols for AND, OR, NOT and logic functions for NAND and NOR

| A | B | X |
|---|---|---|
| 0 | 0 | 1 |
| 0 | 1 | 1 |
| 1 | 0 | 1 |
| 1 | 1 | 0 |

The truth table is identical to that of a NAND gate, so a simple NAND gate would be perfect for an application like this.

It is important to understand that in a logic gate input signals are merely a trigger for the output. In no way does an input 'become' the output. This is a crucial point to remember. Every logic gate has separate power terminals that need to be connected to a power source in order for the logic circuit to function. The current and voltage for the output are drawn from the power source and *not* the input signals.

Logic gates can also be used as counters. This is done by connecting a clock signal to one input of the gate and using the second input terminal for, let's say, a signal from the sensor measuring wheel rotations. By using a simple AND gate, a timed output of the pulse from the wheel sensor can be obtained and used to calculate speed and acceleration. For more detail about counters, see pages 59–60.

### Combinational logic

The use of single gates only caters to simple applications. Most automotive applications require more complex logical operations to be implemented. Complex operations are made possible by using a combination of two or more logic gates. Some large logic functions may require a combination of several gates. Self-tuning injection valves are an example of a large logic function. Electronic control devices are discussed further in Chapter 7.

Of course, for implementing a given logic function, especially a large one, there may be more than one possible combination of logic gates. Where multiple combinations are possible, the cheapest circuit is used, preferably one that uses fewer gates. Along with reducing the cost, fewer gates lowers the risk of mathematical error.

## 4.4    Integrated logic circuits

The integrated circuit (IC) has been a milestone in electronics. Instead of assembling components to make devices, the whole circuit can be integrated into a body of semiconducting material. A piece of such an IC is called a chip. Silicon is the most widely used semiconductor for manufacturing chips. A chip consists of several gates formed by combinations of transistors, capacitors and diodes. Figure 4.6 shows a typical integrated logic circuit.

*Figure 4.6 Integrated logic circuit*

The three main integrated logic circuit technologies are introduced below. In each technology the basic function of logic gates remains the same; the only variations are in performance parameters.

### 4.4.1 IC families

#### Complementary metal oxide semiconductor (CMOS) logic

The CMOS family uses MOSFETs (metal oxide semiconductor field effect transistor) as the main switching devices in the circuit. Among the three technologies mentioned here it consumes the least power. This makes it particularly useful for microprocessor and microcontroller applications where a large number of gates are used.

#### Transistor–transistor logic (TTL)

Bipolar junction transistors (BJTs) are the main switching elements in a TTL circuit. The switching speed is three times faster than a CMOS device, but the power consumption is also higher. However, TTL devices are more stable than CMOS devices, which can be easily damaged from electrostatic discharge. In addition, TTL devices are very cheap to manufacture. TTL chips are widely used in circuits of consumer electronics.

#### Emitter-coupled logic (ECL)

ECL devices are similar to TTL but have much faster switching speeds and consequently consume more power. ECL logic chips are used in specialised electronic applications.

### 4.4.2 Storage in sequential circuits

So far we have discussed combinational circuits. Most systems in practical applications use combinational circuits, along with storage components and a clock pulse to synchronise their operation. Such circuits are called sequential circuits (Figure 4.7).

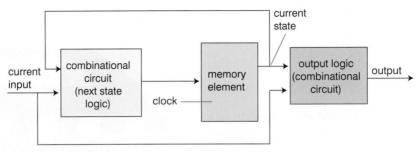

*Figure 4.7 Flow diagram of a sequential circuit*

## Latches

Storage components can maintain and switch between binary states in response to an input signal. Flip-flops are the simplest storage circuit. Flip-flops are constructed from latches. To understand the working of a flip-flop, we first need to understand the latch circuit. The set-reset (S-R) latch is a versatile latch made using cross-coupled NOR (or NAND) gates. Figure 4.8a shows an S-R latch and its truth table. The S and R inputs can be combined into a single output to make a data (D) latch. The D latch removes the undefined state when both inputs are 1. Figure 4.8b shows the two inputs combined to form a D latch.

Latches cannot be used alone as storage elements because their output state changes immediately with a change in input. Described simply, this transparency causes constant state changes in all connected latches for the duration of the clock pulse, 'avalanching' data and causing an unpredictable operation. A flip-flop solves this problem by isolating the input from the output.

## Flip-flops

Flip-flops are constructed by combining two latches. The output of the first latch controls the input of the second. The clock pulse on one latch is the inverse of that of the other at any given instant, hence isolating the flip-flop's output from the input (Figure 4.9 shows a D flip-flop). Each flip-flop can store one bit of data.

(a)

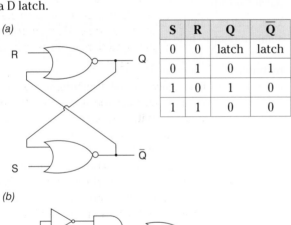

| S | R | Q | $\overline{Q}$ |
|---|---|-------|-------|
| 0 | 0 | latch | latch |
| 0 | 1 | 0 | 1 |
| 1 | 0 | 1 | 0 |
| 1 | 1 | 0 | 0 |

(b)

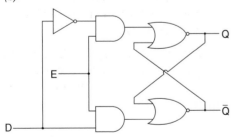

| E | D | Q | $\overline{Q}$ |
|---|---|-------|-------|
| 0 | 0 | latch | latch |
| 0 | 1 | latch | latch |
| 1 | 0 | 0 | 1 |
| 1 | 1 | 1 | 0 |

*Figure 4.8 (a) S-R latch and truth table, (b) D latch and truth table*

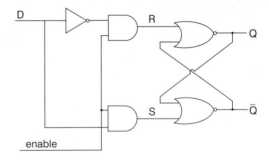

*Figure 4.9 D flip-flop*

The flip-flop is an important basic unit for larger circuits like counters, registers and memories. The J-K flip-flop (Figure 4.10) is perhaps the most useful of all basic flip-flops. It has a range of applications in data transfer, frequency dividers and sequence detectors.

## Registers

A register is made from a set of interconnected flip-flops. Since every flip-flop stores one bit of data, $n$ interconnected flip-flops make an $n$-bit register. Registers are useful for storing data and are an important component of microprocessors in computers. Modern computers use 32-bit and 64-bit registers. Figure 4.11 shows a 4-bit register.

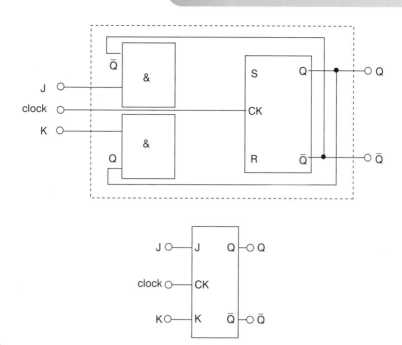

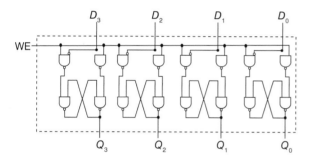

*Figure 4.10  J-K flip-flop*

$D_3$    $D_2$    $D_1$    $D_0$

WE

$Q_3$    $Q_2$    $Q_1$    $Q_0$

*Figure 4.11  4-bit register*

The clock input is common to all four flip-flops and triggers them on the rising edge of the clock pulse. When triggered, the Boolean states of the four $D$ inputs are stored in the 4-bit register. The binary data stored in the register can be accessed at the four $Q$ outputs. The clear (overline) signal is connected to the R inputs of the flip-flops and switches them to logic 0. The clear signal is maintained at logic 1 to prevent it interfering with the normal operation of the register. It is only used when a system reset is required.

## Counters

Counters are logic circuits for counting digital pulses received from another circuit, usually transducers such as motion, temperature and pressure sensors. Data from counters is used to acquire information on various parameters so appropriate responses can be produced manually or automatically.

Counters store numbers using the binary system. The output from counters can be used directly by control devices, as in ignition timing controllers, or be used as input to another circuit. In cases where the numerical output from a counter needs to be displayed, the data is decoded and fed to a seven-segment display and the appropriate light-emitting diodes (LEDs) illuminated. The seven-segment display is an array of LEDs, combinations of which resemble mathematical digits.

Counters are registers that change their binary state in an ascending or descending sequence in response to a clock pulse. In asynchronous counters, the clock

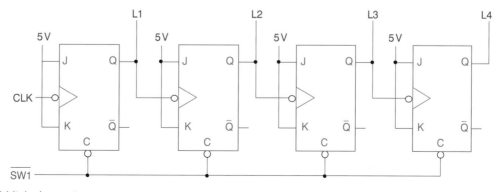

*Figure 4.12  4-bit ripple counter*

pulse is applied to only one flip-flop. Each subsequent flip-flop is clocked by the output of the previous flip-flop. Such counters are called ripple counters. Figure 4.12 shows the circuit layout of a ripple counter.

## 4.5   Logic testers

Logic circuits can be tested and diagnosed using a range of logic testing tools. The most comprehensive logic analysers have a hardware probe that is connected to an external computer and specialised software. These analysers test the circuit in depth and provide detailed information on the performance of each component in report form and the overall efficiency of the circuit in graphical form. In the motor industry, these analysers are used for high-performance vehicles and by racing teams to help fine-tune the electrical components.

High-performance and luxury vehicle manufacturers have specially made logic analysers for their vehicles. These analysers can be purchased through the manufacturer's dealership. Domestic vehicle manufacturers also sell logic testers for their vehicles at their dealership. The complexity of the tester varies according to the make and model of the vehicle.

The most basic logic tester is a simple probe that tests a point in the circuit and identifies whether it is in the high or low logic state. These low-cost testers are also called 'pen probes' and are available at most automotive and electronic dealers. The probe has various connectors and a tip probe, any of which can be used according to the situation. An LED array or a simple digital display shows whether the signal at the test point is low or high.

Logic probes are usually used with a logic pulser. A logic pulser is a signal generator that can deliver digital pulses of various compositions. The pulses are calibrated to not damage the transistors in the logic circuit. Figure 4.13 shows a logic probe and a logic pulser.

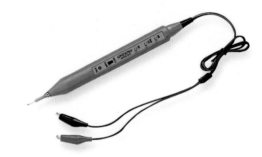

Figure 4.13  Logic probe and pulser

# 5 Sensors

In the modern motor vehicle, including hybrid, hydrogen-fuelled and electric vehicle propulsion systems, the engine management system (EMS) relies on accurate data from digital and analogue sensors working in an adaptive closed-loop network (see page 75). It detects signals from various sensors throughout the vehicle and then, after processing the data, it will either send an instruction to an actuator or store the data in the random access memory (RAM) of the EMS, to be used at some time in the future. Most of this chapter will deal with sensors that are located in engine management systems, anti-lock braking systems (ABS), traction control, temperature monitoring, driver assistance systems, and so on (Figure 5.1). The five main categories are reviewed here:

- Pressure sensors
- Pulse generators: speed/position sensors
- Temperature sensors
- Gas sensors
- Acceleration and vibration sensors

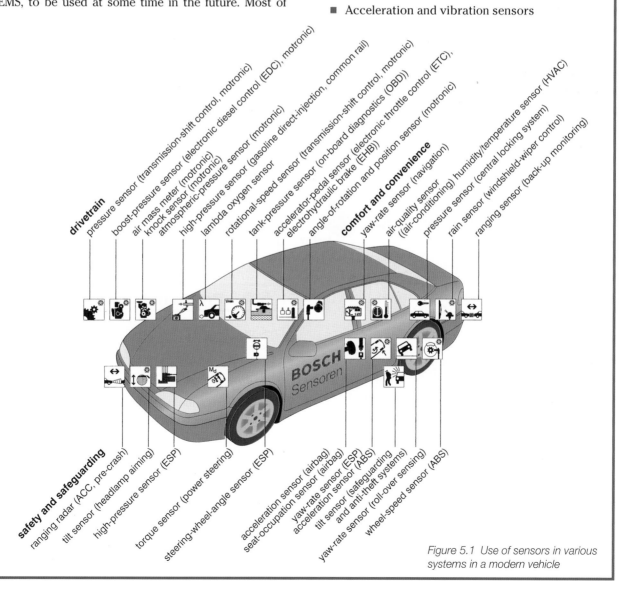

*Figure 5.1 Use of sensors in various systems in a modern vehicle*

## Health and safety best practices

When testing any component on a motor vehicle, it is important to make sure that you and others around you are protected. If you have to carry out dynamic tests, such as running the engine, make sure you are aware of moving parts, hot surfaces and emissions. Also, although most systems use a 12V supply, an ignition system can easily produce voltages in excess of 60,000 V, which can give you a significant shock, so always apply common sense and use the correct personal protective equipment (PPE). All sensors described in this chapter can be tested using a multimeter or oscilloscope to test for an earth, signal and supply.

## 5.1 Types of sensors

All sensors are used to gather information that relates to a particular mechanical action or thermal effect. They are designed to register a specific moment and convert a physical or chemical value into either an analogue or digital electrical signal.

The number of sensors required to control a system efficiently depends on the factors that affect the operation of the system. For example, a simple EMS, as shown in Figure 5.2, has sensor signal inputs to measure crankshaft position, engine speed, engine load through manifold **depression**, engine coolant /air temperature, throttle position and battery supply/reference voltages. These inputs have a direct bearing on the outputs, namely the EMS, ignition, fuelling, idle control and turbo waste gate, as well as an influence on other systems, such as ABS and air-conditioning operations.

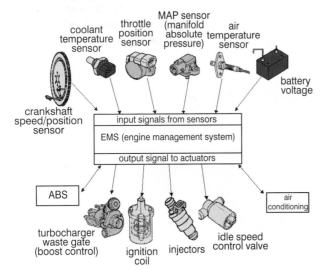

Figure 5.2 *The system has a number of sensors and actuators, so the EMS can perform a number of tasks and control functions, including an influence on other systems*

**Depression**: a pressure lower than atmospheric pressure. (This term is preferred to 'vacuum' because a vacuum suggests that no pressure exists whatsoever.)

Sensors can be:

- active or self-generating (generate their own energy), or
- passive or modulating (require an external electrical supply).

Many sensors have to work in a harsh environment where there is heat, vibration, thermal or mechanical shock, and possibly contamination. However, the sensor has also to fulfil the requirements of size, power consumption and compatibility with other electronic circuits.

Signal input to the EMS should relate closely to the physical quantity the sensor is intended to measure. Once the signal has been transmitted, no amount of signal processing can improve the original data accuracy, so if control precision is expected, the sensor quality must be high. The cost of higher-quality sensors can be eased if demand is high, since cost is associated with manufacturing volume.

For example, the sensors used for emission control have to be accurate and fast acting. They must be monitored for defects and standards throughout their operation, and the system should inform the driver if an error occurs through a malfunction indicator lamp (MIL) on the dashboard.

## 5.2 Pressure sensors

Pressure sensors are used to measure variable pressure. They are mainly static-type pressure sensors and have many applications, such as the monitoring of:

- intake manifold pressure to calculate air/fuel ratio for fuel management
- oil pressure for engine/transmission
- brake fluid pressure
- common rail fuel pressure
- tyre pressure.

### 5.2.1 Strain gauge pressure sensor

When a material is strained, a change in length occurs, which results in an increase of electrical resistance. A solid-state semiconductor is sandwiched between two silicon dioxide layers, into which are positioned four pressure-sensitive resistors arranged along the edges of the silicon diaphragm. Connection to the resistors is by metal bonding pads formed at each corner of the sensor (Figure 5.3). Air pressure sensing requires a vacuum chamber and, in this case, the bonding of a Pyrex plate to one face of the chip under vacuum conditions forms the chamber.

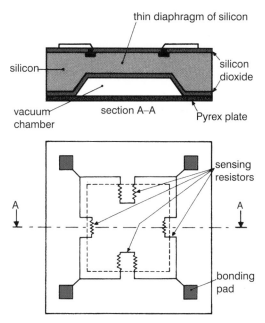

Figure 5.3 Strain gauge pressure sensor

Being of a compact design, the diaphragm thickness is no greater than 250 µm (0.25 mm). Most sensors are directly attached to the inlet manifold.

When load changes within the manifold deflect the diaphragm, the length of each resistor is affected. Because of the arrangement of the resistors, the resistance of two of them increases while the resistance of the other two decreases by an equal amount. The resistance change is then made use of in a Wheatstone full bridge circuit to give an output signal proportional to the pressure (Figure 5.4).

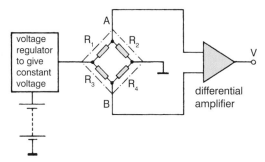

Figure 5.4 Strain gauge circuit using Wheatstone bridge

The four resistors in the strain gauge form the four arms of the bridge. This resistor array is supplied with a constant voltage and the bridge is calibrated so that it is balanced when the strain gauges are undeflected. When pressure is increased, the resistance of $R_1$ and $R_4$ increases and that of $R_2$ and $R_3$ similarly decreases. This unbalances the bridge and gives a difference in potential at AB, which provides an output signal proportional to the pressure.

Using resistors in this form compensates for temperature change. Any increase in resistance due to heat affects all resistors equally, so the bridge balance is maintained over a wide temperature range.

## 5.2.2 Manifold absolute pressure (MAP) sensor

The most common application of a pressure sensor is for engine load monitoring. Originally, a mechanical aneroid capsule type was used for this. It incorporated a signal voltage from a potentiometer, variable inductance or differential transformer. The most common MAP sensors on modern vehicles are the capacitor-capsule MAP sensor and the more recent piezoelectric MAP sensor.

The requirements for these sensors are to monitor the various MAP changes in response to throttle movement. These changes represent the load of the engine. Quality of airflow due to pressure difference depends on the throttle opening, so the throttle must also be fitted with a potentiometer to indicate the throttle angle position.

When the engine is lightly loaded, the MAP is low (i.e. a high depression exists in the manifold) because the throttle is fully closed and the depression is approaching about 0.17 **bar** absolute. This pressure change is both reliable and convenient to use.

During normal loading of the engine, the MAP varies between the following limits:

- High speed, light load, low MAP (high depression) (e.g. 0.4 bar).
- Low speed, heavy load, high MAP (low depression) (e.g. 0 bar).

**Bar**: a unit of pressure. 1 bar (101.3 kPa) is the standard pressure of the atmosphere on an **absolute pressure** scale. On this scale 0 bar means there is zero pressure (i.e. a vacuum).

**Absolute pressure**: this is zero-referenced against a perfect vacuum, so it is equal to **gauge pressure** plus atmospheric pressure.

**Gauge pressure**: this is zero-referenced against ambient air pressure, so it is equal to absolute pressure minus atmospheric pressure. Negative signs are usually omitted. Differential pressure is the difference in pressure between two points.

These limits are 'gauge pressure' values when atmospheric pressure is taken as zero. In other words, the difference between absolute pressure and gauge pressure is the variable atmospheric pressure value. Therefore, the pumping action of the engine (suction effect) has actually lowered the pressure by 0.6 bar.

## Capacitor-capsule MAP sensor

A capacitor consists of two metal plates separated by a **dielectric**. Capacitance is varied by altering the distance between the plates, so this feature can be used in a pressure sensor. The basic construction of a capacitor-capsule MAP sensor is shown in Figure 5.5. It consists of two aluminium oxide plates, which are coated on the inner surfaces with a film electrode, and a lead connected to each electrode.

> **Dielectric**: an electrical insulator material which, when placed in an electric field, prevents an electrical charge from flowing as it would in a conductor; instead, it polarises the positive charge towards the field and the negative charge in the opposite direction.

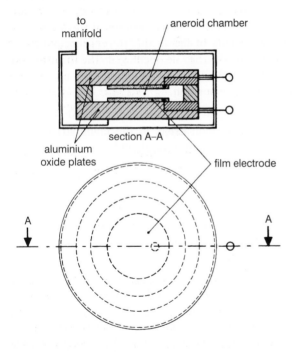

Figure 5.5 Capacitor-capsule MAP sensor

The two plates are held apart by an insulation material shaped in the form of a flat washer to provide an aneroid chamber at the centre. The capsule is placed in a container that is connected by a pipe to the pressure source.

Operation of the unit is achieved by using the change in pressure that is communicated to the sensor. This pressure change deflects the plates and alters the distance between the two electrodes.

## Signal processing for capacitor-capsule MAP sensor

Change in capacitance caused by alteration in the MAP is made to generate an output voltage signal by using various circuit arrangements. One method of signal processing is to use a series resonant circuit (Figure 5.6).

In this arrangement a change in capacitance is made to alter the phase of the frequency produced by an oscillator.

The main circuit consists of an inductor (L), resistor (R), and sensor capacitor (C), which are supplied with alternating current (AC) from an oscillator.

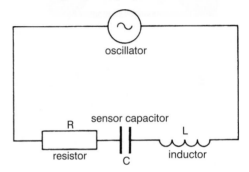

Figure 5.6 Series resonant circuit

The output from the oscillator gives a normal AC waveform, such as those shown in Figure 5.8. If the circuit contained resistance only, the voltage and current peaks would occur at the same time. However, the presence of an inductor or capacitor causes a change in the wave pattern. The inductor has the effect of retarding the current peak, causing it to lag behind the voltage peak, but the capacitor has the opposite effect and advances the current peak ahead of the voltage peak.

At one particular frequency, called the resonance frequency, the effect of the inductor balances the effect of the capacitor. Then the voltage and current are in phase and the current is at a maximum, so the voltage across the circuit is high. This feature has been used for many years to amplify radio waves received by an aerial, where a variable capacitor is used to 'tune' the circuit to the resonance frequency.

Figure 5.7 shows two voltage pick-up points in an LCR series circuit. Voltage $V_1$ is the supply or reference voltage and $V_2$ registers the potential difference (PD) across the resistor R. At the resonance frequency the voltage $V_2$ is proportional to the current in the circuit and in phase with it. The peak voltage at C–D, $V_2$, then occurs at the same instant as the peak voltage, $V_1$, at B–D. In other words, the voltage across the resistor is in phase with the oscillator voltage. The phases coincide at this frequency because the retardation in current due to the inductor equals the advance due to the capacitor.

When the capacitance is altered, the circuit will cease to resonate, so the current will decrease. Also, the time at which there is maximum current through the resistor becomes out of phase with the voltage $V_1$. Since $V_2$ depends on the current passing through R, the phase change produced by the alteration in capacitance is shown by the time difference between the voltage peaks at C–D and B–D (Figure 5.8).

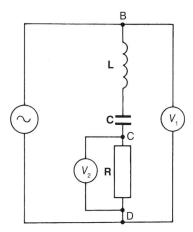

Figure 5.7 LCR series circuit

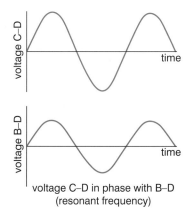

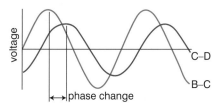

Figure 5.8 Phase change of $V_1$ and $V_2$ due to change in capacitance of LCR circuit in Figure 5.7

Figure 5.9 shows an LCR series circuit used for a MAP sensor. In this case, the frequency and circuit components are tuned to resonate at standard atmospheric pressure. When the pressure is varied, the change in phase between the resistor p.d. and the reference p.d. is measured by a phase detector. This generates an output signal proportional to the change in manifold pressure.

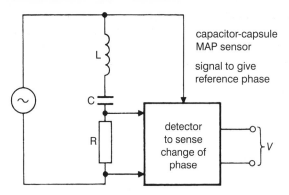

Figure 5.9 LCR circuit for capacitor-capsule-type MAP sensor

## Piezoelectric MAP sensor

This sensor contains a piezoelectric circuit and a crystal that changes its internal resistance when deflected. It converts the pressure change into a signal voltage. This voltage usually functions within a 0–5 V range, although some devices produce a square wave output. The output signal will increase when less depression within the manifold is acting on the sensor.

This form of sensor is commonly used to measure pressure but can also be used to measure acceleration. The data from the MAP signal is used to calculate air density, which the EMS combines with engine speed and air temperature to determine the air mass that will help to establish the correct air/fuel ratio for optimum combustion at that specific moment. In other words, it is there for metering the fuel.

## Fluid pressure sensor

Of this sensor configuration the most commonly used sensor is the diaphragm type, which can be used in monitoring:

- engine lubrication integrity
- automatic transmission oil pressure operation
- hydraulic brake pressure rises
- fuel pressures.

A pressure switch sensor signals when a certain pressure is reached or it initiates a warning message when the pressure drops below a given point. Using a more costly transducer for fluid pressure indication gives an output signal, of digital or analogue form, that is proportional to the pressure. This signal can be processed to indicate to the driver the actual pressure reading.

The diaphragm functions with pressure being exerted to one side, so that it will deflect to a greater or lesser degree depending on the pressure. Low pressure systems require large diaphragms that can easily deflect. As with higher-pressure systems (e.g. diesel common rail systems) the diaphragm would be manufactured of spring steel with a smaller diameter and would only deflect very slightly, plus the sensor would also need to incorporate strain gauge technology (see pages 62–63).

## Tyre pressure monitoring

This system comprises a pressure sensor chip contained in a silicon block. Being a direct pressure measurement, it requires a signal processor and transmitter so that real-time sensing can be transmitted to the driver display within the vehicle. The system also needs a temperature sensor to compensate for pressure variations due to temperature changes.

## Air mass meters

The modern spark ignition (SI) and compression ignition (CI) engines' fuel-injection systems use air mass metering or MAP sensors, as defined previously. On older vehicles a volume flap-type sensor was used but is no longer in production because it restricted airflow within the manifold. There are now two types of air mass sensors:

- Hot wire
- Hot film

### Hot wire/film air mass meters

Air mass meters rely on the cooling effect of air as it passes over a heated wire (hot wire type) or a heated resistor (film type). In the hot wire type, a constant electric current passing through the wire heats it, and then the temperature of the wire will fall as the airflow is increased. Similarly, if a hot wire is kept at a constant temperature, then the amount of current required to maintain this temperature will be governed by the airflow; the larger the airflow, the greater the current.

Both the constant-current and constant-temperature methods use electronic means to measure the temperature. Generally this is done by measuring the change in resistance that occurs when the temperature is changed.

Hot wire systems take into account changes in air density. Atmospheric pressure decreases with altitude, therefore, in an area situated well above sea level, the air mass supplied for a given throttle opening is reduced considerably. Unless this feature is taken into account, the richer mixture received by the engine would cause high exhaust gas pollution.

Figure 5.10a shows the construction of a hot wire of diameter 0.070 mm, which is exposed to air that passes through a tube situated in the air intake. Figure 5.10b shows that the wire is connected into a Wheatstone bridge circuit as described previously. A power amplifier, situated where the galvanometer (an instrument for detecting the presence and direction of an electric current) is placed in a bridge circuit, controls the current supplied to the four arms of the bridge. When a signal shows that the bridge is unbalanced, the amplifier adjusts the heating current to restore the bridge to a balanced state.

Operation of the sensor is based on the constant temperature principle. When air is passing at a constant rate, the supply current holds the hot wire at a given temperature; consequently the bridge is maintained in a balanced state. Any increase in airflow cools the hot wire and causes its resistance to decrease. This unbalances the bridge and, as a result, causes the amplifier to increase the heating current until the original temperature is restored. This increase in the heating current causes a higher voltage drop across $R_M$. By measuring this drop across a precision resistor placed at $R_M$, a sensor output signal is obtained (see Figure 5.10c – the red trace indicating a correct operational trace). The signal shows the heating current but it also indicates the mass of air flowing through the meter.

By relating the air mass meter signal to values stored in a 'look-up' table in the ECU's read-only memory (ROM), the computer can determine the amount of fuel that needs to be injected to give the required air/fuel ratio.

Any alteration in the temperature of the intake air causes the bridge to become unbalanced. Therefore, a compensating resistor wire $R_K$ is placed in the airstream adjacent to the hot wire. The temperature of the 'cold wire' compensating resistor acts as a 'standard'. In operation, the amplifier keeps the hot wire $R_H$ at 100 °C above the temperature of the cold wire.

Heat radiation from a hot wire is decreased when the wire becomes dirty. To avoid this problem, the ECU is programmed to burn off the dirt by heating the wire to a higher than normal temperature for one second every time the engine is switched off.

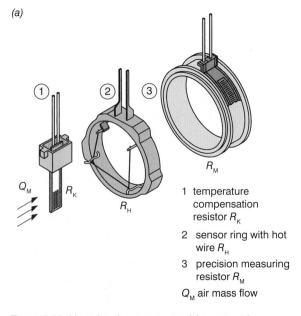

(a)

1 temperature compensation resistor $R_K$

2 sensor ring with hot wire $R_H$

3 precision measuring resistor $R_M$

$Q_M$ air mass flow

*Figure 5.10 Hot wire air mass meter: (a) construction*

(b)

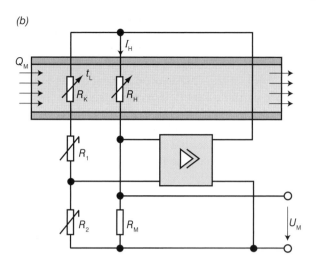

$R_K$ temperature compensation resistor

$R_H$ hot wire heater resistor

$R_M$ measuring resistor

$R_{1,2}$ bridge balance resistors

$U_M$ measurement voltage

$I_H$ heating current

$t_L$ air temperature

$Q_M$ air mass flow

(c)

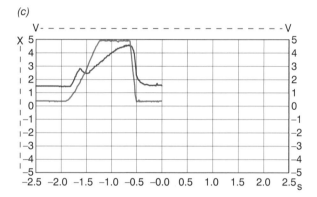

*Figure 5.10 (continued) Hot wire air mass meter: (b) schematic, (c) traces*

A more recent development is the hot film air mass meter. In this arrangement, the wire is replaced by a heated film having integral resistors for airflow measurement and temperature compensation, making it a thermal flow meter. This meter is insensitive to contamination because the sensor elements are made of a ceramic aluminium oxide substrate and the actual film resistor is made of platinum. Using this design does not require a burn-off period. This is an important feature, as the burn-off causes damage to the hot wire air mass meter, causing it to reach a temperature of 1000 °C every time it is deployed. Accuracy is improved as both meters measure actual mass, so no conversion is required within the EMS, although the hot film air mass meter is claimed to be more accurate, robust and reliable than the hot wire air mass meter due to the lack of contamination.

## 5.3 Pulse generators: speed/position sensors

Speed/position sensors, which are magnetically, optically or capacitance generated, are known as pulse generators. They are used in many applications, such as:

- crankshaft angular position for timing of the ignition and injection systems
- crankshaft movement for computation of engine speed for engine management and tachometer operation
- throttle position for fuel injection and automatic transmission systems
- steering angle position
- gearbox output shaft movement for speedometer, odometer and trip computer operation
- axle to body position for indication of axle loading
- maximum wear of brake friction material
- door position for 'door ajar' indication
- road wheel movement/speed for ABS and traction control systems.

### 5.3.1 Variable reluctance sensor

This type of sensor (Figure 5.11) is very robust and consists of a permanent magnet and a sensing coil winding. A steel disc, having a series of cut-away portions, is attached to the driving shaft and is set so that the disc passes between the poles of the magnet.

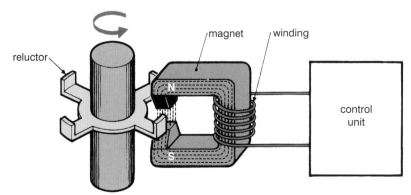

*Figure 5.11 Variable reluctance sensor*

Placing a ferrous metal between the poles of a magnet makes it easier for the flux to link the two poles. This low **reluctance** path gives a high magnetic field intensity.

> **Reluctance**: the term used in magnetic 'circuits' to indicate the circuit's resistance to the 'passage' of a magnetic flux.

Turning the reluctor disc to bring the cut-away portion of the disc between the magnetic poles considerably increases the reluctance of the magnetic circuit. As the permeability of air is much greater than that of the steel, the difficult flux path through the air gives a field of low intensity.

The reluctor disc can be thought of as being like a water tap: it controls the 'flow' (flux) around the magnetic circuit. When the protruding tab of the disc is between the magnetic poles, the tap is open, but when the cut-away portion is in place, the tap is closed.

The sensing signal is generated by the changes that occur in the magnetic flux intensity. When the magnetic flux either increases or decreases, an electromotive force (EMF) is induced in the coil winding. Since the magnitude of the EMF is proportional to the rate of change of the magnetic flux, the faster the change, the greater is the EMF. For example, when the reluctor disc is stationary, no output is obtained. This means that when the variable reluctor sensor is used for ignition the engine timing cannot be set statically.

Figure 5.12b indicates the waveform produced as the reluctor tab is passed through the magnet pole. As the reluctor approaches the pole the EMF builds up to a maximum. When the reluctor tab reaches a point where it is aligned with the pole, such that the flux is at its maximum, the EMF is zero. At this point the rate of change of magnetic flux is zero. After this point has been passed, the magnetic flux decays and an EMF of opposite polarity is generated. The actual shape of the AC pulse wave produced by the sensor depends on the shape of the magnetic pole and reluctor. In general, the wave resembles that shown in Figure 5.12c.

Two crankshaft position sensors are shown in Figure 5.13. Flywheel applications use either a ferro-magnetic pin or a missing tooth to trigger the sensor pulse.

*Figure 5.12 Variable reluctance crankshaft position/speed sensor: (a) crankshaft reluctor disc with a master position reference point (missing tooth), (b) note the different shape of the signal created by the missing tooth, (c) waveform*

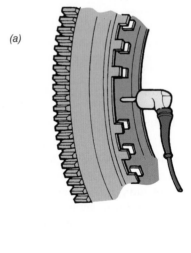

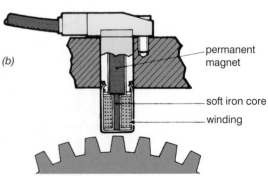

*Figure 5.13 Crankshaft position sensors*

Typical peak-to-peak outputs for this type vary from zero, when stationary, to around 200 V, when the peripheral speed of the flywheel is 60 m/s (metres per second).

In the second sensor (Figure 5.13b) the lobe centre line corresponds to the point where the positive pulse half-wave changes to the negative half-wave.

This sensor has many advantages. It is an active pulse generator, which means it does not need an external voltage supply, so it is possible to reduce vehicle loom cable weight. It also operates over a wide temperature range and has a long life. The disadvantage is that the AC signal is very low at slow speeds and its signal magnitude is variable throughout its operation, whereas the EMS would prefer a constant magnitude signal. Before the EMS can use the signal input it has to convert the AC signal to a digital signal because computers can only work in binary.

## 5.3.2 Direct current-excited inductive sensor

The disadvantage of low output, as given from a variable reluctor sensor is overcome by using a direct current-excited (DC-excited) inductive sensor. This passive type uses DC to excite a field magnet to give a suitable minimum output voltage, such as 2 V peak-to-peak, irrespective of the operating frequency.

Figure 5.14 shows the principle of this type of sensor. It consists of a W-shaped iron core with a field coil wound around the centre leg of the core. The spacing of the other legs is arranged to bridge the teeth of the rotating ferro-magnetic member. In the example shown, the flywheel teeth provide the paths for the flux.

Unless precautions are taken, the generation of eddy currents causes the pulse peaks to alter in relation to the position of the rotating member. This 'phase shift' problem is minimised in this design by using a ferrite material for the magnetic core. A typical phase shift is given as 0.3° over a range of 0–6000 rev/min. Operation of the sensor is achieved by exciting the field magnet with DC from an EMS.

The EMS varies the current to give a constant voltage pulse. At low speeds the excited current is comparatively large, but as the speed is increased the current is reduced. As the flywheel teeth pass the legs of the iron core, the charge in the reluctor path varies the magnetic field intensity and, as a result, it produces an AC pulse in the field winding. This pulse is detected by the EMS, which processes it to provide the output signal.

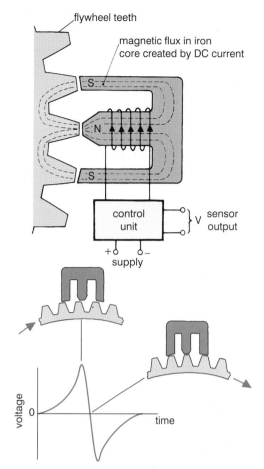

*Figure 5.14 DC-excited position sensors*

## 5.3.3 Hall effect sensor

This passive sensor uses the principle that a voltage is produced when a thin-film semiconductor carrying an electric current is placed at right angles to a magnetic field. This is known as the Hall effect.

The Hall effect is shown in Figure 5.15a. This shows a semiconductor material placed in a magnetic field and supplied with constant current across the material from A to B. Under the influence of a magnetic flux, the electron flow of the current $I$ is deflected as it passes through the semiconductor. This causes a potential difference (PD) across the plate in the direction C–D. This limited Hall voltage of a few millivolts is amplified to induce a signal voltage so that the EMS can interpret its position.

### Ignition speed/position Hall effect sensor

When the Hall effect is used for an ignition speed/position sensor, one method is to use a rotating vane to act as a switch for controlling the magnetic flux (Figure 5.15b). When the vane is in the air gap between the magnet and the Hall integrated circuit

*(a)*

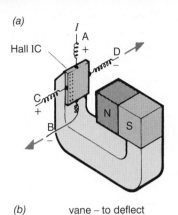

*(b)*

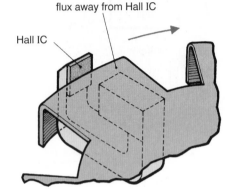

vane – to deflect
flux away from Hall IC

*(c)*

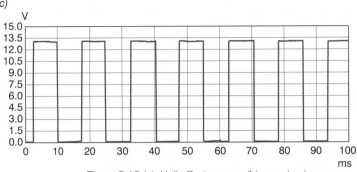

*Figure 5.15 (a) Hall effect sensor, (b) vane in air gap, (c) expected waveform*

(IC), the magnetic field is diverted away from the semiconductor. This 'turns off' the Hall effect and switches the primary ignition circuit on. The time for which the charge flows in the primary is known as the dwell time. This specifically signals the position of the shaft controlling the vane. When the vane leaves, the Hall voltage is re-established and secondary ignition occurs.

The advantage of this sensor is that there is no need for converting the signal because it is already a digital square wave and there is very little fluctuation in the output signal voltage, which remains almost constant. This constant will only change if the magnetic field strength varies the Hall effect voltage; the stronger the field, the higher the voltage.

These sensors are currently favoured within the automotive industry because of accuracy, product life expectancy and cost.

## Steering angle Hall effect sensor

Using electronic stability control (ESC) technology, the system must compare the steering wheel angle and applied braking pressure with the actual vehicle rotary motion and its road speed. This provides a means of retaining vehicle stability and preventing the vehicle from becoming incontrollable. Figure 5.16 shows an exploded view of one design of the Hall effect type of steering angle sensor.

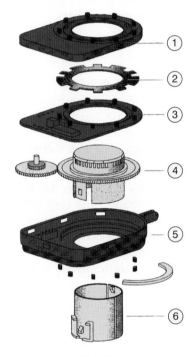

1  housing cover with nine equidistantly spaced permanent magnets

2  code disc (magnetically soft material)

3  PCB with nine Hall effect switches and microprocessor

4  step-down gearing

5  remaining five Hall effect vane switches

6  fastening sleeve for steering column

*Figure 5.16 Hall effect steering angle sensor*

The Hall effect element function is to measure the magnetic field of an adjacent magnet. It uses a magnetic code disc (2) that, when rotating in conjunction with the steering shaft, reduces or even screens off the magnetic field of the individual nine magnets (1), registering in a digital format the angular position through the nine Hall effect switches (3). The remaining five switches (5) register the number of revolutions the steering wheel has been turned through. A ratio of 4:1 is needed for the step down-gear (4) because a steering wheel can rotate a total of four complete turns and the actual position of the steering wheel needs to be established and acknowledged.

## 5.3.4 Reed switch

A reed switch consists of two or more contacts mounted in a glass vial to exclude contaminants. The vial is evacuated of air or filled with an inert gas to reduce damage by arcing.

The switch is operated by a permanent magnet, exposing the reeds of the switch to a magnetic flux, which causes each reed to take up the polarity of the magnetic pole nearest to it. Since the reed polarities are opposite, they will be attracted together (Figure 5.17a). This will close the switch and allow the flow of charge to create the sensor pulse.

It is possible to operate the reed by using a magnet attached to a rotating shaft, but it is more common to keep the magnet stationary and use a mechanical means, such as a toothed wheel, to divert the flux away from the reed when the switch is to be opened (Figure 5.17b). This simple operation is commonly used for speedometers or for indicating a liquid level.

## 5.3.5 Optical optoelectronic sensors

This passive sensor can be used to signal a shaft position, although it is more commonly used for torque and steer angle indication, rain/light sensors and even lane guidance systems.

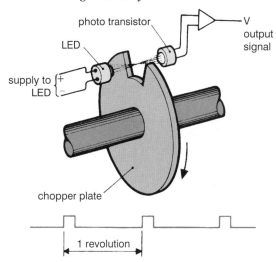

Figure 5.18 Optoelectronic sensor

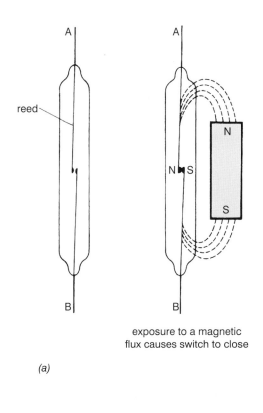

(a)

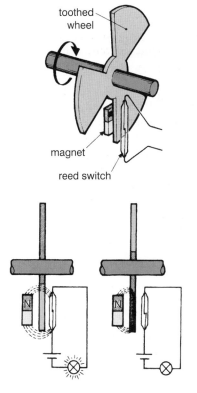

(b)

Figure 5.17 Reed switch

The principle is shown in Figure 5.18. An LED light source is positioned opposite a phototransistor. A chopper plate, in the form of a disc, is attached to the moving shaft.

A slot or hole in the disc allows the light to pass to the phototransistor at the instant when the slot is aligned with the LED. At this point it signals the position of the shaft.

The LED fitted generally has a frequency within the range infrared to ultraviolet, and often lies outside the range of vision of the human eye.

A voltage applied to the LED is set to give a phototransistor output that is sufficient after amplification to signal the EMS. In a case where a transistor–transistor logic (TTL) circuit is used, the typical output voltages will be 2.4V (high level) and 0.2V (low level).

This system has the same advantages as the Hall effect sensor, although contamination of the lenses is a specific problem. However, in operations such as using a turbine to measure fluid flow (where the rotational speed is proportional to the flow rate) an optical sensor is highly practical in converting the motion into an electrical signal.

## Rain and light sensor

Located on the windscreen, this dual sensor is designed to detect rain droplets and activate the windscreen wiper system. The light sensor monitors the various light conditions and will activate lights on or off accordingly.

The rain sensor (Figure 5.19) uses an LED (6) or an infrared light that is emitted at a specific angle, which reflects back to a photodiode (4), and when rain drops form on the screen they alter the signal, activating the wipers. The light sensors (3 and 5) are combined standard and silicon photodiodes, which evaluate various directions of light.

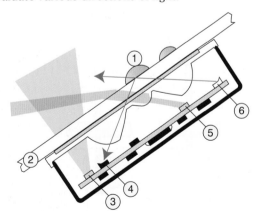

| | | | |
|---|---|---|---|
| 1 | rain drops | 4 | photodiode |
| 2 | windshield | 5 | light sensor, aligned to far distance |
| 3 | ambient-light sensor | 6 | LED |

*Figure 5.19 Rain/light sensor*

## Dirt sensor

This sensor is also fitted with an LED and a photodiode (also known as an opto receiver). This system is used for monitoring dirt on headlamp lenses and, once detected, automatically cleans them. The LED is carefully positioned in the lens away from the direct path of the light source. When dirt particles are present, the infrared beam being emitted is reflected back to the photodiode. The intensity of the light received by the photodiode is proportional to the amount of contamination, and leads to the headlamp washer system being automatically initiated if required.

## Fibre-optic sensor system

Limited space in the vicinity of the sensor sometimes prevents the fitting of a normal type of optical sensor. This drawback can be overcome by using two fibre-optic strands to transmit the light signal from the LED to a phototransistor (Figure 5.20).

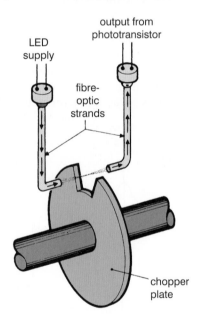

*Figure 5.20 Fibre-optic sensor system*

This light-transmission system offers many advantages for motor vehicles, including:

- saving space
- a very high rate of data transmission
- extra safety because fibre-optic cables do not carry an electrical current
- the possibility of using in hostile environments
- that they do not suffer 'noise' problems (i.e. electrical charges are not induced from surrounding electrical equipment).

## 5.3.6 Capacitance sensor

This type of sensor uses a toothed wheel to form either a plate or the dielectric of a capacitor. Its operation relies on the following principle.

If a parallel-plate capacitor is charged to a given value, the voltage across the plate will:

■ increase as the distance between the plates increases
■ decrease if a dielectric is used instead of air between the plates.

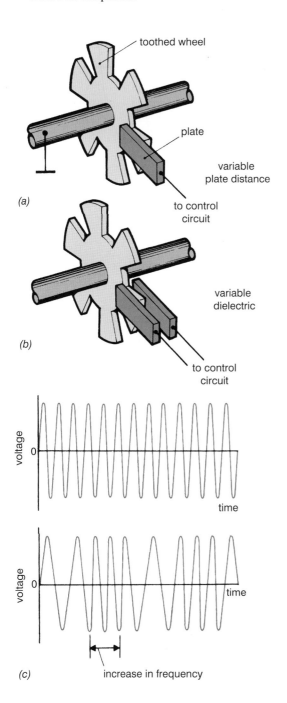

*(a)*

*(b)*

*(c)*

*Figure 5.21  Parallel-plate capacitor*

Capacitance sensors can be designed to use one or other of these two features. They can be excited by means of AC or DC.

Figure 5.21a shows a sensor that produces a signal by varying the distance between the plates. This is achieved by rotating a toothed wheel. Since the plate and the toothed wheel are electrically charged, the movement of the wheel has the effect of changing the distance between the plates. In the case of a DC-excited sensor, this change in voltage provides a pulse, which is processed to give the required output.

The alternative construction uses a dielectric wheel (Fig 5.21b). Rotation of the wheel between the two charged plates varies the voltage across the plates to give the pulse. This sensor can be used for a high rotational speed. However, it is not favoured for use at a lower speed and for detecting zero motion because it is difficult to maintain the plates in a clean state and at a constant electrical charge at such low speeds.

When the sensor is AC-excited, the capacitor forms part of an oscillator circuit. Changes in capacitance due to movement of the toothed wheel result in a change in the frequency (Figure 5.21c). To detect high-speed movement, a high frequency must be used. This can be a disadvantage because this often causes interference with radios and in-car telephones unless the sensor system is adequately screened. Because the screening affects the capacitance of the sensor system, the associated circuitry of the sensor must be situated as close as possible to the sensor.

This type of sensor can be used as a human machine interface (HMI). Where human touch comes into proximity with the capacitance electrodes, an additional capacitance is created (which can be used to detect a physical presence), so it can be used as a touch-sensitive control throughout the vehicle.

## 5.3.7 Throttle position potentiometer sensor

The potentiometer (pot) is a variable resistance sensor that is used for altering electrical potential. One of the simplest arrangements is a variable resistor, as shown in Figure 5.22. In this case, the

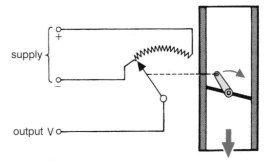

*Figure 5.22  Throttle position sensor*

throttle is connected to a contact blade, which wipes across a resistor coil. As the throttle is opened, the number of resistor coils in the circuit is reduced. This alters the voltage and potential of the output in relation to earth. Figure 5.23 shows a typical sensor.

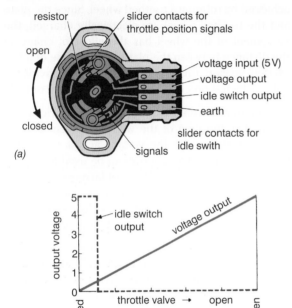

*(a)*

*(b)*

*Figure 5.23 (a)Throttle position potentiometer, (b) expected output*

A constant voltage of 5 V is applied to the sensor. As the contact blades slide along the resistor in accordance with the opening of the throttle valve, the output voltage increases proportionally. This linear signal is transmitted to the EMS, which provides the throttle angle information. This can be used as a comparator with the engine load sensor. The sensor information will also indicate the throttle closed position for idle/overrun conditions, part-load and full throttle.

## 5.4 Temperature sensors

A number of sensors are used on a vehicle to measure temperature. These include measuring:

- engine temperature for ignition, fuel metering and instrumentation
- air intake temperature for fuel metering and vaporisation control
- ambient conditions for driving safety
- transmission fluid temperature
- exhaust temperature for fuel metering.

The majority of temperature sensors use a thermistor, but there are occasions where a thermocouple is used.

## 5.4.1 Thermistor sensor

This type normally consists of a brass bulb, which is in contact with the substance it is sensing. The bulb contains a capsule called a thermistor (see Chapter 2, pages 37–38).

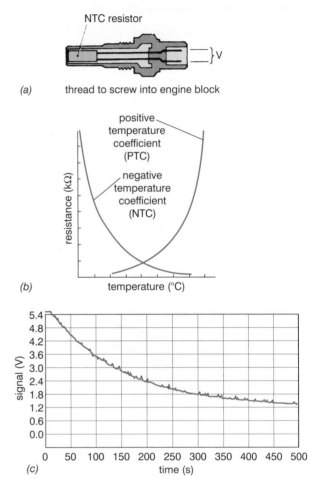

*Figure 5.24 Thermistor sensor: (a) construction, (b) sensor characteristic, (c) negative temperature coefficient signal change over time*

The resistance of common metals increases with temperature. Thermistors that have a sensing capsule that responds in this way are said to have a positive temperature coefficient (PTC). Conversely, a capsule made of a semiconductor material has a resistance that decreases with temperature. These materials, of which silicon is the most common, have a negative temperature coefficient (NTC). Figure 5.24 shows the construction and resistance variation with temperature of a typical sensor as fitted into an engine block to measure the coolant temperature.

In addition to temperature measurement, the thermistor is often used to compensate for temperature changes in an electronics circuit to safeguard semiconductor devices when the circuit components are cold.

## 5.4.2 Thermocouple sensor

The thermistor is excellent for measuring temperature up to about 200 °C. However, above this temperature a thermocouple is normally used.

The principle of a thermocouple is shown in Figure 5.25. It consists of two wires of dissimilar material joined together and connected to a galvanometer. When the hot junction is heated, an EMF is generated, which is registered by the galvanometer. Up to a given temperature, which depends on the metals used (250 °C for copper–iron), the current increases with an increase in the temperature difference between the hot and cold ends of the wires. Indication of temperature is achieved by scaling the galvanometer accordingly.

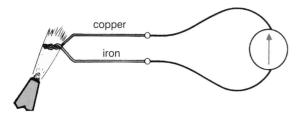

*Figure 5.25 Thermocouple*

A thermocouple can be made by joining many different metals, most commonly nickel–chromium/ nickel–aluminium alloys. These sensors are suitable for a temperature range 0–1100 °C, such as exists in an engine exhaust system and combustion chambers.

## 5.5 Gas sensors

### 5.5.1 Lambda oxygen sensors

Excess oxygen in the exhaust indicates that the air/ fuel ratio is weak (e.g. 20:1). The absence of oxygen shows that the mixture is rich (e.g. 10:1) and exhaust gas pollution of the atmosphere is taking place. The lambda exhaust gas oxygen (EGO) sensor is designed to indicate the effectiveness of the combustion process through measuring the oxygen content in the exhaust gases and then provide information about the fuel mixture composition (i.e. that the air/fuel mixture delivered to the engine is chemically correct).

It enables the EMS to operate effectively, irrespective of the mechanical state of the engine. It also introduces a **closed-loop adaptive control**, which works in the region of a 14.7:1 air/fuel ratio (by mass) or a **stoichiometric ratio of lambda 1** (Figure 5.27). This is maintained throughout all throttle conditions apart from the warm-up phase and snap acceleration, when the system goes open-loop and further enrichment is achieved.

**Closed-loop**: a control system with a feedback loop that automatically changes the output once it detects a difference between its feedback signal and the input signal.

**Adaptive control**: a control system, usually closed-loop, that varies different control signals in order to optimise and maintain a system's performance throughout its lifetime and drive cycle.

**Stoichiometric ratio of lambda 1**: this is equivalent to the ideal air/fuel ratio of 14.7:1. For a lean mixture lambda is greater than 1 and for a rich mixture it is less than 1.

The conventional EGO sensors are the zirconium oxide and titanium oxide types. More recently a wide range (band) sensor has also been introduced.

### Zirconium oxide ($ZrO_2$) sensor

This consists of two porous platinum electrodes separated by zirconium dioxide, which acts like the electrolyte in a battery (Figure 5.26a). At high temperatures this electrolyte becomes conductive, so if oxygen comes in contact with the electrodes, then a small voltage is generated across them. This occurs because oxygen atoms carry two free electrons so the atom carries a negative charge. The $ZrO_2$ attracts oxygen ions, so negative charges build up on the surface of the $ZrO_2$ adjacent to the platinum electrode (Figure 5.26b).

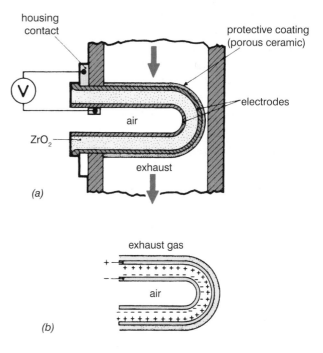

*Figure 5.26 Lambda sensor operation*

The sensor has vents in the outer body as shown, which allow air to come into contact with the internal electrodes. A high voltage signal indicates a rich mixture and low oxygen content.

A signal voltage is produced when the difference is detected between the oxygen in the exhaust pipe and the oxygen in the outside air. The signal voltage varies between 0.2 V and 1 V, depending on the oxygen content in the exhaust gases, and will try to maintain a constant of 500 mV (Figure 5.27).

The time taken for the sensor to respond decreases as the temperature is increased. Common types in use become operational above 300 °C and have a response time of less than 200 ms.

An exhaust gas contains gases other than oxygen. Therefore, these have to be neutralised by conversion to avoid affecting the action of the $ZrO_2$. This duty is performed by the platinum plates. The plates, as stated, are porous and unwanted gases passing through the platinum are oxidised. The platinum is not used up because it is a **catalyst**.

**Catalyst:** a material that enables or speeds up a chemical reaction without being changed itself.

### Titanium oxide ($TiO_2$) oxygen sensor

This sensor contains a ceramic strip covered in titanium dioxide. It also contains a heater element and it changes resistance in relation to the oxygen content. The EMS supplies the sensor with a reference voltage between 5 V and 12 V. This voltage passes through the resistive titanium dioxide and the EMS monitors the signal voltage that returns. The principle is not unlike the operation of coolant NTC electrical circuits.

When there is excess oxygen (lean mixture) the resistance of the titanium is high, in the region of 20 kΩ, and when there is no oxygen (rich mixture) it is about 1 kΩ.

No reference measurements of the outside air are made, and the sensor has to be heated. This means the resistance of the heater element is constantly changing with temperature and this change is monitored by the EMS. The heater is rapidly pulsed on and off by the EMS, as the sensor heats up or cools down, keeping the sensor at its most efficient operating temperature.

### Wide band sensor

The latest variation on the lambda sensor is called the 'wide band' sensor; this was introduced in order to meet the demands of increased fuel economy, lower emissions and improved engine performance.

It is based on a planar zirconia element, which incorporates an electrochemical gas pump.

A feedback electronic circuit controls the gas pump current to keep the output of the electrochemical cell constant, this allows the pump current to directly indicate the oxygen content of the exhaust gas. This sensor type eliminates the lean-rich cycling of narrow-band sensors which allows closer control of the fuel delivery and ignition timing.

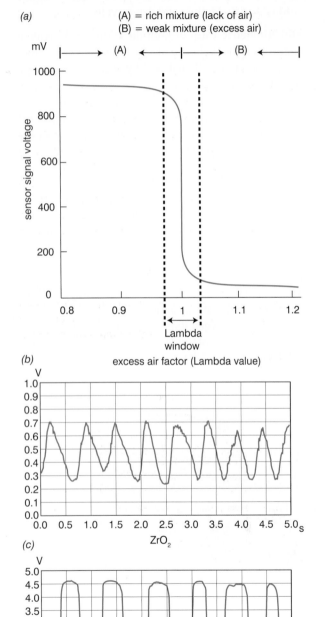

*Figure 5.27 (a) Lambda sensor output voltage, (b) Example waveform for zirconium oxide oxygen sensor, (c) Example waveform for titanium oxide oxygen sensor*

## 5.6 Acceleration and vibration sensors

### 5.6.1 Knock sensors

The main purpose of this sensor is to detect combustion knock (**detonation**) in an engine combustion chamber while advancing the ignition timing.

> **Detonation**: a fault in which spontaneous ignition of the gases compressed in the combustion chamber occurs when these attain high temperature, leading to explosion instead of gradual burning.

#### Accelerometer knock sensor

This sonic sensor has to detect the vibrations from detonation in the frequency range 1–10 kHz. Figure 5.28a shows the basic construction of a knock sensor. The body is screwed into the side of the cylinder block and the piezoelectric crystal is clamped by a seismic mass, which tunes the sensor to the required frequency range.

When detonation occurs in the combustion chamber, the transference of pressure waves through the cylinder block causes the metal particles to be accelerated to and fro. The sensor detects this oscillatory motion by using a piezoceramic semiconductor (as shown in Figure 5.28b), which is fixed to the sensor body. The sound waves vary the compression of the crystal, causing a small EMF of the order of 20 mV/g to be generated by the sensor. This is transmitted to the EMS.

After filtering to remove the unwanted waves, the signal is then averaged and converted to a digital form and, if detonation is detected, ignition timing is retarded accordingly to prevent any excessive damage.

#### Ionisation current sensor

This sensor is built within a spark plug and works with one ignition coil per cylinder, so the plug not only ignites the combustion mixture, but is also used as a cylinder sensor to monitor for detonation.

During combustion, ionised gas is formed from the chemical reaction and raised temperatures. By applying another voltage after the spark, the free ions readily form an ion current, allowing electrical current more readily in proportion to the flame electrical conductivity. By using a measured voltage within a capacitor, it is sent through a current bias circuit and this current is measured over a resistor within the spark plug electrodes forming a bias voltage, which enables the conductivity to be measured. Therefore, the measured current across the electrodes after the spark event reflects the combustion process at that specific moment.

This sensor signal can then be used for knock detection and misfire detection in individual cylinders with minimal influences from vibration and mechanical noise, which makes this sensor more accurate in comparison with the sonic type of knock sensor.

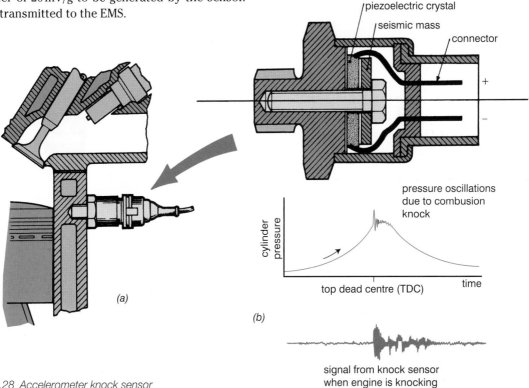

*(a)*

*(b)*

*Figure 5.28 Accelerometer knock sensor*

## 5.6.2 Piezoelectric acceleration sensor

This sensor is incorporated into systems for:

- seat belt pre-tensioners
- airbags
- rollover bars.

Figure 5.29 illustrates a hermetically sealed housing and, internally, a two-layer opposing polarity piezoelectric beam configuration. When a force is applied it induces a mechanical tensile stress to one layer and a compressive stress to the other. During a severe change of vehicle speed it will create an output voltage.

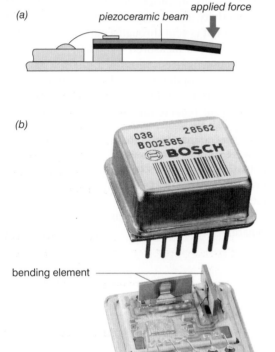

Figure 5.29 Piezoelectric acceleration sensor

## 5.6.3 Piezoelectric yaw rate sensor

It is necessary for modern vehicle operations to incorporate a navigational aid within the vehicle comfort systems, to understand at all times the vehicle location and more specifically its actual movement at that given time. One method is to use four piezo elements and a tuning fork-shaped steel element (Figure 5.30). When the vehicle turns a corner, a voltage is applied to the base piezo elements, which oscillate the upper section of the tuning fork, creating a counter oscillation from the upper piezo elements. This determines the vehicle direction.

In a straight direction no voltage is applied because no forces act on the tuning fork.

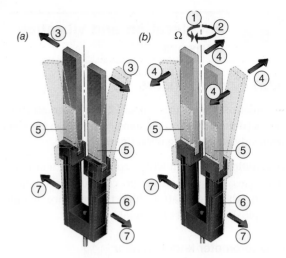

1  tuning-fork direction of oscillation resulting from cornering

2  direction of rotation of the vehicle

3  direction of oscillation resulting from straight-ahead driving

4  coriolis force

5  upper piezo elements (sensing)

6  bottom piezo elements (drive)

7  excitation oscillation direction

$\Omega$  yaw

Figure 5.30 Tuning fork yaw angle sensor

## 5.6.4 Ultrasonic parking sensor

Another application is to incorporate a diaphragm transducer close to a piezo oscillator. This configuration can be used as a parking aid assistant located in the front and rear bumpers (Figure 5.31). The sensors work on the pulse echo principle. In this, the EMS sends a signal to the diaphragm to oscillate (emit ultrasound at a specific frequency). The sound is reflected back from an object, which in turn oscillates the diaphragm that is now at a steady state. These oscillations are transmitted via the piezoceramic element as an analogue signal, which is converted to digital and amplified by the EMS.

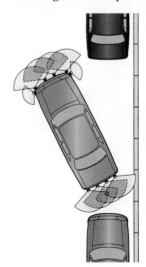

Figure 5.31 Parking sensors

## 5.6.5 Radar detection sensor

This can be incorporated with an adaptive cruise control (ACC). The radar monitors its surroundings by emitting electromagnetic waves for a distance up to 200 m away, and if these strike a surface, they are reflected back to the sensor's internal receiving unit (Figure 5.32). The frequencies of the emitted and received signals are compared through time to calculate the distance and relative speed. Upon detection of a slower moving vehicle in front, the ACC will take action by decelerating to maintain a safe distance.

*Figure 5.32  Radar detection sensor*

## 5.7    Test procedures

All sensors need to be tested using a digital voltmeter or, for greater accuracy, an oscilloscope (always refer to the manufacturer's auto data). A generic test sequence is:

1  Visual check, making sure there is no damage and that all connections are good.

2  Check battery voltage is correct.
3  Check that supply and earth voltage to sensor is as specified by the manufacturer.
4  Check variable signal output is as specified by the manufacturer.

The signal voltage can be analogue or digital and it is easiest to display this dynamic signal with a digital oscilloscope. Some multimeters have a hertz or rpm function that you can use to test a digital signal, however; this is because you are looking for a frequency change in a digital signal, not the voltage change that occurs in an analogue signal.

Some sensors need to reach a specific temperature before the signal begins to switch, namely the lambda sensors and the NTC temperature sensors, which will only change the signal voltage when the engine or transmission oil has begun to warm up.

## 5.7.1 Future technology

Within the foreseeable future and beyond, sensors will increase within many applications. One key area will be an awareness of the actual vehicle surroundings, in terms of its specific location, movement and safety. The accuracy and intelligence of the systems will initiate autonomous driving and detection systems to protect passengers and pedestrians.

Other measures will be:

- monitoring vehicle wheel contact to aid vehicle guidance and electronic vehicle steering assistance
- more accurate torque-sensing for steer-by-wire application
- more precise monitoring of vehicle combustion processes to further improve emissions standards.

Standards of the modern motor vehicle systems have increased the importance of precision control, utilising digital and analogue data to communicate with electrical **actuators**. The actuators implement motion via the engine management system (EMS). This chapter will detail actuators that are engaged throughout the vehicle. There are four main categories of these:

- Linear solenoids
- Linear motors
- Rotary actuators
- Stepper motors

The three main stages of a simple control system are shown in Figure 6.1. The actuator is part of the final stage.

**Actuator**: a device that produces mechanical motion when commanded by an electrical signal.

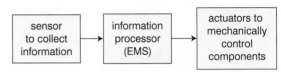

Figure 6.1 Electronic control system

Electrical actuators interface between the EMS and the mechanical motion that needs to be conveyed. They can be either of the following types:

- Linear
- Rotary

The linear type is the more common. In this a force from a linear **solenoid** or motor moves the device in a straight line.

**Solenoid**: a device that converts electromagnetic energy into a linear motion.

## 6.1 Linear solenoids

These solenoids are commonly used in actuating:

- central door locking
- gear shift in automatic transmission systems
- petrol cap locking
- fuel injection.

The solenoids resemble a bar magnet, and consist of an insulated coil winding with a movable armature 'plunger'. This has a sufficient diameter to permit movement along the axis on to a bobbin when there is current (Figure 6.2a). The deactivated plunger is normally returned by a spring.

For long periods of activation, closing and holding coils can be used to reduce current loads (Figure 6.2b). Both coils are active initially until the end of the plunger movement when a pair of contacts are opened disconnecting the higher-current consumer closing coils, just leaving the plunger in position via the holding coils.

Dual direction can be produced by using two coils, placed end-to-end (Figure 6.3). When one coil is energised the plunger moves to the right and when the other coil is energised it returns the plunger. This solenoid is used in some central door locking as it can produce a rapid response with a relatively large force, although its stroke (distance moved in one direction) is limited.

This limitation arises because the force on the plunger is proportional to the square of the distance between the plunger and the pole piece. This is more significant when the air gap is increased. Extension arms are combined with the plunger to make the application suitable for other uses.

### Health and safety best practices

When testing the operation of actuators on a motor vehicle, it is important that you make sure you and others around you are protected. When carrying out dynamic testing, such as running the vehicle, make sure you are aware of moving parts, hot surfaces, high voltages and emissions. Always apply common sense and use the correct personal protective equipment (PPE).

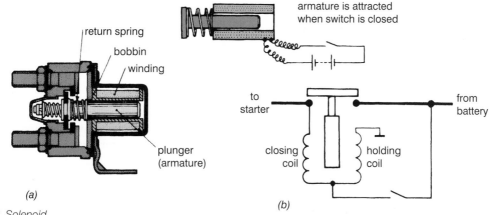

*(a)*

*Figure 6.2  Solenoid*

*(b)*

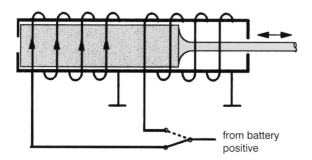

*Figure 6.3  Double-acting solenoid*

## 6.2  Linear motors

The linear direct current (DC) motor uses a powerful permanent magnet to increase the magnetic action, achieving a near-constant force over a longer stroke. As illustrated in Figure 6.4 there are two types:

- Moving winding
- Moving field

### 6.2.1 Moving winding

This has a fixed magnet around which is fitted a hollow armature and coil winding. When a DC current is supplied to the coil, the armature is either pushed or pulled, depending on the direction of the current. This also applies to the moving field type.

### 6.2.2 Moving field

This motor has a static field winding and a moveable magnet to provide the actuating force. The stroke is limited to half the length of the magnet. To be effective, the width of the coil winding should equal the stroke.

Alternatively, using two coils wound in opposite directions does away with the need to change polarity. More specifically, one coil moves the magnet one way and the other coil moves it in the opposite direction. This function can be incorporated in seat base movements and some door actuation.

## 6.3  Rotary actuators

This type of actuator has a permanent magnet compact DC motor. During operation, high speeds need to be generated to produce sufficient output. This tends to reduce reliability and generally, to achieve the desired speed and specific torque, the motor will incorporate a gearbox. In order to reduce cost and weight the gearbox uses plastic gears, although they are weaker than metal components.

Friction is a problem and this is not helped where the motion has to be changed from rotary to reciprocating by means of a flexible rack.

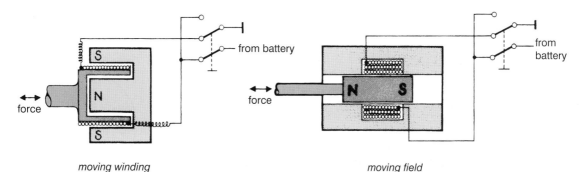

*moving winding*

*moving field*

*Figure 6.4  Linear motors*

Nevertheless, the rotary motion together with its mechanical linkage gives a long-stroke action demanded by many automotive components. The most commonly used are:

- windscreen wipers
- washer pumps
- electric windows and sunroofs
- seat movement
- radio antennae
- fuel pumps.

## 6.4    Stepper motors

A key feature of these rotational motors, or actuators, is that they are brushless so during rotation they can be divided into a number of steps in either direction. The motor responds to electrical DC pulse signals in accordance with the messages it receives from the EMS. Modern applications include precision electronic throttle control and simple mirror adjustment. Each is governed by the angle steps it moves through. Typical angles are 1.8°, 2.5°, 3.75°, 7.5°, 15° and 30°.

The three types of stepper motor are:

- permanent magnet (PM)
- variable reluctance (VR)
- hybrid (combination of PM and VR).

The underlying operating principle of all three motors is the same, but the details vary according to the torque, operating frequency and accuracy of movement required. They are used for:

- idle speed control
- seat positioning
- electronic throttle control
- adaptive cruise control
- variable valve control.

By coupling electronic throttle actuation to adaptive cruise aids, finer control in vehicle stability can be achieved.

### 6.4.1 PM stepper motor

The principle of this type is shown in Figure 6.5a. Here the active **rotor** is a two-pole PM.

The **stator** has two pairs of independent windings ($AA_1$ and $BB_1$) through which currents may be passed in either direction to make the rotor turn through 90° steps.

When current ($I$) is passed to phase winding $BB_1$, the magnetic laws of attraction and repulsion align the rotor with the active poles of the stator (Figure 6.5b). Complete rotation is obtained by applying four electrical pulses of suitable polarity to the motor. Direction of rotation depends on the polarity of the stator during the first pulse (e.g. if the current direction in Figure 6.5b is reversed, the rotor will move in a clockwise direction).

**Rotor**: the rotating part of a motor.

**Stator**: the stationary part of a motor, surrounding the rotor.

Altering the frequency of the step pulses applied to the stator varies the speed of rotation. Also, by controlling the number of pulses, a given angular displacement can be obtained.

By increasing the number of rotor and stator poles, the step angle (°) can be reduced; this is calculated so:

$$\text{Step angle} = \frac{360}{\text{number of step positions}}$$

Each winding has two possible current directions so the number of step positions will always be an even number. PM motors are generally available with basic step angles between 7.5° and 120°.

*(a)*

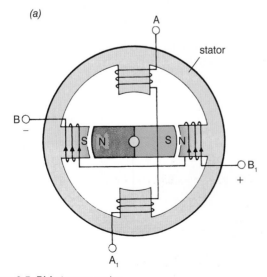

*(b) anti-clockwise rotation in 90° steps*

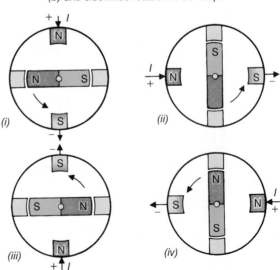

*Figure 6.5 PM stepper motor*

One advantage of this type of stepper motor is that the magnet holds the rotor in place when the stator is not energised. This is called detent torque. Not all stepper motors have this feature, however. Disadvantages include high inertia and the fall-off of performance due to changes in magnetic strength.

## 6.4.2 VR stepper motor

This type has a soft iron rotor with radial teeth and a wound stator having more poles than the rotor. Figure 6.6a illustrates a simplified layout of a three-phase, 15° step angle motor; this has eight rotor teeth and 12 stator poles around which the charge flows in one direction only.

Figure 6.6b shows the winding arrangement for phase 1. When a charge flows through one phase of the stator windings, the rotor aligns itself to give the shortest magnetic path (i.e. the path of minimum reluctance). In each step position, the rotor aligns with four stator poles, giving the motor greater power.

An angular movement of one step from the position shown in Figure 6.6a is obtained by energising either phase 2 or phase 3, depending on the required direction.

For a clockwise motion, the phases would be energised in the order: 3, 2, 1, 3, 2, 1. The rotor is turned through 90° by each of these six current pulses. The time for one complete rotation is governed by the time the control circuit takes to energise the windings sufficiently to move the rotor to the next step.

This type of motor is obtainable with step angles between 1.8° and 15°. It has a fast response because of its low rotor inertia and has a fast stepping rate. As it has no detent torque it is prone to oscillate and resonate unless it is damped externally.

## 6.4.3 Hybrid stepper motor

Most commonly used in industry alongside the PM type, this stepper motor consists of a combination of the VR and PM motors. Figure 6.7 illustrates that the rotor is constructed in a manner similar to that used in an alternator. A PM, with its poles coaxial with the shaft, is sandwiched between two iron claws, having teeth that form two sets of poles.

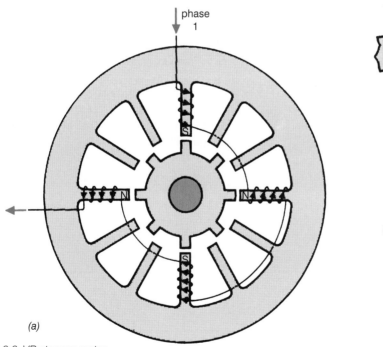

(a)

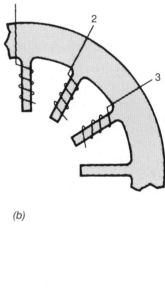

(b)

Figure 6.6  VR stepper motor

---

### VR stepper motor: calculating the number of step positions

The number of step positions ($N$) is calculated using the formula:

where: $N = \dfrac{SR}{S-R}$

$S$ = number of slots in the stator

$R$ = number of slots in rotor

In this case:

$$N = \frac{8 \times 12}{12 - 8} = \frac{96}{4} = 24$$

$$\text{Step angle} = \frac{360}{24} = 15°$$

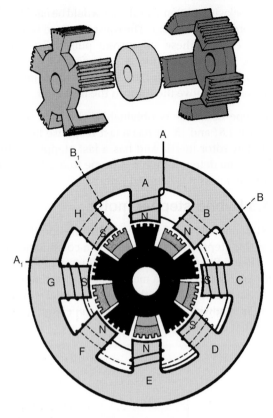

*Figure 6.7 Hybrid stepper motor*

The stator has eight main poles, which are cut to form small teeth on the surface adjacent to the rotor. The operation is similar to the PM type: the rotor aligns itself so that the magnetic reluctance is lowest.

The hybrid stepper motor has stepping angles as low as 0.9°, a high torque, and the ability to operate at high stepping rates. Disadvantages of this type of motor include high rotor inertia and the risk of resonance at some speeds.

### 6.4.4 Stepper motor control

The controlling input to the drive circuit is normally from a digital signal source that all three stepper motor types respond to. Its low power output needs to be amplified to provide a power high enough to drive the motor.

The direction of current through the appropriate stator winding governs the direction of rotor movement, and the speed at which the pulse signals are supplied controls the speed of rotor movement. Taking the PM type as an example, Figure 6.8a shows the pulses that are applied to turn the rotor. Note that the pulses do not overlap and that the speed is controlled by the pulse frequency.

Figure 6.8b shows the pulse pattern needed to move the rotor forward through three steps (270°) and then reverse it to its original position.

## 6.5 Test procedures

All solenoids, actuators and motors need to be tested using a digital volt and ohmmeter, or for more accurate testing an oscilloscope. Always refer to the manufacturer's auto data. A generic test sequence is:

1 Visual check, making sure there is no damage, that all connections are good, and movement can be detected in some application.
2 Check battery voltage is correct.
3 Check coil winding for continuity using an ohmmeter (once the motor has been disconnected).
4 Check that supply and earth voltage to the solenoids, actuators and motors are as specified by the manufacturer.
5 Check AC/DC signal output as specified by the manufacturer.

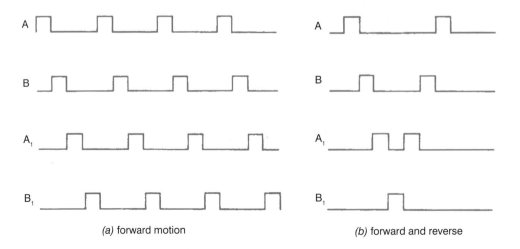

*(a) forward motion*

*(b) forward and reverse*

*Figure 6.8 Pulse signals to control stepper motor*

## Waveforms for stepper motors

Stepper motors are usually either 4- or 5-wire units. When checking their waveforms with an oscilloscope you can use the following diagrams as a reference, although you should still consult the manufacturer's data and recommendations.

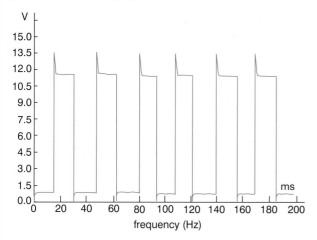

Figure 6.9  4-wire stepper motor expected waveform

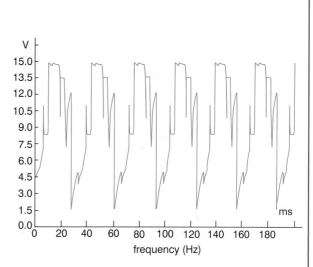

Figure 6.10  5-wire stepper motor expected waveform

The signal voltage can be analogue or digital and it is easiest to display this dynamic signal with a digital oscilloscope. Some multimeters have a hertz or rpm function that you can use to test a digital signal. However, this is because you are looking for a frequency change in a digital signal, not the voltage change that occurs in an analogue signal.

**Embedded systems** were a milestone in electronics that made circuits smaller, cheaper and more efficient. A computer chip is a good way to visualise the idea of an embedded system. The block diagram for a typical embedded system is shown in Figure 7.1. Computers, smartphones and ATMs are all operated by embedded systems.

**Embedded system**: a combination of computer hardware and software designed for a specific application.

The electronic control unit (ECU) in vehicles is also an embedded system. It is the electronic brain which regulates and controls all the electrical systems on board. The ECU is housed in a box and its location on each vehicle varies depending on the make and model of the car. Usually it is installed either in the passenger area or in the engine bay.

At the heart of the ECU lies the microprocessor. The processor is accompanied by a number of memories and communication ports. The ECU controls other electronic modules around the vehicle. Typical modules in a car include the engine control module, transmission control module and suspension control module.

In older cars each module was an isolated component that functioned independently. Modern cars use the central ECU, which makes maintaining and modifying other modules very easy. The modules have their own processing units. These may be microprocessors, or smaller units called microcontrollers.

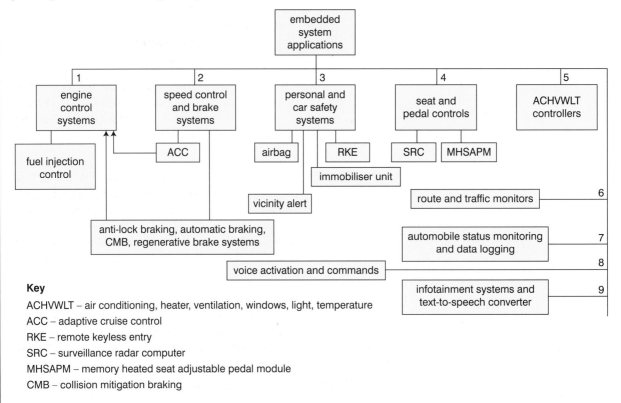

**Key**

ACHVWLT – air conditioning, heater, ventilation, windows, light, temperature
ACC – adaptive cruise control
RKE – remote keyless entry
SRC – surveillance radar computer
MHSAPM – memory heated seat adjustable pedal module
CMB – collision mitigation braking

*Figure 7.1  Block diagram of an embedded system*

## 7.1   The microprocessor

Microprocessors combine all the logic circuits for computer functions into a single integrated circuit (IC). It is a complex circuit consisting of billions of transistors printed on a single piece of silicon. The microprocessor takes digital data signals in binary form at its input, processes the data according to instructions, and then provides a digital output. The microprocessor is the central processing unit (CPU) in a computer.

The number system we use most commonly is called the decimal system. Microprocessors, however, use the binary number system, which makes data processing and storage extremely efficient. (See Chapter 4, pages 54–55 for an explanation of binary numbers and their advantage in electronic applications.)

Binary digits are called bits, for example, the binary number 1011 has 4 bits. Early processors processed data as 4-bit or 8-bit numbers at a time. Subsequent processors were made in multiples of 8 bits. A set of 8 bits is known as a byte. Current processors have either 32-bit or 64-bit formats. They process data arrays much faster, can perform more calculations simultaneously and are more accurate.

The information coming into the processor of a vehicle ECU consists of raw data from transducers, data from modules, data from memory, and instructions from a module, memory or the driver's console.

### 7.1.1 Microprocessor components

The CPU consists of a number of components. Figure 7.2 is a block diagram of a microprocessor's components.

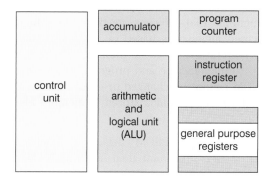

*Figure 7.2  Block diagram of microprocessor*

### Clock

The microprocessor is a sequential circuit (see Figure 4.7 on page 58). The clock in a microprocessor consists of a crystal-controlled chip that generates timed electrical pulses, typically of a frequency above 1 **gigahertz (GHz)**.

**Gigahertz (GHz)**: 1 GHz = 1,000,000,000 Hz (hertz).

### Control unit

The control unit receives the instructions and generates a step-by-step micro-instruction code, which is used by various components to perform the required task. This process is actually the data-hardware border, where the digital signals are translated into hardware operation.

### Arithmetic control unit (ALU)

This unit carries out arithmetic and logic operations on the input data and produces an output. Modern processors include another component called the floating-point unit (FPU). This unit handles mathematical operations on floating-point and complex numbers. Vehicles that have simple electronic systems usually do not need an FPU. Any special cases can be emulated, which may be slower. However, vehicles with more complex electronic systems (e.g. traction control) need specialised FPUs for a better, sharper response.

### Registers

Registers are the data storage 'bins' in a microprocessor. Each bin can store a binary number, the size of which depends on the processor's architecture (e.g. 32-bit processors have 32-bit registers).

Registers are divided into four sections:

- Accumulator
- Program counter
- Instruction register
- General purpose register

### Accumulator

The accumulator stores intermediate results from the ALU. Operations such as binary multiplication consist of several steps, the results of which are stored in the accumulator.

### Program counter

The program counter keeps track of where the processor is in its instruction sequence. The program counter holds memory addresses for the current or next instruction of the computation. The CPU accesses the memory address stored in the program counter at each clock and updates it when a section of code is completed.

### Instruction register

The instruction register contains the instruction that is currently being executed. Typical instructions include arithmetic and logic operations, and store and load commands.

### General purpose register

The general purpose register is used for storing all other information. Data from input, data for output and their memory addresses are stored here. Each number that is stored is called a 'word' and is stored in one 'bin'.

## 7.1.2 Multi-core processors

A multi-core processor is a single embedded device that has more than one independent microprocessor. The presence of more than one processing core speeds up program execution by dividing the workload among the cores. As the automotive industry progresses into the next generation, vehicle ECUs will use multi-core processors for managing the increasing load.

## 7.2    Computers

The CPU serves as the 'thinking brain' of a computer. A standard automotive computer includes several other components, which may be thought of as 'organs'. Figure 7.3 shows the main components of a vehicle computer.

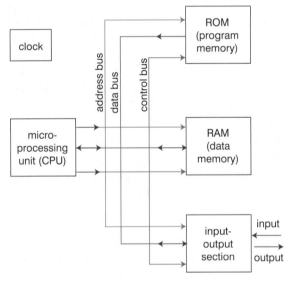

*Figure 7.3  Components of a vehicle computer*

Modern vehicle computer units provide an efficient way to manage and control car functions. Engine, suspension, transmission and other modules can be accessed through the main ECU computer and have their settings changed according to requirements. Before changes are made, performance feedback is acquired from the ECU and analysed. Each module in the car sends its feedback and fault report to the ECU, which stores the data. The data can be accessed and a performance report generated to give an in-depth knowledge on which settings need to be changed. The settings are then programmed in from an external computer via cable through the diagnostic port.

The on-board computer also allows the driver to make various changes through an interface on the driving console. Many cars allow suspension, engine power and traction control changes through such interfaces.

Controlling cabin settings such as lighting, seat position, windows and climate are also made easier.

## 7.2.1 Electronic structure of a vehicle computer

### Memory

Computers store data in digital devices called memories. The basic unit in such a device is a cell, which can store a single bit of binary data. A byte is a set of 8 bits. Most devices use a byte as the smallest storage unit and all larger values are expressed as multiples of 8 (e.g. 64, 256 and 1024). Current memory devices have capacities of several gigabytes (each gigabyte is equal to $10^9$ bytes). Modern memory chips are very small in size. In addition to storage cells, memory chips contain circuits for storing and retrieving information as well. Memories can either be volatile (temporary) or non-volatile (permanent).

### Permanent memory

### Operating memory

The operating memory is used to store core data and instructions. The complete set of fundamental instructions is known as the operating software. The operating software has the same function as in personal computers; it provides a platform for other programs to run and an interface from which a user can access and convey information. The operating memory is used to store data and custom settings defined by a user or automotive engineer. Operating memory has a rewritable structure.

### Dedicated memory

The dedicated memory stores fixed, built-in instructions that do not need to be changed. Dedicated memory is based on read-only memory (ROM) architecture. ROM architectures are very cheap to manufacture and program. Information in the ROM cannot be changed or erased by the CPU. The information remains stored in memory even if the power is switched off.

Programmed ROM (PROM) devices can only store data once, which cannot then be erased. Erasable programmable ROM (EPROM) devices can have their information erased. In an EPROM charged electrons are trapped in cells to represent stored bits. The memory chip lies below a quartz window. When reprogramming is necessary, electrons can be released and data erased by prolonged exposure to ultraviolet light. The EPROM can then be reprogrammed with new data through a PROM programmer. An EEPROM (electrically erasable read-only memory) is used when small amounts of information must be stored to be reused.

## Temporary memory

At a given instant, the microprocessor performs multiple tasks on large quantities of data. The microprocessor's internal registers can only store a limited amount. In such situations the microprocessor uses an external memory called the RAM (random access memory). The RAM is a volatile device, so when the power is turned off the data is erased.

In applications where data frequently changes, the RAM is used instead of a permanent rewritable memory. The RAM gives quicker data transfer rates as compared to a permanent memory. To keep the data safe, the RAM is constantly supplied power even when the engine is not running.

## Communication cables

The microprocessor is linked to the memories and other external components through communication

**Bus**: a communication cable for sending and receiving data.

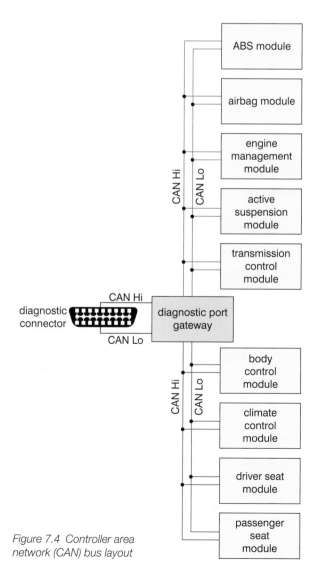

*Figure 7.4 Controller area network (CAN) bus layout*

cables known as **buses**. Each bus can be thought of as a multi-lane highway, which gives an obstacle-free flow of data to and from the microprocessor.

A bus has three separate sections, each of which carries a specific type of signal:

- Data bus
- Address bus
- Control bus

The buses greatly reduce wiring clutter between a vehicle's electronic components. The reduced wiring means that only a single bus runs to each portion of the car (Figure 7.4).

### Data bus

This is responsible for carrying information from sensors and memories to the microprocessor. Normally this bus has eight wires.

### Address bus

This carries memory addresses from the microprocessor to the memories. The memory address is a numerical location for each bit of data stored in the memory. When the microprocessor requires certain stored data, it sends its memory address to the memory chip. Circuits in the memory chip take the address and return the value stored at that location.

### Control bus

This carries instructions from the CPU to other parts of the computer. Instructions may be commands that instruct where to send each batch of data, or which component is being called by the microprocessor.

## Peripheral devices

Peripheral devices help a computer communicate with other electronic components around the vehicle. These devices are an interface between a transducer or actuator and the CPU. The input from most transducers cannot be directly understood by the CPU, as most transducers give an analogue output. Similarly, signals from the CPU cannot act directly on an actuator. Peripheral devices are often either signal processing units or signal monitoring units.

### Signal processing units

Signal processing units are used to convert analogue signals from a transducer into digital signals that can be understood by the CPU. Variations in the analogue signal can be modulated into the amplitude of the digital signal or the frequency of the amplitude signal. The conversion is carried out by a circuit known as an analogue to digital converter (ADC).

The signal processing units also convert the digital signals from the CPU so that they are understood by actuators (motors and pistons). Actuators are operated by varying the analogue signal at their output. In these cases, the signal processing unit decodes the digital signals into an analogue signal using an ADC circuit.

Signal processing units (Figure 7.5) also decode input from the driver's console. Changes in climate, drive terrain and performance settings at the driver console controls are processed into digital signals by them and sent to the CPU for operation.

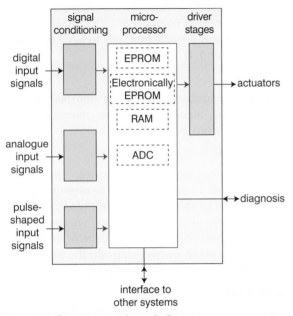

Figure 7.5 Signal processing unit diagram

## Signal monitoring units

The use of these units greatly reduces the workload on the microprocessor. Without signal monitoring units (Figure 7.6), the microprocessor had to constantly receive input from all the sensors and process them. The signal monitoring units act as assistants to the microprocessor. The unit only sends a signal to the microprocessor when the value of the signal from a transducer changes. Therefore, the microprocessor is only interrupted when it actually needs to process input from a transducer. As long as all sensors give a constant reading, the microprocessor is not disturbed.

## Service and maintenance alert systems

At the manufacturing plant, the permanent memory is used to store a code that contains the condition of each component in the car (Figure 7.7). The sensors at the brakes, oil sump and other components send a status signal to the microprocessor at regular intervals. The microprocessor matches these signals with those stored in the memory and estimates when each component needs to be replaced or serviced. Many modern cars display this information at the driver's console in the form of a service date.

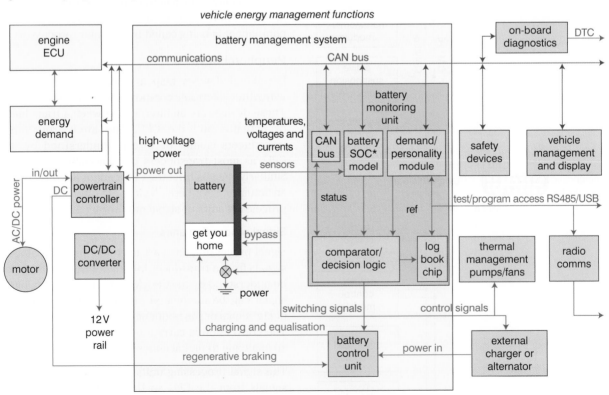

Figure 7.6 Signal monitoring unit diagram

*SOC = state of change

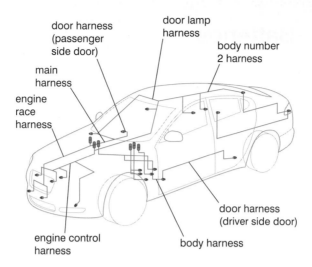

*Figure 7.7  Service control layout*

Signals from some sensors (such as engine temperature) are continuously updated at the driver's panel. Such critical information is usually coupled with a warning sensor. The warning sensor sends out visual and audio warnings when a parameter enters a danger zone.

# CHAPTER 8

# Batteries

This chapter will cover the types, construction and use of low-voltage battery types. The term 'low voltage' is used to describe batteries that produce 12 V for the vehicle electrical system. As the new generation of hybrid and electric vehicles (EVs) are utilising the latest electronic and battery technology to generate in excess of 400 V, these batteries and their use will be covered in Chapter 10.

## Health and safety

Always wear the correct personal protective equipment (PPE) when handling batteries: a face shield or safety goggles, appropriate gloves to prevent acid burns, and an apron or smock to protect your clothes.

### Working with acid

- Acid spills must be cleaned up immediately. A water and baking soda solution will neutralise the effects; the solution should be 1 kg of baking soda to 10 l of water.
- When working with sulphuric acid, ensure that you are in a well-ventilated area with good lighting.
- All acid containers must be clearly marked.

### Dealing with accidents

- If sulphuric acid gets on to skin, flush with copious amounts of water.
- If swallowed, drink large quantities of milk or water, followed by milk of magnesia, beaten eggs or vegetable oil. Do not induce vomiting. Call a doctor immediately.
- For acid in the eyes, flush for several minutes with clean water and seek immediate medical attention.

### Safety while charging

When charging conventional lead–acid batteries, loosen vent caps where possible and ensure the area is adequately ventilated. When conventional batteries are being charged they give off hydrogen and oxygen; a build-up of hydrogen and oxygen in the battery or in the charging area can create an explosion hazard.

- If the battery starts to heat up during charging, STOP! Excessive heat damages the internal plates, and a battery that is too hot can explode.
- Allow the battery to cool and check the charging rate before charging again.
- If a vent tube is fitted, ensure that it is not kinked or blocked, which could cause gases to build up and explode.
- Ensure the charger is correctly connected to the battery: positive charger lead to positive battery post and negative charger lead to negative battery post. Unplug the charger or turn it off before you disconnect the leads; this will reduce the chance of sparks.
- Always connect the negative lead last and remove it first.
- Ensure there is absolutely NO smoking, sparks or flames around charging batteries. Charging gives off hydrogen and oxygen, which explodes if ignited.
- If the ambient temperature is below 3 °C, do not try to charge a battery as the electrolyte may have frozen.
- Charging the battery when still fitted to the vehicle is not recommended.
- Always refer to the manufacturer's data for information about removing the battery from the vehicle.

## 8.1   Battery types

A vehicle battery is the source of electrical energy used to meet the electrical load requirements when the engine is not running. It must 'store' the electrical energy generated and then deliver this energy when it is required by the vehicle systems. A standard lead–acid battery fitted to the majority of vehicles fulfils the storage role using an electrochemical process; the energy delivered by the electrical current produces a chemical change in the battery as it discharges.

The current supplied to a battery is called the charge, whereas the electrical output from a battery is called the discharge.

### 8.1.1 Primary and secondary batteries

If a battery cannot be recharged, it is called a primary battery; an example of a primary battery would be a standard torch battery.

When the chemical process in a battery can be reversed after discharge (i.e. it can be recharged), it is called a secondary battery.

Many years ago it was discovered that when two dissimilar metals were placed close together and immersed in an acid solution, an **electromotive force (EMF)** was produced. This effect can be demonstrated by placing two coins made of different metals in a lemon. If a millivoltmeter is connected across the two coins the meter will register a **potential difference (PD)**. In this case the acidic juice conducts the electrical charges (ions) from one plate to the other.

**Electromotive force (EMF)**: the energy per unit charge that is converted reversibly from chemical, mechanical, or other forms of energy into electrical energy in a battery or dynamo.

**Potential difference (PD)**: the difference in electric potential between two points in an electric field or circuit; it is the work that has to be done in transferring unit positive charge from one point to the other, measured in volts (V).

### 8.1.2 Types of secondary battery

Secondary batteries are generally classified by the materials used to form the plates and the type of electrolyte into which the plates are immersed.

The two main types used on motor vehicles are:

- lead–acid
- nickel–alkaline.

### Lead–acid

This is the type used on the majority of vehicles because it is relatively inexpensive and maintains its performance over a long period of time (four to five years). Because of their construction and the materials used, all of these types of battery are heavy, so care must be taken when carrying and working with them.

The three types of lead–acid battery used on a motor vehicle are: high-maintenance, low-maintenance and maintenance-free. These are looked at in more detail in the next sections of this chapter.

### Nickel–alkaline

This type of battery is a non-acid battery that uses nickel as a plate material. It is larger in size than a lead–acid type and more expensive to produce, but it can withstand prolonged heavy discharge currents without damage. As this type of battery has a very long life, it is used in situations where reliability over a long period of time is the most important requirement. This battery type is looked at in more depth later in this chapter.

## 8.2   Lead–acid high-maintenance batteries

The lead–acid battery is the most commonly used type of battery on motor vehicles; it is capable of supplying the large current (several hundred amperes) demanded by a starter motor, it has a reasonable lifespan of four years or more, and is relatively inexpensive to produce.

Early lead–acid batteries suffered the disadvantages of being large, heavy and needing periodic attention, but modern materials and improved production methods have minimised these factors to such an extent that 'high-maintenance' batteries no longer exist.

The basic construction of a lead–acid battery has remained unchanged for a number of years, but improvements have been introduced to minimise the periodic maintenance required to ensure it is kept in good condition. The more recent designs of lead–acid battery (Figures 8.1 and 8.2) are named low-maintenance and maintenance-free, indicating the work needed to service each type of battery.

The battery consists of a container that houses a number of cells; each cell holds a nominal 2V and is connected in series to the other cells by lead bars to give the required voltage (Figure 8.3).

In a 6V battery three cells are connected and six cells are used for the common 12V unit. Normally, the

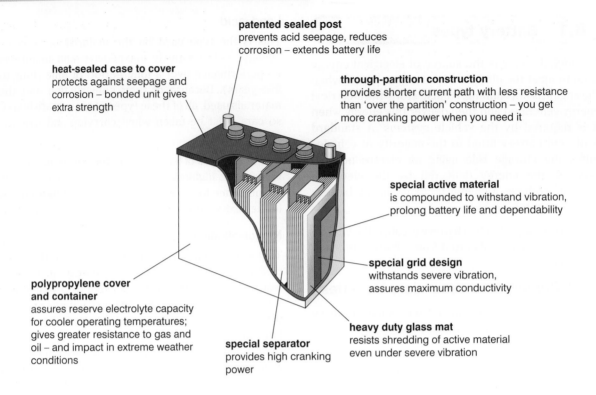

**patented sealed post**
prevents acid seepage, reduces corrosion – extends battery life

**heat-sealed case to cover**
protects against seepage and corrosion – bonded unit gives extra strength

**through-partition construction**
provides shorter current path with less resistance than 'over the partition' construction – you get more cranking power when you need it

**special active material**
is compounded to withstand vibration, prolong battery life and dependability

**special grid design**
withstands severe vibration, assures maximum conductivity

**polypropylene cover and container**
assures reserve electrolyte capacity for cooler operating temperatures; gives greater resistance to gas and oil – and impact in extreme weather conditions

**special separator**
provides high cranking power

**heavy duty glass mat**
resists shredding of active material even under severe vibration

*Figure 8.1  Cut-away of Yuasa lead–acid conventional battery*

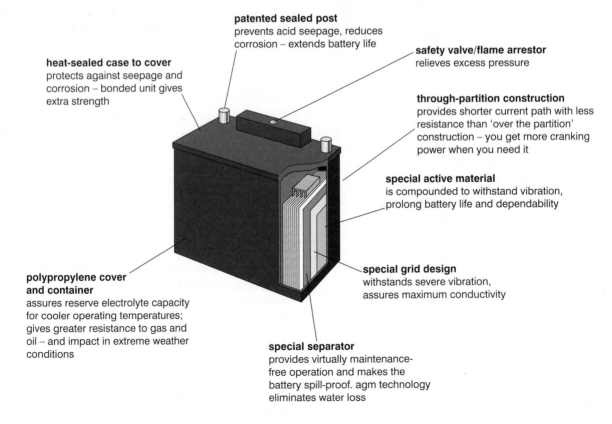

**patented sealed post**
prevents acid seepage, reduces corrosion – extends battery life

**safety valve/flame arrestor**
relieves excess pressure

**heat-sealed case to cover**
protects against seepage and corrosion – bonded unit gives extra strength

**through-partition construction**
provides shorter current path with less resistance than 'over the partition' construction – you get more cranking power when you need it

**special active material**
is compounded to withstand vibration, prolong battery life and dependability

**special grid design**
withstands severe vibration, assures maximum conductivity

**polypropylene cover and container**
assures reserve electrolyte capacity for cooler operating temperatures; gives greater resistance to gas and oil – and impact in extreme weather conditions

**special separator**
provides virtually maintenance-free operation and makes the battery spill-proof. agm technology eliminates water loss

*Figure 8.2  Maintenance-free battery cut-away with absorbed-glass mat (AGM) technology*

connecting bars are internal, with a moulded cover that seals the cells and a removable plug that allows the cells to be topped up with distilled water and also exposes the electrolyte for testing purposes. A small vent hole in the plug or at the end of the case allows for the escape of gas.

Charging a lead–acid battery requires a direct current (DC) power supply. However, during the charging period the electrolyte density will increase and the plate materials will return to their original forms. When the process is complete (i.e. when the battery is fully charged), if the charging current is not removed it will lead to excessive gassing of the cell. The gas produced consists of hydrogen and oxygen and is a highly explosive mixture, so no naked flames or sparks must be produced in the vicinity of a battery at any time.

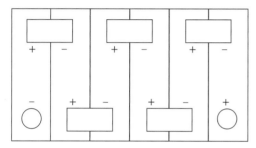

*Figure 8.3 Internal cell connections*

## 8.3 Lead–acid maintenance-free batteries

### 8.3.1 What makes a battery maintenance-free?

Early lead–acid batteries lost water at a high rate due to the charge/discharge cycle, so it was recommended that motorists checked the acid level on a weekly basis. Under normal operating conditions modern maintenance-free batteries need no topping up throughout their life. Battery life has doubled from two years to four or five years over the course of the last 20 years.

In previous battery construction, the grids were made of an alloy of lead with 10 per cent of **antimony**; the antimony gave rigidity to the pure lead plates, which would be too soft on their own. As a result of the charge/discharge process, some of the antimony dissolved in the acid and this resulted in the battery losing water.

**Antimony**: a metal that forms a highly useful alloy with lead, increasing its hardness and mechanical strength. The lead–antimony (PbSb) alloy is used in lead–acid batteries.

As battery technology has improved, the antimony content has been reduced from 10 per cent to 1.5 per cent, which has resulted in batteries that are low-maintenance, needing only yearly attention.

## 8.4 Battery construction

All lead–acid batteries are constructed using the same methods. The difference between low-maintenance and maintenance-free batteries is that the maintenance-free types will normally have 0.1 per cent of calcium added to their plates to harden them; this reduces the amount of water the battery uses during the charge/discharge process, which should remove the need to top up during the battery's lifetime. Maintenance-free batteries will normally be completely sealed except for a small vent hole; this is a safety device that opens when the internal pressure is too high.

### Plates and separators

A battery cell is made up of two sets of lead plates, which are both positive and negative, placed alternately within the cell and separated by an insulating, porous material, such as porous polythene or glass fibre. Each plate is made up of a lattice-type grid of lead–antimony alloy and the active material is pressed into this. The active material is a lead oxide paste electrically formed into lead peroxide (positively charged and chocolate brown in colour) and spongy lead (negatively charged and grey in colour).

Because the surface area of the plates is what determines the maximum discharge current that can be applied for a given time, each cell contains a number of thin plates with each set connected in parallel. This type of connection does not affect the cell voltage.

Modern separators are made of microporous polyethylene; this material has been rigorously tested to ensure that it can withstand the high temperatures and extreme oxidising conditions within the battery. The separator is placed between the positive and negative plates to stop them shorting together. As it is microporous the ions can flow between the positive and negative plates freely.

### Container

Modern mass-produced battery cases are made of translucent polypropylene or a black hard rubber composition. Spaces are formed in the bottom of each cell to collect active material that falls from the plates. This space prevents the material from bridging and short circuiting the plates.

The charge/discharge process is shown in Figure 8.5.

## Electrolyte

In a lead–acid battery, dilute sulphuric acid ($H_2SO_4$) forms the electrolyte in which the plates are immersed.

### Freezing of electrolyte

Because batteries are located within the engine bay or in the rear boot area, the temperature and charge of the electrolyte is important. The freezing point of the electrolyte depends on the state of charge (i.e. it depends on the electrolyte density). When the state of charge reduces, the density of the electrolyte decreases and the acid strength falls; as the electrolyte moves towards a more dilute state the freezing point rises.

The density is measured by comparing the mass of a given volume of electrolyte with the mass of an equal volume of pure water. The ratio obtained is termed its 'specific gravity' (sp. gr.) and is measured by an instrument called a hydrometer (Figure 8.4). Table 8.1 shows the freezing point against the density, or charge, of the electrolyte.

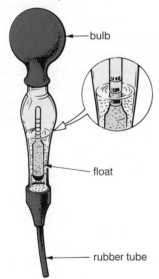

*Figure 8.4 Battery hydrometer*

*Table 8.1 Variation of freezing point with density of the electrolyte*

| Specific gravity | Temperature (°C) |
|---|---|
| 1.000 Discharged | 0 |
| 1.125 Half-charged | −11.2 |
| 1.250 Fully charged | −54.3 |

Table 8.2 shows some hydrometer readings and indicates the state of charge of the battery for the readings.

*Table 8.2 Hydrometer readings for a lead–acid battery*

| Battery state of charge with voltage at specific gravity | | | |
|---|---|---|---|
| Voltage (V) | Specific gravity | State of charge (%) | Discharge (%) |
| 12.66 | 1.265 | 100 | 0 |
| 12.45 | 1.225 | 75 | 25 |
| 12.25 | 1.190 | 50 | 50 |
| 12.05 | 1.145 | 25 | 75 |
| 11.90 | 1.100 | 0 | 100 |

When a battery is fully charged the positive plates comprise lead peroxide ($PbO_2$) and the negative plates are spongy lead (Pb). As the battery discharges, the sulphuric acid reacts with the plates and this changes both plate materials to lead sulphate ($PbSO_4$). Figure 8.5 shows the chemical reactions that take place during the charge/discharge cycle.

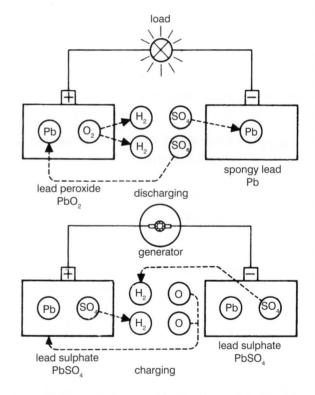

*Figure 8.5 Chemical action when charging and discharging*

During the discharge process the loss of sulphate from the electrolyte to the plates decreases the density of the electrolyte (i.e. reduces the specific gravity); this can be measured using a hydrometer.

Always ensure that the safety items highlighted in the box on page 92 are followed when charging a lead–acid battery.

Some maintenance-free batteries are fitted with a 'green eye' hydrometer built in to the top of the battery; a light yellow or bright green indicator means the battery is fully charged.

If the indicator is dark green, then it is discharged and should be charged before trying to start the vehicle; it may also be jump started at this point. Figure 8.6 shows the state of charge indicator.

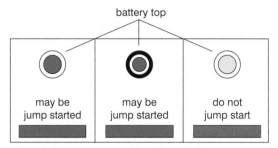

Check the appearance of the charge indicator on top of the battery before attempting to jump start; if it is bright yellow, do not attempt to jump start as this indicates an internal fault.

*Figure 8.6 'Green eye' state of charge indicator built in to some maintenance-free batteries*

### Absorbed glass mat (AGM) batteries

As more vehicles are equipped with stop-start technology to reduce fuel consumption and exhaust emissions, the batteries for these vehicles have to cycle more often than standard batteries and are frequently discharged to a lower level more often. These vehicles are also fitted with the latest brake energy recuperation systems, which can cause high surges of electrical energy to be applied to the battery.

The latest sealed batteries are **recombinant** and use absorbed glass mats (AGM) between the thicker than standard plates. This is a fine fibre boron-silicate glass mat; as the mat is about 95 per cent saturated rather than fully soaked, the battery will not leak acid even if broken.

**Recombinant battery**: a sealed battery that 'recombines' the hydrogen given off by the negative plates with the oxygen given off by the positive plates to produce water. This replaces any moisture lost during the charge/discharge cycle, reducing any need to top up.

### 8.5  Charging and maintenance

The health and safety warnings on page 92 must be followed to ensure the health and safety of all persons in the surrounding area.

Charging of a battery on a vehicle is performed by a generator; also called the alternator (see Chapter 10). This provides an alternating current (AC), which must be rectified to DC at a voltage high enough to overcome the back-EMF and the internal resistance of the battery.

'Sealed' vehicle batteries should be charged only on constant potential chargers or 'smart' chargers. Do not use constant current chargers or boost chargers.

'Sealed' vehicle batteries do not allow any access to the electrolyte, and so cannot be topped up. There are no removable vent plugs or manifolds. The battery is able to vent gases through breathing holes, so strictly speaking it is not sealed.

### 8.5.1 General procedure for all types of chargers

The following gives common information for various types of chargers.

1  Before charging, check the electrolyte levels in all the cells if possible. If these are below the tops of the separators, top up with distilled or deionised water to the tops of the separators. Do not fill to a higher level before charging, but adjust the levels after charging.
2  Remove the vent plugs before charging if you are using a constant current charger or a boost charger (see page 98). There is no need to remove the vent plugs if you are using a constant potential or a smart charger.
3  Check that the charger is switched off.
4  Connect the charger to the battery by connecting the positive lead to the positive terminal first and the negative lead to the negative terminal last.
5  Switch on the charger. See page 98 for the correct charging conditions depending on your type of charger.
6  Stop charging if the battery begins to gas freely (some gassing is normal during the final stages of charging) or if the battery starts to heat up.
7  Switch off the charger.
8  It is safe practice to wait for about 20 minutes for the gases to clear before removing the leads from the battery as this can cause a spark, which may ignite any gasses.
9  Check the electrolyte levels in all the cells and top up if necessary.
10  Refit vent plugs if these have been removed.
11  Wash the battery with hot water and dry it.

## 8.5.2 Types of charger

There are many types of charger available; their working principles and the procedure for using these are given below:

- Constant current chargers
- Constant potential chargers
- Modified constant potential chargers
- Smart chargers
- Boost chargers

### Constant current chargers

These maintain a fixed, constant, preset current throughout the charging period irrespective of the battery voltage.

### Charging procedure with constant current chargers

If charging more than one battery, ideally charge each battery on a separate charger unit.

Charge the battery at the recommended charge rate (check the battery manufacturer's data). If you cannot set the recommended rate, extend or reduce the charging time on a *pro rata* basis. For example, if the recommendation is to charge the battery at 4 A for 6 hours (4 × 6 = 24 Ah), charge the battery for 12 hours if you can only set the charger at 2 A (24/2 = 12 hours).

Measure the open-circuit voltage of the battery; the battery should not have been used or charged for a minimum of 3 hours before checking the voltage.

Check Table 8.3 for a guide time to charge the battery depending on the open-circuit voltage. For example, if the battery has a voltage of 12.16 V, charge it for 10 hours at the recommended charge rate.

*Table 8.3 Charging times*

| Open-circuit voltage (V) | Charging time (hours) |
|---|---|
| >12.40 | 4 |
| 12.31–12.40 | 6 |
| 12.21–12.30 | 8 |
| 12.11–12.20 | 10 |
| 12.01–12.10 | 12 |
| 11.91–12.00 | 14 |
| 11.81–11.90 | 16 |
| 11.71–11.80 | 18 |
| 11.00–11.70 | 20 |
| <11.00 | See 'Over-discharged batteries' |

### Over-discharged batteries

If charging a battery that has been in service and has been over-discharged (below 11 V), a specialist charger, capable of providing a very high initial charging voltage, may be required, and the recommended current may not be initially obtainable. In this case, the current must be monitored and adjusted as necessary during the charge period.

If a battery has become over-discharged, it may suffer from a loss of performance because of irreversible sulphation (growth of large lead sulphate crystals on the plates). Further charging may reduce its potential lifespan.

### Constant potential chargers

These maintain a fixed, constant, preset voltage throughout the charging period. The current cannot be set and will fall as the battery state of charge increases.

### Modified constant potential chargers

In these the voltage and the current are preset. The majority of commercially available chargers, particularly home chargers, are of this type.

### Charging procedure with constant potential and modified constant potential chargers

These chargers are normally designed to charge one battery at a time. Charging must be stopped when the battery is gassing freely and the battery voltage shows no increase over a period of 2 hours. Note that it may not be possible to charge an over-discharged battery using a constant potential charger.

### Smart chargers

The latest generation of smart chargers are able to check and monitor the battery condition and to automatically supply a controlled charge that will charge the battery in the fastest time without damaging or overcharging it.

Some smart chargers have a special setting for calcium batteries and will charge these from flat, which the majority of other chargers are unable to do.

### Charging procedure with smart chargers

Follow the manufacturer's instructions. These chargers should be able to charge over-discharged (below 11 V) batteries; some may also have a special setting for calcium batteries.

### Boost chargers

These provide a very high initial current and are mainly used to put some charge into a flat battery when it is needed urgently. The current falls as the battery state of charge increases, and the battery temperature must be monitored to make sure it does not overheat.

### Charging procedure with boost chargers

- Because of the reduction in battery life, boost charging is not recommended except in exceptional circumstances.
- Never boost charge any battery that is below 11 V as it will be too sulphated to accept a charge; charge normally using the correct charger for the battery type.
- Only use a boost charger that limits the charging voltage to a maximum of 14.2 V and is fitted with a temperature monitor.
- Ensure that the charger manufacturer's instructions are followed.

## 8.6 Battery testing

Modern lead–acid batteries should only be tested using a digital tester. Some manufacturers will only consider any warranty claims if the faulty battery is accompanied with a printout of the test.

The guidance below is generic to digital testers; when using a specific tester, the manufacturer's instructions should be followed. Before testing any battery it should be fully charged and left to stand for 1 hour prior to testing.

1 Connect the red clamp to the positive (+) battery terminal and the black clamp to the negative (−) terminal.
2 The tester display will guide the user through a series of questions to select battery type, voltage, capacity and cold cranking amperes (CCA).
3 Once all of the information has been input, the user will be asked to 'press to start', which will start the battery test procedure. The digital tester will test the internal resistance of the battery using a load test. Once complete, the tester will give one of the following displays/ instructions:
   - Recharge battery and retest.
   - Faulty cell – replace.
   - Load error (this would indicate that there is an electrical component switched on if the battery is still connected to the vehicle).
   - The voltage, CCA, Ah and state of charge, followed by 'good' and 'pass'.

### 8.6.1 Understanding the specifications

#### CCA performance (amperes)

The CCA performance measures the starting performance of the battery. In simple terms, the higher the CCA, the easier it will be to start the vehicle.

#### Reserve capacity (minutes)

The reserve capacity is the amount of time, in minutes, that a battery at 25 °C can deliver a current of 25 A until the voltage drops to 10.50 V (5.25 V for a 6 V battery).

#### Ampere-hour capacity (Ah)

The ampere-hour capacity measures the total amount of electricity stored in a battery. An ampere hour represents the amount of electricity when a current of 1 A passes for 1 hour.

#### Recommended charge rate (amperes)

This is the recommended current level for charging batteries with a constant current charger. The correct manufacturer's data should be checked prior to charging.

## 8.7 Nickel–alkaline batteries

The nickel–alkaline battery is a strong, long-life battery that can withstand higher amounts of charge/ discharge cycles than a lead–acid type. It is more bulky and expensive than the lead–acid battery.

There are two main types of nickel–alkaline battery. The types are classified by their plate material; nickel–cadmium (NiCd), often referred to as 'NiCad', and nickel–iron (NiFe). The NiFe battery is less suitable for automobile use, so it is not considered in this chapter.

### 8.7.1 Nickel–cadmium battery

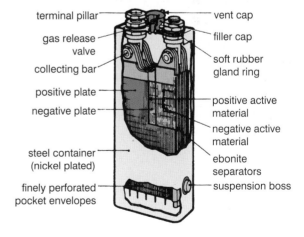

*Figure 8.7 Nickel–cadmium battery*

Figure 8.7 shows a sectioned view of one cell of a NiCad battery. The positive and negative plates are made of a nickel-plated steel frame and a number of flat section perforated tubes, also made of nickel-plated steel, are spot welded to it.

The positive plate tubes are filled with powdered nickel hydroxide and the negative plate tubes are filled with cadmium oxide.

The plates have lugs that attach to collecting bars and a terminal pillar is also fixed to these. The plates are assembled into sets in which the negative plates are interleaved between the positive plates; ebonite rods between the plates prevent electrical contact between them.

In what might be called the traditional construction, each cell is enclosed in a nickel-plated steel container. The terminal pillars pass through rubber gland rings in the cell lid and are secured by nuts. Each cell has a combined filler cup and vent cap.

Five cells are used for a nominal 6 V battery, nine cells for a 12 V, and 18 cells for a 24 V.

As the steel containers are in electrical contact with the positive plates, they must not be allowed to touch one another in the battery crate. Each cell has two suspension bosses welded on opposite sides by which they are located in tough rubber sockets in the crates with gaps being left between the adjacent cells.

### Electrolyte

NiCad electrolyte is a solution of potassium hydroxide (caustic potash, KOH) diluted with distilled water to a specific gravity of about 1.200. The density does not change with the state of charge because it is not chemically combined with the plate material. Instead, the electrolyte acts as a conductor for the electrical current and allows oxygen to pass from the negative plates during charge and return during discharge.

### Charge and discharge

During the charging process the positive plates become oxidised while the negative plates are deoxidised and change from cadmium oxide to spongy cadmium.

When the battery is discharged the action is reversed. The voltage in the cell varies from about 1.4 V to a minimum of 1.0 V during the charge/discharge cycle.

Since the active plate material does not chemically combine with any element in the electrolyte, there is virtually no self-discharge. Therefore, the battery can 'stand' for long periods in either the charged or discharged state without causing damage to the battery.

## 8.7.2 Maintenance of nickel–cadmium alkaline batteries

### Electrolyte

Periodically the electrolyte level in the cells should be checked. If the level is below the manufacturer's recommendations, the cells should be topped up with pure distilled water. Care must be taken to ensure that no trace of acid is allowed to contaminate the cells, so equipment used for lead–acid batteries must not be used on nickel–alkaline batteries.

NiCad electrolyte deteriorates with age, so the electrolyte should be completely replaced about every four years. When a hydrometer shows that the relative density has fallen to about 1.160, replacement is necessary. Exposure to air quickens the ageing process of the electrolyte; therefore, the cell vents must be kept closed except when the level is being checked.

### Battery tests

There is no simple test for the state of charge of a nickel–cadmium alkaline battery as neither the cell voltage nor the relative density of the electrolyte give any useful information.

In vehicle applications, advantage is taken of the fact that the battery cannot be damaged by overcharging so the charging rate should be checked to ensure that it is high enough to provide ample charging. This can be checked by examining the battery from time to time immediately after the vehicle has been running; if the cells are found to be gassing, it can be taken as an indication that the state of charge of the battery is satisfactory.

A further indication is the need for topping up. A reasonable consumption of distilled water is the best indication that the battery is being kept properly charged. Excessive consumption indicates overcharging.

Currently no satisfactory high-rate discharge tester is available for this type of battery, mainly because of the difficulty of obtaining an adequate area of contact with the steel cell terminals.

### General attention

The battery should be kept clean and dry, and periodically the terminals cleaned, fully tightened and lightly smeared with petroleum jelly.

All cell containers should be checked for damage and kept free from fuel oil and hydraulic fluid. The containers should also be checked to ensure that no metal objects bridge the metal cells. The battery should not be discharged below a cell voltage of 1.0 V.

## 8.8    Small batteries

Very small batteries are made to provide back-up power to retain the data in the RAM computer memory at times when the main battery is disconnected. The main types of 'dry' battery are zinc–carbon; this type of cell has been used for many years for low-current domestic items such as torches and toys (Figure 8.8). The cell consists of a zinc case (negative), a rod of carbon (positive) immersed in manganese dioxide, and an electrolyte of ammonium chloride. The EMF is 1.5 V per cell and the capacity is governed by its physical size. The majority of these batteries are not rechargeable and are discarded when discharged.

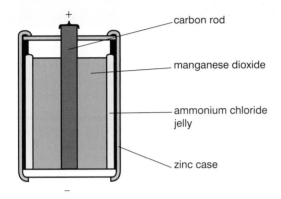

*Figure 8.8  Zinc–carbon battery*

## Other battery types

Modern electronic vehicle systems use batteries of different shapes, sizes and plate combinations, so it is essential to use the type recommended for a given application. In addition to those already covered in this chapter, other types are made that include:

- lithium
- lithium thionyl chloride
- lithium manganese dioxide
- nickel metal hydride
- silver oxide and mercury oxide.

# Vehicle circuits and systems

Electrical components play a principal role in the functioning of a motor vehicle. A standard car contains hundreds of electronic components in several different locations. This means that a car needs a comprehensive electrical circuit that interconnects its components. The sheer number of the components translates into hundreds of wire connections. The easiest way to approach a vehicle's circuitry is to divide the entire electrical sphere into separate systems.

Each system can be thought of as a section of the vehicle's electronics that serves a specific purpose. In this chapter we will identify these sections and describe their functions. We will then look at the wiring in a vehicle, the components of the wiring, circuit protection, modern advances and circuit diagnostics.

## 9.1 Electrical circuits

Figure 9.1 shows an overview of the electrical systems in a standard car.

### Power supply system

The power supply system is the sole source of electric current to all other electronic systems in the vehicle. The power system consists of a generator and a battery. When the engine is running, the generator supplies electricity to all electrical systems. During this time the battery is charged by the generator. Charge stored in the battery is used by electrical components when the vehicle is not running. The main purpose of the battery is to supply electricity to the ignition coils and starter motor to fire up the engine. Secondary functions include security alarms, central locking and emergency lights.

### Engine management system

The engine management system (EMS) consists of modules that regulate ignition timing, fuel mixture and power output. These parameters are adjusted to keep emissions, fuel efficiency and power output within their appropriate limits.

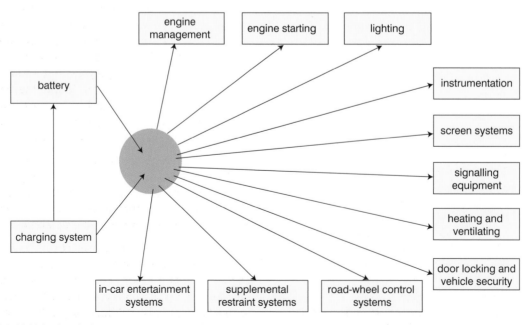

*Figure 9.1 Vehicle electrical systems*

## Ignition system

In older days, car start-up merely meant starting the engine. Today, cars follow a start-up sequence that involves both mechanical and electronic components. The start-up system includes the electronic control unit (ECU), fuel warmer, security module and lastly but, most importantly, the starter motor and ignition coils. Although some of these components are also part of other systems, many start-up problems are due to a malfunction of one of them.

## Lighting system

Lighting includes the head and tail lamps, side lamps, side-mirror lamps and sometimes interior lights (in some cars interior lighting is part of the passenger cabin system). Head lamp intensity needs to be varied depending on the time and situation, such as dipping the main beam in traffic. Similarly, tail lamps change intensity when brakes are applied. These switching circuits are all part of the lighting system. Many cars also have headlamp positioning motors and wipers.

## Instrumentation system

This includes the speedometer, temperature and fuel gauges, rev meter, several warning lamps for brakes, oil, lights and doors, and light indicators. Many new models have a digital display that displays all the information on a single screen. Such displays are connected by a bus to a main module. This module is connected to the main ECU, which receives direct input from sensors around the vehicle.

## Windshield system

Windscreen wipers, washers and defrosting grids on the main windshields and side mirrors are included in this system.

## Signalling systems

Signalling systems include front, rear and side indicator lamps and reverse indicator lamps. The car horn is also part of the signalling system.

## Climate control and ventilation system

This system includes both the cabin equipment and the compressor and heat exchangers in the engine bay. Sensors in the cabin provide temperature and humidity values. The climate control module compares the values to user settings and adjusts the air input from the evaporator (cool air) and heat exchanger (warm air) to cover the deficit. The compressor is located in the engine bay and pumps refrigerant around the cooling system and through the evaporator. It is driven by the serpentine belt (main belt) and a magnetic clutch.

## Locking and security system

The locking and security system is controlled by a module which is linked to the door lock actuators, alarm sirens, motion sensors, wireless unit and engine immobiliser. We will explain this equipment in detail in Chapter 22.

## Drive management system

The drive management system includes modules that control the anti-lock brake system (ABS), traction control system (TCS), electronic stability control (ESC), transmission and suspension. These modern systems have made cars much safer, comfortable and more fuel efficient. These systems are discussed further in Chapter 23.

## Supplemental restraint system (SRS)

Airbags are fitted at strategic locations in the passenger cabin and controlled electronically by a separate module. In many vehicles the restraint system is a totally independent electric circuit; this makes its operation much safer and quicker. The airbags are usually triggered by motion sensors called accelerometers. SRS systems also include seatbelt pre-tensioners.

## In-car entertainment system

Radio, MP3 and DVD players, display screens, audio speakers and user controls are all part of the in-car entertainment system. In simple cars it may consist of a single unit on the dashboard, while in others it may be spread elaborately around the passenger cabin.

## 9.2 Cables

The electrical components in the car need to be connected to the power supply system to form a circuit. For electricity to flow, each component needs a ground connection as well. In most vehicles, the metallic frame of the body serves as the electrical ground. The negative connections of the battery and all electrical components are attached to the metal frame. However, the positive connections are linked using cable wires. The supply cable is known as the feed wire. The main feed wire leaves the battery's positive terminal and splits into various branches, usually through a distributing circuit. The distributing circuit also contains the fuses for each component.

Distributing a car's electrical network into systems in this way is a very helpful way to approach the circuitry. Problems can be tracked down to their systems and diagnosed quickly. Even entire systems can be replaced or upgraded within a few days of work.

Copper cables are used for electric supply wiring to components. The cable consists of a stranded copper core in a rubber coating. Cables to different components in the same area are secured together to form a harness or loom. Harnessing cables makes the electrical layout more organised and easier to protect.

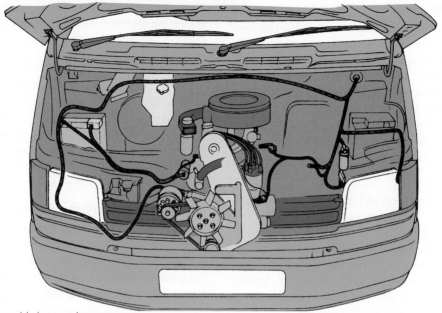

*Figure 9.2 Engine cable loom or harness*

Cables in a harness are taped or spiral taped together to protect against physical factors. In the engine the harness is further protected by convoluted plastic tubing. Within the passenger cabin the harnesses run under the plastic casing on the edges of the roof, floor and side pillars. In other areas of the car the cables run in grooves in the metal body. The cables only leave the harness near each component. Figure 9.2 shows a typical layout of the cable harness in the engine bay.

## Cable varieties

Electrical cables have different technical specifications and dimensions. Each type of cable is distinguished by its wire diameter, strand count, potential drop, current rating and insulation. Using the wrong specification cable will supply a lower (or higher) current and potential to the component, which can be dangerous. Excessive current or potential can damage a component and may cause a fire; insufficient current can also damage the component and cause device failure.

The current in cables causes their temperature to rise. Resistance and heat dissipation are two factors that affect the operating temperature. Harnessing cables can reduce the overall heat dissipation of each cable. This heating problem is solved by running cables side by side instead of using a spiral harness.

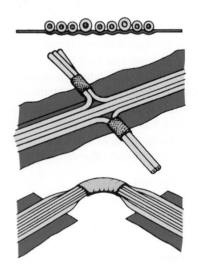

*Figure 9.3 Cables placed side by side*

Manufacturers select cables that save both weight and cost. The safest minimum possible diameter is used for wiring. When repairing electrical wiring, defective cables should be replaced by cables of similar specifications. Table 9.1 shows a list of cable specifications and their applications.

*Table 9.1 Cable ratings and applications*

| Conductor size No. of strands/diam. (mm) | Maximum current rating (ampere) | Application |
|---|---|---|
| 9/0.30 | 5.75 | Lightly loaded circuits |
| 14/0.30 | 8.75 | Ignition circuits, side and tail lamps, general body wiring |
| 28/0.30 | 17.5 | Headlamps, horns, heated rear windows |
| 120/0.30 | 60 | Alternator charging circuit (heavy duty) |

## Cable covering

Electrical cables are insulated with a PVC coat. Rubber is no longer used because it has a lower resistance to oil compounds. PVC is better than rubber because of its higher resistance to both heat and oil compounds. PVC coating is also more durable, and so is sufficient in lesser thickness. This reduces the overall weight of the wiring and saves space.

In addition to PVC, materials such as silicone and PTFE are also used for electrical insulation purposes.

## Cable coding

A vehicle has several cables running through its structure and during diagnosis tracing a single cable can be time-wasting. To help distinguish cables a colour code is followed. The colour code varies from country to country, so the specific code for a vehicle is usually explained in its manual.

*Table 9.2  Wire colour code examples*

| Circuit wiring | BSI colour | Letter code (British) | Letter code (DIN) |
|---|---|---|---|
| Earth wire from component to earth tag | black | B | SW |
| Ignition switched fused supply, e.g. instrument, indicators, brake and reverse lights | green | G | GN |
| Battery supply from fusible link box | brown | N | BR |
| Fused permanent supply, e.g. interior lamps, radio cassette, clock | purple | P | VI |
| Fused supply, e.g. side lamps, interior illumination | red | R | RT |
| Fused supply, e.g. central door locking | slate (grey) | S | GR |
| Fused supply, e.g. headlamps | blue | U | BL |
| Ignition switched supply to passenger compartment fuse box | white | W | WS |

Vehicles made in the UK follow the British Standards Institution's (BSI) recommendation of the AU7 standard for colour coding.

As most diagrams in car manuals are drawn in grayscale, a letter code may be followed to identify the colours. Table 9.2 shows colour code examples for cables.

Each cable has a base colour and a tracer colour. The tracer colour runs as a thin line along the length of the cable. The base colour identifies the main circuit the cable belongs to. The tracer colour identifies the specific location of the cable in the main circuit. Using the colours and the wiring diagram together, cables can easily be identified during diagnosis of the electrical circuitry.

## Circuit numbering

As colours are used to identify cables, similarly numbers are used to identify circuits. This numbering usually follows the German DIN standard. Table 9.3 shows the main numbers used to identify circuits.

*Table 9.3  Number coding: DIN system*

| Circuit No. | Application |
|---|---|
| 1 | Ignition, earth side of coil |
| 4 | Ignition, high-tension output |
| 15 | Ignition, feed (un-fused) |
| 30 | Feed from battery |
| 31 | Earth |
| 51 | Alternator output |
| 54 | Ignition, feed (fused) |
| 56 | Headlamps |
| 58 | Side/tail lamps |
| 75 | Accessories |

## Printed circuit boards

Printed circuit boards (PCBs) are a smart way to make compact, cheap and efficient circuits. Instead of using independent cables, the circuit is printed or etched on a thin board using thin copper lines (Figure 9.4). Electronic components are then soldered into place and the PCB insulated. The PCB is supplied power and connected to external components via cables.

The copper layer of a PCB may develop cracks over time and cause the circuit to break. Small cracks can be repaired by carefully heating the copper around it. If copper degradation is more severe, it is always better to replace the entire PCB instead of repairing it.

PCBs are the core circuit in almost all electrical modules. Windshield wipers, power mirrors, fuse boxes, ECUs and engine management units all have PCB cores.

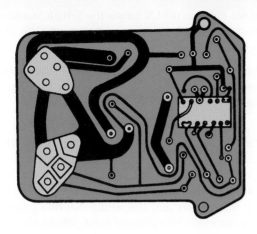

*Figure 9.4  PCB showing wiper circuit*

## Hybrid high-voltage wiring

Hybrid and electrical vehicles have entered the mainstream automotive market. Previously, electrical standards were limited to systems operating under 20 V. Hybrid and electric cars use much higher voltages of 600 V. Cables and connectors in these vehicles are of a much higher rating and the circuitry is very different from that of internal combustion vehicles.

## 9.3  Electrical connectors

Electrical connectors serve as bridges between two electrical components. Different connectors differ from each other in their pinout design, physical shape, size, impedance, insulation, resistance to water and vibration, and their ease of mating.

Several different connectors are used in motor vehicles. These can be divided into cable–component terminals and cable–cable connectors.

### Cable–component terminals

These join cables to other electrical components of the vehicle. Most electrical components have a terminal block, which provides a convenient site to connect cables. The receiving connectors on the terminal vary from component to component. Most such terminals use blade connectors, which are secured using a screw or nut, or simply slid on at the terminal block. On the cable end, the connector is crimped on to the wire. Figure 9.5 shows blade connectors commonly used on a terminal block.

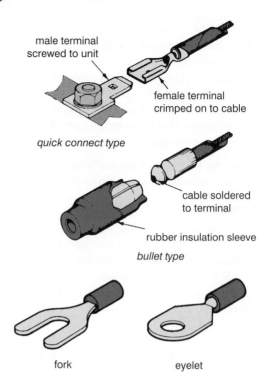

*Figure 9.5  Terminal block and blade connectors*

### Cable–cable connectors

Cable–cable connectors range from simple bullet-and-socket joints to complex precision connectors. The use of connectors depends on the performance requirements of a circuit. Some circuits are very delicate and need their signals to be transmitted with a high degree of accuracy. Cables from some sensors and actuators are a good example. Simple connectors cause electrical fluctuations in the circuit and can cause distortion of signal in the cables. Many circuits in a vehicle operate on very low currents, so factors such as current leakage become very important.

Connectors also need to be insulated against the environment. Direct exposure of wires and terminals can lead to rust and corrosion. Connector terminals are sealed with a rubber diaphragm or annular seal, and the exposed metal is sometimes gold plated. Gold is a good electrical conductor.

For many systems, it is crucial that the connectors perform perfectly at all times. Systems such as airbags are hugely dependent on their connectors working properly. In airbag applications, the connectors may remain dormant for years, yet in the event of a crash, they should handle huge current surges without any problem. In such applications the requirements are very stringent as even a few cases of failure can cause doubts on airbag reliability.

Sophisticated connectors such as these are very sensitive when opened. They should only be handled

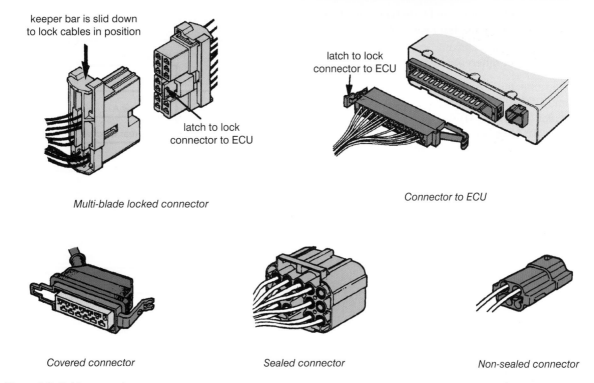

keeper bar is slid down
to lock cables in position

latch to lock
connector to ECU

latch to lock
connector to ECU

*Multi-blade locked connector*

*Connector to ECU*

*Covered connector*

*Sealed connector*

*Non-sealed connector*

Figure 9.6  Cable connectors

if the user has proper understanding of their function and maintenance. Water-proofing seals in connectors are also very sensitive to damage. Water in connectors can cause confusing fault conditions in low-current circuits, which can be hard to diagnose.

Figure 9.6 shows typical cable connectors. Connectors are designed so correct full connections are made. The connectors are keyed to ensure the correct cables are linked together and have a latch or clip to hold the link secure. Connectors reduce the stress on the cables at the mating point and protect the link against jerks and shocks.

## 9.4   Circuit protection

A short circuit or electronic failure can cause a circuit to draw large amounts of current. A large current can heat cables, melt the insulation and possibly cause a fire. Circuit components can also explode and cause serious damage. In less severe cases, short circuits jeopardise the functioning of the electrical component and also drain the battery quickly. A protection device, such as an electromagnetic circuit breaker or a fuse, helps protect circuits from being damaged by short circuits.

### 9.4.1 Fuses

A fuse has a thin length of wire that melts when a large current flows through it. The wire is usually held between two metal arms that make contact with

the supply wire. Figure 9.7 shows some standard automotive fuses. Each fuse serves the same function: to act as a safety switch between the power supply and circuit. Fuses are designed at different current ratings. The fuse wire melts when the current through it exceeds the rating.

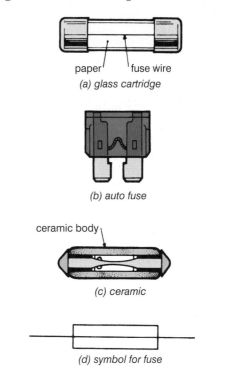

paper     fuse wire
*(a) glass cartridge*

*(b) auto fuse*

ceramic body

*(c) ceramic*

*(d) symbol for fuse*

Figure 9.7  Types of fuses

In automotive applications, the blade-type auto fuse (Figure 9.7b) is used. This thin fuse is manufactured for current ratings relevant to motor vehicle applications in four different sizes:

- Low-profile mini (APS)
- Mini (APM/ATM)
- Regular (APR/ATC/ATO)
- Maxi (APX) heavy-duty

A colour code for the fuse body is used to identify the rating of the fuse (Table 9.4).

*Table 9.4 ATO fuse colour code*

| Colour | Current rating (A) |
|--------|--------------------|
| violet | 3 |
| tan | 5 |
| brown | 7.5 |
| red | 10 |
| blue | 15 |
| yellow | 20 |
| clear | 25 |
| green | 30 |

The blade-type auto fuse is very reliable and gives a consistent performance. Because of this an auto fuse rating can easily be chosen for a circuit based on current usage. Detailed information of the circuit elements is not required.

All the fuses are housed in the fuse box (Figure 9.8), which receives the power from the main feed wire. A blown fuse can be replaced by simply pulling it out and inserting a new one. If the new fuse blows immediately, the circuit should be inspected for short-circuits and repaired.

The majority of short circuits are a result of poor cable mounting or faulty installation of an electrical component. A single faulty component in a system can cause the whole system to shut down. Because of this, many systems have individual fuses for each component. For example, the lighting system has a separate fuse for each headlamp.

In some rare cases, the battery's main cable may short to earth. As a precaution, the main feed wire has a heavy-duty fuse to keep other circuitry safe. These fuses are usually rated between 30 A and 60 A.

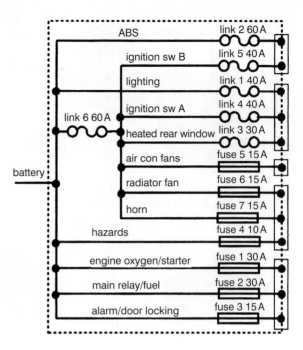

*Figure 9.8 Fuse box circuit*

## 9.4.2 Circuit breakers

In many new vehicles, manufacturers are now installing circuit breakers instead of wire fuses. Circuit breakers and fuses do the same job, but circuit breakers do not need to be replaced. Instead, when a circuit breaker blows, it can be simply reset by means of a lever or switch.

Popular circuit breakers are either thermal or electromagnetic. Thermal circuit breakers use a bi-metallic strip, which heats up and bends when there is a current overload, thus breaking the circuit. Electromagnetic circuit breakers use a current controlled electromagnet to pull a switch that breaks the circuit.

Circuit breakers cost more than a wire fuse, but are much more convenient and easy to use.

## 9.5 Fault diagnosis

A methodical approach to malfunctioning components can help make permanent repairs to faults. After a circuit is identified as being faulty, the next step is to examine its fuses, supply cables, connectors, terminals and electronic elements. Often this inspection will locate a damaged cable, a loose terminal or a short circuited element. However, if this inspection fails, meter tests need to be conducted at diagnostic points as recommended by the manufacturer. The most difficult cases are where more than one factor appears to be responsible. During meter readings, the connectors should not be detached; this helps identify loose connectors, if there are any.

Before conducting a diagnosis, it is important to note the specifics of the circuit in question. This includes the voltage and current requirements, the nature of the circuit, the components involved and which external circuits it is linked to.

## Voltage drop test

Let's take an example of a dim headlamp. The first two thoughts would be: either the lamp is faulty or the battery is faulty. However, neither of them may be true. The voltage drop test helps identify potential drops in the circuit. Under perfect conditions, each leg of a circuit should have a voltage drop as close to 0 V as possible. Corrosion in crimps and connectors can present added resistance and hence a voltage drop.

In this case you start at the headlamp; using the probes you measure the voltage drop at each leg of the circuit (Figure 9.9a). When a significant voltage drop is detected, the two connectors of that leg are separately tested (Figure 9.9b). The connector with the large voltage drop is faulty and should be replaced.

Sealed connectors such as multi-pin plugs are tested using a hook and pin probe (Figure 9.10). The needle-like probe of the device penetrates the insulation to make contact with the wire. The cable must be resealed after testing to prevent admission of water.

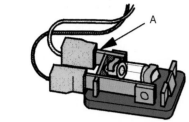

*(a) intermittent resistance at A*

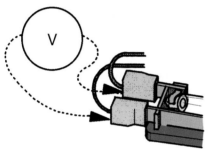

*(b) voltage supply to unit*

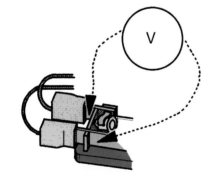

*(c) voltage on lamp side of connectors*

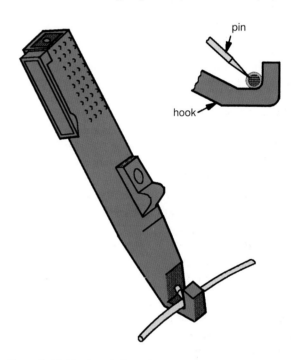

*Figure 9.10 Hook and pin probe*

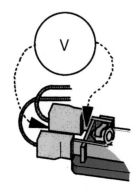

*(d) voltage drop across connector*

*Figure 9.9 Voltage drop test*

# 10

# Generation of electrical energy

A large amount of electrical energy is required to power the electrical consumers in a modern vehicle. The battery will supply this energy when the engine is not running, but when the engine is started the charging system must provide enough energy to run the vehicle's electrical systems and also top up the battery.

## 10.1 Charging circuit principles

Modern vehicles have more electrically operated devices so their charging systems have to provide a much greater output. As well as a high maximum output, the modern generator has to be more efficient and lighter in weight. In the early 1960s these requirements forced manufacturers to change from a dynamo to an alternator. An **electromotive force (EMF)** is generated by moving a conductor in a magnetic field, relative to each other. The parts that move or are fixed indicate the main difference between the two types of generators:

- Dynamo – the magnetic field is fixed and the conductor is moved.
- Alternator – the conductor is fixed and the magnetic field is moved.

**Electromotive force (EMF)**: the force that carries the electrical charge from one point to another in a circuit. It is measured in volts (V).

Figure 10.1 shows the main components for both types of charging system.

In 1831 Michael Faraday demonstrated, by experiment, that electricity could be generated by magnetism. He moved a magnet inside a coil of wire and, using a galvanometer, showed that a current was being

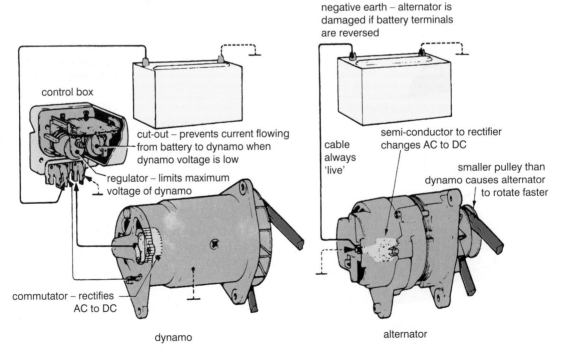

control box

cut-out – prevents current flowing from battery to dynamo when dynamo voltage is low

regulator – limits maximum voltage of dynamo

commutator – rectifies AC to DC

dynamo

negative earth – alternator is damaged if battery terminals are reversed

semi-conductor to rectifier changes AC to DC

cable always 'live'

smaller pulley than dynamo causes alternator to rotate faster

alternator

*Figure 10.1 Vehicle charging systems*

## Health and safety best practice

When working on a vehicle's electrical system:

- make sure that appropriate and proper personal protective equipment (PPE) is used for the task being carried out
- take care of hot and sharp components

- disconnect the vehicle battery if working on high-current components
- be aware of moving parts, drive belts, and so on
- only use equipment that you are trained to use.

generated and that, as the direction of the movement of the magnet changed, so did the direction of the current. His experiment demonstrated that the EMF generated depended on the number of turns in the coil of wire, the strength of the magnet used and the speed that the magnetic field cuts through the coil windings. He concluded:

'An EMF is induced whenever there is a change in the magnetic flux linked with the coil.'

## 10.2   The dynamo

The dynamo consists of a conductor coil that is rotated in a magnetic field (Figure 10.2). The coil is a soft iron armature that is driven via a belt from the engine crankshaft. The electromagnetic field coil surrounds the armature and creates a magnetic field when a current is passed through it. When the engine is running, the armature rotates inside the magnetic field and an **alternating current (AC)** is created in the armature. At the end of the armature is a cylindrical commutator that collects the current and it has carbon brushes running on its contact face, these brushes take the current out to the main output terminals and rectify the current to **direct current (DC)**. The brushes carry the full current of the output and wear out quickly, so will require maintenance. The current to the field windings can be changed to vary the output of the dynamo as it depends on the strength of the magnetic field to induce a strong current in the armature coils. A strong magnetic field will produce a strong output current, whereas a reduced magnetic field will limit the output current of the dynamo.

**Alternating current (AC)**: an electrical current that oscillates between positive and negative charge.

**Direct current (DC)**: an electrical current that remains positively charged.

## 10.2.1 Components of the dynamo

### Control box

The control box for a dynamo is mounted remotely from the dynamo and houses the cut-out and regulator. Although this means that they can be mounted away from excessive heat and vibration, it requires extra wiring and components.

### Cut-out

The cut-out is an electromechanical relay that allows charge to flow from the dynamo to the battery but not back again. This prevents charge from flowing from the battery to the dynamo when the dynamo is not moving or when the dynamo voltage is less than the battery. A faulty cut-out would cause the dynamo to act as a motor – the current in the cables would be too great and the cables would burn. The contact points of the cut-out relay could become burnt out and fail.

### Regulator

The regulator controls the dynamo output to the battery and prevents damage to the dynamo by limiting the output to a safe figure. Regulation is achieved by using electromechanically controlled contacts to interrupt the field current. These contacts vibrate constantly and control the current by varying the closed/open period of each vibration. The contact points can become burnt

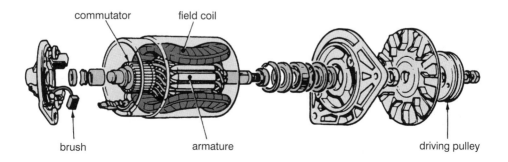

*Figure 10.2 Dynamo*

and fail, either by becoming open circuit and allowing the battery to discharge, or by becoming closed circuit and allowing the battery to become overcharged.

Often, two regulators are fitted side by side; one controls the voltage and the other limits the current. A circuit diagram, showing the current for the field windings (F) and the output current from the dynamo (D) is shown in Figure 10.3.

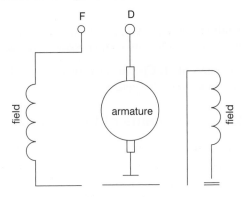

Figure 10.3  Dynamo circuit

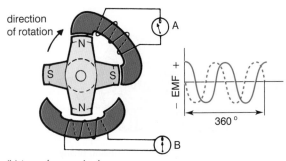

(a) single-phase output

(b) two-phase output

Figure 10.4  Principle of an alternator

## 10.3 The alternator

The principle of an alternator is shown in Figure 10.4a. A shaft and four-pole magnet is fitted adjacent to a stator (stationary section), around which is a conductor coil. This coil is connected to form a simple circuit – in the figure a galvanometer (G) is included to show output. Rotation of the magnet generates an EMF in the stator winding. Since the north and south poles present themselves to the stator in alternate order, the current produced will be AC. Output increases as the speed of rotation increases, but once the speed gets too high the current peaks, which gives protection against current overload. Adding another stator winding in the position shown in Figure 10.4b gives another output, as shown by the graph of EMF. Stator winding B gives an output that is 45° out of phase to winding A; this double-curve pattern is called a two-phase output.

Similarly, if another stator is added and all three are spaced out around a multi-pole magnet, then a three-phase output is obtained (Figure 10.5).

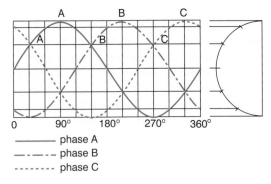

Figure 10.5  Three-phase output

Due to the increase in the number of magnetic poles, each cycle will be shorter; therefore, one revolution of the shaft will produce a large number of AC cycles. Rectification of the current is performed by semiconductor diodes. A single diode (Figure 10.6) gives half-wave rectification, but half of the output is lost.

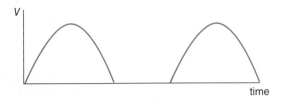

Figure 10.6  Half-wave rectification

Arrangement of the diodes ensures that the current is channelled through the appropriate diodes to give a unidirectional flow to the battery (i.e. full-wave rectification). Besides acting as rectifiers, the diodes also prevent current flow between the battery and the alternator when the battery voltage is higher than the alternator voltage. This removes the need for a cut-out in the charging circuit.

Output voltage control prevents the voltage exceeding a given maximum as this would overcharge the battery and damage the electrical devices in other circuits. Output is controlled by using an electromagnet instead of a permanent magnet for the field. Alternators are fitted with microelectronic solid-state regulators; these control the output accurately to $14.2 \pm 0.2\,\text{V}$.

Compared with a dynamo, an alternator has the following advantages:

- Higher output – rotating parts are more robust so a higher speed of rotation can be allowed. This is achieved by using a drive pulley of smaller diameter, which makes the output greater at low engine speeds (Figure 10.7).
- Lower weight and more compact – the constructional features and improved efficiency allows the required output energy to be given by a smaller unit.
- Less maintenance – output current is not conducted through a commutator and brushes, so breakdown due to brush wear or surface contamination is eliminated.
- More precise output control – the use of a solid-state regulator enables the maximum output limits to be reduced. This permits the use of maintenance-free batteries and other electronic systems that would otherwise be damaged by excessive voltage.
- Requires no cut-out – rectifier diodes serve the same purpose as a cut-out.

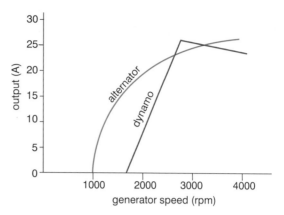

Figure 10.7 Comparison of outputs

Figure 10.8 shows an exploded view of a typical alternator.

This alternator is a three-phase, 12-pole machine that incorporates a rectifier and microelectronic regulator. The lightweight aluminium alloy casing of the alternator contains the following:

- Rotor to form the magnetic poles
- Stator to carry the windings in which the current is generated
- Rectifier packs to convert AC to DC
- Regulator to limit the output voltage

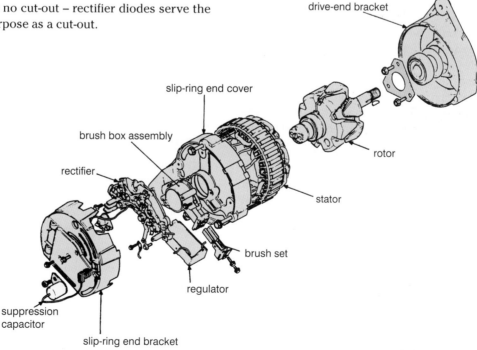

Figure 10.8 Exploded view of an alternator

## 10.3.1 Components of the alternator

### Rotor

The rotor consists of a field winding that is wound around a soft iron core and pressed on to a shaft. Soft iron is used because it becomes magnetised and demagnetised very quickly, which makes it suitable for electromagnets. Each end of the rotor is shaped like a claw to form six magnetic poles: the six fingers on one claw give the north (N) poles and the six fingers on the other claw form the south (S) poles, when a current is passed through the field windings (Figure 10.9).

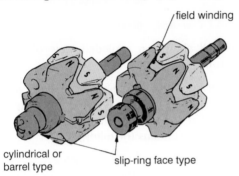

Figure 10.9 Rotor construction

The magnetic excitation winding is made by two carbon brushes that rub on two copper slip rings. Two types of brush arrangement are used:

- Cylindrical or barrel type – two slip rings are placed side by side.
- Face type – two brushes are fitted coaxially with the shaft.

The rotor is belt-driven from the crankshaft through a vee-pulley and Woodruff-type key. Since alternators are suitable for rotational speeds of up to 15,000 rpm, and because the belt tension must be high enough to prevent slip when a large current output is produced, ball bearings are needed to support the rotor. These bearings are packed with lubricant and sealed for life.

Forced ventilation of air through the machine is essential to cool the semiconductor devices and prevent the windings from overheating. Air movement for this ventilation is achieved by a centrifugal fan fitted behind the pulley or inside the alternator.

Figure 10.10 Stator construction

### Stator

The stator is a laminated soft iron member attached rigidly to the casing that carries three sets of stator windings (Figure 10.10). The coils, made of comparatively heavy gauge enamelled copper wire, that form the stator are arranged so that separate AC waveforms are induced in each winding as they are cut by the changing magnetic flux.

The three sets of windings can be interconnected in one of two ways:

- Star connected
- Delta connected

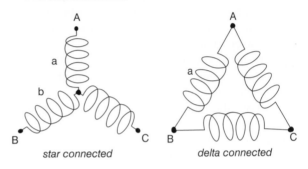

Figure 10.11 Stator windings

Figure 10.11 shows both forms of stator windings. In the star connection, one end of each winding connects to the other two windings and the output current is supplied from the ends A, B and C. The delta connection method is named after the Greek letter delta (Δ) and the output is again taken from points A, B and C. The main operational difference between the two arrangements is in the size of the output. In the star arrangement the voltage between A and B (or two other output points) is the sum of the EMF induced in to windings 'a' and 'b'. Whereas the voltage from the delta arrangement is limited to the EMF induced in winding 'a' only. For a given speed and flux density:

Voltage output from star = 1.732 × Voltage output from delta-wound machine

Although the output from the star arrangement is obtained mainly from two windings, the total EMF is not doubled because only one winding can be positioned at any one time at the point of maximum magnetic flux, hence the value 1.732 (i.e. $\sqrt{3}$).

The energy generated for both arrangements at a given speed is equal, so a comparison of current outputs shows that:

Current output from delta = 1.732 × Current output from star-wound machine

The star arrangement is used on the majority of alternators for light cars. However, where higher current output is needed, the delta-wound stator is preferred.

On some special designs of heavy-duty alternators, the operator can alter the stator windings from star to delta when a large output current is needed, such as a heavy goods vehicle that has a refrigerated trailer, or uses an electric motor to operate a hydraulic crane.

## Rectifier

Most alternators use semiconductor diodes that are arranged to form a bridge network. For a three-phase output, six diodes are needed to give full-wave rectification. These are arranged as shown in Figure 10.12. The diodes are one-way valves, so the current generated in any winding will always pass to the battery via the terminal marked B+. Since a complete circuit is needed to give this DC current, the appropriate earth diode (the negative diode in this case) is fitted to pass current from earth to the active windings.

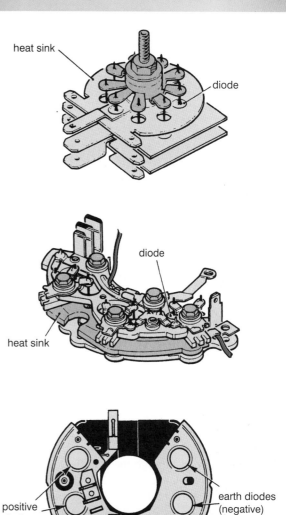

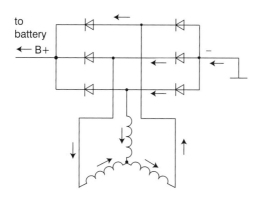

*Figure 10.12  Rectifier circuit*

The action of the diodes can be checked by inserting two arrows adjacent to any two of the stator windings shown in Figure 10.12. Irrespective of the position and direction of the arrows, it will always be possible to trace the circuit between earth and B+. Besides the rectifying function, the diodes also prevent current flow between the battery and alternator when the alternator output voltage is less than the battery voltage. Figure 10.13 shows alternative constructions used to mount the rectifier diodes. In all cases the semiconductors must be kept cool, so it is usual to mount the diodes in an aluminium alloy block or plate called a heat sink. Air pumped through the alternator cools this as well as other internal parts.

*Figure 10.13  Alternative locations for rectifier diodes*

Although the self-excited machine supplies the field current when the alternator is charging, it is not able to provide the initial current to energise the field to start the charging process. This is achieved by utilising the charge warning lamp. The warning lamp sub-circuit fulfils two duties: it provides a signal to warn the driver when the system is not functioning, and also supplies the initial excitation field to the slip rings current.

When the engine is to be started, the ignition is switched on; this connects the lamp to the battery

---

### Health and safety best practice

## Alternator B+ terminal

It must be noted that the cable connected to B+ is live when the alternator is stationary. Before working

on the alternator, either disconnect the battery earth terminal or take some other suitable precaution.

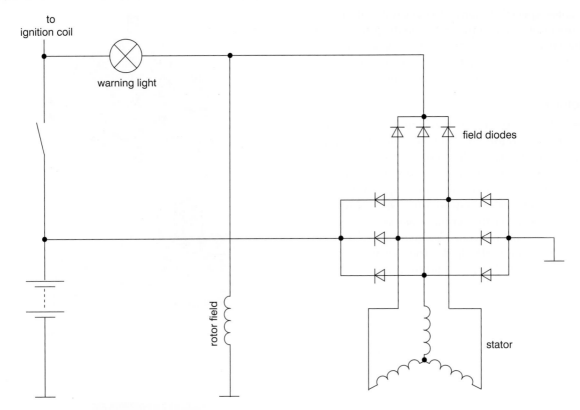

*Figure 10.14 Self-excited field system – nine diodes*

and makes a circuit through the field to earth. At this stage, the lamp is illuminated and the field is excited to the extent controlled by the wattage of the lamp; a typical lamp size is 12V, 2.2W. As the alternator speed is raised, the voltage on the output side of the field diodes is increased. This gradually reduces the voltage applied to the lamp so the light slowly fades and eventually goes out when the output voltage of the alternator equals the battery voltage (i.e. when the alternator cuts-in and starts to charge). When this happens the field diodes will be providing the entire field current. The cutting-in speed, which is normally about 1000rpm, depends on the field current, so if an earlier cutting-in speed is desired, the wattage of the lamp should be increased. In view of the dual role fulfilled by the warning lamp, it will be apparent that if the lamp filament is broken, the alternator will not charge. Figure 10.14 shows the rectifier and field diode arrangement used in a Lucas ACR-type alternator. The cable from the charge indicator warning light connects with the IND terminal on the alternator which is, in turn, joined to the + side of the field.

## Regulator

Output voltage from an alternator must be limited to prevent the battery from being overcharged and to protect the electrical equipment from excessive voltage. On a 12V Lucas machine the regulator sets the alternator voltage to a maximum of 14.2V.

Since this voltage corresponds to a fully charged battery, the alternator must be made to vary its charging current to suit the state of charge of the battery.

Control of the field current is achieved by fitting a regulator on one side (usually the earth side) of the rotor field (Figure 10.15). The regulator uses a power transistor to act as a field-switching device; the current is controlled by the proportion of time that the switch is closed in relation to its open period. When the alternator is below 14.2V the switch is closed, but at the maximum voltage the switch operates and keeps the output voltage at 14.2V, irrespective of the current being generated.

### Surge-protection diode

A surge-protection diode is fitted between the IND and the earth. This is an avalanche diode, which will close at a high voltage. This shorts out the field and prevents the alternator charging, to protect the regulator.

### Regulator construction

The microelectronic regulator is housed within the alternator body. This type is connected by short leads and push-on terminals to the alternator. The principle of a regulator is shown by the simplified circuit shown in Figure 10.16.

This circuit is built around a zener diode (ZD). This type of diode will not conduct any current until a given voltage is reached. When the given voltage is achieved

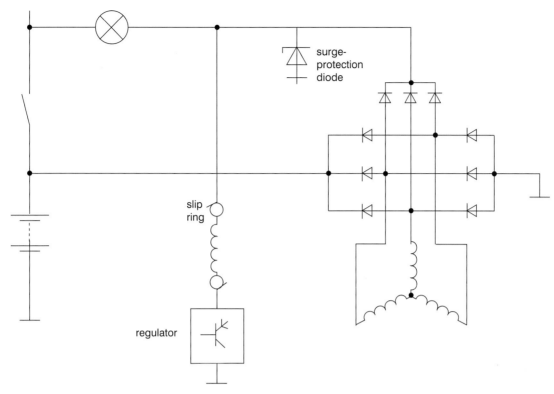

*Figure 10.15  Regulator control of field current and surge protection*

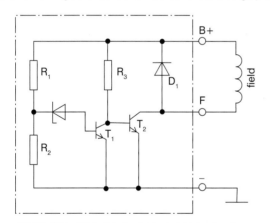

*Figure 10.16  Simplified circuit of a transistorised voltage regulator*

the diode conducts and activates the field-switching transistor. The zener diode operates at a voltage less than 14.2V, so resistors $R_1$ and $R_2$ are fitted to reduce the voltage applied. As in similar electronic control systems, more than one transistor is used; this enables a very small current supplied by the zener diode to be amplified by the driver transistors to a current sufficient to operate the robust power transistor that switches the full field current. When the alternator output voltage is low, current flows from B+ through resistor $R_3$ to the base of $T_2$ and then to earth. Current passing through the base circuit of $T_2$ switches on the transistor and causes the field F to be linked to earth. During this phase, a strong magnetic field is obtained.

As the output voltage reaches 14.2V the diode switches on and passes the current to the base of $T_1$ and allows current to flow freely through $T_1$ from $R_3$, with the result that the base of $T_2$ loses current. $T_2$ is switched off and current through the field winding is interrupted. This sequence is as follows: when the output voltage falls below its operating value, the zener diode switches off; this switches the transistors to re-establish the field circuit. The process continues in rapid succession to give a constant voltage output from the machine. The diode $D_1$ fitted across the field winding prevents a high voltage being applied to $T_2$ when the field is suddenly interrupted by the rapid switching of $T_2$.

## Voltage-sensing circuits

Since the alternator is positioned away from the battery, supplies to other circuits reduce the voltage sensed by the regulator mounted in the alternator. To overcome this, a separate direct lead is sometimes taken from the battery to allow the regulator to sense, without any drop, the battery voltage; this system is called battery sensing. Figure 10.17 shows the circuit for an alternator fitted with a battery-sensed regulator. In this system, the cable connected between the battery and the regulator terminal B+ acts as the sensing lead. Voltage applied to B+ signals the point at which the zener diode starts to conduct.

An alternative system, called machine-sensing, uses an internally connected lead between the regulator and the IND terminal of the alternator. This system

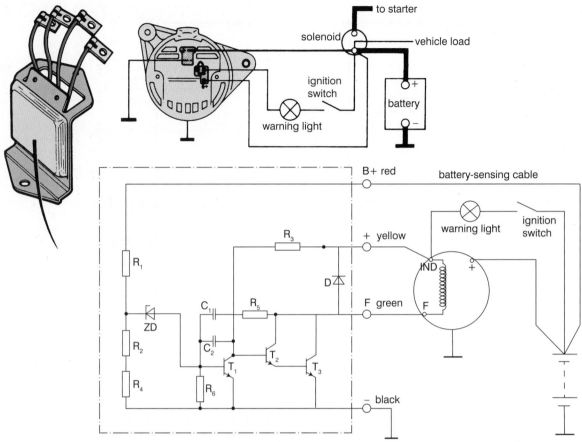

Figure 10.17 *Battery-sensed regulator*

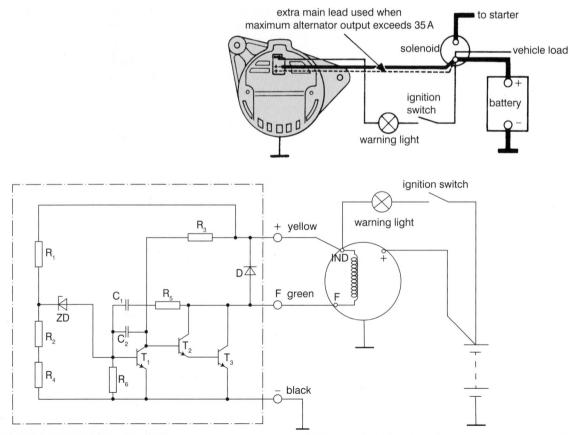

Figure 10.18 *Machine-sensed regulator*

limits alternator output to the regulated voltage, irrespective of external loads placed on the battery. Figure 10.18 shows a typical machine-sensed circuit.

Two additional resistors ($R_3$ and $R_6$) and two capacitors ($C_1$ and $C_2$) are shown. This sub-circuit allows the regulator to oscillate at a frequency controlled by the internal time constant given by the charge–discharge action of the capacitors; this ensures that the transistor $T_3$ is rapidly switched on and off. Output voltage is controlled by varying the ratio of time that it is closed to open (Figure 10.15).

A modern alternator uses machine-sensing and gives a regulated voltage of 14.2 ± 0.2 V. There is a warning light in the instrument panel to warn the driver of faults, such as:

- open-circuit field/worn brushes
- open-circuit regulator
- open-circuit output cable
- broken drive belt
- overcharge through faulty regulator.

Figure 10.19  Compact alternator

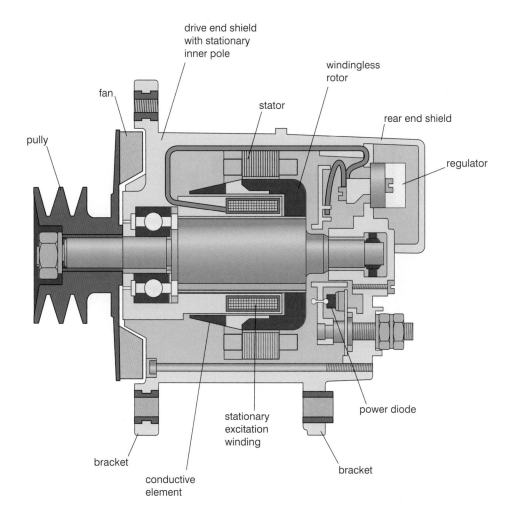

Figure 10.20 Alternator with an air-cooled windingless rotor

## 10.3.2 Other types of alternator

### Double alternator

For vehicles that have an extremely high draw of electrical power a double alternator can be used. This has two electrically and mechanically coupled alternators housed in the same body. It is really two alternators, one mounted behind the other, and sharing the same regulator and rectifier. The drive comes in from the belt pulley and is attached to the rotor. Immediately behind the first rotor is another rotor, which is identical to the first. Behind the second rotor is the brush pack and slip rings that provide excitation current for both rotors. The rectifier and regulator are also mounted at the rear of the assembly. The greater output is useful for vehicles that have a very high electrical consumption, such as luxury coaches.

### Brushless alternator

Another variation of the compact alternator is the brushless alternator which works in a similar way to an alternator that uses brushes to carry the current to magnetise the rotor claws. In a brushless alternator the claws are mounted from one end only and do not oppose each other. The windings for excitation are fitted underneath the claws and are supplied by wiring that enters at the open end of the claws. This does away with the need for carbon brushes and slip ring, which are generally the high maintenance components in the alternator. The magnetic fields created in the excitation winding have an air gap to cross to the claw poles, to magnetise them. There is then a magnet rotating inside the stator windings when the pulley is turned. These alternators can also be manufactured to be liquid cooled (Figure 10.21), which reduces the noise as there is no cooling fan and the whole component is surrounded by a coolant jacket. The electronic components are mounted at the drive end.

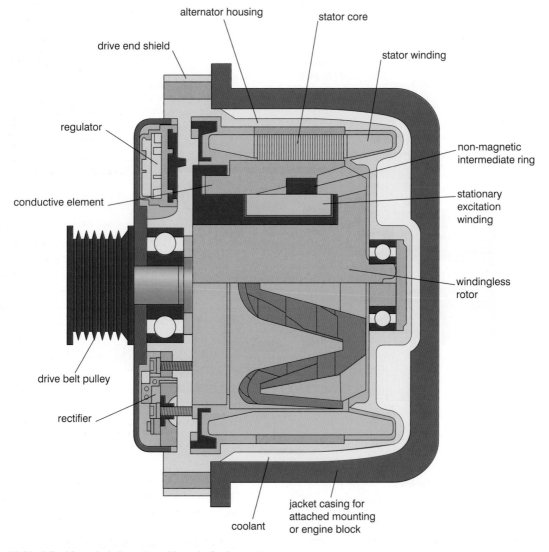

*Figure 10.21 A liquid-cooled alternator with a windingless rotor*

### 10.3.3 External tests on alternator

Very little maintenance is required on a modern alternator other than a check of the tension and condition of the driving belt at 10,000 km (6000 miles) and a brush check at 65,000 km (40,000 miles). At times when an under-bonnet check is being made for general security of all items, the alternator mounting and cable condition should be examined. Fault diagnosis equipment needed for testing a charging system on the vehicle should include:

- DC voltmeter, 0–20 V
- DC ammeter, 100 A.

Many different types of charging system are used so the following is intended to outline the basic method for diagnosing a fault.

1. Battery test – no-charge or low-charge.
2. Drive belt – the condition and tension should be checked. Most vehicles are now fitted with a self-adjusting mechanism which is usually a pre-tensioned spring mounted on an eccentric cam (Figure 10.22b). When the tensioner pulley is rotated the tension is removed and the belt can be removed for inspection. Always ensure you remember how the belt fits around the pulleys before removal, or take a photograph to ensure it is refitted in the correct position.

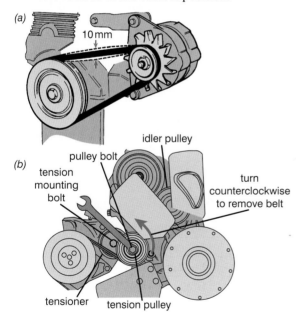

Figure 10.22 (a) Drive belt tension (b) self-adjusting mechanism

3. Visual check – all cables and connections should be checked for security.
4. Cable continuity – the connector is removed from the alternator, the ignition switched on and the voltage checked at each of the leads (Figure 10.23). No voltage at any one lead indicates an open circuit. In the case of the IND lead, the charging light bulb may be defective.

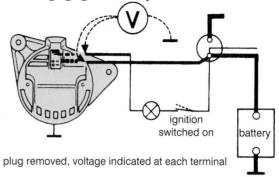

plug removed, voltage indicated at each terminal

Figure 10.23 Check for cable continuity

5. Alternator output – maximum output will not be supplied if the battery is fully charged, so switch on all loads (excluding wipers) for about one minute. With the ammeter securely connected in series with the output lead, the engine is run to about 3000 rpm (Figure 10.24). The output should not be less than the manufacturer's specification.

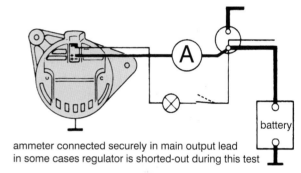

ammeter connected securely in main output lead in some cases regulator is shorted-out during this test

Figure 10.24 Check for maximum output

6. Voltage drop of external circuit – a voltmeter is connected across the insulated output cable from the alternator to the battery. With all loads on (except wipers) the engine is run to about 3000 rpm and the reading is noted. If the voltage drop exceeds 0.5 V on any alternator charging system, it indicates a high resistance in that line (Figure 10.25). Sometimes a similar check is made on the earth line to ensure the voltage drop is 0–0.25 V.

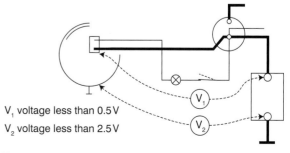

$V_1$ voltage less than 0.5 V
$V_2$ voltage less than 2.5 V

Figure 10.25 Voltage drop of external circuit

7 Regulator operation – a voltmeter is placed across the battery and an ammeter is connected in series with the main output lead(s) (Figure 10.26). The engine is run to about 3000 rpm until the ammeter shows a charging current of less than 10 A. When this occurs, the voltmeter should show a reading of 13.6–14.4 V if the regulator is serviceable.

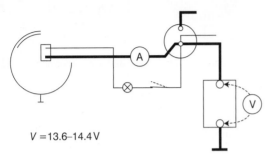

$V = 13.6{-}14.4\,V$

*Figure 10.26 Regulator checks*

### Digital storage oscilloscope tests on an alternator

Faults in an alternator can be diagnosed by using a digital storage oscilloscope (DSO). The patterns shown on the screen will enable the operator to pinpoint the fault (Figure 10.27). The manufacturer's instructions for connection must be followed to avoid damage to components and equipment.

*Figure 10.27 DSO wave pattern*

*Figure 10.28 Typical alternator connections*

## 10.3.4 Requirements of the alternator

The alternator must be able to generate enough electrical energy to power all the required consumers as well as recharge the battery. Energy requirements for systems on a vehicle can be put into three categories:

- Full-time consumers, which are used all the time the vehicle is running.
- Part-time consumers, which are used for long periods of time when the vehicle is running.
- Small-time consumers, which are used only for a short period of time when the vehicle is running.

*Table 10.1 Consumer demand on battery and alternator*

| Alternator supplying energy when the engine is running | | Battery supplying electrical energy when the engine is switched off | |
|---|---|---|---|
| **Full-time consumers** | **Part-time consumers** | **Small-time consumers** | |
| Ignition system 20 W | Navigation system 15 W | Indicators 50 W | |
| Electric fuel pump 50 W | Sound system 30 W | Fog lamps 45 W | |
| Petrol injection 70 W | Obligatory lamps 40 W | Brake lamps 45 W | |
| Engine management 70 W | Headlamps low 110 W | Reverse lamps 45 W | |
| Chassis systems 80 W | Headlamps high 240 W | Power windows each 150 W | |
| Powertrain systems 80 W | Radiator fan 250 W | Heated rear window 120 W | |
| Comfort systems 150 W | Wipers 150 W | Horn 25 W | |
| | | Starter motor 1200 W | |
| | | Washers 50 W | |
| | | Mirrors 20 W | |
| | | Auxiliary heating 750 W | |

The alternator must be powerful enough to generate the required energy but not absorb too much of the engine power to drive it. Alternators are usually rated on their output of amperes, so calculate what size of alternator is required. Power is the product of the voltage required and the amperes generated.

$$\text{Watts (W)} = \text{Volts (V)} \times \text{Amperes (A)}$$

An alternator rated at 130 A would be able to supply $12\,V \times 130\,A = 1560\,W$. When fitting additional electrical equipment to vehicles, it must be taken into consideration whether the alternator will be able to supply the required energy, otherwise the battery will become flat even as the vehicle is being run.

The alternator should be mounted where it can get a supply of air for cooling and away from heavy vibration. If it is rubber-mounted, then it must have a separate earth connection.

## 10.4 Charging in hybrid electric vehicles

A hybrid vehicle is one that uses two sources of energy for torque: an internal combustion engine (ICE) and an electric motor (Figure 10.29) to provide additional torque when it is required. The electric motor is mounted between the engine and gearbox. An all-electric vehicle has no ICE back-up. This vehicle uses brake energy regeneration to charge the high voltage battery.

*Figure 10.29 Bosch generator/motor*

The electric motor is powered by a high-voltage (250–350 V) battery, but when the vehicle is on the overrun, the electric motor can be switched to become a generator of electrical energy to recharge the battery, using the momentum of the moving vehicle to drive it. In this state, the torque required to turn the electric motor, when it is in generating mode, can also be used

to slow the vehicle down. In order that more energy can be regenerated, the braking system must be controlled so that, as the vehicle slows, more retardation is carried out by the generator than the braking system. This is done by the electronic control units (ECUs) for the electric motor and the anti-lock braking system (ABS) interacting to reduce the braking effort of the braking system and increase the amount of electrical energy generated by the electric motor. To work successfully, the systems must interact together according to the vehicle and driver requirements. They should:

- measure driver braking requirements
- make the combined systems work as one unit and operate like the normal vehicle braking system
- operate efficiently, offering stability and comfort
- distribute the braking force between the four wheels for the operating conditions
- adjust the braking force of the braking systems to suit the operating conditions.

When the driver takes their foot off the accelerator pedal, the ABS will recognise that the vehicle is slowing down from the input of the wheel-speed sensors. It signals to the motor/generator ECU, which switches from motor to generator. The ECU monitors the voltage of the battery and puts a torque draw on the motor/generator. This starts to slow the vehicle down. As the driver starts to brake, the ABS and ECU will operate together to determine how much retardation is required (Figure 10.30). If the battery needs a lot of recharging, it will give a high torque draw on the motor/generator and this will cause the vehicle to slow down. If the battery is suitably charged, then further retardation will not come from the generator and the brakes will slow the vehicle as normal. Vehicle stability and wheel slip are monitored and adjustments are made to the systems.

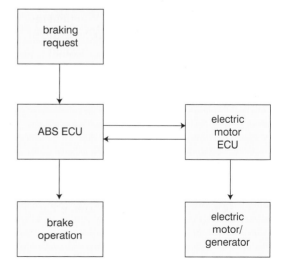

*Figure 10.30 Interface of the regeneration and braking systems*

The internal-combustion engine has undergone many major changes since its beginnings more than 100 years ago. The main components and operation have changed little, but the materials and the control mechanisms have undergone so many changes that the systems now used to control the operation of the engine would be unrecognisable to the original engine and vehicle designers.

The biggest issue for the continued use of the internal-combustion engine is the use of fossil-based fuels and the harmful emissions of greenhouse gases produced when these are burnt. With the advent of modern technology, the internal-combustion engine has been transformed from a gas-guzzling, smoke-belching lump of iron into an extremely efficient piece of machinery, using the very latest lightweight materials and electronic technology. While it is by no means perfect, the changes and improvements in the way fuel is burned and the energy is converted has had major benefits for the manufacturers and the consumers.

This chapter sets out to explain the combustion process for both spark-ignition and compression-ignition engines, and the operations and components that help to improve their efficiency. By understanding the combustion process and the improvements made to its operation over the years, the modern technician will be able to understand why and how these systems operate the way they do and ensure that they are maintained in peak condition for many years to come.

## 11.1 Combustion process

Before a vehicle manufacturer can sell a new model, a vehicle of this type must be tested in a laboratory and a certificate granted by the appropriate authority to show that all exhaust emissions from the vehicle are within the statutory limits.

This is achieved by close control of the combustion process, usually by electronic components and systems, to ensure that the air/fuel mixture is completely burned to produce the maximum power and the minimum emission of pollutant gases.

At the time of publication, all new model types must be approved to the Euro 5 Emissions Standards for limits as shown in Table 11.1.

## 11.1.1 Combustion in a petrol engine

During normal operating conditions the compressed air/fuel, at the **stoichiometric ratio** (14.7:1), is ignited by a high-voltage spark jumping the gap at the electrodes of the spark plug. This produces a flame, which travels across the combustion chamber at a regular and smooth rate (Figure 11.1). The full combustion process takes place within 3–4 ms (milliseconds). The rapid expansion of gas and the increase in pressure and heat within the chamber gives a smooth and steady downward push to the piston. This pressure will be dependent on a number of factors, but can reach 70 bar (1029 psi).

**Stoichiometric ratio**: the ideal air/fuel ratio for the most efficient combustion (14.7:1).

### Health and safety

Modern electronic ignition systems operate on voltages as high as 90,000 V, so extreme care must be taken to reduce the risk of electric shock when working with these systems. Where possible, correctly rated and insulated personal protective equipment (PPE) and tools should also be used. In addition, petrol vapour is extremely flammable, so care must be taken to ensure that there are no leaks from the fuel system when working with running vehicles.

Table 11.1 *European Emission Standards for passenger cars*

| Tier | Date | CO | THC | NMHC | NO$_x$ | HC + NO$_x$ | PM |
|---|---|---|---|---|---|---|---|
| **European emission standards for passenger cars (Category M), g/km** | | | | | | | |
| **Diesel** | | | | | | | |
| Euro 1 | July 1992 | 2.720 (3.16) | – | – | – | 0.970 (1.13) | 0.140 (0.18) |
| Euro 2 | January 1996 | 1.000 | – | – | – | 0.700 | 0.080 |
| Euro 3 | January 2000 | 0.640 | – | – | 0.500 | 0.560 | 0.050 |
| Euro 4 | January 2005 | 0.500 | – | – | 0.250 | 0.300 | 0.025 |
| Euro 5 | September 2009 | 0.500 | – | – | 0.180 | 0.230 | 0.005 |
| Euro 6 (future) | September 2014 | 0.500 | – | – | 0.080 | 0.170 | 0.005 |
| **Petrol (Gasoline)** | | | | | | | |
| Euro 1 | July 1992 | 2.720 (3.16) | – | – | – | 0.97 (1.13) | – |
| Euro 2 | January 1996 | 2.200 | – | – | – | 0.5 | – |
| Euro 3 | January 2000 | 2.300 | 0.200 | – | 0.150 | – | – |
| Euro 4 | January 2005 | 1.000 | 0.100 | – | 0.080 | – | – |
| Euro 5 | September 2009 | 1.000 | 0.100 | 0.068 | 0.060 | – | 0.005 |
| Euro 6 (future) | September 2014 | 1.000 | 0.100 | 0.068 | 0.060 | – | 0.005 |

**Key:**

CO = Carbon monoxide  NMHC = Non-methane hydrocarbons  HC + NO$_x$ = Hydrocarbon + nitrogen oxides
THC = Hydrocarbon  NO$_x$ = Nitrogen oxides  PM = Particulate matter

*(a)* Normal combustion

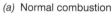
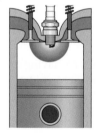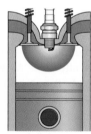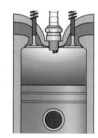

*(b)* Knocking

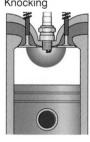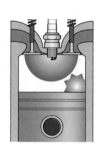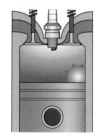

*(c)* Pre-ignition

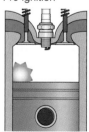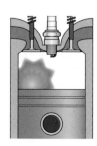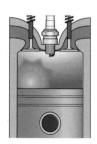

Figure 11.1 *(a) Normal combustion, (b) combustion knock (detonation) and (c) pre-ignition*

## Combustion phases

A **spark-ignition engine** combustion process can be split into three phases:

1 Ignition delay
2 Rapid pressure rise or uncontrolled combustion
3 After burning or late burning

Ignition delay is the period between the spark occurring and the start of the pressure rise above compression pressure (about 20 bar or 294 psi).

Rapid pressure rise is the period when the pressure in the combustion chamber starts to rise above compression pressure to the peak combustion pressure (about 60 bar or 882 psi).

After burning or late burning is the period between the peak combustion pressure, to the point where the exhaust valve opens.

**Spark-ignition engine**: when the method used to ignite the air/fuel mixture is an electric spark jumping the gap on a spark plug.

Power output and economy are strongly influenced by the flame speed, which can be altered by the following:

■ Compression ratio – a high flame speed is obtained when the air and fuel particles are closely packed together. This occurs with a high-compression ratio or when the engine has drawn in a large volume of air/fuel mixture (when the volumetric efficiency is high).
■ Air/fuel ratio – the highest flame speed and power are obtained when the air/fuel ratio is slightly richer than stoichiometric. If the mixture is weaker than stoichiometric, the flame speed and power decrease considerably.
■ Ignition timing – the maximum gas pressure produced during combustion should occur at approximately 12° of crankshaft rotation after the piston reaches **top dead centre (TDC)**. As it takes some time for the burning gas to build up to maximum pressure, the spark must be timed to occur at approximately 12° before the piston reaches TDC. If the spark occurs too early, a rapid burning takes place in the combustion chamber, and the resultant expansion of gas above the piston slows it down before it reaches TDC, reducing the power produced at the crankshaft. This effect can also damage engine components.

**Top dead centre (TDC)**: the point at which the piston is at its highest point in the cylinder bore.

■ Degree of turbulence (swirl) – the movement of the air/fuel mixture within the combustion chamber helps to increase the flame speed. This is influenced by combustion chamber design.
■ Quantity of exhaust gas left in the combustion chamber – any residual exhaust gas left within the combustion chamber will slow down the burning of the fresh mixture. This, in turn, will reduce the maximum combustion temperature. A large number of vehicles are fitted with an exhaust gas recirculation (EGR) system to reduce harmful emissions at certain times when the engine is running.
■ Fuel quality (octane rating) – the octane rating of petrol measures the fuel's ability to resist engine knock. Octane levels in the UK are usually 95 RON, 97 RON or 98 RON (Research Octane Number); the higher the number the higher the resistance to knock.

As well as having an effect on the flame speed, the above factors also have an effect on combustion, knock or detonation.

### Combustion faults in spark-ignition engines

Two combustion faults associated with spark-ignition engines are:

■ combustion knock (often called detonation)
■ pre-ignition.

Both faults reduce engine power and, if not rectified quickly, can cause serious engine damage.

## Octane rating

| Compression ratio | 9:1 | 10:1 | 11:1 | 12:1 |
|---|---|---|---|---|
| RON | 96 | 100 | 104 | 108 |

This table is a guide to the octane number (RON) of the fuel that would be ideal to use for each compression ratio. However, a spark-ignition engine with a compression ratio of 10:1 will still run on 95 RON petrol, although not as efficiently as it would on the higher octane number fuel.

An engine with a compression ratio of 12:1 will normally be a lean burn engine.

## Combustion knock (detonation)

To obtain high power output from the engine a high flame speed is necessary; the quicker the fuel burns, the higher the temperature and pressure of the gas. This requirement suggests that the factors controlling the flame speed should be set to give the highest speed; however, various combustion faults develop if this is attempted. To illustrate this, consider an engine that has a provision for varying the compression ratio. As the compression ratio is increased, the flame speed is increased. When a certain compression is reached, the flame speed increases to the speed of sound and the fuel is no longer burnt in a progressive manner, instead the air/fuel mixture explodes. This condition is called detonation. The compression pressure at which detonation occurs depends on a number of factors, including the grade of petrol used and the design of combustion chamber.

Examination of the combustion process prior to the onset of detonation shows that a portion of the air/fuel mixture furthest away from the spark plugs (the end gas), would not be burning normally. Instead, this pocket of gas, which has been compressed and heated by the gas that has already burnt, will spontaneously ignite and cause a rapid build-up of pressure and noise. This condition is called combustion knock.

Although detonation and combustion knock are two different combustion faults, the effects of both are similar and both conditions are often grouped together. In both cases they occur *after the spark*.

The effects of detonation and combustion knock depend on the severity of the condition, but the main results are:

- 'pinking' – a sound produced by the high-pressure waves; the noise could be described as 'a metallic tapping sound' or the 'sound of fat frying in a pan'
- shock-loading of engine components
- localised overheating – piston crowns can be melted
- reduced engine power.

These effects show that detonation and combustion knock should be avoided. The main factors that promote detonation are:

- compression pressure and grade of petrol – the compression ratio is linked to the fuel used; engines with a high compression ratio require fuel with a higher octane level
- air/fuel ratio – weak mixtures are prone to detonation
- combustion chamber type – the degree of turbulence or swirl and the provision for cooling the end gas has a great bearing on the compression ratio used
- ignition timing – over-advanced ignition promotes detonation
- engine temperature – overheated components increase the risk of detonation.

## Pre-ignition

This condition occurs when the air/fuel charge in the cylinder is ignited by a red-hot particle before it is ignited by the spark plug. The object that causes this to occur could be a carbon deposit or a sharp edge within the combustion chamber. Pre-ignition always occurs *before the spark* and can lead to detonation, melting of the piston crown and other types of damage. An engine suffering from pre-ignition will have a reduced power output and can often be accompanied by a 'pinking' sound.

Pre-ignition of a charge produces a situation where the rising piston is compressing a gas that is trying to expand. This results in a considerable increase in pressure and temperature.

## Running-on

An engine that continues to run-on after the ignition is switched off is caused by the air/fuel charge being ignited by a 'hot spot', such as a spark plug, valve or carbon deposit, which glows and ignites the charge as the piston is around TDC. This condition can be caused by cooling system faults or excessive carbon deposits.

Modern engines run on weaker mixtures to try to reduce emissions of pollutant gases. This causes the combustion chamber and its components to operate at higher temperatures, which can cause hot spots.

Running-on in modern engines is avoided by the use of fuel injection. When the ignition is switched off the current to the injectors is removed and no fuel is injected into the combustion chamber.

## Combustion and fuel requirements

In order to burn efficiently the fuel must be vaporised to form a gas when it is mixed with the air in the inlet manifold or injected into the combustion chamber. The petrol should also have a sufficiently high octane rating to avoid detonation. The use of fuel injectors and closed-loop monitoring to control the amount of fuel entering the engine means that the air/fuel ratio can be more closely controlled to suit a large number of varying engine conditions.

An incorrect air/fuel ratio can cause the problems shown in Table 11.2.

For further information on the use of closed-loop engine management systems (EMSs), catalytic converters and lambda sensors see Chapters 5, 12 and 14.

## Combustion by-products

When a spark-ignition engine is operating correctly, the only by-products of combustion are:

- $CO_2$ (carbon dioxide)
- $H_2O$ (water)
- $N_2$ (nitrogen).

If the engine is not running correctly, the by-products are:

- $CO_2$ (carbon dioxide)
- CO (carbon monoxide)
- HC (hydrocarbons) – unburnt fuel
- $H_2O$ (water)
- $NO_X$ (nitrogen oxides).

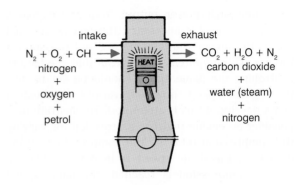

*Figure 11.2  Chemical changes – correct air/fuel ratio*

*Table 11.2  The cause, effect and symptoms of incorrect air/fuel mixtures*

| Fault | Effect | Symptom |
|---|---|---|
| Rich mixture | Incomplete combustion | 1. Black smoke from exhaust |
| | | 2. High exhaust pollution |
| | Slow burning | 1. Low power output |
| | | 2. High fuel consumption |
| | Sparking plugs soon soot-up | 1. Misfiring |
| | | 2. Poor starting |
| Weak mixture | Slow burning | 1. Low power output |
| | | 2. High fuel consumption |
| | | 3. Overheating |
| | Detonation | 1. Pinking (excessive knocking) |
| | | 2. Low power and if condition persists will give blue smoke from exhaust showing piston failure |

## Exhaust gas recirculation (EGR)

When exhaust gases mix with the fresh charge, this reduces the amount of $O_2$ in the fresh charge and increases its temperature. This results in a lower combustion temperature, which decreases $NO_X$ production and also reduces exhaust emissions.

An excessive amount of recirculated exhaust gas results in increased fuel consumption and CO emissions. The amount of recirculated exhaust gas must be controlled accurately to ensure that the combustion chamber receives sufficient $O_2$ to ensure complete combustion.

Excessive amounts of EGR can also cause uneven idle, which in turn creates an increase in HC emissions.

EGR can be implemented in two ways:

- Internal EGR is achieved by altering the valve timing (overlap).
- External EGR uses electronically controlled EGR valves.

As this chapter is concerned with the electronic control of the combustion process, it will only cover the internal EGR method. The external EGR systems are investigated further within Chapters 12, 13 and 14.

## Symptoms of faulty EGR

If there is too much EGR or the timing of the EGR is incorrect, the following symptoms will usually be found:

- Poor idling
- Stalling, especially when starting from cold
- Hesitation and rough running during warm-up
- Surging at cruising speeds, even with warm engine
- Poor acceleration
- Low engine vacuum

## Valve overlap

Large **valve overlap** (early opening of the inlet valve) increases the internal EGR and helps to reduce $NO_x$ emissions. However, as the recirculated exhaust gas limits the amount of fresh air/fuel mixture, this will then lead to a reduction in the maximum torque produced.

**Valve overlap**: the period of time when both the *inlet* valves and the *exhaust* valves are open. This extends from just before TDC to just after TDC (Figure 11.3).

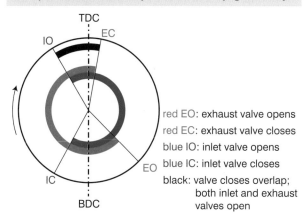

red EO: exhaust valve opens
red EC: exhaust valve closes
blue IO: inlet valve opens
blue IC: inlet valve closes
black: valve closes overlap; both inlet and exhaust valves open

*Figure 11.3 Valve timing diagram showing valve overlap*

## Electronic control of valve timing

Valve timing on modern engines can be controlled electronically to ensure that the timing of the opening and closing of the valves is matched to the engine speed, maximising performance and minimising exhaust emissions. Systems have different names, such as variable valve timing (VVT) and variable valve actuation (VVA). Whatever the name and method of actuation, the desired effect is the same: altering the opening and closing time of the inlet and exhaust valves

**Cam phasing**: the moving of the camshaft from its original opening/closing point to an earlier or later point. The actual time the valve is opened by the cam remains the same.

**Phase angle**: the time period from when the camshaft starts to open the valve to the time when the valve is closed. This time period is measured in degrees of rotation.

during engine operation to increase performance and fuel economy and reduce toxic gas emissions.

There are two ways vehicle manufacturers can operate the control of valve timing:

- Cam phasing
- Cam changing

### Cam phasing

During **cam phasing** the valve timing is altered by rotating the camshaft forward to change the start point of valve opening and the finish point of the valve closing; this is known as the **phase angle**. At higher engine speeds the inlet cam is rotated forward to allow the inlet valve to open earlier. This increases the amount of valve overlap. The advancing of the inlet camshaft is controlled by the EMS.

Basic systems will only rotate the inlet camshaft to open the inlet valve early. If the valve opens early, then it will close early, as the profile of the cam remains the same.

In order to overcome this and improve the performance and efficiency of the internal-combustion engine, some manufacturers use a camshaft with the lobe having a different profile at each end – a three-dimensional (3-D) cam profile (Figure 11.5).

## Control of cam phasing

The electronic control of cam phasing varies according to the manufacturer, but the system operates in one of the following ways:

- Electromagnetic solenoids are switched on and off to allow oil flow in different directions to rotate a vane. The camshaft sprocket is mounted on a helical spline and when pressure is introduced to the vane it rotates and advances or retards the camshaft depending on inputs from the PCM (powertrain control module).
- Electronic control of oil pressure pushes a locating pin forward against a spring; this brings an additional cam lobe into action, which changes the valve opening and closing time. When oil pressure is removed the spring pushes the pin back and the additional lobe no longer acts on the valves (Figure 11.4).

In both of these the PCM receives inputs from the following sensors to determine whether it should operate or not:

- camshaft position sensor
- crankshaft position sensor
- engine RPM sensor
- MAP (manifold absolute pressure).

(For further information on sensors see Chapter 5.)

## Honda VTEC – Operation of Honda variable valve timing

A four-stroke engine goes through induction, compression, combustion and exhaust strokes to generate power. Before the advent of VTEC, the valves controlling the intake and exhaust strokes were operated according to fixed rules.

If the intake valves were made to open a relatively small amount to privilege drivability at low engine speeds, as used in normal driving conditions, the engine would not be allowed to intake enough air at higher engine speeds, sacrificing outright performance. On the other hand, if the intake valves were made to open wide to privilege breathing at higher engine speeds, performance at low engine speeds would be compromised. This is a dilemma that has plagued engines for over a century.

So Honda introduced VTEC: an elegant, simple mechanism switching between high and low valve lift using two cam profiles and two rocker arms per cylinder. The switch is made using hydraulic pressure to push/release the sliding pin, locking/unlocking the middle rocker arm and the other rocker arm.

At low engine speeds, the pin is retracted, disengaging the middle rocker arm. The valves are operated by the two outside, low-profile cams for a low valve lift. At higher engine speeds, increased hydraulic pressure pushes the pin, engaging the middle rocker arm. The valves are operated by the middle, high-profile cam for high valve lift.

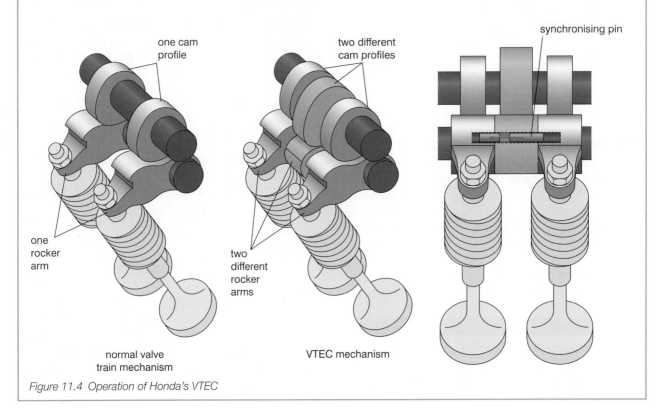

Figure 11.4  Operation of Honda's VTEC

## Helmholtz resonance

If pressurised air is pushed into a cavity, the pressure will build up inside until it equals the external pressure. If the external pressure is then dropped suddenly, the higher pressure inside surges out. This 'pulse' of air moves forward.

If this principle is applied to an air intake system, as the inlet valves open and close, air 'pulses' are created; these pulses also create sound waves, which are heard as intake noise.

The sound waves have a frequency that varies with the speed of the operation of the inlet valves. If the inlet manifold length is matched to the frequency of the sound wave, then at the point when the inlet valve opens, the pressure behind it will be higher than atmospheric and extra air can be drawn into the combustion chamber, which will allow more fuel to be injected and so will generate more power.

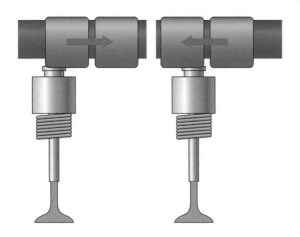

*Figure 11.5  3-D variable cam lobe*

The 3-D camshaft is linked to a hydraulic pump, which uses the engine lubrication oil to push the camshaft across the top of the valve. At one end the camshaft has a cam profile, which will open and close the valve in a certain period that suits the low-speed performance of the engine. At the other end the cam profile will allow the valve to open and close for a duration that is more suited to the high-end performance required. The pressures in the hydraulic system are altered by the electronic control unit (ECU) using readings from load, speed and throttle position sensors and determine the optimum position the camshaft should be in.

### Cam changing

Other manufacturers use systems that have two sets of camshaft lobes, on one camshaft and the ECU. Using readings from the load and speed sensors will determine which set of lobes should be used. These systems also use engine oil and a hydraulic pump to slide the camshaft across the top of the valve. Figure 11.5 shows the stages of low- and high-speed operation.

### Variable length inlet manifolds

A number of manufacturers are now employing variable length inlet manifolds to increase the amount of torque and power at different stages of engine rpm; these systems use the principle of Helmholtz resonance.

Most systems will have two inlet tracts; one is designed to have a resonance at a lower frequency (or low rpm), while at a higher rpm the second tract, with a much shorter inlet length, will be used. This shorter inlet manifold will have a resonance frequency that is higher. The tract that operates at

a higher rpm will have a flap or a valve that will be opened electronically by the engine management ECU. When this will occur is dependent on the input signals from a number of sensors in the EMS.

It is also worth remembering that the actual lengths of the inlet tracts are constrained by physical space. Some manufacturers overcome the issue of space by having two inlet manifolds for each cylinder. The short inlet manifold operates at low speed and the longer one has a valve or flap that opens at higher speed. Both are used at high speed to allow more air to enter the combustion chamber. Figure 11.6 shows the two inlet manifolds for the Ford Duratec 2.5 V6.

*Figure 11.6  Ford Duratec variable length inlet manifolds*

### 11.1.2 Combustion in a diesel engine

The compression-ignition engine has no sparking plug to initiate combustion.

On the induction stroke the compression-ignition engine draws in only air. On the compression stroke the air is compressed and an injector sprays fuel oil into the combustion chamber, just before the piston reaches TDC at the end of the compression stroke. The power stroke is much the same as with a spark-ignition engine; the rapid expansion of gas and heat drives the piston down and rotates the crankshaft. The exhaust stroke is the same as the spark-ignition engine; the piston travels up with the exhaust valve open, pushing the burnt exhaust gases out to the exhaust system.

Because the compression ratio of a combustion-ignition engine is much higher than that used with a petrol engine (16–25:1), the heat generated by the high compression of the air is normally sufficient to ignite the fuel oil as it is sprayed into the chamber.

A special provision must be made when a cold combustion-ignition engine is to be started. This is necessary because the low temperature of

---

**Combustion phases for a compression-ignition engine**

The combustion phases for a compression-ignition engine differ from the spark-ignition engine in that there are four phases:

1  Ignition delay.
2  Rapid pressure rise or uncontrolled burning.
3  Mechanical controlled combustion.
4  After burning or late burning.

the cylinders absorbs the heat generated by the compression of the air. The result is that the injected fuel oil will not ignite. One way of overcoming this problem is to fit a heater plug in the combustion chamber (Figure 11.7). This device is an electrically heated bulb or wire filament, which glows red-hot when in use. Prior to starting a cold engine, the heater plugs are switched on automatically for a few seconds to raise the temperature of the air in the cylinder to approximately 850 °C. Most modern glow plugs can reach this temperature in approximately 4 s.

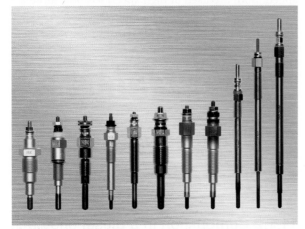

*Figure 11.7 A selection of NGK diesel glow plugs*

Because of the high self-combustion temperature of diesel fuel, diesel (compression-ignition) engines need some form of pre-heating when the engine is cold. The engine is fitted with pre-heater or glow plugs, which are fitted into the pre-combustion chamber or directly into the cylinder head. This heats up the air sufficiently to allow the fuel to self-combust when it mixes with the heated air. The driver turns the key to the 'on' position, a relay switches the glow plugs on and a light displaying a coil on the instrument cluster is illuminated.

If the car engine had been running and the temperature was high enough, the glow plug operating light might not come on. In this case, the driver could turn the key to operate the starter and start the engine without having to wait.

Modern compression-ignition engines use an ECU for the operation of the glow plugs. This ECU will take information from the vehicle's ECU on whether or not glow plug operation is required; this information is based on readings from the engine temperature sensor. When the engine is running, the glow plugs will continue to operate to reduce the amount of smoke emissions and combustion noise, and the ECU will monitor engine speed and load sensors to determine when the glow plugs should be switched off. There is also a time-out setting to ensure that the glow plugs are not switched on too long, as they draw a large amount of current from the power supply.

Diesel exhaust gas emission is affected by the design of the combustion chamber. Engines that have a pre-chamber, or swirl chamber, produce less $NO_X$ than direct-injection engines. However, the direct injection gives increased fuel economy.

Other factors that have an effect on emissions include the start of injection and the atomisation of the fuel. Combustion starts at the start of injection (injection timing). A delay in the timing of injection reduces $NO_X$ emissions, however, an excessive delay results in both increased fuel consumption and HC emissions.

It should be noted that a deviation of as little as 1° of rotation at the crankshaft, at the start of injection, can increase $NO_X$ emissions and HC emissions by as much as 10–15 per cent. This means that extremely accurate injection timing is essential. Recent years have seen the increased use of electronic control systems to maintain the optimum injection timing with a high level of precision.

Common rail systems (CRS) use components that, until now, have been more common on spark-ignition injection systems. More information on this can be found in Chapter 14.

### Inlet charge temperature

As the air drawn into the combustion chamber increases in temperature, so too does the combustion temperature, which leads to an increase in $NO_X$ emissions. **Intercooling** is one means of reducing $NO_X$ emissions and is usually installed to turbocharged engines.

**Intercooling**: a light vehicle intercooler is usually an air to air intercooler which is used to reduce the temperature of the intake air charge from a turbocharger or supercharger. The intake charge can reach temperatures of 150 °C, this means that it is less dense and contains less oxygen.

### Exhaust gas after treatment

The use of catalytic converters in the exhaust system helps to reduce the HC emissions by burning a portion of the HCs bound to the particulates using the excess $O_2$ in the exhaust gases.

The catalytic converters used by spark-ignition engines must operate with a precise stoichiometric mixture. Compression-ignition engines, however, operate with excess air, so conventional catalytic converters cannot be used on compression-ignition engines. The compression-ignition engine uses a diesel oxidation catalyst (DOC). This catalyst uses excess $O_2$ in the exhaust gas to convert CO to $CO_2$ and HC to $H_2O$ and $CO_2$.

### Passive regeneration

If the vehicle is used for spells of motorway or dual carriageway running and the exhaust reaches a high enough temperature, then passive regeneration will burn off the soot contained within the filter.

### Active regeneration

If the ECU detects that the soot build-up within the filter has reached approximately 45 per cent, it makes a small adjustment to the injection timing, which raises the temperature in the exhaust system and initiates regeneration. If there is insufficient time to complete this, then the warning light will illuminate to show that the filter is partially blocked.

This type of catalyst can operate at up to 90 per cent efficiency, which virtually eliminates diesel odour and reduces visible particulate (soot). These catalysts cannot be used for $NO_x$ reduction because of the high concentration of $O_2$ in the exhaust gas.

$NO_x$ emissions from a compression-ignition engine are reduced by the use of EGR (exhaust gas recirculation). The introduction of exhaust gas into the fresh charge has the effect of reducing the combustion temperature, which then reduces the amount of $NO_x$ produced. The EGR system is designed to shut off at low speeds, as it causes the engine to idle erratically, and also at high speeds, as it causes loss of performance.

Particulate filters are also installed in the exhaust system to reduce particulate emissions. Diesel particulate filters (DPF) catch soot in the exhaust gases. As with any filter they have to be cleaned or emptied regularly to maintain performance. For a DPF this process is called 'regeneration'; the collected soot is burnt off at high temperature and leaves only a tiny ash residue. Regeneration may be either passive or active. When the DPF reaches approximately 45% saturation the ECU willl illuminate a dashboard warning light.

*Figure 11.8 Particulate filter warning light*

If the vehicle is driven at speeds of over 40 mph, the ECU will be able to start and complete a full regeneration cycle to clear the filter and the warning light should then go out. Some systems make use of the latest design of glow plug systems and switch the glow plugs on intermittently to assist in the regeneration stage.

Currently, the use of variable valve timing for compression-ignition engines is in the development stage. Any system used for this will be extremely complicated, costly and may not yield sufficient returns in emission reduction to justify the expense.

## 11.2 Non-electronic ignition system

As modern ignition systems are all electronic, this section of the chapter will be consigned to publications more suited to classic vehicles. Some references are made to contact breaker (Kettering) systems throughout this chapter, but only to give the reader a better understanding of a particular feature.

## 11.3 Electronic coil ignition system

### Ignition system requirements

The ignition system for a spark-ignition engine must fulfil the following requirements:

- It must provide a spark of sufficient voltage to ignite the air/fuel mixture in the combustion chamber.
- It must provide this spark at the correct time.
- The system should require little or no maintenance throughout its working life.
- The system should be able to vary the timing of the spark to suit different load and speed conditions.

### Ignition system operation

There are a number of transistorised or electronic ignition systems in current use; in their latest form these are combined ignition/fuelling (engine management) systems. The EMS control of ignition is covered in more detail in Chapter 14.

Components within these systems:

- Battery to provide the low-tension (LT) voltage.

- Ignition on/off switch to provide the initial 12 V to the coil LT circuit.
- Oil-filled cylindrical coil.
- Electronic trigger box.
- Distributor including trigger mechanism, rotor arm and high-tension (HT) leads.
- Spark plugs.

Figure 11.9 shows the main layout of a breakerless electronic ignition system. The distributor unit is similar to a non-electronic unit with the exception that the contact breaker is replaced by an electronic switch called a pulse generator.

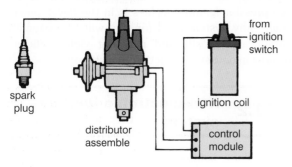

*Figure 11.9  Layout of breakerless electronic system*

As the name suggests, this device generates an electrical pulse to signal when the spark is required. This action is similar to the trigger of a gun – when the trigger is operated the coil fires its HT charge.

The duty of the solid-state control module is to electronically make and break the primary current for the ignition coil. To do this, it must amplify and process the signals received from the pulse generator. In addition to the switching duty, the control module senses the engine speed from the pulse frequency and uses this information to vary the **dwell** time to suit the engine speed. If the dwell time is too short, the primary voltage will be reduced. This will also have a reducing effect on the output of the secondary voltage. (Chapter 14 will give further details of dwell control with EMS.)

**Dwell**: the period of time the primary circuit of the coil has to charge up before the trigger switches off the current to the primary circuit. It can be measured in degrees of crankshaft rotation or percentage of crankshaft rotation.

## Pulse generator

There are three types of pulse generator ignition system:

- Inductive
- Hall sensor
- Optical

### Inductive type

Figure 11.10 shows one type of inductive pulse generator. The permanent magnet and inductive winding are fixed to the base plate and an iron trigger wheel is driven by the distributor shaft. The number of teeth formed on the trigger wheel or reluctor matches the number of engine cylinders.

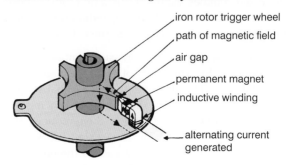

*Figure 11.10  Inductive pulse generator*

When a tooth is positioned close to the soft iron stator core, the magnetic path is completed, which gives a flux flow as shown in the diagram. When the trigger wheel is moved away from the position shown, the air gap between the stator core and the trigger tooth is increased. This larger gap increases the magnetic resistance or reluctance, so the flux in the magnetic circuit is decreased. Generation of an electromotive force (EMF) in the inductive winding fitted around the iron stator core occurs as a result of the change in the magnetic flux, so maximum voltage is induced when the rate of change in flux is greatest. This occurs just before and just after the point where the trigger tooth is closest to the stator core.

Figure 11.11 shows the variation in voltage as the trigger wheel is moved through one revolution. This shows that the build-up of flux gives a positive peak and the decay of flux gives a negative peak. In the trigger position of greatest flux, no EMF is induced into the winding. It is this mid-point of change

## Health and safety

Modern electronic ignition systems operate on voltages as high as 90,000 V. Extreme care must be taken to reduce the risk of electric shock when working with these systems and, where possible, correctly rated and insulated personal protective equipment (PPE) and tools should be used. In addition, petrol vapour is extremely flammable. Care must be taken to ensure that there are no leaks from the fuel system when working with running vehicles.

between the positive and negative pulses that is used to signal that the spark is required. Rotational speed of the trigger wheel governs the rate of change of the flux, so the output of the pulse generator varies from about 0.5 V to 100 V. This voltage variation, combined with the frequency change, acts as sensing signals that can be used by the control module for purposes other than spark triggering. The size of the air gap varies the reluctance of the magnetic circuit, so the output voltage depends on the size of the air gap. Due to the magnetic effect, the gap is checked with a non-magnetic feeler gauge (e.g. a plastic gauge).

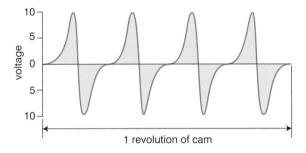

*Figure 11.11 Voltage output from pulse generator*

A Bosch pulse generator operates on a similar principle but uses a different construction (Figure 11.12). This type uses a circular disc magnet with the two flat faces acting as the N and S poles. On the top face of the magnet is placed a soft iron circular pole piece; this has fingers bent upwards to form four stator poles in the case of a four-cylinder engine. A similar number of teeth formed on the trigger wheel make a path for the flux to pass to the carrying plate that supports the magnet. The inductive coil is wound concentrically with the spindle and the complete assembly forms a symmetrical unit that is resistant to vibration and spindle wear.

Some manufacturers do not use a conventional distributor. Citroën has used a single metal slug called a 'target', which is bolted on the periphery of the flywheel, and a target sensor mounted on the clutch housing (Figure 11.13). The target sensor comprises an inductive winding arranged around a magnetic core and is set so that the core is 1 mm ± 0.5 mm from the slug when number 1 piston is just before TDC. The voltage output is similar to other pulse generators, with the exception that in this case the control module (computer) receives only one signal

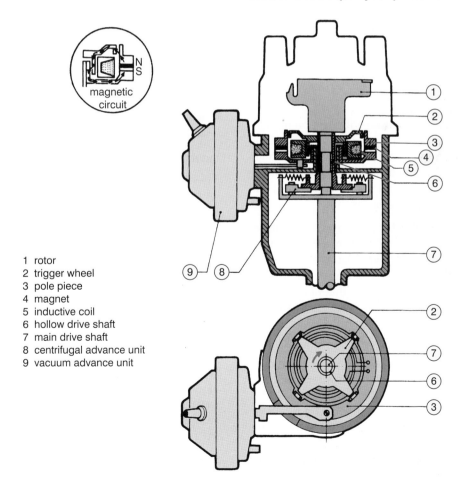

1 rotor
2 trigger wheel
3 pole piece
4 magnet
5 inductive coil
6 hollow drive shaft
7 main drive shaft
8 centrifugal advance unit
9 vacuum advance unit

*Figure 11.12 Pulse generator – Bosch*

pulse per revolution. For control purposes, Citroën fit a second target sensor, of identical construction to the other sensor, adjacent to the starter ring teeth on the flywheel. This sensor signals the passage of each flywheel tooth so that the computer can count the teeth and determine the engine speed. This sets the ignition advance to suit the conditions.

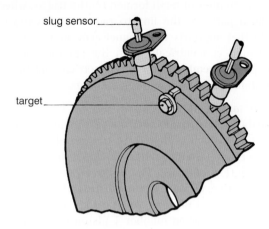

*Figure 11.13 Pulse generator – Citroën*

### Hall sensor type

The Hall effect principle is covered in depth in Chapter 5. This sensor is used to 'break' the primary circuit for the ignition coil. This then allows the induction of the secondary voltage, which is used to ignite the air/fuel mixture.

### Optical pulse type

Although not fitted as original equipment on modern vehicles, the optical pulse generator ignition system was used by manufacturers of some high-performance vehicles and is still readily available as an aftermarket fitment for some older sports and high-performance classic vehicles.

This system senses the spark point by using a shutter to interrupt a light beam projected by a light-emitting diode (LED) on to a phototransistor. Figure 11.14 shows the principle of this type of trigger. An invisible light, at a wave frequency close to that of infrared, is emitted by a gallium arsenide semiconductor diode, and its beam is focused by a hemispherical lens to a width at the chopping point of about 1.25 mm (0.05 in).

A steel chopper, having blades to suit the number of cylinders and wide enough to allow for a suitable dwell period, is attached to the distributor spindle. This controls the time periods that the light falls on the silicon phototransistor detector. This transistor forms the first part of a **Darlington amplifier**, which builds up the signal and includes a means of preventing timing change due to variation in line voltage or due to dirt accumulation on the lens.

**Darlington amplifier**: a pair of linked transistors used to amplify voltages for ignition systems. More information on the use and operation can be found in Chapter 3.

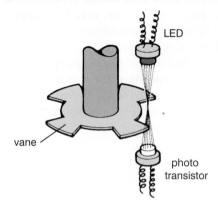

*Figure 11.14 Optical pulse generator*

The signal sent by the generator to the control module switches on the current for the coil primary, so when the chopper cuts the beam, the primary circuit is broken and a spark is produced at the plug.

### Control modules

The control module, or trigger box, is responsible for switching the current of the primary winding of the ignition coil in accordance with the signal received from the pulse generator. Two control systems used are:

- inductive storage
- capacity discharge.

### Inductive storage

This system uses a common primary circuit layout and makes use of a robust power transistor in the control module to make and break the primary circuit.

A typical control module has four important semiconductor stages, which perform the duties of pulse shape, dwell period control, voltage stabilisation and primary switching (Figure 11.15).

### Pulse shaping

The oscilloscope waveform shown at the top of Figure 11.16 represents the output voltage from an inductive-type pulse generator when it is connected to a control module circuit. It should be noted that the full negative wave is achieved only when the generator is tested on an open circuit. After feeding the alternating current (AC) signal to the trigger circuit stage, the pulse is shaped into a direct current (DC) rectangular form, as shown at the bottom of Figure 11.16.

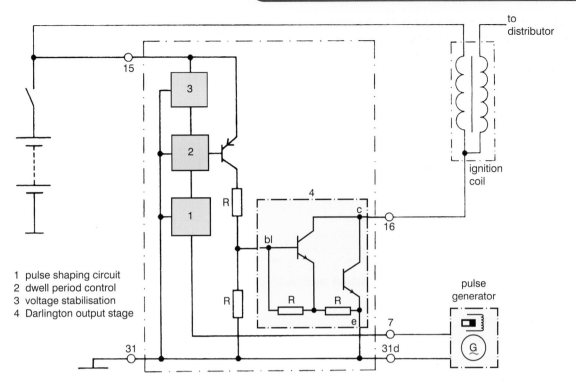

Figure 11.15  Inductive storage control module

1  pulse shaping circuit
2  dwell period control
3  voltage stabilisation
4  Darlington output stage

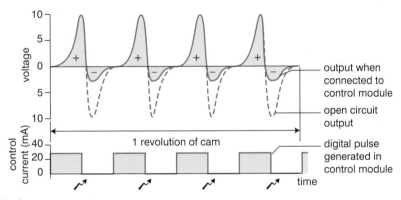

Figure 11.16  Pulse shaping

## Semiconductors

Silicon is the main material used to create most semiconductors. Other materials are used, including germanium, gallium arsenide and silicon carbide, to dope the silicon and create semiconductors that have different conductive and resistive properties. Refer to Chapter 2 for more information.

## Pulse generators

Pulse generators:

- produce a signal to trigger the spark
- are used to sense the speed of rotation
- are either inductive, Hall generator or optical types
- (of the inductive type) have two leads including earth

- (of the inductive type) signal a spark when a tooth on the reluctor trigger wheel lines up with its magnet
- (of the Hall type) have three leads including earth
- (of the Hall type) signal a spark when a vane leaves the Hall integrated circuit chip.

The width of the rectangular pulse depends on the duration of the pulse output from the generator, but the height of the rectangle, or the current output from the trigger circuits, is independent of engine speed.

### Dwell period control and voltage stabilisation

This stage normally varies the dwell period by altering the start of the dwell period. Secondary output is reduced when the dwell period is decreased, so by means of this control feature, the period of time that charge flows through the primary winding of the coil is altered to suit the engine speed.

The voltage supplied to this resistor–capacitor (R–C) network must not vary, even though the supply voltage to the control module alters due to changes in charging output and consumer loads. This control duty is performed by a voltage stabilisation section of the module.

### Primary switching

Switch control of the primary circuit current is normally performed by a Darlington amplifier. Pulse signals received from the dwell period control stage are passed to a driver transistor, which acts as a control current amplifier. At the appropriate times, current from the driver is switched on or off to control the heavy-duty power transistor of the Darlington output stage.

### Pulse processing

Figure 11.17 shows the sequence of events from the time that the original pulse generator's signal is received to the instant of the spark in the cylinder.

The secondary output patterns show the image given when an oscilloscope is connected to the output of an ignition coil forming part of an electronic ignition system.

Vertical and horizontal axes of the cathode ray oscilloscope (CRO) pattern represent voltage and time respectively. Figure 11.18 shows the main features of one secondary discharge. At the instant the primary circuit is broken, the secondary voltage increases until the spark is initiated. When this occurs, the voltage needed to sustain the spark falls until a value is reached, which is then maintained until the output energy is no longer sufficient to support the sparking process. At this point the secondary voltage raises slightly; it then falls and oscillates two or three times as the remaining energy is dissipated in the coil.

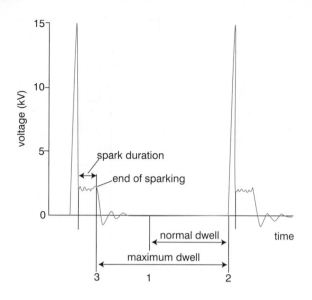

*Figure 11.18 Dwell time in relation to secondary voltage*

### Secondary output control

Disregarding any changes due to mechanical defects, a breaker-triggered system had a constant dwell over the whole speed range. This meant that at high speed the dwell period was too short. As a result, the secondary output was poor owing to the comparatively low primary current.

Use of a low-inductance coil improved the output in the upper speed range, but this type of coil caused erosive wear at the spark plug tip at low engine speeds.

To overcome this problem, a constant energy system is used. This system uses a high-output coil and is electronically controlled to vary the dwell period to suit all speeds. At low speed, the percentage dwell is kept relatively small, but it is lengthened progressively as the speed is increased.

Figure 11.18 shows that at low speed the normal dwell starts at (1) and ends at (2). As the engine speed is increased, the start of the dwell period (i.e. the point at which charge starts to flow in the primary winding) is gradually moved towards the maximum limit (3). Any increase in dwell past point (3) reduces the spark duration because this point represents the end of the sparking discharge period.

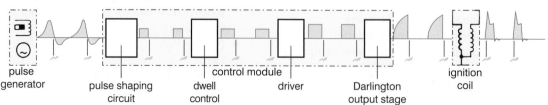

*Figure 11.17 Pulse processing*

Figure 11.19 shows the variation in percentage dwell with engine speed. At idling speed the percentage dwell is set large to provide a high-energy spark to limit exhaust gas emissions, but between idling and 4000 rpm the increase in percentage dwell prevents a reduction in the stored energy. As a result, this gives a near-constant secondary available voltage up to the system's maximum; this is generally about 15,000 sparks/min. When the system is used on six- and eight-cylinder engines it is necessary to reduce the percentage dwell at speeds beyond 5000 rpm. This is because the start of the dwell would otherwise occur before the end of the spark discharge period.

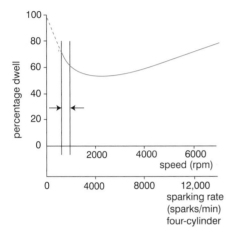

Figure 11.19 *Alteration in dwell to suit engine speed*

To overcome this problem, the control system uses a transistor to switch on the primary current a

given time after the spark has been initiated; a time duration of 0.004 ms is normally sufficient to meet most combustion requirements.

Constant-energy systems using dwell-angle control give an output as shown in Figure 11.20. (The use of the terms 'dwell angle', 'percentage dwell' and 'dwell period' should be noted. In many electronic systems the term 'dwell angle' is inappropriate.)

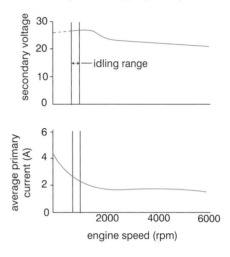

Figure 11.20 *Output from constant-energy system*

### Control module circuit

Having identified the functions performed by a control module, it is now possible to examine a typical circuit.

Fig 11.21 shows a simplified circuit diagram laid out in a manner that can identify the four sections A, B, C and D.

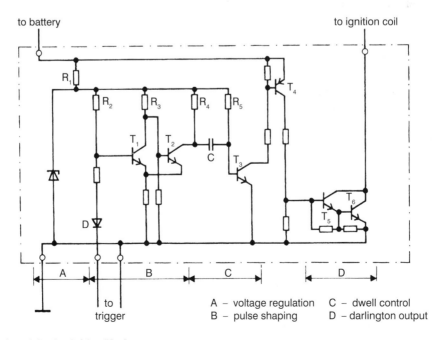

A – voltage regulation    C – dwell control
B – pulse shaping         D – darlington output

Figure 11.21 *Control module circuit (simplified)*

## A Voltage regulation

Voltage stabilisation is performed by the zener diode (ZD). This ensures that the voltage applied to control sections B and C is kept constant and is not affected by voltage variations that take place in other circuits of the vehicle. Voltage drop across a diode is constant so this feature is utilised to provide the regulated voltage to drive the control circuit.

## B Pulse shaping

In the form shown, the two transistors, $T_1$ and $T_2$, produce an arrangement called a Schmitt trigger. This is a common method for converting an analogue signal to a digital signal (i.e. an **A/D converter** for forming a rectangular pulse).

**A/D convertor**: a device that converts an analogue voltage or current to a digital number; this number will be proportional in size to the amount of voltage or current (i.e. the higher the current the higher the number).

Transistor $T_1$ is switched on when the pulse generated by the external trigger is of a potential that opposes current from the battery to the trigger via the diode D.

This causes charge to flow through the base-emitter of $T_1$, which switches on the transistor and diverts current away from the base of $T_2$. The action of this Schmitt trigger causes $T_2$ to be 'off' when $T_1$ is 'on' and vice versa. The voltage at the time of switching is governed by the threshold voltage required to switch on $T_1$. In this application, the switching of $T_1$ occurs at a very low threshold voltage so, for practical purposes, the switching is considered to take place at a point when the trigger potential changes from positive to negative.

## C Dwell control

The coil primary charge flows when the PNP transistor $T_4$ is switched on. This is controlled by $T_3$ so that when $T_3$ is 'on', $T_4$ is also 'on'.

The switching of $T_3$ is controlled by the current supplied via $R_5$ and the state-of-charge of the capacitor C.

All the time the capacitor is being charged with current from $R_5$, so no current passes to the base of $T_3$. During this stage, $T_3$ is switched off.

Only when the capacitor is fully charged will current pass to the base of $T_3$ and switch it on to start the dwell period (i.e. to initiate current in the primary winding of the coil).

The time taken to charge the capacitor dictates the dwell period, so in this case the R–C time constant is determined by the amount that the capacitor is discharged prior to receiving its charge from $R_5$.

At low engine speeds, the transistor $T_2$ will be switched on for a comparatively long time, so this allows the capacitor plate adjacent to $T_2$ to pass to earth the charge it received from $R_4$ when $T_2$ was switched off. At this slow speed, there is sufficient time for the capacitor to fully discharge to a point where the plate potential becomes similar to earth. This causes the capacitor to attract a large charge from $R_5$ when the transistor $T_2$ switches 'off'. Since the time taken to provide this charge is long, the switch on point of $T_3$ will be delayed and a short dwell period will result.

At high speed, the duration that $T_2$ is switched on is short so this only allows partial discharge of the capacitor. As a result, the time taken to charge the capacitor is shorter and the dwell commences at an earlier point and gives a longer period. Interruption of the coil primary takes place when $T_2$ is switched on. This is dictated by the trigger signal so the end of the dwell period always takes place at the same time. At the instant $T_2$ switches on, the capacitor starts to discharge; this causes $T_3$ to switch off to trigger the spark.

## D Darlington output

A Darlington pair is a common power transistor array used for switching large currents (see Chapter 3, page 46). The pair consists of two robust transistors, $T_5$ and $T_6$, which are integrally constructed in a metal case having three terminals: base, emitter and collector. When a forward-biased voltage is applied to the base-emitter circuit of $T_5$, the transistor is switched on. This increases the voltage applied to the base of $T_6$ and when it exceeds the threshold value, this transistor also switches on. When $T_5$ and $T_6$ are switched on, the coil primary is energised, but when $T_5$ is switched off by the switching off of $T_4$, the primary circuit is broken and a spark is generated.

The switching of transistors is summarised as follows:

| Trigger pulse | $T_1$ | $T_2$ | $T_3$ | $T_4$ | Primary | |
|---|---|---|---|---|---|---|
| + | On | Off | On | On | On | |
| – | Off | On | Off | Off | Off | ← Spark |

To make the system suitable for a vehicle, additional capacitors and diodes are fitted to the circuit shown in Figure 11.21. These extra items prevent damage to the semiconductors from high transient voltage and they also reduce radio interference.

## Alternative method of dwell control

Another method of achieving dwell-angle control is to superimpose a reference voltage on to the output signal supplied by the pulse generator (Figure 11.22a).

In this system the triggering of the spark at the end of the dwell period occurs at the change-over point between the positive and negative waves, whereas the start of the dwell period is signalled when the pulse voltage exceeds the reference voltage.

At low speed a reference voltage of 1.5V acts on the dwell-control stage and this rises to 5V at high speed. Figure 11.22b shows that the stronger pulse signal, combined with the higher reference voltage, gives a longer dwell period. No pulse signal is generated when the engine is stationary, so the dwell control cannot operate. This feature ensures that no current can flow through the coil when the engine is idle.

## Integral module

In this layout the control module is mounted on the side of the distributor assembly and connection is made by a four-pin multi-plug built into the distributor body.

External LT cables from the distributor are limited to two leads; these connect with the coil and ignition switch (Figure 11.23). A tachometer, connected to the '–' side of the coil, uses the LT charge pulses of the coil to sense the engine speed.

When fitted initially, the distributor is accurately timed to the engine and, because it has a breakerless construction, no further check of the timing is necessary when the vehicle is being serviced.

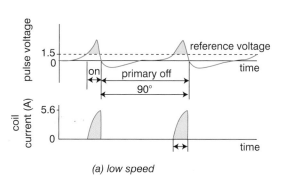

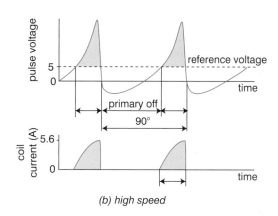

(a) low speed    (b) high speed

Figure 11.22  Use of reference voltage to control dwell

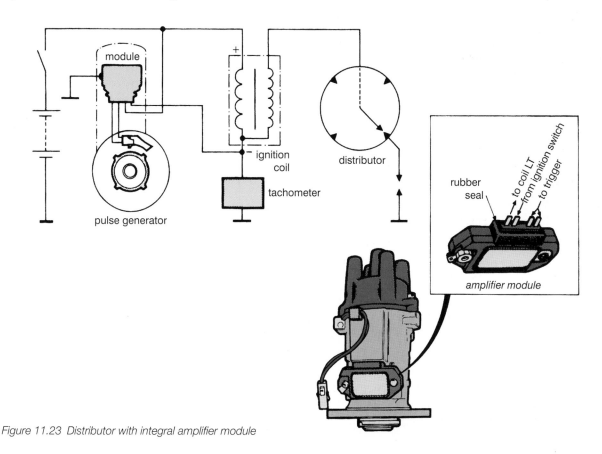

Figure 11.23  Distributor with integral amplifier module

Because the dwell angle is governed by the control module, no check or adjustment is necessary.

## Honda electronic ignition

This system has an inductive-type pulse generator and a control module called an igniter (Figure 11.24). The switching of the coil's primary current is performed by two transistors, a driver transistor ($T_1$) and a power transistor ($T_2$). The pulse generator has a reluctor, shaped in the form of a saw tooth, to produce the AC waveform.

When the ignition switch is closed with the engine stationary, a voltage is applied by $R_2$ to the base of $T_1$. This voltage is above the $T_1$ trigger voltage and, since the resistance of the pulse generator's winding is about $700\,\Omega$, the transistor $T_1$ will be switched on. At this stage, $T_1$ conducts current 'A' to earth instead of passing the current to the base of $T_2$, so $T_2$ is switched off and the primary circuit is open.

Cranking the engine causes an EMF to be generated by the movement of the reluctor. When the polarity of the generator's EMF at the $T_1$ end of the winding is negative, the resistor $R_2$ supplies current, which flows through the winding and diode $D_1$ to earth. At this stage, voltage applied to the base of $T_1$ is less than the trigger voltage, so $T_1$ is switched off. Current

A from $R_3$ is now diverted from $T_1$ to the base of $T_2$, so $T_2$ is switched on and current passes through the primary winding of the ignition coil.

When the EMF from the pulse generator is reversed, the combined effect of the voltage from $R_2$ and the EMF from the pulse generator triggers $T_1$.

This causes $T_1$ to switch on, $T_2$ to switch off to interrupt the primary current, and give a spark at the plug.

Zener diodes, $ZD_1$ and $ZD_2$, fitted at each end of the primary winding, conduct to earth the high-voltage oscillatory currents caused by self-induction. These diodes protect both transistors from high-voltage charges.

## Constant-energy system

Although many of the systems previously described offered some degree of spark energy control, the limits are too wide for modern low-inductance coils. The quick build-up of primary current, achieved by using a primary winding with a very low resistance (less than $1\,\Omega$), makes the low-inductance coil attractive for an electronic system. One drawback of this coil is the high current at low engine speeds, which damages the system unless a current regulator is inserted into the system.

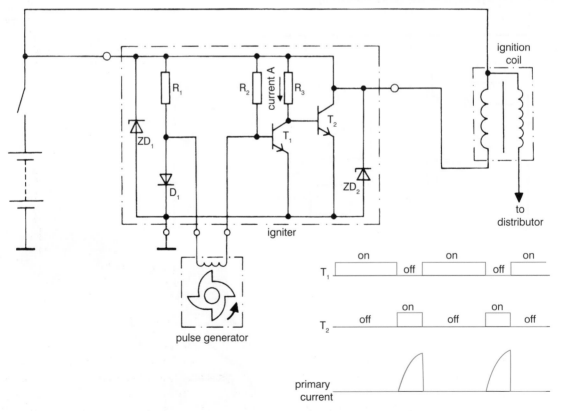

*Figure 11.24 Electronic ignition circuit – Honda*

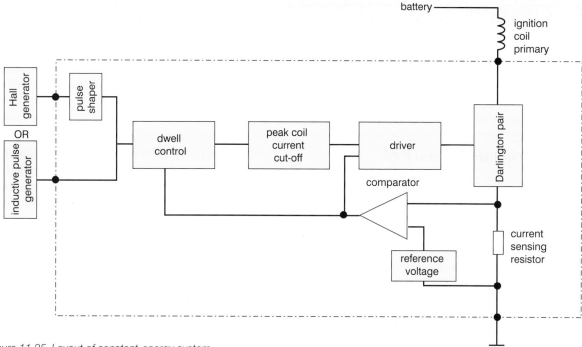

*Figure 11.25  Layout of constant-energy system*

A modern circuit provides current regulation and uses a dwell-angle closed-loop control system to minimise the variation in output energy.

Figure 11.25 shows how the primary current is regulated by a voltage feedback system. Primary circuit switching and current is controlled by a Darlington pair and the voltage drop across a current-sensing resistor provides the feedback signal. The resistor is in series with the primary winding of the ignition coil, so the feedback voltage (as shown by the voltmeter) is proportional to the current. When the current exceeds its rated value, the high feedback voltage signals the system to reduce the input voltage to the Darlington pair; this decreases the collector-emitter current, which drops the feedback voltage and causes the loop-sensing cycle to start again.

Figure 11.26 shows how feedback is used to give closed-loop control for Hall-effect and inductive pulse generators.

Current regulation is achieved by comparing the feedback voltage with a standard reference voltage.

When the two voltages are not equal, a signal is passed to the driver of the Darlington pair, and directs it to alter the input. The dwell-angle closed-loop control system uses the same feedback voltage, but in this case it directs the signal to the dwell control stage. By comparing the sensed voltage with the frequency of the pulse generator (engine speed), the dwell controller can find out whether the coil current is too high or too low. It then makes the necessary dwell-angle alteration to make the primary current correct for the engine speed.

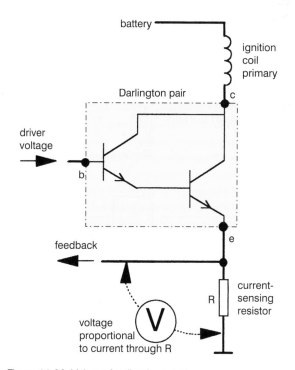

*Figure 11.26  Voltage feedback control*

The continuous monitoring of current and dwell gives a closed-loop control system that maintains the output within the design limits. Dwell-angle control senses engine speed, so this characteristic can be used to interrupt the supply to the ignition coil when the engine is stationary.

## Closed-loop control

This is a term used to describe a voltage feedback arrangement in which the level of the output is controlled by using a monitoring signal from the output to regulate the input.

This is similar to a system managed by a human (e.g. when a constant engine power output is required, the driver has to sense any changes in power and then alter the throttle setting to compensate for the change). In this case of an ignition system, a constant primary current is needed, so when an increase in this current (output) is detected, the input voltage is lowered and vice versa.

### Capacitor discharge ignition (CDI)

The module of this system stores electrical energy of high voltage in a capacitor until the trigger releases the charge to the primary winding of a coil.

In this system, the coil is a pulse transformer instead of being an energy-storage device as is normal (Figure 11.27).

To obtain a voltage of about 400 V for the capacitor, the battery current is first delivered to an inverter (to change DC to AC) and then it is passed to a transformer to raise the voltage. When the spark is required, the trigger releases the energy to the coil primary winding by 'firing' a **thyristor**.

**Thyristor:** a type of transistor switch that, once triggered, continues to pass current through the switch even after the trigger current has ceased.

Sudden discharge of the high-voltage energy to the primary winding causes a rapid build-up in the magnetic flux of the coil and induces a voltage in excess of 40 kV in the secondary circuit to give a high-intensity, short-duration spark.

Although the CDI system is particularly suited to high-performance engines, the spark duration of about 0.1 ms given by this system is normally too short to reliably ignite the weaker air/petrol mixtures used with many modern engines.

Advantages of a CDI system:

- High secondary voltage reserve.
- Input current and output available voltage are constant over a wide speed range.
- Fast build-up of output voltage – since the speed of build-up is about 10 times faster than the inductive type of electronic ignition, the CDI system reduces the risk of the HT current shorting to earth via a fouled plug insulator or taking some path other than the plug electrodes.

To offset the problem of the short spark duration, advantage is taken of the high secondary output by increasing the sparking plug gap to give a larger spark.

The system is normally triggered by pulse generator, using either inductive or Hall effect. The AC signal from the generator is applied to a pulse-shaping

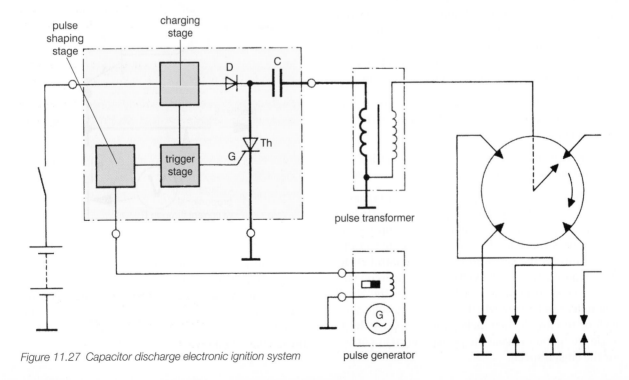

*Figure 11.27 Capacitor discharge electronic ignition system*

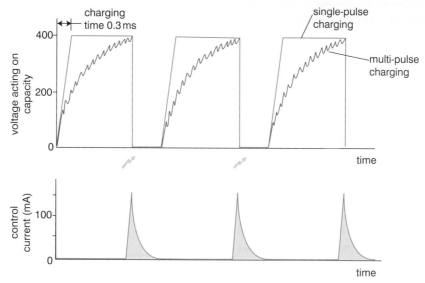

Figure 11.28 Capacitor charging

control circuit, which converts the signal into a rectified rectangular pulse and then changes it to a triangular trigger pulse to 'fire' the thyristor when the spark is required.

A capacitor's ability to store energy is measured in farads (F): μF = 1,000,000th of a farad (microfarad).

Charging of the 1 μF capacitor by the charging stage to a voltage of about 400 V is performed by a voltage transformer, which gives either a single- or multi-pulse output. In both cases a diode is fitted between the charging stage and the capacitor to prevent the charge flowing back from the capacitor.

Single-pulse charging of the capacitor is preferred because it enables the build up to maximum voltage to be achieved in about 0.3 ms, whereas the oscillatory charge given by the multi-pulse is much slower (Figure 11.28).

This short charge-up time overcomes the need for dwell-angle control because the charge time of a CDI system is independent of engine speed. Since the primary winding of the ignition transformer (coil) always receives a similar energy discharge from the capacitor, the secondary available voltage is constant throughout the speed range (Figure 11.29).

Although the external appearance of an ignition transformer of a CDI system is similar to a normal ignition coil, the internal construction is quite different.

Besides being more robust to withstand higher electrical and thermal stresses, the inductance of the primary winding is only about 10 per cent of that of a normal coil.

Since its impedance is only about 50 kΩ, the CDI coil will readily accept the energy discharged from the

capacitor. In view of this, the rise in secondary voltage is 10 times faster. It is this feature that reduces the risk of misfiring due to the presence of HT shunts (i.e. leakage paths such as a fouled sparking plug, which can have a resistance of 0.2–1.0 MΩ).

As the ignition transformer and capacitor form an electrically tuned circuit, it is necessary to fit the recommended type of transformer when replacement is required. Although a standard coil used in place of an ignition transformer will operate without damaging the system, many of the advantages of a CDI system are lost.

Conversely, if an ignition transformer is used with a non-CDI system, damage to control module and transformer will occur immediately the system is used.

The CDI principle is also used in some small engines, as fitted to motorcycles and lawn mowers.

As a battery is not used in these cases, the energy needed by the CDI system is generated by a magneto.

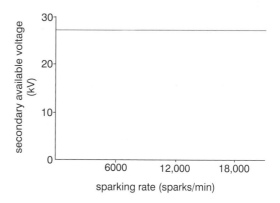

Figure 11.29 Secondary output from CDI system

## 11.4 General maintenance

In some systems (e.g. CDI systems) a high-voltage charge is still stored when the ignition is switched off. Many different systems are in use, so the manufacturer's service manual should be consulted for the specific service and test information, and safety precautions.

Very little routine maintenance is necessary on modern systems because checks on dwell angle and spark timing are no longer required. Also, sparking plug service intervals are extended with these systems.

### Ignition circuit testing (coil and distributor system)

If an engine fails to start, the following basic checks are made to most systems before conducting detailed tests on the control module and pulse generator.

1 Visual checks – check all cables and connectors for security and ensure that the battery is in good condition.
2 Coil output – remove king lead from distributor cap, fit extension and hold with insulated pliers so that the end of the extension is about 6 mm from the engine block.
3 Switch on ignition and crank the engine. A good spark indicates that the fault is beyond the coil HT lead. It is recommended that a high-resistance neon plug tester is used to make sure that the spark does not short to the LT components.
4 If a coil output test shows that the system is defective, the full circuit should be checked. There are many types of coil and distributor system, so the manufacturer's instructions should be consulted where possible.

### Inductive storage with inductive pulse generator

The following description is included to show the general principles; specific manufacturer's data should be used where possible.

### Test 1: Amplifier static test

With the ignition switched on and the engine stationary, voltage readings are taken at points A, B, C and D, as shown in Figure 11.30.

### Test 2: Amplifier switching test

The engine is cranked and the voltage between battery '+' and coil '–' is measured (Figure 11.31). The voltage should increase when the engine is cranked.

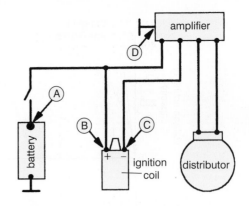

| Static test | | |
|---|---|---|
| Correct reading | A | more than 11.5 V |
| | B | less than 1 V below A |
| | C | less than 1 V below A |
| | D | less than 0.1 V |
| Battery discharged | A | less than 11.5 V |
| | B | correct |
| | C | correct |
| | D | correct |
| Defective switch and/or wiring | A | correct |
| | B | more than 1 V below A |
| | C | more than 1 V below A |
| | D | correct |
| Defective coil or amplifier | A | correct |
| | B | correct |
| | C | more than 1 V below A |
| | D | correct |
| Poor amplifier earth | A | correct |
| | B | correct |
| | C | correct |
| | D | more than 0.1 V |

Figure 11.30 Inductive storage Test 1

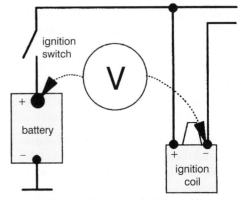

voltage should increase during cranking

Figure 11.31 Inductive storage Test 2

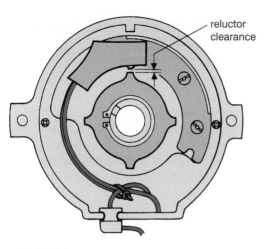

*Figure 11.32 Pulse generator gap*

## Test 3: Pulse generator coil resistance (pick-up resistance)

The pick-up leads from the pulse generator are disconnected at the harness connector and the resistance of the pick-up coil is measured with an ohmmeter. The resistance value depends on the application (a typical value is 2–5 k$\Omega$). If the reading is incorrect, the pick-up is assumed to be faulty, but if the resistance is between the limits, the control module should be changed.

It will be necessary to remove an integral type of control module from the distributor to carry out this test.

## Test 4: Pulse generator gap

If the reluctor pick-up has been disturbed for any reason, the reluctor gap should be checked. The gap

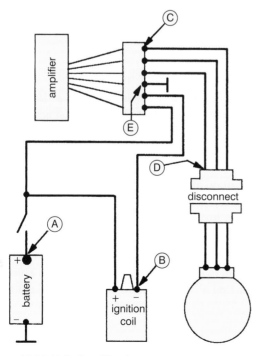

*Figure 11.33 Hall effect Test 1*

depends on the engine type, but a typical gap is 0.2–0.4 mm (0.008–0.016 in). A non-magnetic feeler gauge blade is used for this test (Figure 11.32).

## Test 5: Other components

The remaining parts of the system are checked in a manner similar to that used for a non-electronic system.

## Hall effect pulse generator

### Test 1: Amplifier static test

With the ignition switched on, the engine stationary and the Hall generator plug disconnected, voltage readings are taken at points A, B, C, D and E, as shown in Figure 11.33.

| Static test | | |
|---|---|---|
| Correct reading | A | more than 11.5 V |
| | B | less than 2 V |
| | C | less than 1 V below A |
| | D | less than 2.5 V below A |
| | E | less than 0.1 V |
| Battery discharged | A | less than 11.5 V |
| | B | correct |
| | C | correct |
| | D | correct |
| | E | correct |
| Defective amplifier | A | correct |
| | B | more than 2 V |
| | C | more than 1 V below A or correct |
| | D | more than 2.5 V below A or correct |
| | E | correct |
| Defective switch and/ or wiring | A | correct |
| | B | correct |
| | C | more than 1 V below A |
| | D | correct |
| | E | more than 2.5 V below A or correct |
| Defective amplifier | A | correct |
| | B | correct |
| | C | correct |
| | D | more than 2.5 V below A |
| | E | correct |
| Poor amplifier earth | A | correct |
| | B | correct |
| | C | correct |
| | D | correct |
| | E | more than 1 V |

### Test 2: Amplifier static test

The Hall generator plug is linked as shown in Figure 11.34 and the voltage is checked at the '–' terminal of the coil. If the voltage is more than 1 V below battery voltage, check the coil and if this is serviceable replace the amplifier.

### Test 3: Rotor vane earthing

An ohmmeter is connected between the chopper vane and earth. The resistance should be less than 50 Ω.

### Test 4: Amplifier switching test

A voltmeter is connected to coil '–' and the engine is cranked. The voltage should fluctuate and show a mean value of 2.5–5 V.

### Test 5: Other components

The remaining parts of the system are checked in a manner similar to that used for a non-electronic system.

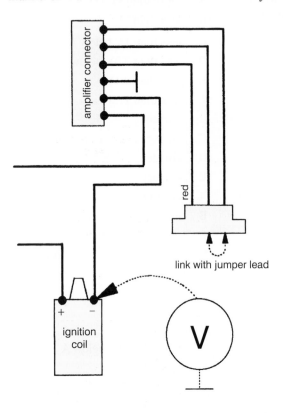

voltage should be more than 1 V below
battery voltage

*Figure 11.34 Hall effect Test 2*

### Constant-energy system

An example of the tests made on a constant-energy system are shown in Figure 11.35.

On a four-cylinder engine, two double-spark ignition coils are fitted to replace the distributor and all of the moving parts it contains; this includes both mechanical and vacuum-ignition advance and retard mechanisms. This system will use a timing point at the crankshaft, which is indicated by the use of a sensor close to a toothed rotor or pulley. A missing tooth in the rotor will indicate the signal for cylinders 1 and 4 to fire simultaneously. As only one of the cylinders will be on the compression stroke, the spark at the other plug will be 'wasted' as it will be on the exhaust stroke. This system called a wasted spark-ignition system.

When the HT voltage flows through the lead to the centre electrode on number 1 spark plug, it creates a spark in that cylinder as it jumps the gap and flows to earth through the earth electrode. As the charge flows to earth in the engine block, it travels through the earth electrode and the spark 'jumps' to the centre electrode in the opposite cylinder. The charge flows in the opposite direction, back through that HT lead, to its starting point, completing the electrical circuit.

### 11.5.1 Operation of the distributorless ignition system

Because there is no distributor, the distributorless ignition system (DIS) uses a number of sensors to trigger the spark at the correct time. Typical system components are:

- crankshaft sensor
- camshaft sensor
- ignition module
- one ignition coil pack for each pair of cylinders.

The crankshaft sensor is usually a Hall effect sensor, which is activated by a missing tooth on the crankshaft rotor for each coil pack. This sensor signal provides ignition timing and engine speed information to the ECU.

The position of the piston relative to TDC is indicated by the camshaft sensor. This information is also used to trigger fuel injection.

When the ignition module receives the signal from the crankshaft and the camshaft sensors, it also receives the signal to instigate a spark from the ECU. This is to ensure that all cylinders fire in the correct sequence. The ECU also controls the ignition dwell time.

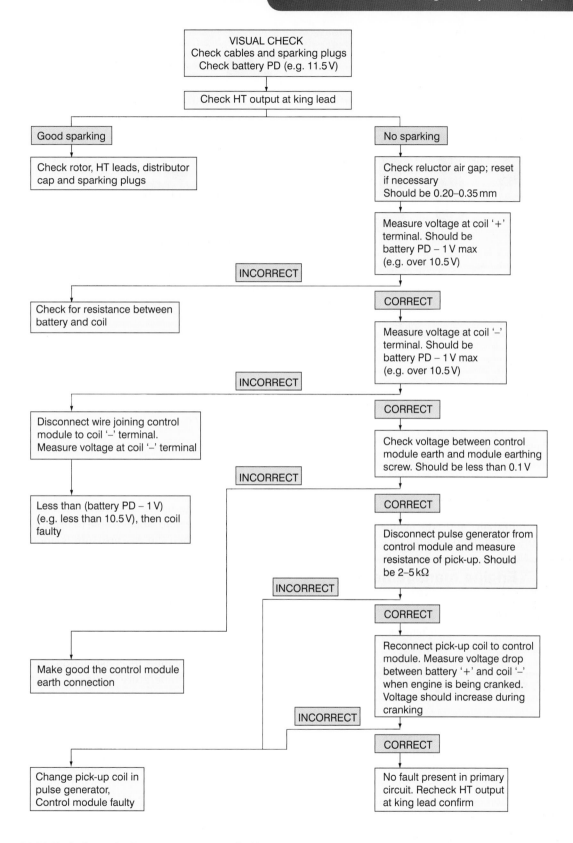

*Figure 11.35 Fault diagnosis chart: constant-energy ignition system*

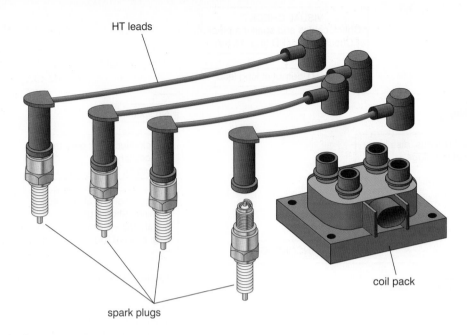

HT leads

coil pack

spark plugs

*Figure 11.36 DIS ignition components*

There are a number of advantages in using a DIS, such as:

- no moving parts
- timing adjustments are electronically controlled
- there are fewer components to accumulate moisture and cause starting problems
- ignition and fuelling are electronically controlled
- the crankshaft and the camshaft position sensors are both no-maintenance sensors.

## 11.6 Engine management system (EMS)

For information and tests on ignition units that are controlled by an EMS see Chapter 14.

## 11.7 Spark plugs

At the heart of every spark-ignition system is the component that provides the spark. Spark plugs have changed very little since the first viable spark plug was invented by Etienne Lenoir in 1860. Many detailed changes have been made since, but the basic construction has remained the same: a highly insulated electrode connected to the HT cable and an earth electrode joined to the plug body.

### 11.7.1 Spark plug requirements

The basic requirement of a spark plug is that a spark of sufficient energy should be produced across the electrodes at all times, irrespective of the pressure and temperature of the gases in the combustion chamber.

Plug operating conditions are severe due to the pressure and temperature of their environment.

### Pressure

Besides withstanding a pressure of 70 bar during combustion, the plug must be able to produce a high-energy spark when the gas pressure is about 10 bar. The voltage required to do this can be as high as 90 kV in modern engines, so adequate insulation is needed to prevent leakage of the electrical energy to earth.

### Temperature

The plug must be capable of withstanding an electrode temperature of between 350 °C and 900 °C for long periods of time. Its construction should keep the electrode temperature between these limits, because if they are exceeded the plug will fail.

Above 900 °C the high temperature of the electrodes causes pre-ignition, whereas below 350 °C carbon will form on the insulator. This will cause 'fouling', which is a term used when the plug allows the electrical charge to short to earth instead of jumping the spark.

In addition to these basic requirements, the plug must be resistant to corrosion, durable, gas tight and inexpensive.

### 11.7.2 Construction

Figure 11.37 shows the main parts of a typical spark plug, it consists of a copper core inserted within the alloy steel centre electrode and an aluminium oxide ceramic insulator, which is supported by a steel shell. Gas leakage past the insulator is prevented by **sillment** compressed powder seals and leakage between the cylinder head and the shell is by means of a gasket or tapered seat. A hexagon is machined on the shell to allow for removal and installation. Ribs formed on the external ceramic increase the length of the flashover path and allow the HT covers to grip tightly preventing the ingress of moisture.

> **Sillment seal**: a gas-tight seal. In spark plug construction, a finely powdered insulator material is placed between the separate parts of the plug and compressed when the plug is constructed. This seal prevents any gas blowing past the plug during the compression/combustion cycle.

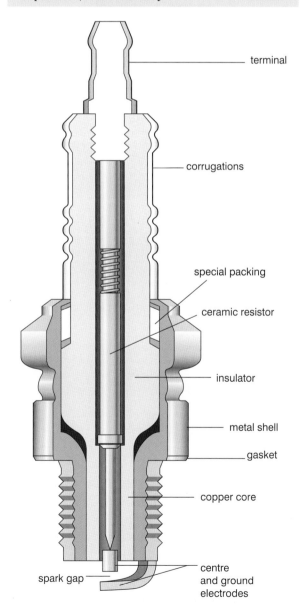

*Figure 11.37  Cut-away of NGK spark plug*

### Plug terms

The length of the thread that screws into the head is called the reach and the diameter of the threaded part indicates the plug size. Common sizes used are 10 mm, 12 mm, 14 mm and 18 mm. Manufacturers use a code to identify their products; the letters and numbers on the insulator give the information listed on the chart in Figure 11.38.

## 11.7.3 NGK spark plugs heat rating

The spark plug heat range has no relationship to the electrical energy transferred through the spark plug. The heat range of a spark plug is the range in which the plug works well thermally. The heat rating of each NGK spark plug is indicated by a number; lower numbers indicate a hotter type, higher numbers indicate a colder type.

Some basic structural factors affecting the heat range of a spark plug:

- Surface area and/or length of the insulator nose.
- Thermal conductivity of the insulator, centre electrode, etc.
- Structure of the centre electrode, such as a copper core, etc.
- Relative position of the insulator tip to the end of the shell (projection).
- The major structural difference affecting the heat rating is the length of the insulator nose. A hot-type spark plug has a longer insulator nose.
- The insulator nose of a hotter spark plug has a longer distance between the firing tip of the insulator, and the point where insulator meets the metal shell; therefore, the path for the dissipation of heat from the insulator nose to the cylinder head is longer and the firing end stays hotter.
- The insulator nose of a hotter spark plug also has a greater surface area that is exposed to more of the ignited gases and is easily heated to higher temperatures.
- A colder spark plug functions in an opposite manner.
- The heat range must be carefully selected for proper spark plug thermal performance. If the heat range is not optimal, then serious trouble can be the result.
- The optimal firing end temperature is approximately between 500 °C and 800 °C.
- The two most common causes of spark plug problems are carbon fouling (<450 °C) and overheating (>800 °C).

## 11.7.4 Firing end appearances

The appearance of the firing end of a used spark plug graphically reflects the condition of an engine, the suitability of the spark plug heat range, and whether or not the fuelling and ignition systems are correctly set.

| B | P | R | 5 | E | S | −11 |
|---|---|---|---|---|---|---|
| Thread diameter<br><br>A – 18mm<br>B – 14mm<br>C – 10mm<br>D – 12mm<br>E – 8mm<br>BC – 14mm<br>BK – 14mm<br>DC – 12mm | P  Projecting insulator type<br><br>M  Small spark plug (CMR6H: Seat height is shorter than CR6HS)<br><br>U  Surface gap, semi-surface gap or supplementary gap (such as BUHW, BURGET) | R  Resistor<br><br>Z  Inductive resistor type | Heat rating<br><br>Hot type<br><br>2<br><br>4<br><br>5<br><br>6<br><br>7<br><br>8<br><br>9<br><br>10 Cold type | Thread length<br><br>E    19.0mm<br>H    12.7mm<br>L    11.2mm<br>EH   19.0mm half-thread<br>M    Bantam type<br>　    BM      9.5mm<br>　    BPM-A   9.5mm<br>F    Conical seat type<br>　    A-F     10.9mm<br>　    B-F     11.2mm<br>　    B-EF    17.5mm<br>　    BM-F    7.8mm | E: Integral terminal<br>CM: Short seat height<br>CS: Oblique ground electrode<br>D: Daihatsu only (BCPR6ED)<br>G, GV: Racing spark plug<br>IX: Iridium IX spark plug<br>IX-P: Iridium? MAX spark plug<br>J: 2 projecting electrodes<br>K: 2 ground electrodes<br>LPG: LGP only<br>N: Thick ground electrode<br>P: Platinum spark plug<br>Q: 4 ground electrodes<br>　(BKR6EQUP: BMW)<br>　(BKR5EQUPA: Nissan)<br>　(BUR9EQP: Mazda)<br>QP: 4 ground electrodes, platinum centre electrode<br>S: Standard type<br>T: 3 ground electrodes<br>U: Semi-surface gap spark plug<br>VX: VX spark plug<br>Y: V-grooved centre electrode<br>YA: Fouling resistant (BA9EYA) | Spark gap<br><br>Nono:　Standard<br>−9:　0.9mm<br>−10:　1.0mm<br>−11:　1.1mm<br>−13:　1.3mm<br>−14:　1.4mm<br>−15:　1.5mm<br><br>−L:　Medium heat rating |
| BK: The length from the plug gasket circuit to the terminal contact on parts using International Standard (ISO) dimensions is 2.5mm shorter than the Japan standard (JIS) BCP type. | | | | | | |

| P | F | R | 5 | A | −11 | |
|---|---|---|---|---|---|---|
| I:  Iridium spark plug<br><br>L:  Long thread reach spark plug<br><br>P:  Platinum spark plug<br><br>Z:  Protruding type spark plug | Mounting thread dimensions Hex. Size<br><br>F    Ø14 × 19mm<br>　    16.0mm<br>G    Ø14 × 19mm<br>　    20.8mm<br>J    Ø12 × 19mm<br>　    18.0mm<br>K    Ø12 × 19mm<br>　    16.0mm<br>M    Ø10 × 19mm<br>　    16.0mm<br>T    Conical seat type<br>　    Ø14 × 17.5mm<br>　    16.0mm<br>　    (Except PTR-A Ø14 × 25mm)<br>U    Conical seat type (BP-FS)<br>　    Ø14 × 11.2mm<br>　    16.0mm<br>Y    Conical seat type (B-FS)<br>　    Ø14 × 11.2mm<br>　    16.0mm | R  Resistor type | Heat rating<br><br>4 Hot type<br>5<br>6<br>7<br>8<br>9 Cold type | A. B. C.<br>Suffix code<br><br>I  One-side iridium spark plug (KR7AI)<br><br>P  One-side platinum spark plug (FR6BP-11) | Spark gap<br><br>None:　Standard<br><br>−9:　0.9mm<br>−10:　1.0mm<br>−11:　1.1mm | (this table shows how to read general part numbers) |

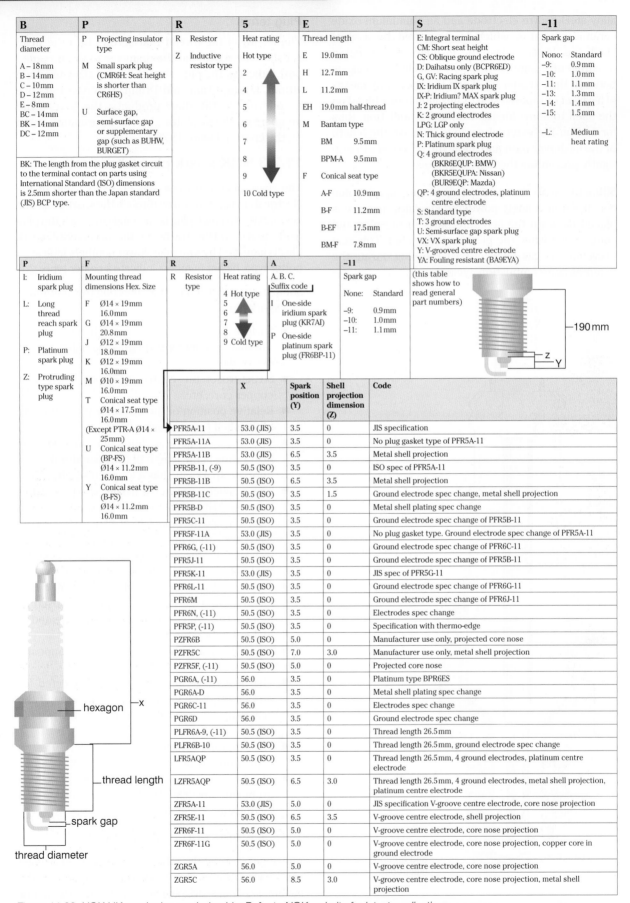

|  | X | Spark position (Y) | Shell projection dimension (Z) | Code |
|---|---|---|---|---|
| PFR5A-11 | 53.0 (JIS) | 3.5 | 0 | JIS specification |
| PFR5A-11A | 53.0 (JIS) | 3.5 | 0 | No plug gasket type of PFR5A-11 |
| PFR5A-11B | 53.0 (JIS) | 6.5 | 3.5 | Metal shell projection |
| PFR5B-11, (-9) | 50.5 (ISO) | 3.5 | 0 | ISO spec of PFR5A-11 |
| PFR5B-11B | 50.5 (ISO) | 6.5 | 3.5 | Metal shell projection |
| PFR5B-11C | 50.5 (ISO) | 3.5 | 1.5 | Ground electrode spec change, metal shell projection |
| PFR5B-D | 50.5 (ISO) | 3.5 | 0 | Metal shell plating spec change |
| PFR5C-11 | 50.5 (ISO) | 3.5 | 0 | Ground electrode spec change of PFR5B-11 |
| PFR5F-11A | 53.0 (JIS) | 3.5 | 0 | No plug gasket type. Ground electrode spec change of PFR5A-11 |
| PFR6G, (-11) | 50.5 (ISO) | 3.5 | 0 | Ground electrode spec change of PFR6C-11 |
| PFR5J-11 | 50.5 (ISO) | 3.5 | 0 | Ground electrode spec change of PFR5B-11 |
| PFR5K-11 | 53.0 (JIS) | 3.5 | 0 | JIS spec of PFR5G-11 |
| PFR6L-11 | 50.5 (ISO) | 3.5 | 0 | Ground electrode spec change of PFR6G-11 |
| PFR6M | 50.5 (ISO) | 3.5 | 0 | Ground electrode spec change of PFR6J-11 |
| PFR6N, (-11) | 50.5 (ISO) | 3.5 | 0 | Electrodes spec change |
| PFR5P, (-11) | 50.5 (ISO) | 3.5 | 0 | Specification with thermo-edge |
| PZFR6B | 50.5 (ISO) | 5.0 | 0 | Manufacturer use only, projected core nose |
| PZFR5C | 50.5 (ISO) | 7.0 | 3.0 | Manufacturer use only, metal shell projection |
| PZFR5F, (-11) | 50.5 (ISO) | 5.0 | 0 | Projected core nose |
| PGR6A, (-11) | 56.0 | 3.5 | 0 | Platinum type BPR6ES |
| PGR6A-D | 56.0 | 3.5 | 0 | Metal shell plating spec change |
| PGR6C-11 | 56.0 | 3.5 | 0 | Electrodes spec change |
| PGR6D | 56.0 | 3.5 | 0 | Ground electrode spec change |
| PLFR6A-9, (-11) | 50.5 (ISO) | 3.5 | 0 | Thread length 26.5mm |
| PLFR6B-10 | 50.5 (ISO) | 3.5 | 0 | Thread length 26.5mm, ground electrode spec change |
| LFR5AQP | 50.5 (ISO) | 3.5 | 0 | Thread length 26.5mm, 4 ground electrodes, platinum centre electrode |
| LZFR5AQP | 50.5 (ISO) | 6.5 | 3.0 | Thread length 26.5mm, 4 ground electrodes, metal shell projection, platinum centre electrode |
| ZFR5A-11 | 53.0 (JIS) | 5.0 | 0 | JIS specification V-groove centre electrode, core nose projection |
| ZFR5E-11 | 50.5 (ISO) | 6.5 | 3.5 | V-groove centre electrode, shell projection |
| ZFR6F-11 | 50.5 (ISO) | 5.0 | 0 | V-groove centre electrode, core nose projection |
| ZFR6F-11G | 50.5 (ISO) | 5.0 | 0 | V-groove centre electrode, core nose projection, copper core in ground electrode |
| ZGR5A | 56.0 | 5.0 | 0 | V-groove centre electrode, core nose projection |
| ZGR5C | 56.0 | 8.5 | 3.0 | V-groove centre electrode, core nose projection, metal shell projection |

*Figure 11.38 NGK UK spark plug symbol guide. Refer to NGK website for latest applications.*

a   Normal condition
An engine's condition can be judged by the spark plug's firing end appearance. If the firing end of a spark plug is brown or light grey, the condition can be judged to be good and the spark plug is functioning correctly.

b   Deposits
The accumulation of deposits on the firing end is influenced by oil leakage, fuel quality and the engine's operating period. Deposits come from:
 - fuel: C (carbon), Pb (lead), Br (bromine)
 - lubricating oil: C, Ca (calcium), S (sulphur), Ba (barium), Zn (zinc)
 - others: Fe (iron), Si (silicon), Al (aluminium).

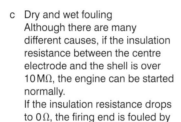

c   Dry and wet fouling
Although there are many different causes, if the insulation resistance between the centre electrode and the shell is over 10 MΩ, the engine can be started normally.
If the insulation resistance drops to 0 Ω, the firing end is fouled by either wet or dry carbon.

d   Lead fouling
Lead fouling usually appears as yellowish brown deposits on the insulator nose and this cannot be detected by a resistance tester at room temperature. Lead compounds combine at different temperatures. Those formed at 370–420 °C have the greatest influence on the resistance.

e   Overheating
After having overheated, the insulator tip is glazed or glossy, and deposits that have accumulated on the insulator tip have melted. Sometimes these deposits have blistered on the insulator's tip.

f   Breakage
Breakage is usually caused by thermal shock due to sudden heating or cooling.

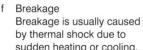

*Figure 11.39 Firing end appearances*

g   Normal life
A worn spark plug not only wastes fuel but also strains the whole ignition system because the expanded gap requires higher voltages. Worn spark plugs also reduce the engine's efficiency, resulting in reduced fuel economy and increased exhaust emissions. The normal rate of gap growth is about 0.01–0.02 mm/1000 km for four-stroke engines and about 0.02–0.04 mm/1000 km for two-stroke engines.

h   Erosion, corrosion, oxidation
The material of the electrodes has oxidised, and when the oxidation is heavy it will be green on the surface. The surfaces of the electrodes are also fretted and rough.

i   Abnormal erosion
Abnormal electrode erosion is caused by the effects of corrosion, oxidation and reaction with lead, all resulting in abnormal gap growth.

j   Lead erosion
Lead erosion is caused by lead compounds in the petrol, which react chemically with the material of the electrodes (nickel alloy) at high temperatures. Crystals of nickel alloy fall off because of the lead compounds permeating and separating the grain boundary of the nickel alloy. Typical lead erosion causes the surface of the ground electrode to become thinner, and the tip of the electrode looks as if it has been chipped.

k   Melting
Melting is caused by overheating. Mostly, the electrode surface is rather lustrous and uneven. The melting point of nickel alloy is 1200–1300 °C.

## 11.7.5 Electrode features

A conventional plug uses nickel alloy for the electrodes to give resistance to corrosive attack by combustion products or erosion from high-voltage discharges. In engines where corrosion and erosion are severe, special materials such as platinum or iridium are sometimes used.

Both electrodes must be robust to withstand vibration from combustion effects and also they must be correctly shaped to allow a spark to be produced with minimum voltage; Figure 11.40a shows the normal electrode shape. Under normal operating conditions, erosion eats away the earth electrode, so after a period of time the earth electrode becomes pointed in shape; Figure 11.40b shows this. In this state it requires a higher voltage to produce a spark. A traditional sparking plug gap was 0.6 mm (0.024 in), but wider gaps are now used for modern engines, which run on a weaker mixture; gaps of 0.8–1.2 mm are not uncommon. These weaker mixtures are more difficult to ignite, so a higher voltage is required. As indicated at the start of this chapter, it is now the norm to have secondary voltages of up to 90,000 V (90 kV).

An auxiliary gap (or booster gap) is used on some spark plug types. This gap is formed between the terminal and the end of the electrode. Its purpose is to reduce the build-up of carbon on the insulator nose and so improve the plug performance when the engine is operated at low power for a considerable time.

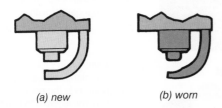

**(a) new**          **(b) worn**

Figure 11.40 (a) Normal shape of the earth electrode, (b) a worn electrode

#### Copper-cored electrode

Increasing the insulator nose length reduces the risk of carbon fouling when the vehicle is operated on short journeys, but when a high vehicle speed is maintained for a long period, the spark plug seriously overheats.

This temperature problem can be overcome by using expensive electrode tip materials, such as platinum, iridium, silver or gold palladium. However, a cheaper alternative is to use copper-cored electrodes to improve the thermal conductivity of the plug (Figure 11.37).

### 11.7.6 The future

At the time of writing, various tests are being carried out on the use of lasers to ignite the fuel in a petrol engine. This system was initially patented in March 2006 and has almost reached the prototype stage.

A team of Japanese and Romanian scientists have demonstrated a laser beam system that can focus two or three beams into the combustion chamber area at various depths, which allows combustion to

start at the same time at different points. This allows a more efficient and complete combustion process with increased fuel economy and reduced emissions.

The major Japanese spark plug manufacturer Denso is working with the team to study this for practical use.

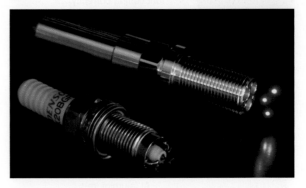

Figure 11.41 Denso spark plug and laser equivalent prototype

### 11.7.7 Waveforms

The ignition secondary picture shown in the example waveform (Figure 11.42) is a typical picture from an engine fitted with electronic ignition. The waveform is an individual secondary HT picture that can be observed one cylinder at a time.

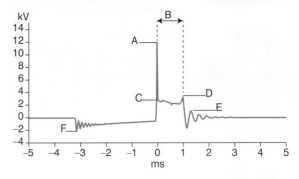

Figure 11.42 Oscilloscope pattern of a correctly functioning spark plug

The secondary waveform shows the voltage required to jump the plug's electrode (A), and (B) the length of time that the HT is flowing across the spark plug's electrode after its initial voltage to jump the plug gap. This time is referred to as either the 'burn time' or the 'spark duration'.

In the illustration shown, it can be seen that the horizontal voltage line in the centre of the oscilloscope (C) is at fairly constant voltage of approximately 3 kV. This voltage is referred to as the sparkline kV. This voltage is the voltage required to maintain the spark flow across the plug's electrode, and is determined primarily by the secondary resistance within the HT circuit. From the 0 ms point on the scope to point D is the spark duration, in this case around 1.0 ms. The waveform is then seen to drop sharply into what is referred to as the 'coil oscillation' (E). The coil oscillation should display a minimum number of peaks (both upper and lower); at least four peaks should be seen. A loss of peaks on this oscillation shows that the coil needs substituting. An example of a faulty coil and the subsequent loss of oscillations can be seen in Figure 11.43. The oscillation seen at point (F) is called the 'polarity peak'. This voltage will be of the opposite polarity to the plug firing voltage as this is created when the magnetic flux is initially built, or at the start of the dwell period.

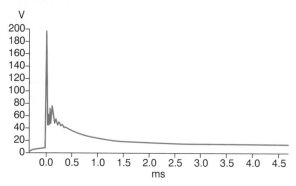

*Figure 11.43 Waveform depicting faulty coil affecting secondary voltage*

The plug firing voltage is the voltage required to jump and bridge the gap at the plug's electrode; commonly known as the 'plug kV' (kilovolts).

The plug kVs will be increased by:

- large plug gaps
- a large rotor air gap
- a break in a plug lead
- a break in the king lead
- worn spark plugs
- a lean mixture
- rotor to reluctor misalignment.

The plug kVs will be decreased by:

- small plug gaps
- low compression
- rich mixture
- incorrect ignition timing
- tracking to earth
- fouled plugs.

A high resistance in the HT lead or the coil lead will not alter the plug kV (however an increase in sparkline kV will be evident). An open circuit lead will increase both the plug kV and the sparkline kV.

Use different voltage ranges for different tests:

- 0–25 kV for plug firing voltages and HT insulation testing.
- 0–50 kV for plug firing voltages on DIS and coil output testing.

# 12

# Engine fuelling petrol injection (spark ignition)

Methods of fuelling the internal-combustion engine have evolved in the last few decades, from the common carburettor to direct multi-point fuel-injection systems. This is mainly due to legislative requirements for emission control. With decreasing costs and increasing reliability, electronic components have flooded the automotive industry.

Following the introduction of Euro 1 in July 1992, carburettors could no longer meet the stringent emission regulations and were phased out. The introduction of Euro 2 in 1996 and Euro 5 in 2009 has meant that vehicle manufacturers have had to develop fuel management systems to meet the continual tightening of emission regulations. These systems are now combined fuel and ignition management systems and use inputs from a number of sensors around the vehicle, which are processed by the engine management ECU. The output signals from the ECU are sent to actuators to provide the spark and injection pulse(s). There are a number of different engine management systems in current use, so manufacturers' specifications and procedures should always be followed.

## 12.1 Metering requirements: air/fuel mix control

Under ideal conditions the air/fuel ratio is 14.7 parts air to 1 part petrol (by weight, e.g. 14.7 g of air are required to burn 1 g of petrol). This proportion is called the chemically correct ratio or **stoichiometric ratio** because when this air/fuel mixture is ignited, it burns

**Stoichiometric ratio**: the ideal air/fuel ratio (14.7:1) for the most efficient combustion.

completely to form carbon dioxide ($CO_2$) and water ($H_2O$). This 14.7:1 stoichiometric ratio is theoretically possible but is rarely completely achieved.

When this air factor, or excess of air, as it is now more commonly called, is used for mixture combustion a certain amount of oxygen is produced. This correct amount of oxygen is regarded as 1 or lambda = 1. The Greek symbol for lambda ($\lambda$) is used to indicate the excess air factor.

From Figure 12.1 it can be seen that when the mixture is correct then lambda = 1 ($\lambda$ = 1). When a richer mixture, such as 12:1, is supplied to an engine, the fuel consumption is increased and lambda is less than 1 ($\lambda$ < 1). Also, with this rich mixture undesirable by-products are exhausted from the engine, such as carbon monoxide (CO), nitrogen oxides ($NO_X$) and unburned fuel (HC).

Less pollution of the atmosphere occurs when the engine is operated on a weaker mixture, such as 18:1. In this case, lambda is greater than 1 ($\lambda$ > 1) as this mixture has excess air. Although slightly weaker mixtures give the best economy, the power output is compromised. In addition, a weak or lean mixture is more difficult to ignite, is prone to detonate (i.e. cause combustion knock) and, since it burns slower, is more likely to overheat the engine.

Despite the many problems associated with a weak mixture, it is still used in order to conform to the stringent statutory regulations relating to exhaust pollution in many parts of the world.

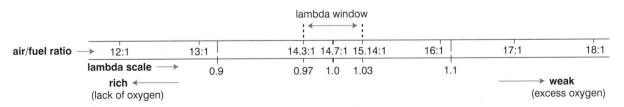

*Figure 12.1 Lambda (excess air factor) compared with the air/fuel ratio scale*

The lambda window shown in Figure 12.1 is a narrow range that gives good performance while lowering CO, HC and $NO_x$. Current VOSA emission regulations for class IV vehicles in conjunction with the European Directive 96/96EC are:

- Lambda = 0.97–1.03
- CO = 0.3–0.5%
- HC = 200 parts per million (ppm).

## 12.2   Types of petrol injection

All spark-ignition engines must be supplied with an air/fuel mixture that is correctly calibrated and thoroughly mixed. This must be accurately controlled to give good economy, high power and an exhaust pollution level that is within the legal requirements for the country in which the vehicle is to operate.

Electronic control of a fuel-injection system provides precise metering of the air/fuel mixture to suit the wide range of conditions under which an engine operates. The sensitivity of an electronic control system gives high engine power and good economy while maintaining as low exhaust emissions as possible. Petrol-injection systems can be divided into three main groups:

- Single-point injection
- Multi-point injection
- Direct injection

Single-point injection has now been phased out, as there were issues with the outer cylinders not receiving sufficient fuel, giving weak and inconsistent air/fuel mixtures. A combination of this disadvantage, tighter controls of emissions and advances in electronics has led to the use of multi-point fuel injection in most vehicles since the early 1990s.

The fuel-injection system can further be split into two subsystems:

- Fuel-delivery system
- Electronic system

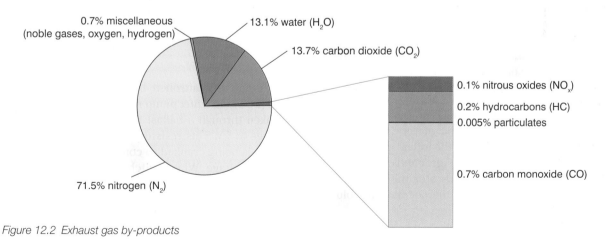

Figure 12.2 Exhaust gas by-products

Table 12.1 Exhaust gas by-products when operating with a stoichiometric air/fuel ratio where $\lambda = 1$

| Not considered harmful | Considered harmful |
| --- | --- |
| Nitrogen ($N_2$) forms 71.5% of exhaust gas | Nitrogen oxide ($NO_x$) forms 0.1% of exhaust gas |
| Water ($H_2O$) forms 13.1% of exhaust gas | Hydrocarbons (HC) form 0.2% of exhaust gas |
| Carbon dioxide ($CO_2$) forms 13.7% of exhaust gas (not toxic, some global warming concerns) | Carbon monoxide (CO) forms 0.7% of exhaust gas |

## Air/fuel mixture

The air/fuel mix supplied to the engine must:

- be of a proportion of 14.7 parts air to 1 part petrol

- produce low levels of CO, $NO_x$ and HC
- be calibrated for economy, performance and meet legislative requirements.

## 12.2.1 Single-point injection

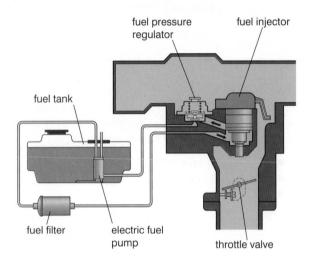

Figure 12.3 Single-point fuel delivery system

First, we will look at the layout, components and operation of the single-point fuel-injection system (Figure 12.3).

### Fuel delivery

The purpose of a fuel-supply system is to provide the injector with adequate fuel at a pressure sufficient to allow the injector to give good atomisation (mechanically breaking up the fuel into fine particles). For a single-point system the fuel pressure operates just under 1 bar of pressure.

### Pump

This is normally a roller cell-type pump driven by a permanent magnet electric motor (Figure 12.4). Rotation of the pump moves the rollers outwards and seals the spaces between the rotor and casing. As the fuel is carried around with the rotor, the combination of the rotor movement and the decrease in volume causes an increase in pressure.

As fuel from the pump passes through the motor it aids cooling of the pump. Although sparks are generated in the motor, combustion does not occur because insufficient oxygen is present in the fuel tank. It is important to remember that when bench testing a fuel pump it should never be energised outside the tank as it could burst into flames.

The pump is designed to supply more fuel than is needed; excess fuel is recirculated back to the tank.

This feature reduces the risk of vapour-lock problems. Two ball valves are fitted in the pump: a non-return check valve at the outlet, and a pressure-limiter valve at the inlet to limit the maximum pressure.

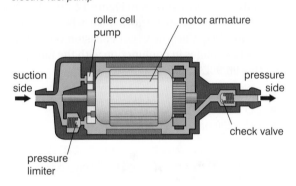

Figure 12.4 Roller cell fuel pump

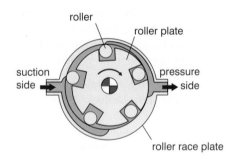

The pump is controlled by the electronic control unit (ECU) via a fuel pump relay. Supply to the pump is taken through a ballast resistor, which drops the voltage to 7 V. This resistor is shorted out when the engine is being cranked to compensate for the lower battery voltage. When switching on the ignition, the pump motor runs for a couple of seconds to fully pressurise the system. After this initial period, the pump is stopped until the engine is cranked.

For safety reasons, an inertia switch is fitted in the electric supply line to the pump relay. This switch opens if it is jolted, so in the event of a collision the pump ceases to operate. The switch can be reset by pushing down a protruding plunger. Modern systems have the inertia switch as part of the fuel relay, which must be replaced if activated.

## Fuel pressure regulator

This controls the operating pressure of the system and is set to maintain a constant pressure difference of 1 bar. The fuel pressure regulator is part of the throttle body.

Two chambers within the regulator are divided by a rubber diaphragm; the top chamber spring acts against the diaphragm. The centre of the diaphragm has a movable plate with a valve to seal it. When fuel enters the lower chamber its pressure pushes against the diaphragm causing a state of equilibrium in both chambers; if the pressure is high enough to move the spring the fuel is returned to the tank, regulating the fuel pressure.

The design feature of this fuel pressure regulator inhibits the formation of vapour bubbles and aids engine hot starts.

## Injector

The function of an injector is to deliver a finely atomised spray into the throat of the intake manifold before the throttle valve (Figure 12.5). In addition, the injector must vary the quantity of fuel to suit the engine operating conditions and evenly distribute fuel to all cylinders. This is achieved by appropriate positioning of the injector and varying the time that the injector is opened.

The required conical spray pattern (cone shape) is obtained by pumping the fuel through a pintle-type nozzle. Fuel flow takes place when the nozzle valve is opened by the energising of the injector's solenoid. Movement of the valve is limited to about 0.06 mm (depending on the system) and the period of time that the valve is open varies from about 1.5 to 10 ms (milliseconds).

## Electronic system

### Throttle body injection

A single-point injection system provides a comparatively simple modern replacement for the carburettor, giving the following advantages:

- More accurate metering of the fuel and air.
- Better atomisation of the fuel over the speed range, especially at part-load.
- Less service adjustments.
- Low production costs.

Figure 12.6 shows the layout of a throttle body injection system. This shows a single solenoid-operated injector situated centrally in the air intake. It is supplied by a pressurised fuel system. Injected fuel is directed into a venturi-shaped region around the throttle, so the increased air speed at this point is used to further break up the fuel. Airflow can be measured by a mass or hot-wire sensor; engine load, speed and temperature are all variants.

The ECU contains a microcomputer so it can easily process data from all sensor variants shown and then control the actuators for precise fuelling. (See Chapters 5 and 6 for an in-depth explanation of sensors and actuators.)

When the engine is started from cold, extra fuel must be injected; this is provided by increasing the frequency of injection. Injector opening is obtained by using a solenoid winding resistance under 3 Ω, for a single-point system. This solenoid overcomes a return spring, which is fitted to hold the nozzle against its seat when it is closed.

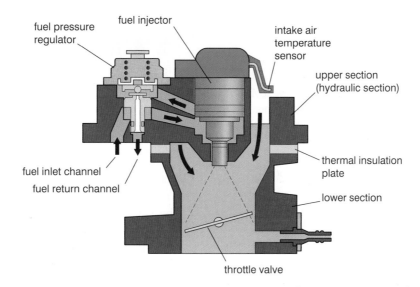

*Figure 12.5 Fuel pressure regulator and injector operation*

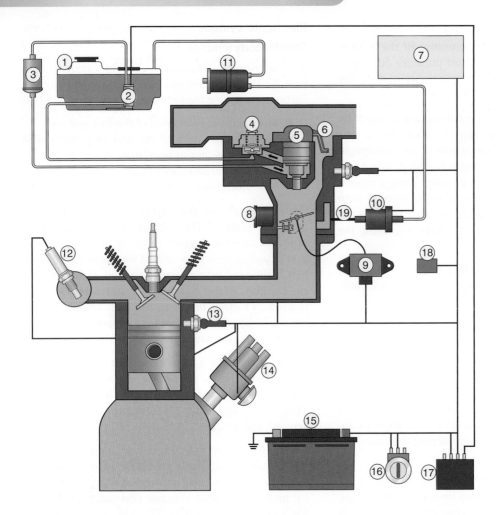

1 fuel tank

2 electric fuel pump

3 fuel filter

4 fuel pressure regulator

5 solenoid operated fuel injector

6 air temperature sensor

7 ECU

8 throttle valve actuator

9 throttle valve potentiometer

10 canister purge valve

11 carbon canister

12 lambda oxygen sensor

13 engine temperature sensor

14 ignition distributor

15 battery

16 ignition start switch

17 relay

18 diagnosis connection

19 central injection unit

*Figure 12.6  Single-point fuel-injection system with sensors and actuators*

## 12.2.2 Multi-point injection

Single-point injection has limits when applied to larger engines with more than four cylinders, as the end cylinders can be robbed of their full charge. Problems with cold manifolds and cylinder walls can result in poor mixing of the fuel and air.

Multi-point systems (Figure 12.7) have one injector per cylinder, situated to give a fuel spray into the air stream at a point just before it enters the cylinder (back of the inlet valve). Injection of fuel at this point ensures that each cylinder receives its full share of fuel, so equal power output from the cylinders is achieved. Unfortunately, the multi-point system is more expensive and complex than the single-point throttle body system.

### Multi-point fuel delivery

The fuel-delivery system for a multi-point injection system is similar to the single-point delivery. However, the delivery pressure is higher, ranging from 1.5 bar (on early multi-point systems) up to 5 bar, depending on the system. The fuel pressure regulator is usually on the fuel rail for a multi-point system.

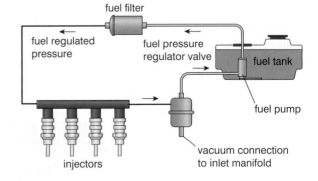

*Figure 12.7  Multi-point fuel system*

### Fuel pressure regulator

The rail pressure is kept constant in a similar manner to the single-point system; the pressure difference (e.g. 3.0 bar) is kept above the manifold pressure, irrespective of the throttle opening. It consists of a spring-loaded diaphragm and ball valve.

Manifold pressure depression depends on throttle opening (i.e. engine load), so when the opening is small the depression encourages more fuel to leave the injector. To compensate for this, the fuel system operating pressure is lowered when the manifold depression increases. This is achieved by connecting one side of the regulator to the induction manifold. At times when the engine is operated under a light load, the regulator valve is slightly opened and the pressure is reduced (Figure 12.8).

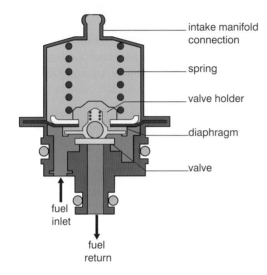

Figure 12.8 Multi-point fuel pressure regulator

Injection of the petrol takes place in the induction manifold. Normally the fuel spray is directed towards the inlet valve. This downstream injection spray is produced by a pressure of about 3 bar, which is either continuous (simultaneous) or timed (sequential). The former method gives an intermittent spray from injectors that open at least once every engine cycle, whereas the continuous method delivers a constant stream of fuel at a rate proportional to the quantity of air that is entering the engine.

## Simultaneous injection

The simultaneous system, when all the injectors on a four-cylinder engine are fired at the same time, was phased out in the late 1990s. For six-, eight- and 10-cylinder engines, the injectors are fired in banks of three, four and five respectively. As these injectors are opened twice every engine cycle, they deliver half the required fuel at each injection phase, so fuel needs to wait for the inlet valve to open. For this reason, this system does not deliver a metered fuel quantity as precisely as a sequential system can.

## Sequential injection

Sequential fuel injection (Figure 12.9) opens the injectors in sequence, like the spark plug firing order (i.e. 1, 3, 4, 2 for a four-cylinder engine), and only once per engine cycle. This system has all the injectors' solenoid valves connected in parallel and the injectors are fired just before the inlet valve

opens, delivering all the required fuel at this time. On overtaking or full load, the injectors can be fired twice per engine cycle, delivering half the fuel on both periods.

The timing of the injectors is controlled by the engine ECU, which is triggered by the camshaft phase sensor.

Modern multi-point systems are controlled electronically, making the system sensitive to changes in temperature and pressure. Together with electrical operation of the pump, this makes the system very different from early types, which were completely mechanical.

**simultaneous injection pattern**

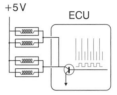

**injection timing**

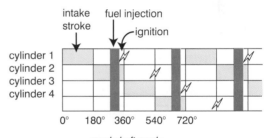

*crankshaft angle*

**sequential injection pattern**

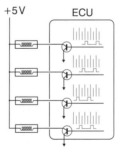

**injection timing**

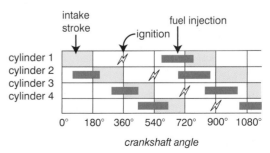

*crankshaft angle*

Figure 12.9 Injector timing for simultaneous and sequential injection on a four-cylinder engine

## Multi-point electronic operation

The electronic operation is controlled by the engine ECU. This unit takes inputs (data) from the sensors then processes them to adjust and manage the system's actuators.

### Sensors

The main sensor inputs from Figure 12.10:

- Mass airflow – this can be a hot-wire or film sensor. It measures air mass directly, so the signal transmitted to the ECU will not need further correction for changes in density and temperature of the intake air.
- Throttle position – this is a variable resistor, which is used as a means for altering electrical potential to give an accurate throttle position.

- Intake manifold pressure – this measures the absolute pressure in the inlet manifold, after the throttle valve.
- Camshaft phase – a Hall sensor that indicates a timing reference for injector firing.
- Lambda – detecting oxygen in the exhaust gas from the engine provides a useful means for controlling the air/fuel mixture.
- Engine speed – this is an inductive sensor, giving engine speed to the ECU.
- Knock – this detects combustion knock (detonation) in an engine combustion chamber.
- Temperature – this thermistor supplies the ECU with the temperature for the coolant and air.

See Figure 12.15 on page 165 for a flowchart on sensor input, and refer to Chapter 5 for further information on sensors.

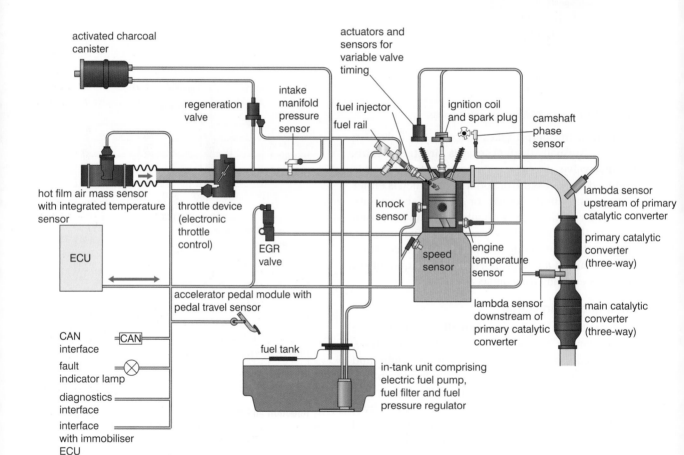

*Figure 12.10 Multi-point fuel-injection system, showing the fuel and electrical/electronic subsystems*

### 12.2.3 Direct injection

The previously explained single- and multi-point systems mix the air and fuel outside the cylinder. The fuelling system for a direct injection system sprays the fuel directly into the combustion chamber (similar to diesel injection). This requires an increased fuel pressure to atomise the fuel and overcome the cylinder pressure, as the injection takes place on the compression stroke (Figure 12.11).

Rapid vaporisation of the fuel draws in the ambient heat, cooling the air in the cylinder and lowering the chamber temperature. This limits the formation of $NO_x$ and helps prevents combustion knock.

Similar in construction to the multi-point system, direct injection has the following additional or modified sensors and actuators:

- Injectors – more robust and quicker to open. This rapid opening is controlled by the ECU via a driver module with 50–100 V to open, and a holding voltage of 7 V.
- Airflow meter/intake manifold pressure – uses a hot film type airflow meter with a manifold pressure sensor to calculate the air mass entering the engine.
- Fuel pressure sensor – this is located on the fuel rail to supply the ECU with fuel pressure.
- Pressure control valve – controlled by the ECU to regulate rail pressure.

### Low-pressure fuel delivery

A low-pressure roller cell pump is fitted in the tank to supply a high-pressure pump with 3–5 bar. This system has a pressure regulator in the fuel tank similar to the multi-point injection systems explained earlier.

### High-pressure fuel delivery

There are two types of high-pressure fuel delivery: continuous and demand-controlled. The continuous system supplies extra fuel to the pressure rail from the high-pressure pump. A pressure control valve allows excess fuel to return to the tank. The demand-controlled system uses a fuel quantity control valve to regulate fuel rail pressure as required.

The high-pressure pump is engine-driven (usually by the camshaft) and increases the fuel pressure to 120 bar. The high-pressure pump is usually of the single-barrel or three-barrel type.

### Single barrel

A single plunger is driven by a camshaft lobe; low-pressure fuel enters the pump and is forced out at high pressure by the single plunger. A pulsation damper is used, as this single-barrel pump creates pressure pulses.

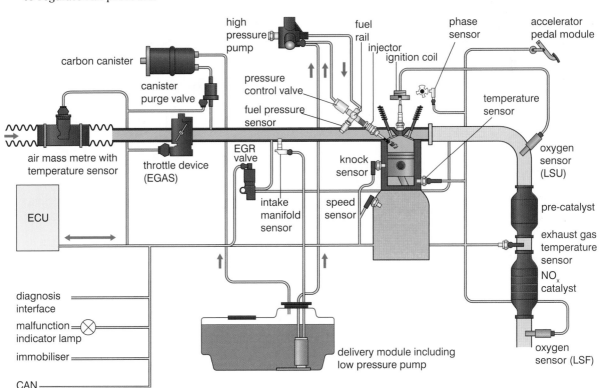

*Figure 12.11 The fuel and engine management arrangement for a direct fuel-injection system*

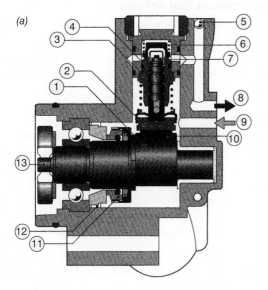

(a)

(b)

1 eccentric element
2 slipper
3 pump barrel

4 pump plunger (hollow
   piston, fuel inlet)
5 sealing ball
6 outlet valve

7 inlet valve
8 high pressure connection
   to rail
9 fuel inlet (low pressure)

10 cam ring
11 axial seal (sleeve seal)
12 static seal
13 input shaft

*Figure 12.12  Three-barrel high-pressure pump*

## Three barrel

The three-barrel pump, shown in Figure 12.12, is driven by the camshaft but has three plungers moved by an eccentric cam. The cam forces the plunger up the barrel, increasing fuel delivery pressure. The overlap from the multiple plungers reduces pressure pulsation.

## Homogenous and stratified charge

For a direct-injection system, the fuel can be delivered by injector timing to produce two types of mixture formation in the combustion chamber, either homogenous or stratified. This is accomplished by firing the injectors, either on the induction stroke or near the end of the compression stroke.

### Homogenous

This is a uniformed mix of the air and fuel; all areas of the combustion chamber are evenly mixed with no pockets of a weak or rich mixture. Most single- and multi-point injection systems run with this charge (Figure 12.13a).

Flame propagation for a homogenous charge is evenly spread for the mixture, as it is at 14.7:1. This gives low emissions and good performance.

### Stratified

Manipulation of the injector timing can supply a stratified charge. This is where a small pocket of rich mixture is focused at the spark plug and the rest of the mixture becomes progressively weaker (Figure 12.13b).

Flame propagation for a stratified charge is uniform for the rich pocket, which heats up the rest of the air to create expansion within the cylinder. The rest of the air can contain a small amount of fuel (weak mixture); it will burn slowly. A stratified mixture will not produce a performance as good as an homogenous charge, but it will achieve good fuel economy.

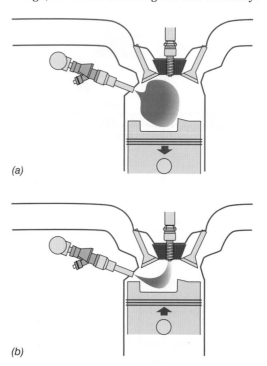

(a)

(b)

*Figure 12.13  (a) Homogenous and (b) stratified mixture formation*

## 12.3  Electronic control

The control system for fuel management must supply the correct quantity of fuel to be injected at the right time. To meet this requirement, the quantity of air entering the system, together with the engine crankshaft position, must be measured accurately. The quantity of air entering the engine dictates the amount of fuel required, and the crankshaft and camshaft position signals indicate when injection should commence. The electronic microprocessor control unit shown in Figure 12.14 is an ECU. The size of modern ECUs is governed by the pin size of the connections – they could be made a lot smaller.

*Figure 12.14  ECU*

### ECU

During recent years, advances made in ECU technology have made it possible for the microprocessor to accurately match the fuel requirements of the engine. This means that the operating performance of a modern system depends largely on the quality of the peripheral components, namely the accuracy and efficiency of the various sensors and actuators that are the inputs and outputs to and from the ECU.

Normally, the ECU consists of a number of integrated circuits and many hybrid modules containing various semiconductors, which are all mounted on one or two printed circuit boards. Input and output signals are communicated by a wiring harness that is connected to the ECU by a multi-pin connector.

The ECU microprocessor interprets the data received from the sensors and, after calculating the duration of the injection time, it signals this message, together with the time of opening, to the injectors (Figure 12.15).

### Digital control

More recent developments use digital control units. These allow quite complex fuelling needs to be stored in a micro-sized silicon chip. One system uses a 5 mm square chip, containing about 5000 transistors, as a part of its control circuitry.

Most digital ECUs store the fuelling requirements in a digital memory, pictorially represented by a three-dimensional map (Figure 12.16). Once the standard pulse has been determined, it is then modified to take into account the conditions that exist at that time, namely engine speed and load. Corrections must also be made for battery voltage, because the action of the injector depends on the voltage applied to it.

Modern ECUs can have this digital memory reprogrammed (re-mapped) for performance or to update software.

### Other features

In addition to the above basic functions, an ECU fitted to a modern injection system incorporates extra control circuits to include the following:

- Cranking enrichment – when the engine is rotated at cranking speed, the ECU provides double the number of injection pulses to satisfy cold-start conditions.
- After-start enrichment – the ECU provides extra fuel by extending the injection pulse duration for a given time after the engine has been started. This feature is provided for all engine temperatures, but the enrichment period is shortened when the engine is hot.

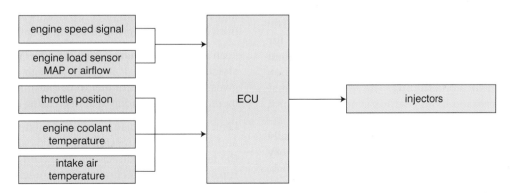

*Figure 12.15  Layout of a simple electronic fuel-injection system. The schematic layout shows the ECU receiving information from sensors and then controlling the fuel injectors*

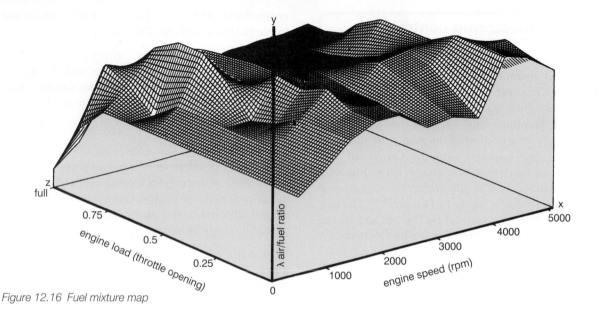

Figure 12.16 Fuel mixture map

- Hot-start enrichment – when the fuel in the fuel pressure rail is very hot, the ECU lengthens the pulse duration to compensate for the change in fuel density.
- Acceleration enrichment/deceleration weakening – signals from the throttle potentiometer and airflow sensor indicate when the engine is accelerating or decelerating. Under these conditions, the ECU enriches or weakens the mixture accordingly, by increasing or decreasing the pulse respectively.
- Full-load enrichment – enrichment is required when the engine is put under full load. When the sensors indicate this condition, the ECU lengthens the pulse duration to the injectors.
- Over-run fuel cut-off – the ECU cuts off the fuel so as to improve economy and exhaust emissions when the programmed conditions are sensed.
- Idle-speed control – idle speed is controlled by a stepper motor energised by electrical pulses supplied from the ECU. A valve moved by the motor varies the quantity of air that is allowed to by-pass the throttle valve. The main engine sensors provide the signals for this feature but extra data is required when the vehicle is fitted with an automatic gearbox and/or air conditioning. The idle speed must be increased if the gearbox is set in drive or if the air-conditioning unit is switched on.
- Fault code storage – the ECU has an electrically erasable programmable read-only memory (EEPROM) to store fault codes for diagnostics. Even if the supply power is lost the fault code will be retained.

## 12.4   Emission control

With the introduction of Euro 5 emission standards, from September 2009 manufacturers have had to cut the environmental impact of $CO_2$ emissions for new vehicles. There have also been economical impacts for the motorist, with rising fuel costs and the linking of road tax to $CO_2$ per g/km, forcing further controls on emissions.

Manufacturers have developed various systems that have helped decrease fuel consumption and cut emissions: variable valve timing, steering assist that operates only when required, active grill shutters to optimise cooling, and enhanced aerodynamics to reduce drag.

The more common methods of emission control will now be explained in more detail.

### Lean burn

The lean burn concept has been around since the mid-1970s, when Chrysler used an electronic lean burn system (ELBS), which was in use up until 1995.

Lean burn engines have a higher air/fuel ratio than the stoichiometric 14.7:1; it can be as high as 22:1. This gives a lean amount of fuel to be burnt in the engine, increasing fuel economy and decreasing emissions.

Lean burn engines use a stratified mixture formation and a higher compression ratio, typically 9.5:1, but the latest gasoline direct-injection (GDI) engines can run at 12.5:1. This technology uses precisely metered fuel control, with the engine designed to create a strong air swirl within the combustion chamber. The concentration of fuel (rich mixture) is at the spark plug tip and the rest of the cylinder's mixture is progressively weaker.

Lean burn engines generate more heat in the cylinder, which in turn increases the amount of $NO_x$ in the exhaust gas. These systems require an expensive $NO_x$ accumulator catalytic converter to reduce the $NO_x$ and cannot run with a standard three-way catalyst.

## Catalytic converter

Catalytic converters were invented by Eugene Houndry to respond to concerns that automobiles' exhaust gas caused smog. The catalyst takes harmful exhaust emissions from the engine and changes them into less harmful gases. There are three main types of catalysts in use today:

- Two-way – a dual-function converter, this converts CO by oxidising it with $CO_2$ and oxidises HC into $CO_2$ and $H_2O$. This catalyst cannot control $NO_x$ and is usually found on diesel vehicles.
- Three-way – this catalyst has three simultaneous functions: it carries out the same functions as the two-way catalyst, with the addition of reducing $NO_x$ to $N_2$ and $O_2$.
- Three-way and air – this carries out the same functions as the three-way catalyst, but has air pumped into it to improve the oxidation process in the converter.

Figure 12.17 shows a modern three-way catalyst with upstream and downstream lambda sensors. The upstream sensor measures the oxygen content for fuelling, while the downstream sensor measures the converter's efficiency. On V6, V8 or V10 engines the sensors are labelled in banks (bank 1 or bank 2). Bank 1 sensors are always on the same side of the engine as cylinder number 1.

## Closed-loop

When the engine runs on a closed loop, the lambda sensor measures the oxygen content in the exhaust gas and feeds this information to the ECU, which in turn makes changes to the fuel quantity entering the cylinders. A closed loop is when the engine

is operating within the lambda window, as close as possible to $\lambda = 1$. The ECU makes these fine adjustments in a continual loop (closed loop) from various sensor inputs, including the lambda.

The engine will run on open loop when cold or under full load; the lambda sensor information will not be calculated by the ECU for fuelling under these conditions.

### Exhaust gas recirculation

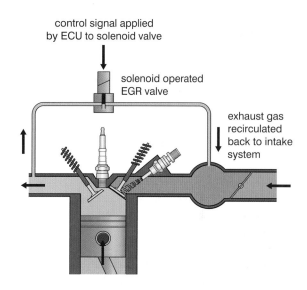

*Figure 12.18 Exhaust gas recirculation (EGR) system*

If a measured amount of hot exhaust gas is reintroduced into the intake system, it has the effect of lowering the combustion chamber temperature. This prevents the formation of $NO_x$.

Recirculation of exhaust gas is controlled by the programming in the ECU; 10–15 per cent can be reintroduced, depending on exhaust and inlet manifold pressures. The ECU opens the exhaust gas recirculation (EGR) valve when the engine is at medium or light load.

The EGR valve in Figure 12.18 is a simple solenoid operating a plunger; it receives a digital signal from the ECU, which is usually a duty cycle to control how far the valve opens.

1 engine
2 lambda oxygen sensor upstream of the catalytic converter (two-step sensor or broadband sensor, depending on system)
3 three-way catalytic converter
4 two-step lambda oxygen sensor downstream of the catalytic converter (only on systems with lambda dual-sensor control)

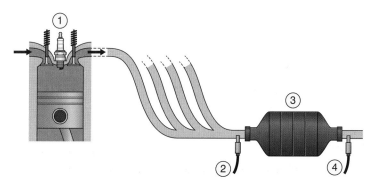

*Figure 12.17 Location of catalytic converter and lambda sensors*

## Secondary air injection

On cold start, the engine requires a richer mixture due to condensing of the fuel in the cold engine. This richer mixture produces higher levels of CO and HC; it also lacks oxygen to heat up the catalyst to operating temperature. Secondary air injection injects air into the exhaust manifold or ports to combust (combine) with the CO and HC to continue to burn them and help heat up the catalyst.

An electric air pump is supplied by a timer relay or the ECU and runs on cold start until the catalyst is at operating temperature. The air is drawn in from the atmosphere and regulated by a check valve, before being introduced to the exhaust system.

## Evaporative control

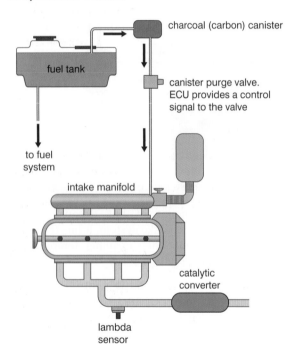

*Figure 12.19 Evaporative emission control (EVAP) system*

An evaporative emission control (EVAP) system vents fuel vapour back into the engine to be combusted along with the fresh charge. This fuel vapour is harmful if vented into the atmosphere; it contributed to about 20 per cent of automotive HC before 1971, after which US regulations prevented fuel vapour in the fuel tank from being vented into the atmosphere.

From the system shown in Figure 12.19, a sealed fuel tank is vented into a carbon canister containing activated carbon granules. These granules are porous and absorb the fuel vapour, until it is sucked into the inlet manifold by vacuum from the engine when the purge valve is opened.

The ECU sends a duty cycle to open or close the purge valve, usually on light throttle when engine load is low.

## Stop-start

This feature switches the engine off when the vehicle is stationary, for example, at traffic lights or in queuing traffic. The system keeps comfort and information systems running via a separate battery and instantly starts the engine when the vehicle has to move. Some systems cut the engine below 15 km/h (forward travel) when the vehicle is slowing down, the engine can be restarted in less than 0.5 s. Some manufacturers claim this saves 10 per cent of fuel for urban driving. The system uses a clutch pedal sensor and a belt-driven starter/generator for smaller engines, or a flywheel starter/generator for larger engines.

> ### 12.5  General maintenance and testing of fuel-injection systems

### 12.5.1 General maintenance

The periodic maintenance of a fuel system involves checking the system for the security of electrical connections and fuel lines. The electrical/electronic system should be checked for wiring and component security and corrosion.

When a maintenance check is carried out, an inspection should be made for fuel leaks under pressure. Fuel-injection systems incorporate a fuel filter, so this must be changed at the appropriate time (e.g. every 48 months or 80,000 km). Direction of fuel flow through the filter is important, so it should be fitted as indicated by the arrow on the filter casing.

As part of a vehicle inspection or service, the engine fault codes should be checked; any stored P codes relate to the powertrain and will affect performance and emissions.

### 12.5.2 Testing the fuel system

Before carrying out specific tests on a fuel-injection system, basic engine checks should be made to ensure that these items are serviceable, such as plugs, timing, air intake, and so on. For safety reasons, it should be noted that any test involving the disconnection of a fuel line must take into account that the line is pressurised to the extent of up to 5 bar for multi-point and 120 bar for direct injection. Fuel pressure should be checked to confirm the condition of the fuel pump and regulator. This gauge connects to the fuel system via a Schrader valve and registers fuel pressure in bar when the engine or pump is running.

## EVAP system fault

Commonly, the purge valve might become faulty, causing the engine vacuum to draw the fuel directly into the engine, enriching the mixture. When inspecting the carbon canister, if it is full of fuel and extremely heavy, this could indicate a possible fault with the purge valve.

## How to depressurise a fuel system

Working on a pressurised fuel system can be dangerous, so the system should be depressurised for components to be removed safely. This can be done easily by removing the fuel pump fuse and starting the engine; this will run until the fuel in the system is used up. As the pump is not running, no fresh fuel is pumped from the tank. The filter, fuel lines, pressure rail and injectors are then purged, depressurising the system.

## Testing electrical/electronic system

As in the case of many other electronic components, ECUs can easily be damaged by workshop test equipment (and personnel), so care must be exercised when testing any part connected to an ECU.

An ECU can be damaged by:

- boost starting – using a high-speed battery charger for starting an engine
- electric welding – induced voltage from an electric welding plant will damage a semiconductor, so disconnect the battery earth to isolate the ECU before any welding
- steam cleaning – heat and steam will damage an ECU.

## Test equipment

Many manufacturers offer a range of portable test equipment for checking the operation of engine management systems to aid fault diagnosis.

One comparatively cheap tester, developed for modern fuel management systems, is a code reader that is plugged into the on-board diagnostics (OBD) socket. This type of tester is simple to use, but it can only be used to read the fault codes (Figure 12.20).

More advanced diagnostic equipment can display live streaming data and can operate actuators and carry out flash programming. This diagnostic equipment has become lightweight and portable, and the technician can see the signals from all the sensors and actuators at a glance.

## Multimeter tests

Fault diagnosis without using dedicated equipment is time consuming but, with the aid of a good digital multimeter and circuit diagram, it is possible to pinpoint the cause of a particular problem. This technique can still be required even when designated equipment is used. Because in many cases designated equipment only indicates the faulty sub-circuit and not the actual defect in this circuit.

Most ECUs are now fairly reliable, so a diagnostic test must start with an examination of all cables and connectors that link the units in the suspect sub-circuit.

Ensure that all connectors are secure and, bearing in mind that many faults in the past were due to bad contacts, it is suggested that each plug is wriggled to improve its conductivity.

In the absence of special equipment, knowledge of the circuit is essential. A wiring diagram must be used to locate terminal connections and numberings. In addition to indicating these cable terminations, it also enables you to estimate the voltage at each point (e.g. the voltage on both terminals of the injector will be about 12 V, the EMF of the battery, when the ignition is switched on and the engine is stationary).

Modern software programs supply digital wiring diagrams that are readily available, easy to find and user friendly. Paper diagrams are becoming obsolete.

*Figure 12.20 Code reader*

## Multimeter tests on petrol-injection systems

These should:

- be made in a logical sequence
- be made with a good-quality calibrated digital meter
- start at the power source where possible
- NOT be carried out until you are satisfied that all connectors and cables are securely fitted

- NOT involve the separation of any connector, especially cables carrying a sensor signal, unless it forms part of the test
- NOT involve resistance tests on any units that may be damaged by the meter current.

Fault diagnosis by substitution can be very costly, because a defect in another part of the circuit may, and often does, destroy the newly fitted unit; as when a cable shorts to earth and blows a fuse.

Tests should be carried out in a methodical manner: start at the source and proceed through the circuit to build up a clear picture of the operation of each part of the circuit. Repair operations should begin by finding out from the driver all the symptoms, before starting on a costly repair that may be unnecessary. Information gained will indicate the suspect area, so tests of this region will be a starting point. In many ways, this verbal analysis is similar to that used by dedicated equipment: the test computer scans all sub-circuits until it recognises that a part of the system is defective.

### Oscilloscope

The switching of digital circuits is too fast for a multimeter or even handheld diagnostic equipment, so an oscilloscope must be used to complete diagnosis of electronic systems.

The oscilloscope can be used to check sensors and actuators; available with two or four channels to process speedy data, it can also store the captured patterns. For testing engine management systems an oscilloscope's library of sensor and actuator patterns can be compared to check the correct function. A laptop, installed with the relevant software and hardware, can be used as an oscilloscope (Figure 12.21).

### Exhaust gas analyser

An exhaust gas analyser (Figure 12.22) can check the performance of the engine and catalyst. A sensing probe is placed in the exhaust tailpipe to sample the gas. This, in turn, is then displayed on the data screen. Commonly used four-gas analysers measure CO, $CO_2$, HC and $O_2$. A more superior five-gas analyser includes the measurement of $NO_X$.

Figure 12.21 Automotive oscilloscope

Figure 12.22 Exhaust gas analyser

## Tips for using a gas analyser for diagnostics

- Carbon monoxide (CO) – indicates partly burned fuel; a high content points to a rich mixture.
- Carbon dioxide ($CO_2$) – measures combustion efficiency; the higher the value the better the combustion.
- Hydrocarbons (HC) – unburned fuel measures engine inefficiency; high readings can indicate a misfire.

- Oxygen ($O_2$) – measures oxygen left after combustion; high levels indicate poor combustion, low levels indicate a rich mixture.
- Nitrogen oxides ($NO_X$) – formed when the combustion chamber temperature is higher than 1300 °C and increase rapidly when above 1800 °C. Abnormally high readings can indicate a faulty EGR valve.

This chapter will deal with the modern high-pressure **common rail direct fuel injection** systems and the electronic systems and sensors used in its operation.

**Common rail direct fuel injection**: the latest version of the fuel-injection system fitted to diesel combustion-ignition engines.

Diesel fuel-injection systems have advanced immeasurably in recent years from the mechanical in-line pumps and mechanical injectors to the modern high-pressure systems we now see. Although the systems now fitted are far more complex, they are also proving to be just as reliable and are delivering less noise and emissions with increased fuel economy and more power (torque).

Early systems would start with a low-pressure lift pump from the tank through a filter and into either a rotary or in-line pump. In-line pumps were normally used for larger heavy vans and trucks. The rotary pump had one rotating element fitted with a number of high-pressure outlets; the number of outlets matched the number of cylinders on the engine. As the pumping element rotated, it pressurised fuel within it. As it rotated further, an opening allowed the pressurised fuel to push along steel pipes to the mechanical injector; the increase in pressure in the system raised the injector needle off its seat and fuel was sprayed into the combustion chamber. When the pressure dropped, a spring pushed the needle back on to its seat again. All of the components were mechanical and operated on the high pressure provided by the mechanical pump. Speed and power were controlled by mechanical governors, which controlled the amount of fuel delivered and the power produced.

Common rail diesel fuel systems operate on far higher pressures than the earlier mechanical systems, and electronic sensors control and monitor temperature, timing, pressure and delivery of the fuel to ensure clean burning of the fuel and significant improvements in miles per gallon. The fuel is delivered from the tank through a filter by a low-pressure pump; this is then pressurised by a high-pressure pump and the pressurised fuel passed into the fuel rail. The pressure is allowed to rise and, if it exceeds a preset pressure, a pressure relief valve opens and allows fuel to flow back to the fuel tank. When the electronic control unit (ECU) determines that one of the electronically controlled solenoid injectors should open, then the fuel is injected into the combustion chamber. The high pressure ensures fine atomisation of the fuel, which ensures a cleaner burn. The latest piezo injectors can open and close so quickly that it is possible to have five injection phases within 1s.

Looking to the future, there will be higher operating pressures and wider use of microelectronics to further boost the already improved power outputs and emission reductions. Some manufacturers are already matching the latest diesel engines with hybrid technology; these production vehicles are returning mileage figures in the region of 75 mpg and current prototypes are boasting figures in the high 100s.

The use of stop-start technology for vehicles fitted with diesel engines is a recent addition and has also helped fuel economy. Although now commonplace on petrol engine vehicles, the use of stop-start on diesels has been restricted, awaiting the advance of the technology that allows the systems fitted to petrol engines to be modified to suit the characteristics of the diesel engine.

Many of the components fitted to diesel engine management systems (EMSs) have been commonplace in petrol EMSs for a number of years; it is only with the recent advances in electronics that these can be used on the compression-ignition diesel engines. This chapter deals with the latest electronic components and systems currently available and will also look to anticipate future developments.

## 13.1 Principles of operation

Diesel engine operation differs from petrol in that on the induction stroke only air is drawn in. The fuel is injected as the piston approaches **TDC**; at this point the compression of the air has heated it up to a temperature above the self-ignition point of the fuel. When the fuel is injected, it self-ignites and burns, releasing the energy required to drive the piston downwards. Most diesel (compression-ignition) engines run on an excess air mixture with the engine speed and power produced controlled by the amount of fuel injected.

**Top dead centre (TDC)**: the highest point of travel for the piston on the compression or exhaust stroke.

At idle, the air/fuel ratio for a non-common rail system can be as much as 145 : 1; at a partially opened throttle (POT) it will be approximately 45 : 1; and at wide-open throttle (WOT) it will be between 17 : 1 and 29 : 1. The main problem with varying the ratio has been that within the combustion chamber the fuel may not be atomised fully. The common rail system with direct injection and the extremely high operating pressures that are commonly found within them have led to better atomisation of the fuel. With the electronic control allowing over five separate injection points, the air/fuel ratio will vary, even between individual cylinders, but will usually be around 22 : 1 for naturally aspirated, turbocharged and supercharged engines. As mentioned before, the possibility of an increased number of injection points and injector patterns that can vary with pressure, mean that fuel can be directed to areas within the combustion chamber that have a weak mixture and withheld from areas that have an already burning rich mixture; this allows better fuel mixing and reduces soot particulates and $NO_x$ emissions.

## 13.2 Electronic diesel control (EDC) pump

The advance of electronics and modern electronic control has allowed a massive improvement in the operation of diesel-fuelled engines; these improvements in control have allowed engine designers to reduce emission and noise levels as well as increase the power output.

The common rail diesel engine with EDC manages the pressure of the fuel, the timing of injection and the duration of the injection period by using inputs from sensors in much the same way as a petrol electronic fuel-injection (EFI) system would.

The principal feature of the common rail system (Figure 13.1) is that the injection pressure is controlled independently from engine speed and fuel quantity injected. Pressure generation and injection are controlled by an accumulator system. This includes components such as fuel lines and injectors.

The pressure is generated by a high-pressure plunger pump. A radial-piston pump is used in passenger cars.

This type of pump requires low torque drive levels, which allow it to generate a high output pressure from a low torque input.

### 13.2.1 First generation pumps

One version of high fuel pressure generation is to have a two-chamber two-pump plunger arrangement; driven by an eccentric cam, which is driven at half engine speed. This type of pump permanently generates the high pressure for the fuel rail maximum system operating pressure, which is 1600 bar.

This pump is a mechanical device by nature but has some electrical control in the form of a fuel metering valve.

## Engine, engine management, and high-pressure fuel-injection components

17 high-pressure pump
18 metering unit
25 engine electronic control unit (ECU)
26 fuel rail
27 rail pressure sensor
28 pressure control valve (DRV 2)
29 injector
30 glow plug
31 diesel engine (01)
M torque

### A Sensors and setpoint generators

1 pedal-travel sensor
2 clutch switch
3 brake contacts (2)
4 operator unit for vehicle speed controller (cruise control)
5 glow plug and starter switch ('ignition switch')
6 road speed sensor
7 crankshaft speed sensor (inductive)
8 camshaft speed sensor (inductive or Hall sensor)
9 engine temperature sensor (in coolant circuit)
10 intake air temperature sensor
11 boost pressure sensor
12 hot film air mass meter (intake air)

### B Interfaces

13 instrument cluster with displays for fuel consumption, engine speed, etc.
14 air-conditioner compressor with operator unit
15 diagnosis interface
16 glow control unit CAN Controller area network (on-board serial data bus)

### C Fuel-supply system (low-pressure stage)

19 fuel filter with overflow valve
20 fuel tank with pre-filter and electric fuel pump (EFP) EFP (presupply pump)
21 fuel-level sensor

### D Additive system

22 additive metering unit
23 additive control unit
24 Additive tank

### E Air supply

32 exhaust gas recirculation cooler
33 boost pressure actuator
34 turbocharger (in this case with variable turbine geometry (VTG))
35 control flap
36 exhaust gas recirculation actuator
37 vacuum pump

### F Exhaust-gas treatment

38 broadband lambda oxygen sensor, type LSU
39 exhaust gas temperature sensor
40 oxidation type catalytic converter
41 particulate filter
42 differential pressure sensor
43 $NO_x$ accumulator type catalytic converter
44 broadband lambda oxygen sensor, optional $NO_x$ sensor

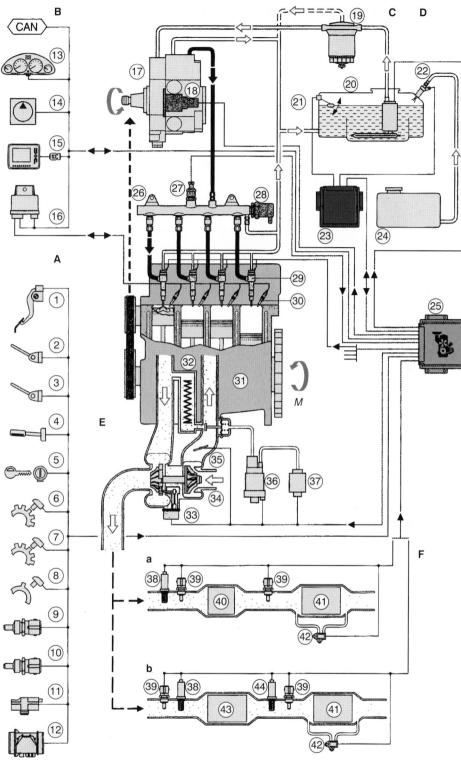

*Figure 13.1 Common rail fuel system*

## 13.2.2 High-pressure pumps: second and third generation

The three-piston high-pressure pump (Figure 13.2) is driven by the camshaft, either directly or via a toothed belt. This type of pump is a feature of the common rail system used in most light vehicles today.

The high-pressure pump is fitted with an electrical pressure control valve to regulate the fuel rail pressure; this is normally mounted on the pump or the fuel rail.

The latest high-pressure pumps also make use of a fuel-quantity control system, which helps to lower the temperature of the fuel within the system. If fuel temperatures reach $116\,°C$, the charge pressure is reduced in order to counteract a further rise in

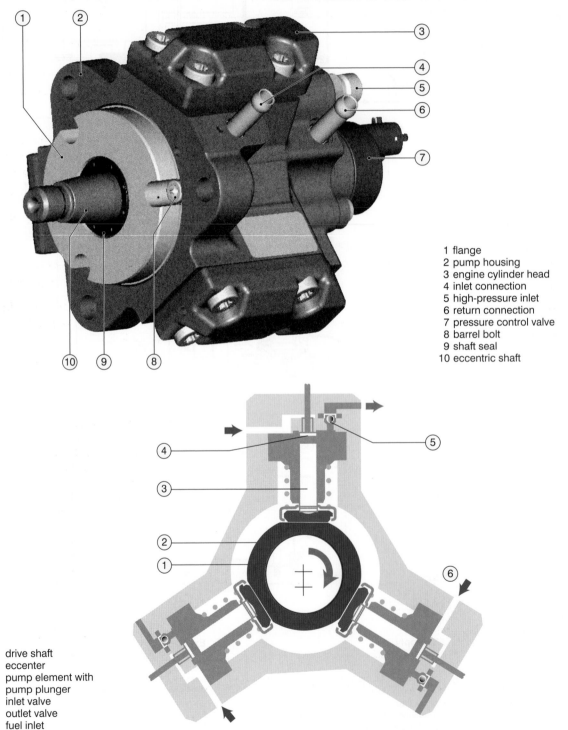

1 flange
2 pump housing
3 engine cylinder head
4 inlet connection
5 high-pressure inlet
6 return connection
7 pressure control valve
8 barrel bolt
9 shaft seal
10 eccentric shaft

1 drive shaft
2 eccenter
3 pump element with
  pump plunger
4 inlet valve
5 outlet valve
6 fuel inlet

*Figure 13.2 High-pressure pump*

temperature. If the temperature drops below 116 °C, the pressure is increased.

The pressure generated by the high-pressure pump pushes the fuel through a pressure-controlled circuit and is applied to the injector. There are a number of different injector types used.

### 13.2.3 Electromagnetic fuel injectors

First generation injectors are of the electromagnetic type. This type of actuator used 12V to open the injector with the fuel pressure helping to lift the needle, overcoming spring force.

The operating voltage of second generation injectors is 120V, generated by a power drive circuit amplifying 12V to 120V.

Upon opening the injector, a current of 20 Amps (A) is applied to the injector coil. This is done to make sure the injector opens quickly, under all operating conditions.

Once the injector is open, to avoid any resonance problems, a damping current of 8A is applied to the coil to avoid injector bounce. The current is rapidly reduced once conditions are met to increase circuit efficiency.

The injector is held open by a holding current of 4A once all other conditions are met, as previously discussed.

This type of fuel injector has a resistance of 2.1 Ω. Its full characteristics are programmed into the EDC system; if replaced with another unit, it must be recoded to the EDC system. These injector types are not serviceable.

The injector is one of the main components in the common rail system; the quantity of fuel injected is controlled by the fuel system pressure and the injector 'on' time.

On early common rail systems, the injection process was controlled by the use of magnetic solenoids fitted to the injectors; these have now been replaced by piezo crystal injectors. The injector uses a stack of piezo crystal plates, which expand extremely quickly when an electric current is applied to them. The speed of opening and closing is approximately twice that of a mechanical injector, which allows five to seven pulses of injection for each combustion cycle and, as there is no mechanical movement within the injector body, any movement is friction-free. The use of pilot injection and multiple injection with piezo injectors (Figure 13.4) allows much closer control of the combustion process. Benefits include a reduction in both noise and exhaust emissions and an increase in the power generated.

By using piezo injectors it is possible to achieve:

- multiple electrical activation up to seven times per cycle
- very short switching times 0.01 ms
- large forces to the current rail pressure
- high stroke precision for rapid rail pressure.

Rail pressure is dependent on engine variables; voltage to injectors also varies depending on variables, which can be 110–148V.

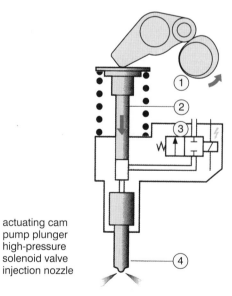

1  actuating cam
2  pump plunger
3  high-pressure
   solenoid valve
4  injection nozzle

(a) unit injector with combined pumping element for a common rail system

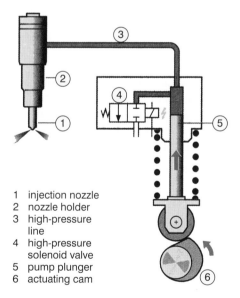

1  injection nozzle
2  nozzle holder
3  high-pressure
   line
4  high-pressure
   solenoid valve
5  pump plunger
6  actuating cam

(b) unit pump system for a common rail system

*Figure 13.3  Mechanical injector types used for early common rail systems*

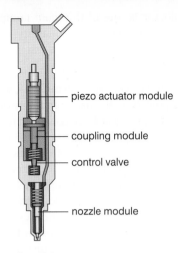

- piezo actuator module
- coupling module
- control valve
- nozzle module

*Figure 13.4 Piezo diesel injector*

High voltage is generated by a power inverter circuit and high-speed switching is carried out by transistors.

Power capacitors that discharge to the injectors are recharged by the injector due to power recuperation.

The next generation of common rail systems will incorporate fuel rail pressures of more than 2000 bar and injectors with variable-injection geometry.

## Euro 4/5/6 emission levels

Emission levels for diesel engine vehicles are covered in Chapter 11.

## Air/fuel ratios

Older diesel fuel systems had air/fuel ratios that were more challenging to control; engine speed governors and axial plungers altered the air/fuel ratio within fixed parameters. These systems used mechanical components for control.

The EDC sensors and actuators now control changes in air/fuel ratios so that diesel fuel systems can be finely controlled for a given engine application, giving air/fuel ratios closer to the stoichiometric value for perfect combustion.

Passenger cars and vans can share a particular engine type, with speed and load characteristics that can be changed by altering the EDC programming.

The accelerator position sensor transfers an analogue signal corresponding to the accelerator position to the EDC. To ensure that the electronic accelerator functions reliably, the accelerator position sensor has two independent potentiometers (P1 and P2). The control unit monitors the two sensors for proper functioning and plausibility. If one sensor fails, the other sensor serves as a substitute.

The accelerator position sensor transfers the driver's inputs to the EDC, which can control torque

output and emission levels depending on software requirements.

Torque-orientated management then decides whether high torque is necessary. This may give a high torque level and a small throttle opening when the engine is under a heavy load, regardless of the driver's foot pedal position.

### Turbochargers and superchargers

It is becoming increasingly common for diesel engine vehicles to be fitted with at least one and sometimes two **turbochargers**. Some vehicles will even have a **supercharger** fitted. The difference between the two is the drive system: a turbocharger is normally driven by the exhaust gases, whereas a supercharger is driven by a belt, either constantly or controlled by an electromagnetic clutch. Both are used to force more air into the combustion chamber; this is called forced induction.

**Turbochargers**: turbines driven by the exhaust gases, forcing air into the combustion chamber and allowing more fuel to be injected and burnt, which in turn generates more power.

**Superchargers**: turbines driven by a belt from the engine, forcing air into the combustion chamber and allowing more fuel to be injected and burnt, which in turn generates more power.

The electronic control on early chargers was restricted to monitoring inlet manifold pressure. If the pressure is too high, the ECU will open a waste gate fitted into the exhaust manifold and the pressure will reduce.

The latest models of turbocharger are fitted with variable geometry turbines (VGT); the ECU can alter the geometry inside the turbine to alter the available boost.

## 13.3 Cold start devices

The first diesel engines had simple **cold start devices** which fell into two categories:

- Cold start via glow plugs.
- Manifold heater via flame injector.

**Cold start device**: a component that is used to preheat the air entering the combustion chamber of a diesel compression-ignition engine. This is required to ensure that the air reaches the self-ignition temperature of the diesel fuel when it is injected into the chamber; the cold start devices also help to reduce smoke emissions from the cold engine.

Both systems needed some form of warm-up injector control, which was usually controlled via a wax thermostat; this is an electrically heated device that shuts off when the engine temperature reaches approximately 50 °C. Power shut-off is determined by a thermostat switch located in the cooling system.

## Glow plugs

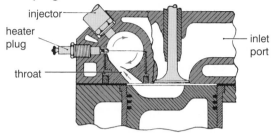

*Figure 13.5 Early glow plug pre-heater system*

Glow plugs had a power supply that fed electrical power to one glow plug per cylinder (Figure 13.6). A relay allowed low power from the battery to flow when the ignition key was switched to the 'on' position. A timing device that switched off the current was incorporated into the system; this would shut down after a predetermined time (normally around 10 s).

For cold start, the user would need to wait for a light to extinguish before cranking the engine. Within this time, the glow plugs would reach a temperature up to 800 °C, which is above the self-ignition temperature of diesel fuel.

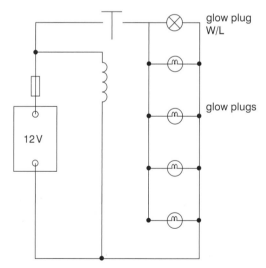

*Figure 13.6 Basic glow plug circuit*

## Flame injector

A large number of commercial vehicles are equipped with flame start systems to aid cold starting. An electrically operated heating element is switched on; once the heating temperature has been reached, a solenoid valve is opened and fuel is allowed to enter the evaporator. The flame produced heats up the

intake air and helps to ease cold starting, particularly at low temperatures.

Flame injector cold start devices (Figure 13.7) consist of a supply feed of diesel from the rotary or in-line diesel injector pump via a metal pipe to an injector. A low current power supply controls the opening and closing of the injector valve.

When the engine reaches a predetermined temperature, the power supply is interrupted and the fuel supply is closed.

*Figure 13.7 Flame start pre-heating evaporator*

Greater demands on cold starting systems, as well as varying operating temperatures, quieter cold running operation, greater emission control and fuel economy mean that modern diesel fuel systems use EDC and the cold start device for warm-up regulation rather than the driver waiting for a given period. Modern methods to heat the diesel combustion chambers use a pre- and post-heating system (Figure 13.8).

During the warm-up phase the use of post-start heating by the glow plugs ensures a cleaner burn of the fuel and there is also a reduction in diesel knock. This helps to reduce the amount of visible smoke from the engine when it is cold, and as the engine runs more quietly during the start-up phase this helps to prolong engine life.

Heating of the air in the combustion chamber can begin upon the user entering the vehicle cabin; delay warm-up time is minimal.

Upon starting the vehicle, ambient air temperature and engine coolant temperature will determine how long after the engine has started that post-heating will continue. This could be up to 60 s after the starting phase has elapsed.

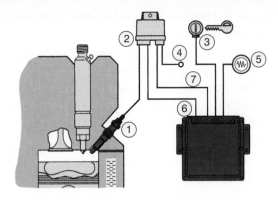

1  sheathed-element glow plug
2  glow control unit
3  glow plug and starter switch
4  to battery
5  indicator lamp
6  control line to the engine ECU
7  diagnosis line

*Figure 13.8 EDC cold start control*

## 13.3.1 The common rail system pilot injection phase

When starting on a cold day (–5 °C) cold starting procedures will be initiated when the ignition is turned on (the latest systems have automatic pre-warm on door entry) in order to pre-warm the combustion chamber. When the ignition switch is turned to the 'on' position, information on coolant temperature, ambient air temperature, accelerator position, fuel pressure, fuel temperature, and so on, are registered with the EDC for the start of combustion. When the key is turned to the start position or the start button is pressed, the starter motor turns the engine over at approximately 70 rpm. A high-pressure chamber in the high-pressure pump delivers slightly more than the minimum pressure required to open the injector (240 bar) and a small amount of fuel is sprayed into the cylinder. A very small quantity of this would be injected between 40° to 90° of the crankshaft angle rotation; this pilot injection phase gives a smoother ignition initiation to the main injection phase, which improves efficiency with the added benefit of a reduction in cylinder noise and emissions.

Other factors that affect the time duration of this phase are:

- engine speed exceeding 2500 rpm
- an injection flow rate above 40 mm$^3$
- a coolant temperature above 18 °C.

The advantage of pre- and post-heating systems include reduced emissions and reduced fuel consumption, as well as smoother and quieter engine operation.

## 13.4 Sensors

As detailed earlier in this chapter, common rail diesel engine management systems share similar sensors and actuators with petrol systems. For example:

- Crank angle sensor
- Camshaft position sensor
- Camshaft sensor
- Coolant temperature sensor
- Manifold absolute pressure (MAP) sensor
- Mass airflow meter hot vane
- Throttle pedal position sensor/actuator
- Brake pedal sensor
- Clutch pedal sensor
- Fuel temperature sensor
- Oil temperature sensor

### Camshaft sensor

The camshaft sensor is used to determine cylinder synchronisation with the crankshaft. Once this is established the EDC can operate the correct injector to inject fuel into the cylinder when the piston is in the appropriate position – this will be determined by the EDC.

### MAP sensor

The MAP sensor is normally connected to the intake manifold. The sensor provides a voltage to the EDC relative to the inlet manifold pressure. This type of MAP sensor uses a diaphragm transducer to measure pressure. The ECU uses the MAP sensor signal for the following functions:

- Maintain manifold boost pressure.
- Reduce exhaust smoke emissions when driving at high altitude.
- Control of the exhaust gas recirculation (EGR) system.

### Mass airflow meter

There are two main types of airflow meter in common use:

- Hot film
- Hot wire

### Hot film

The hot-film air mass meter is a thermal flow meter. A partial airflow from the measuring pipe is fed past the sensor element through a measuring channel in the air mass meter housing.

The ascertained temperature values are evaluated in the evaluation electronics. The system applies a voltage to the hot film; as the air flows across the film the voltage has to be altered to maintain the temperature. This increase or reduction in voltage is the reference for the EDC unit. This voltage is used to calculate the injection period and actual engine torque.

## Hot wire

The hot-wire meter (Figure 13.9) is not as common as the hot film; the flow of air is directed past a heated wire (hot wire), which forms part of an electrical bridge circuit. The current in the wire varies to keep it at a constant temperature higher than that of the intake air. A resistor converts the current used to heat the wire into a voltage signal, which is processed by the ECU as an input signal. A temperature sensor mounted in the airflow meter ensures that its output signal is not influenced by the temperature of the intake air. Each time the engine is shut down, the wire is electrically heated for 1 s to burn off any contamination. As this type of meter has no moving parts it is very reliable.

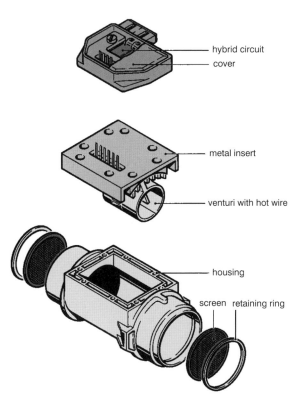

*Figure 13.9 Hot-wire air mass meter*

## Exhaust gas temperature sensor

This sensor is positive temperature coefficient (PTC) by design. For turbocharged engines, the maximum permissible exhaust gas temperature is a key design criterion. To protect the exhaust gas turbocharger and the exhaust manifold, the exhaust gas temperature should not exceed 900 °C for a lengthy period.

The evaluation electronics convert the signal, which the measuring sensor generates into a pulse width modulated (PWM) signal. This is a square wave signal with a fixed frequency and a variable pulse duty factor. If a sender fails, the charge pressure is reduced to a safe level and an emergency enrichment characteristic (engine speed-dependent) is used.

## Inlet air temperature sensor

This is part of the mass airflow meter sensor. The inlet air temperature sensor has a negative temperature coefficient (NTC); when the temperature is low the resistance is high. It has a supply voltage of 5 V from the EDC.

## Coolant temperature sensor

This sensor has a NTC; when the engine is cold the resistance is high and the EDC can ensure cold start enrichment can be initiated.

The signal from the temperature sensor is used for coolant temperature regulation in the coolant circuit; when the temperature reaches a predetermined point the cooling fan is switched on. The signal from the temperature sensor is also used as an input signal for the ECU to calculate injection periods.

## Brake light switch and brake pedal switch

Both switches are encased in one unit; they have a variable resistor fitted to record pedal travel. The information 'brake operated' is required for the following functions:

- Function of cruise control system.
- Safety interrogation of electronic accelerator function (idling speed recognition during emergency running mode of accelerator position sender).

When the brake light switch is open in the 'off' position, this serves as an additional information input for the EDC. When the brake pedal switch is closed in the 'off' position it serves exclusively as an information input for the EDC.

### Self-diagnosis

The two switches are cross-checked for plausibility by the self-diagnosis system; if one is found to be faulty, then the value from the second switch is used.

## Clutch pedal switch

The clutch switches are encased in one unit; they have a variable resistor fitted to record pedal travel.

Incorrect settings, electrical malfunctions or incorrect operation (driver keeps foot on clutch pedal) may result in load change jolts or engine speed overshoots. This can result in the cruise control system switching off or deactivation of the load change functions during the gearshift operation.

The load change function is controlled using ignition angle and throttle valve closing speed.

## Fuel tank and low-pressure fuel supply

All common rail systems have a fuel level sensor fitted; this comprises of a float connected to a rod, which is linked to a potentiometer. As the float rises the resistance decreases ($200\,\Omega$ empty, $20\,\Omega$ full) and as the float level falls the resistance increases.

## Fuel run-dry protocol

The latest common rail fuel systems adopt a run-dry strategy to maintain the fuel prime pressure at fuel run-out. As the components fitted to modern common rail fuel systems operate within very tight tolerances, it is imperative that fuel systems have adequate lubrication under all conditions.

Added to the software is a limp home mode that will be initiated when the fuel warning light is on and the fuel level descends to 4 litres. The EDC will initiate a misfire for 1 mile to warn the operator that the engine is due to shut down. Once shut down, the engine can be restarted but will shut down again after a further mile. The tank must be topped up with fuel to avoid possible system damage.

# 14

# Engine management

An engine management system (EMS) is one of the most important parts of a vehicle. It controls the operation of the engine in terms of performance, economy, reliability and emissions.

To fully understand the large and complex area of engine management and the mechanical systems that it controls, it will be broken down into more simple and manageable sections within this chapter. It should be remembered, however, that all the complex sub-systems within the EMS are interrelated – interacting with each other to allow the engine to operate in its most efficient manner.

## 14.1 Engine systems

Systems within and around an engine are both vast and complex. Their key objective is to control the operation of the engine in order to achieve maximum efficiency, as well as driveability and performance.

Ignition (the spark) and injection (the fuel) are two key examples of sub-systems within the engine's management.

To maintain reliability and to allow for diagnosis and repair, these types of system are separate in their functions, although they are linked in operation by the electronic control unit (ECU), which is effectively the brain of this system and its sub-systems.

### 14.1.1 System function and performance

It is important for designers to produce a system in which the various sub-systems can work in harmony so that the system as a whole can work effectively. When studying engine management, it is important to understand two aspects: function and performance. Firstly, the function of each component within a system and how that system works must be known and understood. Secondly, to understand the system's performance it is necessary to know the operating range of the system and its components. You need to know what each component should be doing under varying conditions, what signal it should be giving, and if not giving a correct signal, why not. This is a common diagnostic problem for technicians working on modern vehicles. Figure 14.1 shows the basic ignition layout.

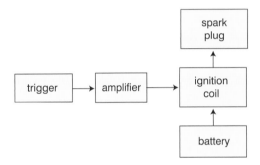

Figure 14.1 Electronic ignition system

### 14.1.2 Control systems

A control system is an arrangement that directs the operation of a main system.

The commands given by the control system should ensure that the main system performs according to a given program. This program will have been devised to achieve a given performance; in the case of an engine, this may be the production of a given output, the achievement of a set economy, or the limitation of a given exhaust by-product.

To achieve a set program within the parameters of the control system's scope, the system must be able to respond quickly and accurately to changes in the operating conditions, maintain a stable control and be able to separate valid input signals from those that are induced into the sensing lines by electrical disturbances (i.e. the system should have '**electrical noise** immunity'). Most systems use appropriate shielding methods in order to reduce any noise issue that could affect the signal that reaches the engine/ECU.

**Electrical noise**: unwanted fluctuating interference with a signal, due to the operation of other nearby circuits and sensors. It can cause an incorrect signal to be read and so alter the output signal of a sensor.

The two main systems of control are:

- open-loop control
- closed-loop control.

### 14.1.3 Open-loop control

This type of control sends commands to the main system but does not have the ability to check or monitor the actual output of the main system (Figure 14.2). Assuming the main system is an engine, then once a control signal has been delivered, the engine will produce its output. However, this output will not always be the same if the engine operating conditions alter. (E.g. if the engine control system does not take into account any ambient conditions such as air temperature, which leads to a change in density, then any variation in this condition will alter the power output and will not be corrected by the control system.)

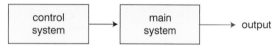

*Figure 14.2 Open-loop control*

Although an open-loop control system is suitable for many applications, it cannot be used where the engine has to operate within narrow limits, for example, where exhaust emissions must be controlled closely to meet environmental legislation requirements (Euro Standards).

Open-loop control is still used for some fuel-supply and ignition systems. In these applications the fuel mixture and ignition timing settings are arranged so that they follow independent programs. Ideally, any change in the air/fuel ratio should be accompanied by an alteration in the timing, but in many cases this is not so. Consequently, the engine performance is lower than expected, economy is poor and high exhaust emissions result. To overcome this problem, all new vehicles produced since July 1992 now use closed-loop control systems.

#### Applications of open-loop control

- Open-loop is often operated during cold starting of an engine as the oxygen sensor installed within the exhaust system is not yet up to operating temperature and is unable to supply reliable data to the computer for controlling the air/fuel ratio. Therefore, mixture control is regulated by a program stored in the ECU.

- In older cars, the less advanced EMS and less strict legislation regarding emission control meant that the air/fuel ratio was controlled by a set of **look-up tables** with no feedback correction signal to optimise fuel metering.

**Look-up tables**: tables of data that have been created to help reduce the time the ECU spends processing incoming data from various engine sensors before sending an output to an actuator. The answers are retrieved from the tables to cut down on calculations. They are most commonly used for ignition and fuelling systems.

### 14.1.4 Closed-loop control

This is similar to an open-loop system but has one very important addition: it has a means for measuring the output of a system and feeding back a signal to allow a comparison to be made between the command signal and the system's output – a form of checking and adjusting to suit any condition.

The feedback signal from the output sensor is passed back to the input where it is compared by use of an error amplifier. This intensifies and processes the signal to allow it to be compared with the input command. If the output differs from that commanded by the input, the command signal is altered until the required output is obtained.

When this control system is applied to an engine, the feedback facility allows any variation in the output to be corrected. This provides a more accurate and stable output than is possible with an open-loop system.

Furthermore, the system can be made to respond quickly and correct any changes in the operation conditions. If these conditions were not compensated for, the output would be very different from that intended, and could result in extensive damage to the engine.

Two forms of closed-loop control are:

- proportional control
- limit cycle control.

A closed-loop proportional control system uses a sensor in the output to generate a signal proportional to the output. Therefore, the magnitude of the feedback signal indicates the system's output.

A closed-loop limit cycle control system uses the feedback to signal when a given limit is exceeded. The output sensor is inoperative during the normal operating range, but when a preset limit is exceeded, the feedback circuit passes a signal back to the input. This allows an alteration to be made to the command input.

This type of control has a number of automotive applications, such as combustion knock and fuel control.

## Applications of closed-loop control

The most common application is the engine fuelling closed-loop system (Figure 14.3). Correct air/fuel ratio is vital to gaining optimum power and low emissions. The optimum ratio, known as the stoichiometric or chemically correct (CC) ratio, is 14.7:1 (based on mass of air to fuel). Either side of this, the conditions are known as lean (>14.7) or rich (<14.7).

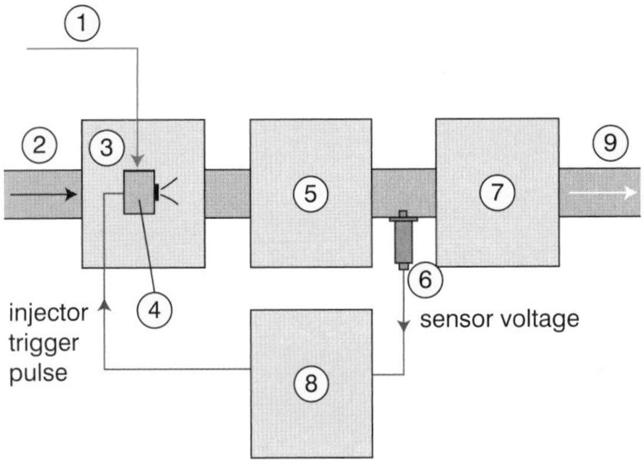

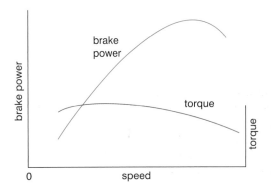

1 fuel
2 air
3 central injection unit
4 fuel injector
5 engine
6 lamda oxygen sensor
7 catalytic converter
8 ECU with lambda closed-loop control
9 exhaust gas

*Figure 14.3 Closed-loop control applied to the engine fuelling system*

This system uses an oxygen ($O_2$)/lambda sensor ($\lambda$) in the exhaust to monitor the air/fuel ratio of the engine. The sensor sends a signal back to the ECU, which informs it of the oxygen content in the exhaust compared with that of the ambient air. From this the ECU can calculate what the air/fuel ratio is and then alter the engine's fuelling and ignition to correct it. Being closed-loop, this system is monitored and altered constantly to stay within the correct parameters.

Open-loop control operates this system on engine start-up, while the lambda sensor heats up. It uses a predetermined fuel map and the system switches to closed-loop when the $O_2$ sensor is up to working temperature (minimum $300\,°C$). This switching can be seen on a diagnostic scanning tool.

## 14.2 Engine mapping

Open-loop digital systems store ignition timing and fuel mixture data in a memory unit of the ECU. The data stored in the individual cells of the computer's memory can be represented graphically by a characteristic map or as a large data table. Information for this 'graph' is obtained by carrying out a series of tests on the engine. The program for these tests is called engine mapping. Engine mapping is carried out by manufacturers during development and design of a vehicle. It is also used by many aftermarket tuning companies when the set data is no longer appropriate for the engine set-up or conditions of use.

These tests measure the performance and investigate the effects of each variable that has some bearing on the output of the engine. When the effects are known, the settings that give the best performance can be determined and noted. This is a time-consuming process, yet one that can yield the most gains in terms of performance and emissions.

A dynamometer (either engine- or chassis-based) is an essential item for these tests since it can be programmed to simulate road conditions. The engine is loaded by means of a 'brake' (operated using a water pump system or eddy current), and the torque, power output, economy and emissions are measured against speed and other factors that have some effect on the engine output (Figure 14.4).

*Figure 14.4 Engine characteristic: full load test (throttle full open)*

## 14.2.1 Engine maps

Performance curves plotted by a computer show graphically the behaviour of the engine when it is subjected to changes in the following:

- Speed
- Load (throttle opening)
- Ignition timing
- Air/fuel ratio
- Engine and ambient temperatures/pressures

A graph is the obvious choice for observation as it is much easier for quick reference, in comparison to a data table. It is, therefore, easy to analyse curve characteristics, such as gradient, maximum and minimum values and, more importantly, any irregularity within the performance of the engine, such as a dip in power or air/fuel ratio.

The performance curves derived from the tests are called engine maps. Some of the more important maps that are analysed are included below.

## Torque vs. consumption loop

This map is obtained by varying the air/fuel ratio and measuring the fuel consumption and torque output for each setting. Speed is kept constant during each test so a series of tests is needed to cover the engine operating range.

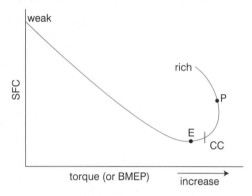

*Figure 14.5 Torque/consumption loop*

Figure 14.5 shows the characteristic fish hook-shaped map, which is obtained when the engine is operated under full load. On the *y*-axis (vertical axis) the specific fuel consumption (SFC) is plotted. These values are obtained from the equation:

$$SFC = \frac{\text{fuel consumption (kg/h)}}{\text{brake power (kW)}}$$

The SFC indicates the quantity of fuel that is needed to produce one unit of power.

*Table 14.1 Power conversion*

| Horsepower | Kilowatts |
| --- | --- |
| 1 hp | 0.735 kW |
| 25 hp | 18.39 kW |
| 50 hp | 36.775 kW |
| 75 hp | 55.16 kW |
| 100 hp | 73.550 kW |
| 125 hp | 91.94 kW |
| 150 hp | 110.32 kW |

The map shows that when the engine is run on a weak mixture, the SFC is high and the torque output is low. As the mixture is enriched, the consumption falls to point E, where maximum economy is achieved. Enriching the mixture past this point gives an increase in torque but at the expense of fuel. Maximum torque and power occur at point P. It will be seen that the stoichiometric ratio of 14.7:1 gives neither maximum torque nor maximum economy. To achieve these outputs, the mixture must be slightly enriched or slightly weakened, respectively.

## Exhaust emission vs. air/fuel ratio

Before exhaust emission regulations were introduced, the mixture supplied was based on the air/fuel ratio required to give either maximum power or maximum economy. Unfortunately the 12–15 per cent enrichment from the stoichiometric ratio to give maximum power also gives a high emission of health-damaging exhaust gases, such as carbon monoxide (CO), hydrocarbons (HC) and nitrogen oxide ($NO_x$).

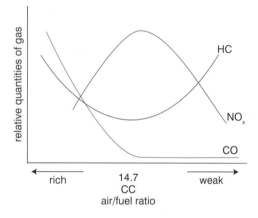

*Figure 14.6 Exhaust emissions*

Figure 14.6 shows the relationship between the formation of undesirable gases and the air/fuel ratio. This map shows the need to avoid operating the engine on an enriched mixture if exhaust pollution is to be kept to a minimum, hence the use of lean-burn engines in modern petrol road cars. Comparing the results shown in Figure 14.6 with Figure 14.5 indicates that lean-burn engines designed to operate with minimum exhaust pollution suffer a considerable increase in consumption and decrease in power if the air/fuel ratio is weakened beyond the economy point E. The tolerance is very small, so close control of fuel metering is needed if satisfactory output, combined with freedom from engine damage, is to be achieved.

## Spark timing and engine performance

The general effects of varying the spark timing are well known. Maximum power over the speed range is achieved when the spark is timed so that maximum gas pressure occurs at 12° after top dead centre (TDC). Reducing the spark advance for a set engine speed reduces the power, increases the fuel consumption and, as a result of the slower burning mixture, overheats the engine. An over-advanced spark also gives poor performance but, in addition, is likely to cause combustion knock (detonation), which quickly damages pistons and causes a high level of noise due to 'pinking'.

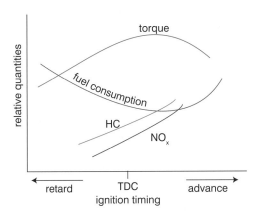

*Figure 14.7 Effect of varying emission timing*

In addition to these effects, spark timing also alters the exhaust by-products. Figure 14.7 shows a map obtained from running an engine at one set speed and load, and altering the ignition timing. This map allows the best setting of the spark to be determined.

### Factors affecting spark timing

Spark timing to achieve a set power depends on three main factors:

- Speed – as the speed increases, the crank moves through a larger angle in the time taken for the gas to burn.
- Load – as the load is increased, the throttle has to be opened a larger amount to maintain a set speed. This increases the gas filling of the cylinder and, as a result of the higher compression pressure, the flame rate is increased and the gas burns more quickly.
- Air/fuel ratio – a weaker mixture takes longer to burn than the stoichiometric ratio.

By using a series of maps, the effects of these three factors can be determined and the optimum timing can be established. The following is a summary of the timing requirements.

The spark timing advance is increased when:

- the engine speed is increased
- the air/fuel ratio is weakened.

The spark timing advance is decreased when:

- the engine load is increased
- the exhaust emission of HC and $NO_X$ is too high.

Fuel mixture requirements are allied to engine load because when the engine is under light load, or if the vehicle is cruising, a weaker mixture is supplied for economy purposes. Conversely, a full-load condition indicates that high engine power is needed, so a stronger mixture has to be provided by the fuel system. Since the air/fuel ratio is dictated by the load on the engine, the spark timing needs only be responsive to load and speed. For this reason, most timing maps are based on these two variables.

### Three-dimensional maps

After performing a series of engine tests at different loads to determine the optimum angle of advance with respect to speed, a large number of maps are obtained. These maps can be reduced to a single map by using the three-dimensional (3-D) form, as shown in Figure 14.8. The three axes of the map ($x$, $y$ and $z$) represent engine speed, spark advance and load, respectively. Accuracy of the timing requirement depends on the number of tests used to construct the map. In the simple map shown, a total of 60 timing settings are used. To determine the spark advance for

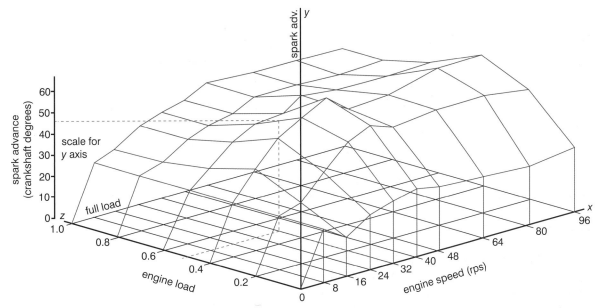

*Figure 14.8 Typical 3-D spark advance map*

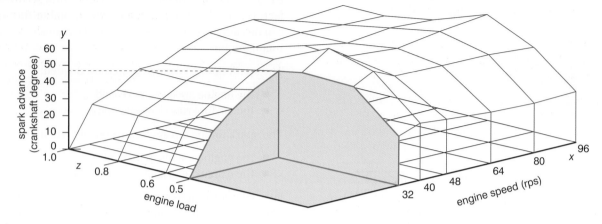

*Figure 14.9 3-D spark advance map showing the spark timing at 32 rps and half engine load*

a speed of 32 rps (revolutions per second) (1920 rpm)) and a half-load condition, the 32 point on the *x*-axis is located and the line from this point is followed until it intersects the half-load line. At this intersection the height of the map indicates the advance. In this case the angle is 46° (Figure 14.9).

### Fuel mixture map

A 3-D map is used to show the fuel requirements of an engine. In this case the three factors are: engine speed (*x*), air/fuel ratio (*y*) and engine load (*z*). Plotting these on the appropriate axes indicates the air/fuel ratio that is needed to suit the conditions of speed and load (Figure 14.10).

This map is often called a lambda map. 'Lambda' is the name of the Greek letter '$\lambda$', which is used to represent the following ratio:

$$\lambda = \frac{\text{Supplied quantity of air}}{\text{Theoretical air requirement}} = 1$$

When the mixture is at the stoichiometric ratio, the value of $\lambda$ is 1. To use a more technical term, $\lambda$ is then the stoichiometric ratio.

Lambda 1 is equal to an air/fuel ratio of 14.7 : 1. To convert it:

$$\lambda = \frac{\text{air/fuel ratio}}{14.7}$$

When $\lambda$ is less than 1, there is insufficient air for combustion (i.e. the mixture is rich). Conversely, when $\lambda$ is more than 1, there is excess air (i.e. the mixture is weak).

To summarise:

- $\lambda = 0.95$ – mixture rich
- $\lambda = 1.00$ – mixture correct
- $\lambda = 1.05$ – mixture weak

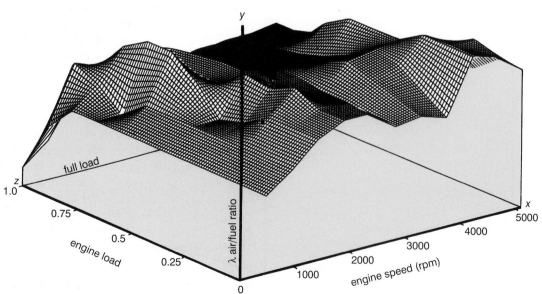

*Figure 14.10 Fuel mixture map*

## 14.3 Open-loop control

Control arrangements based on the open-loop principle have been in common use since the engine was first introduced.

Before about 1935 the driver not only had to manipulate the main controls, but also had to adjust the ignition timing and set the air/fuel mixture. This demanded considerable skill since it involved setting the ignition to a point where the engine was just knock-free and keeping the mixture at the point where it was just rich enough to develop maximum power. In later years, these duties were taken over by open-loop systems. These automatically controlled the ignition and fuel mixture settings in accordance with signals received from engine sources that indicated its speed and load.

### 14.3.1 Ignition timing control

An early development was the introduction of automatic timing by use of a centrifugal timer. This speed-sensitive unit advanced the spark to ensure that maximum cylinder pressure was maintained at about 12° after TDC over the full speed range.

This type of automatic control assumes that the burn time between spark and maximum pressure remains constant in time. Weakening the air/fuel mixture makes this burn time longer, so when economy carburettors came into use in the late 1930s, the weaker mixture delivered by this type of carburettor during part-load operation required a larger advance than that given by the centrifugal timer. This was provided by a load-sensitive vacuum control unit. The spring-loaded diaphragm used the manifold depression to sense engine load and, since the carburettor also used this source for the same purpose, the actions of the ignition timing control and the carburettor were harmonised.

In later years, greater precision of the timing was needed, so electronics were used. This took the form of an ECU, in which the timing requirements are stored in a memory unit. The timing data must relate the timing of the spark to the two factors previously taken into account by the original systems, namely engine speed and engine load (Figure 14.11).

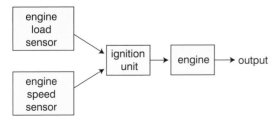

*Figure 14.11 Ignition timing system*

The modern open-loop system is a large improvement over earlier designs, but one drawback is that it has to assume that the engine is in the same condition as that used when the memory was programmed. When this is not so, the timing given by the look-up table in the ECU will be unsuitable for the engine. As a result, emission, economy and power will all suffer and this is unacceptable with modern emission restrictions.

### 14.3.2 Fuel-mixture control

Development of the constant-choke carburettor brought about mixture-compensation systems to correct for enrichment of mixture with increase in load/speed. This was followed by economy systems, which weakened the mixture during part-load operation.

Methods for improving mixture distribution and poor **atomisation** at low speeds received considerable attention from carburettor manufacturers, but the benefits of fuel injection with respect to these problems did not become attractive until stricter emission controls were introduced.

> **Atomisation**: breaking down of fuel into a fine mist spray to allow the air and fuel to mix effectively and allow for better combustion. Modern road cars achieve this using high-pressure fuel injectors, which force the fuel through tiny holes at the end of the injector.

Both carburettor and fuel-injection systems must be capable of sensing engine load and engine speed, so these factors must be measured by the main sensing system. Mechanical and electronic sensing systems suffer the same drawback as the ignition unit: they can only follow the program introduced when the engine is made. Variable factors (e.g. air leaks past the pistons, valve guides, throttle spindles, etc.) are not taken into account, so output will suffer. The introduction of more sensors improves the situation as electronic systems can take into account many more variables than those used with mechanical systems.

### Combined ignition and fuel-supply systems

Previous studies show that both the ignition timing and fuel-supply systems require sensors to measure engine speed and engine load. Duplication of the basic sensors and control electronics is uneconomic, so in many cases the two systems are combined to form a single EMS in which sensors and feedback are shared, avoiding excessive use of sensors, wiring and, ultimately, cost.

Combination of the two systems allows other sensing signals to be used jointly by ignition and fuel systems, so greater precision of control is possible.

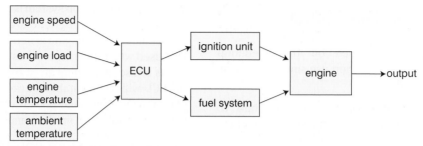

*Figure 14.12  Combined ignition and fuel system*

These additional peripheral devices include the measurement of ambient and engine temperatures, and other factors that affect the operation of the engine (Figure 14.12).

### 14.3.3 Use of engine maps

To achieve precise control of an engine that has no means for feeding back output data, the control system must be programmed with very accurate information relating to the setting that is required for each condition under which the engine is expected to operate.

This program should ensure that the input command produces the expected engine response.

Control maps compiled during the engine development stage show the settings of the main systems in relation to the variables that affect the particular systems. The control data indicated by the maps is programmed permanently into the computer's memory unit.

The computer uses the stored data in various ways. One way is to operate the computer so that it calculates the ignition and fuel mixture settings each time the speed or load conditions change. This computation may take as long as 100 ms to perform and, since this operation may have to be repeated at 50 ms intervals, a quicker method is needed. This is achieved by using look-up tables.

### Look-up tables

A look-up table is a list of related values stored in the memory unit of a computer. This table relates the output settings given by the computer to the input signals received from a given sensor.

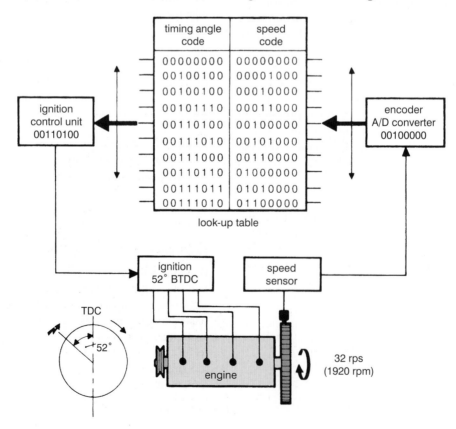

*Figure 14.13  Spark timing look-up table*

The principle used by a computer when it is performing this duty is easier to understand by considering the example of the spark timing look-up table shown in Figure 14.13. This has been constructed from the engine map illustrated in Figure 14.8. To simplify the example, only the speed factor is considered at this stage.

Assuming the engine is running at 32 rps (1920 rpm), the appropriate sensor signals this speed to the ECU. After entering the computer, the signal initially is converted by an encoder into the 8-**bit** digital form 00100000; this is the **binary code** for the number 32.

**Bit**: a binary digit, which may be either 0 or 1.

**Binary code**: a method of representing text or computer-based information using only the numbers 0 and 1. Binary code is made up of a sequence of 8 digits (or bits), each of which can have one of two values: 0 or 1. The sequence can represent up to 256 values, and each of these may stand for a number, letter, symbol or instruction.

The code is then stored in one of the registers of the central processing unit (CPU) and the memory is searched until a similar code is recognised. When the search has been completed and the result verified, the memory unit then issues another binary code, such as 00110100. This is the code that the computer has been programmed to write whenever it reads the code 00100000 (i.e. the matching value in its look-up table). The 8-bit code is the spark timing instruction to the ignition control unit, so, after it has been deciphered, the control unit sets the spark to occur at 52° before TDC.

Although this example is limited to a table of 10 values, a modern computer has a much larger table.

In addition to the spark advance/speed table, extra look-up tables covering other variables are stored in the memory unit. Spark advance depends mainly on load and speed, so the advance given in the engine load look-up table must be added to the value given by the engine speed look-up table. This calculation is performed by the computer very quickly because it involves only the addition of the values given by the look-up tables.

To obtain this method of control, development must progress through the following steps:

1  Mapping of the prototype engine to determine the best settings.
2  Construction of maps to show graphically the required settings to suit the varying operating conditions.
3  Programming the computer's look-up tables with the data contained in the maps.
4  Testing the engine to verify that the computer is giving out control instructions in accordance with the requirements.

### Detailed maps

To achieve the best possible engine performance, the various maps should closely follow the requirements of the engine. This involves the use of maps with many more reference points than those used in Figure 14.8, and the fitting of an engine management computer that has a memory unit of sufficient capacity to store the detailed look-up tables. Without the large

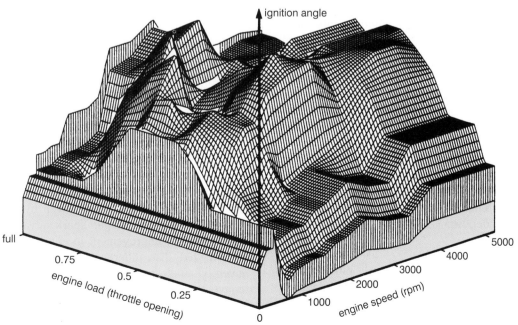

*Figure 14.14 Detailed map for electronic spark advance*

memory capacity to store detailed look-up tables, the gaps in between each data field will mean that the engine will run less efficiently.

An example of a detailed map is shown in Figure 14.14.

## 14.4 Closed-loop control

The accuracy of setting the ignition timing and metering the fuel in an open-loop system is only as good as the mechanical condition of the engine and the program for the control function. Systems using the open-loop principle can only follow a program set-up after testing a prototype engine in a first-class mechanical condition. If the engine is not in a similar condition, then the timing and fuel settings will be incorrect. This problem can be illustrated by highlighting the problem of setting the ignition timing of an older type engine with the aid of a strobe light. Although the timing may be set to the angle recommended by the manufacturer, it may not be the ideal setting for the actual engine being tuned.

These problems can be minimised by using a closed-loop control system. This system can be applied independently to manage ignition and fuel metering or can be combined to give a full engine management system.

### 14.4.1 Ignition control

The correct ignition timing for an engine is where combustion is just free from knock. On modern engines this setting cannot be obtained accurately without special equipment because knock occurs before it can be detected by the human ear (although knock sensors fitted between cylinder walls can be probed to monitor this). Many factors affect the maximum spark advance that can be used before the onset of knock. These include:

- mechanical condition of engine
- compression ratio
- octane rating of fuel
- volumetric efficiency
- throttle opening
- shape of combustion chamber
- air/fuel ratio
- engine temperature
- carbon deposits.

#### What is knock?

Also known as 'detonation' and 'pinking', this unwanted trait occurs in petrol (spark-ignition) engines and when there are a number of uncontrolled combustions of air/fuel pockets once the controlled combustion has commenced. This creates an unexpected shockwave that causes a metallic knocking noise and can be destructive to an engine.

It should not be confused with pre-ignition, which occurs when the air/fuel mixture ignites before the spark plug sparks. This can be due to hot spots on the cylinder walls, a spark plug running too hot or carbon deposits.

To program for all these variables would require a very sophisticated open-loop system having many sensors, together with an elaborate map containing a very large number of ignition angles. This is not possible, so a simpler map is used for normal open-loop systems. This map gives suitable ignition angles to meet general needs but maintains a margin of safety to keep the engine free from knock and damage.

#### Knock control

This safety margin can be reduced with the result that better power and improved emissions can be obtained if a sensitive knock control system is used. With this closed-loop control system, the feedback signal generated by the knock sensor (see page 191, Figure 14.6b) is used to adjust the spark timing so that combustion in the chamber is set to be just knock-free.

It has long been known that a large spark advance is needed to obtain maximum power and economy from an engine, but when the spark is over-advanced, combustion knock will occur. Knock should be avoided for two reasons: the sound is undesirable; and it is likely to cause engine damage, particularly if it occurs when the engine is under heavy load.

Modern lean-burn engines are prone to knock, so when the ignition advance is programmed into a memory unit, a margin of safety is maintained to keep the engine knock-free. In view of this, the advance angle is set considerably less than the ideal. Even so, the engine still enters the knock region if an inferior grade of fuel is used or when engine wear alters the spark advance requirement.

This can be overcome by using a knock limiter to slightly retard the ignition at the first sign of detonation. Engine protection given by this device allows the use of a larger spark advance than is normal, so an improvement in engine performance is achieved. The difference in the spark advance given by an electronic unit with spark control and a conventional mechanical system is shown in Figure 14.15. This graph illustrates how an electronic system can be made to match the ideal requirement more closely.

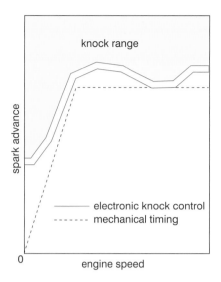

Figure 14.15  Advantage of knock control

A knock control system, as shown in Figure 14.17, consists of a sensor, evaluation circuit, control circuit and an actuator. The knock sensor is mounted on a part of the engine that allows it to detect sound waves transmitted through the engine structure when detonation takes place. A piezo-ceramic disc is the active component of the sound-transducer sensor. This delivers a small voltage signal when it is triggered by pressure oscillations. (See Figure 14.16 for the construction and operation of a knock sensor.)

Initially the timing is set using the data contained in the characteristic map. This basic timing setting is then advanced by the ECU until the knock sensor detects a given degree of knock. When the sensor signals that the engine is knocking, the timing advance is reduced in steps of 1.5 crankshaft degrees until the sensor indicates that the engine is knock-free. The continual repetition of this sequence ensures that the timing for each individual cylinder is maintained at the optimum angle (Figure 14.17).

The analogue signal from the sensor is filtered in a bandpass filter and fed to an integrator. After A/D (analogue to digital) conversion, the signal flow is split up, with one branch leading to the reference signal processing stage. The reference signal generated is the mean value of the previous power strokes. The actual signal is compared in a comparator, which furnishes information about the presence or absence of engine knock for each cylinder. When knock is detected, the control circuit retards the spark in accordance with a given program.

The knock-control system incorporates a safety circuit, which recognises malfunctions of the system. At times when a fault is detected, a warning light on the instrument panel is activated and the ignition timing advance is reduced sufficiently to prevent damage to the engine.

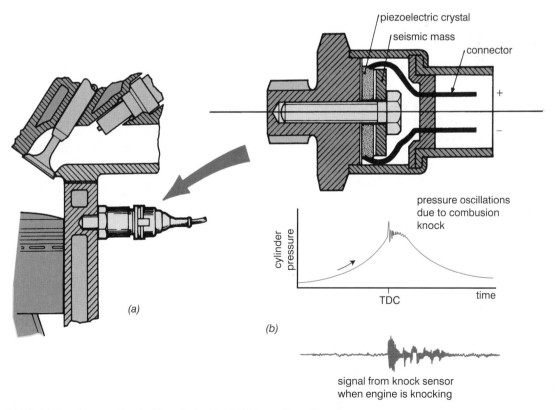

Figure 14.16  (a) Knock sensor located in cylinder block, (b) operation of knock sensor

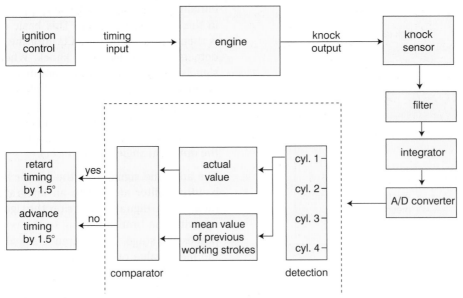

*Figure 14.17 Knock-control system*

## Closed-loop dwell-angle control

This feature is used to ensure that the correct primary current is achieved under conditions of differing battery voltage, engine speed and temperature.

This is particularly important when the engine is cold-started, because at this time the voltage applied to the coil is much lower than normal. To allow for this, a longer time must be allowed for the primary current to build up (i.e. the dwell must be lengthened). Conversely, if the dwell angle is set electronically at too large an angle, then power loss and heating of the ignition system is experienced.

Like other closed-loop systems, the dwell-angle control circuit uses a feedback circuit to signal when the primary current exceeds a predetermined value. When the signal is passed to the dwell-angle control section, the dwell angle is reduced accordingly.

## 14.5 Digital closed-loop ignition control

This system provides the next step in the evolution from the breaker-less arrangements first used on vehicles in the late 1970s.

After a time, moving parts in a conventional distributor drive begin to wear and when any slackness in the drive affects spark timing, some of the advantages of a breaker-less electronic system are lost. The timing variation due to component wear, together with the introduction of more stringent emission and fuel-economy regulations, has forced many manufacturers to use a distributor assembly and ignition control unit that:

- provides optimum spark timing to suit all load and speed conditions; in particular, providing a high degree of advance at light load
- gives a constant energy output over the full speed range as needed by lean-burn engines
- gives a spark timing that allows the engine to operate just clear of the detonation region.

These requirements are achieved by using a solid state, digital control unit to perform the duties undertaken originally by the mechanical advance mechanism (i.e. an electronic system replaces the centrifugal and vacuum control units used previously in a distributor).

Microelectronic memories in which the stored data cannot be changed are called read-only memories (ROMs). Sometimes the manufacturer wishes to buy a standard memory chip and then program it to suit a given application: this is called an EPROM (erasable programmable ROM) and is used when the number of units required is limited.

### 14.5.1 Electronic spark advance (ESA)

Besides controlling the dwell period to suit the engine speed, this unit also varies the angle of advance, by electronic means. A memory chip is programmed with data obtained from prototype engine tests to give the optimum advance needed for the best performance in respect of power, economy, acceleration and emission.

Two main factors dictate the angle of advance: they are speed and engine load. Figure 14.8 shows a typical map of spark advance that is programmed into a memory chip. It is normally shown as a 3-D graph with three axes ($x$, $y$ and $z$) representing engine speed, spark advance and engine load, respectively.

Angle of advance is the 'contour height' from the axis or base of the map to the intersection point obtained from set conditions of speed and engine load. For each step of speed and load, the map shows the spark advance that should be given.

A typical control grid is subdivided into 16 throttle positions (engine load) and 16 engine speed positions, thus providing 16 × 16 or 256 memory calibration points. On more expensive systems, an additional computer program allows each one of these points to give even more control of the timing (512 or even more).

The single-chip minicomputer fitted in the control module needs three basic input signals to allow it to search its memory so that it can trigger the spark at the correct time. These signals relate to engine speed, position of the engine crankshaft, and engine load, which can be sensed by the manifold depression or throttle position. Normally, analogue sensors search out this information and then transmit the electrical signals to the control module. After the signal has been processed, it is converted to a digital form by an A/D converter.

Figure 14.18 shows an alternative method for displaying data stored in a memory unit. The two axes represent the digital signals needed to indicate the correct angle of advance for the engine. For example, when the digital signals received from the speed and load sensors are 3 up and 2 across, the memory output will read 33. After this memory output has been processed, the spark will be triggered 33° in advance of the time when the crank angle sensor sends its reference signal.

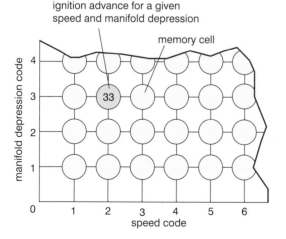

*Figure 14.18 Ignition advance data*

This advance setting is called up after each revolution of the engine, so when the sensors detect a slight change in either the engine speed or load, a suitable alteration in the spark timing is made.

Figure 14.19 shows a first generation digital electronic system. An ESA unit can be made as a discrete (separate) or hybrid module. Hybrid systems lend themselves particularly well to mass production and, since they fulfil other duties besides ignition control, the cost, weight and size are all reduced. In the hybrid system the conductors, contact surfaces and resistors are printed, but most semiconductors and capacitors are soldered in place.

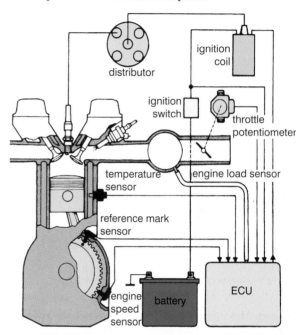

*Figure 14.19 First generation digital electronic system*

The ESA system uses two speed-based inductive sensors, which are either mounted in the distributor or, if greater precision is required, fitted adjacent to the flywheel teeth. One of these sensors monitors engine speed and the other provides a given reference mark, such as 10° before TDC, for the firing impulse.

Engine load can be sensed by a throttle potentiometer or by an inlet manifold pressure transducer, such as a silicon strain gauge type.

Extra sensors may be added to this basic system to further refine the operation of the ECU. These additions often include special transducers to signal the engine temperature and detect the onset of combustion knock (detonation).

A safety circuit is built into the system to protect the engine in the event of a cable break, sensor failure or evaluation circuit fault. To cover these situations, the spark is retarded and an instrument light comes on to warn the driver that a fault is present.

When a knock-control system is used on a turbocharged engine, it can also be arranged to control the turbocharger boost. When the sensor

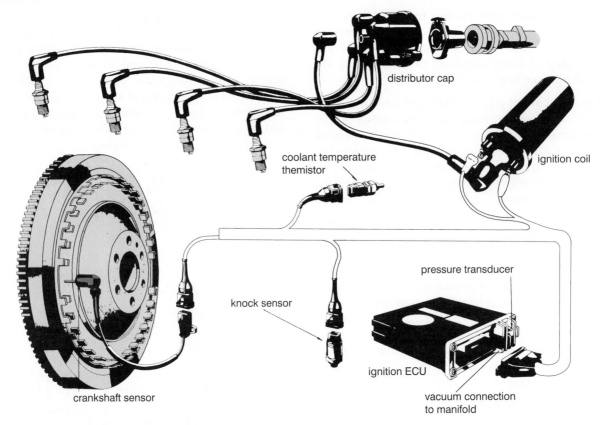

*Figure 14.20  Programmed ignition system*

detects detonation, the spark advance is quickly reduced to take the engine out of the knock region. This is followed by the charging pressure being reduced by the opening of the waste gate valve. When this slower-acting control has taken effect, the spark advance is restored to its optimum setting.

Figure 14.20 shows an early digital system called programmed ignition (PI).

## 14.5.2 Distributorless electronic ignition

Modern ignition systems have eliminated the need for a mechanically operated contact breaker and automatic advance mechanism, so the demand for a bulky distributor unit is questionable. Since the only duty that remains is to distribute high-tension (HT) energy to the sparking plug in the correct firing order, other methods have been developed to take the place of the cumbersome rotor and distributor unit.

One distributorless system uses one HT ignition coil for every two cylinders; so a four-cylinder engine has two coils. Whereas an ordinary coil has one end of its secondary winding connected to the primary, a distributorless system has its secondary winding connected to two sparking plugs, one at each end of the winding (Figure 14.21). Manufacturers use various names for this system, including 'wasted spark' and 'all electronic ignition' (ALI), as well as others. Many

of these help to confuse an outsider until the system is recognised and placed in its general category.

Compared with past methods, a distributorless system has the following advantages:

- Less electromagnet radio interference, particularly at the higher frequencies, which was caused on earlier systems by the unscreened 2kV spark at the rotor gap.
- Less noise because sparking is eliminated.
- No moving parts to wear.
- Fewer cables.

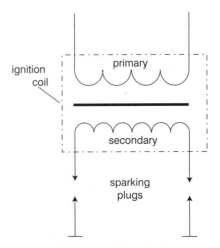

*Figure 14.21  Distributorless ignition system*

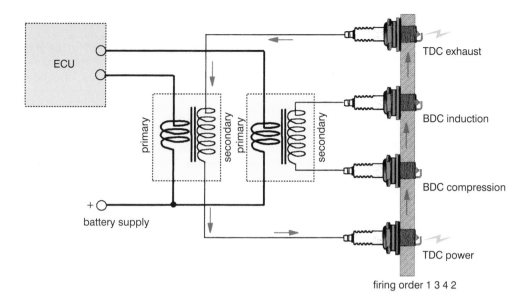

firing order 1 3 4 2

*Figure 14.22 Wasted-spark system*

Figure 14.22 shows the layout of a wasted-spark system suitable for a four-cylinder engine. This is a good descriptive name for the system, because the spark in the cylinder that has just completed its exhaust stroke is not used for combustion: its only purpose is to complete the HT circuit path for its companion sparking plug. The low cylinder pressure at the end of the exhaust stroke means that the voltage required to produce a spark in this cylinder is less than that required at the rotor of the old systems.

The reverse direction of current through one of the two plugs is not ideal, but the slightly higher voltage that is needed for this is well within the capability of the system. Nevertheless, the phasing of the ignition coil should be arranged to give an equal build-up time for each coil. For a four-cylinder engine this is achieved by linking plugs 1 and 4 to one coil and 2 and 3 to the other coil; both coils being of the double-spark type, having a sparking plug connected to each end of the secondary winding.

Engines with an odd number of cylinders have a separate single-spark coil for each sparking plug. This type of coil provides one spark per revolution for two-stroke engines and one spark every other revolution for four-stroke engines. In the latter case, the firing sequence is controlled by a camshaft sensor.

Some systems use a four-spark coil that has two primary windings and one secondary winding. This is connected to the plugs through high-voltage diodes (Figure 14.23). Since the two primaries are wound in the same direction, the opposite polarity of each winding produces a reversing HT current, which is controlled by the diodes to fire two plugs. When the polarity of the secondary winding at point B in Figure 14.23 is positive, for example, diodes 1 and 4 will conduct and produce a spark at plugs 1 and 4. At this instant, the diodes at 2 and 3 block the current.

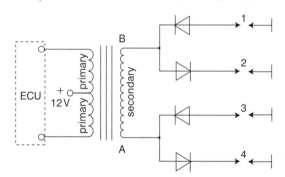

*Figure 14.23 Diode control for HT distribution*

## Ignition coils

Coils used on double-spark and four-spark systems are made wider than a regular coil to accommodate the two HT towers and other connections (Figure 14.24). An externally mounted iron core makes the coil more compact and also provides a securing point for the plastic moulded coil body. For cooling purposes the coil is filled with oil.

*Figure 14.24 Distributorless ignition system (DIS) coil*

Distributorless systems are controlled by an ECU in a similar way to other digital layouts.

## 14.5.3 Coil-on-plug direct ignition system – the modern way

HT leads have caused problems over the years, such as:

- short-circuiting of HT current, either to earth or to leads connected to cylinders with a lower gas pressure
- mutual induction to other HT leads and delicate sensor circuits
- leakage due to damp operating conditions
- radio and TV interference
- suppression difficulties
- conductivity and security of cables, especially when routed in close proximity to a hot exhaust.

Although modern designs of cable have minimised the effects of these problems, it is difficult to guarantee reliability to the standard required by current and future emission regulations. As a consequence, nearly all manufacturers have eliminated all HT leads on their engine by making the sparking plug and ignition coil an integral unit. Each coil-plug unit needs only two LT connections, one to supply battery voltage and the other to provide the ECU trigger signal.

This arrangement means that the problems listed above are overcome, the only drawbacks being the size of the unit and the extra cost (although size is not so much a problem on newer cars as the units are more compact than earlier designs).

*Figure 14.25 Coil-on-plug component*

## 14.5.4 Saab Trionic EMS

Saab has pioneered many systems, such as turbocharging, that are now regarded as standard. As such, its Trionic system must also be considered a piece of great engineering.

The Saab Trionic system is built around a 32-bit Motorola central processor, which is a large step forward from the 16-bit and 8-bit processors used in the past and has provided a platform for other manufacturers to build on. The term '32-bit' indicates the rate at which the computer can handle and process data; 8-bit data processing is much slower so the time taken for a computer to react to any changes in the operating conditions is that much longer. The new processor, which was developed for the American market, can carry out two million calculations a second.

In addition to the new processor, the Trionic system uses a coil-on-plug direct ignition capacity discharge system that also doubles as a knock sensor. A low voltage (80 V) is applied across the sparking plug electrodes after the main firing impulse and measurement of the flow of ions (electrically charged atoms) gives an early and precise warning of the onset of knock. This measurement is taken in each cylinder so greater control over knock is achieved.

In addition to the ignition function, the EMS also controls fuel injection and turbo boost pressure. This integration, together with the 32-bit processor, overcomes the need for the system to revert to standard reference settings during changes in engine operation. Instead, the speed of the computer allows spark timing and injection changes to be made during these transient conditions. This is the type of system that has been adopted by manufacturers worldwide.

> **14.6   Digital closed-loop fuel-injection control**

The need for a closed-loop fuel control system was originally highlighted in the USA when the Environmental Protection Agency (EPA) introduced the Clean Air Act in the early 1970s. This stipulated that vehicles produced in 1975 had to reduce pollution levels by about 90 per cent. Now, in the second decade of the following century, the European Union (EU) has followed this lead and tightens the regulations on a regular cycle. EU directives to member states lay down the timetable for vehicle emission limits that must be met for all new vehicles.

In the UK, the gradual tightening of the statutory emission limits meant that the open-loop fuel control systems could no longer satisfy the requirements and, as a result, closed-loop systems have taken over nearly all forms of engine management control. At an early stage, petrol injection replaced the carburettor and a catalytic converter had to be fitted in the exhaust to meet the legal requirement. This law states that spark-ignition engines require a three-way converter to oxidise CO, HC and $NO_x$ to the required levels. Fitting the catalytic converter had a knock-on effect because this unit is only effective when the exhaust gas is a product of a near-correct air/fuel mixture. Means had to be found to sense and signal to a control system any changes in the combustion process that is caused by incorrect fuelling. To achieve this condition a closed-loop control system was adopted: this system uses a lambda oxygen sensor fitted in the exhaust to provide feedback information about gas content to an ECU.

## 14.6.1 Lambda sensor

The lambda sensor is an oxygen sensor that produces a voltage pulse when no oxygen is present in the exhaust gas; this occurs only when the air/fuel ratio is on the rich side of stoichiometry (the chemically correct ratio).

The system layout is shown in Figure 14.26. This diagram shows the feedback circuit through which the digital pulse signal is conveyed when no oxygen is present in the exhaust gas. The principle of the lambda exhaust gas oxygen (EGO) sensor is described on page 198.

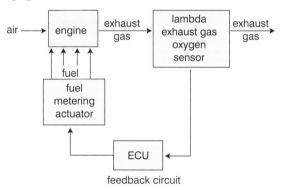

Figure 14.26 Closed-loop fuel control system

When the sensor signals that the oxygen content is below a certain limit, a voltage pulse from the EGO sensor commands the fuel system to decrease the fuel supply so as to weaken the mixture. Shortly after this fuel alteration, the EGO sensor will detect that oxygen is present in the gas. This will cause its voltage output to fall and, as a result, the output from the sensor will change to zero. When the controller discovers that the feedback signal has ceased, it instructs the fuel system to enrich the mixture. Mixture control is obtained by oscillating the mixture between the rich and weak limits and, in this way, the controller is able to keep the air/fuel ratio within a mixture range that

is near correct. Since modern sensors are capable of working to a very small tolerance, with respect to the air/fuel ratio, the risk of severe exhaust emission is considerably reduced; a limit of 0.05 from the required value of 14.7:1 is typical for many sensors.

Figure 14.27 shows the voltage variation when the air/fuel ratio is varied. The abrupt change in voltage, between the point where the excess air factor ($\lambda$) is greater than 1.0 and the point where $\lambda$ is less than 1.0, is the region where the voltage pulse is produced for use as an output signal. This signal gives a limit-control type of cycle so the EGO sensor may be considered as a switch, which opens and closes to signify weak and rich mixtures respectively (i.e. the EGO gives a digital output with the two states, 0 and 1, used to identify the weak and rich mixtures.

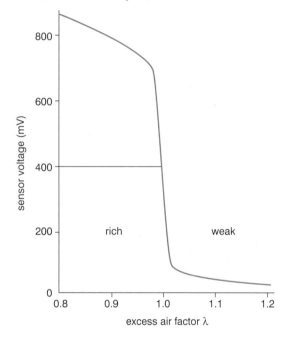

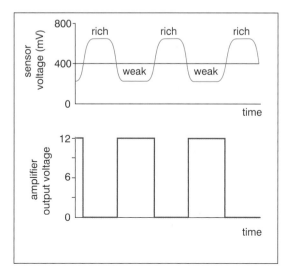

Figure 14.27 Lambda sensor operation

Since this control system is expected to operate very fast, the arrangement used for mixture adjustment must respond to electronic control signals without delay; this can be achieved by using an electronic fuel-injection system.

The EGO sensor does not function efficiently below about 300 °C, so when the exhaust temperature transducer detects that the mean temperature of the exhaust gas is below this minimum temperature, the engine control system is switched to the open-loop mode. This mode is used during cold-starting, when the engine is idling, and at times when the control system detects a fault in the EGO sensor circuit, which can be harmful to the lifespan of the catalytic converter.

During acceleration and deceleration an engine has to operate outside the range of the EGO sensor. At these times, other sensors signal the engine condition and, in response to these signals, older types of ECUs select the open-loop mode until steady conditions are re-established. The EGO sensor will only operate satisfactorily with lead-free fuel.

## Heated lambda sensor

Internally heating the sensor gives more accurate mixture control when the exhaust temperature is below 300 °C. This occurs during cold-starting and when the engine is operated at part-load for long periods.

The heating feature also allows the sensor to be mounted further away from the engine. It is claimed that the cooler position gives this type a life in excess of 100,000 km. This is an improvement, because a sensor mounted close to an engine is exposed to a temperature in excess of its rated maximum (850 °C), during long periods of full-load operation.

Figure 14.28 shows the construction of a heated EGO sensor. The centrally positioned electric heating element, supplied with energy from an ECU, heats the inner surface of the active sensor ceramic. When cold-starting, the heater brings the sensor up to its working temperature in about 30 s.

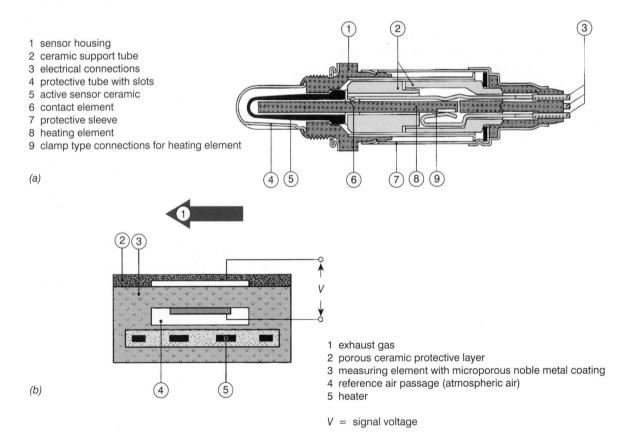

1  sensor housing
2  ceramic support tube
3  electrical connections
4  protective tube with slots
5  active sensor ceramic
6  contact element
7  protective sleeve
8  heating element
9  clamp type connections for heating element

(a)

(b)

1  exhaust gas
2  porous ceramic protective layer
3  measuring element with microporous noble metal coating
4  reference air passage (atmospheric air)
5  heater

$V$ = signal voltage

*Figure 14.28 Heated lambda sensor*

## 14.6.2 Engine control

Besides meeting the rising tide of emission legislation (Table 14.2), the modern vehicle must perform much better than its predecessors.

A potential purchaser expects the power unit to:

- develop high power for its size
- be cheap to operate (in terms of fuel and road tax)
- accelerate briskly
- have good driveability over its speed range
- run smoothly at all speeds
- slow-run evenly without stalling
- start easily when cold and hot
- have a low initial cost.

A modern electronic system allows the engine to achieve these features but, in order to do so, the ECU has to be supplied with far more information than in the past. With these extra inputs, the ECU is able to process the data and decide on the actions that must be taken to achieve the programmed objectives.

Figure 14.29 shows some of the data inputs needed to operate a modern closed-loop control system. If a powerful computer is fitted, the information can be processed quickly: this will overcome the need for the control system to operate on fixed values during changes of engine load or speed, improving the power, economy and driveability.

In the past, the ignition and fuel systems were each controlled separately with their own computers; as a result some inputs were shared. This duplication was necessary because the low-powered computers used took a comparatively long time to process the total data. On some luxury vehicles, more than 10 computers were fitted. The need for shared common inputs, bulky and complex interlinking cables and difficult siting of each computer resulted in poor reliability and slow response times. These early configurations proved that reliability is compromised both by using too many connectors and by parting them unnecessarily. Modern vehicles use a reduced number of ECUs around the vehicle and rely on **multiplexing** and **CAN bus** to allow the fast and efficient control of signals to and from the control units.

**Multiplexing**: the sharing of data between ECUs on a high-speed network. This system allows for the reduction of wires within a vehicle, saving weight, space and cost.

**CAN (controller area network) bus**: developed by Bosch, this system uses a pair of wires (CAN high and CAN low) in order to transmit multiple signals to and from the ECUs in order of high and low priority.

Table 14.2 *European Emission Standards for passenger cars*

| European emission standards for passenger cars (Category M), g/km | | | | | | | |
|---|---|---|---|---|---|---|---|
| Tier | Date | CO | THC | NMHC | $NO_x$ | HC + $NO_x$ | PM |
| **Diesel** | | | | | | | |
| Euro 1 | July 1992 | 2.720 (3.16) | – | – | – | 0.970 (1.13) | 0.140 (0.18) |
| Euro 2 | January 1996 | 1.000 | – | – | – | 0.700 | 0.080 |
| Euro 3 | January 2000 | 0.640 | – | – | 0.500 | 0.560 | 0.050 |
| Euro 4 | January 2005 | 0.500 | – | – | 0.250 | 0.300 | 0.025 |
| Euro 5 | September 2009 | 0.500 | – | – | 0.180 | 0.230 | 0.005 |
| Euro 6 (future) | September 2014 | 0.500 | – | – | 0.080 | 0.170 | 0.005 |
| **Petrol (Gasoline)** | | | | | | | |
| Euro 1 | July 1992 | 2.720 (3.16) | – | – | – | 0.97 (1.13) | – |
| Euro 2 | January 1996 | 2.200 | – | – | – | 0.5 | – |
| Euro 3 | January 2000 | 2.300 | 0.200 | – | 0.150 | – | – |
| Euro 4 | January 2005 | 1.000 | 0.100 | – | 0.080 | – | – |
| Euro 5 | September 2009 | 1.000 | 0.100 | 0.068 | 0.060 | – | 0.005 |
| Euro 6 (future) | September 2014 | 1.000 | 0.100 | 0.68 | 0.060 | – | 0.005 |

**Key:**

CO = Carbon monoxide
THC = Hydrocarbon
NMHC = Non-methane hydrocarbons

$NO_x$ = Nitrogen oxides
HC + $NO_x$ = Hydrogen + nitrogen oxides
PM = Particulate matter

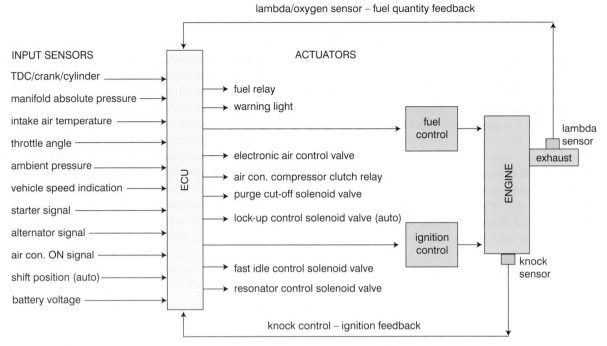

Figure 14.29 Data flow paths

## 14.6.3 Integrated closed-loop control systems

These systems are used on modern vehicles and some of the different arrangements are considered here.

### Hot-wire sensing

Figure 14.30 shows a system similar to that used on Ford Zeta engines. This arrangement uses an engine ECU to manage the ignition and fuel systems. It also incorporates a distributorless HT supply system, self-test fault diagnosis and idle speed control facilities to compensate for changes in the engine load caused by external factors, such as air conditioning, power steering, alternator, clutch pedal actuation and neutral gear selection.

Compared with earlier arrangements, the new management system has a more powerful ECU. This consists of more than a dozen integrated circuits with over 80,000 transistors. The ECU module incorporates:

- a 66 per cent larger memory to store extra calibration data, more advanced mathematical control features (algorithms) and diagnostic information
- a 20 per cent faster controller clock to process information and issue commands more quickly
- more input/output ports (16 instead of 12) to access more variables and export additional instructions.

The system can also handle all the environmental monitoring and fault storage data required for a dealer's diagnostic equipment.

Fuel is injected through a four-hole injector in a sequential pattern that is timed to coincide with the opening of each inlet valve. This intermittent spray method of fuel injection is commonly used because it produces lower emissions.

An ECU used with a sequential electronic fuel-injection (SEFI) system needs an input to signal when each inlet valve is open, as well as a crankshaft sensor to signal engine speed and piston position (by using depressions cast into the rear flywheel face, in this system).

### Pressure-sensed system

In the past, many manufacturers, especially Japanese, used a pressure-sensed EMS. Based on the principle that the engine is a calibrated air pump, the volume of air that passes the throttle is governed by the difference in air pressure on each side of the restriction (i.e. between the air intake and the induction manifold). This pressure difference is measured with a manifold absolute pressure (MAP) sensor.

Signals from this sensor do not take account of the density, so to calculate the mass of air entering the engine, the ECU must know the temperature at each side of the throttle. Two sensors signal this information.

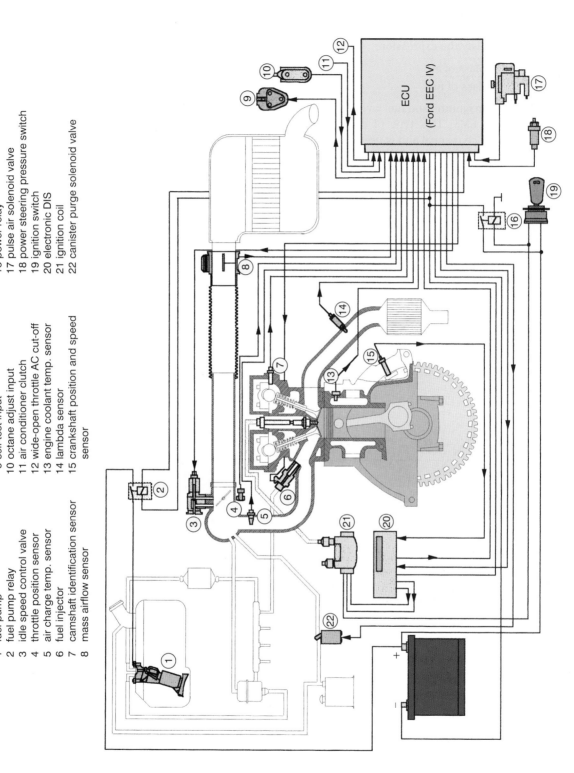

1 fuel pump
2 fuel pump relay
3 idle speed control valve
4 throttle position sensor
5 air charge temp. sensor
6 fuel injector
7 camshaft identification sensor
8 mass airflow sensor

9 self-test input
10 octane adjust input
11 air conditioner clutch
12 wide-open throttle AC cut-off
13 engine coolant temp. sensor
14 lambda sensor
15 crankshaft position and speed
    sensor

16 power relay
17 pulse air solenoid valve
18 power steering pressure switch
19 ignition switch
20 electronic DIS
21 ignition coil
22 canister purge solenoid valve

*Figure 14.30 Hot-wire system using DIS*

In a similar way, the density of the fuel varies with temperature, so by fitting a temperature sensor in the fuel line close to the injectors, the ECU is able to calculate the mass of fuel and set the length of injection pulse to satisfy the expression:

$$\text{Air/fuel ratio} = \frac{\text{Mass of air}}{\text{Mass of fuel}}$$

Figure 14.31 shows an ignition and fuel layout similar to a basic modular EMS. This type of diagram is often found in a service manual and is useful when a particular part needs to be located.

In this system, a rubber pipe connects the manifold to a MAP sensor mounted inside the ECU. This is placed in a cool part of the engine compartment behind the battery.

Operation of the system starts when the ECU receives manifold pressure, speed and throttle position signals. These allow the processor to search the ROM memory for the basic fuel and ignition settings. These values are then modified to take into account the feedback and secondary signals. When these corrections are completed, the ECU sets the length of injection pulse together with the ignition and fuel timing.

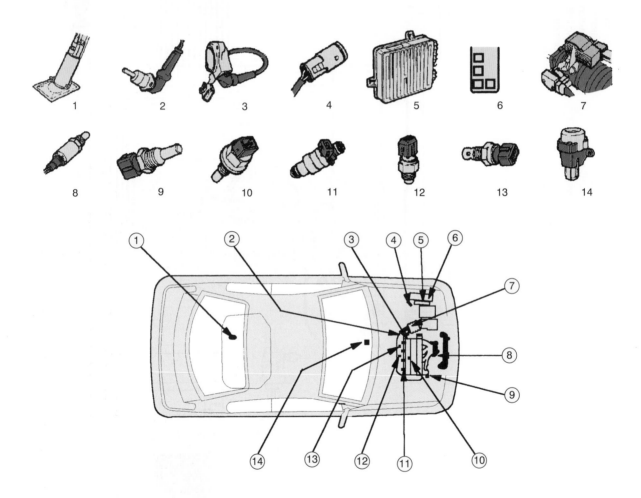

| | |
|---|---|
| 1 fuel pump | 8 oxygen sensor |
| 2 crankshaft sensor | 9 coolant temperature sensor |
| 3 camshaft sensor | 10 knock sensor |
| 4 diagnostic connector | 11 fuel injector |
| 5 ECU | 12 fuel temperature sensor |
| 6 relays; fuel pump, main and oxygen sensor | 13 intake air temperature sensor |
| 7 stepper motor and throttle potentiometer | 14 stepper motor and throttle potentiometer |

*Figure 14.31 Component locations – Rover Modular Engine Management System (MEMS)*

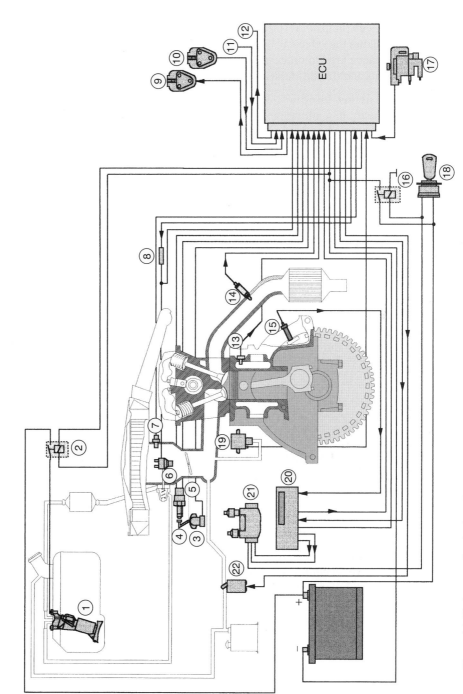

1  fuel pump
2  fuel pump relay
3  throttle position sensor
4  idle tracking switch
5  throttle control motor
6  fuel injector
7  air charge temp. sensor
8  ballast resistor

9  service connector
10 self-test connector
11 neutral drive switch
12 vehicle speed sensor
13 engine coolant temp. sensor
14 lambda sensor
15 crankshaft position and speed
   sensor

16 power relay
17 pulse air solenoid valve
18 ignition switch
19 MAP sensor
20 electronic DIS
21 ignition coil
22 canister purge solenoid valve

*Figure 14.32 Layout of a single-point injection system*

As is usual with modern systems, the ECU has a separate diagnostic connector to enable the record of any intermittent faults stored in its memory to be downloaded. If the computer detects a fault when the vehicle is in use, a back-up (limp home) program comes into operation. This allows the vehicle to be driven, but at a reduced performance level in order to ensure the safety of the occupants and the life of the engine.

Engine idling speed is set electronically by using special test equipment. If a situation arises that causes the speed to change, the ECU signals a stepper motor (an idle control valve) to alter the position of the throttle. This alteration is sensed by the MAP sensor, which results in the ignition timing and fuel delivery being changed to suit the new conditions. The effectiveness of this compensation can be seen when an engine has a defect, such as a faulty sparking plug. In the past this would soon be noticed by the vibration, but with modern systems the ECU attempts to hide the fault by resetting the idling speed.

All injectors, except those fitted to engines with turbos, are arranged to spray simultaneously. Turbo applications and later models operate sequentially. This can be identified by the extra sensor fitted to the camshaft.

Besides catering for basic engine needs, the extra power of a modern ECU allows it to perform other duties, including:

- fuel cut-off when the vehicle is coasting
- over-speed fuel cut-off to protect the engine when maximum speed is reached
- immobilisation of the system, unless it receives a coded signal from an anti-theft device.

## 14.6.4 Single-point injection

Older systems that use one injector to direct its spray into a throttle body are generally controlled in a similar manner to a multi-point system. Compactness and the comparatively low cost of a single-point layout made the system attractive for use on smaller engines before stricter control was required.

### Closed-loop control

Figure 14.32 shows a pressure-sensed closed-loop system arranged around an ECU. This receives primary signals from a crankshaft sensor, an in-built MAP sensor and a throttle potentiometer; together these register TDC position, engine speed, and engine load and throttle position. An oxygen sensor monitors the engine's exhaust gas emissions output and using this feedback signal in conjunction with data received from other sensors, the ECU computes the ignition timing, injection timing and the length of each injection pulse.

### Idling control

Ignition advance, as mapped in the ECU, is varied in response to a cooling temperature sensor and throttle switch to provide stable idling, good driveability and low emissions.

Idle and fast-idle speed is maintained by a stepper motor, as shown in Figure 14.33. This sensitive control continually makes throttle adjustments during idling, so the ignition timing varies with the speed during this period.

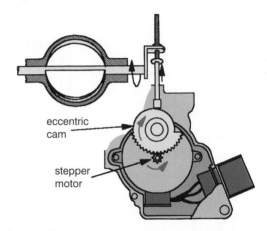

eccentric cam

stepper motor

*Figure 14.33 Stepper motor for idle control valve*

### Coil type

A low-inductance ignition coil with a primary winding resistance of about $0.75\,\Omega$ is used to give high-spark energy throughout the speed range.

### Fuel injection

Fuel delivery to and around the solenoid-operated injector is by means of an electric pump to a common fuel rail. The pump is located in the fuel tank and is supplied with electrical energy from the ECU via a fuel pump relay and inertia switch. The injector sprays fuel when the solenoid is earthed by the ECU. This takes place once per cylinder per cycle (i.e. for a four-cylinder engine twice per crankshaft revolution).

### Manifold heating

To improve fuel vaporisation during warm-up, the system includes an electrically operated manifold heater. This is controlled by the ECU and uses coolant from the cooling system.

### Fuel evaporation

As is normal with modern engines, vapour in the fuel tank is collected and stored in a charcoal canister. This is purged with air into the throttle housing, via a solenoid-operated purge valve, at times when it can be accepted without affecting the performance of either the engine or catalyst. When the engine temperature is above 70 °C and the speed is over

1500 rpm, the valve repeatedly opens and closes, provided the manifold pressure is below 30 kPa.

## 14.6.5 Turbo boost control of spark-ignition engines

A turbocharger is an exhaust-driven air pump used to force air into the engine cylinders instead of relying on atmospheric pressure. Where manifold pressure of a normal aspirated engine is slightly below atmospheric, in a turbocharged engine the pressure is greater. The increase above atmospheric is called boost.

Engine power and torque rise as the boost pressure is increased. However, this must be limited because when the boost is too high, the engine is damaged and high $NO_X$ emissions will occur. Boost limitation is achieved by allowing some of the exhaust gas to by-pass the turbo through a port opened by a valve called a waste gate.

The flap-type gate is operated by a pneumatic cylinder connected by a hose to the induction manifold at a point on the engine side of the throttle. When the maximum boost is reached, the pressure overcomes a spring in the pneumatic cylinder and the gate is opened. In the past, this was the only method used to limit boost pressure, but current emission regulations have meant that a more precise electronic control system is necessary.

Figure 14.34 shows a pneumatically operated waste gate that is actuated by a boost control valve. This solenoid valve is fed from the main relay and earthed by the ECU at times when the valve is to operate.

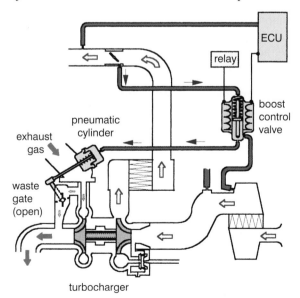

*Figure 14.34 Electronic control of turbo waste gate*

## 14.7 On-board diagnosis (OBD)

Over the past 20 years, EMSs have kept pace with legislation introduced locally to limit vehicle emissions. History shows that European regulations have followed the lead given by the USA (especially California), so this has allowed European manufacturers three or four years grace to develop their products to satisfy future EU legislation. Although the EU sets minimum standards for emission limits, each country is entitled to tighten these limits (e.g. Sweden, which adopts US regulations in full). Also, some manufacturers use strict emission limits to standardise and rationalise their products and thereby minimise export problems across the world.

Since 1992, emission regulations in the USA have been covered by the Clean Air Act (CAA). Under this act, the California Air Resources Board (CARB) and the US Environmental Protection Agency (EPA) introduced one aspect of emission control legislation that has been noted by many countries outside the USA. This new law required that all vehicles manufactured after 1993 have an on-board diagnostics (OBD) facility. In addition, another law (OBD I) specified new test cycles, laid down performance periods and updated emission limits. In 1996, OBD II came into effect: this regulation means European manufacturers have to update their EMSs to match the essential requirements of this law.

### 14.7.1 Requirements of OBD II

Besides giving detailed specifications for emission controls, components and drive cycles, the CAA regulation OBD II requires:

- electronic monitoring of the exhaust system
- indication of emission-related malfunctions by a warning lamp
- rapid heating of the catalyst to reduce pollutant emissions in the warm-up phase (eliminating another form of open-loop control)
- optimisation of the EMS in conjunction with an evaporative emission control (EVAP) system
- CO emission limit maintained for five years or 80,000 km
- provision of a standard diagnostic plug to allow for all repair centres to have access and ability to rectify problems without the need for different types of diagnostic equipment.

Introduction of OBD is intended to extend the useful life of emissions-related components by preventing potentially damaging faults from going unnoticed (hence the warning lamp requirement). Also, the need for the system to adapt fuel and ignition settings to compensate for any defect ensures that the exhaust emissions are kept within the specified limits at all times.

Since engine management now relies on electronic systems, radical modification of the ECU and control arrangement was needed to implement basic OBD requirements. Although management systems provided limp-home and self-diagnosis features as a convenience for the driver and technician, the level of these facilities was well below that required for OBD standards. Some of the main changes that were required are considered at this stage.

## Component defect

On many current systems the total or partial failure of a vital sensor activates the limp-home or limited operating strategy (termed LOS by Ford) facility. This program makes the ECU disregard any signal from a defective sensor and, in its place, substitutes a standard signal. Over the years, the capability of the ECU to operate with a system fault has improved to the extent that the driver sometimes finds it difficult to recognise that the engine has a defect, even though the engine management warning light may be displayed on the instrument panel. Continuous operation in the limp-home mode causes high emissions and destroys the catalytic converter, so modern systems have been programmed to cope with the loss of a sensor by taking a feed from another sensor, which may provide sufficient information to allow that system to work at a better level than the standard limp-home settings.

More precise and regular monitoring of the system is required for OBD. Continuous checking and comparison of one set of sensors against others in the system shows if each part is performing satisfactorily. The measure of airflow is a typical example of this cross-check feature.

One management system with a hot-wire air-mass meter compares the flow through this meter with the value calculated from the throttle valve opening and engine speed. If the results do not compare, the system performs a plausibility check to ascertain which one is faulty. Only after this check is made is an action taken and the fault code generated.

## Combustion defects

Cylinder faults, such as misfiring, are difficult to detect and this is compounded when the oxygen sensor signal associated with combustion faults is wrongly suspected of being faulty. As a result, the ECU substitutes a standard signal with damaging

consequences. In addition, it creates and stores a fault code in its memory, which can be misunderstood by a technician when the vehicle is repaired.

Special means are required by OBD to detect faults such as misfiring. One method is to monitor the rotation of the crankshaft from ignition point to ignition point. When the monitoring system detects an unequal time interval, the fuel supply to the defective cylinder is cut off. As a result, harmful emissions are prevented and catalytic converter damage is avoided. Driving with the engine management light on for a long period of time can cause further damaging problems to the engine if not rectified quickly.

## Catalytic converter defects

Harmful emissions will be exhausted if the converter is ineffective. An OBD system monitors this component by using two lambda sensors, one fitted upstream (on the engine side of the converter) and the other downstream. The upstream sensor performs its normal duty, while the downstream sensor monitors the performance of both the converter and the upstream lambda sensor.

When the signal pattern from both sensors is similar, it shows that the converter is defective. This condition prompts the ECU to activate the driver's warning lamp.

The sensitivity of the upstream sensor deteriorates if it is exposed to excessive heat for a considerable period of time. This condition is detected by comparing the frequency patterns of the two sensors. When the ECU detects from the wave comparison and other sensor plausibility checks that the performance of the main sensor is outside the accepted limits, the limp-home facility and warning lamp systems are activated.

## Other emission-related defects

New management systems designed to meet OBD requirements incorporate extra monitoring facilities to those previously outlined. These include:

- fuel supply – to check that the air/fuel mixture does not deviate from stoichiometric for a long period of time
- secondary air injection – to ensure that air is supplied to the converter only at times when the catalytic converter is below its operating temperature
- exhaust gas recirculation (EGR) – to verify that the system is functioning correctly
- fuel tank emissions – to check the canister purge system.

## 14.7.2 Management systems

Figure 14.35 shows a typical layout of a system designed to meet the US OBD II regulations. Systems such as the Bosch Motronic M5 and Ford EEC V were first introduced in the late 1990s and since then have been improved in different model upgrades.

Other than the addition of the second lambda sensor, the general appearance of OBD II systems does not differ greatly from pre-OBD systems, but the operation is far more involved. All sensors are built to a higher specification and the capability of the ECU is enhanced considerably.

The system shown in Figure 14.35 has a coil-on-plug arrangement to eliminate problems associated with HT leads.

Interesting developments are currently taking place to use the spark plug for cylinder sensing purposes; knock sensing has long been in use. Another system uses the crown of the piston as an earth electrode. With this system it is claimed that ionisation between a single plug electrode and a piston crown provides a monitoring system for detecting cylinder misfires and other combustion faults.

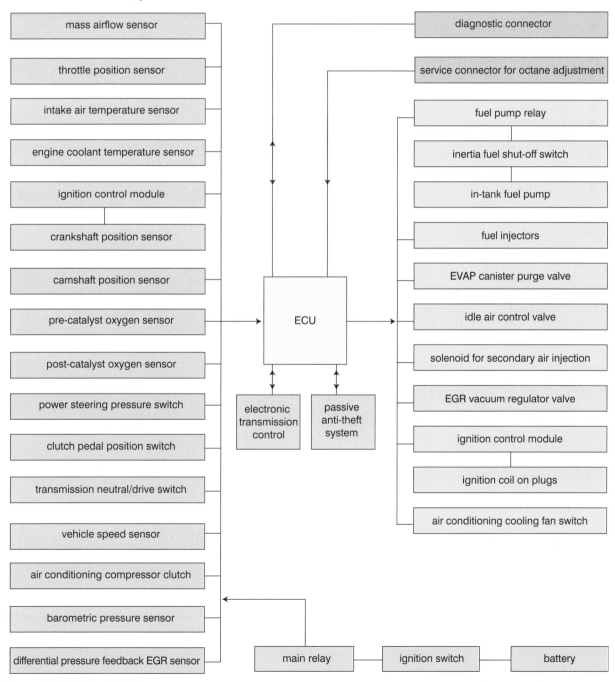

*Figure 14.35 EMS with OBD*

## The ME-Motronic 9.7 system

The latest version of Bosch's engine management system is the ME-Motronic 9.7 system. This is similar to most other combined ignition and fuel management systems. Figure 14.36 shows the sensor inputs and actuator outputs of the ME-Motronic system. The system has the standard two-way diagnostics and controller area network buses, with the CAN bus network communicating with various other systems such as the automatic transmission ECU. The sensor inputs include:

- vehicle speed
- transmission gear
- camshaft position
- crankshaft speed and position
- dual oxygen sensors (located either side of the catalytic converter – 'V' engines have four sensors)
- knock sensor
- coolant temperature
- intake air temperature
- battery voltage
- intake air mass and manifold absolute pressure
- throttle position.

All of the above inputs are standard on all engine management systems; however, the ME 9.7 has an additional input from the accelerator pedal position.

The actuator outputs are also the same as in other recent management systems:

- spark plugs
- injectors
- instrument panel tachometer
- fuel pump relay
- oxygen sensor heaters
- inlet manifold control (i.e. control of the position of valves within dual-tuned length manifolds, or the length of the infinitely variable intake manifolds)
- fuel system evaporative control, secondary air injection and exhaust gas recirculation.

The additional output is to the electronic throttle control actuator.

The additional input and output signals are used to allow the EMS to adjust torque output to the wheels to ensure that the maximum torque is available. This is irrespective of the driver's input on the accelerator pedal.

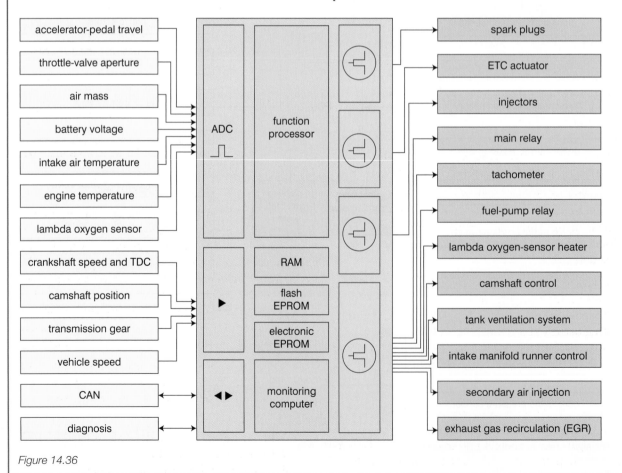

*Figure 14.36*

Modern OBD II systems use a generic set of fault codes (or diagnostic trouble codes, DTC); by far the most popular are those beginning with the letter 'P', which stands for powertrain, and followed by four digits, which reveal a specific problem on the electronic system. Below is a list of how those codes are grouped:

- P0001–P0099 – fuel and air metering and auxiliary emission controls.
- P0100–P0199 – fuel and air metering.
- P0200–P0299 – fuel and air metering (injector circuit).
- P0300–P0399 – ignition system or misfire.
- P0400–P0499 – auxiliary emissions controls.
- P0500–P0599 – vehicle speed controls and idle control system.
- P0600–P0699 – computer output circuit.
- P0700–P0899 – transmission.

## 14.8  Fault diagnosis

Sometimes vehicle performance does not warn the driver of the existence of an engine management fault. At these times the illumination of a 'check engine' lamp on the instrument panel is intended to alert the driver to the problem and suggest that expert attention should be sought as soon as possible.

When the ignition is switched on, the 'check engine' lamp should illuminate for about three seconds while the circuit is being monitored/self-checked. After this initial lamp and system test, the lamp should go out. If this is not so, it indicates that the computer has detected a system fault, the details of which are stored in the random-access memory (RAM) unit in code form. Access to this code is obtained using a fault diagnosis machine or using the flash code readings.

When the system has been accessed, the fault codes stored in the computer RAM will activate the 'check engine' lamp. This assumes the battery has not been disconnected in the interval since the original defect was detected.

Any loss of data due to an interruption in the supply is avoided if the computer incorporates a small battery (or capacitor) to maintain its volatile memory unit. If such a battery is not fitted, it is advisable to connect an external battery to the cigar lighter socket to retain the RAM data while the main battery is disconnected.

### 14.8.1 Lamp flash codes

The flash code diagnosis system used depends on the date of manufacture on the vehicle. One system interrogates the computer memory by connecting a test lamp to the ECU; another uses a LED fitted

to the case of the ECU. This function is no longer used on modern vehicles owing to the availability of diagnostic machines.

The flash code principle can be shown by considering the computer-controlled system used in the past by Toyota. This system monitored 10 possible faults, five of which were capable of producing an engine stall and so in these cases the 'check engine' lamp was illuminated. When a specified test terminal was short-circuited, any fault sensed by the computer from the time that the RAM was last activated caused the panel lamp to flash intermittently in a coded manner. Reference to the manufacturer's service manual allowed the coded message to be translated. Figure 14.37 shows three examples of such lamp behaviour.

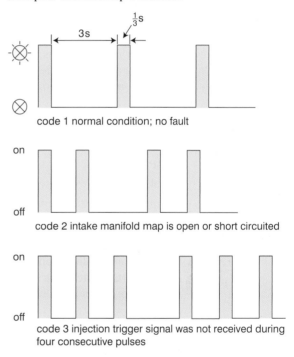

code 1 normal condition; no fault

code 2 intake manifold map is open or short circuited

code 3 injection trigger signal was not received during four consecutive pulses

*Figure 14.37  Fault diagnosis by lamp signal*

Modern management systems then began to use more sophisticated flash codes to communicate the contents of the RAM. These systems allow fault codes to be read from the 'check engine' lamp. When the ignition is switched on the code follows the lamp test. Flash codes can be repeated until the memory has been cleared. This is achieved either by using special test equipment or by removing the main supply fuse to the ECU for the recommended time (e.g. five minutes).

Figure 14.38 shows another example of flash code signals given by the 'check engine' lamp when the ignition is switched on. In this case the lamp behaves as follows:

1 Lights up and stays on for 3 seconds.
2 Goes out for 3 seconds.
3 Lights up and stays on for 3 seconds.

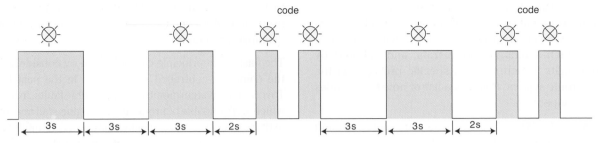

*Figure 14.38 Example of flash code*

4  Goes out for 2 seconds to indicate flash code is to follow.
5  Flash code, which consists of a number of brief flashes, each lasting 0.4 seconds.
6  Goes out for 3 seconds.
7  Lights up and stays on for 3 seconds.
8  Flash code repeated.

Figure 14.38 shows a code having two flashes, so by referring to Table 14.3, the fault area can be identified and further tests can then be made to pinpoint the cause.

*Table 14.3  Toyota flash codes*

| Number of flashes | Probable fault |
| --- | --- |
| 2 | MAP sensor |
| 3 | Intake air temperature sensor |
| 4 | Coolant temperature sensor |
| 5 | Throttle position sensor |
| 6 | Oxygen sensor |
| 7 | Adaptation (modification of fuel setting) including connection of sensors and hoses |
| 8 | EVAP canister purge valve |
| 9 | Control module, internal fault |

These examples show that there are many ways to signal a fault by a flash code, so reference should be made to manufacturer's literature to interpret the code used on a given model.

Although a flash code is a useful diagnostic tool, it must be remembered that a fault in one sensor circuit can affect other parts of the system. When this happens, the flash code may give misleading information. A particular code does not always mean that a component is defective, hence the introduction and use of special test equipment for fault diagnosis.

## 14.8.2 Special test equipment for fault diagnosis

To improve and speed up fault diagnosis, special test equipment has been developed and is in use in both independent and manufacturers' garages. Most vehicle manufacturers specify the diagnostic equipment that their dealer network must purchase and use. These dedicated units range from sophisticated computers to comparatively cheap handheld code readers, and everything in between. In the UK, manufacturers' test figures are not readily available to non-franchised dealers and independents, so if an independent dealer undertakes work on different makes of vehicle, it is often necessary for them to purchase a suitable engine analyser from a general equipment supplier. This is because the manufacturer-specific equipment will most likely be limited to only one make.

The following types of test equipment show what could be used in a franchise and non-franchise workshop for fault diagnosis. Each has its own reason for use, and its pros and cons.

### Manufacturer-specific test equipment

This includes equipment such as Tech 2 (GM), VAG-COM Diagnostic System (VAG Group – VW, Audi, Seat and Skoda), TIS (Toyota) and many others.

These sophisticated systems are built around one specific make of vehicle and can take the form of a handheld device or a stand-alone computer. There is normally a range of slightly different tools that each franchised garage will own.

### Stand-alone computer

These tools have features such as the following:

- Engine analyser and diagnostic search – gives access to the various ECUs on the vehicle via the OBD plug and allows fault codes to be downloaded and displayed on the VDU screen. It also acts as a signal generator to emulate data associated with sensor and actuator operation (actuator tests, etc.).
- Provides a range of meters for volts, ohms and amperes tests, displayed on a backlit LCD screen, with the ability to read from the plug or to scope individual sensors.
- Technical information support – gives immediate access to the latest service information, product manuals, technical data,

schematics, wiring diagrams and other repair documents that would not be available to non-franchised garages.

■ Interactive training – on-screen training programmes for technicians on how to test sensors, common faults and how to troubleshoot running faults.

*Figure 14.39 Bosch KTS stand-alone computer*

With the aid of simple operating instructions displayed on the screen, the technician is able to systematically interrogate and test the vehicle's management systems, diagnose faults and make tuning adjustments. At any time during its use, the data displayed on the screen can be printed or saved for record purposes. This, however, is only of use for one make of vehicle.

Those that use a stand-alone computer, with a CD drive, will be able to run non-manufacturer-specific diagnostic software to allow them to repair other makes and models of car.

The scope facilities can be upgraded by adding dedicated modules to carry out more detailed tests such as engine analysis, and MOT tests for emission and diesel smoke.

## Non-manufacturer-specific test equipment

### Handheld scanner

Portable testers, such as the Launch X431, Snap-on Solus/Ethos/Vantage and Bosch KTS ranges, provide dedicated multi-purpose test instruments that are designed to interface with the car's OBD port and communicate with a multitude of makes and models of vehicles. This non-manufacturer-specific equipment allows for a wide range of use. Although they share the majority of functions, some may still work with one group of vehicles better than others.

When used with the appropriate adapters (keys, cables and plugs), two-way communication with the ECU is obtained. The instrument generally has a keyboard and alphanumeric LCD display to allow the operator to select the test program, key in data and observe test results, which are temporarily retained in the instrument's RAM. In addition to its test functions, the scan tool is able to interrogate the on-board computer to provide information on part number, program version, engine variant and serial number.

When used as a code reader, the scan tool can show a full range of fault codes. Once the fault code is displayed, reference to the manufacturer's manual or other similar equipment, such as Autodata, shows the additional tests that should be made to pinpoint the cause. They may require a particular input signal to the ECU, or some electrical test normally performed by a multimeter. These functions, together with vacuum and pressure measurement, are performed by the one instrument together with actuator tests.

## General engine analysers

In the UK, non-franchised dealers and companies undertaking work on foreign vehicles are often unable to gain access to dedicated test equipment and technical data issued by the vehicle manufacturers. Without this support, repair work and accurate fault diagnosis is impossible unless alternative equipment and technical test data can be purchased from outside sources. This need is filled by companies, such as those listed previously, who manufacture a complete range of vehicle test equipment suitable for detailed fault diagnosis and engine adjustment.

These units offer the technician in-depth problem-solving, reference and scope functions in a powerful computer that can be updated and expanded by loading new software programs to cover new models and testing techniques.

Scope patterns show the performance of the commonly used sensors, injector behaviour and ignition outputs of conventional, wasted-spark, transistorised and full electronic systems.

The equipment is often supported by software that guides the technician through a wide range of diagnostic tests and emission checks recommended for a particular make and model of vehicle.

The LCD-type screens have the capacity to show test results in a variety of formats, including bar graphs.

Also, instructions can be displayed, illustrated with pictures and symbols, to guide the operator through the test sequences; although it may not always be this straightforward when troubleshooting an intermittent fault.

*Figure 14.40 Launch CRecorder*

Figure 14.40 shows the Launch CRecorder. This mobile data logger allows technicians to record live data streams and save intermittent faults and codes on test drives and for up to 24 hours. The recorded data files can be transferred to a PC for further investigation; this is especially suitable for intermittent fauts which can be hard to diagnose.

When returned to the workshop, the recorder can be removed and the information can be analysed further.

### Technical data packages

To overcome the lack of technical information available to non-franchised dealers, software such as Autodata can be purchased on a CD-ROM or online and installed on a computer for use in a workshop. The software covers many vehicle models and contains topics such as test data, maintenance schedules and repair information. In this way, the information can be easily updated when new models are introduced.

### Oscilloscopes

One of the most powerful tools in the technician's kit is the oscilloscope. Modern PC-based oscilloscopes are very accurate and are often the only way to capture an accurate reading from some intermittent faults which occur on sensitive vehicle components. Most oscilloscopes will come with a library of known good waveforms and these can be compared with the readings from the vehicle component being tested. Figure 14.41 shows one type of kit that is commercially available.

*Figure 14.41 Pico automotive oscilloscope kit*

This chapter will cover all areas of the starter motor system. This is a vital function for the motor vehicle on engine start-up, but then becomes redundant for the rest of the time until start-up is required once more.

A starter motor converts electrical energy supplied from the battery into mechanical power. The system must supply sufficient power to enable an engine to be cranked (i.e. turned over) at a speed of about 100 rpm, so as to atomise the fuel and compress the air/fuel mixture sufficiently to start the engine. In addition, the speed must be adequate to allow the momentum of the moving parts to 'carry' the engine over from one firing stroke to the next. It takes a lot of mechanical power to rotate the engine from its stationary position, so the current used can be around 250–500 A, but can reach levels of up to 1500 A, depending on application. As a result, the cables (internal and external) and windings must be heavy-duty in order to cope with this large amount of current.

### Concept of energy

Energy can be transferred into another form of energy but it cannot be created or destroyed. For the starter motor system, the source is the chemical energy stored in the battery, which is changed into electrical energy. This then reaches the starter motor and is converted to kinetic energy (energy of motion) and some of this, in turn, becomes heat and sound energy.

### Power requirements

The power (the rate of energy expenditure) needed to attain a suitable speed depends on the size and type of engine and on the ambient conditions. So to start a warm 1.5 l engine normally requires a power of about 1.2 kW, whereas this is increased to about 4 kW on a cold winter morning owing to the viscosity of the oil (very thick), a reduced amount of electron production in the battery, the fuel's difficulty in vaporising in cold conditions, and the lack of expansion/lubrication of some of the engine components.

### Electrical units

- Voltage – measured in volts (V), this is the potential energy of an electrical supply that is stored as an electrical charge. Voltage effectively pushes the electrons through a circuit.
- Current – measured in amperes (A), this is the flow of electrical charge.
- Resistance – measured in ohms ($\Omega$), this is the ability for a component to resist or prevent current flow.
- Power – measured in watts (W), this is the amount of energy produced or absorbed in a circuit.

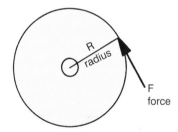

$$\text{torque} = \text{force} \times \text{radius}$$
$$T = F \times R$$

*Figure 15.1 Torque is the product of force and radius*

Power is the product of torque and speed. By definition, torque is a turning moment and is the force exerted at a given radius (Figure 15.1). A starter motor pinion driving an engine flywheel must exert sufficient torque to provide breakaway (i.e. initially move the engine and then accelerate it to the cranking speed). To provide high power, the motor circuit must be of low resistance to enable a current of up to 500 A. The cables and switches must withstand the large load and the motor must be capable of converting the energy in an efficient manner. Naturally, a starting system will not function properly unless the battery can provide the high current that is demanded. Similarly, the battery potential difference (PD) should not fall excessively as this will affect the motor speed.

### What is potential difference (PD)?

This is the difference in electric potential between two points in an electric circuit. This is measured in volts. Energy is required to move a charge around a circuit.

The starter motor uses battery voltage to engage with the ring gear around the edge of the flywheel, which in turn rotates the crankshaft (Figure 15.2). The starter motor and its solenoid operate using electromagnetic principles (see Chapter 1).

### What are the principles of electromagnetism?

A magnetic field is formed when charge flows through a wire (known as a conductor). Conductors will repel when magnetic fields oppose. Therefore, when placed between magnetic poles, the conductor will move (Figure 15.3).

A wire that is looped multiples of times will produce a coil. The charge will then flow in opposite directions on each side of the coil and the magnetic forces

on each side will act in opposite directions. This produces a turning force (torque) and the coil will turn until it is at right angles with the magnetic field (see page 214, Figure 15.4 and Section 15.1.1).

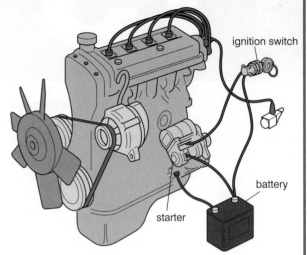

Figure 15.2 Starter motor engine layout

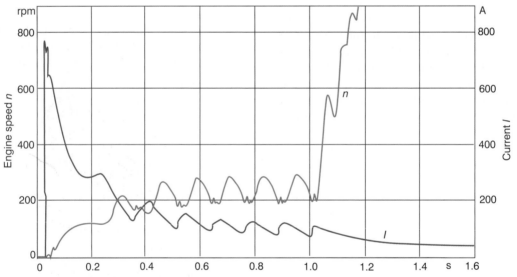

Figure 15.3 Starter motor speed and current during a start process

## 15.1 Types of light vehicle starter motors

Motor vehicles use a direct current (DC) motor (based on the principle described in Chapter 1, sections 1.3, 1.4 and 1.5). In the past, motors with electromagnetic field systems have been popular, but improved permanent magnet (PM) materials have enabled the construction of lightweight and more compact starter motors. Starter motors have

field windings connected in series or series-parallel with the main circuit and **armature**. Since a series-wound motor is capable of producing a high torque at low speed, it is particularly suitable as an engine starter motor.

**Armature**: the revolving component of the DC motor. The armature shaft is supported at each end by bushes pressed into end frames, which locate the armature centrally in the outer casing or yoke of the motor.

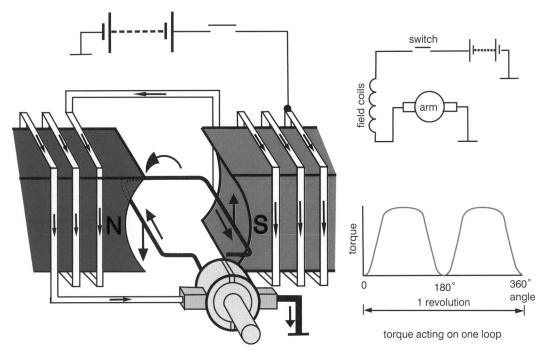

Figure 15.4 Series wound motor

## 15.1.1 Series motor

This type of motor has the thick field coils arranged in series with the armature windings and all the current that passes to the armature also goes through the field. As a result, this gives the strongest possible field. When the switch is closed (Figure 15.4) the combined effect of the current in the armature and field windings distorts the magnetic flux. This generates a torque that pushes the armature away from the field pole. Constant rotation and a steady torque are required, so a number of armature conductor coils are needed. These coils are set in slots around a laminated soft iron core. The end of each coil is soldered to a copper **commutator** segment, which is insulated from the adjacent segments by mica (Figure 15.5). Armature conductors are made in the form of thick copper strips to provide a high current.

> **Commutator**: a sliding electrical connection between the motor windings and the brushes. It is mounted on one end of the armature shaft. The commutator has many segments that are insulated from each other.

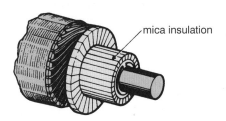

mica insulation

Figure 15.5 Commutator

Comparatively hard brushes are used, often of a composition of carbon and copper, and these are pressed against the commutator by spiral-shaped springs (Figure 15.6).

Figure 15.6 Brush springs

Using a normal armature and commutator allows the brushes to 'feed' the armature conductor that is positioned where the field flux is most dense. When this conductor is pushed away, another conductor takes its place. By using a number of conductors, a near-uniform rotation is obtained. A typical armature has about 30 slots for conductors: the larger the number of slots, the smoother the motion (Figure 15.7).

Figure 15.8 shows the construction of the field coils. These are made of copper or aluminium alloy and are wound in a direction that produces north and south poles. Each coil is bound with tape to provide insulation.

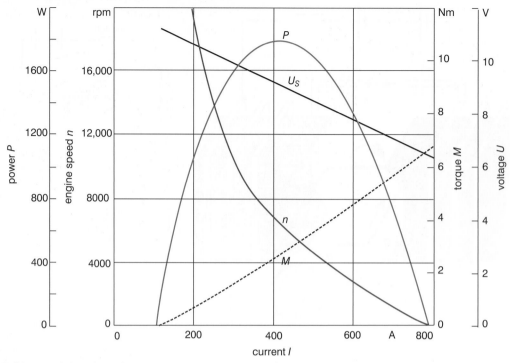

Figure 15.7 *Characteristics of a series-wound motor*

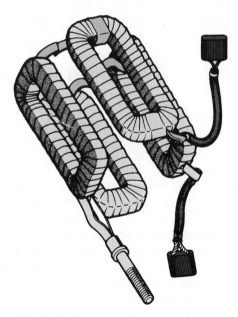

Figure 15.8 *Field coil construction*

for only short periods of time, plain, oil-impregnated sintered bronze brushes are suitable for the armature bearings.

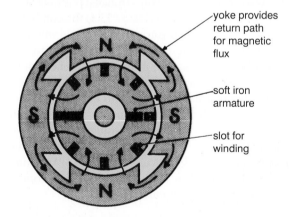

Figure 15.9 *A four-pole, two-brush motor*

In the case of the two-pole field coils shown in Figure 15.8, one end of the coil is connected to a brush and the other end is attached to the starter supply terminal. By using more poles a more powerful motor is obtained. Figure 15.9 shows a two-brush, four-pole motor in which the total magnet strength of the series-wound field is doubled because the current is made to form other field paths. The polarity of the poles is N-S-N-S and the diagram shows how the yoke forms a part of the magnetic circuit. As the motor is in use

A four-pole, four-brush series motor is shown in Figure 15.10. In this design the current from the field is fed to the two insulated brushes, so the reduced brush resistance allows more current. Current is the same throughout the circuit, so two other insulated brushes must also be fitted. Some Lucas starter motors, which use this field-and-brush arrangement, have a wave-wound field system and a face-type commutator (Figure 15.11). This design is more compact and is cheaper to manufacture.

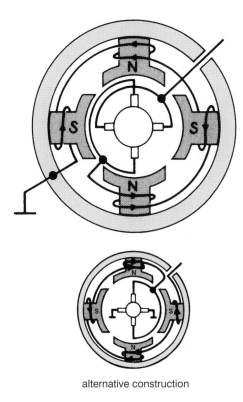

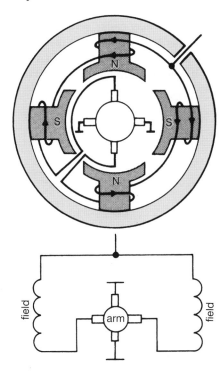

field resistance is achieved with this arrangement, so the motor can handle more current and give a higher torque output.

alternative construction

*Figure 15.10 A four-pole, four-brush motor*

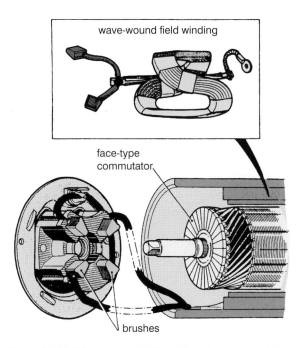

brushes

*Figure 15.11 Wave-wound field and face-type commutator*

## Series-parallel motor

Figure 15.12 shows a series-parallel motor. This has the field coils in series with the armature but connects the two pairs of field coils in parallel. Charge flowing to the armature divides as it enters the motor. Half passes through one pair of field coils and the remainder flows to the other pair. A lower

*Figure 15.12 Series-parallel motor*

## Characteristics of a series motor

Torque output of a motor is directly proportional to the product of magnetic flux and current. In a series motor these are at a maximum at zero speed, so the torque will be at a maximum when the armature is locked. As armature speed is slowly increased, a back-electromotive force (EMF) is generated and this causes the current to gradually decrease. Back-EMF is due to the tendency of the motor to act as a generator. As the armature moves through the magnetic flux, an EMF is induced in the conductors. As the polarity of the induced EMF is opposite to the PD applied to the motor, the EMF acts against the supply PD, hence the term back-EMF. The increase in back-EMF with increase in speed, and in consequence the decrease in current, causes the torque output of the motor to gradually fall. This characteristic makes the series motor very suitable for engine starting. A very high torque is required to give engine breakaway but a much lower torque is needed to overcome the resisting torque of the engine at cranking speed.

The speed of a motor varies inversely to the field strength (i.e. when the field strength is decreased the armature speed is increased). Figure 15.13 shows the effect of load on a starter motor. Under a heavy load the field is saturated, and no large variation in speed occurs with slight alteration in load, but when the load is considerably reduced, the rise in the back-EMF causes the magnetic flux to diminish. This results in a rise in the motor speed. The graph shows that a series motor will overspeed if it is allowed to run free without load: this may cause serious damage to the motor. The efficiency of a starter motor is between the limits of 50–70 per cent. Modern vehicles will, therefore, use series-parallel and PM starters.

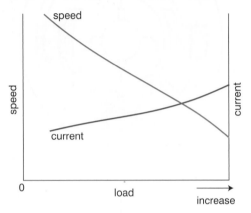

Figure 15.13 Effect of load on a starter motor

### Permanent magnet (PM)

The principle of a PM motor (Figure 15.14) is very comparable to the pre-engaged starter motor, in that the field windings and pole shoes are replaced with high-quality PMs. This gives a reduction in weight of up to 15 per cent. The diameter of the yoke can also

be compacted by a similar amount. These magnets offer continuous excitation and, because of this, the speed and torque characteristic is expected to be constant. Nevertheless, owing to the decrease in battery voltage under load and the low resistance of the armature windings, the characteristics are similar to that of a series-wound motor (Figure 15.15).

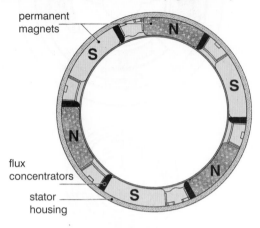

Figure 15.14 PM motor – flux concentrators

A copper and graphite blend is used to make the brushes in two pieces, so that higher copper content is in the power area and higher graphite content is in the commutation area. This gives an improvement in the service life and a reduction in voltage drop, giving higher starter motor power output.

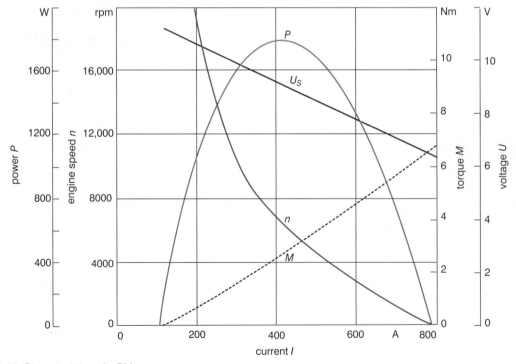

Figure 15.15 Characteristics of a PM motor

## 15.2 Circuits for light vehicle starter motors

Ideally the battery should be situated as close as possible to the motor to minimise voltage drop of the cables. A thick cable is used, such as 37/0.90 (see Chapter 9), and a solenoid is fitted to act as a remote-controlled switch to limit the length of the cable.

Although an insulated-return system is sometimes used, the earth-return arrangement shown in Figure 15.16 is the most common. Since the circuit may have to carry a current of up to 500 A, it is essential that all connections are clean and secure and that the earth-bonding strap joining the engine to the vehicle body is in good condition.

### 15.2.1 Solenoid

A solenoid connects the battery with the starter motor. It is energised when the ignition switch is set to the start position (on some vehicles a starter button is pushed to engage the starter solenoid). On early vehicles, the solenoid was mounted separately from the starter motor.

A solenoid contains field windings and a movable plunger. At one end of the plunger are heavy-duty contacts. These are designed to connect across the heavy-duty terminals.

On modern vehicles, the solenoid is mounted on the starter motor. A shift lever is mounted on one end of the plunger. The lever 'pre-engages' the starter motor pinion gear with the flywheel ring gear.

This common type of solenoid usually contains two separate field windings. The low-current winding connects to ground. The high-current winding connects to the starter motor.

Figures 15.16 and 15.17 show both types of solenoid.

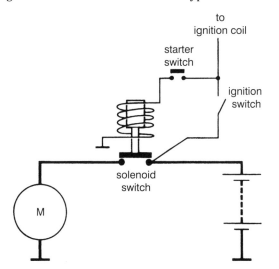

Figure 15.16 Starter motor solenoid

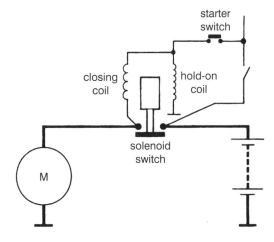

Figure 15.17 Two-coil, single-stage solenoid

The solenoid has copper contacts of adequate area, which are brought together in one stage when the solenoid is energised. When the starter switch is released, a spring returns the solenoid plunger and the contacts are opened (Figure 15.18).

| | |
|---|---|
| 1 solenoid armature | 6 switch contacts |
| 2 pull-in winding | 7 electrical connection |
| 3 hold-in winding | 8 switch contact |
| 4 solenoid core | 9 armature shaft (split) |
| 5 contact spring | 10 return spring |

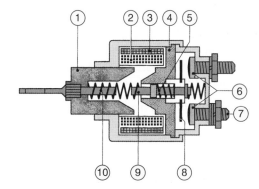

Figure 15.18 Pre-engaged solenoid

Vehicles fitted with an automatic transmission require an additional switch in the solenoid switch circuit. This extra switch, called an inhibitor switch (or neutral safety switch), is set to open and prevents starter operation when a gear is selected.

### 15.2.2 Starter motor immobilisation

A modern anti-theft unit fitted as original equipment normally works in conjunction with the engine management system (EMS). In addition to immobilising the ignition system, these units also isolate the starter motor when the ignition key is removed.

Figure 15.19 shows an example of a circuit that incorporates an anti-theft and engine immobilisation control unit. In this double-fused circuit, the external

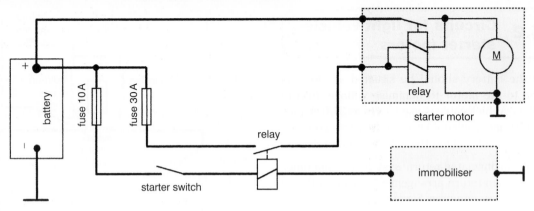

*Figure 15.19 Starter circuit with anti-theft alarm*

relay is energised when the combined ignition/ starter switch is closed to complete the circuit to earth through the anti-theft alarm.

All modern road cars use a chip transponder system, which is integrated into the vehicle's key fob. When inserted into the ignition barrel, the chip is energised by a radio frequency (433.9 MHz set by European Law in 1995) sent from the ignition barrel. Once energised, the chip produces a code that is received and sent to the vehicle's electronic control unit (ECU). If the code is correct, the immobiliser fitted to the vehicle is disarmed and will allow the car to be started. If the code is incorrect, the vehicle will not start and will remain immobilised. Depending on the immobiliser system, this may be done by cutting out voltage to the starter motor, the spark plugs, the fuel pump, or a combination of all three components.

### 15.2.3 Keyless starting

Keyless entry, introduced in 1998 by Mercedes Benz, relies on a radio frequency communicating with the car upon approach. This means that it can unlock doors upon approach and also energise the ignition system when situated anywhere inside the vehicle. This makes de-immobilisation virtually impossible for someone without the key fob and life much easier for the driver of the vehicle when starting the car. The system will usually incorporate a starter button and a brake switch to allow the car to be started.

### 15.2.4 Biometrics

Biometrics is another system that is being implemented on prestige cars to further improve security and immobilisation of vehicles. This system uses fingerprint scanning technology to unlock the car and start the engine. By having a memory database of authorised fingerprints, the system will only allow entry and start-up of the car if the

approved fingerprint can be read. This overcomes the risk of keyless technology whereby the key fob can be stolen and the car driven away by anybody.

## 15.3 Light vehicle starter motor drive mechanisms

On the majority of vehicles, the flywheel is fitted with a ring gear, which meshes with a pinion that is driven by the armature of the motor.

### 15.3.1 Gear ratio

The ratio of the flywheel gear and the starter pinion is governed by the characteristics of the motor. Figure 15.20 shows a typical output for a motor: in this case the maximum power is developed when the motor speed is 1000 rpm. Assuming that the cranking speed required is 100 rpm, then the ratio needed for this motor is given by:

Ratio = motor speed/cranking speed = $\dfrac{1000}{100}$ = 10 : 1

Normally, the pinion has about nine teeth, so the number of teeth on the flywheel is set to give the appropriate ratio; in this case 90 teeth.

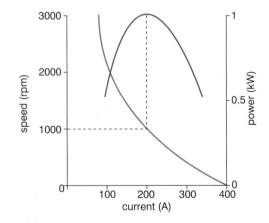

*Figure 15.20 Motor performance*

## 15.3.2 Pinion engagement

The pinion is meshed with the flywheel only when the starter motor is operated. Engagement can be made in one of two ways:

- Inertia engagement (used until the 1980s).
- Pre-engaged drive (used on all cars after the 1980s).

### Inertia engagement

As this type of engagement is becoming obsolete now, only a brief overview will be provided here.

This system uses inertia to provide engagement of the pinion gear on to the flywheel ring gear. As the motor speeds up, the pinion gear is thrown out, since it is mounted on a helical thread. The gear is held in mesh by the force created. It is then disengaged when the engine speed becomes greater than the starter motor speed and the pinion gear moves back along the helical thread.

### Pre-engaged drive

This type was originally introduced for diesel engines, but nowadays it is used on almost all automotive engines.

The pinion engagement is performed by an electrical solenoid, which is integral with the starter motor.

In addition to its mechanical engagement role, the solenoid acts as a relay switch to delay the passage of the full motor current until the pinion has fully meshed with the flywheel. When the engine fires, the pinion does not eject until the driver releases the switch.

This feature overcomes the problem of premature ejection of the pinion during the isolated firing stroke. This achieves better starting and reduced wear of the flywheel teeth (hence the demise of the inertia engagement starter).

After the engine has started, overspeeding of the motor is avoided by using a unidirectional (overrunning) clutch between the pinion and the armature. Figure 15.21 shows the constructional details of one type of pre-engaged motor. A solenoid plunger is connected to an operating lever, which is pivoted to the casing at its centre and forked at its lower end to engage with a guide ring. This ring acts against the unidirectional roller clutch and pinion. Helical splines, formed on the armature shaft, engage with the driving part of the unidirectional clutch. These splines cause the pinion to rotate slightly when the clutch and pinion are moved axially. A strong return spring in the solenoid holds the lever and pinion in the disengaged position. When the starter switch is operated, the two-coil solenoid winding becomes energised and the plunger

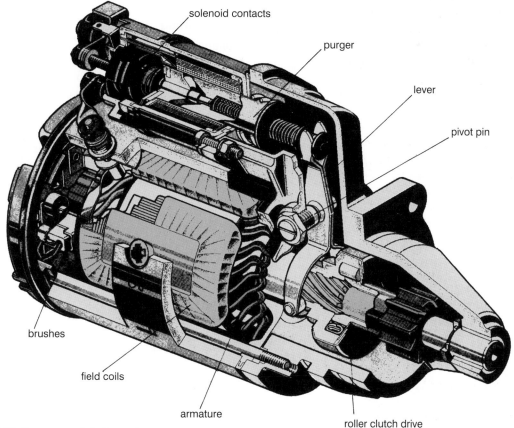

*Figure 15.21 Pre-engaged starter motor*

is drawn into the core. This initial action causes the lower end of the operating lever to move the guide ring and pinion assembly towards the flywheel teeth. This movement, aided by the slight rotation of the pinion, normally gives full meshing of the gears. After this initial action, extra travel of the solenoid plunger causes the main contacts to close: this connects the battery to the motor.

Drive from the armature is transmitted to the unidirectional clutch and pinion by helical splines. Sometimes the initial movement causes the pinion teeth to butt against the flywheel teeth and this prevents full engagement. When this occurs, a spring in the linkage flexes and allows the solenoid plunger to operate the main switch. As soon as the armature and pinion start to move, the teeth engage and the meshing spring pushes the pinion to its driving position. After the engine has fired, the pinion speed will exceed the armature speed. If the motor is still in use, the rollers in the unidirectional clutch will be unlocked and the clutch will slip to protect the motor (Figure 15.22).

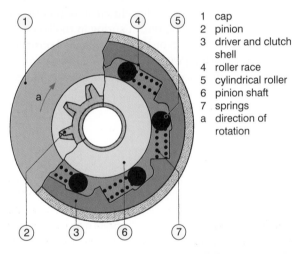

1 cap
2 pinion
3 driver and clutch shell
4 roller race
5 cylindrical roller
6 pinion shaft
7 springs
a direction of rotation

Figure 15.22 Roller-type clutch to protect motor

Release of the starter switch de-energises the solenoid and allows the return spring to open the switch contacts. This occurs well before the pinion disengages and so avoids overspeeding of the motor. Further movement of the plunger causes the operating level to fully withdraw the pinion from the flywheel.

### Armature braking

After disengagement, there is a tendency for a large armature and pinion assembly to continue to rotate because of its momentum. In some starter motors this is prevented by using a disc brake. The driving part of the unidirectional clutch is designed to rub against a part of the casing when the pinion has fully returned. This device minimises noise and tooth wear, which would occur if the starter were operated before the components had come to rest.

### Low-power indexing

As applied to starter motors, indexing means the lining up of the pinion and flywheel teeth to allow full engagement before maximum power is supplied by the motor. Low-power indexing is used on Lucas MSO starter motors. These motors have a two-stage solenoid that enables one field winding to be energised before the other field windings come into operation. The low-powered initial rotation of the pinion reduces the problem of tooth abutment.

### Pinion setting

A pinion of an inertia drive should have the correct out-of-mesh clearance so that it does not contact the flywheel before it starts to revolve. Lucas 5-type drives should have a clearance of about 3 mm.

On some pre-engaged motors, an adjustable pivot pin for the operating lever allows the pinion to be set in the correct position. After energising the solenoid from a 6 V supply, the pin is adjusted until the recommended clearance is obtained between the pinion and end housing (Figure 15.23).

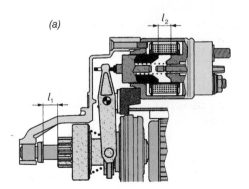

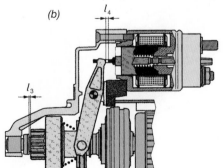

$l_1$ overall pinion travel
$l_2$ solenoid-armature travel
$l_3$ helical travel
$l_4$ free travel

Figure 15.23 Pre-engaged starter – drive engagement: (a) resting position, (b) extended position at end of lever travel

### 15.3.3 PM motor

A significant improvement in the performance-to-weight ratio is achieved by using a PM field system. Used in conjunction with a planetary gear reduction drive, this type of motor is very compact and is suitable for use as a starter motor for a car engine. Figure 15.24 shows the basic construction of a PM motor. This type uses a planetary gear train made of a new plastic steel material. The sun gear is attached to the armature and the output is taken from the three planets that revolve around the inside of a fixed ring gear.

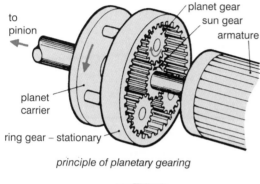

*principle of planetary gearing*

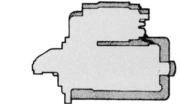

*comparison size – permanent magnet type and conventional type motor*

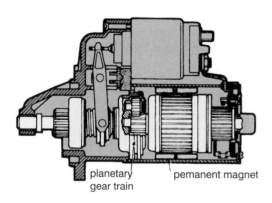

*Figure 15.24  PM starter motor*

### 15.3.4 Stop-start technology

This system came into use in the 2000s and is said to improve fuel efficiency by 5–10 per cent for city cars. Different manufacturers use slightly different systems but the main function is still the same. The idea behind the technology is that when in traffic or stationary for a minimum period of time, instead of wasting fuel by keeping the engine running, the car turns itself off automatically and then restarts as soon as the driver wishes to proceed forward.

Some systems use a starter-alternator, which is basically a starter motor and alternator together in one unit (known as a reversible alternator, see Figure 15.25). Drive is taken from the auxiliary drive belt. This system, adopted by Peugeot, is both faster (400 ms instead of 800 ms) and quieter than a conventional starter motor. A stop-start ECU is integrated to control the system and takes information from a variety of sensors from other ECUs around the vehicle, such as gear position, brake/clutch position, engine temperature, battery voltage and many others. A different type of battery with a higher capacity is also required (around 55 Ah) to cope with having to start the engine numerous times within a short distance and to run all interior functions such as air conditioning and stereo equipment. A warning light is also incorporated in the dashboard to show when the system is active. (See Chapter 8 for further information.)

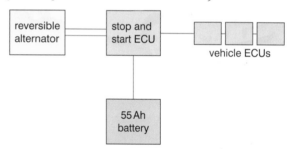

*Figure 15.25  Reversible alternator system*

### 15.3.5 Reversible alternator

This compact unit works as both an alternator and as a starter motor. The starter motor can silently start the engine using the alternator belt as quickly as 0.4 s and provides no vibration. Once started, it automatically reverts to being an alternator. A reversible tensioner allows power to be transmitted in both directions. These units are mainly manufactured by Valeo and Denso.

### 15.3.6 Brushless motors

These starter motors are beginning to be phased into automotive applications. They do away with the carbon brushes and instead rely on electromagnetism to transfer electrical current. An integrated sensor that is coupled with a speed controller is used to control commutation, which is more precise. This type of starter has many advantages over its predecessor:

- No wear and tear (because there are no brushes that can wear down), so the lifetime is increased.
- Greater reliability.
- Reduced maintenance.

- Reduced friction, so less noise and a lower level of radio interference, improving communication throughout the engine bay.
- Space saved, by having no brushes, can be used to make the starter motor more compact, or for more turns of wire and thicker wire, hence less resistance and more power.

### 15.3.7 Hybrid vehicle starting

A hybrid vehicle uses a system that includes both a high-voltage battery and internal-combustion engine power linked to a split powertrain system, which then powers the wheels (Figure 15.26).

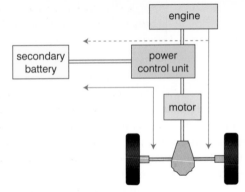

*Figure 15.26 Hybrid vehicle: (a) Toyota Prius, (b) starting system*

To start the engine, an alternating current (AC) motor generator is used, which serves as both a generator for the high-voltage batteries and a starter motor.

The motor contains two magnetically reliant rotor and stator layers. The rotor has six poles with windings, while the stator has nine. The layers are symmetrical, when considering the plane perpendicular to the centre of the motor shaft. Being a three-phase motor, three coil windings from a layer are connected in series, with three windings on the other layer. A stationary reel is present and has field coils wrapped around it. This is positioned between the two stator sets. The reel has a rotating cylindrical core that guides the magnetic field.

Magnetic flux is created by the coils and this travels through the guide and shaft onto the rotor before the stator poles. It then closes itself via the motor housing. With this system, one set of rotor poles is magnetically north, while the other set is magnetically south. The magnetic field is induced in the rotor without the use of brushes. On both sides of the field coil assembly are two rotor and stator sections, having the rotor shaft as its main core, along with a front and end cap, plus the motor's housing. Photo-interrupters are also used at the rear of the motor to detect rotor position.

A photo-interrupter sensor is composed of an infrared emitter on one upright and a shielded infrared detector on the other. By emitting a beam of infrared light from one upright to the other, the sensor can detect when an object passes between the uprights, breaking the beam.

### 15.4 Heavy vehicle starter motors

An engine having a capacity of more than 3 litres needs a starter motor of considerable power, especially if the engine is a compression-ignition (diesel) type. This type of engine must be cranked at a speed of at least 100 rpm to initiate combustion, whereas a petrol engine will usually start if it is rotated at about 50–75 rpm. The compression-ignition engine always draws in a full charge of air and has a very high compression ratio, so the maximum torque required to drive the engine over 'compression' is greater than for a petrol engine. Having passed top dead centre (TDC) the high pressure in the cylinder accelerates the piston rapidly, so this causes both the rotational speed and the resisting torque loading on the starter motor to vary considerably.

To obtain high starting power, many heavy vehicles use a 24 V system. For a given electrical power requirement, the doubling of the voltage, compared with a light vehicle's 12 V system, reduces the current by half. Without the extra 12 V, the current load on the battery and starter circuit would be exceptionally high, especially on a cold morning in winter.

Another problem experienced with large engines is the high torque required to overcome breakaway and inertia of the heavy parts. It needs a strong drive system and the pinion of this system must be fully engaged before full power is applied to the motor.

Two types of motor and drive system are used:

- Axial (sliding armature)
- Coaxial (sliding gear)

## 15.4.1 Axial (sliding armature) starter motor

The main features of this type are its size and robust construction. Engagement of the pinion to the flywheel is obtained by arranging the complete armature assembly to slide axially through the motor casing. Figure 15.27 shows a simplified construction.

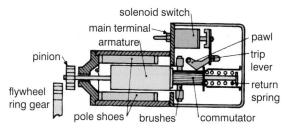

*Figure 15.27 Construction of axial starter*

The motor is shown in the rest position and, in this state, the armature is held by a spring so that it is offset to the field poles. When the field is energised, the armature is pulled to the left and the pinion is slid into engagement with the flywheel.

Figure 15.28 shows the electrical circuit, which incorporates three field windings. The main winding is the usual thick-section, low-resistance winding, which is connected to the armature in series. The auxiliary winding is wound with thinner wire and has a relatively high resistance. It is also connected in series with the armature, but in parallel with the main winding. The holding winding is also a high-resistance winding, but is connected in parallel with the armature as well as with the other windings.

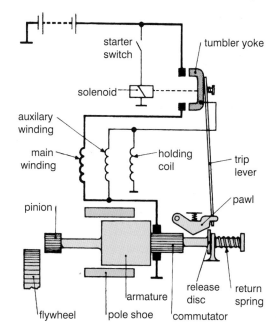

*Figure 15.28 Circuit of axial motor*

The starter is operated through a two-stage solenoid switch, mounted on the starter, and is energised by the driver's switch in the cab. When the switch is operated, the first pair of contacts closes but the second pair is held open by a pawl, which engages in a slot in the trip lever. Only when the pinion is near fully engaged does the pawl allow the second pair of contacts to meet.

Closing the first pair of contacts energises the auxiliary windings, holding windings and armature. This action causes the armature to rotate slowly and move axially to a position where it is central to the field poles. At the same time, the pinion is slid into mesh with the flywheel gear.

When the pinion is near to full engagement, the release disc on the armature strikes the pawl and causes the trip lever to close the second pair of contacts. Charge now flows through the main windings, allowing the motor to develop its full torque.

As cranking speed increases, back-EMF causes the current through the main and auxiliary windings to decrease, especially when the engine fires spasmodically but does not actually start. In this condition, the magnetic strength in the main and auxiliary windings is insufficient to oppose the armature return spring and hold the pinion in full engagement. This is prevented by the holding winding because the current in this winding is not affected by the back-EMF generated by the rotating armature.

After the pinion has de-meshed and the armature has returned, the momentum of the rotating mass tends to keep the armature rotating. This is resisted by the 'generator effect' produced by the interaction of the holding winding and the armature. This electrical reaction to the armature 'brakes' the armature and quickly brings it to rest to enable the driver to re-engage the starter without damage to the gear teeth.

The pinion is connected to the armature shaft through a small multi-plate clutch. This serves two functions:

- It is arranged to slip if the torque applied to it exceeds a predetermined limiting value, thus safeguarding the starter from damage should the engine backfire.
- It is arranged to disengage when the engine starts and drives the pinion faster than the armature, thus preventing the armature being damaged by excessive speed.

## 15.4.2 Coaxial (sliding gear) starter motor

Lucas CAV can offer this type of motor in 12 V or 24 V versions as an alternative to the axial type, whereas Bosch uses it for the heavy end of their range.

As with the axial starter motor, this type moves the pinion into engagement under reduced power and only when it is fully meshed is full power applied. The main difference is in the way the pinion is slid into mesh with the flywheel. Instead of the whole armature assembly moving axially, only the pinion is made to slide into mesh by a solenoid mounted in a housing coaxially with the shaft.

Figure 15.29 shows the main details of the circuit of a coaxial starter motor. The main terminal is connected directly to the battery and the terminal marked 'sol' is connected to the battery via a starter switch in the cab. When this switch is operated, the two-stage solenoid is energised, which moves the pinion into mesh and at the same time closes the first set of contacts, the second set being kept open by a trip lever. At this state, current to the main field is limited by the resistor, so the armature rotates slowly during the engagement period.

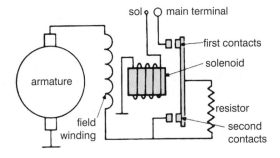

*Figure 15.29 Circuit of coaxial starter*

Just before the fully meshed position is reached, a lever trips the second set of contacts. This action bypasses the resistor, gives full current to the main field and allows the motor to produce its maximum torque.

This design uses four steel balls to lock the pinion sleeve to the shaft to avoid premature ejection of the pinion when the engine fires spasmodically. When the engine starts normally, overspeeding of the motor is prevented by using the centrifugal effect on a set of steel balls positioned adjacent to the locking balls. When a given speed is reached, the outward force on the balls moves the locking collar and allows the pinion to disengage.

A return spring at the flywheel end of the armature shaft assists pinion disengagement and holds the pinion clear of the flywheel while the engine is running.

Bosch sliding-gear motors have the main solenoid placed at the opposite end of the motor to the pinion. This solenoid keeps the pinion in full engagement until the driver releases the starter switch. Drive from the armature to the pinion is transmitted by

a multidisc clutch. In addition to its torque-limiting duty, this clutch also prevents overspeeding by releasing the plates and slipping when the engine starts and overruns the motor.

Some motors use a shunt field winding to limit the no-load speed and others have a brake winding, which comes into action when the driver releases the starter switch.

## 15.5 Maintenance and fault diagnosis

The most important part of a starting system is the battery; if this is not in first-class condition, then the speed will be low and the duration of cranking will be limited (Figure 15.30). It should be noted that a fault attributed to a battery may be due to other factors, such as a defective charging system, a short to earth in another system, or overload of the battery due to driving or seasonal conditions.

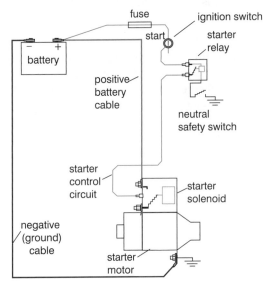

*Figure 15.30 Battery connection to starter motor system*

Attention to warning instruments and observation of the engine's starting performance enables the driver to recognise the initial conditions that soon develop into a major fault.

As a very large current has to be provided by a battery to the starter motor, a drop in the battery PD occurs. When this drop is excessive, the ignition system is 'robbed' and the voltage output of the coil may then be insufficient to give a suitable spark at the plugs (although the starter motor is still functioning, albeit at low speed). This condition can be confirmed when an engine cannot be started with the motor, but can be started easily by 'bump-starting' (rolling the vehicle in top gear and suddenly releasing the clutch). Normally, this problem is associated with a battery fault, but on many modern engines the problem is overcome by fitting a cold-start ballast resistor in the ignition supply lead. In addition to the resistor lead, a separate lead is fitted between a terminal on the starter solenoid and the ignition coil. This lead allows the resistor to be bypassed when the starter is operated.

## 15.5.1 Maintenance

Routine attention should be given to the battery, especially the terminals. All terminals and connectors in the starter circuit should be clean and secure, and earth straps from the engine to the chassis should be checked.

## 15.5.2 Fault diagnosis

If the likely defects of each part of the system are considered, together with the possible symptoms given by each defect, then it is possible to reverse the order and, as a result, the electrician should be able to offer a probable cause of a particular fault.

The parts of the system that cause the main problems and the possible faults are:

- battery – low state of charge or defective
- terminals – high resistance due to corrosion or slackness
- cables – broken or partially broken, especially the earth-bonding strap between the engine and frame
- solenoid – dirty contacts or faulty connection between windings and terminals
- starter switch – high resistance at contacts or broken cables
- motor – brushes not bedding or dirty commutator
- pinion – not meshing or jammed due to a worn flywheel ring gear.

These faults are incorporated in Table 15.1. The second column suggests some initial checks that should be made to enable the actual cause to be diagnosed. Location of the precise cause often requires the use of test equipment.

A starter motor that seizes the engine when the motor is operated indicates that the teeth on the flywheel have worn to the extent that they allow the gears to jam together as they attempt to mesh.

An engine always comes to rest at the start of one of the compression strokes, so the flywheel becomes burred due to pinion entry in these positions. The number of places that wear occurs around the circumference depends on the number of cylinders of the engine. For example:

- four-cylinder engine = two places
- six-cylinder engine = three places
- eight-cylinder engine = four places.

Whereas in the past a spanner was used to wind-out the pinion after it had jammed, on a modern unit it is necessary to slacken off the securing bolts of the motor. In an emergency, it is sometimes possible to free a pinion by rocking the car backwards and forwards with top gear engaged and the ignition off, but this practice may result in a bent armature spindle.

Most starter-ring gears are held on to the flywheel by an interference fit: this involves no fasteners, only the friction of the two parts once pressed together, which will hold the two parts securely. When a new gear has to be fitted, the worn gear is removed by drilling a hole in the gear and then splitting the ring with a chisel. The new ring is preheated to the recommended temperature and, while it is still hot, it is tapped into place, making sure that the chamfer on the teeth is positioned on the side of pinion entry.

### Circuit tests

Before carrying out these checks, the battery condition should be determined by using a hydrometer and heavy-discharge tester. A hydrometer is an easy way to test the level of sulphuric acid in the electrolyte, while a voltmeter can measure the level of charge within the battery.

SAFETY – Be careful not to spill any electrolyte fluid that is stored within the battery. This sulphuric acid is both poisonous and corrosive, and is harmful if it comes into contact with skin and eyes. It can also easily damage painted surfaces.

Tests are made with a multimeter or moving-coil voltmeter (0–20 V range for 12 V system) and all readings are taken when the engine is being cranked (Figure 15.31). To prevent the engine starting, the low-tension ignition circuit should be disconnected or, in the case of a diesel engine, the stop control should be operated.

- Test 1. The meter is connected across the battery and the reading is noted. If the voltage is less than 10 V, the battery is suspect.
- Tests 2, 3 and 4. Readings taken at the switch and just before the motor points should be similar to those in Test 1. If the reading at point 4 shows a voltage drop greater than 0.5 V, then the cause of the resistance should be investigated.
- Test 5. This test measures the voltage drop on the earth side of the circuit. If the reading is greater than 0.25 V, then all earth connections should be checked, especially the engine-bonding strap.

*Table 15.1  Fault diagnosis*

| Symptom | Result of initial check | Possible cause |
|---|---|---|
| Low cranking speed | Lights dim when starter switch is operated | 1  Discharged or defective battery |
| | | 2  Poor connections between battery and solenoid |
| | | 3  Tight engine |
| Starter does not operate | No lights or lights go out when starter is operated | 1  Discharged or defective battery |
| | | 2   Poor connection between battery and solenoid or between battery and earth |
| | | 3  Severe short circuit to earth in starting motor |
| | Solenoid 'clicks' when starter switch is operated; lights unaffected | 1  Poor connection between solenoid and motor |
| | | 2  Broken or insecure earth strap |
| | | 3  Defective solenoid |
| | | 4   Defective motor – most probably commutator or brushes |
| | No 'click' from solenoid; lights unaffected | 1  Defective solenoid |
| | | 2  Defective starter switch |
| | | 3  Poor connections between starter switch and solenoid |
| | | 4  Defective inhibitor switch (auto. transmission) |
| | Repeating 'clicking' from solenoid; lights unaffected | 1  Broken holding coil in solenoid |
| | Repeating 'clicking' from solenoid; lights dim | 1  Discharged or defective battery |
| | Lights dim when starter is operated and engine has seized | 1  Pinion teeth jammed in flywheel |
| | | 2  Engine has seized due to engine problem |
| Starter 'whines' but pinion does not engage | | 1  Dirt on helix (inertia drive) |
| | | 2  Defective pinion engagement system (pre-engaged) |

### Safe practice

Disconnect the earth terminal of the battery before removing a starter motor from an engine. Ensure the radio code and any other coded unit information is available before disconnecting.

After the starter motor has been refitted and the battery reconnected, do not forget to re-programme all coded units, such as radio and ECUs.

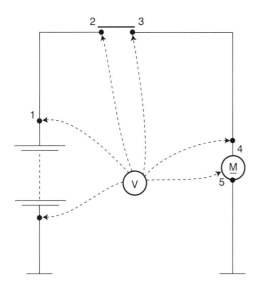

*Figure 15.31 Starter motor circuit tests*

A high resistance at any connection point causes a drop in voltage; this can be verified by connecting a voltmeter across the part of the circuit where the resistance is suspected. If the voltage applied to the starter is lower than specified, the current will be reduced and this will lower the motor's speed and torque.

## Commutator and brushes

If the battery and external circuit are serviceable but the motor fails to operate, then the motor should be removed, dismantled and inspected. The earth terminal of the battery must be disconnected before attempting to remove the motor.

### Commutator

This should be cleaned with a petrol-moistened cloth. Any burnt spots can be removed by using fine glass-paper, but not emery cloth. When a satisfactory surface cannot be obtained, it will be necessary to skim the commutator in a lathe.

### Brushgear

All brushes must move freely in their boxes; the springs must exert sufficient force and each brush should not be less than the specified length. For example, in the case of Lucas motors, the minimum length is 9.5 mm and 8 mm for face-type and cylindrical commutators respectively.

Fitting new brushes involves the soldering of the brush leads to the appropriate connector points. In the case of aluminium alloy field coils, the old brush lead is cut at a given distance from the field and the new lead is soldered to the old lead.

A brush used on a cylindrical commutator must be bedded-in by using glass-paper to cut the brush to the same contour as the commutator.

## Bench-testing the motor

A number of tests can be applied to the motor, as detailed below.

### Light-running test

The power of the motor can be measured under free-running conditions on a test stand. The time taken for this test must be short because the centrifugal effect at the no-load speed can cause damage to the armature windings. An ammeter must be connected in series before the starter motor, while a voltmeter can be connected in parallel before and after the motor.

A Lucas 9M90 motor should 'draw' 840 W from a 12 V supply.

### Running-torque test

The torque can be measured by using a dummy flywheel on a special test bench that loads the motor and simulates the resisting torque of an engine. By noting the output torque $t$ (Nm) and speed $n$ (rev/s), the power (W) is obtained from:

$$\text{Power} = 2\pi nt$$

For example, if:

$\pi = 3.142$

$n = 50\,\text{rev/s}$

$t = 100\,\text{Nm}$

$\text{Power} = 2 \times 3.142 \times 50 \times 100 = 31,420\,\text{W}$

Comparing the output power with the input power allows the efficiency of the motor to be calculated:

$$\text{Efficiency (\%)} = (\text{Output power/Input power}) \times 100$$

For example:

$(31,420/35,000) \times 100 = 89.8\%$ (to 1 decimal place)

### Keyless starting and biometrics

These advanced systems often require the use of a diagnostic tool when a fault occurs, unlike the mechanical issues that are found with the actual starter motor.

With keyless starting/entry, if the key fails, there is often a manufacturer's procedure to gain entry to the car. This is most commonly achieved by removing a cap on the door handle, which hides a key slot that can be used with the small key strip that will be built into the key card.

If the keyless starting system begins to fail, through the drainage of the key card battery, the key card should be placed next to the steering column and the car should start as the radio frequency then only has to travel a small distance to reach a transmitter that communicates with the ECU. When battery replacement is necessary, it may mean that the key has to be re-coded to the car in order to ensure communication takes place.

The system can also be read for fault codes using the appropriate diagnostic tool.

The start/stop switch can also be an area for fault as the simple switch controls the ignition–start–stop procedure.

### Stop-start technology

This system relies heavily on sensors from other areas in the vehicle, so an error in another system will render this technology non-functional until the fault is cured. A diagnostic tool can be used to check for system faults in order to rectify any problem. If a fault occurs, the engine management light will become illuminated and the system will be unavailable for use so that the car can operate in a conventional fashion.

## 15.6 Summary of basic pre-engaged operation

When the ignition switch is set to the start position, electrical charge flows through both of the solenoid windings, creating a magnetic field.

The starter motor (field coils and armature) is connected in series with the high-current winding of the solenoid, so it begins to turn. The magnetic field moves the plunger towards the heavy-duty terminals. At the same time, the shift lever moves the pinion outward. As lever movement continues, the slow-moving pinion gear of the starter motor engages with the flywheel ring gear. At full travel, the heavy-duty contacts join and full current passes to the starter motor. The resulting magnetic field turns the armature, which turns the engine. Once the gears are meshed, the magnetic field produced by the low winding is sufficient to keep the plunger in position. When the ignition switch is set to the run position, the plunger returns to its original position.

In the past, the transmission system was controlled by the driver and used the minimum of electronic assistance. But with growing need to limit the emissions from the internal-combustion engine, the control of the transmission has become computer controlled. The advantages of electronic control include reduced emissions, increased driveability and ease of use, self-diagnosis and reliability. It is more complicated, however, the advantages outweigh the disadvantages.

## What the transmission system does

The function of the whole transmission system is to take the torque from the engine to the wheels. It also needs to:

- provide a temporary neutral
- provide a permanent neutral
- allow for a reverse gear

- give variable torque multiplications for all driving conditions
- change the direction of the drive
- allow for the different wheel speeds while cornering
- be easy to use.

## 16.1 Purpose of the transmission system

The internal-combustion engine used in modern vehicles will only operate well over a limited effective speed range (e.g. 1500–7000 rpm), producing a comparatively low torque (turning effort). If the speed drops below the lower limit, or if the load is too great, the engine will stall and the vehicle will come to rest.

If the vehicle did not have a gearbox, the following disadvantages would soon become apparent:

- Poor acceleration from rest
- Poor hill-climbing ability
- Vehicle cannot be driven at low speeds
- No neutral or reverse

### Poor acceleration from rest

The clutch would have to be slipped for a considerable time to avoid stalling the engine. A road speed of about 24 kph (15 mph) would have to be reached before full engagement could take place and, during this time, the driving force at the wheels (**tractive effort**) would only be slightly greater than the force opposing the motion of the vehicle (**tractive resistance**). The acceleration is governed by the difference between the tractive effort and resistance, and, if this difference is small, the acceleration will be poor.

**Tractive effort**: the force required to move an object or vehicle forwards.

**Tractive resistance**: the opposing force that the tractive effort must overcome to create movement.

### Poor hill-climbing ability

A gradient increases the resistance, which will mean that as soon as a hill is tackled, the engine will slow down and eventually stall. This could be overcome by using a large engine with high **torque** output, but that would be uneconomical.

**Torque**: turning effort. It is calculated as the force applied at a distance from a fulcrum point and is measured in newton metres (Nm). Torque = Force (N) × Distance (m).

### Vehicle cannot be driven at low speeds

As the vehicle speed is decreased, the engine speed will also be decreased. Slipping of the clutch would be necessary to avoid stalling if the vehicle had to be driven at low speeds.

### No neutral or reverse

It would not be possible to keep the vehicle stationary without stalling, so the clutch would always have to be disengaged when the vehicle was not moving. This also makes the vehicle difficult to manoeuvre.

The transmission takes the torque of the engine, variably multiplies it and moves it to the driving wheels.

## 16.2 Transmission types

Transmission in modern vehicles can be broken down into various types:

- Manual
- Semi-automatic
- Fully-automatic
- Continuously variable transmission (CVT)

### Manual

Completely manual transmission is where the driver operates all the functions of the system. It has a lever to change the gears and a pedal to disengage and engage the clutch (Figure 16.1).

Figure 16.1 Vauxhall Vectra six-speed gear lever

### Semi-automatic

With semi-automatic transmission there is a driver-operated gearbox, however, there is no clutch and the drive from the engine passes through a torque converter before passing through to the gearbox. No clutch pedal is fitted.

### Fully automatic

With the fully automatic system there is no clutch and the gearbox is a series of epicyclic geartrains controlled by multi-plate clutches and oil pressure operated valves. These have no clutch pedal and have a lever for the driver to select, but not change gears. There is usually a choice of gears: park, reverse, neutral, drive, 3, 2 and 1 (Figure 16.2).

### Manual or automatic

There are now also systems that are fully manual, in that they have a clutch and a manual gearbox, however the control of the clutch and changing of the gears are carried out by servo motors controlled by the transmission control module (powertrain control module, PCM). There is no clutch pedal but there are normally switches mounted around the steering wheel

Figure 16.2 Typical automatic gear lever

so that the driver can change the gears. The switches operate the servo motors and the gears will change if the operating conditions are suitable (Figure 16.3).

Figure 16.3 Modern gear selector lever with option for automatic or manual gear changing

### Continuously variable transmission (CVT)

A continuously variable transmission (CVT) system is a fully automatic transmission that uses two variably sized wheels and a drive link (either a chain or a belt) between them. An **electronic control unit (ECU)** controls the size of the drive pulley and a variable gear ratio is achieved, allowing for optimum torque, economy or speed. There is no clutch pedal and the driver can select either forward or reverse, neutral or park.

> **Electronic control unit (ECU):** a small computer in the vehicle that uses sensors to find out the state of a component so that it can control another component or system.

## 16.3 History of electronic control

Traditionally, manual gearboxes had no requirements for any kind of electronic control, except for a contact switch when reverse was engaged to operate the reverse lights. The speedometer was driven by a gear connected to the differential. Some manufacturers removed the cable drive for the speedometer and fitted a speed sensor to drive an electronic instrument.

### Electronic speedometer

This system can be actuated by a transistorised pulse generator type of sender unit driven by a short length of flexible cable from the gearbox output shaft. The sensor consists of an electromagnetic coil, a four-bladed rotor driven from the gearbox, and a solid-state circuit incorporating two transistors (Figure 16.4). Two cables are connected to the sensor: one provides a 12V supply from the battery and the other provides an oscillatory voltage of 1.2–6.5V at a frequency of 3.5MHz. When the rotor pole passes the electromagnet, the oscillation is quenched and this produces a signal that oscillates between 1.2V and 6.5V, but then has periods when the voltage is held at 1.2V. This is passed to the logic circuit in the instrument panel where it is converted into a signal of square waveform. The speed of the rotor controls the number of pulses generated per second. A typical application produces 5968.8 pulses per mile, which the logic board converts to give an output to the speedometer display unit of 1.6588Hz per 1mph and 6151 pulses per mile for odometer operation. A stepper motor is often used to drive the odometer.

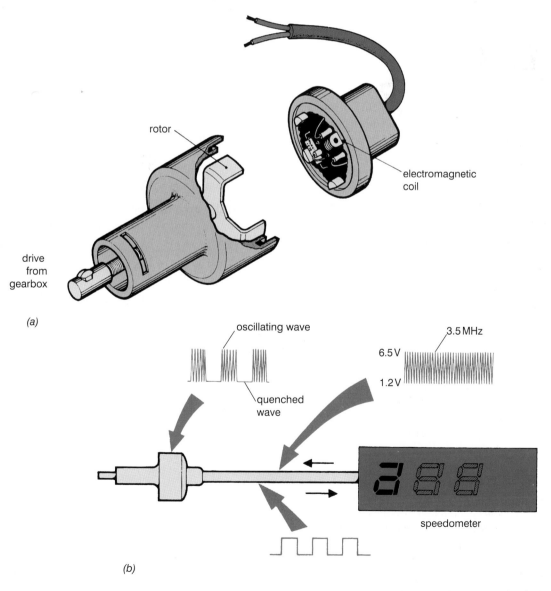

Figure 16.4 Electronic speedometer

In most modern vehicles this function is usually carried out by the wheel-speed sensors, which are part of the anti-lock braking system (ABS) and are mounted at the wheel hubs (Figure 16.5).

*Figure 16.5 Wheel-speed sensor mounted on a hub*

Automatic gearboxes use oil pressure to operate multi-plate clutches to operate epicyclic geartrains to provide ratios and, more recently, electronic valves have been used to control the movement of the oil pressure to give more accurate and precise gear changes. The torque converter (Figure 16.6) is very effective, but as the speeds of the engine and gearbox become closer they become more inefficient. To compensate for this inefficiency, most modern automatic transmission systems use an electronic solenoid-operated clutch to lock the impellor and the turbine together so that they rotate at the same speed. This direct drive through to the gearbox increases the fuel economy of the vehicle by eliminating slip in the torque converter and transferring all the engine torque to the gearbox.

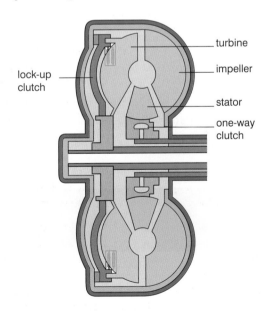

*Figure 16.6 Torque converter with lock-up clutch*

## 16.4  Multiplexing

Modern electronically controlled transmission systems require a lot of information about the state of the vehicle if the **transmission control module (TCM)** is going to make the correct decisions about the selection of gears, control of the gear changes and control of clutch engagement and disengagement. The TCM needs to know about the engine speed, vehicle speed, engine load and braking requirements, as well as informing other systems of the state of the transmission. In order to control these functions, a labyrinth of cables and sensors is required, which occupy valuable space as well as being costly and heavy.

Using a multiplexing or **controller area network (CAN)** system cuts down on the cables and sensors required, and the time needed to pass on the information. The CAN system (Figure 16.8) has been recognised by the International Organization for Standardization (ISO) as the standard for automotive applications that require a baud rate (information transfer speed) of more than 125 Kb (kilobits). Other standards are used for non-essential systems, which do not have to use such a fast rate; they can use a baud rate of about 10 Kb.

**Transmission control module (TCM):** the computer that controls the operation of the transmission. It takes inputs from various sensors around the transmission and the rest of the car.

**Controller area network (CAN):** the network for the passing of information between separate vehicle systems.

The TCM is given information about the state of the engine and all the other systems; it can use this information to control the transmission for optimum driveability and economy. The TCM also passes information about the transmission throughout the vehicle so that all the other systems know about its state at any particular time (Figure 16.7).

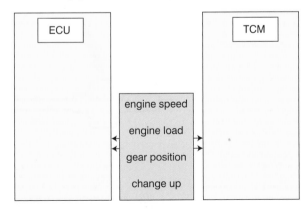

*Figure 16.7 Multiplexing information between ECU and TCM*

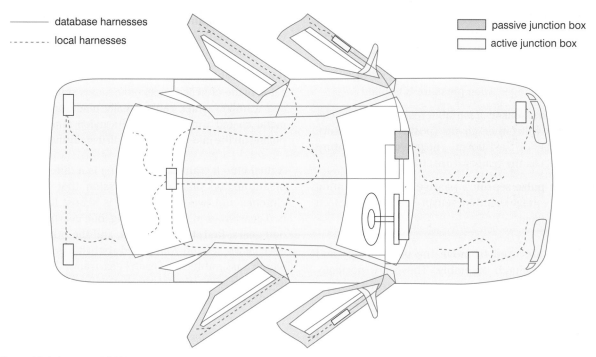

database harnesses
local harnesses

passive junction box
active junction box

*Figure 16.8 Layout of CAN system*

## 16.5 Sensors and actuators used in transmission systems

In this section we will discuss the use of sensors and actuators in the transmission system. For further information on sensors and actuators, refer to Chapters 5 and 6.

The electronic operation of the transmission system imitates the control of other systems. As with any computerised system, it will have inputs, a process and control of outputs. It has a central TCM, which controls the operation of the transmission. The TCM depends on a series of sensors to provide information about the current functioning condition of various components and from that will control various actuators to change the state of the transmission.

The types of sensors and actuators used will depend on the kind of transmission system and the amount of electronic control that it has. A fully manual system has little or no electronic control, whereas a fully automatic system will have many sensors and actuators to control all aspects of the transmission, normally with additional inputs from the driver.

Various inputs are required from sensors that are mounted in systems other than the transmission system and it would be unnecessary and over complicated to have more sensors gathering the same information just for the TCM. The other systems share the information with the transmission system via the vehicle's CAN system.

Engine speed is usually measured, using either a **Hall effect sensor** or an inductive pulse sensor; the sensor will be fitted around the crankshaft. It senses engine speed and basic engine position. For more accurate engine position information a sensor is also mounted around the camshaft. This combination of the two sensors gives accurate information about the speed and position of the engine. The camshaft generally uses a Hall effect sensor.

Engine load is measured by a combination of the air mass meter, the manifold absolute **pressure sensor** and the throttle position sensor. Engine temperature is monitored by a negative temperature coefficient (NTC) **temperature sensor** fitted to the cooling system, and oil temperature sensors fitted to the engine and gearbox.

Vehicle speed is monitored by the wheel-speed sensors for the ABS. It is usually a Hall effect or **inductive pulse sensor** fitted around the wheel hubs.

There may be another speed sensor in the gearbox to measure the speeds of the individual shafts, the input shafts, lay shafts and main shafts, and the epicyclic gear clusters may all have speed sensors on them, depending on the type of transmission system fitted. These are likely to be either Hall effect or inductive pulse and will send a signal back to the TCM.

**Hall effect sensor**: an active (i.e. requiring an input voltage) motion sensor that can sense zero movement as well as movement. It creates a digital signal.

**Pressure sensor**: normally a variable resistor whose resistance changes when pressure is applied.

**Temperature sensor**: a variable resistor sensor. The resistance will either go up (positive temperature coefficient) or go down (negative temperature coefficient) as the temperature changes.

**Inductive pulse sensor**: a passive (i.e. not requiring an input voltage) motion sensor that generates an analogue signal.

Actuators are used to move the gear linkage and operate the clutch assembly. These are normally electric motors, either rotary or linear servo motors.

## 16.6  Clutch electronic control

In the past, the only electronic control associated with the clutch system was a switch on the clutch pedal to signal that the clutch was being operated, usually for the purposes of cruise control. More modern vehicles use an **automated manual transmission (AMT)** system in which the car has a manual clutch, a manual gearbox, and no clutch pedal or gear lever as the operation of these items is done by electric actuators controlled by the TCM. This will use an electric motor to operate the hydraulic system or to pull on a **Bowden cable** to actuate the clutch. When the driver selects a gear, usually by operating a dummy gear lever or a switch on the steering wheel, the TCM will disengage the clutch before actually selecting the gear. As soon as the driver operates the accelerator the TCM will engage the clutch and the vehicle will move off. As the vehicle speed increases, the TCM will disengage the clutch as the gear changes up in the gearbox and then engage the clutch again to continue the drive. The TCM knows which gear is selected by comparing the road-wheel speed to the engine speed. As the car slows down the TCM will operate the clutch actuation and then the gear selector to move down through the gearbox. The times for changes are much shorter than for a driver-operated change. Just before the vehicle comes to a stop, the TCM will finally operate the actuator to disengage the clutch and keep it disengaged until the driver touches the accelerator or selects neutral. The TCM will react to driver changes up and down the gearbox if the conditions are suitable (i.e. it will not change up a gear too soon and have the engine labouring or change into a gear that will have the engine over-revving).

**Automated manual transmission (AMT)**: manual transmission that has all the gear changes controlled by a TCM and carried out by actuators.

**Bowden cable**: a type of flexible cable with an inner cable made of helical steel (sometimes stainless steel) and a hollow outer cable usually made of plastic or metal coated with plastic and a nylon inner surface; pulling on the inner steel cable will usually move a lever.

A dual clutch transmission (DTC) is a different style of automated manual transmission that uses two clutches and two geartrains. It is almost like having two gearboxes in the one casing, one gearbox for the odd gears, first, third and fifth, and the other for the even gears, second, fourth and sixth. It has a separate clutch assembly for each geartrain. The whole gearbox works as one unit and is usually operated in fully automatic mode but with the function for the driver to change gears manually.

The driver selects a gear by operating the gear selector and both the clutch packs will disengage. The TCM operates the electric motors to select the gear then as the driver presses the accelerator then the clutch for that gear cluster, the clutch for the other gear cluster is still disengaged. When the driver changes manually they operate the gear lever; this is a switch that activates the TCM, which in turn will operate the selector servo motors to change the gears, as long as the operating conditions are met.

The clutches used are the smaller diameter multi-plate clutches, similar to the clutches found on motorcycles. Dry multi-plate clutches can be used on smaller engines with a torque output of up to 250 Nm. These can also use less fuel because they do not have the drag on the clutch components of the oil. Wet multi-plate clutches are used with engines that have a higher torque output and run in oil, which helps to maintain a suitable working temperature. The clutches in the Bugatti Veyron can transmit 1250 Nm of torque (Figure 16.9).

*Figure 16.9 Volkswagen Group dual clutch direct-shift gearbox (note two clutches in the bell housing)*

## Fitment of the clutch assemblies in a dual clutch gearbox

One design is to have the two clutches in line, one behind the other, with the forward clutch output shaft running inside the rear clutch output shaft (Figure 16.10).

Mounted right behind the crankshaft, this design has the clutches together, but one is outside the other and the output shaft of the inner clutch will run inside the output shaft for the outer clutch (Figure 16.11).

The latest fitment of the clutch is to have two similar-sized clutches mounted side by side and driven by a gear from the engine crankshaft. The two geartrains run side by side (Figure 16.12).

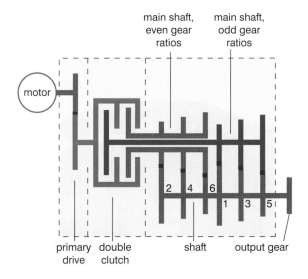

Figure 16.10  Dual clutch gearbox

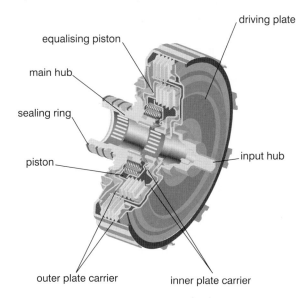

Figure 16.11  Volkswagen dual clutch assembly

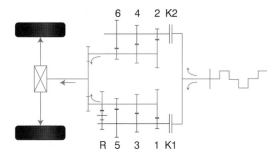

Figure 16.12  Dual clutch assembly mounted side by side

## 16.7  Manual gearbox electronic control

The control of manual gearboxes has been taken over by a TCM, which will now control the gear changes using servo motors. The gearbox itself has not changed and may be exactly the same as previous vehicles, however, the gear change linkage is now connected to three or more electric servo motors, which will move the linkage side to side across the neutral position, or forwards and backwards into and out of the gears. The driver selects the gear by operating a 'dummy' gear selector lever on the floor. The lever has a series of switches on it so that the TCM knows which position the driver has selected.

It will have the following choices:

- P (park) – this holds the gears in neutral and will lock up the gearbox. The car can be started in this position.
- R (reverse) – this is for moving the car backwards. The engine cannot be started in this position and this gear cannot be selected without pressing the footbrake.
- N (neutral) – there is no gear selected but the gearbox is not locked. It should be used when the vehicle is stopped for more than a few seconds, as sitting in gear when the vehicle is not moving will cause the clutches to become very hot and wear. This is because the clutches are held very close to the point of engagement.
- D (drive) – these are the forward gears and selection will be automatically controlled by the PCM. Manual is usually selected from here by moving the gear selector lever to the side. The lever cannot be moved into neutral without pressing the footbrake.
- M (manual) – the lever sits in the central position and is spring-loaded back to this position. When the driver wants to change to a higher gear they will push the lever forwards and, if all the conditions are as required, the gear will be

changed. When down changes are needed the lever is pulled back and the gear will change. When the car is being driven in manual operation the driver may have the choice of changing up and down the gears either by operating buttons on the steering wheel with their thumbs or by pulling paddles behind the steering wheel with their fingertips. This means that manual changes can be made without taking the hands off the steering wheel (Figure 16.13).

*Figure 16.13 Audi A8 controls with gear-change paddles above the centre spokes of the steering wheel*

The rate of change is faster than a driver can make the change; this system is useful in any vehicle that uses manual or automatic transmission presently. Vehicles that require a faster and smoother change for more powerful engines may use a double clutch system, which has been described previously.

## 16.7.1 Direct shift gearbox (DSG)

The DSG uses two multi-plate clutch assemblies, one to transmit the engine torque to the gear cluster for first, third and fifth gears, and the other to transmit to second, fourth and sixth, if fitted. There are three ways in which the clutches are fitted into the geartrain, described earlier in this chapter. The operation of the DSG allows for much faster gear changes; gears can be preselected as the next gear required will be in the gear cluster that is not being used at any particular time. The TCM can select the next gear, depending on whether the vehicle is speeding up or slowing down. Gear changes are then made by the TCM disengaging the current working clutch and engaging the other one. This predictive gear change is much faster than a manual gear change and much smoother as there is minimal time that there is loss of drive through the gearbox. The gear change time for a DSG is about 8 ms (milliseconds) compared to about 60 ms for a sequential manual transmission (SMT) and 150 ms for an automatic change.

The TCM will also allow for different driving modes that can be selected by the driver, either by the selector lever or buttons. It can have sports mode, in which

the TCM will hold on to the lower gears for longer to allow for the use of the engine power at higher engine revs and better engine braking when slowing down. In normal mode, a more relaxed style will allow gear changes to be made sooner to keep the revs lower for a more relaxed, economical drive. The TCM will be programmed with fuzzy logic so that it will adapt to the style of the driver and time gear changes to suit.

The TCM will normally select a gear and change sequentially through the gears by moving from first to second to third and so on when accelerating, and from fifth to fourth to third when slowing. However, if all the operating condition requirements are met, then the TCM will carry out block changes (i.e. from fifth to second gear) to cut down on gear changes or when fast acceleration is required. Block changes can only be carried out from odd to even gears because they are on different gear clusters. A change will not be made to another gear on the same gear cluster. A display on the instrument panel will inform the driver of the driving mode used and the gear selected (Figure 16.14).

*Figure 16.14 Honda instrument cluster including gear selector*

### Controls of a DSG

The DSG normally has a floor-mounted gear selector lever, although a column lever would also be suitable as it is just a switch to activate the TCM. It has selection positions similar to an automatic or automated manual transmission:

- P (park) – this holds the gears in neutral and will lock up the gearbox. The car can be started in this position. The ignition key can only be removed in this position so that the engine cannot be stopped and then restarted when a gear is selected. Both of the clutch assemblies are disengaged. The gear lever will be locked in this position until the brake pedal is pressed.
- N (neutral) – there is no gear selected but the gearbox is not locked. It should be used when the vehicle is stopped for more than a few seconds. The vehicle should not be run in gear for more than this as the clutches run at the point where they are almost engaged and will overheat and wear very quickly if they are kept at this position.

## Fuzzy logic

Fuzzy logic is the ability of a computer program to use a wide range of information to provide a variety of outputs for the information provided.

When a computer monitors all the information it receives, it compares it to an algorithm (a pre-programmed scenario) in its memory. It then chooses the algorithm that is most similar to the information that it has and then operates all the output as it has been programmed to.

For example, if the TCM received signals that the wheel speed is low, the engine is at working temperature and the engine load is high while it is in fouth gear, then it will examine all the available algorithms to see which is most similar to this situation and then change down gear.

A TCM that is using fuzzy logic will also monitor the information that it is receiving from all the other vehicle systems and will take into account their operating conditions.

If it has the situation mentioned above but also gets information that the traction control is operating, then it may not change down a gear until the traction control system stops operating and the vehicle has good traction. It has looked at its own algorithm and then not chosen the obvious operation because it has additional information from another system that would compromise the vehicle.

---

- R (reverse) – this is for moving the car backwards. The engine cannot be started in this position and again the lever cannot be moved out of this position until the brake is pressed and the vehicle is stopped.
- D (drive) – these are the forward gears and selection will be automatically controlled by the PCM. The clutches for both gear clusters will be disengaged and both first and second gears selected. Once the driver presses the accelerator pedal, then the clutch for first gear is engaged and the vehicle moves off. The TCM will monitor operating conditions throughout the vehicle and at a suitable time will disengage the clutch for first gear and engage the clutch for second gear. It will also deselect first gear and select third gear in readiness for the next predicted change. If the driver takes their foot off the accelerator, the TCM predicts that the vehicle is slowing down or stopping and will deselect third gear and reselect first gear again. Manual is usually selected from the drive position by moving the gear selector lever to the side. This can normally be done whether the vehicle is moving or stationary
- M (manual) – the lever sits in the central position and is spring-loaded back to this position. When the driver wants to change to a higher gear they will push the lever forwards and, if all the conditions are as required, the gear will be changed. When down changes are needed the lever is pulled back and the gear will change. The gear lever is usually marked + for changing up the gears and – for changing down the gears. Some vehicles have the manual gear change operated by either buttons on the steering wheel or paddles mounted behind the steering wheel. These allow

the driver to change gear without taking their hand off the steering wheel. If the driver tried to hold on to a gear too long, or wants to change down too soon the TCM will change the gear at a suitable time. The gear change time for manual changes is much slower, as the TCM cannot predict when the driver will decide to make gear changes.

*Figure 16.15  Audi A8 gear selector*

### Advantages and disadvantages of DSG

Advantages:

- Faster gear-change time than conventional automatic or manual gearboxes.
- Smoother gear changes as there is no loss of engine torque during changes.
- Lower fuel consumption as there are fewer losses for pumping oil.

Disadvantages:

- Bigger and heavier gearbox.
- More costly to produce and requires special fluid and maintenance.

## 16.8 Torque converter electronic control

The torque converter is a fluid drive between the engine and gearbox. It is used instead of a mechanical clutch and is not controlled by the driver. It is very efficient when the engine is rotating at a high speed but the gearbox is rotating at a much lower speed. As the speeds of the engine and gearbox get closer together, its efficiency drops as the dynamic pumping action of the oil is reduced and torque output is lost. To prevent this loss of torque, a torque converter lock-up clutch is used to lock the impellor and the turbine together. The clutch must be disengaged when the engine speed and gearbox speed are very different, and engaged as the speeds become the same. The clutch is actuated by a torque converter clutch (TCC) solenoid motor controlled by the TCM. Once the clutch is locked and all of the torque developed by the engine is transmitted to the gearbox input shaft, they rotate at the same speed. The TCC can be controlled to lock up the clutch in any gear to reduce fuel consumption. The TCM needs to know the speed of the impellor and the speed of the turbine at any particular time so that it can control the TCC. The impellor speed is measured by the crankshaft speed sensor as it is connected to the rear of the crankshaft, and the turbine speed is measured by a turbine speed sensor (TSS). The TCM compares the speed of the impellor and the turbine and, when the operating conditions are correct, it will engage the TCC to lock up the torque converter. The TCC can operate at high speed to engage and disengage the lock-up clutch smoothly and progressively for good driveability.

The torque converter also acts as a vibration damper between the engine and gearbox, however, this effect is lost when the lock-up clutch is engaged, so there has to be a torsion vibration damper and the ability to allow controlled slip of the lock-up clutch when there is heavy vibration through the engine or transmission.

## 16.9 Automatic gearbox transmission management

Automatic transmission systems in vehicles have been developed to provide variable gear ratios for torque multiplication, to provide a reverse gear and a neutral, as well as being easy to use for the driver and able to deal with high engine torque. Since the early days of vehicle development, this was carried out by a hydro-mechanical gearbox using oil pressure and a series of epicyclic gears controlled by multiple clutches and brake bands. Development of electronics over the last 30 years has provided the opportunity to have more precise control over the gear changes to reduce emissions and increase driveability. With electronic sensors that will operate at very high speeds and a TCM, with its complex design and ability to consider so many stored algorithms, there now seems an almost infinite number of gear-change patterns.

The integration of the electronic control of the hydro-mechanical operation of the automatic gearbox has made great progress over this period of time. Modern automatic gearboxes offer faster and more reliable gear changes, as well as a smoother drive and reduction of fuel consumption and emissions.

The TCM can control the oil pressure and direction valves in the valve block, as well as controlling electronic solenoids to operate the multi-plate clutches and lock up the torque converter to reduce slip in the system. It can also offer various modes that the driver can select to suit their own driving style and requirements.

Vehicles designed for sports driving can be programmed to hold the lower gears for longer to keep the engine at a higher power output, whereas vehicles designed for economy will change gear earlier to reduce consumption. Modern intelligent computer-controlled systems, which use fuzzy logic in their programming, will monitor the way the vehicle is being driven and change the programme of the transmission so that it will perform in the style that the driver requires at that time. It can be programmed for normal running, sports mode or comfort mode.

### 16.9.1 Inputs

The TCM needs to take information from various sensors within the transmission systems and other vehicle systems before it can control the gear changes. In older vehicles, the TCM only received information that would allow it to make gear changes from the transmission system itself. These would include oil pressure, gear lever position and kick-down.

Modern TCMs will receive information from other vehicle systems, such as the engine management, cruise control and the ABS. This is done using the CAN or similar protocol (discussed earlier in this chapter).

#### Wheel-speed sensor

This input to the ABS system is also used for the TCM to determine the speed of the vehicle so that it can determine the timing of gear changes. It lets the TCM know whether the vehicle is speeding up or slowing down.

## Engine load sensors

The engine load sensors (air mass, manifold absolute pressure, throttle position), along with the wheel-speed sensors, are the main inputs for most TCMs to make decisions for gear changes. By comparing the engine speed, engine load and vehicle speed, the TCM can determine which gear is currently engaged, if the vehicle is accelerating or slowing down and how much torque the driver requires. If the TCM gets signals for a high engine load and low wheel speed, this would suggest that a lower gear is required for the driving conditions, so the TCM would change down. The signals produced by all the sensors are monitored all the time to make sure that all the gear changes happen at the correct time. It can also determine whether the vehicle is travelling uphill (high engine load with no increase in vehicle speed) or cruising (low engine load and steady vehicle speed) so that it alters its gear-change pattern accordingly.

## Transmission fluid temperature (TFT) sensor

This lets the TCM know the temperature of the automatic transmission fluid (ATF) so that the oil pressure in the valve blocks and solenoids can be modified in relation to the changing viscosity of the oil as it heats up. Diagnosis of the oil condition can be made by measuring the current draw of oil pressure solenoids at a certain temperature, measuring its viscosity at that temperature (as oil that has a lower viscosity will require a lower current to open the solenoid than oil with a higher viscosity).

## Kick-down switch

This is mounted at the accelerator pedal and lets the TCM know that the driver has pushed the pedal down past full throttle. The TCM knows that a high power is required and will measure the engine speed, engine load and road speed, and change the gear down to a more suitable gear if it is required (Figure 16.16).

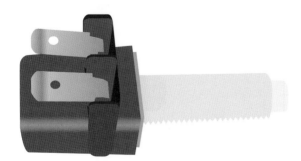

*Figure 16.16  Contact switch for kick-down switch*

## Brake light switch

This is mounted at the brake pedal and is used to let the TCM know that the vehicle is slowing down

so that it can be ready to change down the gears to assist with engine braking. When the vehicle is stopped, the TCM will only allow the gear lever to be moved in and out of park and reverse when the brake pedal is activated.

*Figure 16.17  Contact switch for brake pedal switch*

The TCM will also receive an input from the traction control system (TCS) so that it knows how frequently the TCS is being used. If the TCS is used a lot, such as on snow or loose sand, the TCM will select a higher gear to pick away and change up the gears earlier to reduce torque at the wheels.

## Pressure sensors

These are mounted in the gearbox to monitor pressure in the various oil lines. The TCM will then open and close valves at high speed to maintain the required pressure in the line. They are also used to diagnose any problems in the valve block and lines.

## Cruise control

The TCM receives signals from the cruise control module to let the TCM know that it has taken control of the throttle.

## 16.9.2 Outputs

The purpose of the TCM is to make the correct gear changes at the correct time, so all the outputs are to oil pressure solenoids, solenoids for the multi-plate clutches to change the gears and the torque converter lock-up clutch in the gearbox.

Oil pressure solenoids are used to control the oil pressure in the oil lines. The TCM will vary the duty cycle to open and close these very quickly, which will control the pressure and direction of the oil in the valve block.

## Pressure control solenoids

Previous versions of automatic transmissions used the same oil pressure throughout the whole system as there was only one solenoid to control the pressure; however, modern automatic transmissions use a larger number of solenoids to control the pressure in different parts of the gearbox. This is done by varying the duty cycle (how fast the valve is opened and closed) of the solenoid valve. If the oil pressure for the gear change clutches is too high, then the vehicle will have a harsh, jerky gear change and if the pressure is too low, then the gear changes will be slow and the clutches can overheat, which will wear out the clutches and burn the oil.

### Shift lock

Many automatic transmissions lock the gear selector lever via a shift lock solenoid to stop the gear selector lever from being moved until the brake pedal is depressed.

The TCM and the ECU for the engine have constant information flowing between them about the running state of the vehicle and can make adjustments to the running very quickly. When the TCM is about to make a gear change, the engine ECU will retard the ignition to reduce the torque from the engine to give a smoother gear change and reduce shock through the vehicle. The TCM will also monitor the working of the transmission and will alert the driver to any service

requirements, via a service lamp in the instrument cluster. It also works together with the engine ECU and the ABS and traction control ECU to improve driveability when using these systems (Figure 16.18).

## 16.10 Continuously variable transmission (CVT)

CVT provides an infinitely variable number of gear ratios within its operating range. This offers a lot of advantages for the operation of the vehicle. It makes it possible to have exactly the correct ratio for any given driving condition. CVT can allow the engine speed to be maintained at a specific range (i.e. its most efficient in terms of torque, power or economy). There is no loss of torque during gear changes as it has no individual gears, so it accelerates smoothly without jerking. In stop-start traffic it is far more comfortable to drive as there is no clutch or gear shift requiring constant attention, and low engine speed keeps the noise at more acceptable levels. When the driver pushes the accelerator pedal hard

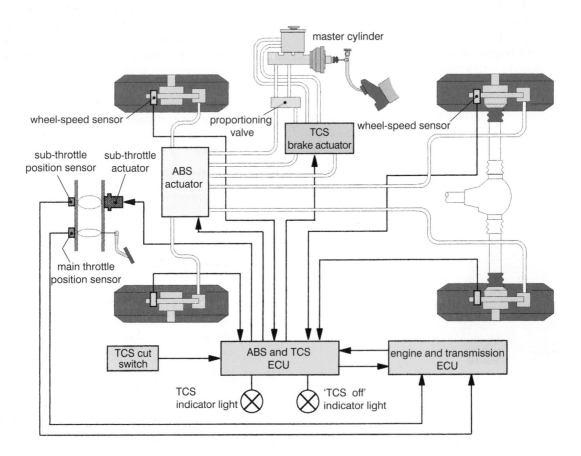

*Figure 16.18 Interaction with engine and traction control system*

to the floor the transmission can keep the ratio low to give maximum engine power. At cruising speeds it can select a high ratio to give better economy and lower exhaust emissions.

Electronic control of the CVT system can also offer switchable modes to the driver. The TCM will use measurements from sensors mounted on the engine to get the engine speed, sensors on the wheel hubs to get the vehicle speed, throttle body, manifold absolute pressure and air mass sensors to get the engine load, and gear selector to control the actuators in the gearbox.

The direct shift controller is mounted in the hydraulic valve control panel on the gearbox. Its function is to control the amount of oil pressure applied to the clutch assemblies. It can supply pressure up to 4000 kPa and can operate at high speed to give fast, smooth engagement and disengagement of the clutches (Figure 16.19).

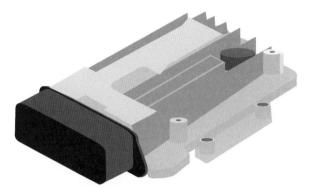

*Figure 16.19  Bosch direct shift controller*

The variable transmission solenoid is mounted in the hydraulic control plate of the automated transmission. It is a bleed-type pilot control valve, which is available with different characteristic lines (normally low or normally high) (Figure 16.20).

*Figure 16.20  Bosch variable transmission solenoid*

The electro-hydraulic modules are usually very robust and may come complete with integrated actuators, electrical plug-in connectors and terminals, and transmission connections. Sensors can be integrated in the module, for example, speed, pressure or temperature. Mounting the fully contained module on to the transmission control plate is a simple matter and has advantages with respect to costs, handling, and simplicity of wiring. Furthermore, the reduction in the number of components and interfaces improves the system's reliability, and so further increases the quality of the whole system.

## 16.11 Light hybrid powertrain technology (starter–generator)

A hybrid electric vehicle (HEV) is a vehicle that uses two different sources of propulsion, either singly or together, to provide more efficiency and economy than a conventional vehicle without the distance restriction of a full electric vehicle (EV), which uses batteries that are charged up from an external source.

The sources of propulsion commonly used are an internal-combustion engine and a high-voltage (HV) battery, which is used to add torque to the engine by an electric motor. The batteries are charged by using the inertia of the vehicle to produce regenerative braking and a generator, driven by the engine. The generator can also be used to power the electric motor to drive the vehicle under light-load conditions. A smaller internal-combustion engine is used because the electric motor provides additional torque under high engine load conditions. Emissions are lower than a conventional vehicle and are lowered further by the use of the stop-start technology.

Hybrid vehicles can be described as being one of two kinds:

- Full hybrid
- Stop-start hybrid

### Full hybrid

A full hybrid uses a small-capacity petrol engine as the main source of energy and has an electric motor to supply additional torque when a higher engine load is required. The electric motor can be used as the main source of energy when there is enough battery power and the engine load is low, such as cruising and low-speed manoeuvring. This electric-only driving mode further reduces fuel consumption and emissions under some driving conditions.

## Stop-start hybrid

Stop-start hybrids use the same technology and have the same benefits as full hybrids but, in addition, have a system to further reduce fuel consumption. It does this by switching off the petrol engine when the vehicle is stopped for more than a few seconds and all the operator and vehicle conditions are met, such as at traffic lights, and automatically restarts it when the driver presses the accelerator pedal to move. Most manufacturers achieve this by using a conventional starter system, up-rated to be able to deal with the additional starts. The system is controlled by an ECU, which receives data from the wheel-speed sensors (so it knows when the vehicle is stopped), engine speed sensor, engine load sensors, brake pedal sensor, parking brake switch and throttle position sensor. When the ECU has the information that the vehicle has stopped, the engine is at idle and the brake pedal is depressed, then the engine is stopped by switching off either the fuel injectors or the ignition coils. When the driver removes their foot from the brake pedal and touches the accelerator pedal, the ECU activates the starter system. This system starts the engine much faster than a manual start as all the other systems are primed and the engine is already at working temperature. If the battery voltage is too low, or there are too many electric consumers being used, the engine will not switch off. The driver can normally switch the whole system off.

On vehicles fitted with automatic transmission, an additional oil pump may be required to maintain pressure when the engine is stopped. This makes sure that there is minimal delay between the start operation and the vehicle being ready to drive away. The additional pump is primed just before the engine switches off. This means that both the engine-driven mechanical pump and the electric pump are running for a short period of time and oil pressure is maintained during the stop-start process.

It is claimed that stop-start technology can reduce fuel consumption and emissions by up to 10 per cent.

The following requirements have to be met for the stop-start systems to operate.

Operator conditions:

- Transmission is in neutral
- Vehicle is stationary
- Service brake is applied
- Accelerator and clutch pedal are not being operated

Vehicle conditions:

- Stop-start system is switched on
- Engine is at operating temperature
- Ambient temperature is between 0 °C and 30 °C
- At least 10 mph has been achieved at least once since the vehicle started the journey
- Air conditioning is switched off
- Windscreen is not fogged, so it does not need to use the windscreen blower or air conditioning
- Brake pressure is okay
- Battery has a suitable voltage.
- Bonnet is closed
- Driver's door is closed
- Driver's seatbelt is buckled
- Steering angle is not changed
- Reverse is not engaged

Most stop-start hybrids use a conventional starter system to start the engine; however, some smaller engine vehicles use the generator. When the engine needs to be restarted, the ECU connects the battery to the generator to 'back feed' it. This turns the generator, which is now being operated as an electric motor, and it rotates the engine to start it. This method depends on the strength and durability of the generator drive belt, so it is only used on small engine applications. The vehicle may or may not have a conventional starter system for driver-operated starts.

The electric motor/generator may be built on to the engine crankshaft, taking the place of the engine flywheel. This system removes the conventional starter motor and all the engine starts are carried out by the generator. The starting time is reduced and it is virtually silent in operation (Figure 16.21). A brushless motor can be used as this will operate as an electric motor to assist the ICE but can also be used as a generator when extra torque is not required.

*Figure 16.21 Bosch electric motor/generator*

Mazda has devised a new system that provides fast and consistent starts for their direct petrol injection engines. When the engine stops, sensors make sure

## Brushless motor design

The brushless motor design is a small simple arrangement that has no commutator to take the excitation current into the rotor. It has an external rather than an internal rotor, which is made up of several permanent magnets. The inner stator contains coils of wire that cause the rotor to turn and also to generate electricity when the rotor is rotating. This requires electronic control of the current to the coils of wire to make sure that they can operate as either a generator, by having the movement of the rotor generate electricity in the coils, or as a motor, by supplying current to the coils so they will push the rotor around in the method of an electric motor. This electronic control means that it can change from being a generator to being an electric motor as it runs (Figure 16.22).

*Figure 16.22 Honda brushless generator/motor*

that it stops in a position where there is a fresh induction charge in one cylinder. When the engine needs restarting there is an injection of fuel and it is then ignited by the spark plug. The expansion of the burning fuel on top of the piston is used to turn the engine and get it running. The engine is started in about 350 ms, which is about half the normal starting time. The stop position of the engine is noted so that the same cylinder is not used every time.

## 16.12 Electronic differential and four-wheel drive control

The construction and operation of the differential has not changed since the introduction of electronic control, however, control of the operation of the differential and four-wheel drives has now been introduced. Previous high-performance and off-road vehicles suffered from the effect of the differential when they lost traction of one wheel. All the drive went to that wheel and drive was lost. This happened during hard acceleration and if the vehicle was on soft ground, sand or snow. Limited slip differentials were introduced to reduce this effect and were very successful; however, this added weight and complexity to the vehicle. Four-wheel drive vehicles with three differentials, one on each axle and one in the transfer box, might have had differential locks on each to make sure that the transfer of torque was not lost. These systems were generally vacuum-operated and were prone to leaks, seizures and wear.

On modern vehicles with high-speed data transfer systems, traction is controlled not by the TCM and transmission system but by the ABS system. When the ABS ECU senses that one wheel is rotating faster than the others (i.e. wheel slip), it alerts the engine ECU, which will reduce the torque output of the engine either by retarding the ignition timing, closing the throttle butterfly slightly or reducing the injection time. It can do any of these singly or a combination of all three of them. This will stop the difference in wheel speed and the original engine values are restored, unless wheel slip is detected again. If the wheel speed difference is great, then the ABS ECU can operate the brake for the wheel that is slipping until the wheel rotates at the same speed as the other wheels. All of these operations are carried out in milliseconds and, in many cases, the driver will not even be aware that it is happening, except perhaps for a lamp lighting up in the instrument cluster. This system has the advantage that it required no extra components, weight or complexity, it requires only that the ECUs for the ABS and engine are reprogrammed to allow this to happen.

Control of four-wheel drive has not really changed, in the point of view that the vehicle will still have differentials at the front and rear axles and a method of connecting them. Instead of having a centre differential, most light four-wheel drive vehicles have an oil-controlled multi-plate clutch built into the rear output of the front axle differential or at the input of the rear differential. When wheel slip is sensed by the wheel-speed sensors, the TCM will operate the oil pump to apply pressure to connect the multi-plate clutch. This will transfer torque to the rear wheels for increased traction. The oil pump is pre-charged so that it can engage the clutch very quickly, in about 150 ms, so that any loss of traction from the front wheels can be compensated for by the rear wheels. It will also provide four-wheel drive from start-up and when the vehicle is accelerating. Control of the torque to the rear wheels is managed by partially or fully engaging the multi-plate clutch. This constant high-speed monitoring of the four-wheel drive systems means that all four wheels are only driving when they are required, which reduces noise, wear and emissions.

## 16.13 Transmission diagnostics

Make sure that all health and safety procedures are adhered to when carrying out diagnostic work on vehicles. Use a logical method of diagnosis and take care especially when working on high-voltage vehicles. Make sure that the correct personal protective equipment (PPE) for the task is worn and that necessary precautions have been taken.

When it comes to fault diagnostics of the transmission system, it is always worthwhile to check all the basic components first. Has the clutch burnt out? Is there enough oil in the transmission? Are all the electrical connections clean and secure, including earths?

Modern transmission systems are controlled by a TCM. The diagnostic functions that are built into the PCM monitor the transmission. If a fault is detected within the system, the PCM will record the fault and an applicable numerical fault code will be stored in the PCM memory. In most cases, if a sensor has failed then the PCM will recognise this and substitute a typical value for the reading for that sensor. This will allow the system to still function, however, it will not perform to its maximum potential. This is known a limited operating strategy (LOS) and the driver of the vehicle will be informed that there is a service requirement by the lighting of a lamp on the instrument cluster. To access the fault code it is necessary to connect diagnostic test equipment to the vehicle. The test equipment reads the information stored within the PCM's memory and will give an indication of the area where the fault exists. Most manufacturers' and after-market diagnostic equipment has a function for guided fault finding, which, with the workshop manual for the vehicle, will guide the technician through a set logical test sequence to determine the fault. As most equipment now also has vehicle information, a built-in multimeter and perhaps an oscilloscope, testing and diagnosis is made much quicker and easier. When the diagnostic equipment indicates a fault code it is still necessary to test the component and wiring for correct operation to make sure that suitable rectification can be made to the vehicle. As all the electronic components are controlled by the PCM, they are connected so the diagnostic equipment can be used, via the PCM, to check resistances of the components, operate the components and collect operating voltages of the components. All of these are required to make fast and accurate diagnosis of the components individually and of the system as a whole.

## 16.14 Summary

The progress that has been made in the field of electronics over the last 30 years has played a major part in the development of motor vehicles. Performance and economy have increased to such an extent that would have been impossible without electronics. Safety and ecological features have also been increased to protect life and the environment. The electronic control of the transmission has contributed to all of these features and has increased vehicle driveability, smoother and quieter gear changes, and reduced driver fatigue. With the introduction of electric and hydrogen fuel cell vehicles there will be a reduced requirement for the full transmission systems that are available today, however, any vehicle will always have the need of transmission. There will always be a need for variable torque control, neutral and reverse.

# CHAPTER 17

# Vehicle lighting systems

Lights are a basic electrical component in motor vehicles. The primary use of lights is to assist the driver and other drivers in poor visibility and darkness. This chapter is in three parts:

- Lighting circuit layout
- Lamp construction
- Maintenance and fault diagnosis

External lights are required by law. The detailed regulations identify the minimum required lamp devices and also the maximum number and intensity allowed. Very low lighting can make driving difficult at night, while very intense lighting can blind oncoming traffic and also compromise road safety. In Britain, the Vehicle and Operator Services Agency (VOSA) supervises mandatory road worthiness tests (MOTs) to ensure vehicles meet road safety requirements. The MOT also includes a lighting inspection and issues an approval certificate.

## 17.1 Lighting circuit layout

The lighting system consists of several circuits, each of which consists of a group of lamps. The main circuits are:

- side and rear lamps – this also includes illumination lamps for the number plate, glove compartment, driver's console and instrument panel
- headlamps and main driving lamps – the circuit switches between high and dipped beams in response to driver input
- tail/rear lamps – these guard the rear of the vehicle at night and under poor visibility
- auxiliary driving lamps – these include fog lamps to help reduce headlamp glare and spot lamps for long-distance illumination
- reversing lamps – these serve to illuminate the road to assist the driver when driving backwards, and also caution other drivers of the movement
- brake lamps – these alert drivers behind when the vehicle slows down
- passenger cabin lamps and door lamps
- instrument panel lamps – these indicate the status of vehicle units and warn against any system faults
- indicators and hazard lamps – these flash to signal direction change and hazard situations.

## 17.1.1 Circuit arrangement

The lamps within each circuit are connected in a parallel arrangement. Parallel connections give full illumination by giving each lamp the full intended voltage supply. Series connections result in a voltage drop after every component. The separate circuit paths for each lamp also mean other branches function normally if any branch fails.

To reduce wiring clutter, lighting systems use the metallic body of the car as the ground (or return) for their circuit. The earth return connections within the car body need to be clean and sure. Car manufacturers mark suitable earth points on the metal body. Connections should be checked by a voltage drop test.

There are two ways to represent a lighting circuit on paper (Figure 17.1):

- Locational diagrams – these show each lamp and its connections on a vehicle map. This is helpful in showing individual components and their locations, but tracing a single circuit using the diagram can be difficult. Most car manuals include separate circuit diagrams for each part and also a compact circuit diagram.
- Compact circuit diagrams – these show only the connections and structure of lamps and power supplies.

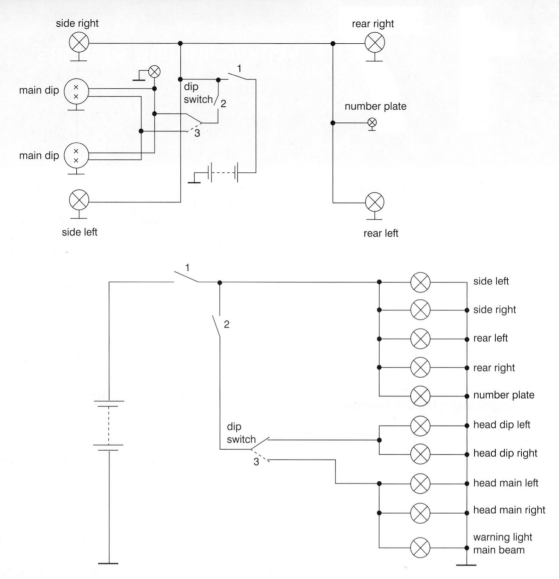

*Figure 17.1  Circuit layout diagrams*

## Circuit protection

The lighting system does not use a common fuse. A common fuse will disconnect all lights even when a single component short circuits. Because of this, separate fuses are used for each headlamp and tail lamp. Less important lights are usually given a common fuse to reduce wiring clutter. Figure 17.2 shows the layout of a fused lighting circuit.

## 17.2   Lamp construction

Illumination lamps are of several types. The most popular type is the incandescent filament lamp. These lamps use a metal wire that emits light on heating up. The metal used for the wire and the structure of the reflecting material affects the light quality and colour.

## Light intensity

Light intensity is a measure of the power of radiated light and its range of illumination. Light intensity is measured in candelas (cd); 1 cd is roughly equal to the illumination power of a candle. Illumination is the quantity of light falling on a surface. Illumination is measures in lux (lx) or metre candles (mc); 1 lx is the illumination provided by a 1 cd lamp at a distance of 1 m. Illumination varies according to distance and intensity. It is directly proportional to intensity and inversely proportional to the square of the distance between a point and the light source.

### Filament lamps

Figure 17.3 shows a standard filament lamp. Filament lamps normally use a tungsten filament. The filament is held by a wire support and enclosed in a glass bulb.

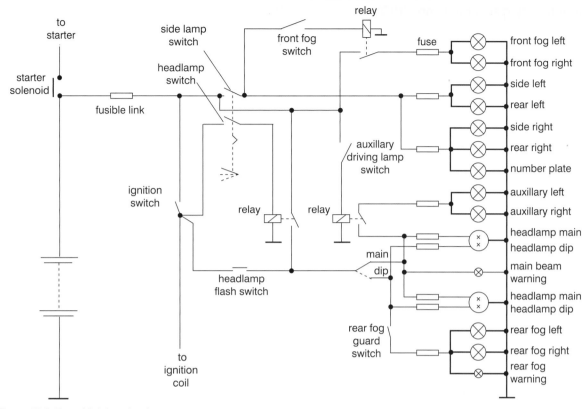

*Figure 17.2 Fused lighting circuit*

The glass bulb is fixed to the brass casing, which also holds the power terminals. High-power lamps have an inert gas (usually argon) to prevent oxidation of the filament. Low-power lamps often have a vacuum glass bulb.

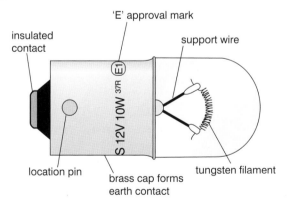

*Figure 17.3 Filament lamp*

When supplied with power, the tungsten filament starts to heat up to reach its operating temperature. At the operating temperature, a white light is produced. A lower power will emit light of lower intensity; higher power supplies can vaporise the tungsten.

Glass bulbs of headlamps are filled with halogen gas at a slightly higher pressure. Within the bulb, the tungsten filament is wound into a double helix. Both these features increase the light intensity of the headlamp.

## Light-emitting diodes (LEDs)

LEDs have, until recently, been used mainly for warning lamps on the instrument panel. LEDs are small devices enclosed in an epoxy lens with a light-emitting semiconductor. As electrons pass through the semiconductor their energy levels change. This releases energy in the form of photons. The energy of the emitted photons determines the colour of the light. LEDs (Figure 17.4) are very cheap and are available in several colours. The majority of manufacturers now use LEDs for rear marker lamps, rear brake lamps and auxiliary driving lamps.

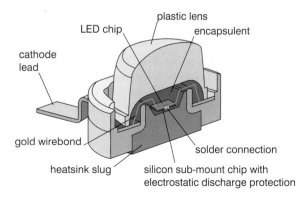

*Figure 17.4 LED*

## High-intensity discharge lamps (HID)

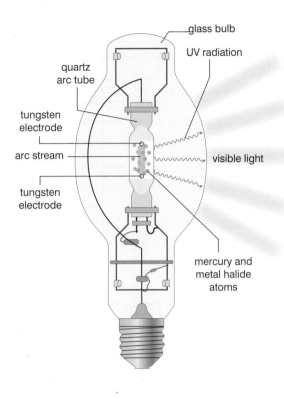

*Figure 17.5 HID lamp*

HID lamps produce light by generating an electric arc between two tungsten electrodes. The setup is housed in a quartz or alumina tube, which contains a gas and metal salts. The gas helps initiate the arc; the arc heats the tube and causes the metal salts to evaporate and form plasma; this boosts the light intensity of the lamp and also reduces power consumption. HID lamps (Figure 17.5) are power-efficient but take time to reach their operating state. However, they emit light of very high intensity, which can cause problems for oncoming traffic. MOT tests have guidelines for the beam patterns and light intensities from HID lamps to help keep roads safe.

### Reflectors

Headlamp reflectors are designed to direct light rays into a beam. The beam should ideally have parallel rays to give maximum range and illumination. A basic reflector has a smooth and highly polished parabolic aluminium surface (Figure 17.6).

In a **parabolic** reflector, the filament needs to be placed at the focal point in order to give a parallel reflected beam. Convergent beams reduce the range and divergent beams cause excessive glare on other traffic. The tip of a headlamp is opaque so light from the tip does not interfere with the beam.

**Parabolic**: Parabolic reflectors are curved so that light from the bulb bounces off the reflector and is focused forward at a controlled level and pattern.

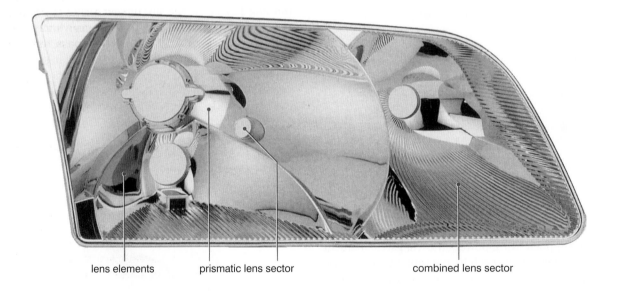

*Figure 17.6 Reflector design*

## Lens

Headlamps have a glass lens to help direct the light beam and spread the illumination properly. The main beam needs to have a long range while the dip beam needs to be low-level and requires a wide profile. The lens is moulded to accommodate the proper focus for each beam. Figure 17.7 shows a rectangular headlamp lens.

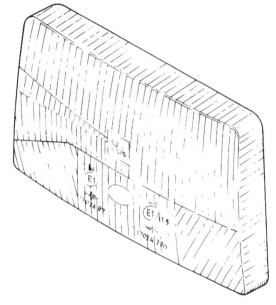

*Figure 17.7  Headlamp lens*

The lens is required to spread the light from the main beam to the dip beam in a smooth gradient. This allows the driver's eye to quickly adjust during movement and not be blinded by the intensity of the main beam. A badly designed lens can cause stress on the eyes during night driving.

## Dip beams

The dip beam is either formed by a twin filament bulb, or by a separate bulb in the headlamp. In a twin filament bulb, the second filament is placed slightly ahead of the focal point of the reflector and has a beam deflector underneath. This causes the reflected beam to converge, and the deflector gives the beam a wide profile. Headlamps with a separate bulb for the dip beam work in a similar way. The filaments or bulbs are switched by the dip lever near the steering wheel.

The reflectors in modern vehicles are a combination of circular and triangular reflectors. Each model has a different design because of the different shape for the headlamps. These are known as homofocal reflectors.

## Auxiliary lamps

Auxiliary lamps are fitted under the main headlamps. Fog lamp beams have a sharp cut-off and their beam is directed towards the ground. Spot lamps have a parallel beam that illuminates objects in the distance.

## Tail lamps

Rear lamps use filament bulbs and are generally of a low wattage, but at least 5W. Newer car models use LED tail and brake lamps. The LED lamps are more visible and aesthetically pleasing than filament lamps.

The lamp units, according to European law, have to be:

- between 1500 mm and 350 mm from the ground
- spaced at least 500 mm apart
- positioned to ensure that the distance between the edge of the vehicle and the area illuminated is not less than 400 mm.

It is also a requirement that the rear number plate is illuminated. The bulb illuminating the number plate should not be visible if you are viewing it from behind the vehicle.

## Stop lamps

Two stop lamps are required, with wattage of between 15W and 36W. Generally, this means that a 21W bulb will be used. The lamps must illuminate a red diffused light. They are marked with an 'E' to show that they are European standard approved lenses. The lamps have to be positioned so that they are between 150 mm and 350 mm from the ground and symmetrically they are at least 400 mm apart.

## Fog lamps

These are high-intensity lamps that are designed to be visible from behind the vehicle if conditions are poor, such as in heavy rain, extreme road spray, fog and falling snow. Usually one or two rear lamps are fitted and have a separate switching system from the front fog lamps. They need to be:

- positioned between 250 mm and 1000 mm from the ground
- positioned more than 100 mm from any stop lamp
- on the vehicle's offside or centred, if one lamp is fitted
- symmetrical, if two lamps are fitted.

## Reversing lamps

These are designed to conform to statutory regulations. No more than two lamps can be fitted to the vehicle, with a total wattage per lamp of 24W. These lights come on automatically when the driver engages reverse gear.

## Interior lighting

Numerous lamps are fitted as integral parts of the lighting system in order to illuminate when the vehicle doors are opened. Many of the interior lamps are now fitted with time delay units. This enables the driver and passengers to fasten their seat belts before the lights go off. Some systems automatically switch on the interior lights when the ignition system is turned off. Most vehicles also have map lights in order to allow the driver or passenger the use of a light source. Other lights are designed in such a way so that the driver is not distracted by them. Most vehicles also have additional interior lights designed to illuminate storage areas, such as the boot or glove compartment.

## 17.3 Maintenance and fault diagnosis

The vast majority of lighting system faults are caused by the failure of either a bulb or a fuse. By carefully examining a blown bulb an indication can be given to show where the problem originated, for example, a mirroring effect on the glass of the bulb would show poor earthing.

### Lamp circuit failures

Blown fuses need to be replaced with fuses of the correct rating. In cases where the new fuse blows straight away, the fault needs to be identified and located before fitting another fuse. Bulb failures require replacement bulbs. It is good practice not to touch the glass surfaces with the fingers, but to fit the bulb using a clean cloth.

Wiring checks may be necessary if the bulb or fuse is not the cause of the problem.

It is usually the case that earth problems are the root cause of issues with lighting circuits. It is good practice to check the earth connections first. It is also a wise precaution to check that the right bulb

has been installed. Figure 17.9 shows a flow chart for fault diagnosis for lighting systems.

### Headlamps

In order to conform to legislation and to pass an MOT, the headlamps not only need to provide good illumination for the driver, but also need to be correctly aligned. Figure 17.10 shows an optical beam setter, which is designed to check the horizontal and vertical aim of the beam. This equipment enables the mechanic to accurately set the lamp using adjusters. The aligner is set level and positioned parallel with the front of the vehicle. The lamps are then switched on and light rays from the lamp pass through condenser lenses and are reflected by a mirror on to a small screen.

It is also possible to adjust the headlamps without using specialist equipment. If the vehicle is placed on level ground at a given distance in front of a vertical screen, then, providing the car is positioned correctly, the tyre pressures are correct, the suspension is settled and the aiming board is marked out properly, it is possible to adjust the horizontal and vertical alignment. Figure 17.11 shows how to set the headlamp alignment without using special equipment.

An increasing number of vehicles are being equipped with self-adjusting headlamps, which make use of LIN communication systems to move the beam for optimal driver vision and safety in ensuring that oncoming traffic is not dazzled. This is particularly important if the vehicle is fitted with HID headlamps.

A basic system will incorporate self-levelling of the headlamps to accommodate loads, and may even include a sensor for measuring the light from oncoming traffic. If the headlamps are on main beam and the sensor detects a preset amount of light it will automatically dip the headlamps.

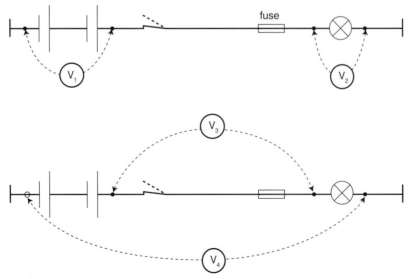

*Figure 17.8 Voltmeter checks on a simple lighting circuit*

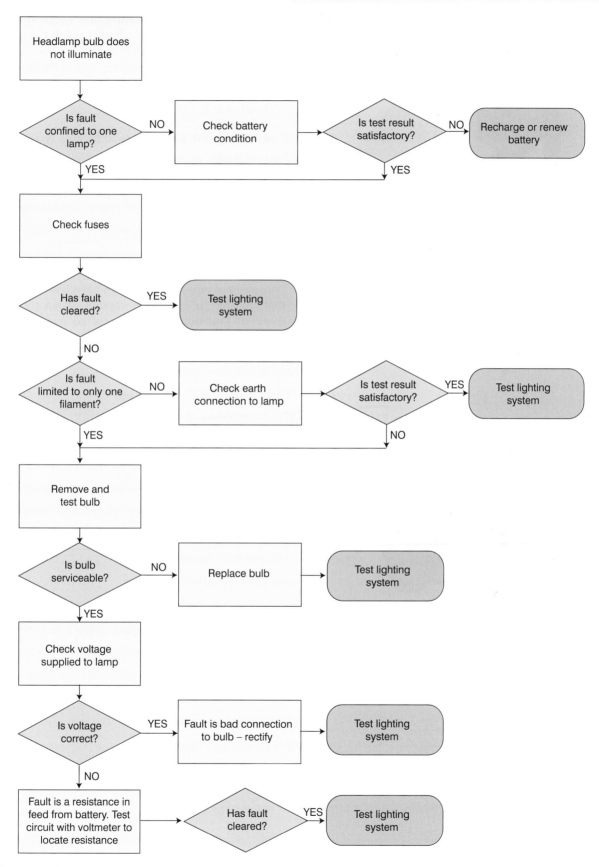

*Figure 17.9 Fault diagnosis flowchart for lighting circuits*

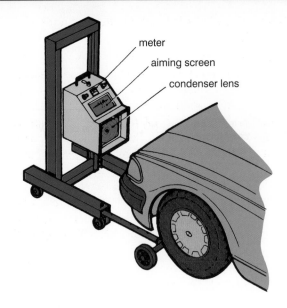

Figure 17.10 Optical beam setter

The latest system incorporates the onboard GPS system fitted to vehicles and adjusts the lighting to the curvature of the road ahead. The system makes use of up to three micro-stepping motors connected to each headlamp; each stepper motor has its own function:

- Up and down control
- Swivelling control
- AFS control (advanced front lighting system)

AFS systems make use of the LIN low-speed communications system (19,200 kbs). This is down to cost and because headlamp direction control is not a safety-critical system, this compares to CAN which has a communication speed of up to 1 Mbs, and is used for safety systems.

### Self-levelling and adaptive headlamps

These newer types of headlamps have level sensors that are able to determine whether or not the car is tilted. Traditionally, when cars go over bumps with their headlamps on, the headlamps will briefly point upwards. So viewed from the front, the car's

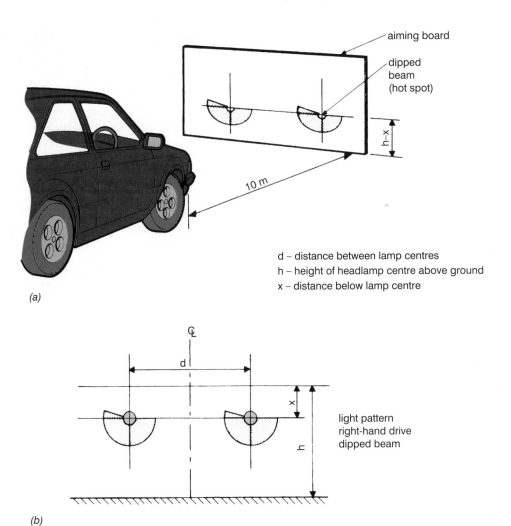

d – distance between lamp centres
h – height of headlamp centre above ground
x – distance below lamp centre

*(a)*

*(b)*

Figure 17.11 Setting headlamp alignment without special equipment

headlamps will appear to flash, when in actual fact they are temporarily pointing upwards and into the eyes of oncoming drivers. Headlamps with a self-levelling system have electric servo motors. These ensure that the headlamps are always aimed at the road, regardless of the position of the vehicle. These types of headlamps are gradually becoming a requirement for all new vehicles, although at present they are only available as optional extras.

Not only do these self-levelling and adaptive headlamps handle bumps in the road, but they also aim to illuminate curves in the road. The adaptive headlamp responds to signals from a sensor, known as a steering wheel angle sensor. Tiny bi-directional motors swivel the headlamps. This allows them to rotate up to 15° to the right or left.

It is also now possible for the adaptive headlamps to be controlled by GPS. The road ahead is plotted and a control unit anticipates curves in the road, which enables the adaptive headlamps to illuminate the curves. It can also determine the optimum brightness and light intensity, even before the driver turns into that curve.

A new development related to adaptive brake lamps should eventually allow drivers following a braking vehicle to see how hard the brakes are being applied. The harder the brakes are being pressed the more the brake lamps will shine; in other words, this is a progressive system. Small touches of the brakes will show a relatively dim brake light, while a heavy brake will show a bright brake light.

## Automatic operation in low ambient light conditions

These systems are designed to provide light-sensitive, automatic on and off control of the lamps, which are normally controlled by the headlamp switch. The system is based on a light-sensitive photocell sensor or amplifier assembly along with a headlamp control relay. In normal operations the photocell, which is usually mounted in the upper instrument panel pad or in the grill panel, responds to ambient light. If the light level decreases, the light sensor's resistance increases. Once the resistance has reached a pre-set level the amplifier then applies power to the headlamp relay coil. This triggers the headlamps, exterior lamps and illumination on the instrumentation. These lamps will remain on until the ambient light level has increased.

There are other systems that have two sensors; one monitors the intensity of the ambient light above the vehicle and another to the front of the vehicle. There are also automatic headlamp dimmer switches. These switch from high to low beam when the intensity of the light at the photocell increases. This means that the lamps will respond to the light from the headlamps of an approaching vehicle or the tail lamps of a vehicle up ahead. It is possible to adapt the sensitivity to meet specific driving conditions.

Many of these systems also have headlamp delays, which enable the headlamps to remain on, for up to three minutes usually, after the vehicle has stopped and the ignition has been turned off.

*Figure 17.12 Adaptive brake lamps*

*Figure 17.13 Automatic low ambient headlights*

# CHAPTER 18

# Instrumentation

This chapter looks at various aspects of instrumentation: the basic vehicle instrumentation and display; the various systems involved in vehicle condition monitoring; electronic driver displays; and the maintenance of systems and fault diagnosis.

## 18.1 Vehicle instrumentation and displays

Not long ago instrument panels were fairly basic. They would have:

- a speedometer, which incorporated an odometer that registered the mileage covered
- a fuel contents gauge
- an engine temperature gauge
- an engine oil pressure gauge or warning lamp
- signal lamps indicating battery charge (ignition warning lamp), directional indicator operation and headlamp main beam.

Even the most basic vehicles today have enhanced versions of these instrumentation systems. Only older vehicles or vintage cars still have mechanically operated instruments and even then the speedometer is often electrically operated.

Over time, newer displays and signals have been introduced. These all provide the driver with vital information in order for them to judge whether the vehicle is operating normally or whether there is a malfunction in one of the vehicle systems.

Over the last couple of decades, advances in electronic technology have radically altered the way in which the instrumentation panel works, how it looks and the nature of the whole system that lies behind it. The vast majority of the instruments and systems are electronic. Some of the displays are still relatively basic, but the dashboard now has an enormous number of different warning features and lamps.

Figure 18.2 Car instrument panel

What has become of vital importance is the layout of the display. The driver needs to be able to notice,

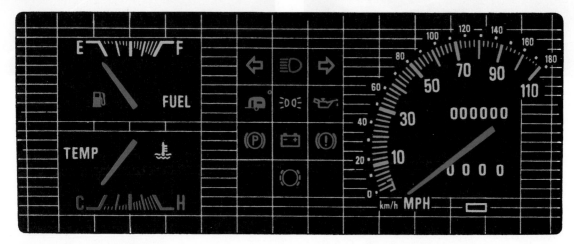

Figure 18.1 A basic instrument panel

understand and act upon the information being displayed. It is often a question of the display giving too much information or displaying information that could distract or confuse the driver. However, there are a number of essential pieces of information that need to be shown on an instrument panel:

- Speedometer
- Odometer
- Engine speed or rev counter
- Fuel gauge
- Engine temperature gauge
- Low oil pressure warning
- Generator warning lamp, or alternator charging lamp
- Lamps for indicators
- Lamp showing status of headlamp main beam (e.g. full or dipped)

### 18.1.1 Gauge and warning systems

There are a number of essential gauge and warning systems that form the basic information given on a display panel. Many vehicles have advanced features but they are often just a natural development of the basic systems.

#### Fuel contents gauge

Originally, fuel gauges were similar to an analogue multimeter and used a moving-iron, cross-coil gauge. Essentially, a float mechanism activated a variable resistor; in this way the current in the gauge circuit altered as the level of fuel in the tank altered. On the instrument panel the amount of fuel in the tank was indicated. One of the problems with this early system was that fuel surging caused apparent changes in the gauge showing the amount of fuel.

A newer system was introduced that was based on a thermal system in which a bi-metal element was heated up by the current in the gauge circuit (Figure 18.3). This bi-metal element would then deflect the display needle. The needle would deflect more when the bi-metal heated up and there was more current. This system relied on having a voltage stabiliser to regulate the voltage to the gauge assembly; otherwise the gauge readings would not be accurate. This system got over the problem of fuel movement, as it simply did not react quickly enough. The stabiliser has a bi-metal element. The supply voltage is switched on and off to ensure that there is a voltage of between 5 V and 10 V at all times.

These types of system may still be seen in older vehicles, but for some time electronic units, which are better able to regulate voltage, have been used. Usually the electronic stabilisers provide voltage to more than one gauge, such as the fuel and the temperature gauges.

In the thermal-type fuel-level gauge circuit the following takes place:

1  The sender unit, being a potentiometer that is connected to the float arm, ensures that when there are changes in fuel level the position of the wiper alters, which in turn alters the resistive value.
2  The gauge circuit's current changes.
3  Consequently, the display changes.

Newer systems with modern sender units are robust and accurate. They are even able to deal with different shapes of fuel tank.

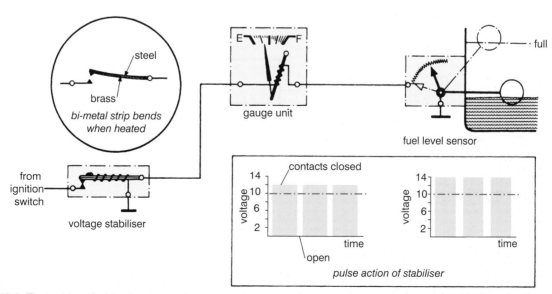

*Figure 18.3 Thermal-type fuel-level gauge*

## Engine temperature gauge

Essentially, the gauge movement is the same as fuel-level gauges. The key difference is the fact that the gauge sender unit has a resistor element that is mounted inside a brass screw-in body (Figure 18.4). The resistor is a negative temperature coefficient (NTC) resistor, which is thermally sensitive. Therefore, it changes its resistance in line with changes in temperature. In other words, the NTC element's resistance decreases if the engine temperature increases. The driver will see the gauge on the display panel move towards 'hot' as a result of the fact that when the engine's temperature increases there is a higher current in the circuit, which deflects the needle towards 'hot'.

## Engine oil pressure warning

A warning lamp on the display panel will light in the event of low oil pressure. The switch is actually in the oil gallery of the engine and operates under full oil pressure. This means that the contacts in the switch are closed in their dormant state. The engine pressure opens up the switch as the pressure is applied to the diaphragm. This means that the engine oil pressure warning lamp will come on if the ignition key has been partially turned but the engine is not running, or if there is a drop in engine oil pressure (Figure 18.5).

The threshold for the oil pressure switch has to be set at a low level of 0.5 bar, or 7 psi. This is essential because otherwise there would be persistent false faults. Inside the engine of a normal vehicle, the oil pressure is likely to undergo a huge variance as a result of environmental factors, in addition to the speed of the vehicle and the load it is carrying. This does mean, however, that this type of engine oil pressure system is relatively basic. It is designed so that it does not show a warning if the engine is hot or the vehicle is travelling at high speed or pulling a heavy load.

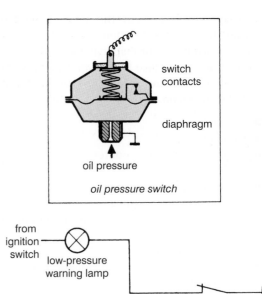

Figure 18.5 Spring-controlled diaphragm-type oil pressure indicator

As a result, several oil pressure switches are often fitted to more modern vehicles. Each of these, placed in different parts of the engine, have a range of pressure thresholds. These are often connected to a circuit that evaluates the information received from the different switches. This, in turn, is linked to a warning lamp.

## Battery warning lamp

When the ignition is turned on, but before the engine starts running, a lamp will illuminate on the display panel. This is often referred to as an ignition warning lamp. In the past, vehicles that did not have an electronic ignition system faced a potentially damaged ignition coil as a result of overheating.

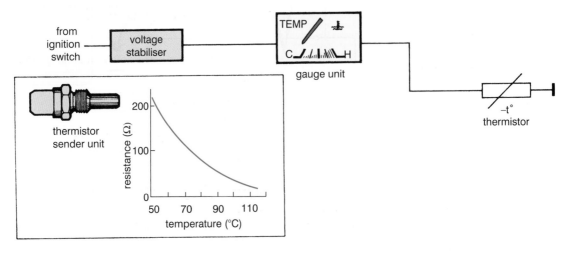

*Figure 18.4 Thermal-type engine-temperature gauge*

The difficulty with the system is that if there is a problem with the alternator, the lamp is not often illuminated. The lamp itself on the control panel is often referred to as a charge warning lamp. It is connected to the ignition supply on one side and it is earthed through the generator rotor via the electronic regulator (before the engine is running). The generator charges the battery as soon as the engine starts and the circuit is turned off via the regulator. All the driver knows is that the generator is actually working.

### Tachometer/engine speed indicator

This part of the display is designed to show the engine speed and is often referred to as a rev counter. The purpose of this indicator is to alert the driver if the engine is being over-revved. The display is a graduated dial with a danger zone noted. The idea is that the driver can look at the engine speed and then assess the optimum level at which the gears need to be changed. Earlier systems used the ignition circuit to show engine speed.

Analogue or digital displays can show the engine speed. Usually an electronic counter notes how frequent the ignition pulses are. This is a direct indication of the speed of the engine. In modern vehicles, engine speed is displayed by an electronic control unit (ECU) with a pulse train output.

### Vehicle speed indicator

Electronic speedometers have replaced the older cable versions; these mechanical instruments were driven by a cable from the gearbox output shaft. Unscrupulous car dealers could therefore find ingenious ways of reversing mileage readings. This is much less of a problem now that there are electronic odometers. It is relatively simple to check that the displayed mileage on the control panel is legitimate, as the same information is now stored in the transmission control systems.

Different makes of vehicle use different types of speedometer display; there are analogue or digital versions. Speed measurement is measured in different ways:

- A sensor or electronic pulse generator can be fitted to the differential.
- A sensor or electronic pulse generator can be fitted to the gearbox output shaft.

The pulse generator or sensor is designed to pick up on the movement of the teeth on a pulse ring (exactly the same as engine speed sensing). A microprocessor monitors the time taken between each of the edges of the teeth. The sensor produces a pulse train that has a frequency that is proportional to speed in both analogue and digital systems. The microprocessor already knows the right calibration in order to establish vehicle speed. An output driver circuit then sends this information to the control panel.

## 18.1.2 Instrument symbols

Since the majority of vehicle makes are sold in different countries around the world, it has been necessary to introduce a standard set of instrument symbols. This ensures that there is no misunderstanding or misinterpretation. The following table shows the symbols and their meanings.

*Table 18.1 Instrument panel symbols*

| Symbol | Information provided |
|--------|----------------------|
|        | Brake warning lamp |
|        | Turn signal/hazard indicator lamp (green) |
|        | High beam indicator lamp (blue) |
|        | Charge warning lamp |
|        | Door open reminder lamp |
|        | Hazard warning flasher indicator lamp |
|        | Low washer fluid warning lamp |
|        | Oil pressure warning lamp |
|        | Glow plug indicator lamp |
|        | Heated rear window indicator lamp |
|        | Rear fog light indicator lamp |
|        | Low fuel warning lamp |
|        | Stop/tail warning lamp |

## 18.2 Vehicle condition monitoring

A condition monitoring system for a vehicle comprises a central control unit and numerous remote data acquisition modules. Each of the modules is connected to the central control unit by a single wire. This wire carries a multitude of inputs and is connected to local condition-sensing transducers. Each data acquisition module serves to store data representing signals received at its inputs. The central control unit prompts the modules in turn and each module, when prompted, transmits its stored data to the central control unit over the respective single wire. The system provides a simplification of the wiring and connectors required between various transducers and the central control unit, which operates displays showing the condition of the transducers.

In the past, it was generally recommended that vehicles undergo more frequent routine servicing and maintenance. However, it is now commonplace for service intervals to be in excess of 20,000 miles. This means that there is a greater likelihood of specific components wearing out and fluid levels dropping in between services.

Condition monitoring has, therefore, become an essential part of the overall driver information systems. Over time, each manufacturer has identified specific issues that may routinely crop up and have incorporated these into their monitoring systems. Across each manufacturer's range of vehicles there may be other levels of sophistication, as a result of issues being noted for specific models.

The idea of vehicle conditioning monitoring systems is to warn the driver regarding a range of issues, which include (but are not exclusive to) the following:

- Failure of bulbs
- Wear on brake pads
- Level and condition of engine oil
- Other essential fluid levels (e.g. screen wash and brake fluid)
- Anti-lock braking systems (ABS)
- Supplementary restraint systems (SRS)

Much of this monitoring and subsequent feedback to the driver is achieved by placing a number of sensors and then linking them to a vehicle on-board diagnostic system (OBD). This means that the vehicle itself, or rather the sensors and the OBD together, monitor the condition of various systems and areas and can effectively self-diagnose.

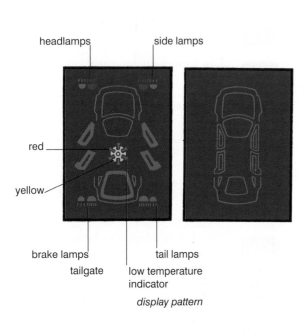

*display pattern*

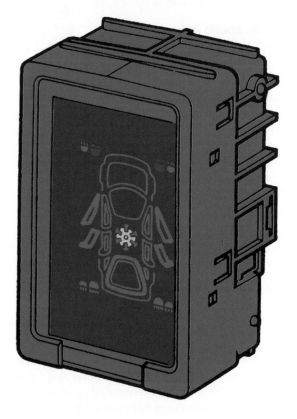

*graphic display model*

*Figure 18.6 Graphic display unit*

The OBD needs to be able to monitor the vehicle's exhaust emissions, as this is a statutory requirement for modern vehicles. Typically, the system uses a range of different warning lamps. These are shown on a graphical display. This display shows all of the monitored areas of the vehicle and when there is an issue with a specific location this is lit up on the graphical display.

The basic vehicle condition monitoring system has the following features:

- Signals from sensors at various points around the vehicle are monitored by a microprocessor.
- The majority of the sensors are simply switches and only transmit a signal stating that the condition is 'OK' or 'not OK'.
- The system needs to be reliable so it self-detects any wiring faults and informs the driver.
- As the system is fully integrated, it runs continuous system self-checks and is seen as being a much more reliable system than a series of individual warning circuits.

All the following types of condition-monitoring use sensors. These are the basic systems and more sophisticated vehicles may have additional features and checks linked to the OBD.

## Bulb failure

Traditionally, a reed switch was put into a circuit in order to monitor the current. This had two or more contacts. The contacts were mounted within a glass vial. The vial itself was filled with an inert gas, which would help to prevent arcing. The switch was closed by either permanent or electromagnetic flux. In the case of electromagnetic flux, a coil around the switch actually created the magnetic field.

The reed switch is located close to the lamp unit, inside a bulb monitoring unit. Each individual lighting circuit would have its own reed switch. When the circuit is activated the reed switch contact closes. This produces a circuit path to light the relevant part of the display panel. Should the bulb actually fail, then the appropriate part of the display does not light up, therefore warning the driver.

## Tyre pressure monitoring

It is vital that the vehicle has the correct tyre pressure. Incorrect tyre pressure not only has a marked effect on fuel economy, but it also affects both the stability of the vehicle and the safety of the occupants. It has become increasingly important to ensure that the vehicle is able to monitor tyre pressures, in

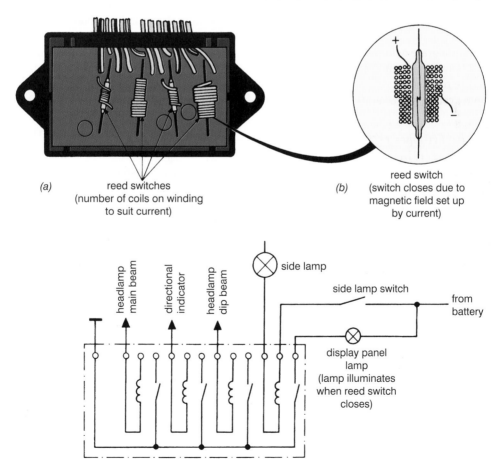

*Figure 18.7 Bulb failure module*

order to reduce tread wear. Tread wear, of course, is associated with aquaplaning in wet conditions, reduced handling, tyre failure and the inability of the vehicle to make sudden stops.

Vehicles in the USA are required to have a tyre pressure monitoring system (TPMS) to reduce the number of accidents caused by low tyre pressure. It is a legal requirement in the UK that vehicles with runflat tyres are fitted with a TPMS.

The TPMS has a number of key features:

- A display shows the tyre pressures, indicating whether they are too high or too low.
- Four wireless tyre pressure sensors linked to an in-car display unit.
- The driver is alerted should the tyre pressures fall below a pre-set level. The warnings are given as both visual and audible prompts.
- There is an emergency tyre pressure leakage alert system. This activates if the tyre pressures drop by more than 1.5 psi over a period of 12 s.
- The actual tyre pressure sensors are battery-operated and tamper-proof; the batteries usually have a lifespan of around two years.
- The sensors are able to be set from around 1.5 psi.
- The sensors check the tyre pressure every 4 s and send updates on the data to the monitoring system at five-minute intervals.
- The sensors operate using a direct current (DC) voltage of between 8 V and 24 V and monitor the temperature of the tyre.
- The whole system can operate with up to eight sensors.

There are two distinct types of TPMS. The first is a direct system (Figure 18.8), with the following key features:

- Pressure sensors and transmitting systems are fitted or attached to the wheels of the vehicle.
- A receiver inside the vehicle evaluates the data from the sensors and then displays the information to the driver, in the event that the tyre pressure falls below a particular level.
- It is a highly accurate system and considered a reliable way to determine if a tyre is under-inflated.
- The system is made up of a number of pressure sensors, an analogue to digital (A/D) converter, a microcontroller, a system controller, an oscillator, a radio frequency transmitter, a low-frequency receiver and a voltage regulator for battery management.

The second type is an indirect system (Figure 18.9), which has speed sensors in the ABS system of the vehicle. The system compares the rotational speed of each wheel. If a tyre has lower pressure, then it will rotate a different number of times per mile than one operating under the correct pressure. The on-board computer in the vehicle will receive data regarding any discrepancies. There will be a problem if all the tyres are losing pressure at the same rate, as this will not be registered. Some later Audi and Volkswagen models are able to pick up on these potential discrepancies and problems.

The system uses a controller area network (CAN) bus system to cope with the interchange of data. This is what links the various electrical components. It has become a standard installation and is relatively low cost. Mercedes introduced CAN bus for their engine management systems (EMSs) and it was used in conjunction with their power system ECUs.

The CAN bus system is now used to link together body control modules. Each of the modules is connected by a separate CAN bus with a second CAN bus dedicated to dealing with important data, such as the ABS. The slower body control CAN buses run at a speed of around 125 kbits/s, whereas the higher speed networks run at around 500 kbits/s.

The CAN bus is rather like a serial bus system. It has the capacity to be able to transmit and receive data at the same time. A transmitter sends data on to the system. This is received by all of the other nodes. Each node has an individual address. If the data travelling from a transmitting node does not relate to another node, then it is discarded or ignored. If the receiving node is the intended destination, then the message is accepted and acted upon (processed). It is also a feature of the system that high-priority information is dealt with first, so that it can be analysed and acted upon immediately.

The CAN bus system is very reliable and it has excellent error detection capabilities. If there is a node error, then an evaluation is made as to the status of the error and what action needs to be taken. With a normal serial system, if one node fails then the whole system fails. In a CAN bus system there are multiple systems in order to reduce this possibility. This eliminates the likelihood that if there is a simple error on one of the nodes, such as the boot locking mechanism, the car would fail to start when the ignition key was turned.

### Brake lining wear

Another system has been developed in order to alert the driver of safety issues arising out of wear to the brake linings. This has become increasingly important as a result of the longer periods required between services.

Figure 18.10 shows two different sensor systems used for brake lining wear. Figure 18.10a illustrates the open-loop system, consisting of a simple sensor linked

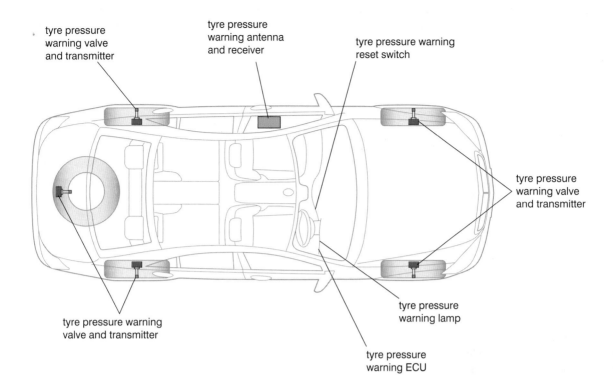

tyre pressure
warning valve
and transmitter

tyre pressure
warning antenna
and receiver

tyre pressure warning
reset switch

tyre pressure
warning valve
and transmitter

tyre pressure warning
valve and transmitter

tyre pressure
warning lamp

tyre pressure
warning ECU

Figure 18.8  Direct TPMS system

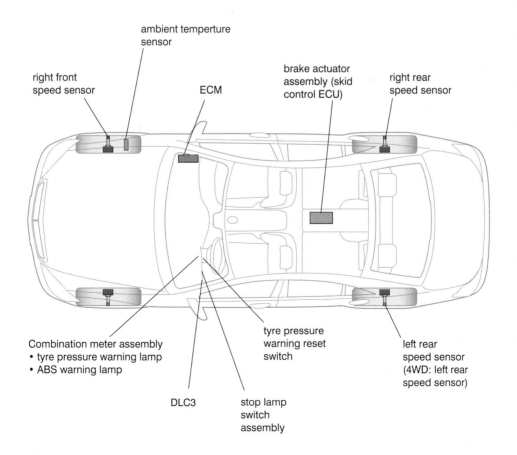

ambient temperture
sensor

right front
speed sensor

ECM

brake actuator
assembly (skid
control ECU)

right rear
speed sensor

Combination meter assembly
• tyre pressure warning lamp
• ABS warning lamp

tyre pressure
warning reset
switch

left rear
speed sensor
(4WD: left rear
speed sensor)

DLC3

stop lamp
switch
assembly

Figure 18.9  Indirect TPMS system

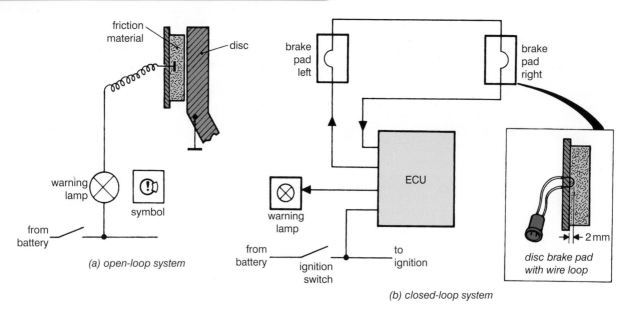

Figure 18.10 Sensor system for brake lining wear

to a wire loop and then to a warning lamp, which gives an indication that the brake pads need to be replaced. It is only activated when the pad wear has reached a point at which replacement is essential. The major problem with this type of open-loop system is that if there is a fault in the basic circuit to the warning lamp, or the warning lamp connection with the battery has failed, then the warning lamp will not illuminate. In such cases the driver will have no idea that the brake lining has reached a critical stage.

Figure 18.10b illustrates the closed-loop system, which is a much more reliable system. An ECU makes a check of the integrity of the circuit when it is switched on. The driver is immediately alerted if one of two things has occurred:

- One or more of the pads are actually worn.
- The circuit has failed.

In both instances, the ECU will switch on the warning lamp on the display panel to alert the driver.

In this system arrangement the sensing loop is buried in the friction material. When the friction material is ground away to its limit of 2 mm the wire is cut. The brake sensors are arranged in series with each other and the two cables forming the closed circuit loop are connected to the ECU. The processor is designed to pass a current for a duration of around 5 s to the lamp on ignition switch-on, in order to verify the integrity of the system. Once the initial check period has been completed, illumination of the warning lamp will indicate to the driver that brake inspection is necessary. Should the brake check indicate that the pad material is serviceable, then this indicates the presence of an open circuit somewhere in the circuit path; this will have to be located. If the external circuit

is found to be satisfactory and the warning lamp still remains on, this points to a fault in the ECU itself. This usually means that the ECU will have to be replaced. It is possible that damage can be caused to the ECU if current from an ohmmeter is allowed to pass through it. To avoid this, the unit should always be disconnected when checking the external circuit.

### Engine oil level

In order to get an accurate reading of the engine oil level it is necessary for the engine to be at a particular temperature. Equally, to get an accurate reading using a dipstick the oil temperature needs to be cold and the vehicle itself on a level surface. Figure 18.11 shows the most straightforward method using what is known as hot-wire measurement.

The hot wire is at the tip of the dipstick. The system works in the following way:

1. The wire element on the dipstick is immersed in the oil.
2. The element is heated up and the resistance is measured.
3. The resistance will change if the element is heated up but there is no oil present in order to dissipate the heat.
4. These measurements are monitored by the circuit.
5. If there is a problem, the warning lamp will be illuminated.

There are, however, problems with this basic system:

- There is a requirement that the connections are sound.
- The sensor and the wiring in the dipstick can be easily damaged, so care has to be taken when being handled.

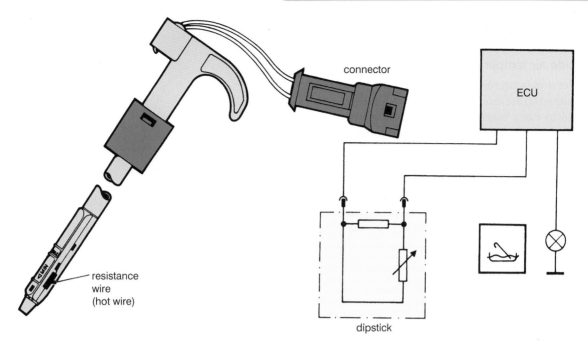

*Figure 18.11 Engine oil level sensor*

These problems have been largely dealt with by effectively replacing the dipstick with sensors. These are placed in the housing of the engine sump. They are considered to be a far more reliable means by which not only the oil level can be assessed, but also the quality of the oil. They have become an integral part of the overall vehicle conditioning systems. Once again, the measurement of not only oil level but the condition of the oil allows the driver to have knowledge of the oil in the engine between longer service periods.

### Essential fluid levels

In order to monitor the current levels of essential fluids it is usual that a float-type switch mechanism is used. The float-type switch system measures the current levels of washer fluid, coolants and brake fluid. Figure 18.12 illustrates how the float-type switch is connected to the ECU battery and warning lamp. It also shows a more detailed diagram of the process of the switch closing when the float drops.

Key characteristics of these float-type switches:

- The switch part is usually a reed-type device.
- The float has a magnet incorporated.
- If the magnet moves away from the reed switch, a warning lamp is triggered. This happens because the reed switch has opened and has effectively broken the circuit.

This type of simple circuit is considered to be extremely reliable. Most vehicles have a test system, which takes place when the ignition is turned on for the first time. The circuit is tested in order to ascertain

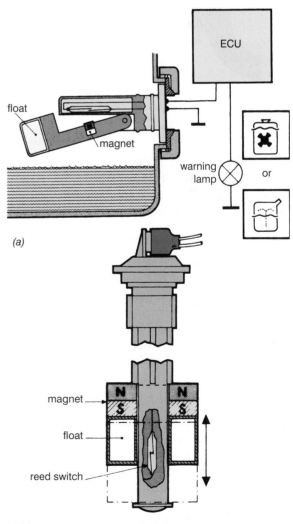

*Figure 18.12 Float system switch*

whether the circuit has retained its integrity and that the warning lamp is functional.

## Outside air temperature

In order to measure the outside temperature a thermistor is mounted on the exterior of the vehicle. The thermistor is able to carry out a temperature reading, which in turn is relayed via an evaluation circuit to the display panel inside the car. The system often incorporates an additional warning feature. It will light up a yellow or orange warning lamp if the temperature is sufficient to suggest that there may be ice. Alternatively, it could light up as a red warning if the temperature is below $0\,°C$ and there is a danger of black ice and even more hazardous driving conditions (Figure 18.13).

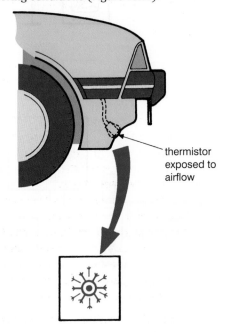

*Figure 18.13  Air temperature sensor*

The whole system is relatively straightforward. The thermistor is an NTC type, which means that it is a resistor. The resistance value of the resistor changes when the temperature it is exposed to changes. Unlike the majority of conductors whose resistance increases with temperature (PTC), these semiconductors reduce their resistance as temperature increases (Figure 18.14).

The system works in the following way:

1  The electronic evaluation circuit (in the display panel) receives data on the thermistor's resistance through a potential divider circuit.
2  The display panel then shows the temperature reading.
3  If necessary, additional warning lamps are illuminated to indicate hazardous temperatures (particularly if the temperature has dropped below $0\,°C$).

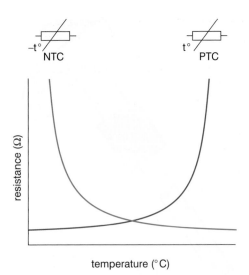

*Figure 18.14  Thermistor characteristics*

## 18.3  Electronic driver displays

In modern vehicles the basic functions of the instrument panel are similar for most makes and models. The panel itself receives data input either via a data bus or by direct signal input. The signal processing and calculation is then executed by a microprocessor. The microprocessor then outputs the measured value to the indicator device driver.

Display technologies tend to fall into two categories: they are either active or passive display systems. The essential difference between the display systems is:

- active systems emit light
- passive systems reflect light.

There are a number of different display systems, such as:

- light-emitting diode (LED)
- liquid crystal display (LCD)
- vacuum fluorescent display (VFD)
- DC electroluminescence (DCEL)
- cold cathode fluorescence lamp (CCFL)
- head-up display (HUD).

Mechanical instruments and warning lamps were widespread across all makes and models. However, the advances in microcontroller technology that have been incorporated into modern vehicle systems have reduced the reliance on conventional mechanical instruments and warning lamps.

Key characteristics of the modern electronic driver display are as follows:

- The display panel is a microcontrolled sub-system.

- It is designed to provide the driver with feedback.
- It is connected to the vehicle network communication system.
- It receives data from a number of sensors to which it is wired around the vehicle.
- The display on the panel itself may still be analogue and simple, but it is far more sophisticated and reliable than the mechanical systems that were used previously.

Vehicle manufacturers have had to tread a careful path in replacing systems and warning lamps with these new technologies. Most have not wished to be too revolutionary in their redesign of display panels; even the most sophisticated electronic systems are actually displayed in a fairly straightforward and recognisable manner (Figure 18.15).

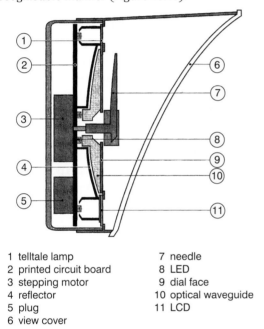

| | |
|---|---|
| 1 telltale lamp | 7 needle |
| 2 printed circuit board | 8 LED |
| 3 stepping motor | 9 dial face |
| 4 reflector | 10 optical waveguide |
| 5 plug | 11 LCD |
| 6 view cover | |

*Figure 18.15 Instrument cluster*

However, while the electronic displays may look like their mechanical predecessors, they have a huge number of advantages:

- The displays are often clearer and more attractive.
- They are designed so that the driver can read, process and act upon the information in front of them.
- There is far less reliance on mechanical parts in the systems that could fail or wear.
- The display panel can essentially prioritise what is being displayed to the driver (e.g. a warning that an essential fluid level has dropped below the recommended level, or the fuel level is low).
- As there is less reliance on mechanical moving parts, the display system itself can be far more stylish and compact.

As already mentioned, regardless of the sophistication of the vehicle, the functions of the instrument panel remain largely the same:

1 The display panel receives a series of inputs.
2 These inputs are routed to the display panel via either direct signal inputs or a data bus.
3 A microprocessor processes the signals and carries out necessary calculations.
4 The microprocessor then sends measured values to the indicator device driver.
5 The indicator device driver could be a display gauge, such as a speed indicator or rev counter, an indicator lamp or a simple dot matrix display showing external temperature or the range of the vehicle based on current fuel levels.

As shown in Figure 18.16 the various types of sensor are linked to the system via a connector. They are largely reliant on having a power supply. Once the data reaches the microcontroller or processor the software then deals with the data and routes the result of the calculations to the appropriate driver display type.

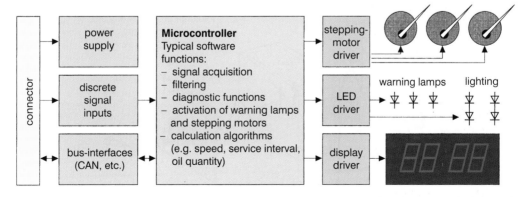

*Figure 18.16 Signal processing in a microprocessor-based instrument cluster*

Systems such as these have developed in order to provide the driver with a wide range of information. Each vehicle has its own on-board intelligent diagnostic system. Manufacturers set up the systems in order to cope with their preferred service intervals, as well as having identified key diagnostic functions that need to be incorporated into the system and relayed to the driver.

As already mentioned, the ways in which the driver sees the data in the form of a display differs and are usually identified as being either active or passive, according to the way in which the display elements deal with light.

### Light-emitting diode (LED)

An LED consists of seven basic segments (Figure 18.17). LEDs are very reliable, they have a long lifespan and, as they are simple to integrate into circuits, they are widely used in display panels. They are often used in order to provide a warning lamp or as backlighting. LEDs are active light sources and can be produced in a number of different colours.

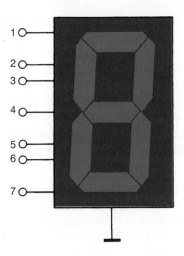

*Figure 18.17 Figure-of-eight display with seven-segment LEDs*

### Liquid crystal display (LCD)

Because LCDs require little power they are ideal for larger display modules. However, they are passive so backlighting is needed. Key features of LCDs are as follows:

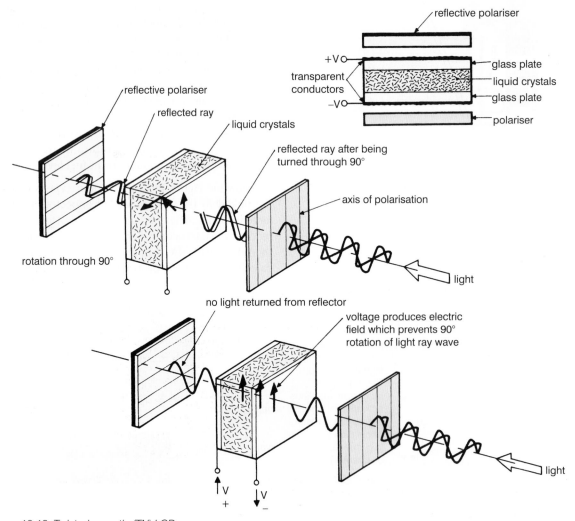

*Figure 18.18 Twisted nematic (TN) LCD*

- They can operate using either positive or negative contrast. This means that they can show up as light figures on a black background using negative contrast, or black on light for positive.
- The LCD consists of twisted, elongated, liquid crystal modules sandwiched between glass plates. The conductors are transparent. This is known as twisted nematic LCD (TN LCD).
- The modules, along with the plates and the conductors, create a layer or light valve. If a voltage is applied to the conductors, then polarised light can pass through the layer. Essentially, this works like a valve.

Although the TN LCD (Figure 18.18) can provide simple display elements, there are more advanced versions of LCD technology that can provide more complex graphical displays. These include:

- super twisted nematic (STN) LCD, which is used in monochrome displays and has moderate resolution
- double layer super twisted nematic (DSTN) LCD, used in colour displays where a higher resolution is required
- thin film transistor (TFT) LCD, which is capable of providing a high-quality image in colour at high resolution.

In motor vehicles the TFT LCDs are used for:

- reversing camera display
- GPS displays
- vehicle control and system switches.

In the last example, these displays are multifunctional. There is a driving zone, which has all of the driving-based controls and a comfort zone, which uses a controller to regulate the atmospheric heating and other systems within the vehicle.

## Vacuum fluorescent display (VFD)

The illustration (Figure 18.19) shows a VFD display element being used for a digital number display, in this case a seven-segment figure.

VFD has largely been superseded by other systems, but it was initially used to provide the display for digital speedometers, showing either bar graphs or numerals. It was considered to be a first generation electronic technology. The essential workings of the systems are as follows:

- Each segment has a filament.
- The filament operates as a cathode.
- The cathode emits electrons.
- It has a phosphor anode and a control grid, which is designed to even out the electron flow.
- All of these elements are inside a vacuum glass envelope.
- When an electric current heats up the tungsten wires of the cathode it emits electrons.
- Under normal circumstances the electrons would move directly to the grid, which has a positive charge. But a voltage is applied to a segment of the anode, giving it a positive potential, and as a result electrons pass through the grid. They hit the anode and this action causes it to glow.
- Each time the display needs to illuminate something in particular the segments of the display are arranged in a suitable manner.

## Cold cathode fluorescence lamp (CCFL)

While most laptop computers, for example, have LCD panels, they are lit with built-in fluorescent tubes, positioned above, behind or beside the LCD panel, which provide a backlight. Most laptops use a CCFL

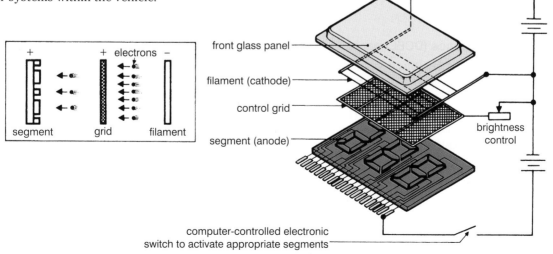

*Figure 18.19 Vacuum fluorescent display*

for this backlight. It can provide bright, white light and its temperature does not raise much above the ambient temperature. This means that it is ideal to be used in conjunction with LCDs, as their low heat generation does not damage the CCFL or the LCD.

CCFLs are incredibly thin and are driven by a tiny control board. They are, however, susceptible to damage and do not like rough treatment.

In a vehicle environment they are often used for black screen displays. This enables the display to have a good contrast. It also means that they can be used with tinted screens or covers.

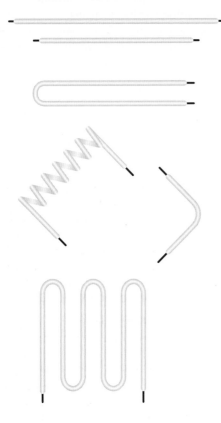

Figure 18.20  Examples of long-life CCFLs

## DC electroluminescence (DCEL) panel

In DCELs illumination takes place when voltage is applied. DCELs are solid state. They are similar to an LCD cell, with the liquid crystal layer replaced by a zinc sulphide-based compound. The system has many advantages over the LCD and, in addition, provides a display by emitting light instead of relying on reflected light. The DCEL is an active light source and has uniform light distribution.

Many different colours can be produced by an electroluminescent panel. The system can operate either by DC or alternating current (AC). In many cases the DC electroluminescent panel is used to provide backlighting for an LCD display.

## Head-up display (HUD)

Although drivers of modern vehicles do not have to contend with the bewildering amount of data, information and warnings that pilots of helicopters and modern jets have to contend with, there is still the issue of the time adjustment of the eyes when moving from the road to the display panel. Typically, this process takes an average driver 0.5 s. This is simply for the eyes to refocus either from the road to the display panel or from the display panel back to the road.

During this very short period of time the driver is unable to pay direct attention to either the display panel or the road. Clearly, in a military aircraft, for example, half a second could be the difference between life and death; while this is not as critical a time period in a motor vehicle, it could still lead to problems.

The solution that was applied to aircraft pilots was to project an image of the most important data directly into the field of vision of the pilot, so that they would not have to move their eyes up or down and could focus entirely on the job at hand. This meant coming up with a system that could project a virtual image of the display system, hence the term 'head-up', meaning that the requirement to look down or to move the head was eliminated.

The key aspects of the HUD system as applied to a motor vehicle can be seen in Figure 18.21.

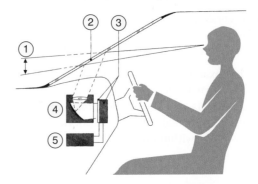

| | |
|---|---|
| 1  virtual image | 4  optical system |
| 2  reflection in windshield | 5  electronics |
| 3  LCD and lighting (or cathode ray tubes, VFD) | |

Figure 18.21  Head-up display

Although the HUD is complex, it works on the following principles:

- An image of the display is projected on to the windscreen; this is a reflection created by the optical image generator.
- The optical image generator can use a combination of illumination technologies, including active or passive systems.

- The image itself is projected on to a part of the windscreen that will not obscure vital visual information that the driver is picking up from the external environment. This often means that the optical image generator will project the image on to the corner of the screen.
- The information displayed only includes the most vital information; typically this is safety related. It is not usually the case that the system provides standard information that would otherwise be found on the display panel.

## 18.4 Driving displays, maintenance and fault diagnosis

With increasingly smart on-board systems that can monitor the vehicle's condition and relay this information via the display panel to the driver, a great deal of fault diagnosis can be readily identified. The maintenance of the systems can then follow either as a routine service matter, or as an interim measure in the case of component failure.

### Driver displays

Electronic display units use numeric readouts, alpha-numeric prompts, quasi-analogue gauge patterns and bar graphs. These signal to the driver various operating conditions and warnings of specific faults. Irrespective of the type of display, many electrical connections are needed to supply the various rectangular bars or dot images that form the display. The standard seven-segment displays (Figure 18.17) require seven electrical connections to form one digit. So for the display of vehicle speed a three-digit stack would require 21 connections plus a number of auxiliary lines.

This is an expensive and bulky layout, but it can be reduced by multiplexing, where all of the digits in the stack effectively share the same electrical connections (Figure 18.16).

Rapid cycling of the driving current between the digits illuminates only one digit at any one time. This cycling action is achieved by making the driving circuit earth each connection independently. Since the human eye retains an image for a short time the impression is that each digit is lit continuously. Flicker is avoided by switching each display segment on and off many thousands of times per second.

### Data sampling

Although the majority of data is transmitted using digital systems, it can actually be displayed in either digital or analogue format. The digital signalling has some distinct advantages compared to that of analogue:

- Digital signals are transmitted as a series of binary pulses. This means that they are less likely to be affected by noise interference or the corruption of the signal during the transmission process.
- Only a relatively small bandwidth is required in order to send the digital signals.
- The result is that more information can be sent on the system at the same time, making the overall system far more flexible.

A computer can deal with only one item of information at any one time. In order to handle the numerous pieces of data that are being fed into it, a multiplexing technique is often used in order to separate out the various signals. We have already seen how the principles of this system work.

In standard wiring diagrams the multiplexer is shown as a switch (M). The purpose of the multiplexer is to select the signal source and then to convey the data to the computer for processing.

Once the processing has taken place the signal has to be transmitted to the correct display area of the display panel, at the right time. This is achieved by fitting a smaller switching device, called a de-multiplexer (shown in diagrams as D). The de-multiplexer is fitted to the computer output. The two switches need to be timed to ensure that the display matches the appropriate sensor.

The switching time between subsequent signals that are received from given signal sources will depend on the rate at which an individual signal varies. Some data from signal sources will indicate that the actual data varies very little over a short period of time. Other data sources will indicate a sudden change in conditions. In other words, quantities such as the content of the fuel tank or the temperature of the coolants are likely to change very slowly. On the other hand, data related to the vehicle's speed or the engine speed are likely to rapidly change. These differences require some data sources to be sampled more often than others. As a result, the sampling of the fuel content level would not be as frequent as checking the vehicle's speed.

In addition to the variable sampling periods, a system must also allow for the longer time that may be needed by the computer to process some items of data. Some of the data will contain long strings of information and take considerably longer for processing. Control functions to deal with these different types of data are programmed into the microprocessor or computer.

## System configuration

A typical instrumentation system incorporates analogue displays. These could be on/off warning lamps and digital seven-segment displays. We have already seen how a six-instrument configuration can involve three types of display operated by a single computer system. Sensor signals are converted into 8-bit two-level digital codes by the A/D unit and are then supplied to the central processing unit (CPU) by the multiplexer. After processing, the de-multiplexer outputs the signals in an 8-bit or on/off form to drive the appropriate area of the display unit.

## Vehicle computer control

The vast majority of modern motor vehicles have at least one computer in overall control. Computers are also necessary in order to control other vital functions:

- The control of the air/fuel mixture through either a feedback carburettor or via electronic fuel injection.
- Ignition timing.
- Climate control.
- Automatic transmission.
- Anti-theft devices, including immobilisation.
- Seat adjustment.
- Steering wheel adjustment.

While most of these computer-controlled systems are highly reliable, they are not infallible. As with the majority of systems, the reliability of the whole is entirely dependent upon the reliability of the weakest link in the chain, which invariably are the sensors. If the sensors fail or provide inadequate or incorrect data, then the computer will act accordingly and respond to what it perceives to be the problem.

## Limp home mode

Limp home mode refers to a situation where, under normal circumstances, it would be advisable to halt the vehicle and carry out essential maintenance or repair. However, the on-board computer system, while highlighting a fault, allows the vehicle to run under limited conditions. It will not allow the vehicle to be driven to excess, reducing the revs or speed, for example.

The computer system will override a failed sensor or a sensor that is giving a warning in order to allow the driver to get the vehicle either home or somewhere that it can be looked at. For example, the engine warning lamp will flash, which is a continual reminder that potential damage is still being done to the engine as the car is still running.

This system was originally introduced because some of the early sensors provided the computer with incorrect data. Rather than allow the driver to be stranded, the computer would allow the car to continue to run, albeit under restricted circumstances. Whether the fault is real or there is an error can be ascertained under proper conditions in the workshop, as the fault code is stored in the memory of the computer.

As computer systems have become more sophisticated, they do not automatically switch to limp home mode, even though a critical warning lamp may have been illuminated. Often, the computer would substitute a reading between the minimum and maximum parameters of the sensor in order to ensure that it still runs despite error codes.

Ultimately, the way in which the computer responds will be dependent on exactly what a particular sensor is indicating. It will also, of course, depend on where that sensor is located and how critical the system is that it is monitoring. On the majority of vehicles, even a critical warning will disappear if the sensor begins to send normal readings back to the computer. There are, however, some exceptions. Some makes and models of vehicles will flash up the check engine warning lamp if the driver has failed to tighten the petrol cap properly. Other vehicles will not turn off warning lamps even after normal readings and will require a workshop technician to use a scan tool to eliminate the light.

When a computer takes over in limp home mode in some makes and models, it will control the transmission. In switching to limp home mode the driver will only be able to engage second gear, thereby limiting the top speed of the vehicle. They will be able to engage reverse. This system is specifically designed to reduce the amount of potential damage, particularly to the engine, when the check engine warning lamp has been illuminated.

## Fault code readers

The majority of modern vehicles have built-in diagnostic systems. These are either On-Board Diagnostics II (OBD II) or the European On-Board Diagnostics (EOBD).

### OBD II

In order to diagnose engine problems and to control their functions specifically to meet emission standards, OBD systems began to be introduced. The majority of vehicles built in America since the 1990s certainly have these systems.

By linking the OBD system to a computer it is possible to receive real-time data on fuel consumption and emissions monitoring. In fact, it is now no longer necessary to even use a laptop, as handheld devices do exactly the same job. Most modern vehicles use an engine ECU, which is

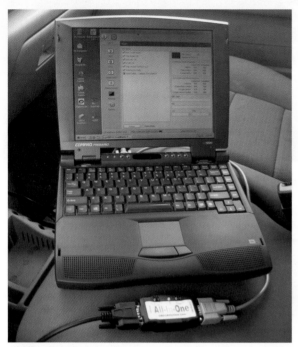

*Figure 18.22 Laptop computer used to interrogate OBD II system*

a computer designed to ensure that both the engine and the transmission run in an efficient manner and, at the same time, keep exhaust emissions down to a minimum (or at least the permitted amount).

It would be impossible for most drivers to be able to make the correct settings to ensure that their vehicles run at optimum efficiency. As a result, the sensors linked to the engine ECU send signals to allow the ECU to make tiny tweaks to the ignition timing, the fuel injection setting and other parameters. There is a pair of oxygen sensors, which are located in the exhaust system. One is usually fitted before the catalytic converter and the other after it. The first sensor sends signals back to the ECU on the cylinder's combustion efficiency. The ECU can then make adjustments designed to lower emissions by changing the air/fuel mix. The second sensor provides data about the efficiency of the catalytic converter. The system works in the following way:

1 If a sensor detects something outside normal values, the engine ECU records it with a fault code.
2 This fault code, or diagnostic trouble code (DTC), switches on a lamp that indicates a malfunction. The nature of the malfunction will determine the action that will need to be taken.

Fault codes can be retrieved via a scanning tool. This will identify the precise nature of the fault and corrective action can then be taken.

### EOBD

The European On Board Diagnostics software was installed by manufacturers to monitor and diagnose faults in vehicle engine management systems to ensure compliance with the regulations brought in by the EU for petrol and diesel engined vehicles.

# Screens and window systems

## 19.1 Wiper systems

The basic requirement for the wiper system is the removal of water and dirt from the windscreen. The screen must be kept clear enough to provide suitable visibility regardless of vehicle speed or weather conditions.

### 19.1.1 Screen cleaning

#### Wiper blades

The wiper blades are made from a rubber component with a screen contact thickness in the region of 0.1 mm. They are mounted on metal wiper arms and are pulled against the screen by a spring. The aerodynamic properties of the wiper have become more important and so have led away from the conventional metal blade holder (Figure 19.1a) to the now more common 'flat' wiper blade (Figure 19.1b). This design reduces wind drag and cuts down on wind noise.

*(a)*

*(b)*

*Figure 19.1 (a) Conventional wiper blade, (b) flat wiper blade*

#### Wiper linkage or drive system

There are various methods used to drive wiper blades; the most common types use a mechanical linkage system. Figure 19.2 shows the layout of a typical wiper system. A worm on the armature drives a worm wheel, which is connected to a crank to provide the **reciprocating** action needed to oscillate the wiper blades. The gearing gives the speed reduction and the torque increase needed to drive the wiper blades. On modern vehicles, pedestrian safety has a major impact on the wiper linkage used.

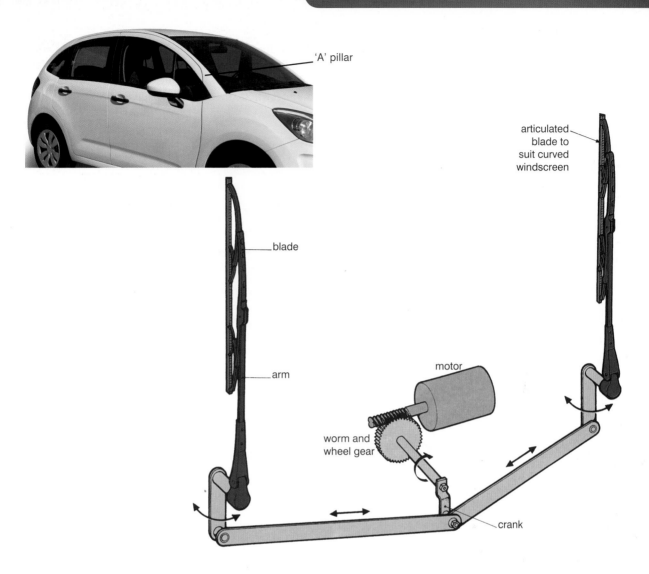

*Figure 19.2 Layout of a typical wiper linkage system*

It is becoming equally popular for wiper blade arms to be mounted to the outside of the linkage near the 'A' pillar (see Figure 19.2) so as not to cause impact injuries as can happen when mounted towards the centre of the vehicle. Wiper arms can also be parked in the upright position behind covers mounted on the 'A' pillars.

**Reciprocating**: having a forward and backwards motion.

## Other drive systems

Some manufacturers have begun to use a system in which each wiper arm is driven by its own electric motor. The twin-motor wiper system synchronises the two drives electronically and integrated sensors monitor the precise movement of the wiper arms. This allows each individual wiper arm to change direction, ensuring that the wiper sweeps close to the 'A' pillar, clearing the maximum field of view.

In addition, this system has the added road safety benefit of the wipers being parked below the bonnet line due to its more compact design. This improves aerodynamics and also reduces the risk of injury to pedestrians and cyclists in an accident.

## Wiper motors

The most common type of motor used on the wiper system is the permanent magnet type. The motor consists of an eight-slotted armature, which is mounted on self-lubricating sintered bushes. Two carbon brushes, set 180° apart, rub on an eight-segment commutator. Two strong permanent magnets are bonded with an adhesive to the steel yoke. This is sometimes coated externally with a non-ferrous metal to resist corrosion. Rubber seals are fitted at the joint faces of the motor to exclude moisture and a polythene pipe vents the gases formed by arcing at the brushes.

## Two-speed operation

Two-speed operation is generally achieved by using an extra brush. The third brush is thinner than the main brushes and is set as shown in Figure 19.3a.

When the switch supplies current to B, a low wipe rate of about 50 wiping cycles per minute is obtained; this is increased to about 70 wiping cycles per minute when the supply is delivered to terminal C.

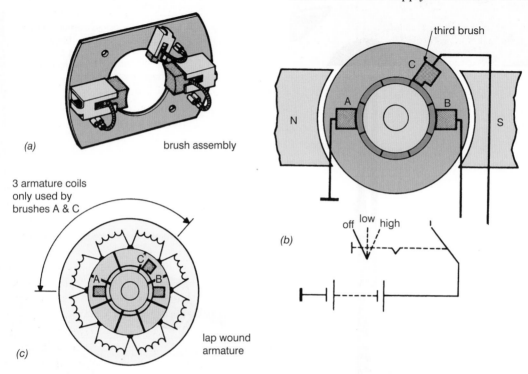

*(a)* brush assembly

3 armature coils only used by brushes A & C

lap wound armature

*(c)*

*(b)*

Figure 19.3 Two-speed wiper operation including third brush

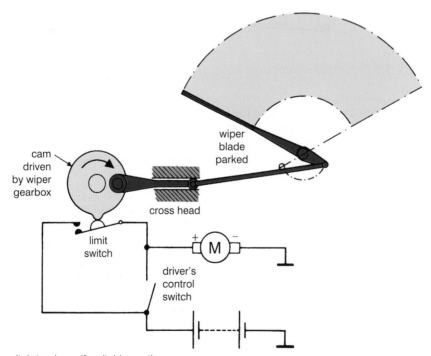

wiper blade parked

cam driven by wiper gearbox

cross head

limit switch

driver's control switch

Figure 19.4 Limit switch to give self-switching action

The rise in speed is due to an increase in the current in the motor. When brushes A and C are used, fewer armature windings are involved and, therefore, the lower resistance gives a higher current and a higher rotational speed. As the speed is increased a rise in back-electromotive force (EMF) reduces the current. The shorter armature path between brushes A and C is shown in Figure 19.3b. Figure 19.3c shows the interconnection of the coils of a lap-wound type of armature normally used for a wiper motor.

High speed should not be used when there is a heavy load on the wiper blade, e.g. in heavy snow or on a windscreen that has been swept clear of water and is dry.

### Self-switching action

When the wiper is not required, the blades should be set so that they are at the end of their wiping stroke. The driver may find it difficult to stop the blades in this position so a limit switch is fitted to achieve this requirement. This automatic switch is controlled by the gearbox of the wiper motor and is arranged to open only when the wiper blades are at one end of their stroke.

Figure 19.4 shows the principle of the limit switch. If the driver switches off the motor in any position other than that shown, the limit switch continues to supply current until the 'park' position is reached. Even with this switch, the blades do not always come to rest at the correct place owing to the momentum of the moving parts. This problem is overcome by using an action called regenerative braking. When the driver has switched off the motor, another set of contacts on the limit switch is arranged to connect the positive brush to earth, shorting out the two main brushes (Figure 19.5). At this point the current generated by the moving armature creates a load on the armature, which gives a braking action and quickly brings the motor to rest.

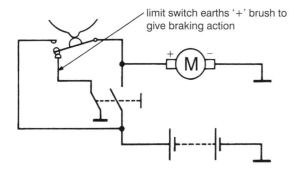

limit switch earths '+' brush to give braking action

*Figure 19.5 Regenerative braking*

### Self-parking wipers

On some vehicles the wiper blades are parked off the windscreen. This provision can be achieved by switching the circuit so that after the motor has stopped the current through the armature is reversed. When the brush polarity of a permanent magnet motor is changed, the armature rotates in the opposite direction. By arranging the gearbox linkage so that reverse motion extends the wiping stroke, the movement is made to park the wiper blades well away from the glass screen. In today's vehicle, this function is commonly controlled by the wiper electronic control unit (ECU) or by the body ECU.

### Intermittent wipe

Spray from passing vehicles and light drizzle conditions require the screen to be wiped infrequently, so all vehicles have a switch position to provide this facility. When selected, this setting will allow the wiper system to complete a single sweep every few seconds. The desired time period can be set by the driver to meet changing weather conditions. To overcome the regenerative braking provision on a permanent magnet-type motor, a current pulse of comparatively long duration is needed to rotate the armature sufficiently to move the limit switch from its 'braked' position. Older vehicles use a relay-controlled circuit to provide this function. An example circuit diagram is shown in Figure 19.6. The time period between pulses is governed by a circuit that is controlled using an R–C network or timer microprocessor. (An R–C network is a device made up of resistors and capacitors. For more details of how these work see Chapter 1.) This control method is now being replaced by electronic control, using an ECU, which is sometimes also referred to as a central control unit (CCU). (See the following section.)

Figure 19.6 shows the two main brushes, marked + and –, interconnected through the two switches and relay contacts 1. Regenerative braking takes place when the contacts are set in this position. When current is supplied to terminal A, the relay is energised and the contacts are closed. This connects the negative brush to earth and causes the motor to operate, irrespective of the position of the limit switch. If at this stage the supply is disconnected from A, the relay will open and the contacts 1 will close. Since the limit switch is earthed, the motor will continue to operate until the earth contact at the limit switch is broken.

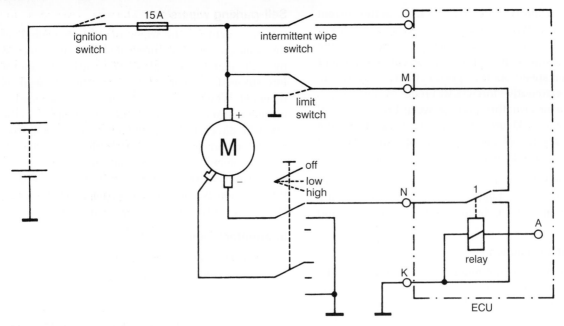

Figure 19.6 Intermittent wipe control circuit

## 19.1.2 Electronically controlled wiper systems

### Electronic control of wiper system

On today's vehicles electronically controlled wiper systems have been added by numerous manufacturers. An electronic wiper motor in this type of system incorporates integrated control electronics within the wiper motor. A major advantage of this system is the ability to reverse the wiper motor direction. This gives reciprocating action without the need for complicated wiper linkages. An added advantage of this system is that a greater swept area of the screen can be achieved

(Figure 19.7). Electronically controlled wiper systems can be linked to other vehicle systems, for example automatic headlight systems and automatic operation of rear wiper when reverse gear is selected by the driver. Linking the control unit to other systems not only cuts down on wiring behind the dash but also gives the driver extra comfort features. These added features include:

- automatic rain-sensing
- intermittent wipe (electronically controlled)
- automatic start of rear wipe when reverse is engaged
- front wash wipe
- rear wash wipe.

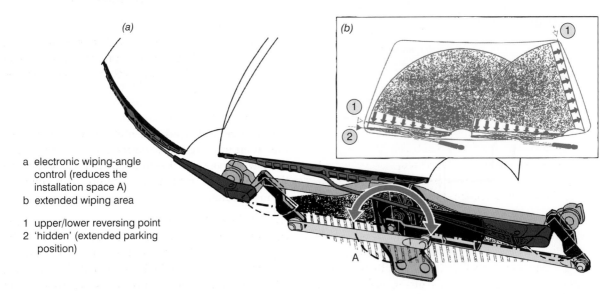

a electronic wiping-angle control (reduces the installation space A)
b extended wiping area

1 upper/lower reversing point
2 'hidden' (extended parking position)

Figure 19.7 Electronically controlled reversing wiper motor system

## Automatic rain-sensing

Sudden changes in road or weather conditions can leave a driver with reduced visibility for a few seconds while switching on the wiper system. Rain-sensing wiper systems are now commonplace on vehicles. The systems use a rain sensor usually mounted at the top of the windscreen by the interior mirror. This sensor monitors rainfall and this data is used by the ECU to activate the wiper system. One method of monitoring rainfall is by using the principle of total internal reflection. A light-emitting diode (LED) is shone at an angle of approximately 45° on to the windscreen from inside the rain-sensing unit. When the glass is wet, less light is reflected back to the photodiode due to **refraction**. Under this condition the wipers are turned on. When the screen is dry the light from the LED returns to the photodiode without any major change to its intensity. Vehicles with this system have an 'AUTO' position on the wiper selector switch. Vehicles fitted with a rain-sensing device usually have automatic headlight function integrated into the system (see Chapter 17). The rain sensor can also be used by the central locking system and vehicle security system to close windows and the sunroof if rain is detected. A typical rain-sensing unit is shown in Figure 19.8.

**Refraction**: the bending of light as it passes from one substance to another.

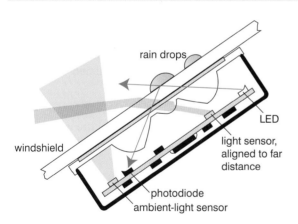

*Figure 19.8  Rain sensor*

There are some variations of rain-sensing devices used by manufacturers. One such sensor works in an identical manner as just described, but instead of employing an LED light an infrared beam is directed at 45° to the screen by an emitter. The workings of this sensor are still based on the principle of refraction.

Some of the latest forms of rain sensors make use of the piezo properties of certain crystalline minerals. These types of sensors are capable of acoustically detecting individual raindrops, and can also distinguish between raindrops and hailstones. The sensor is made up of a stainless steel cover, which is attached to the **piezoelectric** detector. Raindrops hit the steel cover causing the generation of elastic waves. These waves are transferred to the piezoelectric sensor via the plate. When such mechanical stress is placed upon the piezoelectric material, a voltage is generated. These voltage pulses created by the piezoelectric material contained in the sensor are filtered and amplified before being digitised. A microprocessor system is used to analyse the data obtained against preset parameters relating to raindrop size.

**Piezoelectric**: producing an electrical charge when mechanically deformed or, conversely, changing size when an electric field is applied.

### Intermittent wipe (electronically controlled)

This feature allows the driver to not only select the intermittent position on the switch, but gives them greater control and enables the selection of time delay in between wipes. The time difference is achieved by the driver selecting the required time delay using a variable resistor on the wiper stalk. This variable resistor usually has five settings, ranging from approximately 3 s delay with a resistance of 500 Ω, to a delay in the region of 15 s with a resistance of 5400 Ω. It should be highlighted that this time delay can be as great as 40 s on some vehicles. Due to the networking of ECUs the time delay can also be linked to vehicle speed. As vehicle speed increases, the control system will decrease the time delay in between wipes.

### Automatic start of rear wipe when reverse is engaged

If the front wipers are in the 'on' position and the driver selects reverse gear, the control unit automatically switches the rear wiper on. The rear wiper will continue to sweep until the front wipers are turned off or reverse gear is deselected.

### Front wash wipe

When the front washer system is operated the wipers will be energised by the control unit and will continue to wipe for approximately 5 s after the driver releases the washer switch.

### Rear wash wipe

As with the front wash wipe, the rear wiper will be energised when the driver operates the rear washer system. On most vehicles the wiper will continue to sweep a number of times after the washer switch has been released.

As mentioned earlier in this chapter, some manufacturers are using separate motors to drive the front wiper arms. The electronic control for this type of system is incorporated in the electronically controlled wiper system. A computer program is used to count the revolutions of the motors using the park limit switch as a reference point. This is then used by the control unit to synchronise the two motors. Communication for this system is via the controller area network (CAN) or local interconnect network (LIN) bus.

## Wiper blade pressure control

Wind pressure on the wiper blades can increase significantly at high speeds and can cause the wipers to lift off the screen and judder. Setting the pressure too high at low speed can deform the contact area of the blade. The wiper blade pressure control system is designed to prevent this from happening. Sensors in the pressure control system allow the ECU to determine the air stream velocity and the intensity of the rain. The ECU evaluates this data and, in turn, passes an appropriate signal to a servo motor. When greater pressure is required the servo motor is activated and moves the actuating rod against the pivoted wiper arm causing an increase in pressure on the blade against the screen. The system can respond quickly to any change in the driving conditions.

## Rear wiper

Rear wipers are generally less complex than front wipers. Usually using one wiper there is no need for any linkage system. Instead, a reversing motor is normally used giving a wiping arc up to 180° if required. Rear wiper systems still offer the same functions as front systems, these include:

- intermittent wipe
- wash/wipe operation.

It should be noted that the motor uses the same technology and self-switching action as the front wiper system.

## 19.2 Washer systems

Vehicles are required by law to have a screen washer so that the driver's vision through the windscreens is not impaired. The vehicle will fail the annual MOT inspection if the washer system does not provide enough liquid to clear the windscreen in conjunction with the wipers. The water or cleaning fluid is sprayed on to the windscreen by two or more jets operated by a pump, which is powered electrically. Depending on the manufacturer, there may be separate pumps for the front and rear windscreen or one may serve both. There may also be a separate washer and wiper system for the headlamps.

Headlamp cleaning systems are common on modern vehicles. Not only are these systems essential to keep the headlamps free from dirt, but they are mandatory if the vehicle has gas-discharge headlamps fitted.

There are two main systems that are commonly fitted:

- Wash/wipe system
- High-pressure wash system

### Wash/wipe system

This system is identical to the windscreen washer and wipe system. However, there is one major drawback that has made this a less desirable system: the wiper blades are only effective if the headlamp lens is flat, limiting designers to basic lens designs.

### High-pressure wash system

This system is preferred as it is suited to more complex headlamp lens designs. The system uses high-pressure fluid to remove dirt from the lens. The system also has the added benefit of being more cosmetically pleasing as the washer nozzles can be located in the bumper and only become visible when the system is operated. The washer nozzles rise up due to the pressure generated by the washer pump causing high-pressure water to be aimed directly at the headlamp lens.

Both of the above systems operate when the vehicle's headlamp system is switched on and the windscreen washer system is activated.

### Washer pump

Figure 19.9 shows the design of the washer pump. This is a small centrifugal pump operated by a stalk on the steering column, which switches on a motor of permanent magnet type. A current of about 3A is

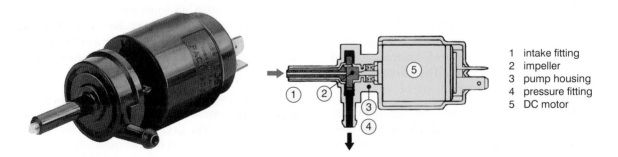

1 intake fitting
2 impeller
3 pump housing
4 pressure fitting
5 DC motor

*Figure 19.9 Washer pump design*

enough to drive the pump with a flow rate of around 0.75 litre per minute (Figure 19.10). The pump is guarded with an inlet filter and takes water from a reservoir, which may hold up to 4 litres of fluid.

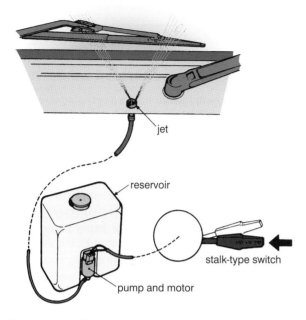

*Figure 19.10 Windscreen washer system*

Various refinements can be embodied in the wash system, including:

- timer to control the wash period
- timer programmed to give a controlled wipe/wash action following the touch-operation of the washer switch (see 'Front wash wipe' on page 278)
- integration of the washer outlets with the wiper blades to eliminate spray problems
- heating the washer fluid before it is applied to the screen to minimise risk of freezing
- heating elements in washer jets to prevent freezing.

CAN-controlled wash/wipe systems will use a separate motor on each of the front wipers which allows the arms to be synchronised and will offer additional functions not available on a standard system. The following are some of the additional features:

- Alternating rest position
- Speed-dependent wiper stage reset
- Speed-dependent intermittent delay
- Service and winter position
- Bonnet contact
- Anti-blocking function
- Prewash
- Synchronisation function
- Tip wiping stage 2
- Follow-up wash after wash/wipe function
- Follow-up wipe cycle
- Wiper control for rear window

### Alternating rest position

In order to prevent damage to the wiper blades, the wiper arms move upwards slightly every second time they are switched off.

### Speed-dependent wiper speed

If the road speed drops below approximately 4 km/h, the wiper speed will be reduced by one stage; when the road speed increases above approximately 8 km/h, the wiper speed returns to the selected stage.

### Speed-dependent intermittent delay

There are four adjustable intermittent phases and each one is dependent on the road speed of the vehicle. The delays between the individual wiper movements vary from 1.28 seconds to 24 seconds at speeds of 4 km/h to 150 km/h.

### Service and winter position

When the vehicle is parked and within 10 seconds of switching the ignition off the wiper switch is switched to the tip wiping position, both wipers will move to the edge of the windscreen. This function will not operate when the bonnet is open.

### Bonnet contact

If the bonnet is open the wipers will not operate.

### Anti-blocking function

If the wiper system detects that the wipers are blocked (this is monitored by the amount of current drawn) the system will attempt to resolve this five times. If it is unable to move the blockage, the wipers will remain in the rest position and the blockage will have to be removed manually.

If the wiper blades are frozen to the windscreen, the wipers will attempt to break free five times; if unsuccessful after the fifth attempt, the system will shut down.

### Prewash

If the wash/wipe function is operated at speeds of less than 120 km/h, there will be a prewash period of approx. 0.8 seconds, during which only the washer pump will operate.

### Synchronisation function

If the ignition is switched off and the wipers are not in their rest position, they will be moved automatically to the rest position on turning the ignition on again.

### Tip wiping stage 2

If the tip wiping function is operated for more than two seconds, the wiper is automatically switched to the second stage of operation.

### Follow-up wipe after wash/wipe function

If the wash/wipe function is operated for longer than 0.5 second, the follow-up wiping function will be actuated three times. If the operation time is less, the follow-up wipe is operated twice.

### Follow-up wipe cycle

If the vehicle speed is greater than 2 km/h, the wiper function is operated once more 5 seconds after the last wash/wipe.

### Wiper control for rear window

Rear window wiper actuation features three operating modes:

- Reverse wipe
- Rear intermittent wipe
- Rear window wash/wipe operation

### Reverse wiping

The reverse wiping function operates the rear window wiper to clear the screen when the front windscreen wiper is switched on and reverse gear is selected.

### Stage 1 or 2 rear intermittent wipe

Conditions for activation:

- Ignition switched on.
- Windscreen wiper is in intermittent stage 1 or stage 2. Identification of the selected stage is communicated via the CAN data bus.
- Reverse gear or R-selected (automatic). Identification is via the reverse light switch or via the gear selector position, the automatic

gearbox control unit, the drive train CAN data bus and the data bus diagnostic interface. This system will only operate if the tailgate is closed. Identification of this is via the wiper system central control unit.

## 19.3 Window closure systems

### 19.3.1 Electrically operated windows

Electric window applications use a permanent magnet motor for each window. The motor is operated via a three-position rocker switch to enable the polarity to be changed to give up-and-down motion of the window glass. The driver's panel has four main window switches, one for each window, and an isolation switch to disconnect the supply to the rear windows. Early systems incorporated relays in the control circuitry, which are now being phased out and replaced by more sophisticated ECU-controlled systems. (See section 19.3.2 'Electronically controlled window systems'.)

Drive between the motor and the window glass is by means of a gearbox or window regulator; this amplifies the torque sufficiently to raise the window, which is more difficult to undertake than the downward motion. It is not uncommon to also find a flexible rack or cable assembly used by some manufacturers. Figure 19.11 shows both systems. The drive system also includes a self-locking worm reduction gear. This is incorporated to ensure the window glass cannot be forced down. To

**Power-window drives**

1 drive motor
2 guide rail
3 driver
4 link mechanism
5 Bowden cable

*(a) system with link mechanism*　　　　*(b) system with Bowden cable*

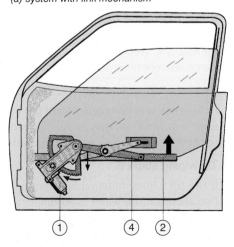 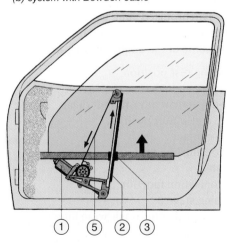

*Figure 19.11 Electric window drive mechanisms (cable and link)*

## Thermal protection device

This is used to protect circuits in systems, such as electric window systems, and is often built into the motor. It can be one of two types:

- Mechanical bi-metal strip – the bi-metal strip is formed using two layers of different metals. If excessive current passes through the bi-metal strip, the two metals heat up at different rates causing the strip to bend and break the contacts. When left to cool the device resets itself by returning to its original shape (see Figure 19.12).
- Solid state positive temperature coefficient (PTC) type device – a polymer PTC is a type of thermistor, its resistance increases as its temperature increases. In its normal state the polymer PTC is in the form of dense crystals with many carbon particles packed together. This gives good conductivity. When heated from excessive current the material expands and allows the carbon particles to move away from each other. This is now said to be in its

'tripped' state as electricity cannot flow. When current is stopped the device will cool and the carbon particles become tightly packed again.

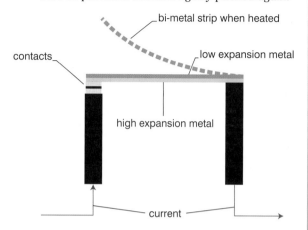

Figure 19.12 Mechanical bi-metal thermal trip

Both these devices automatically reset and are often referred to as 'cycling' circuit breakers.

---

protect the system components, for example, motor and wiring loom, a thermal protection device is fitted to the circuit. This is often built into the body of the motor in the form of a thermal trip or remotely via thermal circuit breakers. This protects the system from damage if the switch is operated for too long or the window is jammed, for example, with ice.

Figure 19.13 shows a circuit for electric operation of a rear passenger window; the remainder of the circuit has been omitted for simplicity. The motor in this layout is supplied directly via the ignition switch. The additional rear window switch enables a passenger to adjust the window, but this control can only be operated when the driver's isolation switch is closed. Either switch can operate the motor as the system is effectively a parallel circuit.

## 19.3.2 Electronically controlled window systems

With the introduction of more sophisticated electronically controlled systems, more manufacturers are moving towards systems that use microprocessors to control window operation. In these types of systems a speed and position sensor is used so the control unit knows the actual speed of the motor, its direction of rotation and the exact position of the window glass. In this system the control unit is located in the door with the motor and forms localised intelligence for the system. It is normal for these control units to communicate with

other body systems via the CAN or LIN bus and can provide the following features:

- One-touch or one-shot up or down
- Anti-pinch (back off) feature
- Inch up or down
- Lazy lock

### One-touch or one-shot up or down

The window drives in the chosen direction until another direction is chosen or the motor stalls. To achieve this, the ECU needs to know the position of the window glass, and uses an additional commutator located on the motor armature. This produces a signal, via two brushes, which is proportional to the motor speed. Thus the ECU can determine the position of the glass by counting the pulses received from the additional commutator. Alternatively, some vehicles use Hall effect sensors to monitor position and speed.

Whichever system is used, it is important that the window one-touch is programmed correctly if the glass or motor has been removed. This is normally done by operating the glass fully down and holding the switch and then sending the glass up and holding the switch again for a few seconds.

### Anti-pinch (back off) feature

To prevent entrapment in a closing window, the anti-pinch feature is present. The rate of change of speed of the motor is monitored and if it is detected

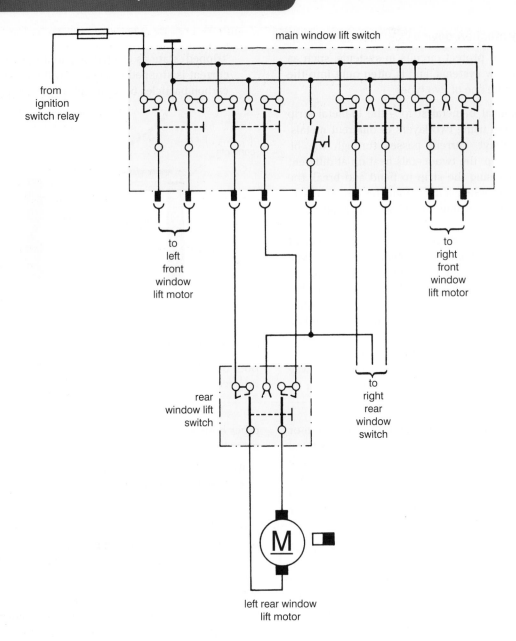

from
ignition
switch relay

main window lift switch

to
left
front
window
lift motor

to
right
front
window
lift motor

rear
window lift
switch

to
right
rear
window
switch

M

left rear window
lift motor

*Figure 19.13  Circuit for electric windows*

as falling below a preset threshold when closing, the ECU will reverse the direction of the motor until the window glass is halfway down.

### Inch up or down

The desired window glass height is selected manually by operating this switch for short periods.

### Lazy lock

This allows all the windows, sunroof and doors to be secured by integrating the keyless entry and security system with the window systems. When the keyless entry is operated a signal is sent to the window control unit to close all the windows.

## 19.4    Heated screens

### 19.4.1 Heated rear screen

Most cars are fitted with an electrically heated rear screen to clear and/or prevent condensation. The heating element consists of a wire or strip element bonded to the interior surface of the glass.

Figure 19.14 shows the basic layout of a heated rear screen circuit. Effective de-misting of the window requires a high amount of power. This can be as high as 180 W when the screen is cold. A normal heated rear screen will draw 10–15 A of current.

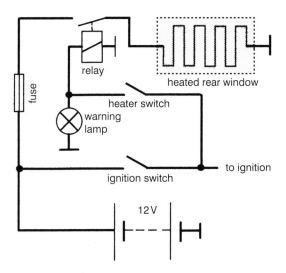

Figure 19.14 Heated rear screen circuit

Using this amount of power means the circuit requires a relay; this minimises the voltage drop in the cable and reduces the load on the switch. In addition, the extended use of the rear screen heater places an extra load on the engine via the alternator. This can have a major effect on the emissions and also the economy of the vehicle. Most modern vehicles will include a timer in the heated rear screen circuit. This timer will switch off the heated rear screen after 10–15 minutes, regardless of driver input. It should also be noted that many modern vehicles will automatically reset the heated rear screen to the 'off' position once the ignition has been switched off ensuring less draw on the battery during the next start-up cycle.

Vehicles with stop-start technology and hybrid vehicles have the ability to automatically switch off the heated rear screen if the vehicle's engine is not running or the alternator has a low output. The alternator and battery status is constantly monitored by the central ECU fitted to control body electronics

in this type of system. However, to remind the driver that the heated rear screen is in operation, either a warning lamp is incorporated in the switch or a heater window symbol is displayed on the instrument panel. It should also be noted that it has become common practice for vehicles to be fitted with heated door mirrors and that these are operated via the same switch as the heated rear screen.

The elements are normally positioned across the rear screen to defrost the main area of the screen and the rest position of the rear wiper blade if fitted.

### 19.4.2 Heated front screen

Many vehicles are now equipped with heated front screens. This technology has to include more discreet heating elements as not to impair the driver's vision. The system consists of micro-thin elements that are bonded in between the glass layers. These micro-thin elements cover a large surface area and so draw high amounts of current. For this reason a timer function, as fitted on heated rear screens, will be utilised. The heated screen may be disabled if the central control unit determines it is compromising the battery or charging system performance.

## 19.5 Mirrors

### 19.5.1 Electrically operated door mirrors

Adjustment of a door mirror is difficult for the driver, especially the setting of a mirror on the passenger door. This task is made easier by using an electrical control system.

Figure 19.15 shows a typical circuit diagram for the control of two door mirrors. Each mirror is electrically adjusted by two reversible permanent magnet motors fitted behind the mirror glass. One

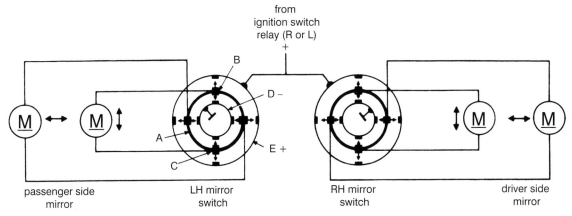

Figure 19.15 Electrically operated door mirrors

motor controls the vertical tilt of the mirror and the other the horizontal operation. Each mirror is set by means of a single switch. This system uses either a joystick-type switch or a flat cursor-type switch. Before operating the direction switch the driver must select which mirror they intend to adjust via a simple slide switch.

When the switch is depressed to vertically tilt the mirror, the switch cage A is moved downwards and the two contacts B and C make a circuit with the – and + surfaces, D and E.

Conversely, when the switch stalk is moved upwards, B contacts the positive surface and C contacts the negative or earth surface. In this switch position, the potential applied to the vertical tilt motor is opposite to that given when the switch was in the previous position. This causes the motor and mirror glass to move in the opposite direction.

### Automatic foldaway mirrors and reverse tilt action

Many modern vehicles now take advantage of the networked systems and offer extra convenience features. Two such features are:

- automatic foldaway mirrors
- reverse tilt action.

### Automatic foldaway mirrors

This system uses a permanent magnet motor housed in the door mirror casing to automatically fold the door mirrors in when the central locking system is operated. The system can also be manually operated by the driver from inside the vehicle via a switch usually located with the door mirror adjustment joystick or cursor cluster.

### Reverse tilt action

This is a system whereby the mirror glass in the door mirrors automatically tilts downwards when the driver engages reverse gear. This improves the driver's visibility of the rear quarter panel areas while reversing the vehicle; the mirrors may normally be positioned higher and wider for general driving conditions.

## 19.5.2 Heated door mirrors

Moisture on mirrors can impair safety, so a heating element placed behind the mirror glass improves the mirror image when driving conditions are poor. As mentioned earlier (see page 285), connecting the mirrors in the same circuit as the heated rear screen overcomes the need for a separate switch. This also means the mirrors are governed by the same timer as the heated rear screen.

## 19.5.3 Interior mirror

Automatic-dimming interior mirrors monitor light levels from the headlamps of vehicles travelling behind. If the headlight intensity reaches a preset limit, the interior mirror will darken the mirror glass to prevent the driver being dazzled from the glare of the headlights.

The interior mirror dim function utilises a transparent, electronically conductive material that becomes increasingly impervious to light when current is applied to it. This material is located between the actual mirror reflector and the outer glass. The mirror unit also contains a forward-facing photoelectric cell and a rear-facing photoelectric cell. The forward-facing cell monitors ambient light levels and the rear-facing cell monitors light levels from behind the vehicle. If bright light hits the rear-facing cell while the front cell is only open to low level light, then the photoelectric cells generate the required signal, the electrically conductive layer darkens and the bright light from the rear no longer dazzles the driver (Figure 19.16).

This system of photoelectric cells is often integrated with the lighting system and offers the benefit of automatic dipped-beam operation when ambient light levels fall.

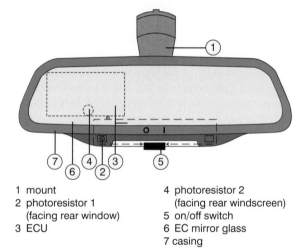

| 1 mount | 4 photoresistor 2 |
| 2 photoresistor 1 | (facing rear windscreen) |
| (facing rear window) | 5 on/off switch |
| 3 ECU | 6 EC mirror glass |
| | 7 casing |

*Figure 19.16 Automatic-dimming interior mirror*

### 19.6 Maintenance and fault diagnosis

### Maintenance of the wiper and washer system

Good clear visibility is essential for safe driving, so for this reason a check on the operation of the wipers and washers is included in the annual MOT test. Inspection of the system generally ensures the screen is clean and the wiper and washer systems are functioning correctly.

## Window closure systems

Maintenance of window closure systems is minimal. Windows should be kept clean and window run channels clear of foreign items. Switches should be kept clear of dirt and moisture. More in-depth diagnostics, for example, checking wiring to the motor involves removal of the door panel trim. Other checks may include inspection of the regulator mechanism if the window fails to operate. An example of a test sequence when the left-hand side rear window fails to close is shown in Table 19.1.

## Heated screens

The most common fault with heated screens is damage to heating elements. Elements often become damaged from objects placed in the vicinity of the rear screen or while cleaning the glass.

## Mirrors

Mirrors should be kept clean to ensure vision is not affected. Switches for electric mirrors should be kept clean and free from moisture.

## Diagnosis of electrical circuits

With the improvements and more common use of electrical systems, reliability has improved over the years. However, if an electrical fault is present on a system, it is important that a logical approach is used by the technician to ensure a thorough inspection is carried out and the correct diagnosis is reached. The following keys points should always be followed:

- Ensure you are familiar with the system being diagnosed.
- Always check most accessible components first.
- Always work logically.
- Never overlook the obvious.

If a complex electrical system is being investigated, the use of wiring diagrams will be necessary.

Often diagnostic flowcharts will be available and should be followed closely (see Figure 19.17 for an example).

With the common use of ECU-controlled systems and networking of ECUs, diagnostic scanners may be used to access diagnostic trouble codes (DTCs). Retrieval of such codes can often be a starting point for diagnosis. Other equipment used for diagnostics may include:

- multimeter
- oscilloscope
- test light or test probe.

When carrying out diagnostic procedures with test equipment it is crucial that the technician knows how:

- the system should operate
- to connect test equipment correctly
- to interpret test results and readings.

As already discussed, working in a logical sequence is crucial when diagnosing an electrical fault. Figure 19.18 shows where a technician would connect a multimeter when carrying out an inspection on a wiper motor circuit if the motor failed to operate on any speed. The positive probe of the multimeter would be connected to the terminal marked Ⓐ at the motor and the ground probe should be connected to terminal marked Ⓑ. If the motor is switched on but no voltage is present at the terminal, then a problem with the supply voltage must be investigated. This again should be done using a methodical and logical approach. An example of this would involve first checking the fuse. This can be done by removing the fuse and carrying out a continuity check across the fuse. If the fuse has continuity, then the wiper switch and wiring should be checked. A wiring diagram should be followed closely to ensure the technician investigates the correct wiring and tests the wiring at the correct terminals.

Table 19.1 *Test sequence when left-hand side rear window fails to close*

| Test | Result – Yes | Result – No |
| --- | --- | --- |
| Do front windows operate? | Check that driver's isolation switch is on | Proceed with test |
| Is fuse serviceable? | Proceed with test | Replace |
| Does right-side rear window operate? | Proceed with test | Check continuity from isolation earth switch to rear window switch and check feed to rear window switch |
| Expose left-hand-side switch: is supply voltage 12 V? | Proceed with test | Check continuity between left- and right-hand switches |
| Measure output voltage from left-hand switch in up and down mode: is voltage 12 V? | Fault is in limit switch or motor | Fault is in switch |

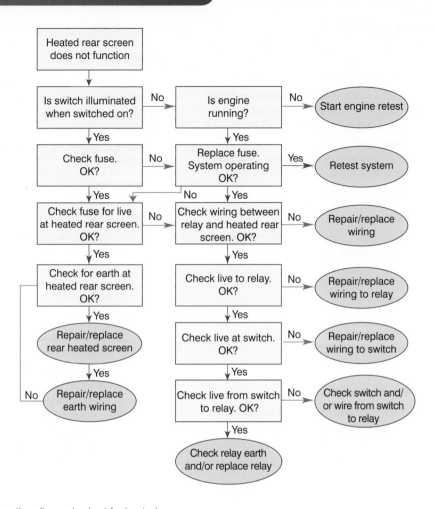

*Figure 19.17  Troubleshooting diagnosis chart for heated rear screen*

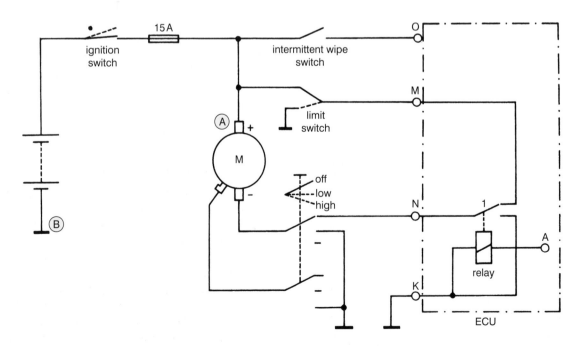

*Figure 19.18  Wiper motor circuit including points to connect a mulitmeter*

# 20

# Signalling equipment

According to the Road Vehicles (Construction and Use) Regulations 1986 all motor vehicles travelling over 20 mph must be fitted with an audible warning device (horn), which must give out a continuous note that is neither too loud nor too harsh in sound.

Under the Road Vehicles Lighting Regulations 1989 all vehicles must be fitted with three indicator lamps on each side of the vehicle that flash at the same time and with a flash rate (or frequency) of 60–120 flashes per minute.

A visual indicator must also be fitted for the driver.

This chapter deals with the following signalling devices:

- Horns
- Direction indicators
- Maintenance and fault diagnosis

## 20.1 Horns

Horns can be sub-divided into three types:

- High-frequency (HF) – the most common
- Wind-tone – similar to high-frequency
- Air horn – trumpet

Most horns are electrically operated and the note is produced by:

- magnetic vibration of a diaphragm
- pumping air past a diaphragm into a trumpet.

The note produced should have a 'musical' quality, aimed at minimising the sound being annoying to the ear. To this end, two horns are often fitted:

- One horn emits a high-pitched note to overcome traffic noise.
- The other emits a low-pitched note for distance travel of sound.

These two notes blend together (harmonise) to produce a sound that is not audibly too harsh, but nonetheless penetrating.

### High-frequency (HF) horn

Electromagnetic action causes a steel diaphragm to vibrate and sets up oscillation in a tone disc. The diaphragm vibrates at 300 Hz (300 cycles per second) and the disc oscillates at 2000 Hz (2000 cycles per second). Harmonising together, these frequencies produce a sound that meets the requirements of a horn.

Figure 20.1 shows how the required oscillatory movement of the diaphragm is produced by the action of the magnetic field winding in an iron core.

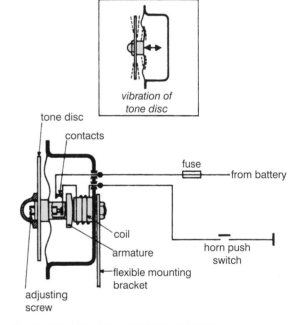

Figure 20.1 High-frequency horn and circuit

When the horn push switch is pressed:

1 A circuit is formed that allows a current of 4 A to flow around the coil.
2 This produces a magnetic flux that attracts the armature towards the coil.
3 The armature will then move a distance, set by the adjusting screw.
4 The contacts open, causing the supply to be cut to the coil and the magnetic field around the coil to collapse. Due to the natural spring action of the diaphragm, the armature returns to its original position, which causes the contacts to close again.

This cycle repeats for as long as the horn is pressed.

## Wind-tone horn

These use a similar action to the HF horn to produce initial diaphragm movement. However, the oscillations produced are used in this instance to vibrate or to resonate a column of air in a trumpet. This is similar to the way sound is produced in a wind instrument (Figure 20.2).

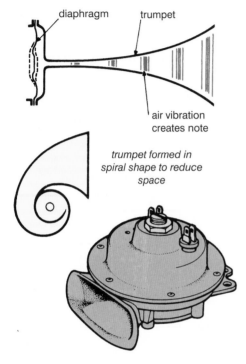

*Figure 20.2  Wind-tone horn*

Note that the pitch is governed by trumpet length. Since this needs to be fairly long, the trumpet is usually shaped in a spiral form, to conserve space. Again, two horns are normally fitted for harmonic resonance, in order to produce a pleasing, non-harsh sound.

Flexible mounting of horns is needed to limit transmission of external shocks. Such shocks could affect the sound quality of the horn note.

Horns, particularly wind-tone horns, can consume currents in excess of 10A. To prolong the life of a horn switch, a relay is generally fitted in the circuit. This buffers the switch from the supply (Figure 20.3).

## Air horn

This uses a trumpet-type design. Air is forced through by an electrically driven air pump. Trumpet air column vibration is started by a diaphragm valve, which is fitted at the end of the trumpet.

Pressing the horn switch causes the air compressor pump to discharge air into the pressure chamber in the horn. The air pressure causes a deflection in the centre of the diaphragm and allows some air into the trumpet. The air forced into the trumpet causes a slight pressure change in the chamber and causes the diaphragm to close. The cycle is then repeated.

Again, the quality of the pitch and note produced are governed by diaphragm vibration rate and trumpet length.

## 20.2    Direction indicators

Direction indicators are amber-coloured flashing lights that warn other road users of a driver's intention to turn left or right, or to overtake. Figure 20.4 shows the typical layout of a directional indicator circuit.

In the case of vehicle breakdown, there is the separately switched hazard warning feature.

All signal indicators should be capable of functioning simultaneously. Each directional indicator light must:

- be sited so that it is visible through a given angle
- carry the appropriate 'E' marking for its position
- have a bulb rated between 15W and 36W.

In a typical directional indicator circuit, a circuit is created when the switch is moved to the left or right. The current is then supplied to the appropriate lamps. The regular interruption of the current caused by the flasher unit produces the flashing light. The flasher unit is situated on the battery side of the switch.

Three types of flasher used to be in common usage:

- Thermal
- Capacitor
- Electronic

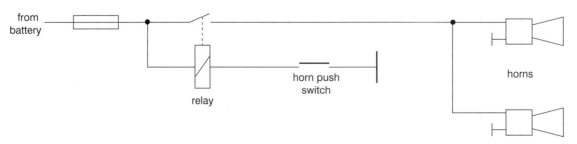

*Figure 20.3  Horn circuit with relay*

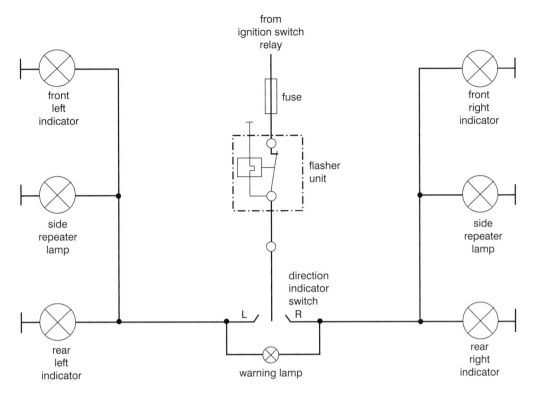

*Figure 20.4  Directional indicator circuit*

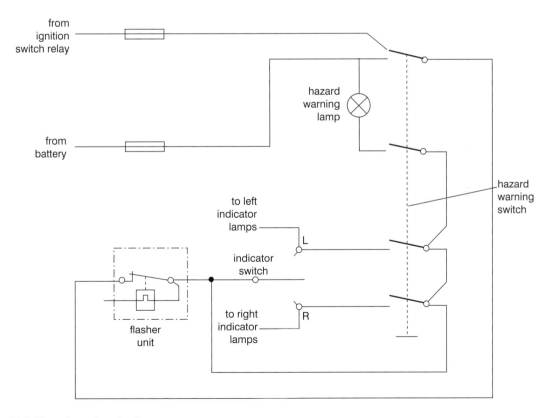

*Figure 20.5  Hazard warning circuit*

*Figure 20.6 Typical indicator bulb*

However, modern vehicles no longer use thermal and capacitor types as electronic control is preferred. It became clear that the older thermal units, which heated a bi-metal element, were much less reliable and efficient than electronic flasher units. A typical electronic flasher unit can be seen in Figure 20.7.

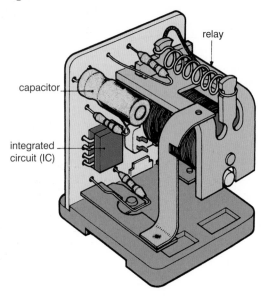

*Figure 20.7 Electronic flasher unit*

## 20.2.1 Electronic flasher units

Electronic flasher units are more efficient than the thermal pulse generator types. The electronic types meet international standards that include the provision of an audible and visual warning system when a bulb has failed. Bulb failure is indicated by

arranging the lamps to flash at twice the normal rate or by using an extra warning lamp.

Many electronic systems work on the principle of a stable multivibrator. Figure 20.7, for example, shows a type that could handle a directional indicator signal load of up to 98 W without altering flash frequency. Additionally, it provides a hazard warning signal for hours of continuous use.

Electronic flasher units normally use an electromagnetic relay to control the current to the signal lamps. This method is better than transistor switching because, in addition to giving an audible signal, it is not affected by the high-voltage spikes that are generated during the switching operation. In fact, the relay contacts give very little voltage drop compared to a transistor. The drop across the relay contacts is only around 10 per cent of that of a transistor. However, transistor switching is still ideal for high-speed applications. The relay is preferred when slow speed, heavy current switching is required.

The basic construction of a typical flasher unit, such as a Lucas FL19, consists of a printed circuit board, which carries an integrated circuit (IC), capacitor, relay and three resistors (Figure 20.8).

The IC chip has three main sections:

- Oscillator
- Relay driver
- Lamp failure detector

A zener diode in the IC regulates the operating voltage of the chip. This ensures that the flash frequency remains constant over a supply voltage range of 10–15 V.

Timer control for the oscillator is achieved by using the charge/discharge action of the capacitor (C). This operates in conjunction with the resistor ($R_1$) to give an R–C time constant for a flash frequency of 90 flashes per minute with a 50-50 off-on signal time.

1. The pulses from the oscillator pass to the relay driver. This is a Darlington amplifier that provides the current pulses in order to energise the relay coil.
2. Transient protection of the output transistor is achieved by fitting the diode across the collector–emitter of the power transistor. This allows the self-induced charges in the relay coil to bypass the transistor.
3. The lamp failure detector senses the voltage drop across the resistor $R_2$. The resistor senses the current passing to the signal lamps via the relay contacts. In the event of a lamp failure the current will cause the voltage drop (IR drop) across the resistor to decrease.

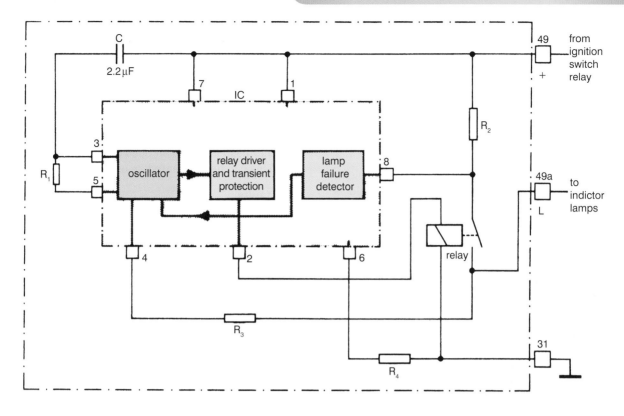

*Figure 20.8 Electronic flasher unit circuit*

**4** This reduced voltage will cause the detector to alter the resistance of the R–C time constant and, as a result, the frequency of the flashing will be doubled.

## LED flasher signals embedded in side-mirrors

Many cars now have light-emitting diode (LED) visual flasher signals embedded in their side mirrors. These provide the following advantages of sighting:

- When a car is in the blind spot, LEDs illuminate faster than incandescent bulbs (0.5 s faster).
- At high speeds, this apparent small time difference is a big advantage considering the distance travelled.
- Collisions are less likely as extra time and space is provided.

## LEDs for rear light clusters

Because LEDs have faster switching time and they have a longer life they have been used for brake lights for some time. Many newer vehicles have switched over entirely to LEDs for rear light clusters. The additional warning time provided by LEDs means they are considered to be far safer. Their use for brake lights in particular means a far shorter delay.

However, if LEDs are not pulsed at a quick enough frequency, they can produce ghost images. Retrofitting of LED bulbs is problematic, as LED brake and rear

lights will not flash using thermal flasher units due to their extremely low current use. An electronic flasher unit is required. These must be LED-compatible.

The key advantages of LEDs are as follows:

- High reliability and long service life
- Low energy consumption and lower operating voltage
- Less heat produced in the illuminated field

LEDs are becoming an established technology for many newer vehicles. They are being applied to rear lights, brake lights and indicators. The technology is only just becoming available for making them suitable for main headlights. However, Audi's A8 does use LED arrays for its running lights for daytime (Figure 20.9).

*Figure 20.9 LED day running light on a VW vehicle*

## 20.3  Maintenance and fault diagnosis

### 20.3.1 Horns

Horns are often positioned in an exposed place behind the radiator grill, so special attention is needed to avoid the ingress of moisture.

Most faults are due to cable and connector problems. When a fault is present a visual check should be followed by a voltmeter test. This should determine whether the potential difference (PD) applied to the horn is correct.

It is good practice to keep the horn circuit diagram. If this is not available, then a vehicle service manual is necessary. As a rule of thumb, however, the following steps to check a horn fault are recommended:

1  Check the circuit fuse; if this is blown, replace it.
2  Open the bonnet of the car and get someone else to press the horn button from inside. If there is no sound or a weak sound, then touch the horn with your hand and see if there is a vibration.
3  In order to adjust the horn, find the adjustment screw.
4  Earth a jumper wire and, while pressing the horn button, touch the horn with the other end of the wire. This will check to see whether the earthing is a problem.

If these steps fail, then the horn needs to be detached from the vehicle and connected directly to the battery. If the horn is still not working, then it will need to be replaced.

### 20.3.2 Direction indicators

A flasher unit is considered faulty if it fails to operate when full voltage is applied to it. When a substitute unit is fitted into the circuit the fault should be eliminated, providing the remainder of the circuit is serviceable. The most common faults are:

■ bulb failure
■ loss of earth at the lamp.

These faults are diagnosed by observing the rate of flashing. However, it is the type of flasher unit that governs whether the rate will be slower or faster.

Earth problems are often caused by a bad connection of the earth cable. This can normally be detected by a visual check.

Assuming the bulbs are serviceable, a system that does not flash is due to an open circuit in the supply line. This can be pinpointed by using a voltmeter.

### LED faults

LED bulbs are available in a number of different colours. They are amber for indicator bulbs and red for tail or brake bulbs. As LEDs run on a much lower wattage, there are sometimes issues with false bulb failure warnings. A simple system is often employed to deal with this persistent problem by installing a resistor. In fact resistors are the probable cause of faults on an LED circuit, so resistor checks are recommended.

The resistor value is calculated by subtracting the LED voltage drop from the supply voltage and then dividing this by the LED's operating current requirement. If the supply voltage is equal to the voltage drop, then the resistor is not usually needed.

LEDs can be bought with built-in series resistors, which can solve many of the potential problems.

Electrical test equipment would normally be a digital multimeter set to measure volts in the 0–20 V range, it can also be used to check resistance of cables and earths including the value of resistors fitted to systems. Another piece of test equipment is the logic probe – this can be used to check the operation of electronic components and circuits. When testing with the logic probe, the green LED will light with a high voltage (over 4.5 V) and the red LED will operate on low voltages (0.5–4.5 V). In addition to the high and low-level indication, the LEDs will pulse off and on with a pulsed circuit.

# 21

## Heating, ventilation and engine cooling

## 21.1 Fan and heater motors

Until recently, motors used to operate the engine cooling fan and the heating ventilation system were of similar construction, in many cases the same model. The motor normally used was a two-pole permanent magnet (PM) type with two brushes set at 180°. Figure 21.1 shows a typical PM-type motor. This type was also commonly used for window operation, seat adjustment and many other general applications.

The continued use of electrical controls on modern vehicle heating and ventilation systems has required manufacturers to look at different designs to meet system needs. As a result, brushless motors are

Figure 21.1 PM-type motor

### Health and safety best practices

- Refer to section 21.4 for EU legislation regarding handling and working on air conditioning systems.
- Use care when working in the vicinity of engine cooling fans – they can operate without warning even after the engine has been switched off.

- Beware of scalding – always ensure the cooling system pressure has been released and the system has cooled down before any system components are removed.

becoming more popular, owing to their increased efficiency and reliability, along with more accurate control of supply voltage through the motor's own control electronics.

## 21.1.1 Brushless motor design

The theory of operation is the same as the PM type: two magnetic fields operate together and, in doing so, result in rotational movement. The main difference in design is that the rotor consists of PMs and the stator is wound (Figure 21.2). This is often referred to as 'inside out' technology, because the construction is the opposite to that of the direct current (DC) PM motor.

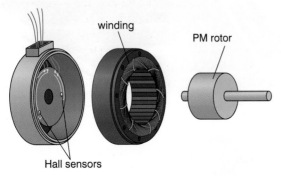

*Figure 21.2  Simplified brushless motor construction*

## 21.1.2 Brushless motor operation

Figure 21.3 illustrates the three stator windings and their location adjacent to the PM rotor. Each of these windings is equally spaced around the centre rotor to allow them to maximise their respective magnetic fields. The number of windings and corresponding magnets on the permanent rotor can vary depending on application.

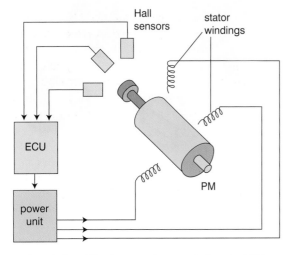

*Figure 21.3  Simplified diagram of stator windings and PM rotor*

The stator windings are then sequentially turned on and off to produce magnetic fields that attract the PMs of the rotor and, in doing so, produce a rotational motion. To ensure that the windings are energised at the correct time, Hall sensors are located at the end of the rotor shaft. These Hall sensors generate output signals referencing rotor position and motor speed and relay them to the electronic control unit (ECU), which is normally located on the motor end casing. The ECU analyses these signals through its circuitry and sends an output signal to energise the stator windings, increasing or reducing current as required.

## 21.2  Heating and ventilating control

### 21.2.1 Heating and ventilation fan

Most systems use a centrifugal-type fan to boost the airflow into the interior of the vehicle (Figure 21.4).

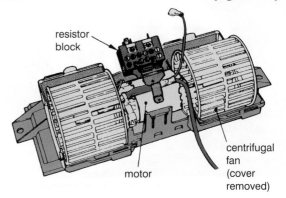

*Figure 21.4  Heating and ventilation fan*

Variable motor speeds are generally required, which are achieved by changing the voltage applied to the motor. This can be done using a variable resistor, a resistor network, or a programmed ECU that supplies the motor with the required voltage using a frequency modulated signal with a variable duty cycle.

Figure 21.5 shows a circuit for a three-speed operation. Moving the switch through the three positions – low, high and boost – shorts out a resistor at each stage and steps up the applied voltage.

Heater controls and the various vents and air blending doors are controlled in a number of different ways depending on manufacturer and the complexity of the system. Cable and lever operation is still produced, along with some pneumatic systems that utilise vacuum produced in the inlet manifold or through an engine driven pump on diesel vehicles. Furthermore, the introduction of automatic climate control has seen the electric stepper motor appearing in more systems.

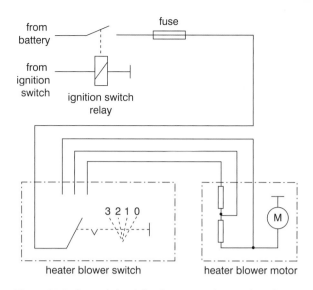

*Figure 21.5 Control circuit for three-speed operation of heating and ventilation fan*

## 21.2.2 Maintenance

Each system is fused so this is the first check to make if the system fails to operate. Most systems now include the control of heating and ventilation together with climate control and will store fault codes within the body ECU should the system fail to operate correctly. This will require the technician to access the on-board diagnostic facility through the diagnostic plug with a suitable scanning tool and check for any relevant fault code. There may also be a facility within the scanning tool to access live data or perform actuator tests, which will assist in the diagnosis of a system fault.

## 21.3   Electric sunroof

Operation of the sunroof is controlled through a multi-position switch that acts as a 'polarity changer' to give the required rotation of the motor, with an adjacent relay reducing the current carried by the switch. The movement of the roof panel is achieved through use of a rack that is driven by a pinion gear.

This is driven by a reversible PM motor after passing the drive through a gearbox to increase the torque.

Often the gearbox incorporates an extra rack to control the switching mechanism. This uses a switch to limit the travel of the roof panel and another switch to insert a resistance in series with the motor to reduce the speed of movement as the roof approaches the limits of its travel.

With developments in electronic control, body ECUs now regulate current as the roof tilt or slide operates, removing the possibility of injury should someone become trapped in the roof. The comfort close feature available on some vehicles allows the sunroof to be closed along with windows, and doors locked through use of the remote control, which also sets the immobiliser and alarm system. An additional feature linked to the operation of the windscreen wipers on some vehicles closes the sunroof, with some manufacturers also reducing the maximum tilt of the roof once the vehicle reaches a preset speed.

## 21.4   Air conditioning

An air conditioning system provides cool and dehumidified air, fresh or recirculated, to the interior of the vehicle. The cooling effect is obtained by blowing air through a cold evaporator unit to control the temperature of the interior. Since the construction and operation of an air conditioning system is described in *Fundamentals of Motor Vehicle Technology 6th Edition Book 2*, the treatment in this chapter is confined to the electrical control system.

### 21.4.1 Control of a basic system

Figure 21.6 shows the main layout. In this system the temperature of the evaporator is controlled by the flow of refrigerant (currently R134a) around the system. This flow is initiated by a belt-driven compressor that is engaged to the engine by an electromagnetic clutch (Figure 21.7) in response to a relay-controlled supply signalled from the driver via the engine ECU.

---

**Safe practices**

Before any system tests are carried out, the manufacturer's information should be consulted to identify the system type and test procedures, to reduce the risk of damaging sensitive components.

---

**Health and safety warning**

From July 2010 the UK minimum requirement of technicians working on mobile air conditioning systems is to hold a refrigerant handling qualification that meets EC Regulations 307/2008 or revised edition.

Contact with air conditioning refrigerant can cause serious injury and, if released into the atmosphere, has a damaging impact on the environment. Refer to the manufacturer's manual before disconnecting any part of the refrigeration system.

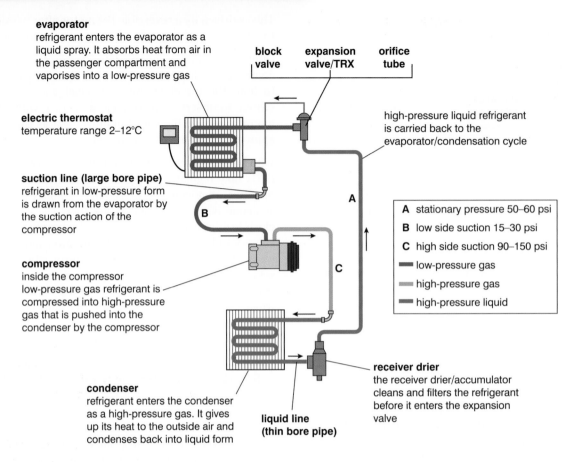

**evaporator**
refrigerant enters the evaporator as a liquid spray. It absorbs heat from air in the passenger compartment and vaporises into a low-pressure gas

**block valve**  **expansion valve/TRX**  **orifice tube**

**electric thermostat**
temperature range 2–12°C

high-pressure liquid refrigerant is carried back to the evaporator/condensation cycle

**suction line (large bore pipe)**
refrigerant in low-pressure form is drawn from the evaporator by the suction action of the compressor

**B**

**A**

A  stationary pressure 50–60 psi

B  low side suction 15–30 psi

C  high side suction 90–150 psi

━━ low-pressure gas

━━ high-pressure gas

━━ high-pressure liquid

**compressor**
inside the compressor low-pressure gas refrigerant is compressed into high-pressure gas that is pushed into the condenser by the compressor

**C**

**receiver drier**
the receiver drier/accumulator cleans and filters the refrigerant before it enters the expansion valve

**condenser**
refrigerant enters the condenser as a high-pressure gas. It gives up its heat to the outside air and condenses back into liquid form

**liquid line (thin bore pipe)**

*Figure 21.6  Schematic layout of air conditioning system*

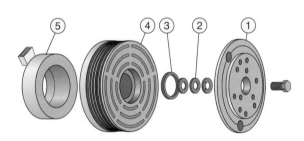

- A magnetic clutch is used to connect or disconnect the drive to the compressor.
- When voltage is applied to the clutch field coil (5), the clutch plate (1) (which is connected to the compressor shaft) is drawn into contact with the pulley (4) and the compressor rotates.
- When voltage is disconnected from the clutch field coil (5), the clutch plate (1) is released and the compressor ceases to rotate.
- The compressor clutch clearance on some models may be adjusted with shims (2).
- The clutch field coil (5) is normally held in position with a snap ring (3)
- Compressors are lubricated by oil held in the compressor and mixed with the refrigerant.

*Figure 21.7  Electromagnetic clutch*

Compressing the refrigerant generates heat; this is dissipated by a condenser placed next to the engine radiator. When the airflow through the condenser is insufficient, electrically driven cooling fans, connected in series for normal cooling, come into operation. The temperature of the evaporator is primarily controlled by a thermostatic expansion valve, but if the evaporator temperature falls low enough for ice to form on the fins, a thermostatic switch, mounted on the fins, will open. This causes the ECU to disengage the compressor clutch.

A pressure switch is fitted to prevent damage to the compressor. This senses the pressure in the line between the condenser and drier and sends a signal to the engine ECU to activate a control circuit when the pressure is:

- below 2.0 bar – a drop to this pressure indicates leakage so the electromagnetic clutch disengages the compressor; when pressure rises above 2.4 bar the clutch is re-engaged
- above 1.9 bar – cooling is increased by energising relays that connect the two cooling fans in parallel

- above 2.7 bar – if this high pressure is reached with maximum cooling (due to possible blockage), the clutch is disengaged until the pressure drops to 2.1 bar.

Some systems replace the thermostatic expansion valve with a fixed orifice tube (Figure 21.8) to control the high-pressure liquid as it leaves the condenser. The flow of refrigerant is controlled by switching the compressor on or off and so is not temperature sensitive like the thermostatic expansion valve.

Further developments of this design have introduced a variable orifice valve, which is preset for high vehicle speeds but also temperature sensitive to reduce the need to control the compressor as refrigerant temperatures change.

Dual air conditioning has been introduced by some manufacturers who produce multi-passenger vehicles. These systems often utilise both the expansion valve arrangement along with the fixed orifice valve to control the overall system for two separate temperature zones. Figure 21.9 shows the dual system.

## 21.4.2 ECU control

In addition to the basic control of the air conditioning system, the ECU adjusts the idling speed of the engine to compensate for the extra load when the compressor is in use. Also the compressor disengages when:

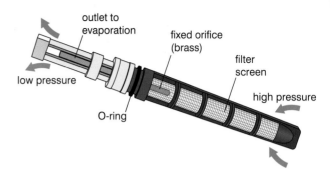

*Figure 21.8  Fixed orifice tube*

- the vehicle is accelerated with a near fully opened throttle
- the oil temperature in the compressor is very high
- engine speed exceeds 5000 rpm to protect the hoses of the air conditioning system.

## 21.4.3 Driver controls

The air conditioning system works in conjunction with the interior heater controls, so when the system is switched on, the fan, air entry mode, air distribution and temperature are all operated in the same manner as that used for the heater.

## 21.4.4 Control circuit

The system is normally controlled by the engine ECU because engine adjustments must be made to allow for the extra load on the engine.

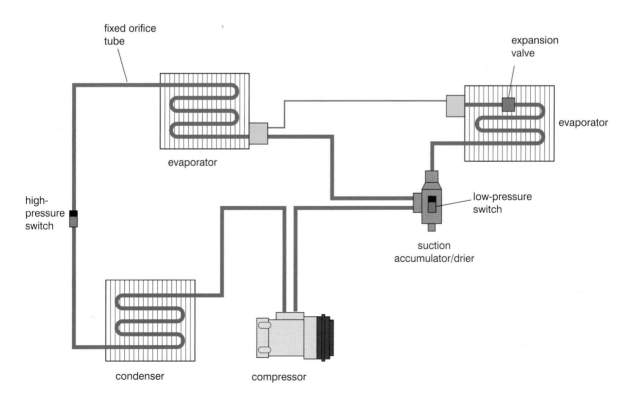

*Figure 21.9  Dual air conditioning system*

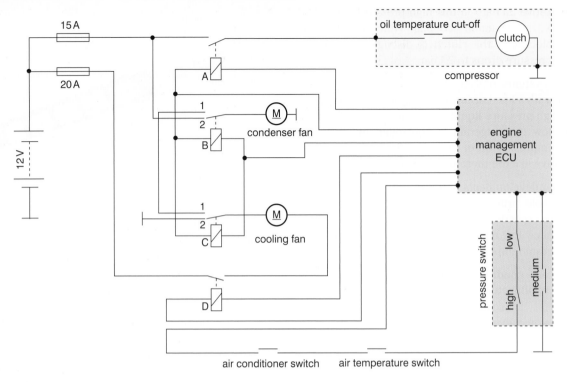

Figure 21.10  Air conditioning circuit (simplified)

Figure 21.10 shows a simplified layout of an air conditioning circuit. Four relays are used in this circuit: one to control the compressor clutch and three to control fan operation. With relays B and C both set in position 1, the two fans are in series, but when the relays are set in position 2, both fans operate at high speed.

## 21.5   Climate control

To allow for the constant changes in temperature and overall quality of air within the vehicle passenger compartment(s), automatic climate control systems are being fitted by many manufacturers. This facility allows the heating and air conditioning to be controlled in single or multiple zones by a panel on the fascia through a controller area network (CAN) bus system (Figure 21.11).

The control system overview in Figure 21.12 shows the main components of an automatic climate control

Figure 21.11  Climate control panel

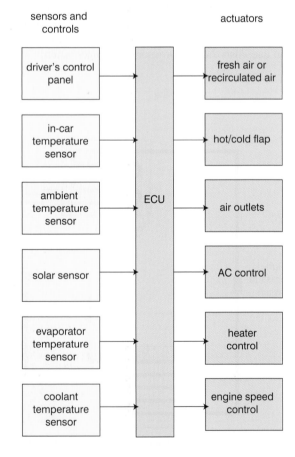

Figure 21.12  Schematic layout of climate control system

system. Signals from the various monitoring sensors and control panel switches are passed to a processor in an ECU. After computing any differences between panel setting and input data, the ECU makes the necessary correction by energising the appropriate actuators. This closed-loop system monitors the air quality and temperature in all zones, ensuring it reaches the preset target as soon as possible and then remains constant for passenger comfort.

## 21.5.1 Electronic temperature and air quality control

Figure 21.13 shows the layout of an air mix and distribution unit for climate control. Exterior air entering the cabin is passed through a filtration system, which is normally a pollen filter or an active carbon filter. The following sensors pass information to the ECU to ensure air quality and temperature is maximised.

■ Air quality sensor – this metal oxide semiconductor (MOS) sensor is located adjacent to the exterior air intake filter. The air quality entering the cabin is then measured by the sensor and is closely monitored by the ECU. If the air is found to be of poor quality (possibly polluted by exhaust fumes) then the ECU directs the various control flaps to move to the recirculation mode, ensuring poor quality air is not directed to vehicle interior. This mode reverts back as soon as good quality air can be passed through the filtration system, ensuring optimum air quality is maintained at all times.

■ Sun load sensor – these sensors can be infrared, photo diode or solar cells and are normally located adjacent to the windscreen, where they measure sunlight. The sensor will also incorporate a temperature sensor to measure cabin temperature.

■ Temperature sensors – these sensors will be either a negative temperature coefficient (NTC) or positive temperature coefficient (PTC) type semiconductor, and will be located within the airflow ducts or passenger compartment measuring air as it is directed into the passenger areas.

The ECU analyses the inputs from these sensors and will then energise the stepper motors controlling the flap positions of the air blend doors. This allows cold air that has passed through the air conditioning evaporator to mix with recirculated air from the passenger's compartment or warmed air that has passed through the evaporator and the heater matrix. This blended mix of air can then be passed through a distribution door, which is also actuated by a stepper motor controlled by the ECU. Control of the fan within the system is also dependent on the ECU and the input signals it receives.

Many systems will incorporate a diagnosis facility within the control panel allowing information to be displayed. Further information will also be available through the serial link diagnostic plug to access fault codes and data stored by the ECU.

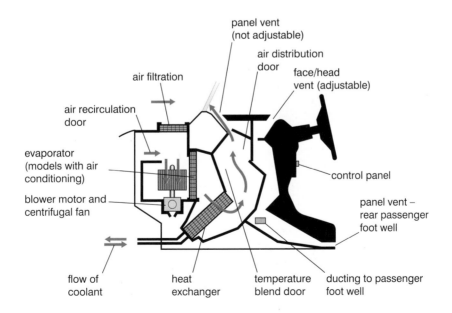

*Figure 21.13 Air mix and distribution unit for climate control*

## 21.6 Engine cooling fans

*Figure 21.14 Electric cooling fans*

A cooling fan driven by an electric motor instead of a belt is advantageous because:

- it saves energy – the fan can be switched off when not needed
- it is easy to accommodate, especially for transverse engines
- it gives close control over engine operating temperatures.

Figure 21.14 shows a typical installation. A plastic fan impeller is fitted to the armature shaft of the motor and the assembly is situated to provide the appropriate air movement through the radiator.

The control circuit (Figure 21.15) uses a bi-metal-type thermal switch located at the radiator side of the thermostat housing. This switch operates the fan when the coolant temperature reaches about 90 °C and switches it off when the temperature drops to about 85 °C. In the layout shown, the current for the motor is supplied from an ignition switch relay. This relay energises when the ignition is switched on.

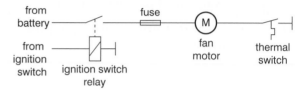

*Figure 21.15 Control circuit for engine cooling fan*

More recent models now incorporate electronic control of the cooling system to provide improved fuel mileage in certain throttle ranges, and reduced exhaust emission levels. Cooling system and fan operation are controlled by the engine ECU using an electronic 'map', similar to the fuel and ignition map seen in Chapter 14; this allows the engine temperature to be matched to the engine load, allowing the engine to run more efficiently.

There are two circuits for the coolant: a small circuit and a large circuit. The large circuit normally includes the oil radiator for the automatic transmission system and the engine oil cooling radiator (where fitted).

This system eliminates the need for a cooling system thermostat fitted to the engine block. The main component of the system is the coolant distributor

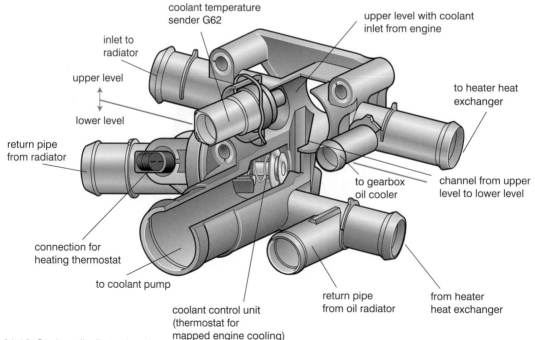

*Figure 21.16 Coolant distributor housing*

housing (Figure 21.16), and this housing controls the flow of coolant using an integrated electronically controlled coolant control unit (thermostat) and monitors the temperature by use of the coolant temperature sensor fitted to the housing.

The coolant control unit is of the wax pellet design but incorporates an ECU-controlled electric heating element for rapid melting of the wax to open the unit and allow either hot or cold coolant to flow to where it is required. The unit operates normally at a higher temperature than older wax pellet units at 110 °C.

The electronic control of the coolant flow allows for faster warm-up of the engine and also provides a supply of warm air more quickly to the passenger compartment. The system is connected using a CAN bus communication system from the ECU and will take information from a number of sensors to determine whether to use the small cooling circuit or the large one and also whether or not to operate the cooling fans.

The sensors include:

- engine speed
- air mass flow meter
- coolant temperature sensor
- radiator outlet temperature sensor
- interior temperature selection control
- temperature flap position switch.

The actuators in the system are:

- mapped engine-cooling thermostat
- radiator fan control unit
- radiator fan 1 and 2
- coolant two-way cut-off valve.

### Starting from cold

Once the engine is started and running, the coolant pump circulates the coolant. The coolant flows from the cylinder head to the top level of the distributor housing and travels along a channel down to the lower level. The electronic thermostat is positioned so that only the small cooling circuit to the coolant pump is available. The coolant heats up quickly.

### Engine full throttle

When the engine is operated at full throttle a higher cooling capacity is required. A current is supplied to the heating element in the thermostat in the coolant distributor housing, opening the return flow from the radiator. The small cooling circuit is closed simultaneously because both circuits are linked mechanically. The coolant pump feeds coolant to the radiator through the upper level in the distributor housing after it flows from the cylinder head.

# 22

# Door locking and vehicle security

## 22.1 Central door locking

Central door locking systems allow all doors to be locked and unlocked simultaneously. Many systems also include boot (tailgate) unlocking functions.

The central door locking system is controlled by the body ECU. This uses the CAN bus system to communicate with the smaller node ECUs in each door to control the locking, unlocking, entry and lazy lock systems.

### 22.1.1 Actuators

The locks are operated by an electro-mechanical system, which may be based on one of the following types of actuator:

■ Electromagnetic solenoid.
■ Motor.
■ Pneumatic.

### Solenoid type

Figure 22.1 shows a solenoid locking unit. Current in the locking coil creates a magnetic field that pulls the magnetic plunger towards it and locks the door. Current in the unlocking coil pulls the plunger into the unlock position. Figure 22.2 shows the central locking circuit with solenoid actuators.

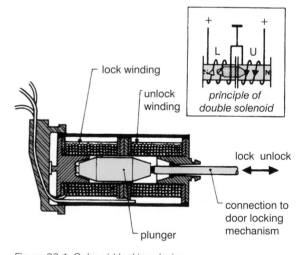

Figure 22.1 Solenoid locking device

### Motor type

A linear or rotary electric motor is used to switch the lock between positions. Linear motors change operational direction by a change in voltage polarity. Rotary motors use a crank arm to switch the lock position. Polarity change is not needed; instead the rotation needs to be calibrated and controlled.

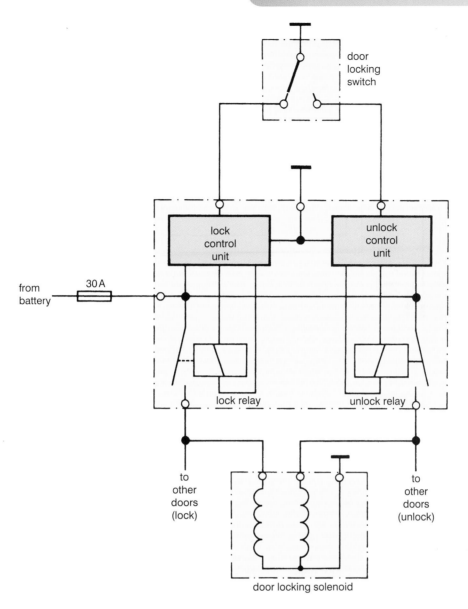

*Figure 22.2 Central door locking circuit with solenoid actuators*

## Pneumatic type

The locking mechanism is operated using air pressure. The locks are connected through tubes to a central pump, which generates air pressure or vacuum to lock or unlock the doors. This method is very silent, but has major drawbacks and, apart from a few models, is practically obsolete.

## 22.1.2 Circuit structure

Figure 22.3 shows the circuit layout for a simple central locking system.

## 22.1.3 Remote access and keyless entry

Most standard cars today include a radio-controlled central locking system. An unlocking remote is integrated into the car key or used as a key chain. The vehicle can

be locked or unlocked via the remote. Central locking locks doors automatically in some models when the gears are engaged or the car picks up speed.

Keyless entry is another emerging technology; luxury and sports cars already use this system. Keyless entry cars have a wireless key. When the key comes within a certain range, the engine immobiliser disengages and the doors unlock. Drivers can activate the ignition by pressing a button or turning a knob.

Various biometric security companies are developing products for automotive applications. Fingerprint, iris and brain recognition are main research areas. Fingerprint authorisation has been very successful in the security industry. Fingerprint sensors are used in buildings, laptop computers and airport security. In a motor vehicle, the sensor is mounted near the

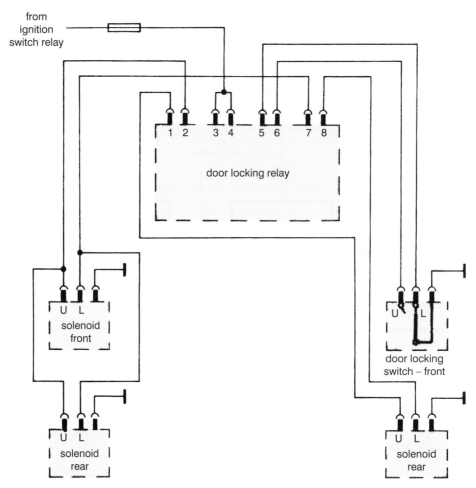

*Figure 22.3 Circuit layout for a simple central locking system*

key slot on the car door. Fingerprint activated remote devices are also becoming popular for keyless entry. Iris and brain recognition technologies are being researched for use in motor vehicles.

## 22.2    Engine immobilisers

In the past, an engine **immobiliser** used to be a novelty item. Now manufacturers are required to fit such systems in all production cars by law. Engine immobilising is controlled by the electronic control unit (ECU), which disarms the fuel and ignition circuits when activated. The immobilisation trigger is electronic and can be controlled either through a manual switch or automatically.

**Immobiliser**: a device to prevent unauthorised persons from starting or running the engine of a vehicle.

Modern cars have factory-fitted engine immobilisers. These are usually automatic and controlled by radio signals from a radio transmitter built into the key or key fob. Receivers mounted in the vehicle receive signals from the transmitter and send proximity

information to the ECU. When the key is close to the driver's console, the ECU disengages the immobiliser. The immobiliser is automatically engaged when the key leaves the area near the driver's console.

Another engine immobilising technique is to disconnect the power supply to the starter motor. This technique was used in cars before the ECU-controlled engine immobilisers became common. In many older models manual immobilisers still use this technique. A hidden switch in the vehicle is used to disengage the immobiliser.

Figure 22.4 shows a layout of the engine immobiliser in modern vehicles. The ECU is usually protected by a back-up battery. This counters attempts to steal the vehicle that involve disconnecting the main battery to silence alarms and disarm the immobiliser.

Older vehicles could be started by 'hot-wiring' the ignition circuit. In these vehicles, the key slot was the only defence against thieves. The key tumbler could be forced out to gain access to the wiring. Ignition wires could be contacted manually to start the engine. Modern engine immobilisers act on the fuel supply so a hot-wiring attempt does not start the engine.

**Immobiliser with interrupt circuits**

1 transmitter (remote control)
2 immobilser ECU
3 receiver (remote control)
4a microcomputer
4b microcomputer with battery connection
5 relay

6 central door locking system
7 status display
8 starting system
9 engine management ECU
10 electric fuel pump (gasoline engine)
   or fuel supply (diesel engine)

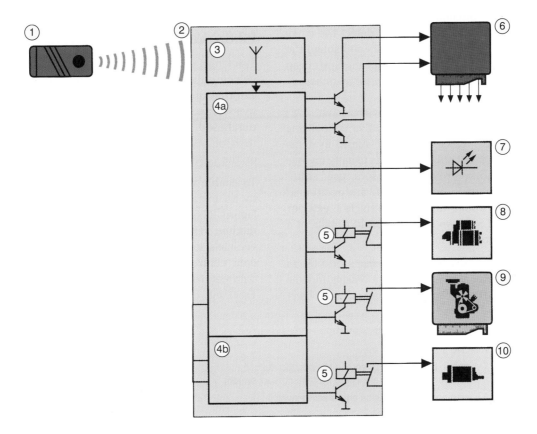

*Figure 22.4 Sensors monitoring vehicle*

## 22.3 Vehicle security systems

Vehicle security systems include alarm systems, vehicle tracking systems and vehicle data loggers.

### 22.3.1 Alarm systems

Vehicles not only need to be protected against carjackers, but also against thieves who intend to steal items present inside the vehicle. An effective warning system should send out a signal immediately.

Alarm systems use sensors mounted on the vehicle to determine whether to sound the alarm. Several types of sensors can be used to detect security breaches on the vehicle. If there is any inconsistency in the parameters being monitored, the system initiates audio and visual alerts.

Early alarm systems included motion sensors, ultrasound sensors, voltage drop sensors and infrared

sensors. Motion sensors were used both to protect against vehicle theft and theft of items within the vehicle. The sensor would send out a signal whenever sudden or prolonged movement was detected. These sensors were very sensitive. The alarm could be triggered by sharp sound waves, causing noisy disturbances in public parking places. New models seldom use this type of alarm system.

Ultrasonic systems used ultrasound transmitters and sensors to monitor the passenger cabin. Movement in the cabin would cause a disturbance in the otherwise constant signal and would trigger the alarm. Infrared sensors functioned in a similar way. A transmitter focused an infrared beam on the receiver. The alarm would trigger if the beam's transmission was disturbed.

Voltage-drop sensors supplied the vehicle's outer body with a constant electric potential. A person touching the vehicle would change the potential and trigger the alarm.

## ECU-controlled alarms

Modern cars use a very smart system to secure the vehicle. As discussed in Chapter 7, the ECU controls all the vehicle sensors; this includes sensors that detect whether a door or window is open or closed. As the ECU monitors these parameters, it is very easy to design an alarm system that is operated by the ECU.

Should someone attempt to enter the vehicle using the doors or windows, the ECU will detect the entry through the door and window sensors and sound the alarm. Although this is a very smart, reliable and cheap alarm system, it is only useful for vehicle breaches.

## Proximity sensors

A number of car-related crimes involve vandalising or damaging the vehicle's exterior. Alarm systems for protection against such situations usually involve proximity sensors. Proximity sensors use either infrared or ultrasonic nodes, which are positioned at strategic locations under the vehicle's exterior body. Figure 22.5 shows the layout and details of a proximity sensing system.

Each node transmits a beam that reflects off objects nearby and returns to the node. A processing module (usually the ECU) determines the distance of each object from the vehicle. Using this data, the alarm system is informed when any object is in contact with the vehicle.

The vehicle's proximity system serves another major function: parking assistance. While parking, the system guides the driver by signalling the distance of the vehicle from objects nearby. Basic parking sensors do this through audio beeps. More advanced systems provide a visual picture on the driver's console.

## 22.3.2 Vehicle tracking systems

Tracking systems provide information on the vehicle's location by transmitting information to an external unit. Usually tracking services are offered by insurance and security companies and need to be purchased separately. The company can assist car theft or insurance claims by providing information on the vehicle's location against a timeline.

To enable vehicle tracking, a tracking device needs to be installed at a secure point on the vehicle. Figure 22.6 shows the components of a tracking module. The GPS records the coordinates of the vehicle's location, which is sent to the company's data centre by the GSM module. A server at the data centre logs the information against a timeline. Tracking companies provide users with a web

**Alarm system (example)**

*protected areas: basic system*

(1) doors, boot, filler cap, engine bonnet, glove compartment (central locking system, contact switch)

(2) starting system (ignition and starting switch)

(3) car radio

*protected areas: auxiliary systems*

(4) passenger compartment (ultrasonic field)

(5) wheels, overall vehicle (vehicle-tilt sensors)

*alarm components:*

(6) remote control (transmitter)

(7) ECU (receiver)

(8) direction-indicator lamps or low beam (flashing signal)

(9) horn (audible signal)

*Figure 22.5 Layout of a proximity system*

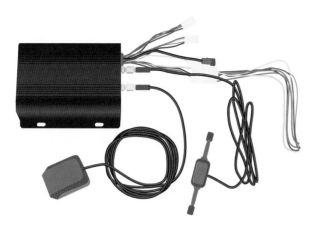

*Figure 22.6 Components of a car tracking module*

account where they can view their vehicle's tracking information. The information can also be requested via text message, email or telephone.

Figure 22.7 shows a diagram representing information transfer of vehicle tracking systems.

Apart from vehicle security applications, tracking systems are also useful for managing commercial transport fleets. Operators can keep track of the location of vehicles in the fleet and manage dispatch and routing. The system is also used in buses to trigger announcements and to change destination signs on the bus.

### 22.3.3 Vehicle data-logging systems

The ECU stores vehicle performance information in a memory to help in performance diagnosis during vehicle service (see Chapter 7). A data-logging system functions in a similar way, except that the purpose of storing information is different. In the case of accidents or vehicle theft, information from the data-logging system can be helpful in making insurance claims and providing evidence in court settlements.

The data-logging module is the black box of a vehicle. It stores information such as vehicle location, altitude, speed, yaw angle, pitch angle and throttle position. A detailed list of parameters is shown in Figure 22.8. The information is stored temporarily and sent to a central server in batches for permanent record.

Like tracking systems, data-logging systems are purchased from a separate provider. Insurance companies offer significant discounts on vehicles that have a tracking and data-logging system installed.

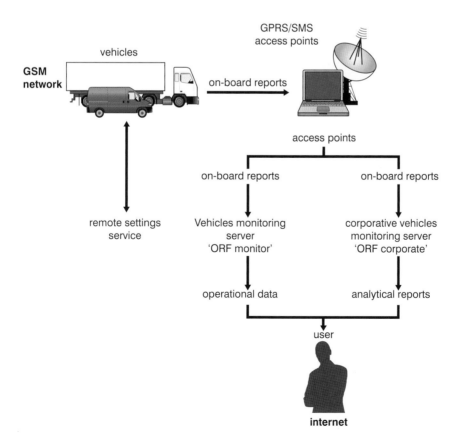

*Figure 22.7 Information flow in vehicle tracking systems*

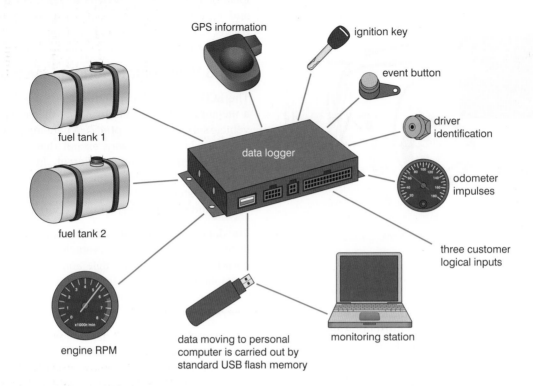

*Figure 22.8  Parameters stored by data log modules*

# 23

# Road wheel control systems

This chapter will explain the wide range of safety systems that are installed in modern road cars in order to make driving both easier and safer for the driver, passengers and other vehicles on the road.

The systems mentioned within this chapter ensure that the car's braking, cornering and acceleration are all controlled in a manner that assists the driver in handling the vehicle.

## 23.1 Cruise control (CC)

Driving a vehicle on a long stretch of road, such as a motorway, within a set speed range can be both a tiring and boring experience. CC is an electronic system that takes over this function and keeps the vehicle at a constant speed, regardless of any change in wind or road gradient.

CC is fitted to many vehicles, either as an optional upgrade or as a standard fitment. Although many manufacturers use their own designed systems, they are all relatively similar.

Adaptive CC (ACC) and the use of **drive-by-wire** throttle systems have also seen an improvement in this technology most recently.

**Drive-by-wire**: a system that uses a position sensor located on the throttle pedal to feed a **signal** to the **electronic control unit** (ECU), which then sends a voltage that is proportional to the pedal movement to control an electric motor on the side of the throttle body, thus removing the need for a cable.

**Signal**: a voltage output from a sensor. There are two types: the analogue form, which produces a sine wave; and the more modern digital form, which produces a square wave that can be read directly by the ECU.

**Electronic control unit (ECU)**: also known as an ECM (electronic control module), this is a compact unit that controls one or more systems.

### 23.1.1 Basic operation

This closed-loop system uses a relatively simple set of components (Figure 23.1).

- The control unit is the 'brain' of this system and takes inputs from the driver control switches and feedback from a speed sensor to regulate the speed of the vehicle via an output voltage to the throttle **actuator**. It consistently provides feedback in order to keep the car at the correct speed.
- The driver command controls now have a multitude of functions and can normally be found on the face of the steering wheel (Figure 23.2) or with the use of a stalk protruding from the steering column. The controls normally consist of:
  - ON/OFF to power up the system or disable it
  - SET to allow the car to maintain its current speed
  - RESUME to allow the car to resume the most recent SET speed if the system is interrupted by a brake/clutch switch or cancelled by the driver
  - + and – to allow the driver to accelerate and decelerate the car with the use of the switches, without interrupting the system and deactivating it.
- The actuator controls the throttle flap position, which subsequently controls vehicle speed. This can be operated either electronically or pneumatically via a vacuum unit; each system can operate the flap smoothly and in both directions.

### Electronic control unit (ECU)

This is a box full of microprocessors and other electronic components that can perform calculations and make decisions. It receives data from sensors and driver commands and compares it with data stored in the module's memory. Modern vehicles have multiple ECUs for controlling electrical systems and sub-systems.

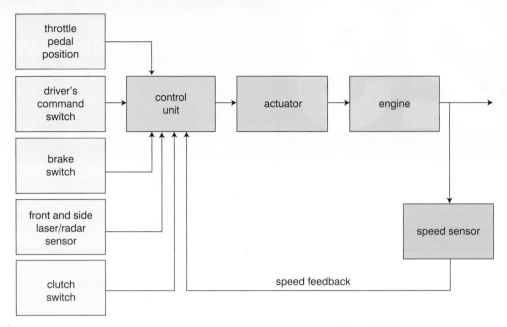

*Figure 23.1 CC system*

- Brake and clutch switches are present in this system and act as cut-off. These are vital and will cancel the CC if the driver presses either pedal.
- The speed sensor takes a reading either from the speedometer or from one of the four wheel-speed sensors in order to ensure the car is travelling at the appropriate set speed.

**Actuator**: a mechanical device for moving or controlling a mechanism or system. It is operated by a source of energy, usually in the form of an electric current, hydraulic fluid pressure or pneumatic pressure, and converts that energy into some kind of motion.

Whereas earlier systems used a throttle cable to connect the pedal to the throttle body and the vacuum unit essentially pulled on the throttle cable, modern systems are now fitted with drive-by-wire technology. This uses a throttle pedal position sensor that relays a voltage to an ECU and then to an electronic motor on the side of the throttle body, which will have a throttle position sensor (TPS) fitted in order to control it. This removes the need for any mechanical connection and allows for greater control of other systems.

The operation of cruise control on a diesel-engined vehicle is carried out by the engine management system ECU; this makes use of the fuel injection control module to switch off injection and reduce power/speed based on inputs from various sensors around the vehicle.

*Figure 23.2 CC switches on a steering wheel*

ACC has also been recently introduced and simply uses front laser or radar sensors to monitor the distance to the vehicle in front and automatically alters the speed of the vehicle to keep a minimum headway distance from the car in front – removing the need for the driver to apply the brakes and reset the speed over and over again. Further developments to this system allow for the addition of features such as:

- lane deviation detection
- anti-collision.

Lane deviation detection can provide a warning system, such as a noise, a warning light, or a light torque input to the steering wheel, to alert the driver that the vehicle may be going out of the lane without indication. This system uses radars on the sides of the vehicle. (These can also sense if there is an object in the blind spot of the mirror and alert the driver once again.) They read and locate lane markings, and a forward-facing camera can also find the centre line of the lane to further enhance lane deviation detection sensitivity.

Anti-collision uses the forward-facing camera mentioned previously either to warn the driver that they may be approaching the vehicle in front too quickly or, in more advanced systems that are integrated with the anti-lock braking system (ABS), it can apply the brakes in order to reduce the chance of a collision. The throttle control unit may also be integrated so that the brakes do not need to overcome the engine power before slowing the car.

### 23.1.2 Fault diagnosis

The ECU for this system will store any fault codes that it generates from self-tests and these can be retrieved by using a suitable piece of diagnostic equipment. Actuator tests can also be carried out on more advanced tools to see if the throttle flap can move through its range on demand. If a fault is detected, the engine management light (EML) will be illuminated and the system may deactivate.

## 23.2 Anti-lock braking system (ABS)

This key safety feature is found on nearly all modern road cars. It was introduced in 1978 by Bosch and is now, in most instances, fitted as standard (mandatory in the EU from 2004). It prevents:

- brakes from locking up
- tyres from skidding on the road
- loss of steering.

The system operates when wheel lock is detected, usually during an emergency stop or when braking hard on a wet or loose surface. ABS allows the driver to remain in control of the vehicle and avoid the risk of any accident. It can sometimes increase stopping distances, but this increase may be necessary in order for the driver to stay in control of the vehicle.

### 23.2.1 Basic operation

Four wheel-speed sensors monitor the individual speeds of each wheel via an ECU. When the ECU detects that any wheels may be locking up, the modulator unit is activated to operate one of its valves. This valve releases the pressure from the line going to that wheel. The valve then reopens to allow pressure to be applied to that wheel again until the maximum **traction** point is exceeded. The cycle will occur over and over to maintain grip and stability with the pressure release–apply–release–apply sequence occurring at up to 16 times per second. This usually results in a pulsating feeling from the brake pedal when in operation.

> **Traction**: the friction between the road surface and the tyres, which can be affected by tyre condition, road condition and weather conditions. A loss of traction can be dangerous as it causes a loss in control for the driver.

Light and heavy vehicles (HVs) both use similar techniques, except that HVs use compressed air instead of the standard hydraulic system used on light vehicles.

### 23.2.2 Components

These are shown in Figure 23.3.

#### Wheel-speed sensors

These use a magnetic pickup (fixed to the suspension upright), which reads a rotating toothed wheel connected to the hub, constant velocity (CV) joint or brake disc. (See Chapter 5 for more information on sensors.) Each sensor feeds back a voltage to the ECU, which converts this voltage into a corresponding speed for the ECU to determine whether wheel lock is occurring. The alternating current (AC) voltage created by inductive sensors, such as the one described, produces a voltage that is proportional to the rotation of the wheel, so the faster the wheel turns, the greater the voltage. This analogue sensor is gradually being replaced by a Hall effect sensor that is digital.

#### ABS modulator unit

This is located between the master cylinder and the brake assembly at the wheels, and its purpose is to control line pressure to the brake calipers or wheel cylinders. Modern systems have eight solenoid valves (two for each wheel) and a pump. Reservoirs hold fluid to aid increases or decreases in pressure.

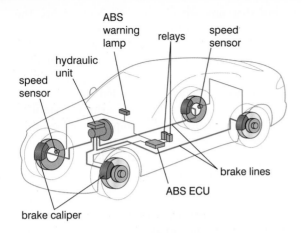

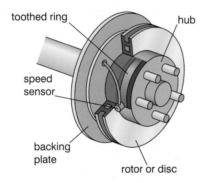

*Figure 23.3 ABS layout*

## Valves and pump

These are shown in Figure 23.4 and work in the following manner:

1 In position 1 (pressure build) the valve is open; pressure from the master cylinder is passed through to the brake calipers or wheel cylinders via the modulator to allow normal braking pressure to be achieved.

2 In position 2 (pressure maintain) the inlet valve shuts the line, isolating that brake from the master cylinder. This stops the pressure from rising further if the driver pushes the brake pedal harder.

3 In position 3 (pressure reduction), when wheel lock is occurring, the outlet valve releases some of the pressure via the return pump, so fluid is forced back in the direction of the master cylinder. This is when the pedal will pulsate and the pump will be heard.

4 As the valves can release pressure from the brakes, there needs to be a way to return the pressure in order to stop the wheel speed increasing during a stop. The ECU then requires pressure to be reapplied by commanding the modulator valves to position 1 once more.

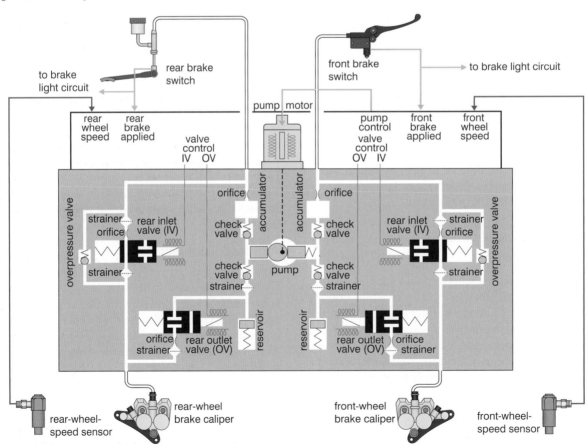

*Figure 23.4 ABS system and modulator internals for a motorcycle*

## Inductive sensors

The sensor generates one output pulse per tooth. The pulse amplitude is a function of the air gap, together with the toothed ring's rotational speed, the shape of its teeth, and the materials used in its manufacture. Not only does the output signal amplitude increase with speed, but so does its frequency. This means that a minimum rotational speed is required for reliable evaluation of even the smallest voltages.

Any metal particles that get attracted to the sensor casing because of the magnetic field must be cleaned off to avoid any chance of miscalculation. Maintaining the correct air gap (distance between sensor and toothed wheel) is also vital for the system to operate effectively. (See Chapter 5 for more information on inductive sensors.)

### ABS ECU

This controls the system and is often found as part of a unit with the modulator. This makes constant calculations and commands the modulator to increase, decrease or maintain braking pressure in order to use maximum braking efficiency without locking the wheels.

Another form of wheel-speed sensor that is now being widely used is what is known as an active wheel-speed sensor. This type of Hall effect sensor helps increase performance, durability and low-speed accuracy. Most vehicles with active sensors still use a toothed wheel, which acts as the trigger mechanism for the sensor. Some use a magnetic encoder in place of a traditional wheel. In either case, the result is a digital square wave signal that changes only in frequency and not amplitude.

To reduce space and improve reliability, manufacturers are installing the magnetic encoder inside the wheel bearing assembly. Care must be taken when installing a new bearing to ensure it is fitted the correct way round or the ABS/TCS systems may not operate correctly.

In this system, the ABS ECU sends the battery voltage to the sensor to give it power. The sensor, in turn, supplies the ECU with a constant 7 mA (milliamp) signal using a signal return circuit. Depending on the toothed ring or magnetic encoder position, this 7 mA signal is turned on or off. The output of the sensor sent to the ECU is a direct current (DC) voltage signal with changing current levels. The ECU monitors the changing digital signal from each wheel-speed sensor and is interpreted as wheel speed. For testing purposes, an input wire will provide its power (up to 12 V dependent upon the system) and an output wire will provide a varying resistance, dependent upon wheel speed.

This sensor type is able to sense a minimum wheel rotation of 0 mph while the inductive sensor requires a speed of approximately 2 mph to register a signal. The air gap sensitivity is also a lot less on this sensor so that in the harsh environment where it is installed there is less chance for error to occur.

### Care of sensors

When working around the brake and wheel assembly, it is important to ensure that the wheel-speed sensor and associated wiring are taken care of. It is also important that the sensor is always fastened in place where specified by the manufacturer, in order to avoid any possible damage.

## 23.2.3 Further developments

Electronic brake force distribution (EBD) controls the brake pressure to the rear wheels and alters it as weight transfer occurs to the front of the car under heavy braking. This replaces the old mechanical pressure-reducing valve (PRV), which allows less pressure to more lightly loaded rear wheels of a conventional road car. It is always coupled with ABS, sometimes with electronic stability control (ESC) (see page 318), and allows each corner of the car to employ maximum braking effort, often reducing the need for the ABS system to stop the wheels from locking.

Brake assist is another technology that works with ABS and also ACC. This helps the driver slow the car during an emergency stop by sensing that the car needs to stop quickly, through driver reactions, brake pedal pressure, and ACC sensors, and uses the ABS to apply full braking force to the car. Some systems also use the brake booster (either controlled via the **engine vacuum** or an electronic motor) to exert maximum braking force. Adaptive systems can also learn the driving technique of the driver in order to more easily recognise when an out-of-character braking situation is occurring.

**Engine vacuum**: the vacuum used to move the diaphragm in a braking servo. It is caused in the inlet manifold, as the intake stroke of a piston causes a pressure difference between either side of the throttle flap and the Earth's atmospheric pressure.

## 23.2.4 Fault diagnosis

The ABS system has a self-checking function and will illuminate a warning light for approximately 4 s when the ignition is turned on, before deciding whether the system passes its self-test. If a fault is detected, a fault code will be stored that can be read by a diagnostic machine, which can also carry out actuation tests to check operation. The ABS warning light will also stay illuminated. If a major fault is found with the ABS, the solenoids are cut off so that the system does not operate at all and normal braking can still function. When in use, the light will illuminate and the brake pedal will pulsate, with the steering wheel also being affected by vibration.

Testing of a wheel-speed sensor can be carried out using a multimeter to test for voltage and resistance when stationary and when revolving, dependent upon which sensor is used. Additionally, an oscilloscope can look at its waveform – refer to the manufacturer's data for precise figures. Wheel speeds can also be read off a suitable diagnostic tool to pinpoint which wheel-speed sensor is causing a problem.

## 23.3 Electro-hydraulic brakes

This new technology uses brake-by-wire to further utilise electronics and enhance the engagement and control of all road wheel control systems (Figure 23.5).

A **potentiometer** is used to monitor the position of the brake pedal; this then relays a voltage to a control unit, which converts the voltage into a pressure and commands an electrically driven hydraulic pump complete with a high-pressure accumulator. The pump (fitted with actuator solenoids) acts on information from the control unit and provides pressure to each brake line. This removes the need for a brake servo and direct connection or plumbing to the brake pedal. A module is also fitted to the pedal to give it the same feel it would have if operating a normal master cylinder.

> **Potentiometer**: a sensor that alters its resistance according to its position, so its output voltage changes with position change.

The system also allows for ABS, traction control (see page 315) and other systems to work together more efficiently, aiding safe driving. No kickback will be felt through the driving controls when the ABS is activated and some systems have the ability (with the use of other sensors) to apply more pressure to the wheels with more load on them (i.e. when cornering) to reduce stopping times.

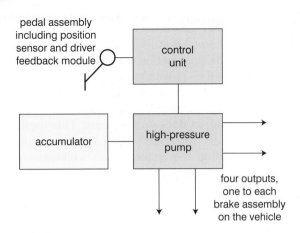

*Figure 23.5 Layout of electro-hydraulic brake system*

At the time of writing, this technology is still in its early days and most systems have a back-up master cylinder in case there is an electrical failure.

### 23.3.1 Electric parking brakes

Electric parking brakes are becoming common. A switch on the dashboard operates an ECU to drive an electric motor on the side of the handbrake caliper. When the ECU senses throttle or clutch movement, it will release the handbrake automatically. This system also receives data from the wheel-speed sensor to ensure the handbrake is only applied at very low speeds so that accidental operation cannot occur.

In the future, **electromechanical** systems may replace hydraulic systems, with each caliper being controlled by an electric motor. But so far these systems are only in development.

> **Electromechanical**: a type of system that uses mechanical and electronic principles to operate. This normally functions with an electronic system controlling a mechanical motor's operation.

## 23.4 Automatic transmission control

Modern automatic transmission is electronically controlled in the same way as most other systems in a vehicle. (See Chapter 16 for operational information on this system.) Its function is to control the mechanical components inside an automatic transmission system.

The ECU for this system will take into account many engine and vehicle parameters (particularly load and speed), including inputs from the driver.

All of this information will be computed and calculated in order to control:

- vehicle speeds at which gear change occurs
- lock-up clutch timing
- hydraulic pressures over operating range
- reduction of engine torque during gear shifts.

Different driving modes, such as 'sport' and 'economy', can also be selected via a switch or button, in order to change the driveability of the vehicle. Modern vehicles now also incorporate systems that allow for semi-automatic use, in which the driver can control the change of gears via buttons on the steering wheel, paddles behind the steering wheel or a **sequential mode** on the gear stick.

**Sequential mode**: a mode of gear selection in which the conventional manual 'H' gate is replaced with a simple 'push–pull' mode of selection. This is common in high-performance cars.

The transmission ECU is now commonly part of the engine ECU as both systems require inputs from some of the same sensors.

The ECU collects data from sensors and compares it with data held in its memory. It then decides which actuators in the hydraulic system must be energised to select the appropriate gear (Figure 23.6).

## 23.4.1 Inputs and outputs

Inputs include the following:

- Wheel/vehicle-speed sensor – used to determine when a gear change is necessary and to know when to decouple the torque converter when the vehicle is stationary in order to save fuel.
- Kick-down switch – used to determine when the throttle has been fully depressed, it will change down to the lowest possible gear, based on inputs from other sensors, to use maximum power and torque. It is now generally superseded by the TPS.
- TPS (throttle position sensor) – used to monitor gearshift patterns and calculate the best time to up- or downshift, depending on driver input. The use of this sensor is vastly superior to its predecessor, the kick-down switch, as it allows greater control of the transmission system.
- Input-speed sensor (ISS) – used to monitor input shaft speed to the torque converter to determine slippage across the transmission system and, therefore, control the torque converter lock-up clutch.
- Transmission fluid temperature sensor – used not only for diagnostic purposes but to monitor oil viscosity to alter line and solenoid pressures accordingly.

- Brake light switch – used to determine whether a downshift is needed to use engine braking and to release the shift lock mechanism and allow the driver to select a different driving mode, such as reverse, park or drive.
- CC (cruise control) and traction control data link – uses data from these systems to modify shift patterns and gear selection in order to improve fuel efficiency and keep the car stable in all situations.
- Pressure switch – used to detect line pressures for diagnostic purposes.

Outputs include the following:

- Shift lock – system used to stop gear selection from being changed without the brake pedal being depressed.
- Shift solenoids – used to activate gear changes.
- Pressure control solenoids – used to control the precise pressure of the system to ensure effective and smooth operation of the system. If the pressure is too high, then the shift will feel rough, while a pressure that is too low will result in the clutch overheating.
- Torque converter clutch solenoid – regulates the torque converter, which provides engine torque to the transmission and provides a torque multiplication function.
- Output to engine ECU – relays information to the engine ECU that allows the engine power to be momentarily cut or limited during shifting, which is particularly useful when the engine is under heavy load.
- Output to driver instrumentation – can provide indication of a fault and also display gear selection and shift modes for driver convenience.

## 23.4.2 Other types of automatic transmission

The continuously variable transmission (CVT) is an electronically controlled automatic transmission system with drive and driven pulleys, joined with a steel belt. The CVT provides non-stage speeds forward and one reverse.

Its electronic control system consists of the powertrain control module (PCM), sensors and solenoid valves. Shifting is electronically controlled for comfortable driving under all conditions.

The PCM controls the pulley ratio via the solenoids. The PCM, which receives input signals from the various sensors and switches located throughout the vehicle, actuates the CVT drive pulley pressure control valve and CVT driven pulley pressure control valve to change pulley control pressure.

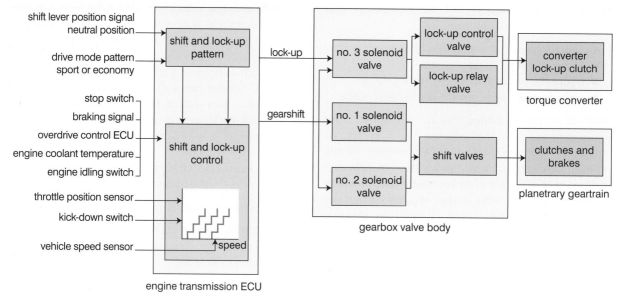

*Figure 23.6 Automatic transmission system*

The pulley ratio is changed upon pressure control valve changes, which alter the gear ratio.

Power split transmission (PST), also known as electric variable transmission, is a system used on hybrid vehicles to provide two possible power inputs (mechanical via the engine and electric) to produce one output. More information can be found on both CVT and PST systems in Chapter 16.

### 23.4.3 Fault diagnosis

As with all other sections in this chapter, fault codes will be stored and the ECU can be interrogated by a diagnostic tool.

## 23.5 Traction control

This system is used to stop the loss of traction that can occur under acceleration. This can be due to a slippery or loose surface.

The traction control system, introduced in 1986 by Bosch, can be easily integrated with ABS. Its components are similar to those of Figure 23.3 with the addition of another ECU (unless it is integrated into another ECU) and a throttle control system (which adapts to the drive-by-wire system easily).

### 23.5.1 How traction control works

Wheel-speed sensors are used to signal when a wheel starts to spin under acceleration (Figure 23.7). The ECU then uses its power to be able to carry out any of the following (dependent upon system):

- Apply brakes to the wheels that are spinning – with the use of ABS.
- Reduce engine power by controlling the throttle flap.
- Retard the ignition timing.
- Cut a number of fuel injectors.
- Shift to a higher gear (automatic only).
- Alter torque bias between front and rear axle (four-wheel drive only).

Traction control can often be overcome with the use of a button in the cockpit of the car. If switched off, a warning light will appear on the instrument panel to remind the driver that the system is disabled. It will default to 'On' when the engine is started and will flicker when it is in operation during wheel spin.

These systems are now also available on motorcycles, along with ABS.

*Figure 23.7 Result of no traction control*

## 23.5.2 Fault diagnosis

Fault codes and diagnostic tools will enable interrogation of any issues with this system.

### 23.6 Electronic stability control (ESC)

ESC is easily incorporated with other systems in this chapter, such as ABS and traction control. It also carries other names such as electronic stability program (ESP) and vehicle stability control (VSC).

This system's function is to ensure that the car is travelling in the direction that the driver intends. This basically means that it limits the car's ability to **understeer** or **oversteer** (Figure 23.8).

**Understeer**: an unstable condition in which the front tyres lose grip and the car does not go in the direction of the front wheels.

**Oversteer**: an unstable condition in which the rear tyres lose grip and attempt to overtake the front of the car.

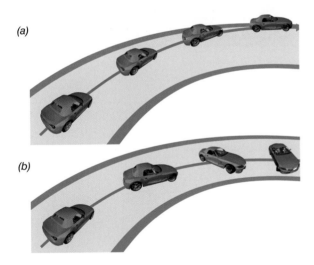

*(a)*

*(b)*

*Figure 23.8 (a) Understeer and (b) oversteer*

### 23.6.1 How ESC works

ESC works in a similar manner to the systems mentioned previously and also relies on similar components. Four wheel-speed sensors are used along with functions from a common ECU that controls the majority of road wheel control systems. Other input sensors include steering angle, yaw/lateral acceleration, and other vital driver inputs such as throttle and brake.

If the car begins to break traction and either understeer or oversteer, the input sensors relay information back to the ECU. This then stabilises the vehicle with use of the brakes (via the ABS modulator) or the engine power (reducing the throttle and cutting the ignition).

As electronics in vehicles advance it is becoming easier to allow these kinds of system to work in harmony together and create a safer environment on the roads. Studies show that 40 per cent of all accidents occur from skidding, so the use of these systems should keep the roads safer by reducing the risk of accidents.

### 23.6.2 Active yaw control (AYC)

Mitsubishi designed AYC, a similar performance-designed system, and introduced it in one of their car models in 1996. This system uses an electronically controlled rear differential for the four-wheel drive car. With the use of a host of sensors, it has the ability to transfer torque to and from each side of the axle in order to control understeer and oversteer. The yaw angle is the difference between the direction the car is going and the way it is actually pointing. It is normally observed as a vertical axis through the centre of the car from the roof to the floor, just like a spinning top.

### 23.6.3 Fault diagnosis

As ESC works hand-in-hand with the previous systems outlined, the diagnosis process is also carried out in the same manner.

### 23.7 Tyre pressure monitoring system (TPMS)

This system monitors tyre pressures in order to keep the occupants safe. It can utilise the wheel-speed sensors mentioned previously, and can also put the car into 'limp home' mode, reducing the risk of an accident caused by travelling at unsafe speeds with a flat tyre.

TPMS is a legal requirement with run-flat tyres, in which the stiff side walls can mask the fact that the tyre pressure is low. It can also help to ensure that tyre life is maximised, in terms of uneven wear, and can help economise on fuel by ensuring that tyre rolling resistance is not increased. From 2012 it will be an EU requirement that all new vehicles have a TPMS fitted.

### 23.7.1 How TPMS works

The system works in one of two ways, depending on the manufacturer.

#### Direct system

This monitors the actual tyre pressure of each of the four wheels, using four pressure sensors attached to the bottom of the tyre valve (behind the wheel face). These sensors then send a signal to a receiver that can show tyre pressure and even temperature on the driver display system. Renault use this system for their Laguna and other larger vehicles in the range.

### Indirect system

This uses the wheel-speed sensors to monitor the rotational speed of each of the tyres and notes when it has changed over a period of time. Therefore, this does not strictly monitor tyre pressure, but indicates a pressure change indirectly by detecting a contraction of the tyre. For example, a tyre with a circumference of 220 cm travels 220 cm for every full rotation. If the pressure drops and the circumference reduces to 180 cm, the tyre will need to rotate faster to cover the same distance as the other tyres. When this happens, the system illuminates a warning light on the dashboard. Once the tyre pressures have been checked and the tyres reinflated, the system must be reset via the trip computer to learn the new values. This type is fitted on the new BMW Mini range.

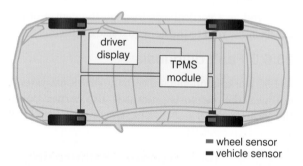

■ wheel sensor
■ vehicle sensor

*Figure 23.9 Basic TPMS layout*

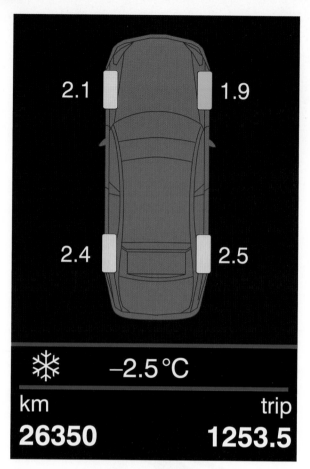

*Figure 23.10 Driver display for TPMS*

By law, all new vehicles manufactured in the UK since 1987 (1967 for front seats only) must be fitted with three-point seat belts for forward-facing seats, except for the central rear seat, which can use a two-point lap strap. These belts must be worn by the driver and all passengers unless a special exemption is granted.

In addition to this legal requirement, nearly all mass-producing vehicle manufacturers have some form of supplemental restraint system (SRS) fitted. Although airbags are not required by law, members of the public strongly prefer purchasing a car with a number of airbags for obvious safety reasons. A series of tests can be carried out using the European New Car Assessment Programme (NCAP), which rates vehicles for safety; without the use of airbags a vehicle would be rated poorly.

The systems are used to protect the occupants inside the vehicle and comprise two main elements:

- Airbag.
- Seat belt pre-tensioners.

## 24.1  Airbags

Airbags (Figure 24.1) were introduced in 1980 for the driver and in 1988 for the front-seat passenger, by Mercedes Benz. An SRS airbag is most commonly found installed in the steering wheel and the front passenger dashboard area, where it serves to give protection in the event of a frontal impact. Other types of airbags have since been introduced:

- Side torso airbags were introduced by Volvo in 1995.
- Kia first used knee airbags in 1996.
- BMW introduced the curtain airbag in 1997, with Toyota producing a rear curtain in 2008.
- Mercedes started to use the seat belt airbag in 2009.
- Motorcycle manufacturer Honda was the first company to use an airbag in 2006 on its Gold Wing.

When a severe impact occurs, a sensor sends a signal to the control unit and this then inflates the airbag. An airbag inflates almost instantaneously, taking approximately 30 ms (milliseconds) to achieve this after being triggered. After around 100 ms, the airbag begins to deflate in order to provide the occupants space to move and allow them to see clearly around and outside the vehicle.

There are many types of airbag in modern vehicles:

- Front – found in the steering wheel and dashboard to protect from frontal impacts.
- Side – to protect the torso area from injury in a side impact. They are found in the side of the seat or B pillar.
- Curtain – to protect the upper body and head from injury from colliding with the side window. They are usually found above the side window in the head lining.
- Knee – to prevent injury to the legs in a frontal impact. They are normally only for the driver and are in the lower part of the dashboard.
- Seat belt – to spread the load and help reduce whiplash. They are part of the webbing of the belt.
- Motorcycle – found on larger motorcycles around the fuel tank area and in the upper sections of motorcycle jackets.

### Health and safety issues

SRSs are classed as explosives and must be stored in an approved steel cabinet that is registered with the local authority if removal from the vehicle is necessary. Always handle SRS components with care and ensure that the manufacturer's procedures are followed when carrying out testing or any removal/refitting procedures on airbag systems.

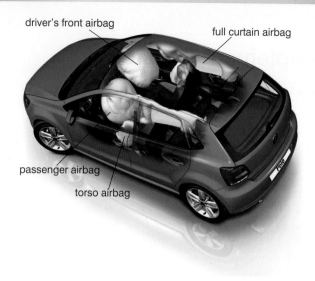

*Figure 24.1 Full curtain, torso and both driver and passenger airbags deployed*

All airbags are electronically controlled and some vehicles are equipped with 'smart airbags' (see page 324), which are much more advanced.

Figure 24.2 shows the main components and circuit diagram of an airbag system:

- Front impact and safing sensors.
- Electronic control unit (ECU).
- Airbag module.

## 24.1.1 Front impact and safing sensors

The front impact and safing sensors, responsible for triggering the airbag, are deceleration sensors and detect sudden forward deceleration or impact. They are connected in series in order to ensure that inflation occurs only when both are operated. (If they

were connected in parallel, then mishandling the sensor while removing the bumper from the vehicle could set off the airbag.) There are generally two types of sensor:

- Coil spring and ball – the ball is attached to a coil spring and once a specific G-force is reached (around 4 g), the spring stretches far enough to touch the contacts and create a circuit to provide a voltage to the airbag module (Figure 24.3).
- Magnet and ball – the magnet holds the ball and, on impact, the ball flies forward to hit the contacts and creates a circuit, acting like a switch (Figure 24.4).

The impact sensors are normally found around the front of the vehicle, near the bumper or wing areas, while the safing sensor is found in the control module or towards the rear of the car. The arrangement is normally specific to the manufacturer, so wiring diagrams must also be considered in order to identify correct colouring systems.

## 24.1.2 Electronic control unit (ECU)

The airbag ECU is one of many highly intelligent computers fitted to a vehicle. In this system, the main components include:

- centre/safing sensor – this acts as a trigger for the airbag, and works in tandem with the front impact sensors in order to complete the circuit required to inflate the airbag(s)
- a back-up power supply – this uses a capacitor to keep the airbag system powered for about 150 ms when the main power source is interrupted

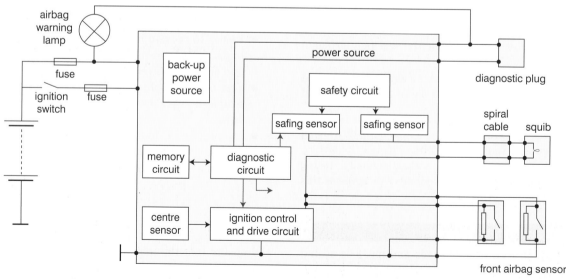

→ indicates monitoring facility

*Figure 24.2 Simplified airbag circuit*

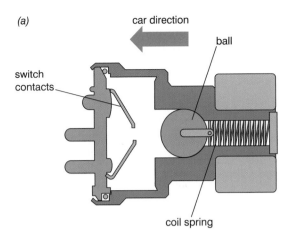

*(a)*

car direction

ball

switch contacts

coil spring

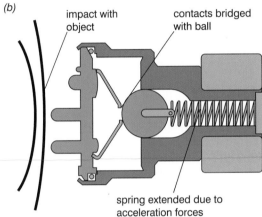

*(b)*

impact with object

contacts bridged with ball

spring extended due to acceleration forces

Figure 24.3 A coil spring and ball sensor: (a) in an open state before impact, (b) in a closed state upon impact

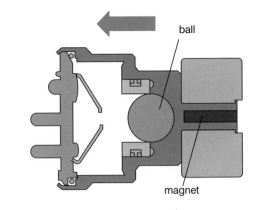

*(a)*

ball

magnet

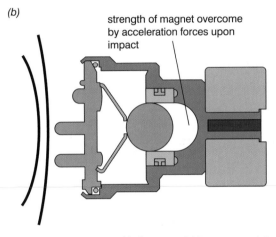

*(b)*

strength of magnet overcome by acceleration forces upon impact

Figure 24.4 A magnet and ball sensor: (a) in an open state before impact, (b) in a closed state upon impact

- trigger circuit – this is the 'brains' of the system, particularly in modern road cars with smart airbags (see page 324). Sensors relay messages to this part of the ECU so it can make a decision on how and when to deploy each airbag. The decision will be based upon stored information in the **ROM**
- diagnosis/memory module – this works in conjunction with the SRS indicator lamp to warn of any potential faults. This lamp (Figure 24.5) is illuminated when the ignition is on, to show that the system is operable, and should go out once the engine is started. It is a self-testing system, so if a fault is found the light will remain illuminated and store a fault code in the memory.

**ROM**: read-only memory, a type of data storage that cannot be modified and is used as a reference database.

### 24.1.3 The airbag module

The airbag module (Figure 24.6) is found in the centre of the steering wheel, in the passenger dashboard area, and wherever else the airbags are installed. It contains the igniter squib and gas-generating pellets (usually sodium azide or ammonium nitrate), which produce a large volume of nitrogen gas (N). This is all housed within the nylon fabric airbag.

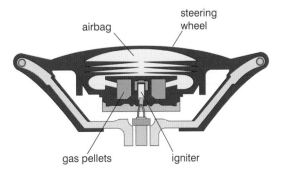

airbag

steering wheel

gas pellets

igniter

Figure 24.6 Airbag module contents

Figure 24.5 Airbag warning lamp

To be activated, a very small amount of current (1–3 A) is applied to the squib. The ignited charge is fired and heat is produced, which causes the pellets to generate nitrogen to inflate the bag.

### 24.1.4 Smart airbags

Smart airbags are commonly fitted to new vehicles and can adapt and alter their inflation parameters to suit the type of crash that is occurring.

These have dual-stage inflation features that allow for two levels of inflation, depending on the severity of the impact. They can monitor crash and occupant characteristics in order for the ECU to deploy the airbags in the best way possible. A separate set of sensors monitors seat position, seat belt status and crash properties, such as speed and direction, in order to create the safest environment for the occupants. To avoid unnecessarily setting off the airbags, seat sensors in the seat base can also determine whether someone is in the seat. This then allows the ECU to determine whether or not to deploy that airbag in an accident.

### 24.1.5 Fault diagnosis

This is carried out using the appropriate diagnostic tool that is capable of communicating with the particular make of car. Fault codes can be accessed from the ECU memory to help solve the problem. Always refer to the manufacturer's instructions for further information on handling and inspection of these units.

## 24.2    Seat belt pre-tensioners

In the event of a front-end impact, vehicle occupants are subjected to a very large inertia force, which can exceed 40 times the weight of their bodies. To improve the chance of surviving a collision of this order, the occupants must be securely restrained to a strong structure (i.e. the vehicle body).

Wearing a conventional seat belt improves safety considerably, but the need to allow the occupants freedom of movement generally means that the belt tension does not prevent a person being thrown through the windscreen. Vehicle designers now realise that, in the interest of safety, seat belts must be tightened during the time that the large inertia force is acting.

This important **pyrotechnic** safety feature activates before the airbag in order to seat the occupants in the correct position before the airbag is deployed. A pre-tensioner takes up any slack in the belt webbing and firmly fastens the occupant against their seat to provide the safest environment possible. Normally, the airbag ECU will control the seat belt pre-tensioners using the components from one system for the other. A gas generator and squib are used again, in the same way as for an airbag – as with an airbag, these must be replaced if activated. The gas is used in a belt-tightening mechanism, such as a piston-driven cylinder (Figure 24.7). This can retract the webbing in the belt reel or, alternatively, it can provide tension by contracting the buckle towards the floor of the car by connection to a steel cable (Figure 24.8). These systems can be used in both the front and rear seats of a vehicle.

**Pyrotechnic**: using a chemical reaction to produce gas and subsequently heat for the use of SRS in vehicles.

The other types of seat belt pre-tensioner are as follows:

- Mechanical pre-tensioners – these use an inertial wheel with a pendulum device, which moves under the rapid deceleration of the crash to lock the belt into place. Such mechanisms can often be detected by giving a sudden tug on the belt. A mechanical pre-tensioner will automatically lock the belt into place, with the intention of limiting occupant travel in the event of a crash.
- Electrical pre-tensioners – these replace the mechanical means of sensing deceleration (the pendulum) with an electrical device. This may or may not be tied into the airbag ignition circuits.

---

**Safe practice**

DO NOT measure squib resistance when fault diagnosing this system with an ohmmeter, as the small current it supplies to the squib could trigger the airbag.

---

**Health and safety**

Legally, a child sitting in a rear-facing child restraint cannot sit in the front passenger seat with an active airbag deployed unless the airbag is disarmed. Most manufacturers now provide a switch to disable the airbag if required.

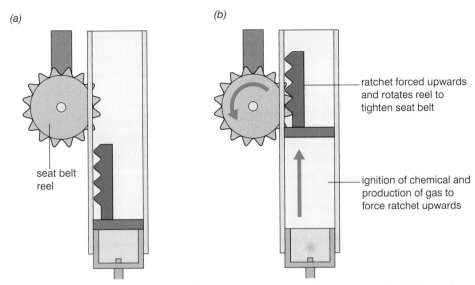

Figure 24.7 Webbing reel tensioner: (a) in normal state, (b) with pyrotechnic reaction causing reel to tighten in the event of a collision. The seat belt reel retracts to keep the occupant firmly seated in the vehicle

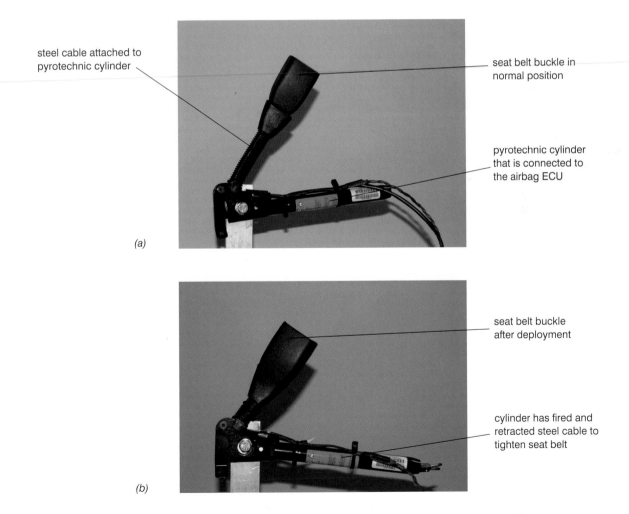

Figure 24.8 Principle of operation of a buckle tensioner: (a) in normal state, (b) once deployed. These two photographs show the situation before and after a collision. As you can see from (b), the seat belt buckle has pulled down and this will fasten the occupant firmly in their seat

## 24.3 Rollover protection system (ROPS)

The purpose of this system is to protect the passengers in the event that a convertible vehicle rolls over. The rollover hoops or bar can be fixed in place but active ROPS uses a pyrotechnic method, as with the airbags and seat belt pre-tensioners, to push the hoops or bar above the standard position to provide maximum safety to the occupants in milliseconds (Figure 24.9). Volkswagen uses a spring and ratchet system that relies on a solenoid (operated by the airbag ECU) so that it can be reset without replacing any components. Crash sensors and gyroscopes are needed to use this safety system.

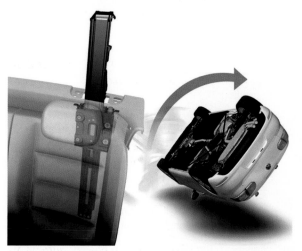

Figure 24.9 Volkswagen ROPS, showing the headrests extended upwards to protect the occupants in the event of the car rolling over

## 24.4 Summary

These systems are all used for one purpose: to ensure the safety of all the occupants within the vehicle. Airbags, seat belt pre-tensioners and ROPS all share common information through the same sensors and ECU and, in most cases, are discharged using a pyrotechnic charge. They are generally not reusable systems and will need to be replaced if the vehicle is repaired for road use.

# 25

## In-car entertainment and communication equipment

The average person spends a significant amount of time in their vehicle on a daily basis. In-car entertainment systems provide passengers with recreation media for the duration they spend in the vehicle.

A decade ago, in-car entertainment was limited to standard radios and audio cassette players.

Today, vehicle entertainment is a growing industry with numerous electronic products. In addition to entertainment equipment, vehicles also have communication facilities and allow integration with personal communication electronics.

In this chapter we will discuss modern entertainment and communication facilities in motor vehicles.

## 25.1 Radios

### 25.1.1 Radio waves

Radio waves have been used for communication for a long time. The UK has a radio network with a choice of entertainment and information channels. Radio programmes are broadcast from a studio; the audio is then converted to a digital format and transmitted to a wide area. Radio signals are 'catapulted' by booster stations, thus allowing transmission to a large area. Strategically placed booster stations enable complete radio coverage over the whole country.

The fundamental radio signal is the carrier wave. In order to transport information, the amplitude or frequency of the carrier wave is modified. This is called modulation.

#### Amplitude modulation (AM)

This type of modulation involves alteration of the amplification pattern of the carrier wave to represent the digital signal being transmitted. AM signals have a range advantage as they can travel long distances. However, the audio quality of AM signals is not very good as the signal can carry limited audio frequencies and can easily be distorted. AM waves are often used by state news channels and international radio channels due to their range.

#### Frequency modulation (FM)

This type of modulation varies the frequency of the carrier wave according the pattern of the digital signal being transmitted. FM signals have a shorter range and lose strength over long distances. The audio, however, is of a high quality and clear of disturbances. This is why FM waves are used to broadcast most entertainment channels.

### 25.1.2 Radio units

The main radio device is customarily installed in the middle of the front console and is referred to as the 'head unit'. This central location for the vehicle's radio existed since the early years of motoring. The head unit contains the control interface for the radio and an liquid crystal display (LCD) or analogue display. The vehicle radio system is illustrated in Figure 25.1.

Car models before 2005 had a metallic antenna to receive radio signals from the surroundings. The antenna could be collapsed or slid into the vehicle body, either manually or by an electric motor. Metal antennas were eventually replaced by a better technique that integrated the radio antenna into the roof or the rear windshield's defroster.

Standard controls on a head unit allow the user to change audio volume, modify audio quality, search for radio channels (tuning) and save the channels in the radio's memory for quick access. Most head units have six channel store buttons for quick access.

#### Radio interference

Radio signals are transmitted through air and so are vulnerable to electromagnetic disturbances. Such disturbances are often location-specific, for example in a covered car park or near electricity pylons. Continuous disturbance in a vehicle's radio reception hints toward an internal fault. Such disturbance is often due to problems in the radio antenna. The antenna should not be in contact with any other metallic object or electronic cables. Loose antenna connections can also cause noise in radio reception.

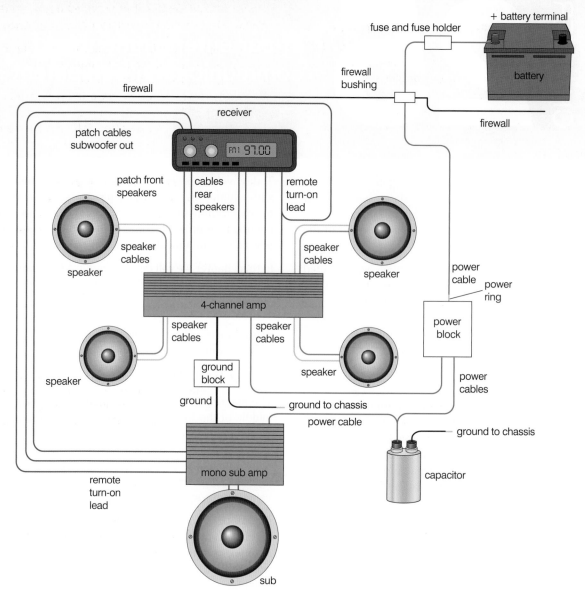

*Figure 25.1 Radio components and location*

## 25.2 Playable media

Many mid-range family cars have factory-fitted entertainment systems that allow visual and audio media to be stored and played. DVD is a common format for video media and the MP3 format is popular for audio media. The head unit contains several ports and slots that are used to transfer media to the vehicle's entertainment unit. A standard media unit is shown in Figure 25.2.

Systems are usually a compromise of cost over quality and, increasingly, more vehicle owners are upgrading the original system and fitting bigger and better speakers with amplifiers and capacitors to boost the sound at all frequencies.

*Figure 25.2 Vehicle media unit – Toyota Avensis*

## Head unit and amplifier

The head unit is the most important part of the system. A good-quality head unit that can handle up to 100 W is reasonable; a four-speaker system and the head unit can handle 100 W, where each speaker should output up to 25 W, providing the speakers can handle it. A good-quality amplifier with reasonably good output is better than a low-quality one with high output.

## Speakers

The speakers must be able to accept their share of the power, depending on the output from the head unit and amplifier; four good-quality speakers will provide a better sound than eight poor-quality ones.

## Cables

For quality sound reproduction, the components of a sound system must be connected with high-performance cable. Wire is normally rated in size using the AWG system (American Wire Gauge); Table 25.1 shows the cable size and current carrying capacity of the wire for certain lengths of cable.

Opinion on the best type of wire to be used for speakers (e.g. braided, air core or oxygen-free) is divided; choice is often down to personal preference and research. Speaker wire must be flexible and heavily insulated. It should be noted that replacing manufacturer-fitted systems may mean the loss of some functionality (e.g. systems may be integrated to the vehicle clock, and some replacement systems will not allow the use of steering wheel controls).

## Disc loaders

These have largely replaced the dated cassette tape players. The latest types accept CDs of various storage formats. Media from the discs is played directly and is not stored in the vehicle's memory for technical reasons.

As changing a disc while driving can be hazardous (especially as a disc should only be handled at the edge), a multidisc auto-changer may be fitted. This is a magazine that holds a number of discs, which can be selected and changed at the touch of a button. They can be fitted into the rear boot compartment or under one of the front seats, depending on the size.

Various options are available when replacing an older CD player or upgrading the head unit. These are dictated by the space available to accommodate the head unit. If the unit is to be fitted in the standard DIN aperture, the choice of replacement may be limited. Alternatively, the CD unit may be mounted separately. Many CD players (or CD/tuners) have a 50 W integral amplifier; in these cases a four-speaker system of about 100 W is necessary if the full benefit of a CD is to be gained.

## USB ports

These allow users to connect flash drives, external computers and smartphones to transfer and store media files in the vehicle's memory. The port is also used to change settings and rearrange playlists of media stored in the vehicle.

## SD card slots

These enable users to connect an external memory card containing media files. SD cards are a convenient method for carrying media files. Such cards can also be used to extend the vehicle's internal memory dedicated to in-car entertainment.

*Table 25.1  Cable gauge and current capacity*

| Current | Length of run (in feet) | | | | | | | |
|---|---|---|---|---|---|---|---|---|
| | 0–4 | 4–7 | 7–10 | 10–13 | 13–16 | 16–19 | 19–22 | 22–28 |
| | Cable gauge | | | | | | | |
| 0–20 A | 14 | 12 | 12 | 10 | 10 | 8 | 8 | 8 |
| 20–35 A | 12 | 10 | 8 | 8 | 6 | 6 | 6 | 4 |
| 35–50 A | 10 | 8 | 8 | 6 | 6 | 4 | 4 | 4 |
| 50–65 A | 8 | 8 | 6 | 4 | 4 | 4 | 4 | 2 |
| 65–85 A | 6 | 6 | 4 | 4 | 4 | 2 | 2 | 0 |
| 85–105 A | 6 | 6 | 4 | 2 | 2 | 2 | 2 | 0 |
| 105–125 A | 4 | 4 | 4 | 2 | 2 | 0 | 0 | 0 |
| 125–150 A | 2 | 2 | 2 | 2 | 0 | 0 | 0 | 0 |

## 25.3 Display screens

Display screens also serve as output devices for media and communication systems. LCD screens are the most popular type used in cars today. The screens are usually mounted on the front console for the front seats and behind the headrests of the front seats for the rear passengers. In larger sports utility vehicles (SUVs) and people carriers, the screens may fold down from the roof.

LCDs installed in vehicles have screen sizes of less than 9 inches. The screen is linked to either the head unit, which includes the radio and media player, or to a separate media unit. Mid-range family saloons and higher-priced luxury and sports vehicles have factory-fitted LCDs on the head unit. Figure 25.3 shows an LCD system for a family saloon.

Under Regulation 109 of the Road Vehicles (Construction and Use) Regulations 1986, it is an offence to drive a motor vehicle on a road if the driver is in such a position as to be able to see, whether directly or by reflection, a television screen showing anything other than information:

- about the state of the vehicle or equipment
- about the location of the vehicle and the road on which it is located
- to assist the driver to see the road adjacent to the vehicle
- to assist the driver to reach the destination.

## 25.4 In-car telephones and mobile integration

### 25.4.1 In-built phones

For many people, their vehicle is also their office. In the past, in-car telephones were bulky pieces of equipment; modern cars offer very convenient and smart communication facilities. In-car telephones are now integrated with the vehicle's computer. With the popularity of cellular communication, a GSM module is installed into the vehicle and is managed by its computer. Cellular network providers issue a subscriber identity module (SIM) to customers. The SIM is a small integrated chip that contains information and data necessary for logging into the cellular network. Cars that have an in-built cellular device have a slot for the SIM. This slot is usually near the steering wheel or on the centre console. Once the SIM is inserted, the vehicle's computer contacts the cellular network. The in-car telephone then functions the same way as a regular cell phone.

### 25.4.2 Bluetooth connectivity

Cars that do not have an in-built cellular phone may have the ability to connect with one. Connectivity can be done through a Bluetooth connection or via USB cable.

Bluetooth is a wireless technology that allows efficient short-range connections between devices. The technology is common in mobile phones and

*Figure 25.3 LCD system in a vehicle*

computers. Car manufacturers worked alongside cell phone manufacturers to develop devices that would allow a mobile phone to pair with the vehicle's computer. In this way, the cell phone can be controlled through the vehicle's systems and make it easier for the driver to connect while driving.

The cell phone can be controlled using an interface built into the steering wheel or by using the vehicle's computer console. While calling, the vehicle's speaker system serves as the audio output for the call. A microphone installed in the steering wheel serves as the audio input. Bluetooth connectivity has made driving safer as the driver can keep both hands on the wheel while talking. However, this feature is not common to all cars. A number of accidents every year are caused by the use of cell phones while driving.

The latest technology fitted to vehicles incorporates Bluetooth connectivity between the latest generation smartphones and the in-car entertainment system; this connectivity allows interaction of both devices to provide digital music, satellite navigation and hands-free communication.

## 25.5  Vehicle computer console and navigation

### 25.5.1 Computer console

Vehicles that use a computer to control their systems have an interface to communicate with the driver and take inputs. Compared with a standard desktop computer, the computer console of a vehicle serves both as the monitor and the keyboard. The interface is a touch-sensitive LCD mounted on the centre console. This is supplemented by a control joystick or knob, usually near the gear lever, that helps the user make inputs.

Vehicle computers provide a central platform from where all the vehicle's functions are controlled. This includes the climate control, drive settings, comfort settings, media and entertainment, and communication. Figure 25.4 illustrates the functions of the vehicle computer.

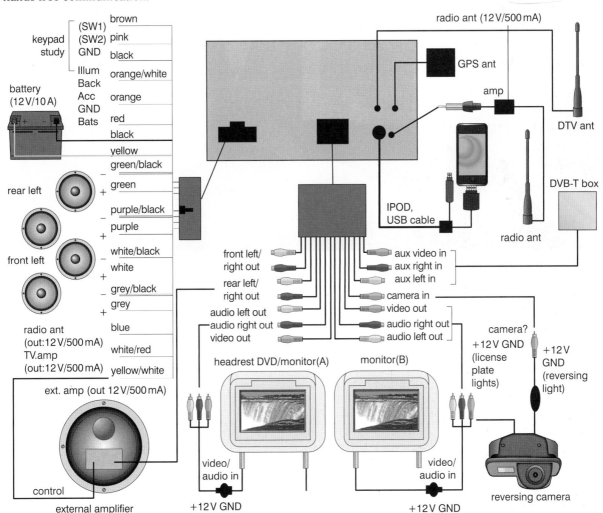

*Figure 25.4  Vehicle computer network diagram*

## 25.5.2 Global positioning system (GPS) devices

Global positioning system (GPS) devices provide navigation assistance to drivers. The system is controlled and displayed by the vehicle computer screen. The service is either provided by the manufacturer through a third party or sometimes needs to be purchased separately.

The GPS displays the current location of the vehicle on a map. Figure 25.5 shows typical displays shown by a GPS. The overhead map was used in earlier versions of GPS services. Now most devices provide a street view, which is much easier to comprehend and follow.

The main function of GPS devices is to assist drivers in finding a suitable route to their destination. Users programme their desired destination into the GPS and are provided with the possible routes. The user then selects their preferred route and the route is highlighted on the map. Most GPS devices also have a digital assistant, which provides audible directions as the driver progresses on the journey.

*Figure 25.5  Global positioning system (GPS)*

# 26

# Other electronic applications

Electronic systems in vehicles are continuously being upgraded and new innovations introduced. Systems that were once at the cutting edge of high-specification vehicles are now commonplace in regular models.

This chapter looks at the various types of auxiliary systems, the increasingly complex nature of multiplexing and looks ahead to future developments in automotive systems.

## 26.1 Auxiliary systems

Many of these systems have been driven by the development of sensors and microprocessing systems. Just as sensors are applied to systems, such as cruise control or parking assistance, equally they are used within the vehicle to make improvements to the overall driving experience.

### 26.1.1 Seats

#### Electric seat adjustment

In luxury vehicles electric seat adjustment or positioning is commonplace. The precise preferred position for specific drivers can be stored in the memory when the systems are controlled by a microprocessor electronic control unit (ECU). The stored data can also remember the preferred steering column position and that of external mirrors.

Some systems may have up to seven electric servo motors. These will deal with the height of the seat, cushion depth, backrest tilt, head restraint, lumber support and the longitudinal positioning of the seat. The system can also deal with the positioning of the seat belt anchor points, in order to make the driver more comfortable and safer in the event of a collision.

Figure 26.2 shows a typical layout that uses four adjustment motors. The driver can store their seat position data in the memory of the ECU using a control interface. When the driver enters the vehicle, the ECU can be activated and the correct seat positions for that driver are restored.

#### Electric seat heaters

These are usually only provided for the front seats and consist of thermostatically controlled heating elements in the backrest and seat pad. The occupant of the seat can select whether the heating elements are turned on and whether they want a high or low setting. These systems were originally introduced by Saab on the first 900 series in 1979 but are now available in many other vehicle types. The use of seat heating has been associated with reductions in back pain as a result of long-distance driving.

### 26.1.2 Steering

#### Power-assisted steering

Power-assisted steering is now fairly commonplace and is especially helpful in low-speed manoeuvring. Far more sophisticated versions of **electric power-assisted steering (EPS)** are gradually being introduced. Electrically powered hydraulic steering can replace systems that use drive belts and pulleys.

**Electric power-assisted steering (EPS)**: a system that uses an electric motor to assist the driver in turning the wheels. EPS systems are controlled by the vehicle ECU.

Tests have shown that these newer systems produce a huge saving in fuel consumption because of the reduction in effort required from not driving pulleys and belts.

There are, in effect, four different types of EPS systems:

- Column assist – where a power assist unit, a controller and torque sensor are fitted directly to the steering column.
- Pinion assist – where the power assist unit is fitted to the steering gear pinion shaft.
- Rack assist – where the power assist unit is fitted to the steering gear rack.
- Direct drive assist – where the power assist unit and the steering gear rack are one unit.

Actuators for
1    backrest curvature
2    backrest angle adjustment
3    seat-cushion depth adjustment
4    head-restraint height adjustment
5    seat-height adjustment
6    longitudinal seat positioning

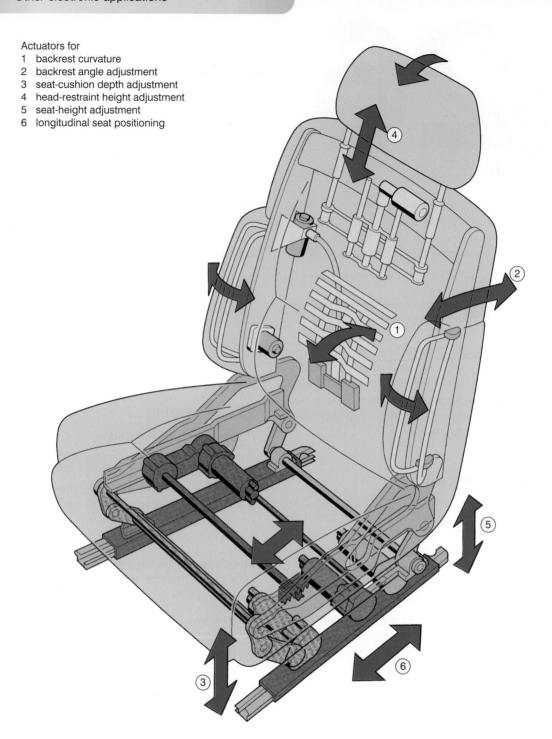

*Figure 26.1  Seat incorporating electromechanical adjustment*

All of these systems receive second-by-second feedback information from sensors, which are fed to the control unit. The steering system then reacts to the external environment, incorporating weather and changes to the road surface and other factors. It can even adapt to the driver. These are known as active controls.

Steering wheels directly connected with the front wheels are hard to turn, especially at low speeds. The driver's physical force is used solely to overcome the weight of the steering assembly and the friction between the wheels and the surface. A power-steering system eases the driver's work by providing the force needed to turn the wheels.

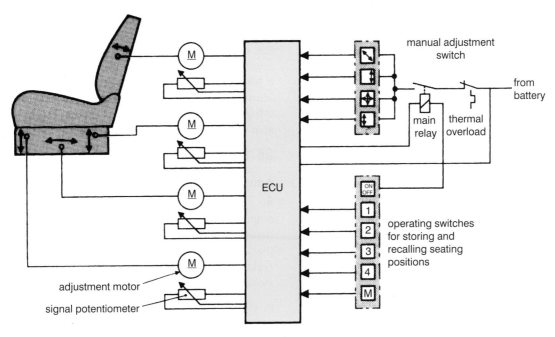

*Figure 26.2  Electric seat adjustment*

In earlier vehicles, power steering was purely pneumatic/mechanical. The assembly consisted of a rotary pump, pistons and valves. The rotary pump was driven by the engine and pumped oil into the pistons. The valves regulated oil flow to the pistons. Turning the steering wheel altered the aperture of the valves. The problem with purely mechanical power steering is that it provides the same level of sensitivity at high speeds as at low ones (i.e. very little force is needed to turn the wheels by a large angle). As a result, manoeuvring at high speeds is difficult. EPS solves this problem completely.

EPS systems vary in type. The following types are described below:

- Electro-hydraulic
- Servo assist
- Drive-by-wire

### Electro-hydraulic

These systems are very similar to mechanical power-steering systems, except that the motor is driven electrically instead of by the drive belt of the engine (Figure 26.3). This allows the speed of the motor, and hence the applied force, to be controlled.

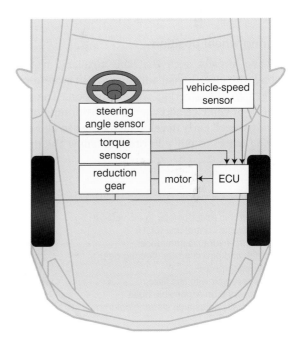

*Figure 26.3  Electro-hydraulic steering system*

## Electric power-assisted steering

Some of the sensors used in an EPS system are:

- torque
- yaw
- speed.

These are usually Hall effect, potentiometers, inductive and piezoelectric (Figure 26.3).

## Servo assist

Servo assist systems use a servo motor to assist the driver in turning the steering wheel. The amount of assistance varies according to vehicle speed.

## Drive-by-wire

In these systems the steering wheel is mechanically isolated from the wheels. The wheels are turned by an electric motor, depending on the turn angle of the steering.

In all these systems, the ECU determines how much assistance the motor or servo needs to provide. The ECU calculates the assistance using vehicle speed and turning angle of the steering wheel. Drive-by-wire systems are the latest concept introduced to commercial vehicles. Although such systems have been in use in aircraft (known as fly-by-wire), their use in vehicles is relatively new. On paper, drive-by-wire systems give the best statistics but many drivers complain of the lack of 'feel'. Several car manufacturers are currently researching and perfecting feedback motors that will provide drive 'feel' by imparting counter-forces on the steering wheel.

## Steering wheel position

We have already seen that the auxiliary systems dealing with electric seat adjustment can incorporate changes to the steering wheel position. The vast majority of vehicles allow manual positioning of the steering wheel. Early developments were to allow the steering wheel to move in order to allow the driver

to get in and out of the vehicle more easily. This function would only be activated as an option once the ignition key had been removed. The ECU that controls the newer systems can return the wheel to a pre-set position once the ignition key is inserted. More usually, however, steering wheel adjustment is integrated into an overall system that incorporates seat position and mirror positioning.

## 26.1.3 Suspension

### Adaptive damping system (ADS)

An adaptive damping system (ADS) aims to automatically adjust the optimal ride firmness dependent on the road surface, the driving style and the load of a vehicle. It has become a standard on certain types of Mercedes Benz vehicles. The aim of the system is to improve the driving comfort (Figure 26.5).

In effect, the system developed for Mercedes Benz combines ADS and pneumatic suspension (Airmatic suspension). Each of the shock absorbers can be individually adjusted to deal with the current driving circumstances. There is a steering angle sensor, three accelerometers (on the body of the vehicle) and an anti-lock braking system (ABS) speed sensor on each of the wheels, as well as a brake pedal sensor. Collectively, the sensors continually measure both the lateral and longitudinal acceleration. The ECU then works out the optimum damper setting for each of the wheels. It transmits this data to actuator valves within the gas pressure shock absorbers. The changes

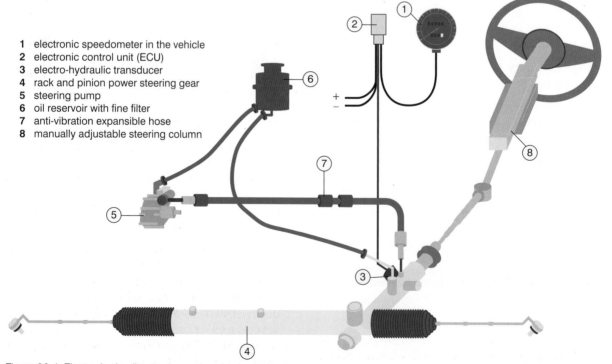

1  electronic speedometer in the vehicle
2  electronic control unit (ECU)
3  electro-hydraulic transducer
4  rack and pinion power steering gear
5  steering pump
6  oil reservoir with fine filter
7  anti-vibration expansible hose
8  manually adjustable steering column

*Figure 26.4 Electro-hydraulic steering system*

*Figure 26.5  ADS on a Mercedes Benz S400 Hybrid*

are instantaneous as the valves are able to switch between a series of preset damping characteristics.

### Active suspensions

Active suspensions use actuators to apply counter-force on the wheels to modify ride quality. The original concepts for such systems were developed by Lotus and Renault and tested on their racing cars in the 1980s. Modern cars have either hydraulic actuated or electromagnetic actuated systems.

Hydraulic actuated systems use a hydraulic pump to develop pressure on a piston. The piston acts on the wheels and controls their firmness and rebound rates. The hydraulic pumps are controlled by the ECU, which receives data from vertical acceleration sensors mounted on the wheel assembly, and vehicle speed and acceleration sensors.

Electromagnetic actuated systems use linear motors instead of hydraulic actuators. Electromagnetic systems are much more precise and considerably fast when compared to their hydraulic counterparts. They are also power-efficient, easier to diagnose faults and need less maintenance.

## 26.2    Multiplexing

### 26.2.1 Principles of multiplexing

Multiplexing involves replacing conventional cables that carry currents with a data bus. The bus needs only one or two wires in order to transmit signals around the vehicle. Additional components and circuitry are needed to code and decode signals at the end of each bus.

Multiplex networks connect ECUs and sensors. Multiplexing divides up what would otherwise be a very complex communication channel into a series of low-level channels, which allow signals or data to be transferred either from sensors to ECUs or from an ECU to another ECU (Figure 26.6).

### 26.2.2 Drive-by-wire systems

This is technology that aims to replace the more traditional mechanical control systems with electronic control systems comprising sensors, actuators and computers. The more generic term used is 'by-wire technology' and has its roots in the earlier fly-by-wire technology used for aircraft.

In 2001, based on a Bosch design, Mercedes introduced a new electro-hydraulic braking system. It used a sensor to work out the brake input of the driver. A computer processed the signal and calculated the optimum brake pressure for each wheel on a vehicle. There was, of course, a conventional brake system as a backup.

The other major development is the throttle-by-wire system. Normally, the driver's pressure on the foot pedal via a cable controls airflow into the engine. The throttle-by-wire system is replaced with an electronic throttle control using an electrically actuated valve (butterfly), which is controlled via the engine's own control module. The first ever throttle-by-wire system was introduced in 1980 by Chevrolet.

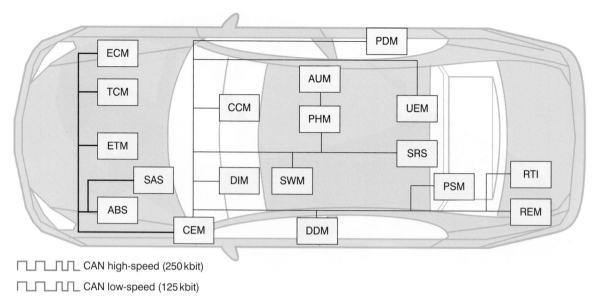

⊓⊔⊓⊔⊓⊔   CAN high-speed (250 kbit)

⊓⊔⊓⊔⊓⊔   CAN low-speed (125 kbit)

*Figure 26.6  Example of a car multiplex system*

## 26.2.3 Controller area network (CAN)

CAN was developed by Bosch, although there are other network technologies. The idea is that the individual ECUs are connected in parallel to the CAN bus system. The connections to the bus are called nodes. Using a protocol known as the multi-master system, each node has equal priority, so access to information on the bus is available to every ECU at the same time. Even if one node fails, all of the other connected nodes are still operational.

Each ECU is connected in parallel to the bus. The connections are known as transceiver modules. Each of these transceivers is a transmitter and also a receiver amplifier. The transceiver converts data in serial form into electrical signals. It also converts the electrical signals back into serial data. This allows each ECU to send and receive information. The information is converted into a binary number and then electrically transmitted through the CAN data bus. When it arrives at another ECU the bit stream is converted into a format that can be processed.

When the data is received at a node it is checked for errors. Assuming no error is discovered then a confirmation is sent back to the transmitter. The message is now processed and checked to see if it is of importance to that ECU or node. If it is relevant it is retained and copied into the memory of the processor.

Each time a message is sent on the bus it begins with an identifier. The identifier indicates the message's priority. The bus deals with the higher priority messages first. If a node cannot gain access to the bus, it switches to receive mode. Once the bus is free, it then attempts to transmit the message once again. If a node detects an error in transmission, then it will contact other nodes by transmitting an error frame. This means that the message from that node is rejected by the other nodes. If the node continues to send errors, then that ECU will be switched off automatically.

Figures 26.8–10 show how engine ECU data is transmitted to the dash panel insert. In this case:

- the data value is acquired by the engine ECU
- the data is then stored in the ECU's memory pending transmission
- the data moves to the transmit mailbox
- when the data is ready for transmission an electronic flag is raised
- the data is then converted to incorporate an identifier, the actual data, a checksum (error protection) and a message acknowledgement
- when the bus is free the data is then transmitted.

## 26.2.4 Local interconnect network (LIN) data bus system

LIN was developed as a lower cost alternative to CAN by a number of vehicle manufacturers, including Volvo and Audi. A LIN network is controlled by a master node. All of the other nodes are slaves and it is the master node that ensures that there is no data collision.

It is not designed to replace CAN, but rather to be complementary to it. Generally speaking it deals with basic vehicle functions, such as central locking, where only a modest bandwidth is required. Universal asynchronous receiver transmitter (UART) hardware is used on a single wire serial communication protocol.

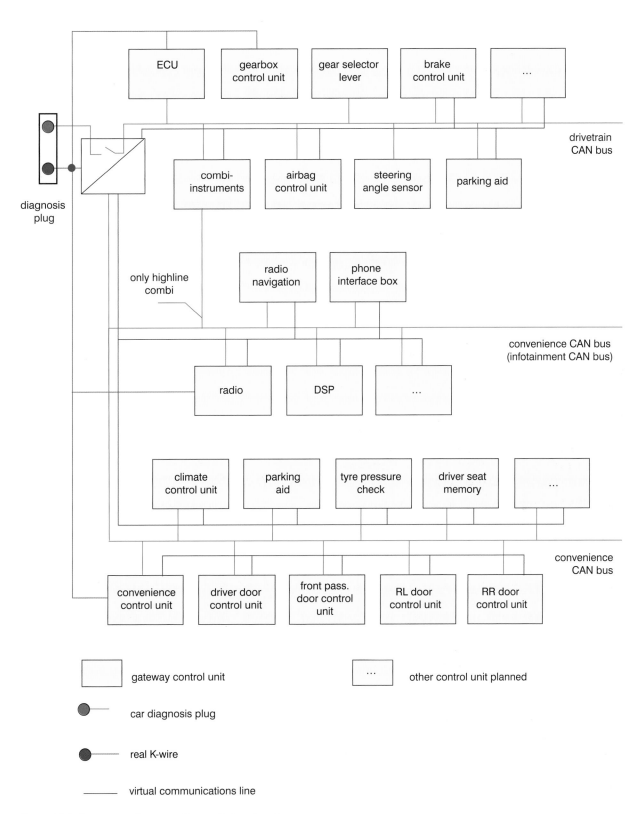

Figure 26.7 Bus system incorporating multiple networks

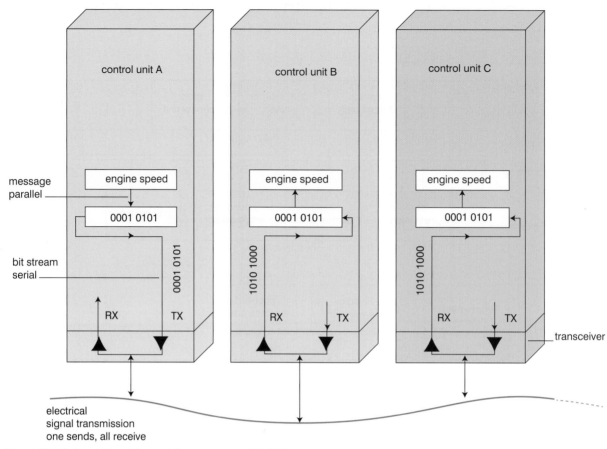

*Figure 26.8  Information exchange of a message on the CAN bus*

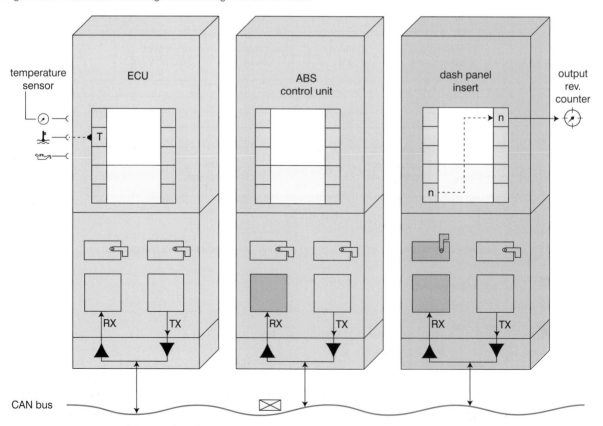

*Figure 26.9  CAN bus data receive*

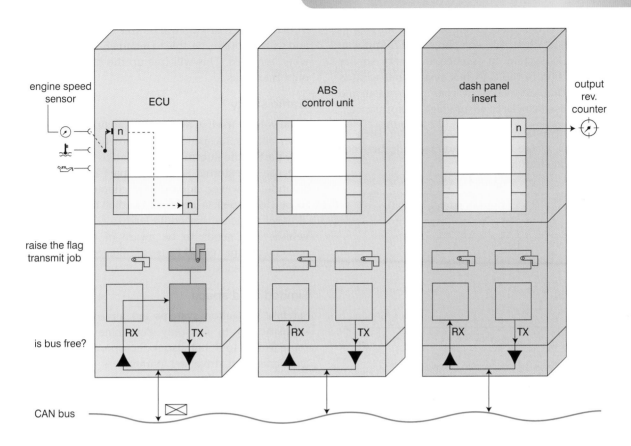

*Figure 26.10 CAN bus data transmission*

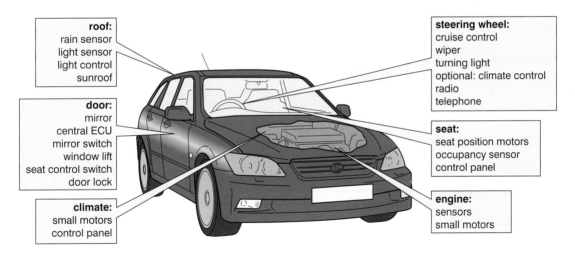

*Figure 26.11 Typical applications for LIN*

It has a relatively low transmission speed (20 kbit/s) and usually a LIN network has 12 nodes. It is a very cost-effective system and is considerably cheaper in terms of the use of hardware compared to CAN.

## 26.2.5 FlexRay

A relatively new development is FlexRay, which is another bus system developed by a number of vehicle manufacturers, including BMW and Volkswagen. FlexRay was specifically designed for automotive needs and aims to anticipate future needs in vehicle control applications. As such, it uses a higher bandwidth than the other systems, which allows real-time performance tweaks as a result of real-time data transmission and reaction. The system has a high level of error detection and diagnosis. It is designed to be extendable in anticipation of future upgrades of vehicle systems. Bus access is collision-free.

The system is designed to support data moving at rates of 10–20 Mb/s; this compares to 125 kbit/s in a CAN or LIN system. In essence, it is very similar in construction to the CAN bus system but what is different is that each of the ECUs has independent and resynchronised clocks to ensure high performance.

The key advantages of FlexRay can be seen in Figure 26.12, where a comparison is made between LIN, CAN and FlexRay.

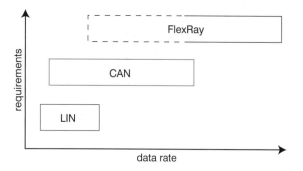

*Figure 26.12 Relative performance comparison of bus systems*

The key advantages are that FlexRay can handle both active and passive safety systems. It can also deal with collision avoidance and provide assistance systems for drivers. It is superior to CAN for a number of reasons:

- It can cope with a data rate of up to 20 Mb/s.
- It can handle synchronous and asynchronous data transfer.
- It can provide data for real-time performance.
- It can prioritise messages.
- It has a high error detection capability.
- It has an independent mechanism to contain errors.

The FlexRay communication system appears to have a limited time in the automotive industry as faster ethernet communication systems are likely to take over.

## 26.3  Future developments

The development of improved vehicle communication systems allows the future development of other systems in vehicles and the use of software. Aside from developments in the luxury car market, where electronic applications will continue to be developed in order to enhance both safety and the driving experience, there are more general trends.

### 26.3.1 Autonomous and semi-autonomous driving

The use of sensors should enable the vehicle to carry out routine driving tasks, such as motorway driving or driving in congested areas, without intervention from the driver. Drivers will be able to set parameters and will, of course, be able to manually override them when required. This will free up the driver to carry out other tasks.

### Traffic safety

If the vehicle itself is aware of its position relative to other objects, its speed and its direction, then this is only part of the information needed to ensure safety. The use of external sensors is part of the overall solution. However, additional technology will need to be developed in order to predict the behaviour of other vehicles that could lead to a collision. The vehicle also needs to be aware of other sudden movements that could cause a collision, such as ice patches or pedestrians.

### Limited road space

Satellite navigation systems are already sufficiently sophisticated to not only determine the shortest route from A to B, but also to incorporate congestion avoidance and driver-set parameters (e.g. avoiding motorways). Satellite navigation systems are already being developed that have a detailed knowledge of traffic patterns. They also have access to real-time data that reveals whether there is parking space available at the intended destination. It is, therefore, perfectly plausible to interrogate a system and receive an answer that will detail the optimum time to undertake the journey, how congestion can be avoided and where the nearest parking is to the destination.

### Real-time data streams

Many of these systems rely on high-performance, real-time sensors and electronic architecture within the vehicle that can process streaming data. This will require a high-performance data network. As far as vehicles are concerned, ethernets are probably the most logical way forward. The systems within the vehicle need to be highly integrated and very functional. There is also a cost and space consideration. It is suggested that a system known as time triggered ethernets is the most likely way of overcoming these considerations.

### 26.3.2 'Green' vehicles

The basic problem behind electric vehicles at the moment is the storage of electrical energy, which at presents limits their range. Once the vehicle industry has produced a viable solution to this it is undoubtedly the case that electric cars will become all-electric. It is likely that they will have dual voltage levels and use full by-wire technology, including brake-by-wire.

*Figure 26.13 Triac 'green' vehicle*

### Hybrid and electric vehicles

Vehicle electronic systems have a huge part to play in the development of the various hybrid vehicles. Typically this will include:

- automatic engine stop and start if the vehicle is motionless
- a regenerative braking system that charges batteries
- a cleaner engine that has reduced emissions
- replacement of mechanical parts with lighter, electronic parts to reduce vehicle weight and improve aerodynamic design.

It is believed that stop-start technology alone can reduce fuel consumption by up to 15 per cent. Regenerative braking also reduces fuel consumption by as much as 25 per cent (although hydraulic regenerative braking claims up to 45 per cent).

The operation of the regenerative braking system is as follows. In a standard hydraulic braking system brake pads generate friction when the pads are pressed against the brake discs to slow or stop the vehicle. Additional friction is produced between the vehicle tyres and the road surface. This friction converts the kinetic energy into heat.

However, with regenerative brakes the electric motor that drives the vehicle does most of the braking. When the driver presses on the brake pedal of an electric or hybrid vehicle, the electronic sensors detect this and put the vehicle's electric motor into reverse. This causes the motor to run backwards, slowing the car's wheels. When running backwards, the motor now acts as a generator, producing electricity which charges the vehicle's high-voltage (600 V) and low-voltage (12 V) batteries.

Regenerative braking is most effective in stop-and-go driving situations; the braking system still retains the hydraulic braking system in case of a breakdown in the regenerative system.

It is important for drivers to be aware that the brake pedal 'feel' will be different; in some cases the pedal travel may be further than the driver is used to.

### 26.3.3 Other developments

There are other major developments in electronics technology, many of which are being directly applied to mainstream models as well as hybrid and electric vehicles (EV). These include:

- position sensors on the engine and chassis
- temperature sensors
- power module inverters for pumps
- lane assist systems – warning the driver by an audible signal or steering vibrations if the vehicle begins to veer off the lane it is in
- electronic injectors – the physical structure of the injectors changes in response to electronic signals from the ECU, resulting in significant improvement in fuel efficiency and acceleration
- launch control – offered in most sports cars, the system electronically controls launch from rest to give optimum acceleration and low wheel spin
- auto stop-start – switches off the engine when the vehicle stops temporarily (e.g. at a traffic light) to save fuel. The engine turns on again when the driver releases the brake or presses the gas pedal
- keyless-go – removes the need for using a key for unlocking the doors and starting the engine. Although this system has existed for a long time, it has been made much more efficient. Automatic boot release is a recent option, which helps while loading luggage
- surface learning – this is a fairly recent research area to enable the vehicle to 'learn' the surface it is driving on. The suspension, braking and traction control can be better adjusted, thus improving both safety and ride comfort.
- automatic self parking – this system has been introduced recently on some high-end models. The vehicle is equipped with sensors or cameras around the vehicle which 'measure' the space as the driver passes it. The driver selects the 'park assist' and the vehicle will park itself with no input from the driver. If the brake, steering or accelerator are touched during the operation then the vehicle will switch off the 'park assist'.

# Index

# Acknowledgements

The author and publisher would like to thank the following for permission to reproduce photographs:

**Alamy/Drive Images**: 16.14; **BMW Group UK**: 16.3; 17.13; 25.3; **Bosch**: 1.55; 5.29b; 10.29; 12.14; 12.20; 12.22; 13.2; 14.25; 14.39; 16.21; 19.9; **Daimler AG**: 17.12; **DASHWARNINGLIGHTS.CO.UK/Peter Marshall**: 24.5; **Denso Europe**: 10.28; **Donald MacAndrew**: 10.19; 16.1; 16.13; 16.15; **elise-shop. com**: 1.52; 16.17; **Ford Motor Company**: 23.2; **Fotolia/Anatoly Abyshev**: 2.16l; **Fotolia/fotografci**: 2.0; **Fotolia/Micah Jared**: 23.7; **Fotolia/Petr Vaclavek**: 2.16r; **Fotolia/Robert Wilson**: 19.2; **Garmin**: 25.5; **Getty Images**: 26.13; **Good Will Instrument Co., Ltd**: 1.54; **GW Instek**: 4.13; **iStockphoto**: 19.0; 19.1a; 21.0; 21.11; 22.0; **John Taylor**: 16.5; **Kevin J. McClafferty, Southwestern Collision Analysis**: 24.8; **Launch Tech UK**: 14.40; **NGK Spark Plugs (UK) Ltd**: 11.7; 11.39; **OBD Diagnostics Inc, www.obd2allinone.com**: 18.22; **Osram**: 20.6; **Peter Laurence**: 11.6; **Pico Technology Ltd, www.picotech.com**: 12.21; 14.41; **Shutterstock/timy**: 18.2; **Stephen Maidment**: 21.1; **Takunori Taira**: 11.41; **Tektronix, www.tektronix.com**: 1.53; **Toyota**: 15.26a; 25.2; **Volkswagen**: 16.2; 19.1b; 20.9; 24.1; 24.9.

The author and the publisher would also like to thank the following for permission to adapt or reproduce illustrations:

4.7 Copyright © 2008 **www.electronicdesignworks. com**. All rights reserved; 4.12 © 1997–2005 **New Jersey Institute of Technology**; 5.1, 12.6, 13.4, 13.8 © Copyright 2011 **Robert Bosch LLC**; 5.10c, 5.12c, 5.25c, 5.27b, 5.27c, 6.9, 6.10, 11.42 **created using Picoscope**; 7.1 from *Embedded Systems: Architecture, Programming and Design* by Raj Kamal, published by **Tata McGraw-Hill Publishing Co**, New Delhi (2009); 7.4 Copyright © **Omitec Limited**. All rights reserved; 7.6 Copyright © **Woodbank Communications Ltd** 2005; 8.1, 8.2 © Copyright 2012. All Rights Reserved. **Yuasa Battery, Inc.**, Laureldale, PA; Tables 11.1, 14.2 © **DieselNet.com**; 11.1 Copyright © 1996–2012 **Web Publications Pty Limited**. All Rights Reserved; 11.37, 11.38 © 2010 **NGK Spark Plugs UK**; 11.4 from 'How Camshafts Work' by Karim Nice. Copyright © 1998–2012 **HowStuffWorks, Inc**; 13.7 © Copyright 2011 **BorgWarner BERU Systems GmbH**, Ludwigsburg, Germany. All rights reserved; 17.5 © 2012 **Midway Industries LLC**; 18.8, 18.9 © 2008–2012 **Toyota Motor Sales U.S.A., Inc**; 22.7 © **JV Technoton**, 2002–2012; 21.9, 21.13 adapted from *Automotive Air Conditioning and Climate Control Systems*, Steven Daly © 2006, with permission from **Elsevier**; 21.16 © **Volkswagen AG**, Wolfsburg. All rights reserved; 22.8 Copyright © 2008, **GuardMagic**; 23.4 from **F650.com**; 24.3, 24.4, 24.6 © **LJ Media Presentations**; 24.7 Copyright © 1998–2012 **HowStuffWorks, Inc**; 25.1 Copyright © 1996–2012, **Crutchfield New Media, LLC** All rights reserved; 26.4 from **www.fanaticars.com**; 26.5 Copyright © 2012 **LMS International**; 26.6 Copyright © 1995–2012. **Nikkei Business Publications, Inc**. All rights reserved.

Every effort has been made to trace the copyright holders but if any have been inadvertently overlooked the publisher will be pleased to make the necessary arrangements at the first opportunity.

Though many of the drawings are based on commercial components, they are mainly intended to illustrate operational principles. For this reason, and because component design changes so rapidly, no drawing is claimed to be up to date. Readers should refer to manufacturers' publications for the latest information.

Manufacturers use many different electrical layouts and it is impossible in a book of this size to include all of them. The layouts and circuits chosen for treatment are intended to establish the working principle of a typical system. With this introduction other systems can be studied and understood.

Although an outline of test procedures is given, no claim is made that the material in the book represents the approved tests applicable to a certain model or type of vehicle. Rapid changes in electronics mean that vehicle manufacturers must be referred to for this service.

Many diagrams have been simplified to help the reader and, in most cases, the graphical symbols used conform to the recommendations made by the British Standards Institution in BS 3939 and the International Electrotechnical Commission EN60617 (IEC).